Lecture Notes in Computer Science 12668

More information about this subseries at http://www.springer.com/series/7412

Alberto Del Bimbo · Rita Cucchiara ·
Stan Sclaroff · Giovanni Maria Farinella ·
Tao Mei · Marco Bertini ·
Hugo Jair Escalante · Roberto Vezzani (Eds.)

Pattern Recognition

ICPR International Workshops and Challenges

Virtual Event, January 10–15, 2021
Proceedings, Part VIII

 Springer

Editors
Alberto Del Bimbo ⓘ
Dipartimento di Ingegneria
dell'Informazione
University of Firenze
Firenze, Italy

Stan Sclaroff ⓘ
Department of Computer Science
Boston University
Boston, MA, USA

Tao Mei
Cloud & AI, JD.COM
Beijing, China

Hugo Jair Escalante ⓘ
Computational Sciences Department
National Institute of Astrophysics,
Optics and Electronics (INAOE)
Tonantzintla, Puebla, Mexico

Rita Cucchiara ⓘ
Dipartimento di Ingegneria "Enzo Ferrari"
Università di Modena e Reggio Emilia
Modena, Italy

Giovanni Maria Farinella ⓘ
Dipartimento di Matematica e Informatica
University of Catania
Catania, Italy

Marco Bertini ⓘ
Dipartimento di Ingegneria
dell'Informazione
University of Firenze
Firenze, Italy

Roberto Vezzani ⓘ
Dipartimento di Ingegneria "Enzo Ferrari"
Università di Modena e Reggio Emilia
Modena, Italy

ISSN 0302-9743   ISSN 1611-3349   (electronic)
Lecture Notes in Computer Science
ISBN 978-3-030-68792-2   ISBN 978-3-030-68793-9   (eBook)
https://doi.org/10.1007/978-3-030-68793-9

LNCS Sublibrary: SL6 – Image Processing, Computer Vision, Pattern Recognition, and Graphics

This Springer imprint is published by the registered company Springer Nature Switzerland AG
The registered company address is: Gewerbestrasse 11, 6330 Cham, Switzerland

Foreword by General Chairs

It is with great pleasure that we welcome you to the post-proceedings of the 25th International Conference on Pattern Recognition, ICPR2020 Virtual-Milano. ICPR2020 stands on the shoulders of generations of pioneering pattern recognition researchers. The first ICPR (then called IJCPR) convened in 1973 in Washington, DC, USA, under the leadership of Dr. King-Sun Fu as the General Chair. Since that time, the global community of pattern recognition researchers has continued to expand and thrive, growing evermore vibrant and vital. The motto of this year's conference was *Putting Artificial Intelligence to work on patterns.* Indeed, the deep learning revolution has its origins in the pattern recognition community – and the next generations of revolutionary insights and ideas continue with those presented at this 25th ICPR. Thus, it was our honor to help perpetuate this longstanding ICPR tradition to provide a lively meeting place and open exchange for the latest pathbreaking work in pattern recognition.

For the first time, the ICPR main conference employed a two-round review process similar to journal submissions, with new papers allowed to be submitted in either the first or the second round and papers submitted in the first round and not accepted allowed to be revised and re-submitted for second round review. In the first round, 1554 new submissions were received, out of which 554 (35.6%) were accepted and 579 (37.2%) were encouraged to be revised and resubmitted. In the second round, 1696 submissions were received (496 revised and 1200 new), out of which 305 (61.4%) of the revised submissions and 552 (46%) of the new submissions were accepted. Overall, there were 3250 submissions in total, and 1411 were accepted, out of which 144 (4.4%) were included in the main conference program as orals and 1263 (38.8%) as posters (4 papers were withdrawn after acceptance). We had the largest ICPR conference ever, with the most submitted papers and the most selective acceptance rates ever for ICPR, attesting both the increased interest in presenting research results at ICPR and the high scientific quality of work accepted for presentation at the conference.

We were honored to feature seven exceptional Keynotes in the program of the ICPR2020 main conference: David Doermann (Professor at the University at Buffalo), Pietro Perona (Professor at the California Institute of Technology and Amazon Fellow at Amazon Web Services), Mihaela van der Schaar (Professor at the University of Cambridge and a Turing Fellow at The Alan Turing Institute in London), Max Welling (Professor at the University of Amsterdam and VP of Technologies at Qualcomm), Ching Yee Suen (Professor at Concordia University) who was presented with the IAPR 2020 King-Sun Fu Prize, Maja Pantic (Professor at Imperial College UK and AI Scientific Research Lead at Facebook Research) who was presented with the IAPR 2020 Maria Petrou Prize, and Abhinav Gupta (Professor at Carnegie Mellon University and Research Manager at Facebook AI Research) who was presented with the IAPR 2020 J.K. Aggarwal Prize. Several best paper prizes were also announced and awarded, including the Piero Zamperoni Award for the best paper authored by a student, the BIRPA Best Industry Related Paper Award, and Best Paper Awards for each of the five tracks of the ICPR2020 main conference.

The five tracks of the ICPR2020 main conference were: (1) Artificial Intelligence, Machine Learning for Pattern Analysis, (2) Biometrics, Human Analysis and Behavior Understanding, (3) Computer Vision, Robotics and Intelligent Systems, (4) Document and Media Analysis, and (5) Image and Signal Processing. The best papers presented at the main conference had the opportunity for publication in expanded format in journal special issues of *IET Biometrics* (tracks 2 and 3), *Computer Vision and Image Understanding* (tracks 1 and 2), *Machine Vision and Applications* (tracks 2 and 3), *Multimedia Tools and Applications* (tracks 4 and 5), *Pattern Recognition Letters* (tracks 1, 2, 3 and 4), or *IEEE Trans. on Biometrics, Behavior, and Identity Science* (tracks 2 and 3).

In addition to the main conference, the ICPR2020 program offered workshops and tutorials, along with a broad range of cutting-edge industrial demos, challenge sessions, and panels. The virtual ICPR2020 conference was interactive, with real-time live-streamed sessions, including live talks, poster presentations, exhibitions, demos, Q&A, panels, meetups, and discussions – all hosted on the Underline virtual conference platform.

The ICPR2020 conference was originally scheduled to convene in Milano, which is one of the most beautiful cities of Italy for art, culture, lifestyle – and more. The city has so much to offer! With the need to go virtual, ICPR2020 included interactive **virtual tours** of Milano during the conference coffee breaks, which we hoped would introduce attendees to this wonderful city, and perhaps even entice them to visit Milano once international travel becomes possible again.

The success of such a large conference would not have been possible without the help of many people. We deeply appreciate the vision, commitment, and leadership of the ICPR2020 Program Chairs: Kim Boyer, Brian C. Lovell, Marcello Pelillo, Nicu Sebe, René Vidal, and Jingyi Yu. Our heartfelt gratitude also goes to the rest of the main conference organizing team, including the Track and Area Chairs, who all generously devoted their precious time in conducting the review process and in preparing the program, and the reviewers, who carefully evaluated the submitted papers and provided invaluable feedback to the authors. This time their effort was considerably higher given that many of them reviewed for both reviewing rounds. We also want to acknowledge the efforts of the conference committee, including the Challenge Chairs, Demo and Exhibit Chairs, Local Chairs, Financial Chairs, Publication Chair, Tutorial Chairs, Web Chairs, Women in ICPR Chairs, and Workshop Chairs. Many thanks, also, for the efforts of the dedicated staff who performed the crucially important work behind the scenes, including the members of the ICPR2020 Organizing Secretariat. Finally, we are grateful to the conference sponsors for their generous support of the ICPR2020 conference.

We hope everyone had an enjoyable and productive ICPR2020 conference.

Rita Cucchiara
Alberto Del Bimbo
Stan Sclaroff

Preface

The 25th International Conference on Pattern Recognition Workshops (ICPRW 2020) were held virtually in Milan, Italy and rescheduled to January 10 and January 11 of 2021 due to the Covid-19 pandemic. ICPRW 2020 included timely topics and applications of Computer Vision, Image and Sound Analysis, Pattern Recognition and Artificial Intelligence. We received 49 workshop proposals and 46 of them have been accepted, which is three times more than at ICPRW 2018. The workshop proceedings cover a wide range of areas including Machine Learning (8), Pattern Analysis (5), Healthcare (6), Human Behavior (5), Environment (5), Surveillance, Forensics and Biometrics (6), Robotics and Egovision (4), Cultural Heritage and Document Analysis (4), Retrieval (2), and Women at ICPR 2020 (1). Among them, 33 workshops are new to ICPRW. Specifically, the ICPRW 2020 volumes contain the following workshops (please refer to the corresponding workshop proceeding for details):

- CADL2020 – Workshop on Computational Aspects of Deep Learning.
- DLPR – Deep Learning for Pattern Recognition.
- EDL/AI – Explainable Deep Learning/AI.
- (Merged) IADS – Integrated Artificial Intelligence in Data Science, IWCR – IAPR workshop on Cognitive Robotics.
- ManifLearn – Manifold Learning in Machine Learning, From Euclid to Ricmann.
- MOI2QDN – Metrification & Optimization of Input Image Quality in Deep Networks.
- IML – International Workshop on Industrial Machine Learning.
- MMDLCA – Multi-Modal Deep Learning: Challenges and Applications.
- IUC 2020 – Human and Vehicle Analysis for Intelligent Urban Computing.
- PATCAST – International Workshop on Pattern Forecasting.
- RRPR – Reproducible Research in Pattern Recognition.
- VAIB 2020 – Visual Observation and Analysis of Vertebrate and Insect Behavior.
- IMTA VII – Image Mining Theory & Applications.
- AIHA 2020 – Artificial Intelligence for Healthcare Applications.
- AIDP – Artificial Intelligence for Digital Pathology.
- (Merged) GOOD – Designing AI in support of Good Mental Health, CAIHA – Computational and Affective Intelligence in Healthcare Applications for Vulnerable Populations.
- CARE2020 – pattern recognition for positive teChnology And eldeRly wEllbeing.
- MADiMa 2020 – Multimedia Assisted Dietary Management.
- 3DHU 2020 – 3D Human Understanding.
- FBE2020 – Facial and Body Expressions, micro-expressions and behavior recognition.
- HCAU 2020 – Deep Learning for Human-Centric Activity Understanding.
- MPRSS - 6th IAPR Workshop on Multimodal Pattern Recognition for Social Signal Processing in Human Computer Interaction.

- CVAUI 2020 – Computer Vision for Analysis of Underwater Imagery.
- MAES – Machine Learning Advances Environmental Science.
- PRAConBE - Pattern Recognition and Automation in Construction & the Built Environment.
- PRRS 2020 – Pattern Recognition in Remote Sensing.
- WAAMI - Workshop on Analysis of Aerial Motion Imagery.
- DEEPRETAIL 2020 - Workshop on Deep Understanding Shopper Behaviours and Interactions in Intelligent Retail Environments 2020.
- MMForWild2020 – MultiMedia FORensics in the WILD 2020.
- FGVRID – Fine-Grained Visual Recognition and re-Identification.
- IWBDAF – Biometric Data Analysis and Forensics.
- RISS – Research & Innovation for Secure Societies.
- WMWB – TC4 Workshop on Mobile and Wearable Biometrics.
- EgoApp – Applications of Egocentric Vision.
- ETTAC 2020 – Eye Tracking Techniques, Applications and Challenges.
- PaMMO – Perception and Modelling for Manipulation of Objects.
- FAPER – Fine Art Pattern Extraction and Recognition.
- MANPU – coMics ANalysis, Processing and Understanding.
- PATRECH2020 – Pattern Recognition for Cultural Heritage.
- (Merged) CBIR – Content-Based Image Retrieval: where have we been, and where are we going, TAILOR – Texture AnalysIs, cLassificatiOn and Retrieval, VIQA – Video and Image Question Answering: building a bridge between visual content analysis and reasoning on textual data.
- W4PR - Women at ICPR.

We would like to thank all members of the workshops' Organizing Committee, the reviewers, and the authors for making this event successful. We also appreciate the support from all the invited speakers and participants. We wish to offer thanks in particular to the ICPR main conference general chairs: Rita Cucchiara, Alberto Del Bimbo, and Stan Sclaroff, and program chairs: Kim Boyer, Brian C. Lovell, Marcello Pelillo, Nicu Sebe, Rene Vidal, and Jingyi Yu. Finally, we are grateful to the publisher, Springer, for their cooperation in publishing the workshop proceedings in the series of Lecture Notes in Computer Science.

December 2020   Giovanni Maria Farinella
                                                                                          Tao Mei

Challenges

Competitions are effective means for rapidly solving problems and advancing the state of the art. Organizers identify a problem of practical or scientific relevance and release it to the community. In this way the whole community can contribute to the solution of high-impact problems while having fun. This part of the proceedings compiles the best of the competitions track of the *25th International Conference on Pattern Recognition (ICPR)*.

Eight challenges were part of the track, covering a wide variety of fields and applications, all of this within the scope of ICPR. In every challenge organizers released data, and provided a platform for evaluation. The top-ranked participants were invited to submit papers for this volume. Likewise, organizers themselves wrote articles summarizing the design, organization and results of competitions. Submissions were subject to a standard review process carried out by the organizers of each competition. Papers associated with seven out the eight competitions are included in this volume, thus making it a representative compilation of what happened in the ICPR challenges.

We are immensely grateful to the organizers and participants of the ICPR 2020 challenges for their efforts and dedication to make the competition track a success. We hope the readers of this volume enjoy it as much as we have.

November 2020

Marco Bertini
Hugo Jair Escalante

ICPR Organization

General Chairs

Rita Cucchiara	Univ. of Modena and Reggio Emilia, Italy
Alberto Del Bimbo	Univ. of Florence, Italy
Stan Sclaroff	Boston Univ., USA

Program Chairs

Kim Boyer	Univ. at Albany, USA
Brian C. Lovell	Univ. of Queensland, Australia
Marcello Pelillo	Univ. Ca' Foscari Venezia, Italy
Nicu Sebe	Univ. of Trento, Italy
René Vidal	Johns Hopkins Univ., USA
Jingyi Yu	ShanghaiTech Univ., China

Workshop Chairs

Giovanni Maria Farinella	Univ. of Catania, Italy
Tao Mei	JD.COM, China

Challenge Chairs

Marco Bertini	Univ. of Florence, Italy
Hugo Jair Escalante	INAOE and CINVESTAV National Polytechnic Institute of Mexico, Mexico

Publication Chair

Roberto Vezzani	Univ. of Modena and Reggio Emilia, Italy

Tutorial Chairs

Vittorio Murino	Univ. of Verona, Italy
Sudeep Sarkar	Univ. of South Florida, USA

Women in ICPR Chairs

Alexandra Branzan Albu	Univ. of Victoria, Canada
Maria De Marsico	Univ. Roma La Sapienza, Italy

Demo and Exhibit Chairs

Lorenzo Baraldi   Univ. Modena Reggio Emilia, Italy
Bruce A. Maxwell   Colby College, USA
Lorenzo Seidenari   Univ. of Florence, Italy

Special Issue Initiative Chair

Michele Nappi   Univ. of Salerno, Italy

Web Chair

Andrea Ferracani   Univ. of Florence, Italy

Corporate Relations Chairs

Fabio Galasso   Univ. Roma La Sapienza, Italy
Matt Leotta   Kitware, Inc., USA
Zhongchao Shi   Lenovo Group Ltd., China

Local Chairs

Matteo Matteucci   Politecnico di Milano, Italy
Paolo Napoletano   Univ. of Milano-Bicocca, Italy

Financial Chairs

Cristiana Fiandra   The Office srl, Italy
Vittorio Murino   Univ. of Verona, Italy

Contents – Part VIII

WMWB - TC4 Workshop on Mobile and Wearable Biometrics 2020

EndoTect: A Competition on Automatic Disease Detection in the Gastrointestinal Tract

The 2nd Grand Challenge of 106-Point Facial Landmark Localization

ICPR2020 Competition on Text Detection and Recognition in Arabic News Video Frames

Competition on HArvesting Raw Tables from Infographics

ICPR 2020 Competition on Text Block Segmentation on a NewsEye Dataset

The 2020 CORSMAL Challenge: Multi-modal Fusion and Learning for Robotics

Pollen Grain Classification Challenge

WAAMI - Workshop on Analysis of Aerial Motion Imagery

Workshop on Analysis of Aerial Motion Imagery (WAAMI)

Workshop Description

WAAMI is a forum for researchers working on analysis of aerial motion imagery. In recent years, there has been an exponential increase in aerial motion imagery due to advances in airborne sensor technologies, rising adoption of manned and unmanned aerial vehicles (UAVs), and emergence of new applications associated with these technologies including aerial surveillance, traffic monitoring, search and rescue, disaster relief, and precision agriculture. We are witnessing a growing need for robust aerial image and video analysis capabilities to take full advantage of this data and to address the pressing needs of its applications. Novel methods, particularly those relying on artificial intelligence/machine learning (AI/ML) approaches, coupled with rapid advances in computational hardware (more powerful, lighter weight, lower energy, lower cost computing platforms) are revolutionizing the image processing, pattern recognition, and computer vision fields. The aim of this workshop was to solicit papers from academia, government, and industry researchers with original and innovative works on all aspects of analysis of aerial motion imagery to address the needs in a diverse set of application areas. Of particular interest to this workshop was analysis of aerial wide area motion imagery (WAMI) that is characterized by very large (few square miles) ground coverage. WAMI enables large scale surveillance and monitoring for extended periods of time, but suffers from unique challenges such as hundreds to thousands of moving objects per frame, small object sizes, parallax, and lower frame rates.

The WAAMI 2020 workshop was held online in conjunction with the 25th International Conference on Pattern Recognition (ICPR 2020). The papers presented covered different aspects of aerial video analysis such as, person and vehicle detection from aerial videos, remote liveness detection, 3D point cloud generation and registration, landcover segmentation, data fusion and interpretability prediction, and modeling and simulation frameworks for airborne camera systems.

We would like to thank Kannappan Palaniappan, Heesung Kwon, Filiz Bunyak, Priya Narayanan, and Hadi Aliakbarpour for co-chairing the workshop, and the WAAMI Program Committee, who made the workshop possible. We would also like to thank ICPR conference for hosting our community, and ICPR workshop chairs Giovanni Maria Farinella and Tao Mei for their help and support.

Organization

General Chairs

Kannappan Palaniappan   University of Missouri, USA
Heesung Kwon   Army Research Laboratory, USA
Filiz Bunyak   University of Missouri, USA
Priya Narayanan   Army Research Laboratory, USA
Hadi Aliakbarpour   University of Missouri, USA

Program Committee

Sanjeev Agarwal   USARMY CCDC C5ISR, USA
Arslan Basharat   Kitware, USA
May Casterline   Nvidia, USA
Diego Faria   Aston University, UK
Adel Hafiane   INSA Centre Val de Loire, France
Chandra Kambhamettu   University of Delaware, USA
Guoyu Lu   Rochester Institute of Technology, USA
Rengarajan Pelapur   Thermo Fisher Scientific, USA
Mahdieh Poostchi   Samsung Electronics, USA
David Portugal   University of Coimbra, Portugal
Surya Prasath   University of Cincinnati, USA
Rao Raghuveer   USARMY CCDC Army Research Laboratory, USA
Walter Scheirer   University of Notre Dame, USA
Guna Seetharaman   Navy Research Labaratory, USA
Omar Tahri   Université Bourgogne, France
Zhangyang (Atlas) Wang   Texas A&M University, USA
Wenjun Zeng   Microsoft Research, China

Additional Reviewers

Noor Al-Shakarji   Ekincan Ufuktepe
Joshua Fraser   Shizeng Yao
Ke Gao

Fine-Tuning for One-Look Regression Vehicle Counting in Low-Shot Aerial Datasets

Aneesh Rangnekar[1]($\boxtimes$) (iD), Yi Yao[2], Matthew Hoffman[1], and Ajay Divakaran[2]

[1] Rochester Institute of Technology, Rochester, NY, USA
aneesh.rangnekar@mail.rit.edu
[2] SRI International, Princeton, NJ, USA

Abstract. We investigate the task of entity counting in overhead imagery from the perspective of re-purposing representations learned from ground imagery, e.g., ImageNet, via feature adaptation. We explore two directions of feature adaptation and analyze their performances using two popular aerial datasets for vehicle counting: PUCPR+ and CARPK. First, we explore proxy self-supervision tasks such as RotNet, jigsaw, and image inpainting to re-fine the pretrained representation. Second, we insert additional network layers to adaptively select suitable features (e.g., squeeze and excitation blocks) or impose desired properties (e.g., using active rotating filters for rotation invariance). Our experimental results show that different adaptations produce different amounts of performance improvements depending on data characteristics. Overall, we achieve a mean absolute error (MAE) of 3.71 and 5.93 on the PUCPR+ and CARPK datasets, respectively, outperforming the previous state of the art: MAEs of 5.24 for PUCPR+ and 7.48 for CARPK.

Keywords: Proxy self-supervision · Low-shot aerial dataset · Vehicle counting

1 Introduction

Tremendous progress has been made in the last few years with respect to aerial scene representation learning - from datasets (DeepGlobe [7], xView [19], DOTA [37], SkyScapes [4]) to better network architectures (RA-FCN [25], ROI transformer [9], SCRDet [38]). Most of these approaches are developed for either object detection or semantic segmentation. [1,2,22]. Recently there has been developing interest in entity counting via regression, as opposed to commonly used via detection, is highly motivational as it requires comparatively fewer parameters while achieving similar, if not better, accuracy, especially for crowded scenes. However, regression-based entity counting has been explored mostly using ground imagery [20,22,24,28]. In this paper, we focus on entity (e.g., vehicle) counting from overhead imagery without relying on any localization information.

© Springer Nature Switzerland AG 2021
A. Del Bimbo et al. (Eds.): ICPR 2020 Workshops, LNCS 12668, pp. 5–18, 2021.
https://doi.org/10.1007/978-3-030-68793-9_1

More specifically, we try to answer the question: *what can we do to improve feature representations pretrained on ground imagery, e.g., ImageNet, for aerial vehicle counting?* In the same line of Aich and Stavness [1], we start by fine-tuning a pretrained VGG-16 network [34] on PUCPR+ and CARPK datasets and use it as our baseline. Singh *et al.* showed that a network trained with self-supervised semantic inpainting was able to outperform its ImageNet pretrained counterpart on aerial semantic segmentation by learning domain specific features [35]. Hence, it is possible to use self-supervision for improved feature learning in the aerial domain. However, PUCPR+ and CARPK contain only 100 and 989 images respectively in the training sets making it difficult to perform full-fledged self-supervision from scratch. Since background categories such as vegetation, roads and buildings dominate the content of these datasets, the likelihood of learning vehicle-specific features is lower than that of background categories.

In order to learn meaningful features and cope with vehicle-specific sample scarcity within the datasets, we propose to adapt representations pretrained using ground images under the premise that features learned from ground images capturing color, texture, edges can be reused for entity counting in aerial images. We investigate two alternative approaches for feature adaptation: 1) **proxy self-supervision tasks:** we apply the self-supervision tasks to the ImageNet pre-trained VGG-16 network instead of its randomly initialized version (Sect. 3.1) and 2) **network modifications:** we experiment with squeeze and excitation blocks and active rotating filters as means for feature re-calibration (Sect. 3.2). We achieve better performance than the state of the art in regression-based entity counting. Comparing to detection-based approaches, our methods are more promising since they achieve counting while bypassing precise localization, which requires more complex network architecture to support the computation and large amounts of annotations to support the training.

2   Related Work

Vehicle counting has been tackled previously by using various approaches - from object detection [3,5,13,14] to regression and matching [1,2,22]. The former set of approaches involve designing complex networks with extensive hyper-parameter search (for example, the anchor scales, anchor ratios, learning rate), while the latter set are prone to making the training in an orderly fashion for the network to capture the dataset space. Hsieh *et al.* released two datasets captured from a drone - PUCPR+ and CARPK - with bounding box annotations, and used spatially regularized constraints to increase the localization performance [6,14]. Goldman *et al.* proposed the soft-IOU (intersection over union) layer as the third head of the RPN detection alongside object score and coordinates to help resolve densely packed object detections [13]. Amato *et al.* adapted the YoloV3 for aerial detection by jointly training the layers for maximizing the use of ImageNet and dataset-specific layers [3,8,32]. Cai *et al.* proposed the Guided Attention Network (GA-Net) which consists of foreground and background attention blocks, learned explicitly to extract discriminative features within the imagery. They also propose a new method for data augmentation, to switch between different times of the day using brightness and Perlin noise, which leads to considerable boost in detection performance [5, 29].

Aich and Stavness proposed the first approach for one-look regression on the dataset - they combined count regression with heatmap regulation of the network [1] . In their approach, the network is trained on two loss functions - an L1-loss for minimizing the count and a Smooth L1-loss for minimizing the corresponding class activation map with the ground truth object locations placed as Gaussians. We denote the network trained with and without heatmap regulation as VGG-GAP-HR and VGG-GAP in Table 1 respectively. Aich and Stavness further replaced the global average pooling layer at the end of VGG-16's convolutional backbone with a global sum pooling layer to achieve resolution invariance [2]. Lu et al. formulated counting as a template matching problem by learning a density map prediction over samples from the ImageNet VID dataset [22, 33]. They minimized the matching between a single snapshot of the object of interest and the whole frame, where the network was trained with weighted L2 loss on the output density map with the ground truth locations (similar to [1]). They used domain adapters to shift from the ImageNet-VID dataset to the CARPK dataset for vehicle counting [31].

Self-supervised Learning. has attracted a lot of research interest [18, 21, 35] in computer vision community as it is able to extract context directly from the design of pretext tasks as the supervisory signals, instead of relying on extensive labeling. Kolesnikov, Zhai and Beyer [18] explored the quality of representations learned from rotation [12], exemplar [11], relative patch locations [10] and jigsaw [26] using ImageNet [8] and Places205 [39] datasets. Singh et al. improved the performance of a ResNet-18 network trained from scratch by adding a self-supervised semantic inpainting loss wherein the network is forced to learn overhead-specific features for correctly filing the masked out regions [35]. Liu et al. [21] improved the performance of crowd counting networks by leveraging unlabeled data with a ranking loss - given two areas sampled from an image in a concentric manner, the network has to ensure that the count predicted for the smaller area is *smaller* than the count predicted for the larger area.

3 Methodology

We establish a baseline for vehicle counting by removing the last set of convolutional layers from VGG-16 network, pretrained on ImageNet, and retrofitting a single fully connected layer that predicts the final count (VGG-GAP [1]). Our focus, herein, is to *improve* the baseline performance by re-calibrating the features learned using ground imagery towards vehicle counting in satellite imagery. To this end, we describe the two unique approaches we investigated (summarized in Fig. 1). One, a data-driven or indirect scheme, encourages suitable features to be learned via introducing proxy self-supervised training. The other directly selects or imposes suitable feature properties via introducing additional network layers. While self-supervision has been widely studied as an unsupervised

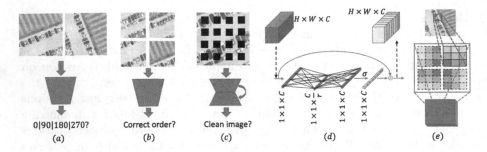

Fig. 1. An overview of all methods experimented in this paper: (a) shows crops with rotation invariance, (b) jigsaw solver, (c) semantic inpainting, (d) squeeze and excitation block, (e) active rotation filters.

representation learning method for various downstream tasks, its application to adapting features from ground imagery to aerial imagery has not been attempted at large, especially for scenarios with sparse annotation. Besides, the effectiveness of indirect and direct adaptation via self-supervision and network modification, respectively, has not been thoroughly investigated and compared in literature. We will address these two issues in this paper.

3.1 Proxy Self-supervision Tasks

Rotation Invariance (RotNet): Proposed by Gidaris *et al.* - the authors create four different copies of a single image by transposing and flipping it and then train a convolutional network to predict the geometric transform applied to the image from its original setting [12]. This helps the network learn informative features and focus on the most salient object in the scene as well as gauge its default appearance. However, we cannot directly apply the task to aerial imagery as there is no *de-facto* default appearance setting - for example, cars can be present with front facing the north or south direction and yet both are plausible settings. Hence, we modify the task and minimize the loss as shown in Fig. 1(a):

$$loss(X_i, \theta) = -\frac{1}{K} \sum_{y=1}^{K} log(F^y(g(X_i|y), X_i|\theta)), \tag{1}$$

where X_i is the sampled image from the dataset and $\{g(\cdot|y)\}_{y=1}^{K}$ applies the geometric transformation with label y to image X_i. $F^y(\cdot)$ and θ indicate the predicted probability distribution over y and the model F's learnable parameters respectively. We convert the problem into a siamese network - where the network receives an image and its rotation version as inputs and is tasked with predicting the rotation used to generate the rotated input. Following [12], we use 0, 90, 180, and 270° as the options for $g(\cdot)$ and discuss the rest of implementation details in Sect. 4.2.

Jigsaw Solver: proposed by Noroozi and Favaro to learn contextual representations by training the convolutional network to solve jigsaw puzzles [26]. This task helps the network to learn discriminative features as it has to find appropriate features that can place the randomly shuffled set of K patches (K = 9 by default) in the correct order. Practically, we implement this approach by minimizing the loss as shown in Fig. 1(b):

$$loss(X_i, \theta) = -\frac{1}{K} \sum_{y=1}^{K} log(F^y(g(X_i|y)|\theta)), \tag{2}$$

where $\{g(\cdot|y)\}_{y=1}^{K}$ splits the image X_i as per the tile configuration $y = (A_1, A_2, \ldots, A_9)$. The original paper used a subset of 1000 permutations based on high Hamming distance, and we use 15 of those combinations in our approach as we did not find using more permutations being a good trade-off in training time and network performance.

Semantic Inpainting: We use the Least squares generative adversarial networks (LS-GAN) with perceptual loss to learn the task of filling in the holes randomly placed within an image (Fig. 1(c)) [16,23]. Our motivation for this task is to encourage learning features that are based on strong contextual and relational information - for examples, if there are pixels to be filled around a red car, how do we make the network aware of what color would be filled in the corresponding pixels? We use a fixed hole grid of 4 × 4 centered around a mask of 12 × 12 with replications instead of random masks - unlike other datasets that contain a wide distribution of images, the datasets PUCPR+ and CARPK have a *slightly fixed* area of focus and hence we use fixed masks with extensive image rotations to capture better variance.

3.2 Network Modifications

Squeeze and Excitation Blocks: introduced by Hu *et al.*, these blocks perform feature re-calibration by adaptively weighting each channel of the feature maps (Fig. 1(d)) [15]. We hypothesize not all ImageNet-learned features contribute to aerial imagery, and hence apply SE blocks as channel attention over the features for adaptation. Assuming $\mathbf{v}_{H \times W \times C}$ is the output of a convolutional block where W, H, and C represent the height, weight, and channel, respectively, the squeeze operation applies a global average pooling layer to aggregate the channel-wise responses $\mathbf{z} = \{\mathbf{z}_c\}$ as

$$\mathbf{z}_c = \mathbf{F}_{squeeze}(\mathbf{v}_c) = \frac{1}{H \times W} \sum_{i=1}^{H} \sum_{j=1}^{W} \mathbf{v}_c(i,j), \tag{3}$$

where i, j, c are the indices for height, weight, and channel, respectively. The squeezed representations $\mathbf{z}$ are passed through two fully connected layers parameterized by $W_1 \in \mathbb{R}^{\frac{C}{r} \times C}$, $W_2 \in \mathbb{R}^{C \times \frac{C}{r}}$ to compute the inter-channel dependencies in the excitation operation as

$$\mathbf{s} = \mathbf{F}_{excite}(\mathbf{z}, W_1, W_2) = \sigma(W_2\delta(W_1\mathbf{z})), \tag{4}$$

where δ, σ and r represent the ReLU non-linearity, the sigmoid activation and the reduction ratio respectively. Finally, the initial features are scaled by the inter-channel weights to obtain the final scaled features as $\widetilde{\mathbf{v}} = \mathbf{s}\cdot\mathbf{v}$. We experimentally insert SE block after the last max pooling layer and before the last convolutional layer choose $r = 2$ to maximize the network prediction performance and minimize changes to the network architecture.

Active Rotating Filters: proposed by Zhou *et al.* and further developed by Wang *et al.* to produce rotation-invariant filters [36,40]. Active Rotating Filters (ARF) generate feature maps with orientation channels - during the convolution, each filter rotates internally and produces feature maps to capture the receptive field layout from K different orientations (for example, $K = 4 \rightarrow 0, 90, 180$, and $270°$ - Fig. 1(e)). This improves the generalization capacity of the network by learning for orientations that have not been seen before with significantly less need for data augmentation and hence, ARFs are a naturally viable candidate for aerial imagery where objects do not follow a default orientation. To assimilate all the gathered orientation information, Zhou *et al.* proposed ORAlign which calculates the dominant orientation and assigns the features in its favor [40]. Wang *et al.* developed it further into S-ORAlign with concepts from SE blocks and fixing the backpropogation to work with constant learning rate [36]. Experimentally, we adopt ARFs with S-ORAlign in our approach for feature adaptation by imposing the desired orientation invariance for improved performance in vehicle counting.

4 Experiments and Results

4.1 Datasets

The PUCPR+ dataset contains images captured from an altitude at a slanted view of a parking lot. It is a subset of the PUCPR dataset [6] and has images under different weather conditions including sunny, cloudy and overcast. This dataset contains 100 training images and 25 test images. The number of car instances varies from zero to 331 in the training set and from one to 328 in the testing set. The CARPK dataset was released along with the PUCPR+ dataset in [14]. It is the first large-scale aerial dataset for vehicle counting in parking lots under diverse location and weather conditions. This dataset contains 989 training images and 459 test images. The number of car instances varies from one to 87 in the training set and from two to 188 in the testing set. CARPK differs from PUCPR in two ways - 1) it has a diverse location setting compared to images in PUCPR overlooking the same region at all times and 2) it has a more complex count distribution. The images in both datasets are at 720×1280 resolution.

4.2   Experimental Settings

We use Pytorch for evaluating all proposed approaches on the PUCPR+ and CARPK datasets [14,27]. We drop the last set of convolutional layers from the VGG-16 network following previous works [1,14] with the presumption to have just enough downsampling to perceive all vehicles in the scene at the last feature map.

We downsample the images by a factor of 2: $720 \times 1280 \rightarrow 360 \times 640$ for all experiments, since we observe negligible performance difference between these two resolutions (this is also consistent with the approach adopted by VGG-GAP [1]). We also split 10% of the training set as validation set using stratified sampling so that the error metrics are more informative as compared to random sampling. We use the validation set for hyperparameter search and final model selection across all epochs. We train our networks on the task of count regression for 30 epochs with a learning rate of $1e - 4$ and then 20 more epochs at a learning rate of $1e - 5$ with a batch size of 16. Unless mentioned otherwise, we use the Adam optimizer [17] in all our experiments. We apply random horizontal flip, random vertical flip, and color jittering to both datasets. In addition, we observe that the orientation of vehicles in CARPK has more variance as compared to PUCPR+. Hence, we add data augmentation in the form of transposing the image to account for more car orientation, which we refer to as transposed augmentation in the following discussion).

For the proxy self-supervision tasks, we sample 10 random patches within [72 $\times$ 72, 90 $\times$ 90] resolution per image. For rotation invariance and jigsaw solver tasks, we train on a batch size of 50 for 30 epochs - we use an initial learning rate of $1e - 3$ and drop the learning rate by a factor of 10 at 15th and 23rd epoch. For semantic inpainting, we use an initial learning rate of $2e - 4$ for the generator and $2e - 5$ for the discriminator. We observed that the discriminator learns at a faster rate and to even the curve, we use stochastic gradient descent (SGD) as the optimizer for the discriminator. We train the networks for 30 epochs after which, we discard the discriminator and use the encoder from the generator for count regression fine-tuning.

5   Evaluation Metrics

We use the Mean Absolute Error (MAE), Root-Mean-Sq. Error (RMSE), %Overestimate (%OA) and %Under-estimate (%UA) for reporting all results:

$$MAE = \frac{\sum_i |y_i - x_i|}{N}, RMSE = \sqrt{\frac{\sum_i (y_i - x_i)^2}{N}}, \tag{5}$$

$$\%OA = \frac{\sum_i |y_i - x_i| I_{[(y_i - x_i)>0]}}{\sum_i x_i} \times 100, \%UA = \frac{\sum_i |y_i - x_i| I_{[(y_i - x_i)<0]}}{\sum_i x_i} \times 100, \tag{6}$$

Table 1. Performance of different methods on PUCPR+ and CARPK datasets. We highlight the best results in each group of methods - detection vs. regression - in bold.

Frameworks	PUCPR+		CARPK	
	MAE	RMSE	MAE	RMSE
Detection				
LPN (1000 proposals) [14]	8.04	12.06	13.72	21.77
YOLOv3 [32]	5.24	7.14	7.92	11.08
Soft-IOU [13]	7.16	12.00	6.77	8.52
GA-Net [5]	3.28	4.96	4.61	6.55
YOLOv3 - Amato [3]	**1.80**	**2.74**	**3.73**	**5.11**
Regression				
VGG-GAP [1]	8.24	11.38	10.33	12.89
VGG-GAP-HR [1]	5.24	6.67	7.88	9.30
Class agnostic counting [22]	–	–	7.48	9.99
Proposed methods	**3.72**	**6.32**	**5.93**	**7.90**

where y_i, x_i are the predicted and actual counts for the image sample i and N is the total number of image samples. Hence, we not only get an overall network performance from Eq. 5, but also get a comparative count of over limit and under limit predictions from Eq. 6. We use MAE as the primary metric of interest throughout our results discussion.

5.1   Results

We discuss the performance of our best performing method in comparison with other published methods in Table 1 and ablation study in Table 2. Our method achieves the best performance among regression-based methods [1]. While we observe about 2–3 increase in MAE and RMSSE with respect to the best performing detection-based method, our method requires only half the computation complexity and can be trained without the need of localization annotation, which is known to be expensive to acquire. This clearly demonstrates the effectiveness of our method for entity counting using aerial datasets with sparse annotation.

Table 2 compares the performance of our methods with different configurations on PUCPR+ and CARPK. We report results with transposed augmentation for CARPK. For PUCPR+, most of the configurations under study, both feature adaptation via self-supervision and feature selection via network modification, produce a better performance than the pretrained baseline. Particularly, RotNet-based self-supervision produces the most improvement followed by semantic inpainting and ARFs, demonstrating the efficacy of representation adaptation. We show activation maps from pretrained baseline and RotNet-trained network in Fig. 2. We observe that the latter version has finer activation

Table 2. Ablation study of all approaches discussed in Sect. 3 on PUCPR+ and CARPK datasets using a baseline VGG-16 ImageNet-pretrained network. We highlight the best results in bold with MAE as the metric of interest.

Task/Blocks VGG-16	PUCPR+				CARPK			
	MAE	RMSE	Over-est (%)	Under-est (%)	MAE	RMSE	Over-est (%)	Under-est (%)
Pretrained	5.84	8.51	2.58	1.15	6.88	9.40	0.85	5.80
Rotation	**3.72**	**6.32**	**1.00**	**1.38**	7.81	10.02	2.10	5.45
Jigsaw	4.56	6.07	2.35	0.56	9.05	11.64	3.35	5.40
Inpainting	4.16	6.33	1.96	0.69	6.31	8.25	2.70	3.40
SE Block	5.76	9.50	1.45	2.22	**5.93**	**7.90**	1.79	**3.94**
ARF	4.12	5.84	1.89	0.74	12.38	15.83	0.77	11.99

details as compared to the ImageNet-pretrained network. This is learned via proxy self-supervision tasks without using any localization information.

For more complex scenes in CARPK, we have two key observations if transposed augmentations is not used:

- the pretrained baseline gives an MAE of 11.5 ± 1.4. This demonstrates the simple effectiveness of understanding the training and test data distribution and adjusting with data augmentation. We also observe in Fig. 3 that the activations for vehicles have lower intensities when transposed augmentations are not used, especially in cases where the orientations do not match the training set distribution.
- RotNet and SE blocks gives an MAE of 9.3 ± 1.2 and 10.2 ± 0.7 respectively, thus proving that feature adaptation is essential for aerial imagery adaptation.

However, with transposed augmentation, we notice that only semantic inpainting and SE blocks, which are complementary to transformation-based augmentation can further improve the performance (Table 2). This further validates our hypothesis that not all ImageNet-learned features contribute to complex aerial imagery and feature adaptation is essential for good performance.

Additionally, we also performed an ablation study where we trained the network from scratch with rotation invariance as self-supervised task. The network trained from scratch without any self-supervision or localization information achieves an MAE of 124.75 on PUCPR+. The network with RotNet-based self-supervision achieves an MAE of 17.05. Although this does not match the MAE of 3.72 on a RotNet-based ImageNet-pretrained, self-supervised learning still leads to a significant difference in the MAE performance and hence strengthening the scope for aerial self-supervised learning. Figure 4 shows the comparison of three networks on the first convolutional layer - two of them based on pretrained ImageNet features and the third on self-supervised RotNet. We observe that the values of the pretrained and RotNet-proxy VGG-16 networks are identical for weights and biases. This visually confirms our hypothesis towards feature re-usage between the ground and aerial imagery as the weights appear to be looking for the same early set of features. For the network trained from scratch with RotNet as a self-supervised learning task, it is harder to interpret the

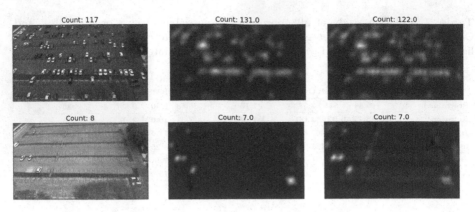

Fig. 2. Exemplar activation maps for images from the PUCPR+ dataset: input image with ground truth count (left), activation maps from pretrained network (middle), and activation maps from the network finetuned with rotation invariance proxy task (right).

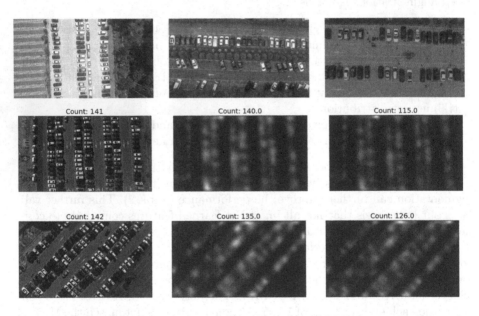

Fig. 3. Exemplar activation maps for images from the CARPK dataset observing the differences based on using orientation-based augmentation. The first row shows images sampled from the training set. Rows 2 and 3 display input image (left), activation maps from network with (middle) and without transposed-image augmentation (right) respectively.

information stored - however, we can still observe that the network is looking for some information towards edges and color given there is not a single weight that is monochromatic.

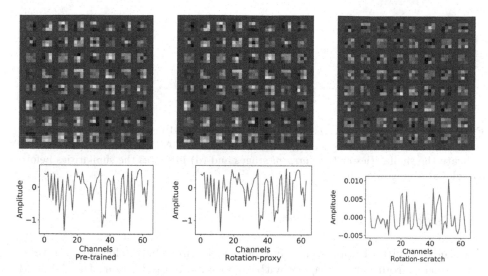

Fig. 4. Comparison between networks trained on PUCPR+ dataset. Top and bottom rows: weights and biases of the first convolutional layer from VGG-16. Left column: pre-trained ImageNet. Middle column: trained with RotNet proxy. Right column: trained with RotNet from scratch.

To further understand where the networks actually differ, we use singular vector canonical correlation analysis (SVCCA) [30] to compare the activations of the two networks on the fixed set of input images from the dataset. SVCCA uses a combination of singular value decomposition and canonical correlation analysis for interpreting similarity within different sets of feature maps without accounting for filter orderings. From Figs. 5, 6, we observe that the activations differ post the second max pooling further strengthening our hypothesis of feature re-usage.

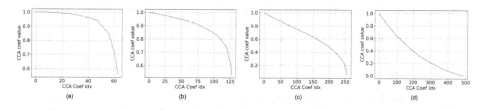

Fig. 5. CCA similarity amongst different layers of VGG-16 comparing the activations of pretrained and RotNet proxy on PUCPR+ dataset. (a), (b), (c) indicate the similarities at the *maxpool* stages and (d) indicates the similarities before the global average pooling layer.

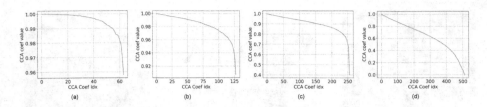

Fig. 6. CCA similarity amongst different layers of VGG-16 comparing the activations with and without transposed-image augmentation on CARPK dataset. (a), (b), (c) indicate the similarities at the *maxpool* stages and (d) indicates the similarities before the global average pooling layer.

6   Conclusion

We study a suite of approaches that help in learning better features for vehicle counting from aerial imagery with small scale datasets. Our study showed that different adaptation approaches induce different amounts of performance improvement depending on data characteristics. With a suitable adaptation scheme, we achieved substantial performance improvement on both PUCPR+ and CARPK datasets.

Acknowledgements. This research is based upon work supported in part by the Office of the Director of National Intelligence (ODNI), Intelligence Advanced Research Projects Activity (IARPA), via 2018- 18050400004. The views and conclusions contained herein are those of the authors and should not be interpreted as necessarily representing the official policies, either expressed or implied, of ODNI, IARPA, or the U.S. Government. The U.S. Government is authorized to reproduce and distribute reprints for governmental purposes notwithstanding any copyright annotation therein.

References

1. Aich, S., Stavness, I.: Improving object counting with heatmap regulation. arXiv preprint arXiv:1803.05494 (2018)
2. Aich, S., Stavness, I.: Object counting with small datasets of large images. CoRR abs/1805.11123 (2018). http://arxiv.org/abs/1805.11123
3. Amato, G., Ciampi, L., Falchi, F., Gennaro, C.: Counting vehicles with deep learning in onboard UAV imagery. In: 2019 IEEE Symposium on Computers and Communications (ISCC), pp. 1–6. IEEE (2019)
4. Azimi, S.M., Henry, C., Sommer, L., Schumann, A., Vig, E.: Skyscapes fine-grained semantic understanding of aerial scenes. In: The IEEE International Conference on Computer Vision (ICCV) (2019)
5. Cai, Y., et al.: Guided attention network for object detection and counting on drones. arXiv preprint arXiv:1909.11307 (2019)
6. De Almeida, P.R., Oliveira, L.S., Britto Jr., A.S., Silva Jr., E.J., Koerich, A.L.: Pklot-a robust dataset for parking lot classification. Exp. Syst. Appl **42**(11), 4937–4949 (2015)

7. Demir, I., et al.: Deepglobe 2018: a challenge to parse the earth through satellite images. In: 2018 IEEE/CVF Conference on Computer Vision and Pattern Recognition Workshops (CVPRW), pp. 172–17209. IEEE (2018)
8. Deng, J., Dong, W., Socher, R., Li, L.J., Li, K., Fei-Fei, L.: ImageNet: a large-scale hierarchical image database. In: CVPR09 (2009)
9. Ding, J., Xue, N., Long, Y., Xia, G.S., Lu, Q.: Learning ROI transformer for oriented object detection in aerial images. In: Proceedings of the IEEE Conference on Computer Vision and Pattern Recognition, pp. 2849–2858 (2019)
10. Doersch, C., Gupta, A., Efros, A.A.: Unsupervised visual representation learning by context prediction. In: Proceedings of the IEEE International Conference on Computer Vision, pp. 1422–1430 (2015)
11. Dosovitskiy, A., Springenberg, J.T., Riedmiller, M., Brox, T.: Discriminative unsupervised feature learning with convolutional neural networks. In: Advances in Neural Information Processing Systems, pp. 766–774 (2014)
12. Gidaris, S., Singh, P., Komodakis, N.: Unsupervised representation learning by predicting image rotations. arXiv preprint arXiv:1803.07728 (2018)
13. Goldman, E., Herzig, R., Eisenschtat, A., Goldberger, J., Hassner, T.: Precise detection in densely packed scenes. In: Proceedings of the IEEE Conference on Computer Vision and Pattern Recognition, pp. 5227–5236 (2019)
14. Hsieh, M.R., Lin, Y.L., Hsu, W.H.: Drone-based object counting by spatially regularized regional proposal networks. In: The IEEE International Conference on Computer Vision (ICCV). IEEE (2017)
15. Hu, J., Shen, L., Sun, G.: Squeeze-and-excitation networks. In: Proceedings of the IEEE Conference on Computer Vision and Pattern Recognition, pp. 7132–7141 (2018)
16. Johnson, J., Alahi, A., Fei-Fei, L.: Perceptual losses for real-time style transfer and super-resolution. In: Leibe, B., Matas, J., Sebe, N., Welling, M. (eds.) ECCV 2016. LNCS, vol. 9906, pp. 694–711. Springer, Cham (2016). https://doi.org/10.1007/978-3-319-46475-6_43
17. Kingma, D.P., Ba, J.: Adam: a method for stochastic optimization. arXiv preprint arXiv:1412.6980 (2014)
18. Kolesnikov, A., Zhai, X., Beyer, L.: Revisiting self-supervised visual representation learning. arXiv preprint arXiv:1901.09005 (2019)
19. Lam, D., et al.: xview: objects in context in overhead imagery. arXiv preprint arXiv:1802.07856 (2018)
20. Lempitsky, V., Zisserman, A.: Learning to count objects in images. In: Advances in Neural Information Processing Systems, pp. 1324–1332 (2010)
21. Liu, X., Van De Weijer, J., Bagdanov, A.D.: Leveraging unlabeled data for crowd counting by learning to rank. In: Proceedings of the IEEE Conference on Computer Vision and Pattern Recognition, pp. 7661–7669 (2018)
22. Lu, E., Xie, W., Zisserman, A.: Class-agnostic counting. In: Jawahar, C.V., Li, H., Mori, G., Schindler, K. (eds.) ACCV 2018. LNCS, vol. 11363, pp. 669–684. Springer, Cham (2019). https://doi.org/10.1007/978-3-030-20893-6_42
23. Mao, X., Li, Q., Xie, H., Lau, R.Y., Wang, Z., Paul Smolley, S.: Least squares generative adversarial networks. In: Proceedings of the IEEE International Conference on Computer Vision, pp. 2794–2802 (2017)
24. Marsden, M., McGuinness, K., Little, S., Keogh, C.E., O'Connor, N.E.: People, penguins and petri dishes: adapting object counting models to new visual domains and object types without forgetting. In: Proceedings of the IEEE Conference on Computer Vision and Pattern Recognition, pp. 8070–8079 (2018)

25. Mou, L., Hua, Y., Zhu, X.X.: A relation-augmented fully convolutional network for semantic segmentation in aerial scenes. In: Proceedings of the IEEE Conference on Computer Vision and Pattern Recognition, pp. 12416–12425 (2019)
26. Noroozi, M., Favaro, P.: Unsupervised learning of visual representations by solving jigsaw puzzles. In: Leibe, B., Matas, J., Sebe, N., Welling, M. (eds.) ECCV 2016. LNCS, vol. 9910, pp. 69–84. Springer, Cham (2016). https://doi.org/10.1007/978-3-319-46466-4_5
27. Paszke, A., et al.: Pytorch: an imperative style, high-performance deep learning library. In: Wallach, H., Larochelle, H., Beygelzimer, A., d' Alché-Buc, F., Fox, E., Garnett, R. (eds.) Advances in Neural Information Processing Systems, vol. 32, pp. 8024–8035. Curran Associates, Inc. Red Hook (2019)
28. Paul Cohen, J., Boucher, G., Glastonbury, C.A., Lo, H.Z., Bengio, Y.: Countception: counting by fully convolutional redundant counting. In: Proceedings of the IEEE International Conference on Computer Vision, pp. 18–26 (2017)
29. Perlin, K.: Improving noise. In: Proceedings of the 29th Annual Conference on Computer Graphics and Interactive Techniques, pp. 681–682 (2002)
30. Raghu, M., Gilmer, J., Yosinski, J., Sohl-Dickstein, J.: Svcca: singular vector canonical correlation analysis for deep learning dynamics and interpretability. In: Advances in Neural Information Processing Systems, pp. 6076–6085 (2017)
31. Rebuffi, S.A., Bilen, H., Vedaldi, A.: Efficient parametrization of multi-domain deep neural networks. In: Proceedings of the IEEE Conference on Computer Vision and Pattern Recognition, pp. 8119–8127 (2018)
32. Redmon, J., Farhadi, A.: Yolov3: an incremental improvement. arXiv preprint arXiv:1804.02767 (2018)
33. Russakovsky, O., et al.: Imagenet large scale visual recognition challenge. Int. J. Comput. Vision 115(3), 211–252 (2015)
34. Simonyan, K., Zisserman, A.: Very deep convolutional networks for large-scale image recognition. arXiv preprint arXiv:1409.1556 (2014)
35. Singh, S., et al.: Self-supervised feature learning for semantic segmentation of overhead imagery. In: BMVC (2018)
36. Wang, J., Liu, W., Ma, L., Chen, H., Chen, L.: Iorn: an effective remote sensing image scene classification framework. IEEE Geosci. Remote Sens. Lett. 15(11), 1695–1699 (2018)
37. Xia, G.S., et al.: Dota: a large-scale dataset for object detection in aerial images. In: Proceedings of the IEEE Conference on Computer Vision and Pattern Recognition, pp. 3974–3983 (2018)
38. Yang, X., et al.: Scrdet: towards more robust detection for small, cluttered and rotated objects. In: Proceedings of the IEEE International Conference on Computer Vision, pp. 8232–8241 (2019)
39. Zhou, B., Lapedriza, A., Khosla, A., Oliva, A., Torralba, A.: Places: A 10 million image database for scene recognition. IEEE Trans. Pattern Anal. Mach. Intell. 40(6), 1452–1464 (2017)
40. Zhou, Y., Ye, Q., Qiu, Q., Jiao, J.: Oriented response networks. In: Proceedings of the IEEE Conference on Computer Vision and Pattern Recognition, pp. 519–528 (2017)

Generative Data Augmentation for Vehicle Detection in Aerial Images

Hilmi Kumdakcı, Cihan Öngün[✉], and Alptekin Temizel

Graduate School of Informatics, Middle East Technical University, Ankara, Turkey
{hilmi.kumdakci,congun,atemizel}@metu.edu.tr

Abstract. Scarcity of training data is one of the prominent problems for deep networks which require large amounts data. Data augmentation is a widely used method to increase the number of training samples and their variations. In this paper, we focus on improving vehicle detection performance in aerial images and propose a generative augmentation method which does not need any extra supervision than the bounding box annotations of the vehicle objects in the training dataset. The proposed method increases the performance of vehicle detection by allowing detectors to be trained with higher number of instances, especially when there are limited number of training instances. The proposed method is generic in the sense that it can be integrated with different generators. The experiments show that the method increases the Average Precision by up to 25.2% and 25.7% when integrated with Pluralistic and DeepFill respectively.

Keywords: Data augmentation · Vehicle detection · UAV · Drone

1 Introduction

Computer vision applications on drone images are gaining importance with the need for automated analysis of increasing amounts of image data captured by drones. Object detection and image recognition tasks for vehicles and pedestrians, are at the heart of many applications such as surveillance. On the other hand, processing of aerial images comes with different challenges as the objects are relatively small and the data collection process is costly and done in uncontrolled environments, limiting the number of images in the datasets. Detection of small objects is generally handled by modifications on the detection network. For the lack of sufficient data, data augmentation techniques are used. Recently, Generative Adversarial Networks [6] and Variational Autoencoders [8] have been shown to generate realistic synthetic images. In this paper, we propose a data augmentation method using these generative networks.

Typically, the number of annotated instances in aerial image datasets are relatively low compared to the common datasets such as COCO [10] and Pascal VOC [5]. In this work, we aim to improve vehicle detection performance in aerial images by synthetic data augmentation on training images. The proposed

© Springer Nature Switzerland AG 2021
A. Del Bimbo et al. (Eds.): ICPR 2020 Workshops, LNCS 12668, pp. 19–31, 2021.
https://doi.org/10.1007/978-3-030-68793-9_2

framework consists of a generator, which generates candidate samples, and an independent detector which evaluates the quality of the samples. The framework is independent from the generator network models, and any generative network capable of image inpainting can be integrated.

2   Related Work

Data augmentation plays a key role in many data-driven neural network tasks such as object detection and object classification. Until recent advances, for visual tasks, data augmentation is mainly provided with spatial and intensity based modifications of images or instances. Even though it is not a guaranteed way of improving performance of a model, classical data augmentation methods are widely accepted as a primary solution to overcome scarcity of data because of ease of implementation. These techniques are mostly useful and applicable for almost all object detection tasks. These methods can be mainly grouped as geometrical and color based transformations. Each transformation method has its own advantages and might work better than other techniques under different conditions and for different data distributions. When the main requirement for the model is robustness to varying illumination, color based illuminations might work perfectly even for small scale datasets. If the angle of the object changes during inference, geometric transformations might be much more helpful to improve the performance. Okafor et al. [13] used multi-orientation data augmentation to improve the classification of single aerial images of animals. They transform an input image to a new single image containing multiple randomly rotated versions the input image. Chen et al. [1] used data augmentation for CNN-based people detection in aerial images. They applied image rotation, perspective transformation and border padding on aerial images. The main disadvantage of these methods is that they are not adding any distribution by discovering features of the data. If the task is to detect or classify classes when training set lacks necessary variety, this can not be considered as a good solution.

In addition to the traditional data augmentation methods, a number of recent approaches focus on data augmentation by copying existing object instances onto the existing training images [3,4,9]. In [9], the ideal locations to place an object together with the best fitting pose of an instance for that scene are estimated. The idea is to provide locations for inserting objects into semantic maps using semantic segmented images to train generator network, since the purpose is placing generated objects visually plausible places in semantic maps, this idea is not defined as an augmentation for detection or classification tasks. In [3,4], a matching score between an object and an image is calculated for augmentation. To prevent boundary artifacts, they use segmented annotated instances while choosing their data to be augmented. These set of methods are based on copying instances into different images without generative modelling. PSGAN [14] handles this contextual instance insertion problem by using a neural network based architecture having two discriminators and one generator. One of the discriminators is responsible for generating the instances and the other generates suitable patches for the generated instances. It uses spatial pyramid pooling layer to generate varying size instances. However, this approach has to deal with instances with artifacts due to the nature of generative networks. VS-GAN [21] also uses a 2 stage discriminator strategy for vehicle detection using least square loss in generator, and validates the augmentation with YOLOv3 and RetinaNet detectors. Since it is required to generate high quality synthetic samples, it was trained with a large scale dataset having car instances. DetectorGAN [11] has added a detector network into the generator-discriminator loop of PSGAN network to have more realistic outputs. This approach is highly dependent on training the discriminator branch which might require training parameters to be changed per subject. Another approach [7] for medical studies keeps geometric and intensity information intrinsically while generating instances. In aerial images, [12] to ours augments aerial images using image-to-image translation by conditional GANs. It is based on mapping the layout into another one while keeping instances which requires layout annotation. In our framework, we don't propose a new generator model but use generator and detector modules separately which is a generic approach for the problem. It prevents the generator overfitting and provides diverse and realistic augmentations. Also with the given parameters, cost and quality trade-off can be arranged.

3 Background

The proposed method consists of a generator network and a detector network. The generator network is expected to generate new instances that fits the given background and the detector network must be able to detect corresponding instances with bounding boxes. The networks must be generic networks that can work with different instance classes. For the experiments, we have selected Pluralistic Image Completion as generator network and Tiny YOLOv3 as detector network. In this section, we explain the selected networks and performance metrics for the experiments.

3.1 Pluralistic

Pluralistic Image Completion [20] is an algorithm for one-to-many image completion tasks. In image completion, there is usually only one ground truth training instance per label which results in generated samples having limited diversity. To overcome this, Pluralistic uses two parallel paths, one is reconstructive and the other is generative, both are supported by GANs. The input images are partially masked to create synthetic holes. The algorithm generates diverse, realistic and reasonable images with completed holes. Let us define the original image as I_g, the partially masked image as I_m, and the complement image as I_c. While the classical image completion methods attempt to reconstruct the ground truth image I_g in a deterministic fashion from I_m, Pluralistic aims to sample from $p(I_c|I_m)$. The reconstructive path combines information from I_m and I_c, which is used only for training. The generative path infers the conditional distribution of masked regions for sampling. Both of the paths follow Encoder-Decoder-Discriminator architecture. We used Pluralistic network as the generator model to generate car instances on given backgrounds.

3.2 Tiny YOLOv3

YOLO [16] is a state-of-the-art, real-time object detection system. It uses a single optimized end-to-end network to predict bounding boxes and class probabilities directly from full images in a single pass. YOLOv1 introduced the concept of directly regressing object coordinates from the image instead of using region proposal networks such as Faster-RCNN [18]. Starting from YOLOv2, the system used anchor boxes for regressing object coordinates. YOLOv3 is trained with a different class prediction loss formula and makes detection at three different scales.

We used Tiny YOLOv3 [17] for experiments which is a smaller version for constrained environments. Since the aim of the proposed method is not to get the best detection performance among different models but to improve the performance of a base model by augmentation, we selected it considering its relatively low training/inference time.

3.3 Metrics

There are 2 common metrics for evaluating the detection performance. Intersection over union (IoU) is used for evaluating localization performance. It is the ratio of overlap (intersection) of predicted and ground-truth locations over union of predicted and correct locations (Eq. 1) where B_g and B_p are the ground truth and predicted bounding boxes of the object.

$$IoU(B_g, B_p) = \frac{|B_g \cap B_p|}{|B_g \cup B_p|} \tag{1}$$

The result is between 0 and 1 indicating the ratio of correct prediction. If the prediction score is above the threshold, it is counted as a correct prediction.

Average Precision (AP) is the area under the precision-recall curve. It is commonly used to evaluate detection performance. Considering the correct predictions as true positives (TP), incorrect predictions as false positives (FP), and no predictions for an instance as false negatives (FN), we can formulate precision, recall and AP as in Eq. 2:

$$precision = \frac{TP}{TP + FP} \qquad recall = \frac{TP}{TP + FN} \qquad AP = \int_0^1 p(r)dr \tag{2}$$

4   Proposed Method

The proposed method consists of 2 stages: training and augmentation. Training stage involves independent training of a generative network and a detector

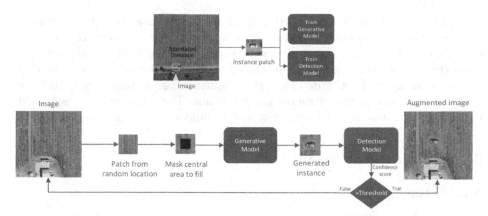

Fig. 1. Schematic of the proposed method. Top: Training stage, Bottom: Augmentation stage

network. At the augmentation stage, the generative network is used to generate new samples and the detector is used to assess the feasibility of these samples for augmentation. An augmented training set is formed using the samples which are deemed feasible after this assessment. This training set then can be used during training of a detector to improve the detection performance. The schematic of the proposed framework is shown in Fig. 1.

4.1 Training Stage

The generator and detector networks are trained with image patches since the aim is to generate patches containing new instances. Both networks are fed with the same patches, extracted around the object instances from the training images. At the end of the training stage, the generator network learns to generate realistic instances on the given patches. The detector is trained with bounding box annotations and the best network parameters which has the highest average precision is selected for the augmentation stage.

4.2 Augmentation Stage

At this stage, the aim is to generate new object instances on the original images. First, 96×96 patches from random locations are extracted and their central 48×48 areas are masked. If the masked holes intersect with the existing instances, the patch is discarded and a new image is used for the patch extraction. The patches are fed into the trained generative model to generate synthetic object instances, which are expected to be located at the center of the patches. Then, the generated data is fed to the detector to evaluate whether the generated sample is acceptable to use for augmentation. For this purpose, the confidence score of the detector model, which reflects the confidence in identifying the generated instance, is used. The generated sample is accepted if the confidence score

is higher than the predetermined threshold. If the generated sample is not realistic or it has artifacts, it is expected to have a low confidence score. In this case,
the augmentation stage starts over with the next image from the training set
since the current image may not be suitable for augmentation. If the generated
sample is accepted by the detector, the original image is augmented with the
generated instance at the extracted patch location. The augmented set is formed
by adding a predetermined number of new instances into the raw train set.

5   Experimental Results

5.1   Setup

Dataset. We used Vehicle Detection in Aerial Imagery (VEDAI) [15] dataset
which has 1272 RGB color images at 1024×1024 resolution. All images are
annotated with bounding boxes for labels such as car, boat and motorcycle. We
have selected "car" instances for our experiments. There are a total of 1377 car
instances in the dataset. Object instances larger than 48×48 pixels (less than
3% of all instances) are discarded as mentioned below. We divided the dataset
as 500 and 772 for training and testing respectively. Only a part of the training
set was used for experiments since we aim to improve the performance on small
training datasets. 96×96 patches have been extracted around car instances from
the training images which have a total of 490 car instances. The images have
been down-scaled to the default input resolutions for performance evaluation.

Patch Size Selection. We analyzed the instance sizes in the dataset to select
the appropriate patch size. The histogram of all instances in the dataset are
shown on the left side of Fig. 2. As can be seen from this figure, 48×48 area
covers more than 97% real instances with the best quality generated samples
and we selected the instance size as 48×48 considering the best coverage and
quality. Larger areas would cover all instances, but, in that case, most patches
would have unproportionately large background area compared to the area of
generated instances. In [20], it is reported that image completion works the best
when the original image is double the size of the generated part. Hence, we
selected the patch size as 96×96. The experiments show that generative models
fail when the patch size is larger and generation time increases exponentially.
Also, the boundary artifacts are more pronounced when patch sizes are smaller.

Generator. Pluralistic algorithm has been used with its original implementation[1]. It uses Residual Blocks as the building block of the system. Each Residual
Block consists of two convolutional layers and a residual connection with a convolutional layer. Encoder has 5 Residual Blocks. Decoder and Discriminator
have 5 and 6 Residual Blocks respectively with an attention layer in the middle.

---

[1] https://github.com/lyndonzheng/Pluralistic-Inpainting.

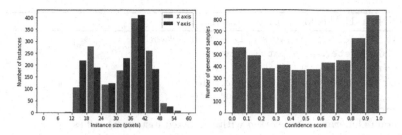

Fig. 2. Left: Histogram of instance sizes for all instances in the training dataset. Right: Histogram of confidence scores for 5000 generated samples.

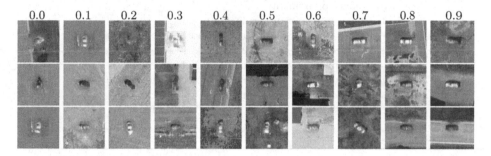

Fig. 3. Examples from generated samples with corresponding confidence scores.

Training of this network takes around 3 h for 200 epochs on an NVIDIA GTX 1080 TI GPU.

The model is able to generate realistic and diverse outputs without mode collapse. To see the distribution of the generated samples, we generated 5000 samples and evaluated it with the detector. Some examples from generated samples are shown in Fig. 3 and the histogram of confidence scores can be seen on the right side of Fig. 2. The equal-ranged histogram bins exhibit no large difference, indicating a good diversity over generated samples. Also it shows that the generator does not overfit to detector vulnerabilities.

Detector. Tiny YOLOv3 has been adopted as the detector module. It has 13 convolutional layers and the first six layers are followed by max-pooling layers. The official implementation has been used with the pretrained weights obtained by training on ImageNet [2] and default parameters for 96×96 resolution. The pretrained weights provides faster convergence, more stable training and better generalization. It also prevents overfitting due to single class training. We trained it for 2000 epochs and for 96×96 patches, the training takes less than 1 h on the same GPU. For performance evaluation, it is trained with the default input size of the network (416×416) which takes around 7 h. Workflow of the proposed method is summarized in Algorithm 1.

Algorithm 1: Workflow of proposed method

---

input : Generative Network g, Detection Network d

$w \leftarrow 96$ // Determined patch size

Training Stage:

    for $j \leftarrow 1$ **to** *Number of instances* **do**

    | $p_j \leftarrow$ Extract $w \times w$ instance patches

    end

    Train Generative Network g with extracted instance patches $p_{1...n}$

    Train Detector Network d with extracted instance patches $p_{1...n}$

Augmentation Stage:

    for $j \leftarrow 1$ **to** *Augmentation count* **do**

        Select an image to augment

        $p \leftarrow$ Extract patch from random location

        Skip to another image if p intersects with another instance

        $p \leftarrow$ Mask the central $w/2 \times w/2$ area

        $p' \leftarrow$ Generate instance with Generative Network $g(p)$

        $o \leftarrow$ Evaluate generated instance with Detector Network $d(p')$

        if $o >$ *Acceptance threshold* **then**

        | Augment the image with the generated instance

        end

    end

5.2   Results

We first conducted an experiment to determine the best parameters for the networks by augmenting 500 images with 1000 generated instances. The result of this experiment can be seen in Table 1 for different confidence thresholds and IoU values. Confidence threshold decides if the generated sample is good enough to augment. When there is no threshold ($= 0.0$), the result is the worst as expected since all generated samples are augmented regardless of their quality. In this case, the process is also completed in 1000 iterations as there are no rejected samples. Considering the average of IoU values, the best threshold value is 0.9. At this threshold, it takes 5902 iterations to generate 1000 accepted instances, i.e. 1 sample is accepted from every ∼5.9 generated samples. It takes significantly long time and the diversity of the accepted samples is low. The augmented dataset does not contribute to the robustness and the generalization performance of the detector and may cause overfitting because of the lack of diversity. The second best threshold 0.4 provides a good balance between average precision and the number of iterations. It also has the best precision for the default IoU value (0.5). Considering the execution time and the diversity of the accepted samples, we selected 0.4 as the acceptance threshold.

There are two main factors for the evaluation of augmentation performance: number of training images and number of synthetic car instances. We have tested the system with varying number of training images to observe the performance of the system. The number of training images has been selected to be 200, 300, and 400, where they contain 251, 334, and 424 car instances respectively.

Table 1. Average Precision results for different confidence thresholds and IoU values where 500 images are augmented with 1000 instances. Augmentation iterations indicate the number of trials to reach 1000 accepted instances.

Acceptance threshold	IoU				Augmentation iterations
	0.2	0.5	0.7	Average	
0.0	56.20	36.11	7.26	33.19	1000
0.1	55.55	40.67	7.97	34.73	1172
0.2	55.42	39.51	9.23	34.72	1288
0.3	56.23	39.65	8.76	34.88	1423
0.4	56.38	44.16	10.31	**36.95**	1709
0.5	56.04	44.05	10.08	36.72	1818
0.6	56.16	42.29	10.81	36.42	2189
0.7	57.63	43.41	9.57	36.87	2667
0.8	57.64	43.15	9.90	36.90	3498
0.9	57.08	43.81	10.57	**37.15**	5902

The number of training instances are increased by adding 1 or 2 new instances per image by augmentation, i.e. when there are 400 training images, we added 400 or 800 synthetic object instances (cars) to approximately increase the existing number of instances by a factor of 2× and 3×. Note that all of the synthetic object instances are placed on the original images, keeping the number of images the same. As per above example, there are still 400 images but they have higher number of object instances than they originally have.

The results shown in Table 2 reveals that the performance of the detector network improves with the generative augmentation in all cases compared to the baseline (i.e. when there is no generative augmentation). Average Precision at IoU > 0.5 performance increases by 17.8%, 25.2% and 16.7% respectively when there are 200, 300 and 400 images in the dataset and they are augmented with 2 new instances per image. Examples from the augmented dataset can be found in Fig. 4 where it can be seen that the augmented instances are realistic, diverse and coherent with the rest of image. Both visual and quantitative results demonstrate that the proposed method can be used as an augmentation strategy to improve the performance especially when there are limited number of training images.

5.3 Additional Experiments

We have conducted additional experiments to show that the proposed method can also be used with different generator models. DeepFill [19] is a generative inpainting network. The model is a feed-forward, fully convolutional neural network which can process images with multiple holes at arbitrary locations and with variable sizes. It has 2 autoencoders, the first one is for coarse inpainting and the following one is for refining the coarse generation. Two discriminators

Fig. 4. Raw training images (left) are augmented with 2 separate car instances (middle). Augmented samples are highlighted with red arrows and their zoomed versions are shown on the right. (Color figure online)

are used for local and global evaluation. It uses contextual attention and gated convolutions. The official DeepFill implementation provided with the paper has been used for experiments. The proposed workflow has been integrated with DeepFill as generator instead of Pluralistic. Some examples of generated samples are shown in Fig. 5 and the results can be seen in Table 3 for 0.9 detector acceptance threshold. Average Precision at IoU > 0.5 increases by 25.1%, 25.7%

Table 2. Detection performances (AP) with the selected parameters.

Dataset images	Augmented instances	IoU	
		0.2	0.5
200	–	49.85	31.43
200	200	52.15	37.65
200	400	51.71	37.04
300	–	53.76	33.25
300	300	55.39	39.76
300	600	56.01	41.62
400	–	55.46	36.14
400	400	56.03	40.24
400	800	56.02	42.18

Table 3. Detection performances (AP) when DeepFill is used as the generator model.

Dataset images	Augmented instances	DeepFill
200	–	31.43
200	200	35.96
200	400	39.31
300	–	33.25
300	300	38.93
300	600	41.81
400	–	36.14
400	400	38.73
400	800	45.40

Fig. 5. Examples of generated samples with DeepFill.

and 25.6% respectively when there are 200, 300 and 400 images in the dataset and they are augmented with 2 new instances per image. It can be seen that the proposed method results in performance improvement for the detector model with similar gains to the variant with the Pluralistic, showing that the method can be used with different generative models.

6   Conclusion

In this paper, we proposed a generative augmentation framework for improving the performance of object detection in aerial images for small datasets. The proposed method consists of a generator to generate instances at random locations and an independent detector to evaluate the feasibility of the generated instances for augmentation. The proposed method is generic and it can work with different generator and detector models. While we evaluated the method with Pluralistic and DeepFill, in the future, use of different generative models can be investigated. The experiments in this paper were based on a single instance class (i.e. cars). In the future, it can be extended to provide augmentation for multi-class detection problems by generating instances for multiple classes at once.

References

1. Chen, H., Liu, C., Tsai, W.: Data augmentation for CNN-based people detection in aerial images. In: IEEE International Conference on Multimedia Expo Workshops (ICMEW), pp. 1–6 (2018)
2. Deng, J., Dong, W., Socher, R., Li, L.J., Li, K., Fei-Fei, L.: ImageNet: a large-scale hierarchical image database. In: IEEE Conference on Computer Vision and Pattern Recognition (CVPR) (2009)
3. Dvornik, N., Mairal, J., Schmid, C.: Modeling visual context is key to augmenting object detection datasets. In: Proceedings of the European Conference on Computer Vision (ECCV), pp. 364–380 (2018)
4. Dvornik, N., Mairal, J., Schmid, C.: On the importance of visual context for data augmentation in scene understanding. IEEE Trans. Pattern Anal. Mach. Intell., 1 (2020). https://doi.org/10.1109/tpami.2019.2961896
5. Everingham, M., Van Gool, L., Williams, C.K.I., Winn, J., Zisserman, A.: The pascal visual object classes (voc) challenge. Int. J. Comput. Vis. **88**(2), 303–338 (2010)
6. Goodfellow, I., et al.: Generative adversarial nets. In: Advances in Neural Information Processing Systems (NIPS), pp. 2672–2680 (2014)
7. Han, C., et al.: Learning more with less. In: 28th ACM International Conference on Information and Knowledge Management (2019). https://doi.org/10.1145/3357384.3357890
8. Kingma, D., Welling, M.: Auto-encoding variational bayes. In: International Conference on Learning Representations (ICLR) (2014)
9. Lee, D., Liu, S., Gu, J., Liu, M.Y., Yang, M.H., Kautz, J.: Context-aware synthesis and placement of object instances. In: Advances in Neural Information Processing Systems (NIPS), pp. 10393–10403 (2018)
10. Lin, T.Y., et al.: Microsoft COCO: common objects in context. In: Fleet, D., Pajdla, T., Schiele, B., Tuytelaars, T. (eds.) ECCV 2014. LNCS, vol. 8693, pp. 740–755. Springer, Cham (2014). https://doi.org/10.1007/978-3-319-10602-1_48

11. Liu, L., Muelly, M., Deng, J., Pfister, T., Li, L.J.: Generative modeling for small-data object detection. In: IEEE/CVF International Conference on Computer Vision (ICCV) (2019). https://doi.org/10.1109/iccv.2019.00617
12. Milz, S., Rudiger, T., Suss, S.: Aerial GANeration: towards realistic data augmentation using conditional GANs. In: Proceedings of the European Conference on Computer Vision (ECCV) (2018)
13. Okafor, E., Smit, R., Schomaker, L., Wiering, M.: Operational data augmentation in classifying single aerial images of animals. In: IEEE International Conference on INnovations in Intelligent SysTems and Applications (INISTA), pp. 354–360 (2017)
14. Ouyang, X., Cheng, Y., Jiang, Y., Li, C.L., Zhou, P.: Pedestrian-synthesis-GAN: generating pedestrian data in real scene and beyond (2018)
15. Razakarivony, S., Jurie, F.: Vehicle detection in aerial imagery: a small target detection benchmark. J. Vis. Commun. Image Representation **34**, 187–203 (2016)
16. Redmon, J., Divvala, S., Girshick, R., Farhadi, A.: You only look once: unified, real-time object detection. In: IEEE Conference on Computer Vision and Pattern Recognition (CVPR) (2016). https://doi.org/10.1109/cvpr.2016.91
17. Redmon, J., Farhadi, A.: Yolov3: an incremental improvement. arXiv preprint arXiv:1804.02767 (2018)
18. Ren, S., He, K., Girshick, R., Sun, J.: Faster r-cnn: towards real-time object detection with region proposal networks. IEEE Trans. Pattern Anal. Mach. Intell. **39**(6), 1137–1149 (2017). https://doi.org/10.1109/tpami.2016.2577031
19. Yu, J., Lin, Z., Yang, J., Shen, X., Lu, X., Huang, T.S.: Generative image inpainting with contextual attention. arXiv preprint arXiv:1801.07892 (2018)
20. Zheng, C., Cham, T.J., Cai, J.: Pluralistic image completion. In: IEEE/CVF Conference on Computer Vision and Pattern Recognition (CVPR) (2019). https://doi.org/10.1109/cvpr.2019.00153
21. Zheng, K., Wei, M., Sun, G., Anas, B., Li, Y.: Using vehicle synthesis generative adversarial networks to improve vehicle detection in remote sensing images. ISPRS Int. J. Geo-Inf. **8**(9), 390 (2019). https://doi.org/10.3390/ijgi8090390

City-Scale Point Cloud Stitching Using 2D/3D Registration for Large Geographical Coverage

Shizeng Yao[1](✉) [ID], Hadi AliAkbarpour[1], Guna Seetharaman[2],
and Kannappan Palaniappan[1]

[1] Department of Electrical Engineering and Computer Science,
University of Missouri - Columbia, Columbia, MO, USA
`syyh4@mail.missouri.edu`
[2] US Naval Research Laboratory, Washington, D.C., USA

Abstract. 3D city-scale point cloud stitching is a critical component for large data collection, environment change detection, in which massive amounts of 3D data are captured under different times and conditions. This paper proposes a novel point cloud stitching approach, that automatically and accurately stitches multiple city-scale point clouds, which only share relatively small overlapping areas, into one single model for a larger geographical coverage. The proposed method firstly employs 2D image mosaicking techniques to estimate 3D overlapping areas among multiple point clouds, then applies 3D point cloud registration techniques to estimate the most accurate transformation matrix for 3D stitching. The proposed method is quantitatively evaluated on city-scale reconstructed point cloud dataset and real-world city LiDAR dataset, in which, our method outperforms other competing methods with significant margins and achieved the highest precision score, recall score, and F-score. Our method makes an important step towards automatic and accurate city-scale point cloud data stitching, which could be used in a variety of applications.

Keywords: 3D stitching · City-scale · Registration · Geographical coverage

1 Introduction

Point cloud data (PCD) stitching is the task of combining two or more point clouds, which only share relatively small overlapping areas, into one larger point cloud model by estimating the relative transformation between them. This task has been gaining more importance due to the massive amounts of 3D data, which only have small partial overlapping areas, are captured from various sensors at different times and locations under different poses or local coordinate systems.

Though One of the basic underlying techniques of point cloud data stitching, point cloud registration, has been studied well through several decades and

A. Del Bimbo et al. (Eds.): ICPR 2020 Workshops, LNCS 12668, pp. 32–45, 2021.
https://doi.org/10.1007/978-3-030-68793-9_3

(a) Point cloud of Columbia dataset 1   (b) Point cloud of Columbia dataset 2

(c) Automatically stitched result using the proposed approach

Fig. 1. This paper proposes a novel point cloud data stitching system for city-scale datasets, that firstly detects overlapping areas among multiple point clouds, then stitches them into one 3D model for larger geographical coverage. Both 3D point clouds in the top row were generated using CM/PMVS [5,6], the two point clouds share 38.39% overlapping areas between each other. All point clouds are visualized using *CloudCompare* [7].

became an essential part of many computer vision algorithms such as 3D object matching [1], localization and mapping [2], dense 3D reconstruction of a scene [3], and object pose estimation [4], a difficult yet fundamental task in point cloud data stitching still exists, which is to determine the overlapping areas in each point cloud, which in many cases could be a relatively small percentage of the whole point cloud coverage. This becomes even more severe when applying point cloud data stitching on city-scale data of urban environments since all point clouds share very similar structures and it is hard to accurately determine the true overlapping area. Without accurately estimating the overlapping areas in each point cloud, modern point cloud registration algorithms fail to complete the task due to mismatching of 3D points (examples can be found in Sect. 4).

In this paper we propose a novel point cloud data stitching system, that addresses this issue and accurately stitches multiple city-scale point clouds that only share small overlapping areas into one 3D model with the help of a 2D image mosaicking technique. Our system not only could handle colorful point clouds reconstructed by 3D reconstruction algorithms, but also color-less LiDAR data captured at different times and locations under different local coordinate systems. Our system consists of three components.

The first component is a module, which creates 2D orthographic views for each city-scale point cloud. The second component applies a 2D image mosaicking technique to mosaic those orthographic views such that the scale between different point clouds can be estimated and the 3D overlapping areas can be determined. The third component estimates multiple transformation matrices between each pair of point clouds based on only the overlapping areas using multiple point cloud registration algorithms and selects the best transformation matrix among all estimations. Once the final transformation matrix is selected, all point clouds are transformed into one common coordinate and form the final result.

The performance is quantitatively evaluated based on realistic city-scale LiDAR data, in which our system outperforms all other point cloud registration algorithms. The key contribution of this paper is the development of the first two modules, which could accurately estimate overlapping areas between different point clouds, such that automatic and accurate point cloud stitching can be performed on large city-scale datasets. The rest of this paper is organized as follows: Sect. 2 presents the related works. Section 3 presents our proposed approach for point cloud data stitching. Experimental results are presented in Sect. 4, and Sect. 5 concludes the paper.

2   Related Work

Our method employs 2D image mosaicking techniques together with 3D point cloud registration techniques to accomplish this task.

2D image mosaicking is a fundamental task in computer vision and has been studied for decades [8–10]. Feature-based image registration techniques mainly match sparse key-points provided by feature descriptors in order to find transformation relationship between multiple images given some area of overlap. The choice of descriptor plays a vital role in determining robustness and efficiency of mosaicking algorithms. One of the earliest mosaicking algorithm is AutoStitch [11] with robust SIFT [12] features. SURF [13] features are reported to be as robust as SIFT and more efficient in terms of time complexity. Many other feature descriptors have also been selected for mosaicking process due to their unique strength, such as KLT feature [14], Harris Corner feature [15], and ASIFT feature [16]. In this study, we look for an efficient and robust feature descriptor particularly for city-scale point cloud data of the urban environment, which is a difficult work due to its challenges. For example, each model covers several square kilometers area with very similar contents. Wide range of objects such as long roads and massive buildings. Occlusion due to the presence of building and shadows add a further twist in these datasets. Thus we take advantage of very robust descriptors such as SURF as our 2D image mosaicking feature descriptor.

Much research also has been done on the topic of 3D point cloud registration: one of the oldest and most widely used algorithms, Iterative Closest Point (ICP) [17,18], is based on an iterative matching process where point proximity establishes candidate point pair sets. Given a set of point pairs, then rigid transformation that minimizes the sum of squared point pair distances can be calculated efficiently in closed form. Many variants of ICP have also been developed including A.V. Segal *et al.* [19], which combined the ICP and *point-to-plane* ICP algorithm into a single probabilistic framework called Generalized-ICP (GICP) to improve performance while maintaining the speed and simplicity of ICP. Later, M. Korn *et al.* [20] integrated L*a*b color space information into the GICP algorithm, which improved the registration result without having an immoderate impact on the runtime. R.B. Rusu *et al.* proposed a 3D feature descriptor named Fast Point Feature Histograms (FPFH), which describes the local geometry around a point for 3D point cloud datasets and can be used for 3D registration [21]. In this study, we take advantage of all modern 3D registration algorithms and select the one which estimates the best transformation matrix.

3 Proposed Approach

Recently, massive amounts of 3D point cloud data are directly or indirectly captured from various active sensors (i.e., LiDAR, depth cameras, and reconstructions based on 2D imagery) but at different times and locations under different poses or local coordinate systems. We proposed a novel system, which can stitch multiple city-scale point clouds of urban scenes with only small overlapping areas into one larger point cloud, which has larger geographical coverage. Our system firstly creates 2D orthographic views for each city-scale point cloud, then applies a 2D image mosaicking technique to locate the overlapping 3D areas while estimating the scales between different point clouds. After obtaining the overlapping areas, we use only these areas to apply 3D registration techniques to find the best transformation matrix to stitch each point cloud into one common coordinate as our final result. A demonstration of our system can be found in Fig. 2.

3.1 2D Orthographic View Generating

Due to the fact that different point clouds were captured under different situations, the majority of the datasets may not have realistic real-world coordinates.

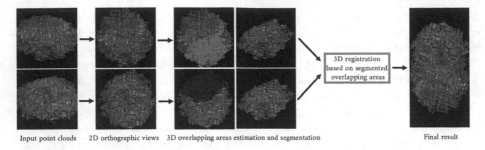

Fig. 2. Our framework consists of three main blocks: 1) 2D orthographic view generating, 2) 3D overlapping area estimation and segmentation, and 3) 3D registration based on segmented overlapping areas.

For example, a point cloud may be rotated around certain origin and the whole model could be facing in a wrong direction. To create 2D orthographic views for these datasets, we firstly correct the normal for each point cloud: one plane is fitted into each point cloud using singular value decomposition (SVD) [22]. We treat this plane as the ground plane, then rotate the point cloud in 3D space and adjust its normal until the normal changes to (0,0,1), which means the point cloud is facing directly into the sky. We then collapse each point along z-direction down to the ground plane and create a 2D image from this ground plane. The color value of each pixel on this plane equals the color of the highest 3D point at this (x,y) location.

3.2   3D Overlapping Area Estimation and Segmentation

After obtaining the 2D orthographic views, we detect SURF feature points on each view and apply feature matching between each pair of the views. Due to the similar underlying structures and potential mismatching in each view, we only keep *good* matches, which have matching scores higher than a predefined threshold value. We then perform 2D image mosaicking using only the good matches together with RANSAC [23]. Figure 4 shows the *good* matches between the two orthographic views in Columbia dataset. In total, we obtained 13 *good* matches in this dataset, and 9 out of them were correct. We used all 13 matches to perform 2D image mosaicing, during which the 4 incorrect matches were discarded by RANSAC.

After applying 2D image mosaicking, we estimate the scale between the two point clouds first, then compute and segment the 2D overlapping areas from each orthographic view. Based on the 2D areas, we trace back and locate the 3D overlapping area in each point cloud. Those 3D overlapping areas are then segmented out and used for 3D transformation matrix estimation (Fig. 5 bottom row).

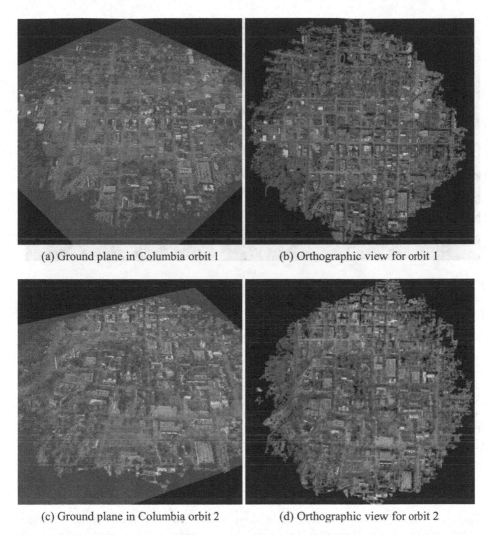

(a) Ground plane in Columbia orbit 1   (b) Orthographic view for orbit 1

(c) Ground plane in Columbia orbit 2   (d) Orthographic view for orbit 2

Fig. 3. A ground plane is fitted into each point cloud (marked in green color in the left column). After adjusting the normal of the ground plane, a 2D orthographic view can be generated (the right column) (Color figure online).

3.3 3D Registration Based on Segmented Overlapping Areas

Once the 3D overlapping areas among multiple point clouds are determined and segmented, we estimate multiple transformation matrices between them using each the following four algorithms only based on the segmented overlapping areas:

– ICP [17,18]
– Generalized-ICP (GICP) [19]

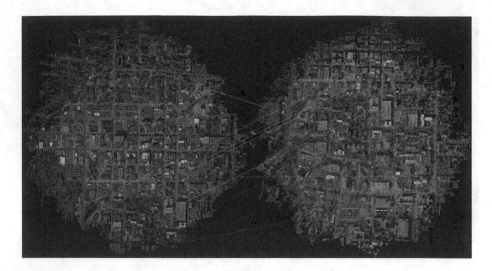

Fig. 4. This figure shows the *good* matches between the two orthographic views, which are indicated by colorful line segments. The 4 mismatches are discarded later by RANSAC [23]. (Color figure online)

- Color Supported Generalized-ICP [20], if color information is available
- Fast Point Feature Histograms (FPFH) [21]

After obtaining four transformation matrices, our system transforms the overlapping area of the source point cloud into the target point cloud coordinate using each of the matrices and calculates the Root Mean Square Error (RMSE) (Eq. 1) between the overlapping areas.

$$RMSErrors = \sqrt{\frac{\sum_{i=1}^{n} \left(P_{target} - P_{source}\right)^2}{n}} \qquad (1)$$

The matrix with the least RMSE is then selected as the final transformation matrix. Our system then uses this matrix to transform the source point cloud into the target point cloud coordinate and merges the two point clouds into one larger model. Depending on the floating-point number precision of the point locations, two point clouds usually do not have multiple points at the exact same location after transformation. However, if this situation happens, we keep only one point at this location and assign the average color to it. An example of our final result can be found in Fig. 6.

4   Experimental Results on Real-World Data

To evaluate our proposed method, we compared our results with all modern 3D point cloud registration algorithms on both reconstructed point clouds and LiDAR data. We also quantitatively evaluated our method versus other algorithms using LiDAR groundtruth data.

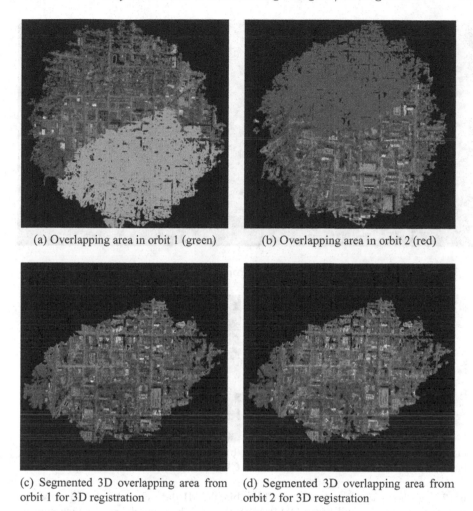

(a) Overlapping area in orbit 1 (green)   (b) Overlapping area in orbit 2 (red)

(c) Segmented 3D overlapping area from   (d) Segmented 3D overlapping area from
orbit 1 for 3D registration   orbit 2 for 3D registration

Fig. 5. The 3D overlapping areas from the two point clouds are shown in the top row
(green area and red area). The two cropped areas are shown in the bottom row, which
will be used for 3D registration in the next module. (Color figure online)

4.1   Reconstructed Point Clouds on Columbia Dataset

Two different circular orbits of 2D Wide-Area Motion Imagery (WAMI) [24] were
captured in Columbia, Missouri, USA by TransparentSky [25]. Each orbit covers approximately 1 km^2 area, and the two orbits share a 38% overlapping. We
then used a well-known open-source tool *CM/PMVS* [5,6] to generate two point
clouds using the two orbits of imagery. An example of the Columbia WAMI
dataset and the reconstructed point cloud of it can be found in Fig. 7. The
reconstructed point cloud from orbit 1 contains 3.15 million 3D points, and the
reconstructed point cloud from orbit 2 contains 6.30 million 3D points. Our pro-

Fig. 6. The final model generated by proposed approach on Columbia dataset.

(a) First frame of Columbia WAMI dataset, or- (b) Reconstructed point cloud model using
bit 1   *CM/PMVS* [5,6] on Columbia dataset, orbit 1

Fig. 7. (a) shows the first frame of Columbia WAMI dataset, orbit 1. (b) shows the
reconstructed point cloud using CM/PMVS [5,6] on the same dataset, which contains
3.15 million 3D points.

posed method requires a similar scale between multiple point clouds. To achieve
this, we firstly upscale/downscale each point cloud to a near-world scale, meaning each unit in point cloud roughly represents 1-meter distance. Since initially,
we're using a 2D matching technique to roughly locate the overlapping areas,
noise, and occlusion created by the MVS algorithms are not hurting the final
result.

When creating the 2D orthographic views of the point clouds, since we're
stitching multiple city-scale models, we set the image resolution to 2 m, meaning
each pixel in 2D views represents 2-meter distance in real world. To apply our
proposed method on smaller objects, the resolution can be increased for better
performance.

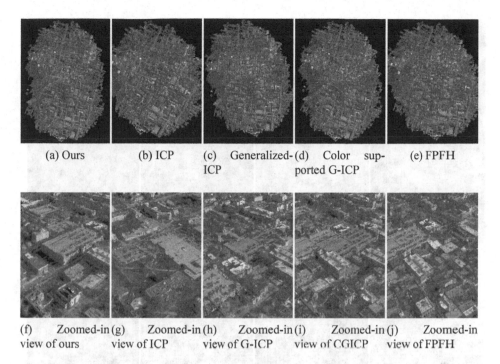

(a) Ours   (b) ICP   (c) Generalized-(d) Color sup-   (e) FPFH
                               ICP   ported G-ICP

(f)   Zoomed-in (g)   Zoomed-in (h)   Zoomed-in (i)   Zoomed-in (j)   Zoomed-in
view of ours   view of ICP   view of G-ICP   view of CGICP   view of FPFH

Fig. 8. Point cloud stitching comparisons on Columbia dataset. From left to right: ours, B. Eckart *et al.* [18], A.V. Segal *et al.* [19], M. Korn *et al.* [20], and R.B. Rusu *et al.* [21]. All other methods fail while only ours accurately stitches the two point clouds.

Figure 8 shows the stitched result from the proposed approach as well as the results from the four most common point cloud registration algorithms including B. Eckart *et al.* [18], A.V. Segal *et al.* [19], M. Korn *et al.* [20], and R.B. Rusu *et al.* [21]. For all four common algorithms, we set the theoretical overlap as 38.39% before tests such that the comparisons are in fair condition. Figure 8 bottom row shows a zoomed-in view from each result, from which we could clearly notice that only the proposed approach is able to produce a reasonable result while all other algorithms fail to stitch the two point clouds due to similar underlying structures and mismatching the 3D points.

4.2   Columbia LiDAR Dataset

We also performed our point cloud stitching approach on a realistic city-scale LiDAR dataset, which was kindly provided by Boone County Government, Missouri. This LiDAR dataset covers a $4.89\,\mathrm{km}^2$ area and the aggregate nominal pulse density of it is $2.1\,\mathrm{pts/m}^2$. In total, this LiDAR dataset contains 8.86 million scanned 3D points. This dataset is then randomly divided into 4 sub-volumes for quantitative evaluations in our experiments. Each sub-volume contains 1.43

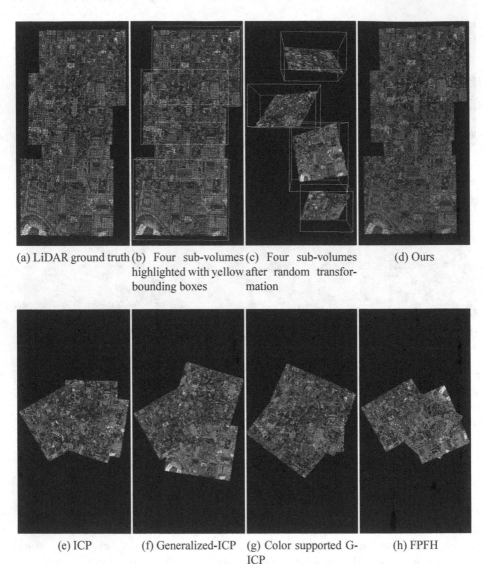

(a) LiDAR ground truth (b) Four sub-volumes (c) Four sub-volumes   (d) Ours
                          highlighted with yellow after random transfor-
                          bounding boxes   mation

        (e) ICP   (f) Generalized-ICP (g) Color supported G-   (h) FPFH
                                              ICP

Fig. 9. Point cloud stitching comparisons on the Columbia LiDAR dataset. Top row from left to right: ground-truth, the four sub-volumes extracted from ground-truth (each area is highlighted with a yellow bounding box), the four sub-volumes after applied a random transformation, and result from Ours. Bottom row from left to right: result from B. Eckart *et al.* [18], result from A.V. Segal *et al.* [19], result M. Korn *et al.* [20], and result R.B. Rusu *et al.* [21]. All other methods incorrectly stitches the four point clouds while only ours successfully stitches the four point clouds. (Color figure online)

million–2.49 million 3D points, and each pair of two sub-volumes share a 10%–30% overlap. A different random 3D transformation (translation and rotation) is then applied to each of the sub-volumes to simulate the realistic situations. The LiDAR dataset is shown in Fig. 9(a), in which the color of each 3D point represents the LiDAR return value, and the 4 sub-volume point clouds extracted from the LiDAR dataset are shown in Fig. 9(b), where each sub-volume point cloud is highlighted using a yellow bounding box. The 4 sub-volume point clouds after random transformation are shown in Fig. 9(c). Figure 9 shows that only our proposed method is able to stitch the 4 point clouds correctly while all other methods fail the task completely without generating any meaningful results.

We quantitatively evaluate our proposed method versus other algorithms using the evaluation methodology proposed in *Tanks and Temples* MVS benchmark [26]. The precision score $(P(d))$, recall score $(R(d))$, and F-score $(F(d))$ are calculated using Eq. 2 (d is set to 0.7 m, which is the same as the *Ground Sample Distance* in this LiDAR dataset).

$$P(d) = \frac{100}{|R|} \sum_{r \in R} [e_{r \to G} < d]$$

$$R(d) = \frac{100}{|G|} \sum_{g \in G} [e_{g \to R} < d] \qquad (2)$$

$$F(d) = \frac{2P(d)R(d)}{P(d) + R(d)}$$

The quantitative evaluations on Columbia LiDAR dataset about our proposed method and all the other four algorithms can be found in Table 1, which shows that our proposed method outperforms other methods with significant margins and achieves the highest precision score, recall score, and F-score among the five approaches, which indicates the importance of overlapping area estimation, and demonstrates our ability of stitching city-scale point cloud data automatically and accurately without the need of any odometry (e.g. INS or GPS).

Table 1. Quantitative evaluations of point cloud stitching methods for the Columbia LiDAR dataset (d is set to 0.7 m, which is the same as the *Ground Sample Distance* in this LiDAR dataset).

Method	Precision $P(d)$	Recall $R(d)$	F-score $F(d)$
Ours	**94.12**	**97.95**	**96.00**
B. Eckart *et al.* [18]	29.10	24.16	26.40
A.V. Segal *et al.* [19]	26.04	22.89	24.36
M. Korn *et al.* [20]	19.86	14.63	16.85
R.B. Rusu *et al.* [21]	24.19	24.42	24.30

5   Conclusions

In this paper, we proposed a novel point cloud stitching pipeline for city-scale point clouds of urban scenes. The proposed pipeline consists of three main components, which fully utilizes 2D image mosaicking techniques together with 3D registration techniques. This pipeline uses 2D image mosaicking techniques to locate the overlapping 3D areas among multiple point clouds first, which is our key contribution and demonstrated to be very critical based on the experiments, then applies 3D registration techniques for better transformation matrix estimation. Experiments on Columbia reconstructed point clouds and Columbia LiDAR data show that our proposed approach could successfully stitch multiple city-scale 3D models as long as they share at least a 10% overlapping area. The quantitative evaluations show that our method outperforms competing methods by a huge margin and achieved 94.12 as precision score, 97.95 as recall score, and 96.00 as F-score. This proposed technique can be used for a variety of applications, such as city-scale data collection, construction design, environment change detection due to constructions or natural disasters.

Acknowledgments. This work was partially supported by awards from U.S. Army Research Laboratory W911NF-1820285 and Army Research Office DURIP W911NF-1910181. Any opinions, findings, and conclusions or recommendations expressed in this publication are those of the authors and do not necessarily reflect the views of the U.S. Government or agency thereof. The authors also would like to thank Steve Suddarth at Transparent Sky LLC [25] for capturing Columbia 2D imagery dataset, and Boone County Government, Missouri for providing the LiDAR data covering Columbia, Missouri.

References

1. Besl, P.J., McKay, N.D.: Method for registration of 3-D shapes. In: Sensor Fusion IV: Control Paradigms and Data Structures, vol. 1611, pp. 586–606. International Society for Optics and Photonics (1992)
2. Campbell, D., Petersson, L.: An adaptive data representation for robust point-set registration and merging. In: Proceedings of the IEEE International Conference on Computer Vision, pp. 4292–4300 (2015)
3. Chen, Y., Medioni, G.G.: Object modeling by registration of multiple range images. Image Vis. Comput. **10**(3), 145–155 (1992)
4. Chetverikov, D., Stepanov, D., Krsek, P.: Robust Euclidean alignment of 3D point sets: the trimmed iterative closest point algorithm. Image Vis. Comput. **23**(3), 299–309 (2005)
5. Furukawa, Y., Ponce, J.: Accurate, dense, and robust multiview stereopsis. IEEE Trans. Pattern Anal. Mach. Intell. **32**(8), 1362–1376 (2009)
6. Furukawa, Y., Curless, B., Seitz, S.M., Szeliski, R.: Towards internet-scale multiview stereo. In: 2010 IEEE Computer Society Conference on Computer Vision and Pattern Recognition, pp. 1434–1441 . IEEE (2010)
7. Cloudcompare 3D point cloud and mesh processing software. https://www.danielgm.net/cc/. Accessed 10 Mar 2020

8. Brown, L.G.: A survey of image registration techniques. ACM Comput. Surv. (CSUR) **24**(4), 325–376 (1992)
9. Zitova, B., Flusser, J.: Image registration methods: a survey. Image Vis. Comput. **21**(11), 977–1000 (2003)
10. Aktar, R., Aliakbarpour, H., Bunyak, F., Seetharaman, G., Palaniappan, K.: Performance evaluation of feature descriptors for aerial imagery mosaicking. In: (2018) IEEE Applied Imagery Pattern Recognition Workshop (AIPR), pp. 1–7. IEEE (2018)
11. Brown, M., Lowe, D.G.: Automatic panoramic image stitching using invariant features. Int. J. Comput. Vis. **74**(1), 59–73 (2007). https://doi.org/10.1007/s11263-006-0002-3
12. Lowe, D.G.: Distinctive image features from scale-invariant keypoints. Int. J. Comput. Vis. **60**(2), 91–110 (2004). https://doi.org/10.1023/B:VISI.0000029664.99615.94
13. Bay, H., Tuytelaars, T., Van Gool, L.: SURF: speeded up robust features. In: Leonardis, A., Bischof, H., Pinz, A. (eds.) ECCV 2006. LNCS, vol. 3951, pp. 404–417. Springer, Heidelberg (2006). https://doi.org/10.1007/11744023_32
14. Lucas, B.D., Kanade, T., et al.: An iterative image registration technique with an application to stereo vision, Vancouver, British Columbia (1981)
15. Harris, C.G., Stephens, M., et al.: A combined corner and edge detector. In: Alvey Vision Conference, vol. 15, no. 50, , pp. 10–5244. Citeseer (1988)
16. Morel, J.-M., Yu, G.: ASIFT: a new framework for fully affine invariant image comparison. SIAM J. Imaging Sci. **2**(2), 438–469 (2009)
17. Eckart, B., Kim, K., Troccoli, A., Kelly, A., Kautz, J.: MLMD: maximum likelihood mixture decoupling for fast and accurate point cloud registration. In: 2015 International Conference on 3D Vision, pp. 241–249. IEEE (2015)
18. Eckart, B., Kim, K., Troccoli, A., Kelly, A., Kautz, J.: Accelerated generative models for 3D point cloud data. In: Proceedings of the IEEE Conference on Computer Vision and Pattern Recognition, pp. 5497–5505 (2016)
19. Segal, A., Haehnel, D., Thrun, S.: Generalized-ICP. In: Robotics: Science and Systems, vol. 2, no. 4, p. 435, Seattle, WA (2009)
20. Korn, M., Holzkothen, M., Pauli, J.: Color supported generalized-ICP. In: 2014 International Conference on Computer Vision Theory and Applications (VISAPP), vol. 3, pp. 592–599. IEEE (2014)
21. Rusu, R.B., Blodow, N., Beetz, M.: Fast point feature histograms (FPFH) for 3D registration. In: 2009 IEEE International Conference on Robotics and Automation, pp. 3212–3217. IEEE (2009)
22. Söderkvist, I.: Using SVD for some fitting problems. University Lecture (2009)
23. Huber, P.J.: Robust Statistics, vol. 523. Wiley, Hoboken (2004)
24. Palaniappan, K., Rao, R.M., Seetharaman, G.: Wide-area persistent airborne video: architecture and challenges. In: Bhanu, B., Ravishankar, C., Roy-Chowdhury, A., Aghajan, H., Terzopoulos, D. (eds.) Distributed Video Sensor Networks. Springer, London (2011). https://doi.org/10.1007/978-0-85729-127-1_24
25. Transparent sky LLC. https://www.transparentsky.net. Accessed 20 Sept 2019
26. Knapitsch, A., Park, J., Zhou, Q.-Y., Koltun, V.: Tanks and temples: benchmarking large-scale scene reconstruction. ACM Trans. Graph. **36**(4), 1–3 (2017)

An Efficient and Reasonably Simple Solution to the Perspective-Three-Point Problem

Qida Yu$^{(\boxtimes)}$ (ID), Guili Xu (ID), and Jiachen Shi (ID)

College of Automation Engineering, Nanjing University of Aeronautics
and Astronautics, Nanjing 211106, China
{qidayu2007,guilixu,JCShi}@nuaa.edu.cn

Abstract. In this work, we propose an efficient and simple method for solving the perspective-three-point (P3P) problem. This algorithm leans substantially on linear algebra, in which the rotation matrix and translation vector are parameterized as linear combinations of known vectors with particular coefficients. We also show how to avoid degeneracy when performing this algorithm. Moreover, we present an approach to roughly remove invalid solutions based on the orthogonal property of the rotation matrix. The proposed method is simple to implement and easy to understand, with improved results demonstrating that it is competitive with the leading methods in accuracy, but with reduced computational requirements.

Keywords: Computer vision · Perspective-three-point (p3p) · Linear algebra

1 Introduction

The perspective-n-point (PnP) problem is aimed at determining the absolute pose (rotation and translation) of a fully calibrated camera from only a single view, by using n ($n \geq 3$) correspondences between known points in space and their projections on the image plane. It has numerous applications in the computer vision, photogrammetry, robotics, and augmented reality fields [1].

In particular, $n = 3$ is the minimal case for the PnP problem, which has up to four solutions [2]. The minimal P3P problem was first investigated by Grunert [3] in 1841, and has been of academic and practical interest since then. In algebraic geometry, the P3P problem can be interpreted as finding intersections of three quadrics [4], a circle and a ruled quartic surface [5], or two ellipses in the projective plane [6]. In practice, this kind of solver is used alternatively when it is difficult to extract sufficient feature points from textureless objects, or it can be used together with random sample consensus (RANSAC) to remove outliers from thousands of noisy data samples [4]. Both of these application scenarios require an efficient, accurate, and simple P3P solution.

© Springer Nature Switzerland AG 2021
A. Del Bimbo et al. (Eds.): ICPR 2020 Workshops, LNCS 12668, pp. 46–59, 2021.
https://doi.org/10.1007/978-3-030-68793-9_4

Existing commonly used solutions to the P3P problem can be divided into the following two categories: classical (triangulation) methods and direct methods. Early works were systematically analyzed and compared by Haralick *et al.* [7] in 1991. A milestone in the classical methods was the work of Gao *et al.* [8], in which the first complete analytic solution to the P3P problem was given, and the nature of various possible solutions was carefully characterized. Generally, classical methods first determine the distance between the camera center and three reference points by solving a quartic equation based on the law of cosines, then recovering the camera pose by aligning two triangles respectively described in the world and camera frames using the singular value decomposition (SVD) algorithm. One drawback to these classical methods is that their numerical accuracy highly relies on the computed distances. Furthermore, the implementation of SVD is quite time-consuming. Another milestone was the recent work of Persson *et al.* [6], which presented a novel triangulation method that can be solved by finding the sharpest root of a cubic polynomial.

A new geometric approach that directly computes the rotation and translation of a camera without triangulation was proposed by Kneip *et al.* [9] in 2011, and provides higher speed and accuracy than do the classical methods. To our best knowledge, it is the first direct method reported in the existing literature. Inspired by [9], Masselli *et al.* [10], Banno [11], Ke *et al.* [12], and Nakano [13] also put forward direct methods based on geometric or algebraic approaches. [9] and [12] parameterized the camera pose with an angle, while [10,11], and [13] derived a quartic polynomial with respect to a distance or a distance ratio. Though all these methods are direct and all the rotation and translation parameters can be linearly calculated after obtaining the intermediate variables, they do not directly solve for the rotation and translation parameters. Thus, the performance of P3P solvers can be further improved.

In this paper, we propose a novel direct method to the P3P problem, in which the rotation and translation are elegantly parameterized using linear combinations of two entries in a rotation matrix with three known vectors. Moreover, we show how to avoid degeneracy of the parameterization method used in this study. Because there is no need for intermediate variables, this technique has simpler formulations and fewer computing operations, and thus achieves a comparable numerical accuracy to that of competing methods, but with reduced computational requirements.

The rest of the paper is organized as follows. After a brief outline of the P3P problem in Sect. 2, we detail the proposed method in Sect. 3. Then the experimental results are presented in Sect. 4. Finally, conclusions are drawn in Sect. 5.

2   Problem Formulation

To be clear, throughout this paper, we use italic, bold lower-case, and bold upper-case letters to represent scalars, vectors, and matrices, respectively.

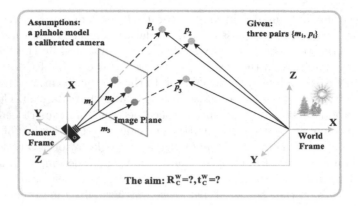

Fig. 1. The setup of the P3P problem.

The setup of the so-called P3P problem is illustrated in Fig. 1. Suppose that we have three 3D reference points $\{\mathbf{p}_i\}_{i=1}^3$ and their corresponding bearing measurements $\{\mathbf{m}_i\}_{i=1}^3$ such that $\|\mathbf{m}_i\| = 1$, where $\mathbf{p}_i$ and $\mathbf{m}_i$ are expressed in the world frame and camera frame, respectively. Based on the pinhole model of a calibrated camera, for each correspondence, we have:

$$d_i \mathbf{m}_i = \mathbf{R}_C^W \mathbf{p}_i + \mathbf{t}_C^W, \quad i \in \{1, 2, 3\}, \tag{1}$$

where d_i denotes the distance between the i-th reference point and the camera center, and the rotation matrix $\mathbf{R}_C^W \in SO(3)$ together with the translation vector $\mathbf{t}_C^W \in \mathbb{R}^3$ define the transformation from the world frame to the camera frame. The task is then to estimate the unknown $\mathbf{R}_C^W$ and $\mathbf{t}_C^W$ from the given $\{(\mathbf{p}_i, \mathbf{m}_i)\}_{i=1}^3$ using Eq. (1).

3 Proposed Method

3.1 Definition of a New Intermediate Coordinate Frame

To do this, our first step is to establish a new intermediate coordinate frame with $\{\mathbf{p}_i\}_{i=1}^3$, where $\mathbf{p}_1$ is set to be the new origin, the ray $\overrightarrow{\mathbf{p}_1 \mathbf{p}_2}$ coincides with the positive x-axis, and $\mathbf{p}_3$ lies in the xy-plane. In this case, its coordinate axes, i.e., $\mathbf{n}_x$, $\mathbf{n}_y$, and $\mathbf{n}_z$, are given by:

$$\mathbf{n}_x = \frac{\mathbf{p}_2 - \mathbf{p}_1}{\|\mathbf{p}_2 - \mathbf{p}_1\|}, \tag{2}$$

$$\mathbf{n}_z = \frac{\mathbf{n}_x \times (\mathbf{p}_3 - \mathbf{p}_1)}{\|\mathbf{n}_x \times (\mathbf{p}_3 - \mathbf{p}_1)\|}, \tag{3}$$

$$\mathbf{n}_y = \mathbf{n}_z \times \mathbf{n}_x. \tag{4}$$

Then we can transform $\{\mathbf{p}_i\}_{i=1}^3$ into the newly-defined frame, using:

$$\mathbf{p}_i' = \mathbf{N}^T(\mathbf{p}_i - \mathbf{p}_1), \quad i \in \{1, 2, 3\}, \tag{5}$$

where $\mathbf{N} = [\mathbf{n}_x, \mathbf{n}_y, \mathbf{n}_z]$ is a transformation matrix. Finally, we get:

$$\mathbf{p}_1' = \begin{bmatrix} 0 \\ 0 \\ 0 \end{bmatrix}, \mathbf{p}_2' = \begin{bmatrix} a \\ 0 \\ 0 \end{bmatrix}, \mathbf{p}_3' = \begin{bmatrix} b \\ c \\ 0 \end{bmatrix}, \tag{6}$$

where $a = \mathbf{n}_x^T(\mathbf{p}_2 - \mathbf{p}_1)$, $b = \mathbf{n}_x^T(\mathbf{p}_3 - \mathbf{p}_1)$, and $c = \mathbf{n}_y^T(\mathbf{p}_3 - \mathbf{p}_1)$. This technique, which was also used in some previous works [9] and [11], can make the point coordinates sparse, thus simplifying the subsequent derivation.

3.2 Formulation of New Transformation Equations

The next goal is to consider the P3P problem in this intermediate frame. Using the same geometry, it can be described as:

$$d_i \mathbf{m}_i = \mathbf{R}_C^o \mathbf{p}_i' + \mathbf{t}_C^o, \quad i \in \{1, 2, 3\}, \tag{7}$$

where

$$\mathbf{m}_i = \begin{bmatrix} x_i \\ y_i \\ z_i \end{bmatrix}, \mathbf{R}_C^o = \begin{bmatrix} r_1 & r_2 & r_3 \\ r_4 & r_5 & r_6 \\ r_7 & r_8 & r_9 \end{bmatrix}, \mathbf{t}_C^o = \begin{bmatrix} t_x \\ t_y \\ t_z \end{bmatrix}. \tag{8}$$

Writing Eq. (7) in matrix-vector form provides:

$$\mathbf{M}_1 \mathbf{v}_1 = \mathbf{0}, \quad \mathbf{M}_1 \in \mathbb{R}^{9 \times 12}, \tag{9}$$

where

$$\mathbf{M}_1 = \begin{bmatrix} 0 & 0 & 0 & 0 & 0 & 0 & 1 & 0 & 0 & -x_1 & 0 & 0 \\ 0 & 0 & 0 & 0 & 0 & 0 & 0 & 1 & 0 & -y_1 & 0 & 0 \\ 0 & 0 & 0 & 0 & 0 & 0 & 0 & 0 & 1 & -z_1 & 0 & 0 \\ a & 0 & 0 & 0 & 0 & 0 & 1 & 0 & 0 & 0 & -x_2 & 0 \\ 0 & 0 & a & 0 & 0 & 0 & 0 & 1 & 0 & 0 & -y_2 & 0 \\ 0 & 0 & 0 & 0 & a & 0 & 0 & 0 & 1 & 0 & -z_2 & 0 \\ b & c & 0 & 0 & 0 & 0 & 1 & 0 & 0 & 0 & 0 & -x_3 \\ 0 & 0 & b & c & 0 & 0 & 0 & 1 & 0 & 0 & 0 & -y_3 \\ 0 & 0 & 0 & 0 & b & c & 0 & 0 & 1 & 0 & 0 & -z_3 \end{bmatrix} \tag{10}$$

is a 9×12 coefficient matrix whose entries are known and $\mathbf{v}_1 = [r_1, r_2, r_4, r_5, r_7, r_8, t_x, t_y, t_z, d_1, d_2, d_3]^T$ is a vector to be solved. Equation (9) serves as the starting equation system of the solver proposed by Banno [11]. However, it is not in the simplest form as it contains $\{d_i\}_{i=1}^3$, which is not the objective of the P3P problem. To improve this, we eliminate d_i from the first two equations in Eq. (7) by taking pairwise divisions, and get:

$$\frac{x_1}{z_1} = \frac{t_x}{t_z}, \quad \frac{y_1}{z_1} = \frac{t_y}{t_z} \tag{11}$$

$$\frac{x_2}{z_2} = \frac{ar_1 + t_x}{ar_7 + t_z}, \quad \frac{y_2}{z_2} = \frac{ar_4 + t_y}{ar_7 + t_z}, \tag{12}$$

$$\frac{x_3}{z_3} = \frac{br_1 + cr_2 + t_x}{br_7 + cr_8 + t_z}, \quad \frac{y_3}{z_3} = \frac{br_4 + cr_5 + t_y}{br_7 + cr_8 + t_z}. \tag{13}$$

After arranging Eqs. (11–13) and combining them in matrix-vector form, six linearly-independent equations with nine unknowns are obtained:

$$\mathbf{M}_2\mathbf{v}_2 = \mathbf{0}, \quad \mathbf{M}_2 \in \mathbb{R}^{6\times 9}, \tag{14}$$

where

$$\mathbf{M}_2 = \begin{bmatrix} 0 & 0 & 0 & 0 & 0 & 0 & 1 & 0 & -\frac{x_1}{z_1} \\ 0 & 0 & 0 & 0 & 0 & 0 & 0 & 1 & -\frac{y_1}{z_1} \\ a & 0 & 0 & 0 & -a\frac{x_2}{z_2} & 0 & 1 & 0 & -\frac{x_2}{z_2} \\ 0 & 0 & a & 0 & -a\frac{y_2}{z_2} & 0 & 0 & 1 & -\frac{y_2}{z_2} \\ b & c & 0 & 0 & -b\frac{x_3}{z_3} & -c\frac{x_3}{z_3} & 1 & 0 & -\frac{x_3}{z_3} \\ 0 & 0 & b & c & -b\frac{y_3}{z_3} & -c\frac{y_3}{z_3} & 0 & 1 & -\frac{y_3}{z_3} \end{bmatrix}, \tag{15}$$

and $\mathbf{v}_2 = [r_1, r_2, r_4, r_5, r_7, r_8, t_x, t_y, t_z]^T$. Compared to $\mathbf{M}_1$, the size of $\mathbf{M}_2$ is smaller, which obviously can facilitate the algebra.

3.3   A Novel Parameterization Method

With Eq. (14), the first two columns of $\mathbf{R}_C^o$ and $\mathbf{t}_C^o$ can be parameterized by three parameters:

$$\mathbf{v}_2 = \alpha_1\mathbf{u}_1 + \alpha_2\mathbf{u}_2 + \alpha_3\mathbf{u}_3, \tag{16}$$

where $\{\mathbf{u}_i\}_{i=1}^3 \subset \mathbb{R}^9$ denotes a basis for $N(\mathbf{M}_2)$ (the nullspace of $\mathbf{M}_2$). After this, a common approach is multiplying $\frac{1}{\alpha_i}$ at both sides of Eq. (16) to further reduce one parameter. However, this may introduce degeneracies when α_i is equal to or very close to zero (this may happen in practice as the elements of $\mathbf{R}_C^o$ and $\mathbf{t}_C^o$ could be zero), which will result in a poor numerical accuracy.

To avoid this, we propose a novel parameterization method. As d_i represents the distance between a 3D point and the camera center, its value obviously should be positive and not close to zero. Hence, we instead adjust the scale by multiplying $\frac{1}{d_1}$ at both sides of Eq. (7). This provides:

$$\begin{bmatrix} t_x \\ t_y \\ t_z \end{bmatrix} = \begin{bmatrix} d_1x_1 \\ d_1y_1 \\ d_1z_1 \end{bmatrix}. \tag{17}$$

From the above displacement, Eqs. (12) and (13) can be rewritten as:

$$\frac{x_2}{z_2} = \frac{a\frac{r_1}{d_1} + x_1}{a\frac{r_7}{d_1} + z_1}, \quad \frac{y_2}{z_2} = \frac{a\frac{r_4}{d_1} + y_1}{a\frac{r_7}{d_1} + z_1}, \tag{18}$$

$$\frac{x_3}{z_3} = \frac{b\frac{r_1}{d_1} + c\frac{r_2}{d_1} + x_1}{b\frac{r_7}{d_1} + c\frac{r_8}{d_1} + z_1}, \quad \frac{y_3}{z_3} = \frac{b\frac{r_4}{d_1} + c\frac{r_5}{d_1} + y_1}{b\frac{r_7}{d_1} + c\frac{r_8}{d_1} + z_1}. \tag{19}$$

Similarly, we combine them in matrix-vector form, and get:

$$\mathbf{M}_3\mathbf{v}_3 = \mathbf{d}, \quad \mathbf{M}_3 \in \mathbb{R}^{4\times 6}, \mathbf{d} \in \mathbb{R}^4, \tag{20}$$

where

$$\mathbf{M}_3 = \begin{bmatrix} a & 0 & 0 & 0 & -a\frac{x_2}{z_2} & 0 \\ 0 & 0 & a & 0 & -a\frac{y_2}{z_2} & 0 \\ b & c & 0 & 0 & -b\frac{x_3}{z_3} & -c\frac{x_3}{z_3} \\ 0 & 0 & b & c & -b\frac{y_3}{z_3} & -c\frac{y_3}{z_3} \end{bmatrix}, \tag{21}$$

$$\mathbf{v}_3 = [s_1, s_2, s_3, s_4, s_5, s_6]^T, \tag{22}$$

$$s_1 = \frac{r_1}{d_1}, s_2 = \frac{r_2}{d_1}, s_3 = \frac{r_4}{d_1},$$
$$s_4 = \frac{r_5}{d_1}, s_5 = \frac{r_7}{d_1}, s_6 = \frac{r_8}{d_1}, \tag{23}$$

and

$$\mathbf{d} = \begin{bmatrix} \frac{x_2 z_1}{z_2} - x_1 \\ \frac{y_2 z_1}{z_2} - y_1 \\ \frac{x_3 z_1}{z_3} - x_1 \\ \frac{y_3 z_1}{z_3} - y_1 \end{bmatrix}. \tag{24}$$

Equation (20) is a non-homogeneous linear system, and $\mathbf{v}_3$ can be parameterized by only two parameters:

$$\mathbf{v}_3 = \beta_1 \mathbf{b}_1 + \beta_2 \mathbf{b}_2 + \mathbf{b}_3, \tag{25}$$

where $\mathbf{b}_3 \in \mathbb{R}^6$ is a particular solution to Eq. (25), and $\{\mathbf{b}_i\}_{i=1}^2 \subset \mathbb{R}^6$ is a basis for $N(\mathbf{M}_3)$. This parameterization yields a similar formulation as Eq. (16) (if we set $\alpha_3 = 1$), but it is more compact and the degeneracy is avoided. Now, our goal is to find such $\mathbf{b}_1$, and $\mathbf{b}_2$, and $\mathbf{b}_3$.

To accomplish this, we divide the augmented matrix $\mathbf{M}_4 = [\mathbf{M}_3, -\mathbf{d}]$ into a 4×4 matrix and a 4×3 matrix, i.e., $\mathbf{M}_4 = [\mathbf{M}_{4l} | \mathbf{M}_{4r}]$. As $\mathbf{M}_{4l}$ is invertible, we can calculate $\mathbf{b}_1$, $\mathbf{b}_2$, and $\mathbf{b}_3$ using:

$$\begin{bmatrix} \mathbf{b}_1 & \mathbf{b}_2 & \mathbf{b}_3 \\ 0 & 0 & 1 \end{bmatrix} = \begin{bmatrix} -\mathbf{M}_{4l}^{-1} \mathbf{M}_{4r} \\ \mathbf{I}_{3 \times 3} \end{bmatrix} \tag{26}$$

as

$$\mathbf{M}_4 \begin{bmatrix} \mathbf{b}_1 & \mathbf{b}_2 & \mathbf{b}_3 \\ 0 & 0 & 1 \end{bmatrix} \begin{bmatrix} \beta_1 \\ \beta_2 \\ 1 \end{bmatrix} = [\mathbf{M}_{4l} | \mathbf{M}_{4r}] \begin{bmatrix} -\mathbf{M}_{4l}^{-1} \mathbf{M}_{4r} \\ \mathbf{I}_{3 \times 3} \end{bmatrix} \begin{bmatrix} \beta_1 \\ \beta_2 \\ 1 \end{bmatrix}$$

$$= (-\mathbf{M}_{4r} + \mathbf{M}_{4r}) \begin{bmatrix} \beta_1 \\ \beta_2 \\ 1 \end{bmatrix}$$

$$= \mathbf{0}_{4 \times 1}, \tag{27}$$

where

$$
\mathbf{b}_1 = \begin{bmatrix} b_{1,1} \\ b_{2,1} \\ b_{3,1} \\ b_{4,1} \\ b_{5,1} \\ b_{6,1} \end{bmatrix} = \begin{bmatrix} \frac{x_2}{z_2} \\ \frac{b(\frac{x_3}{z_3} - \frac{x_2}{z_2})}{c} \\ \frac{y_2}{z_2} \\ \frac{b(\frac{y_3}{z_3} - \frac{y_2}{z_2})}{c} \\ 1 \\ 0 \end{bmatrix} ,
\tag{28}
$$

$$
\mathbf{b}_2 = \begin{bmatrix} b_{1,2} \\ b_{2,2} \\ b_{3,2} \\ b_{4,2} \\ b_{5,2} \\ b_{6,2} \end{bmatrix} = \begin{bmatrix} 0 \\ \frac{x_3}{z_3} \\ 0 \\ \frac{y_3}{z_3} \\ 0 \\ 1 \end{bmatrix} ,
\tag{29}
$$

$$
\mathbf{b}_3 = \begin{bmatrix} b_{1,3} \\ b_{2,3} \\ b_{3,3} \\ b_{4,3} \\ b_{5,3} \\ b_{6,3} \end{bmatrix} = \begin{bmatrix} \frac{-\frac{x_1}{z_1} + \frac{x_2}{z_2}}{a/z1} \\ \frac{a(-\frac{x_1}{z_1} + \frac{x_3}{z_3}) + b(\frac{x_1}{z_1} - \frac{x_2}{z_2})}{ac/z1} \\ \frac{-\frac{y_1}{z_1} + \frac{y_2}{z_2}}{a/z1} \\ \frac{a(-\frac{y_1}{z_1} + \frac{y_3}{z_3}) + b(\frac{y_1}{z_1} - \frac{y_2}{z_2})}{ac/z1} \\ 0 \\ 0 \end{bmatrix} .
\tag{30}
$$

From the components $b_{5,1}$ and $b_{6,2}$, we can get $\beta_1 = s_5$ and $\beta_2 = s_6$. With Eq. (25), the remaining parameters in $\mathbf{v}_3$ can be linearly represented by s_5 and s_6.

Because $\mathbf{R}_C^o \in SO(3)$, i.e., $\mathbf{R}_C^{oT} \mathbf{R}_C^o = \mathbf{I}_{3\times3}$ and $\det(\mathbf{R}_C^o) = 1$, where $\det(\cdot)$ denotes the determinant of a square matrix, we have:

$$
r_1 r_2 + r_4 r_5 + r_7 r_8 = 0,
\tag{31}
$$

$$
r_1^2 + r_4^2 + r_7^2 - r_2^2 - r_5^2 - r_8^2 = 0,
\tag{32}
$$

$$
r_1^2 + r_4^2 + r_7^2 = r_2^2 + r_5^2 + r_8^2 = 1.
\tag{33}
$$

Getting the expressions of s_1, s_2, s_3, and s_4, respectively, from Eq. (25), and then substituting them into Eqs. (31) and (32) result in two quadratic equations:

$$
g_0 s_5^2 + g_1 s_5 s_6 + g_2 s_5 + g_3 s_6 + g_4 = 0,
\tag{34}
$$

$$
h_0 s_5^2 + h_1 s_5 r_8 + h_2 s_6^2 + h_3 s_5 + h_4 s_6 + h_5 = 0,
\tag{35}
$$

where

$$g_0 = b_{1,1}b_{2,1} + b_{3,1}b_{4,1},$$
$$g_1 = b_{1,1}b_{2,2} + b_{3,1}b_{4,2} + 1,$$
$$g_2 = b_{1,3}b_{2,1} + b_{2,3}b_{1,1} + b_{3,3}b_{4,1} + b_{4,3}b_{3,1},$$
$$g_3 = b_{1,3}b_{2,2} + b_{3,3}b_{4,2},$$
$$g_4 = b_{1,3}b_{2,3} + b_{3,3}b_{4,3}$$
$$h_0 = -b_{1,1}^2 + b_{2,1}^2 - b_{3,1}^2 + b_{4,1}^2 - 1, \tag{36}$$
$$h_1 = 2b_{2,1}b_{2,2} + 2b_{4,1}b_{4,2},$$
$$h_2 = b_{2,2}^2 + b_{4,2}^2 + 1,$$
$$h_3 = -2b_{1,3}b_{1,1} + 2b_{2,3}b_{2,1} - 2b_{3,3}b_{3,1} + 2b_{4,3}b_{4,1},$$
$$h_4 = 2b_{2,3}b_{2,2} + 2b_{4,3}b_{4,2}$$
$$h_5 = -b_{1,3}^2 + b_{2,3}^2 - b_{3,3}^2 + b_{4,3}^2.$$

In Eq. (34), s_6 can be expressed as:

$$s_6 = -\frac{g_0 s_5^2 + g_2 s_5 + g_4}{g_1 s_5 + g_3}. \tag{37}$$

After substituting Eq. (37) into Eq. (35), a quartic polynomial in s_5 can be finally derived:

$$k_0 s_5^4 + k_1 s_5^3 + k_2 s_5^2 + k_3 s_5 + k_4 = 0, \tag{38}$$

where

$$k_0 = h_0 g_1^2 - h_1 g_0 g_1 + h_2 g_0^2,$$
$$k_1 = 2h_0 g_1 g_3 - h_1 g_0 g_3 - h_1 g_1 g_2 + 2h_2 g_0 g_2$$
$$\quad + h_3 g_1^2 - h_4 g_0 g_1,$$
$$k_2 = h_0 g_3^2 - h_1 g_1 g_4 - h_1 g_2 g_3 + 2h_2 g_0 g_4$$
$$\quad + h_2 g_2^2 + 2h_3 g_1 g_3 - h_4 g_0 g_3 - h_4 g_1 g_2 + h_5 g_1^2, \tag{39}$$
$$k_3 = -h_1 g_3 g_4 + 2h_2 g_2 g_4 + h_3 g_3^2 - h_4 g_1 g_4$$
$$\quad - h_4 g_2 g_3 + 2h_5 g_1 g_3,$$
$$k_4 = h_2 g_4^2 - h_4 g_3 g_4 + h_5 g_3^2.$$

To solve Eq. (38) analytically, we can employ either Ferrari's method as in [9] and [12], or the eigenvalue-based method (corresponds to *roots* function in MAT-LAB). Once the up-to-four roots for s_5 are determined, s_6 can be calculated by substituting s_5 into Eq. (37). To improve the accuracy, two iterations of Newton's method are applied on Eq. (38) to polish the roots. In addition, since $|r_i| \leq 1$, it follows that $|s_5| \leq \frac{1}{d_1} \leq \frac{1}{d_{min}}$, where d_{min} represents the minimal working distance (in meters) between an object and the camera, which can be known from the camera settings. This can be used to roughly remove invalid solutions.

Algorithm 1: The proposed method

Input: $\mathbf{p}_i$: three world points,
         $\mathbf{m}_i$: three bearing measurements
Output: $\mathbf{R}_C^W$: the rotation of the camera,
          $\mathbf{t}_C^W$: the translation of the camera
1 Convert world frame to intermediate object frame
2 Compute $\{\mathbf{b}_i\}_{i=1}^2$ and $\mathbf{b}_0$ from Eq. (26)
3 Compute the coefficients of Eqs. (34) and (35)
4 Compute the coefficient of Eq. (38)
5 Find n (up to four) solutions to Eq. (38)
6 (Optionally) Polish roots and remove invalid solutions
7 **for** $i = 1$ to n **do**
8 | Compute s_6 from Eq. (37)
9 | Compute the reamining parameters in $\mathbf{v}_3$ from Eq. (25)
10 | Recover d_1 from Eq. (40)
11 | Compute $\mathbf{R}_C^O$ and $\mathbf{t}_C^O$ from Eqs. (17) and (23)
12 | Reover the pose from Eqs. (41) and (42)
13 **end**

3.4   Retrieving the Pose

After attaining s_5 and s_6, the remaining four parameters in $\mathbf{v}_3$ can be easily computed from Eq. (25). Based on Eq. (33), the scale factor d_1 can be determined by:

$$d_1 = \sqrt{\frac{2}{s_1^2 + s_2^2 + s_3^2 + s_4^2 + s_5^2 + s_6^2}}. \tag{40}$$

Plugging d_1 into Eqs. (17) and (23), we can get t_x, t_y, t_z, r_1, r_2, r_4, r_5, r_7, and r_8, respectively. The ignored parameters r_3, r_6 and r_9 are obtained by a cross product of $[r_1, r_4, r_7]^T$ and $[r_2, r_5, r_8]^T$. Finally, the absolute pose of the camera is recovered by:

$$\mathbf{R}_C^W = \mathbf{R}_C^O \mathbf{N}^T, \tag{41}$$

$$\mathbf{t}_C^W = \mathbf{t}_C^O - \mathbf{R}_C^W \mathbf{p}_1, \tag{42}$$

and the proposed method is summarized in Algorithm 1.

4   Experimental Results

4.1   Experimental Setup

We compare numerical accuracy, noise sensitivity, and running time of the proposed method with those of the current state-of-the-art, including the solvers of Gao [8], Kneip [9], Banno [11], Ke [12], and Persson [6] in synthetic scenes. To generate synthetic data, a virtual camera is set to the following properties:

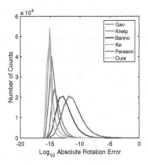 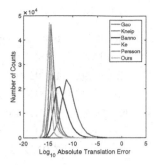

Fig. 2. Numerical accuracy of the proposed method and competing solvers.

a resolution of 640 × 480, a focal length of 800 pixels, and the principal point located at the image center. The world points are randomly distributed in a $[-2, 2] \times [-2, 2] \times [4, 8]$ box in the camera frame, and are then transformed to the world frame by a random rotation and translation. In this case, d_{min} is equal to 4. All the methods are implemented in MATLAB and run on a laptop with Intel Core i7-7700, 2.8 GHz CPU and 8 GB memory on Windows 10. The source codes are available as supplemental materials.

4.2 Numerical Accuracy

For numerical accuracy, rotation and translation errors between the ground truth and the estimate are estimated by computing the norm of the absolute difference of rotation and translation, respectively. We perform 10^5 trials without additional noise attacking the coordinates of image points to assess the numerical accuracy of different solvers. The distribution curves, mean and maximum of rotation and translation errors are presented in Fig. 2, Table 1 and Table 2, respectively. As illustrated, compared to the competing solvers, the entire distribution curve of the proposed method is more concentrated in the smallest errors, and the maximal error of the proposed method is in the second place (see Table 2). Additionally, the proposed method has its mean errors up to 10^{-13}, which is one order of magnitude better than others. These results imply that the proposed method is the most numerically accurate. Because Gao's solver needs to triangulate the points before recovering the pose, and because Banno's solver arrives at a univariate quartic equation using the Gröbner basis technique [14], which may encounter numerical issues [15], these solvers exhibited poorer results than the others in terms of numerical accuracy.

4.3 Noise Sensitivity

To investigate noise sensitivity, rotation errors are measured by the absolute differences of Roll-Pitch-Yaw angles, while translation errors are estimated in the absolute differences of X-Y-Z distances. To evaluate the performance of different solvers against image noise, different levels of zero-mean Gaussian noise

Table 1. Mean errors of different solvers

Method	Rotation error	Translation error
Gao [8]	7.38E−05	2.26E−04
Kneip [9]	1.98E−10	1.00E−09
Banno [11]	3.54E−08	4.05E−08
Ke [12]	5.75E−11	3.69E−10
Persson [6]	2.14E−12	2.60E−12
Ours	**7.01E−13**	**3.65E−13**

Table 2. Maximal errors of different solvers

Method	Rotation error	Translation error
Gao [8]	1.63	6.57
Kneip [9]	1.50E−05	7.92E−05
Banno [11]	1.50E−03	1.52E−03
Ke [12]	2.19E−06	1.57E−05
Persson [6]	**3.68E−08**	7.22E−08
Ours	5.53E−08	**1.74E−08**

with standard deviations varying from 0 to 5 pixels (step 0.1) are added to the image points. In total, 10^4 independent trials are carried out at each level, and the results are shown in Fig. 3. From the last two columns of the figure, we can find that all solvers are stable when noise exists, since errors increase approximately in a line with increasing image noise for all solvers and no big peaks are presented. The first two columns of Fig. 3 indicate that triangulation methods (Gao and Perrson) provide evaluations with lower accuracy in both rotation and translation errors than direct methods for the case where there is image noise. This could be understood, because error in triangulation methods is first propagated to the distances between the world points and the camera center, then to the camera pose. In this case, error is enlarged. The proposed method, along with Kneip, Banno, and Ke's solvers, do not encounter this problem and achieve comparable performance against varying noise. It is important to note that to make a fair comparison, root polishing is not used here for any solver.

4.4 Computational Time

To test the computational time, we perform 10^5 independent runs and calculate the average time for each solver. The average time over 10^5 trials for the proposed method is 109.3 μs, while those for Gao, Kneip, Banno, Ke, and Persson 's solvers are 309 μs, 150.8 μs, 123.8 μs, 133.9 μs, and 171.1 μs, respectively. Among the competing solvers, the proposed method is the fastest. It is respectively 64%,

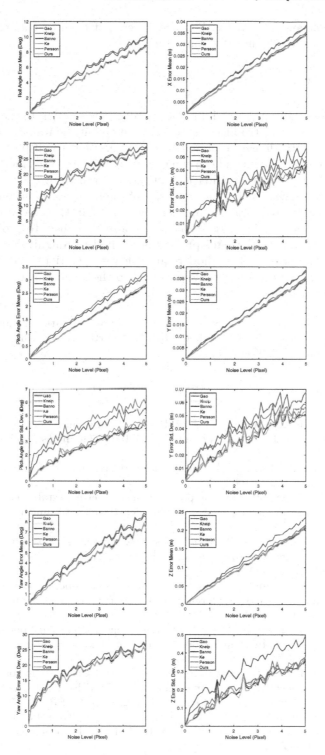

Fig. 3. Mean error and standard deviation of the camer pose against varying image noise for different solvers.

28%, 12%, 18%, and 36% faster than the solvers put forth by Gao *et al.*, Kneip *et al.*, Banno, Ke *et al.*, and Persson *et al.*

5 Conclusion

In this paper, we have presented an efficient algebraic solution to the P3P problem. Unlike the solver introduced in [11] that represent the rotation matrix and translation vector as linear combinations of a basis for a nullspace with three distance between 3D points and the camera center, the presented method parameterizes them using linear combinations of three known vectors with two entries of the rotation matrix. In this case, the size of the involved coefficient matrix is smaller (d_i is eliminated) and the problem can be elegantly solved without using the Gröbner basis technique. In addition, we also show how to avoid degeneracy during parameterization and propose a method to roughly remove invalid solutions. As the presented method requires fewer operations and has simpler formulations, it offers a comparable accuracy to the leading methods but with less computational time.

Acknowledgment. This work was supported partly by the National Natural Science Foundation of China under Grant 62073161, and partly by the China Scholarship Council under Grant 201906830092.

References

1. Lepetit, F., Moreno-Noguer, V., Fua, P.: EPnP: an accurate o(n) solution to the PnP problem. Int. J. Comput. Vis. **81**(2), 155–166 (2009). https://doi.org/10.1007/s11263-008-0152-6
2. Finsterwalder, S., Scheufele, W.: Das Rückwärtseinschneiden im Raum. Verlag d. Bayer. Akad. d. Wiss. (1903)
3. Grunert, J.A.: Das pothenot'sche problem, in erweiterter gestalt, nebst bemerkungen über seine anwendung in der. Archiv der Mathematik und Physik, 238–248 (1841)
4. Fischler, M.A., Bolles, R.C.: Random sample consensus: a paradigm for model fitting with applications to image analysis and automated cartography. Commun. ACM **24**(6), 381–395 (1981)
5. Nister, D.: A minimal solution to the generalised 3-point pose problem. In: IEEE Computer Society Conference on Computer Vision and Pattern Recognition (CVPR), June 2004
6. Persson, M., Nordberg, K.: Lambda twist: an accurate fast robust perspective three point (P3P) solver. In: The European Conference on Computer Vision (ECCV) (2018)
7. Haralick, R.M., Lee, D., Ottenburg, K., Nolle, M.: Analysis and solutions of the three point perspective pose estimation problem. In: IEEE Computer Society Conference on Computer Vision and Pattern Recognition (CVPR), pp. 592–598 (1991)
8. Gao, X.S., Hou, X.R., Tang, J.L., Cheng, H.F.: Complete solution classification for the perspective-three-point problem. IEEE Trans. Pattern Anal. Mach. Intell. **25**(8), 930–943 (2003)

9. Kneip, L., Scaramuzza, D., Siegwart, R.: A novel parametrization of the perspective-three-point problem for a direct computation of absolute camera position and orientation. In: IEEE Computer Society Conference on Computer Vision and Pattern Recognition (CVPR), pp. 2969–2976 (2011)
10. Masselli, A., Zell, A.: A new geometric approach for faster solving the perspective-three-point problem. In: 2014 22nd International Conference on Pattern Recognition (ICPR), pp. 2119–2124 (2014)
11. Banno, A.: A P3P problem solver representing all parameters as a linear combination. Image Vis. Comput. **70**, 55–62 (2018)
12. Ke, T., Roumeliotis, S.I.: An efficient algebraic solution to the perspective-three-point problem. In: IEEE Conference on Computer Vision and Pattern Recognition (CVPR), pp. 4618–4626 (2017)
13. Nakano, G.: A simple direct solution to the perspective-three-point problem. In: British Machine Vision Conference (BMVC) (2019)
14. Kukelova, Z., Bujnak, M., Pajdla, T.: Automatic generator of minimal problem solvers. In: Forsyth, D., Torr, P., Zisserman, A. (eds.) ECCV 2008. LNCS, vol. 5304, pp. 302–315. Springer, Heidelberg (2008). https://doi.org/10.1007/978-3-540-88690-7_23
15. Byröd, M., Josephson, K., Aström, K.: Fast and stable polynomial equation solving and its application to computer vision. Int. J. Comput. Vis. **84**(3), 237–256 (2009). https://doi.org/10.1007/s11263-009-0235-z

Modeling and Simulation Framework for Airborne Camera Systems

Marc-Antoine Drouin[1], Jonathan Fournier[2(✉)], Jonathan Boisvert[1],
and Louis Borgeat[1]

[1] National Research Council Canada, Digital Research Center, 1200 Montreal Road,
Ottawa, ON K1A 0R6, Canada
{marc-antoine.drouin,jonathan.boisvert,louis.borgeat}@nrc-cnrc.gc.ca
[2] Defence Research and Development Canada, Valcartier Research Center,
2459 De la Bravoure Road, Quebec, QC G3J 1X5, Canada
jonathan.fournier@drdc-rddc.gc.ca

Abstract. Full Motion Video (FMV) and Wide Area Motion Imagery
(WAMI) systems have been used extensively in the recent years to collect overhead imagery to produce value-added geospatial products. In
order to better understand the limitations of these systems and to define
the best flight conditions under which they can be operated, an integrated modeling and simulation (M&S) framework named Sensair was
developed. This paper presents how this tool can be leveraged to simulate
data collections with airborne camera systems using different parameters
under varied conditions. Sensair can simulate realistic large-scale environments with moving vehicles and generate representative FMV and
WAMI high-resolution imagery. The built-in interactive analysis tools
enable the study of the different factors impacting the application of
computer vision algorithms to aerial images. This paper presents Sensair's M&S capabilities and describes use cases where the framework is
used to perform tasks that include 3D reconstruction and the generation of an image dataset to support the evaluation of vehicle detection
approaches.

Keywords: Wide Area Motion Imagery (WAMI) · Full Motion Video
(FMV) · Modeling and simulation · Structure from Motion · Vehicle
detection

1 Introduction

In the recent years, Full Motion Video (FMV) and Wide Area Motion Imagery
(WAMI) systems have become reliable tools to collect overhead imagery to support different tasks such as aerial surveillance, traffic monitoring and disaster
response. These systems, which we will refer to as Airborne Camera Systems
(ACS) in the remainder of this paper, do, however, have performance limitations due to their inherent design and the flight conditions under which they
are operated. In order to better understand these limitations in the context of

© Crown 2021
A. Del Bimbo et al. (Eds.): ICPR 2020 Workshops, LNCS 12668, pp. 60–74, 2021.
https://doi.org/10.1007/978-3-030-68793-9_5

specific application tasks and to optimize the use of the ACS, repeated data collection experiments under different trajectories and settings have to be conducted. As this approach proves to be costly and time-consuming in practice, considerable gains can be achieved by combining the outputs of modeling and simulation (M&S) tools with real data to characterize and optimize the performance of ACS for specific applications.

In order to support this combined approach, the National Research Council Canada (NRC) and Defence Research and Development Canada (DRDC) have teamed up to develop an integrated and interactive M&S framework named Sensair. This tool enables the generation and simulation of different scenarios where configurable ACS can perform data collection under varied flight parameters and conditions. The built-in integrated analysis tools allow analysts to study the impact of different alternatives on the capability to perform tasks such as 3D reconstruction and vehicle detection using the simulated imagery. Sensair has several interactive tools that enable to study challenging data collection scenarios that cause performance issues for several computer vision algorithms.

A key example is terrain 3D reconstruction. This refers to the capability of generating a 3D model of a given environment using the imagery collected with an ACS. This process depends on a precise computation of the camera geometry of the ACS sensor in 3D space in order to generate accurate 3D models using Multi-view Stereo (MVS) techniques. Depending on the type of ACS, navigation aiding sensors such as GPS and Inertial Measurement Units (IMU) can be leveraged to perform this task. However, due to the fact that these sensors have intrinsic errors, it is common to combine their output with a Structure from Motion (SfM) pipeline to recover the camera geometry of the ACS sensors. Diverse applications of SfM and MVS to earth sciences are presented in [4,14,24]. M&S tools like Sensair enable analysts to better understand and evaluate how these approaches impact the 3D reconstruction results and allow them to optimize the acquisition pipeline.

Another possible use of imagery collected with FMV and WAMI ACS consists in performing traffic analysis in different urban environments. This enables to gather information on patterns of life which can then be used, for instance, to efficiently plan the routes of emergency response teams. Traffic analysis requires the capability to accurately detect vehicles in collected imagery. Similarly to the 3D reconstruction case, this requires to precisely know the camera geometry for each collected image. Knowing the camera geometry enables the application of approaches such as temporal background subtraction [2,25] to detect moving vehicles. In addition to allowing users to analyze the impact of different camera configurations and aircraft trajectories on vehicles detection techniques, Sensair also supports the generation of simulated vehicles with predetermined trajectories which enables the validation of the detection techniques under varied traffic conditions.

The remainder of this paper is divided as follows. Section 2 presents the related work. This is followed by an overview of Sensair capabilities in Sect. 3. Then, Sect. 4 describes the M&S of camera geometry and sensor platform.

Finally, Sect. 5 and 6 present experimental results, associated discussion and final remarks.

2   Related Work

Using simulated imagery to test and evaluate computer vision approaches has been a popular research topic over the last few years. Different types of simulation frameworks have been developed to support this effort. In [22], a drone simulation platform based on Unreal Engine (UE) was developed to support research in the field of deep learning and reinforcement learning for autonomous vehicles. In [19], UE is used to build a UAV simulator to evaluate real-time object tracking approaches. The game engine is also used in [5] to generate an annotated virtual image dataset for different types of environments. While simulators usually use 3D models with computer generated textures, simulated aerial image datasets can be generated with real ortho-photos [16]. This is the approach that is presented in this paper.

Simulation frameworks can be used to assess the performance of 3D reconstruction approaches using aerial imagery. In [9], Fournier *et al.* presents a workflow that combines imagery of a real scene with simulated images to study the performance of SfM. In [23], UAV imagery datasets are generated using the Blender modeling tool to assess the accuracy of SfM software. In [17], Lindner uses the Gazebo simulator to assess a multi-view path planning probabilistic approach that estimates the quality of reconstructed 3D models. A similar approach is applied in our work to simulate large scale urban environments. In [7], a feature extraction and tracking simulator enables the generation of synthetic 2D features to test and compare different SfM pipelines. In [15], simulated UAV data collections are processed with photogrammetry software to study the influence of image-based and geo-referencing parameters on the output of the SfM process. This is in line with our goal to develop tools to study the constraints and limitations applicable to the different stages of the SfM pipeline.

Aerial simulators can also be used to generate representative synthetic image datasets for WAMI systems. This approach is explored in [6] where a basic WAMI simulator enables the generation of simulated images based on configurable sensor model and flight parameters. Recent research papers often use the WPAFP[1] or CLIF[2] datasets to evaluate the performance of their vehicles detection and tracking approaches applied to WAMI imagery [1,21,26,27]. While the CLIF datasets does not contain annotation for vehicles, the WPAFP dataset contains metadata defining the location of moving vehicles. One issue with these datasets is that they were collected over only one region of interest at a specific date and time which prevent the development of generic detection algorithms. In [12], Griffith *et al.* attempts to address this issue by generating simulated wide area imaging sensor data based on trajectories generated using the SUMO traffic simulator along with representative terrain models. Our simulation framework

---

[1] https://www.sdms.afrl.af.mil/index.php?collection=wpafb2009.

[2] https://www.sdms.afrl.af.mil/index.php?collection=clif2007.

aims at providing similar capabilities while using photo-realistic 3D models. It also provides tools to inject synthetic data at the different stages of the vehicle detection and tracking pipeline to identify challenging scenarios.

3   Simulator Capabilities Overview

The Sensair M&S tool was primarily developed to study the influence of data collection parameters and hardware components selection on the capability to generate valuable geospatial products from aerial images collected with ACS. One of its key features is the capability of generating image sequences collected with simulated ACS that closely match their real counterparts.

Sensair was developed in C++ using the Qt framework[3] and OpenScene-Graph[4]. It was designed to run on both Windows and Linux platforms equipped with a NVIDIA video card.

In order to enable the reproduction of realistic large-scale environments, Sensair integrates advanced multi-resolution rendering techniques [3]. Figure 1 shows examples of such environments along with the corresponding generated synthetic imagery. Several formats of 3D terrain models are supported including Digital Elevation Models (DEM) which can be used to generate geospatial metadata associated to the simulated images (Fig. 1, bottom-left).

Sensair supports the inclusion of moving objects in the simulation (e.g. vehicles or drones). Their trajectories can either be imported from tools such as the Simulation of Urban Mobility (SUMO) multimodal traffic simulation package [18] or manually generated using a trajectory edition utility. This capability allows users to simulate different patterns of life in varied conditions. An example of generated vehicle trajectories is depicted in the bottom-right image in Fig. 1.

ACS with different camera configurations can be simulated with Sensair. This enables testing FMV and WAMI ACS with varied parameters including optical sensors with a resolution of more than 400 megapixels and cameras with specific intrinsic parameters. Navigation aiding sensors with accurate error models, such as IMU and GPS, can also be added to the simulation to create realistic image data collection experiments.

Several types of aircraft trajectories can be selected including orbits, survey mode and manual patterns. The trajectory parameters such as the altitude, speed and camera pointing location can be adjusted using the application's graphical user interface (GUI). It is also possible to import aircraft trajectories generated with other simulation tools as well as real aircraft trajectories flown during actual data collection experiments. Sensair includes several real-time input and output interfaces which enable it to be used as a digital twin for a real ACS and aircraft. It is possible for external applications to control the simulated platforms and sensors via web-based and TCP/IP remote control interfaces. Also, the generated imagery can be output in real time via different protocols including STANAG 4609 H.264, HD-SDI and a custom binary data format. This capability has been

---

[3] https://www.qt.io.

[4] http://www.openscenegraph.org.

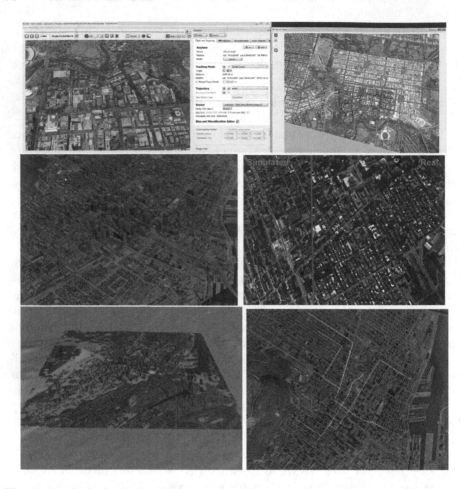

Fig. 1. Top Left: Sensair's main window showing a 3D model of Adelaide, Australia. Top Right: An overview of the complete Adelaide 3D model which comprises a high-resolution 3D model (highlighted in red) overlaid on a detailed ortho-photo. Middle Left: A view of a 3D model of Montreal, Canada. Middle Right: An image of Montreal generated by simulating a large-format camera. The left side of the figure shows a part of a simulated image generated with parameters selected to match a reference image shown on the right. Bottom Left: Image of the Montreal model with a Digital Elevation Model (DEM) shown in gray. Bottom Right: Trajectory of moving vehicles within the Montreal 3D model during a simulation. (Color figure online)

used in the past to simulate a real gyro-stabilized camera gimbal controlled via a TCP/IP connection that outputs video feeds via an HD-SDI connection. The different available interfaces could make it possible to integrate Sensair with other M&S frameworks such as the Robot Operating System (ROS) [20]. Figure 2 gives an overview of the different features implemented in Sensair.

Simulated entities	Image processing	Imaging Sensors
- Vehicles, drones (3D models)	- Style transfer (real to synthetic)	- Configurable optics
- Trajectory (SUMO, generation tool)	- Range image generation	- Configurable camera pose
- Terrain (DEM, 3D models)	- Feature matching	- Variable zoom and focal lengths

Interfaces	Camera geometry	Sensor platform
- Video streaming	- Epipolar geometry assessment	- Land and airborne platforms
- Images and trajectory recording	- Homography assessment	- Configurable trajectory
- Remote control interface and API	- Monte Carlo simulation	- Simulated GPS and IMU

Fig. 2. Overview of the features included in Sensair.

4   Camera Geometry and Sensor Platform

It is often desirable to precisely understand how the selection of flight parameters, sensor characteristics, and terrain can affect the performance of computer vision pipelines applied to ACS imagery. Those pipelines are usually composed of several processing steps. The first step generally consists in extracting and matching features in pairs of images (first column in Fig. 3).

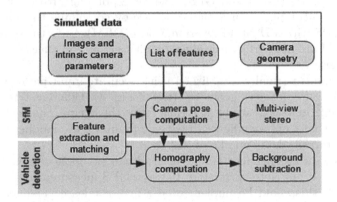

Fig. 3. Simulation injection points into the SfM and vehicle detection pipelines.

These features are used to recover the camera geometry (second column in Fig. 3). For the SfM pipeline, the camera geometry corresponds to the relative pose (position and orientation) of the camera for each image used in the 3D reconstruction. In the case of a vehicle detection pipeline, the camera geometry is the projective transformation (homography) required to register the images to one another. The final step of the pipeline is based on the recovered camera geometry. For the SfM pipeline, this step corresponds to the application of a multi-view stereo approach, while for the vehicle detection pipeline it consists of the background subtraction stage (last column in Fig. 3). Sensair can generate simulated data that can be injected at every step described previously using several uncertainty sources which are shown in Fig. 4.

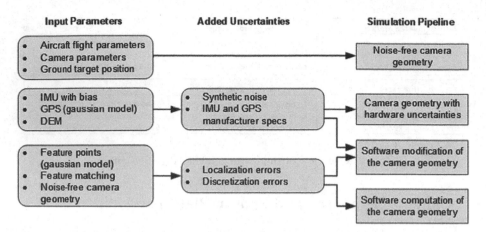

Fig. 4. Overview of the different input parameters and noise model that can be included in the proposed simulation and modeling pipeline.

The camera pose can often be estimated using a combination of inertial measurements units (IMU) and GPS. The corresponding projective transform can generally be computed for a planar surface by combining the outputs of an IMU and a GPS with a Digital Elevation Model (DEM). Unfortunately, as IMU, GPS and DEM are not perfect it is expected that errors will affect the estimated camera geometry.

The baseline is normally established using accurate input parameters which result in a noise-free camera geometry (top of Fig. 4). Different types of errors can then be introduced to study how each affect the overall pipelines. The first type of errors that can be configured relates to the navigation aiding sensors and the available terrain data (middle of Fig. 4).

As of now, an independent Gaussian error can be applied to GPS receiver measurements. While auto-correlation between GPS measurements is currently not simulated, this could be implemented a future release. The generation of GPS measurements can be configured with variable distribution and acquisition rates to match the specifications provided by the manufacturers.

In the case of gyroscopes and accelerometers contained in IMU, the error accumulates over time. For these components, the error is modeled by performing random walks and integration, and adding biases according to the specifications provided by the manufacturers.

DEM can also induce bias due to inaccuracy in elevation and limited spatial resolution. Sensair can load DEM with different resolutions and accuracy to evaluate the impact of this type of error.

In addition to navigation aiding sensors and DEM, the camera geometry can be computed and/or improved using approaches based on feature matching in image pairs. Sensair can generate synthetic feature points in image space that can be used to compute camera geometries. It is also possible to add Gaussian noise and discretization error on those features. This corresponds to the bottom part of Fig. 4.

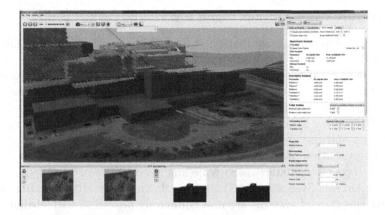

Fig. 5. Graphical interactive tool use to compute the tolerance on camera geometry error for the SfM pipeline applied to a given scenario. The main window displays a possible reconstruction from the synthetic images showed as a color-coded surface. Colors represent the misalignment of the epipolar geometry computed using a GPU-based Monte-Carlo simulation. (Color figure online)

In several cases, common processing pipeline fails to perform as expected because the selected flight parameters result in an unreliable estimation of the multi-camera geometry. Sensair includes interactive tools that can be used to quantitatively understand how a given combination of camera parameters, navigation aiding sensors, flight parameters, and image processing can affect the quality of the camera geometries that can be recovered. These tools can generate intermediate data in addition to simulated imagery to evaluate data processing pipelines. For a specific scene geometry, it is possible to determine the set of data collection parameters that will generate the minimum amount of parallax that is still sufficient to compute valid camera geometries for the SfM pipeline. The same interactive tools can also be used to determine the parameters resulting in the maximum tolerable amount of parallax that still enables the generation of valid camera geometries for a vehicle detection pipeline. In this case, it is possible to compute the maximum height of buildings in the scene to keep the reprojection error and the amount of occlusion under a manageable threshold. Figure 5 presents a view of a tool that can be used to assess the level of misalignment of epipolar lines [13]. This tool can be used to predict when the misalignment will cause a MVS algorithm to fail.

5 Experimental Results

The capabilities of the Sensair simulation framework were assessed via two experiments. The first one involved a multistage validation approach applied to the

SfM process. For the second experiment, a simulated aerial image dataset was generated to support the development of moving vehicles detection methods.

5.1   Structure from Motion Using FMV

Sensair has been used in combination with real imagery to evaluate the applicability of the SfM pipeline to different configurations of ACS. For one of these configurations, an ACS equipped with navigation aiding sensors coupled with cameras with a narrow field of view is used to collect oblique aerial imagery at high altitudes. This configuration is challenging because it requires the use of lenses with very long focal lengths. Also, the shallow angle between the camera's principal axis and the ground's normal makes 3D reconstruction very sensitive to accurate estimation of the relative poses between the camera images [9]. This differs from typical systems where wide-angle cameras are installed on small Unmanned Aircraft Systems (UAS) that are flown at low altitudes. Images collected with this type of systems are now commonly processed with available SfM pipelines [4,14,24].

While the results presented in this section are related to the ones presented in [9], the focus here is on the use of a 4-stage analytic procedure available in Sensair to perform a systematic investigation of complex computer vision workflows applied to challenging data acquisition scenarios.

In the first stage of the analysis, Sensair can perform Monte-Carlo simulations to evaluate the influence of different error sources on the 3D reconstruction process. This capability was used to identify a very challenging scenario where common SfM methods are expected to fail. The resulting scenario is described in Table 1. A Monte-Carlo simulation was also performed to evaluate a modified implementation of an SfM algorithm where the relative orientation provided by an IMU was used without refinement while the position of the platform, estimated using a GPS, was refined [9]. We named this algorithm SfM+Gyro. Results obtained with the Monte-Carlo analysis predicted that this scenario is less challenging for SfM+Gyro than SfM (see Table 2). All simulations were performed with Sensair at an interactive frame rate.

Table 1. Imaging parameters of the challenging scenario. The values are given for the scale model and for the corresponding real environment.

	Scale model (1:220)	Real size equivalent
Camera altitude	2.67 m	587 m
Target ground distance	11.89 m	2615 m
Target distance	12.12 m	2680 m
Camera field of view	2.4°	2.4°
Target area	0.45 m × 0.30 m	99 m × 66 m
Target height variation	0.12 m	26 m

For the second stage of the analysis, synthetic images were generated with Sensair and processed with both the SfM and SfM+Gyro pipeline. For this experiment, the SfM pipeline combined the outputs generated with Visual SfM [28] and the PMVS2 dense multi-view stereo matcher [10,11]. The SfM+Gyro pipeline described in [9] also used PMVS2. Both pipelines share the same feature extraction and matching modules (see Fig. 3). The results confirmed the Monte-Carlo analysis: the scenario is geometrically too unstable to be used with SfM modules using a common pose estimation procedure.

As shown in Fig. 3, Sensair can inject synthetic data at different points in the SfM pipeline. Using this capability, it was identified that, even when provided a list of valid image features, the pose estimation module was not able to compute valid camera poses. Tests performed with other SfM pipelines generated similar results.

Table 2. The standard deviation on the feature position is 0.3 pixel and 160 feature pairs are used. The Monte-Carlo simulation built into our software performs the computation two cameras at the time in order to preserve the interactivity of the software.

	Bias	Standard deviation
SfM	7.5 pixel	30 pixel
SfM+Gyro	1.2 pixel	0.1 pixel

The third stage involved using real imagery to validate the results obtained in the simulation. The same flight geometry and camera parameters used in Sensair were replicated to generate real imagery using a scale model. The scale model, shown in Fig. 6, was built from a commercially available z-scale train set and represents a small village with a railway. The description of this scale model is given in Table 1. Sensair contains a companion tool that can simulate the outputs of navigation aiding sensors. This tool was used to generate the datasets presented in this section. The image acquisition was performed using a 12-megapixel Point Grey Grasshopper monochrome camera. The scale model was installed on a turntable to simulate a data collection performed with an aircraft orbiting around the scene.

20 spherical photogrammetric targets were installed around the scale model. The precise position of the sphere's centers were then measured using a FARO arm. Based on these measurements, the companion tool was used to precisely compute the camera geometry associated with each image (the mean reprojection error for the spheres centers was 0.47 pixel). This enabled an accurate simulation of the navigation aiding sensors.

Ten sets of ten images at ten degrees intervals were acquired for this experiment. Both the basic SfM and the SfM+Gyro pipeline were applied to the collected imagery. Results obtained during the first two stages of the analysis were confirmed. As it can be seen in Fig. 6, the basic SfM approach failed to generate a valid 3D reconstruction, while the SfM+Gyro pipeline was able to generate a valid 3D model of the scene. Additional tests on the generated 3D models would be required to quantitatively assess the performance of the 3D reconstruction.

Ideally, a fourth stage of analysis would be performed using imagery collected with an actual ACS. The methodology presented in [8] could then be leveraged to create large-scale reference models with known uncertainty for evaluating the performance of SfM approaches using aerial images.

Fig. 6. Top: Example of an image of the scale model used for reconstruction. Bottom left: Result obtained using a popular SfM pipeline [10,11,28]. Bottom right: dense reconstruction model obtained using the SfM+Gyro pipeline [9]

5.2   Generation of a Simulated WAMI Dataset for Vehicle Detection

A simulated data collection over Montreal, Canada was performed to test the workflow required for Sensair to generate a representative WAMI dataset over a given urban environment. One of the reasons for selecting this particular city is that a large amount of geospatial data is made available on the city's Open Data portal[5]. The selected region of interest is an area of $36\,km^2$ centered on the Montreal Central Business District (CBD) (top left image in Fig. 7). Vehicle trajectories in this area were generated using the OpenStreetMap Web Wizard tool that is part of the SUMO traffic simulation framework. Both cars and trucks were added to the simulation using a *through traffic factor* of 50 and a *count* of 100. This resulted in 867 unique trajectories over a period of 21 min (top right image in Fig. 7).

The trajectories were imported into Sensair and overlaid on top of a textured 3D model of Montreal purchased on the 3D CAD Browser website[6]. Each trajectory was assigned a 3D model of a vehicle from a database of 8 vehicles.

---

[5] http://donnees.ville.montreal.qc.ca/.
[6] https://www.3dcadbrowser.com/.

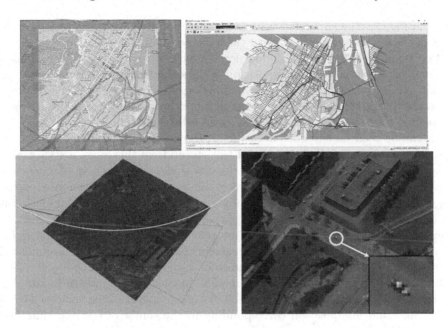

Fig. 7. Top left: Simulated region of interest. Top right: Trajectories generated in SUMO. Bottom left: Footprint of a single WAMI Camera. Bottom right: Simulated car added on the 3D model with a zoomed view of the car.

As the 3D model is geo-referenced, the imported trajectories aligned relatively well with the underlying terrain. However, an issue was identified with this approach. SUMO assumes a flat terrain when generating the trajectories. When these trajectories are imported into Sensair, the vehicles are assigned an altitude which is relative to the highest height of the 3D model. This results in situations where vehicles climb over overpasses instead of passing underneath them. We expect to fix this issue in the future.

The selected virtual WAMI ACS used for the simulation normally has four 29-megapixel cameras. However, due to the limited size of the Montreal 3D model, only one camera centered on the CBD was simulated. In the near future, we expect to replace our model of Montreal with a new one covering a larger area which will enable the simulation of the four cameras.

The simulated aircraft was configured to fly at an altitude of 15,000 ft along an orbit trajectory with a radius of 2 nautical miles. In order to match the specifications of a realistic WAMI ACS, a 60 mm lens was used and the frame rate was adjusted to 1.5 Hz. With this configuration, the expected average Ground Sample Distance (GSD) is 50 cm. An overview of the generated camera footprint is shown in the bottom left image in Fig. 7.

Sensair generated the full-resolution images at 0.1 Hz on an Intel Core i7 2.9 GHz with 32 GB of RAM and a NVIDIA P5000 Quadro graphic card. A sample image generated during the simulation is shown in the bottom right

image in Fig. 7. The simulated vehicle highlighted in yellow has a resolution of
4 × 8 pixels which is consistent with the expected GSD.

The 3D model used for the simulation is textured with images which already
have embedded shadows. As the position of the sun associated to these images is
unknown, it was decided not to cast shadows on the simulated vehicles to ensure
consistency with the model. However, this could be modified in the future as it
is expected that shadows have an impact on vehicle detection approaches.

As can be seen on the bottom of Fig. 7, the color reproduction of the simulated images has an artificial look and feel. To address this issue, a style transfer approach based on histogram matching was developed. This approach was
applied to the generated images using a limited number of references aerial
images captured over Montreal. A sample result is shown in the middle right
of Fig. 1. The left side of the figure shows part of an image simulated using
parameters selected to match one of the reference images shown on the right.
As can be visually assessed, the style transfer that was applied to the simulated
image results in a close match with the color map of the real image.

In addition to the simulated color images, associated ground-truth data can
also be generated with Sensair. This includes image masks of the vehicles as well
as the pixel and geo-position corresponding to the center of the bounding box
of the vehicles in the images.

The objective is to use the Montreal simulated dataset to test and evaluate
approaches for image registration and vehicle detection and tracking in WAMI
images. This will be done using the same methodology as described in the previous section where synthetic intermediate outputs will be generated to evaluate
the different steps of common vehicle detection and tracking pipelines.

6   Conclusion

The Sensair M&S framework presented in this paper provides tools to study
the factors impacting the processing of aerial images using computer vision
approaches. The analysis tools are specifically useful for examining scenarios
where the camera geometries are close to degenerate configurations.

One of the presented use cases demonstrates an integrated multi-stage simulation pipeline that studies the applicability of the SfM 3D reconstruction process
to aerial imagery. Having access to interactive analysis tools enables to better
understand complex pipelines such as SfM in a way that would not be possible by only using real imagery. We believe that integrated approaches based
on interleaving simulated and real-world experiments will be key in developing
efficient computer vision algorithms applicable to aerial imagery.

Another area where Sensair has proved to be a strategic tool is for the simulation of airborne data collection in varied urban environments. Its capability
to generate realistic aerial images with moving vehicles for this type of environment will undoubtedly be useful to develop efficient vehicle detection and tracking approaches. Here again, a smart integration of real annotated datasets with
simulated ones will enable the development of solutions that will be applicable

to a larger number of different environments and to imaging sensors operating in diverse conditions.

Future plans for Sensair include further developing its set of input and output interfaces to enable a more direct integration with existing imagery analysis software applications.

Acknowledgments. The development of the Sensair software and associated companion tools would not have been possible without the contribution of Philippe Massicotte, Shawn Peter, Michel Picard and Pengcheng Xi.

References

1. Abdelli, A., Choi, H.J.: A four-frames differencing technique for moving objects detection in wide area surveillance. In: 2017 IEEE International Conference on Big Data and Smart Computing (BigComp), pp. 210–214. IEEE (2017)
2. AlSaadi, A.H., Swamidoss, I., Almarzooqi, A., Sayadi, S.: Analysis of different background subtraction methods applied on drone imagery under various weather conditions in the UAE region. In: Dijk, J. (ed.) Artificial Intelligence and Machine Learning in Defense Applications, vol. 11169, pp. 181–193. International Society for Optics and Photonics, SPIE (2019)
3. Borgeat, L., Godin, G., Blais, F., Massicotte, P., Lahanier, C.: Gold: interactive display of huge colored and textured models. In: ACM SIGGRAPH 2005 Papers, SIGGRAPH 2005, pp. 869–877. ACM, New York (2005)
4. Carrivick, J.L., Smith, M.W., Quincey, D.J.: Structure from Motion in the Geosciences. Wiley, Hoboken (2016)
5. Chen, L., Liu, F., Zhao, Y., Wang, W., Yuan, X., Zhu, J.: VALID: a comprehensive virtual aerial image dataset. In: 2020 IEEE International Conference on Robotics and Automation (ICRA), pp. 2009–2016. IEEE (2020)
6. Cheng, B.T.: A simulation of wide area surveillance (WAS) systems and algorithm for digital elevation model (DEM) extraction. In: SPIE, vol. 7668, p. 76680A (2010)
7. Degol, J., Lee, J.Y., Kataria, R., Yuan, D., Bretl, T., Hoiem, D.: FEATS: synthetic feature tracks for structure from motion evaluation. In: 2018 International Conference on 3D Vision (3DV), pp. 352–361. IEEE (2018)
8. Drouin, M.A., Beraldin, J.A., Cournoyer, L., MacKinnon, D., Godin, G., Fournier, J.: A methodology for creating large scale reference models with known uncertainty for evaluating imaging solution. In: Proceedings of the 2014 Second International Conference on 3D Vision-Volume 02, pp. 137–144. IEEE Computer Society (2014)
9. Fournier, J., Drouin, M.A., Borgeat, L., Boisvert, J.: Image-based modeling from images collected with an airborne EO/IR sensor platform. In: NATO STO-MP-SET-241, pp. 12A–3. NATO (2017)
10. Furukawa, Y., Curless, B., Seitz, S.M., Szeliski, R.: Towards internet-scale multi-view stereo. In: 2010 IEEE Conference on Computer Vision and Pattern Recognition (CVPR), pp. 1434–1441. IEEE (2010)
11. Furukawa, Y., Ponce, J.: Accurate, dense, and robust multiview stereopsis. IEEE Trans. Pattern Anal. Mach. Intell. **32**(8), 1362–1376 (2010)
12. Griffith, E.J., Mishra, C., Ralph, J.F., Maskell, S.: A system for the generation of synthetic wide area aerial surveillance imagery. Simul. Model. Pract. Theory **84**, 286–308 (2018)

13. Hartley, R., Zisserman, A.: Multiple View Geometry in Computer Vision. Cambridge University Press, Cambridge (2003)
14. Iglhaut, J., Cabo, C., Puliti, S., Piermattei, L., O'Connor, J., Rosette, J.: Structure from motion photogrammetry in forestry: a review. Curr. For. Rep. **5**(3), 155–168 (2019)
15. James, M.R., Robson, S., Smith, M.W.: 3-D uncertainty-based topographic change detection with structure-from-motion photogrammetry: precision maps for ground control and directly georeferenced surveys. Earth Surf. Process. Land. **42**(12), 1769–1788 (2017)
16. Jurevičius, R., Marcinkevičius, V.: A data set of aerial imagery from robotics simulator for map-based localization systems benchmark. Int. J. Intell. Unmanned Syst. **8**, 177–186 (2019)
17. Lindner, S.: Optimization based coverage path planning for autonomous 3D data acquisition. Ph.D. thesis, Heidelberg University (2020)
18. Lopez, P.A., et al.: Microscopic traffic simulation using SUMO. In: The 21st IEEE International Conference on Intelligent Transportation Systems. IEEE (2018)
19. Mueller, M., Smith, N., Ghanem, B.: A benchmark and simulator for UAV tracking. In: Leibe, B., Matas, J., Sebe, N., Welling, M. (eds.) ECCV 2016. LNCS, vol. 9905, pp. 445–461. Springer, Cham (2016). https://doi.org/10.1007/978-3-319-46448-0_27
20. Quigley, M., et al.: ROS: an open-source robot operating system. In: ICRA Workshop on Open Source Software, Kobe, Japan, p. 5, no. 3.2 in 3 (2009)
21. Robinson, G., Zhang, D.: Object detection in wide area aerial surveillance imagery with deep convolutional networks. In: Research Experience for Undergraduates in Computer Vision 2016 (2019)
22. Shah, S., Dey, D., Lovett, C., Kapoor, A.: AirSim: high-fidelity visual and physical simulation for autonomous vehicles. In: Hutter, M., Siegwart, R. (eds.) Field and Service Robotics. SPAR, vol. 5, pp. 621–635. Springer, Cham (2018). https://doi.org/10.1007/978-3-319-67361-5_40
23. Slocum, R.K., Parrish, C.E.: Simulated imagery rendering workflow for UAS-based photogrammetric 3D reconstruction accuracy assessments. Remote Sens. **9**(4), 396 (2017)
24. Smith, M., Carrivick, J., Quincey, D.: Structure from motion photogrammetry in physical geography. Prog. Phys. Geogr. **40**(2), 247–275 (2016)
25. Sommer, L.W., Teutsch, M., Schuchert, T., Beyerer, J.: A survey on moving object detection for wide area motion imagery. In: 2016 IEEE Winter Conference on Applications of Computer Vision (WACV) (2016)
26. Sommer, L.: Systematic evaluation of moving object detection methods for wide area motion imagery. In: Proceedings of the 2015 Joint Workshop of Fraunhofer IOSB and Institute for Anthropomatics, Vision and Fusion Laboratory, p. 153 (2016)
27. Vella, E., Azim, A., Gaetjens, H.X., Repasky, B., Payne, T.: Improved detection for WAMI using background contextual information. In: 2019 Digital Image Computing: Techniques and Applications (DICTA), pp. 1–9. IEEE (2019)
28. Wu, C.: Towards linear-time incremental structure from motion. In: 2013 International Conference on 3D Vision-3DV 2013, pp. 127–134. IEEE (2013)

On the Development of a Classification Based Automated Motion Imagery Interpretability Prediction

Hua-mei Chen[1], Genshe Chen[1(✉)], and Erik Blasch[2]

[1] Intelligent Fusion Technology, Inc., Germantown, MD 20876, USA
gchen@intfusiontech.com
[2] MOVEJ Analytics, Dayton, OH, USA

Abstract. Motion imagery interpretability is commonly represented by the Video National Imagery Interpretability Rating Scale (VNIIRS), which is a subjective metric based on human analysts' visual assessment. Therefore, VNIIRS is a very time-consuming task. This paper presents the development of a fully *automated motion imagery interpretability prediction*, called AMIIP. AMIIP employs a three-dimensional convolutional neural network (3D-CNN) that accepts as inputs many video blocks (small image sequences) extracted from motion imagery, and outputs the label classification for each video block. The result is a histogram of the labels/categories that is then used to estimate the interpretability of the motion imagery. For each training video clip, it is labeled based on its subjectively rated VNIIRS level; thus, the required human annotation of imagery for training data is minimized. By using a collection of 76 high definition aerial video clips, three preliminary experimental results indicate that the estimation error is within 0.5 VNIIRS rating scale.

Keywords: Motion imagery interpretability · VNIIRS · National Imagery Interpretability Rating Scale · Deep learning · 3D-CNN

1 Introduction

The pervasive use of still and video imagery from advanced imaging sensors and computing systems produces a desire to quantify the interpretability of imagery. Hence, the Video National Imagery Interpretability Rating Scale (VNIIRS) has been developed. The VNIIRS defines different levels of interpretability based on the types of tasks an analyst can perform with videos of a given VNIIRS rating. The VNIIRS concept assists imagery analysts to perform demanding interpretation tasks as the quality of the imagery increases. Users of motion imagery exploit the interpretability of motion imagery as a guide to determine its relevance value. However, the availability of increasing volumes of motion imagery data makes it infeasible to rely on human analysts for rating all the motion imagery.

The VNIIRS standard is documented in *Motion Imagery Standards Board* (MISB) Standard 0901.2 [1]. A concurrent recommended practice MISB RP 1203.3 describes

© Springer Nature Switzerland AG 2021
A. Del Bimbo et al. (Eds.): ICPR 2020 Workshops, LNCS 12668, pp. 75–88, 2021.
https://doi.org/10.1007/978-3-030-68793-9_6

two equations, including 1) a video quality equation that predicts the overall appearance of the video and 2) the VNIIRS interpretability estimation equation, or *Motion Imagery Quality Equation* (MIQE) [2], that predicts the VNIIRS rating of a given video based on resolution, blur, noise, camera/platform motion, overall contrast, foreground contrast and motion, and artifacts. The difference between task-based interpretability and appearance-based video quality is defined by ITU-T Recommendation P. 912 [3]. MIQE has been previously used for the development of an automated VNIIRS assessment system [4, 5] as well as the General Image Quality Equation (GIQE) [6, 7]; however, experience has shown that measurements of interpretability from engineering metrics are not easily reconciled with measurements of interpretability from human analysts [8, 9].

The *value of aerial motion imagery* depends on the resolution, quality, and intended use. Standard aerial imagery typically involves a single camera pointing towards a region of interest from which to determine the dynamic content. The interpretability of such aerial imagery compounds for situations such as wide-area motion imagery (WAMI) where multiple cameras are collocated and the images are stitched together to increase the field of view. WAMI exploitation from aerial collects includes multi-object detection [10], coordinated target association [11], distributed processing [12], multi-object tracking [13], and image mosaicking [14]. The ability for aerial imagery to support operational needs of registration, detection, recognition, classification, and identification requires intelligent methods for processing. Examples inherent in any imagery processing pipeline is image compression with effects of image quality [15], interpretability degradation [16], and multiview reconstruction [17]. Additional motion imagery developments of semantic labeling [18] and tensor methods [19] enable fusion on different types of aerial imagery. For example, synthetic aperture radar (SAR) for moving targets [20] utilizes the NIIRS, but can be enhanced for a VNIIRS and advancements in deep learning [21].

This paper describes a fully automated VNIIRS estimation approach without resorting to MIQE. The idea is to cast VNIIRS estimation as a video classification problem and develop an advanced machine learning (ML) 3D convolutional neural networks (CNNs). To realize the ML approach, the video clip is segmented into many short, small video blocks (VBs). The classification result is a histogram of predicted labels/categories that can be used to estimate the VNIIRS level of the test video clip.

This paper is organized as follows. In Sect. 2, the VNIIRS standard is reviewed. Section 3 present works that are related to the present study. The *automated motion imagery interpretability prediction* (AMIIP) approach is detailed in Sect. 4, followed by experimental results in Sect. 5. Conclusions are provided in Sect. 6.

2   Video National Imagery Interpretability Rating Scale and Motion Imagery Quality Equation

Measures of visual interpretability are used in various ways: [1]

- By users to describe a user's visual interpretability needs
- By mission planners in predictive equations
- By users to measure visual interpretability of collected images
- By developers to assess sensor design and image interpretability

The VNIIRS is designed to quantify the interpretability of motion imagery through a set of pre-defined criteria for seven orders of battle or content domains[1]. Each of the written criteria contains the following five components: Analyst Task (such as 'track' or 'confirm'), Object of Interest, Associated Activity or Behavior, Environment, and optional Object Reference Examples. We refer to the criteria as the *VNIIRS components* in this paper. For instance, the following criterion is provided to define the level 5 VNIIRS rating in CULTURE content domain: *"Track the movement of - a car, SUV, van, or light truck- driving independently - on roadways in medium traffic - (mid & full-size cars & trucks: 5 m – 6 m length)."* The VNIIRS has interpretability levels ranging from 3 to 11, and each content domain has at least one task defined for each of the nine VNIIRS level.

Both sensor design parameters and imaging conditions affect the VNIIRS rating of Motion Imagery. For example, the sensor design parameters are relative edge response (RER), signal to noise ratio (SNR), *peak SNR* (PSNR) resolution or frame size, and compression are sensor design parameters; while the imaging conditions are *ground sample distance* (GSD), atmospheric conditions, target illumination, object and camera motion, and amount of clutters. Attempts have been made to objectively predict the VNIIRS based on these factors, and the result is *motion imagery quality equation*, or MIQE [2], which expresses the instantaneous interpretability estimate for the k_{th} frame as a function of resolution (in term of ground sampling distance, GSD), blur (in terms of relative edge response, RER), noise (in terms of peak signal to noise ratio in dB, PSNR), camera/platform motion, overall contrast, foreground contrast and motion, and artifacts as:

$$I_k = 14 - \log_2 GSD_k - \log_2\left(1/_{RER_k}\right) - \exp(0.5 \cdot (PSNR_c - PSNR_k)) \qquad (1)$$

$$-\Delta I_{camara} - \Delta I_{contrast} - \Delta I_{movers} - \Delta I_{artifacts}$$

where $PSNR_c$ is the critical point which has been experimentally determined to be 26 dB. Interesting readers are referred to [3] for the detailed definition of each involved variable as well as the recommended implementations.

3 Related Work

The current study is related to deep learning-based no-reference video quality assessment (NR-VQA). The goal of NR-VQA is to estimate the mean opinion score (MOS) of the video. In [3], video quality is formally defined as a metric of five levels: 1. Bad; 2. Poor; 3. Fair; 4. Good; and 5. Excellence. Nevertheless, other standardized quality ratings also exist, such as a continuous scale ranging from 1.0 to 100.0, but Huynh-Thu *et al.* [22] noted that there are no statistical differences between the different scales used for the same visual stimuli.

Among varies NR-VQA schemes [23–27], the work proposed by Varga [28] mostly resembles the work presented in this paper in the sense that both works cast video quality or interpretability prediction as a classification problem. Nevertheless, there are

---

[1] This is based on the standard MISB ST 0901.2. However, in the newest standard MISB ST 0901.3, criteria are defined for three orders of battle.

several differences. 1) In [28], Two-dimensional deep convolutional neural networks are employed to extract frame-wise feature vectors followed by varies element-wise fusion strategies to form video-level feature vector, while AMIIP utilizes a 3D CNN for feature extraction. 2) In [28], there is only one classification task involved in each video clip; while in the AMIIP approach, a large number of small video blocks (VBs) are extracted from each video clip and classification is performed on each VB. Finally, 3) in [28] a support vector regressor is employed to map the temporally pooled video-level feature vectors to perceptual quality scores, while AMIIP employs a simple linear classifier for classifying the encoded feature vector for each VB.

Another closely related area is video analysis through spatiotemporal features such as action recognition and content-based video classification. The spatiotemporal features in [29] for action recognition are learned by performing 3D convolutions on an image block of size 60 (H) × 40 (W) × 33 (D) which in turn is obtained by stacking five channels[2] of the input video block of size 60 (H) × 40 (W) × 7 (F). In [30] for content-based video classification, different strategies for extending the connectivity of a CNN in time domain are proposed and compared, including Late Fusion, Early Fusion and Slow Fusion, in addition to the base line Single Frame. In [31], a general-purpose spatiotemporal feature learning scheme, known as C3D, is proposed. C3D features the use of small 3×3×3 convolution kernels in all layers making it an appealing scheme for end-to-end deep learning applications. The AMIIP deep convolutional neural network is based on the C3D network structure with some modifications to accommodate the specific input sizes for the application. Specifically, AMIIP doubles the number of convolutional layers from Conv3a to Conv5b and adds Conv6 in the network architecture. Due to the deeper CNN architecture, to avoid the vanishing gradient problem [32], the concept of residual blocks is employed to build Conv3a to Conv5b network blocks. The details of the 3D CNN architecture are illustrated in Fig. 2. The imagery analysis is to maintain situation awareness [33] through an interpretability index demonstrating classification performance.

4   Methodology

The workflow of the proposed automated motion imagery interpretability prediction (AMIIP) method is shown in Fig. 1 which consists of three stages: Video Block (VB) Generation, 3D-CNN Based VB Classification, and VNIIRS Prediction. In the first stage of *VB Generation*, a large number of small video blocks are generated from the center part of the video, which is the part of the video that analysts focus on. In the second stage of *VB Classification*, each video block is fed into a 3D-CNN based classifier for label prediction. The result is a frequency histogram, which is then used for VNIIRS prediction at the third stage for *VNIIRS Prediction*. The details of each stage are provided next.

4.1   Video Block Generation

As shown in Fig. 1, the first stage of the proposed approach is video block generation. The output of this stage is a large number of fixed sized image volumes employed as

---

[2] The five channels are defined as gray, gradient-x, gradient-y, optflow-x and optflow-y.

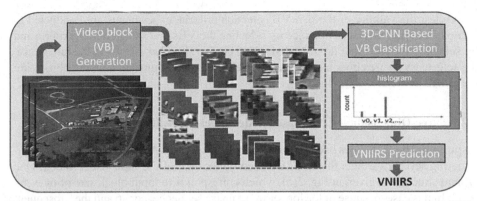

Fig. 1. Overview of the proposed automated motion imagery interpretability prediction (AMIIP) approach with (1) video block generation, (2) video block classification, and (3) VNIIRS prediction based on aggregate video block processing

inputs to the subsequent 3D CNN. There are at least two reasons that support the use of small video blocks instead of using the entire video. 1) Motion is an important cue for an image analyst to subjectively assign a VNIIRS level. To capture the information pertaining to motion, a reasonable number of consecutive frames need to be grouped instead of just three frames as employed by Tran *et al.* in [31] or seven frames by Ji *et al.* in [29]. As a result, the spatial extent has to be small enough in order to have a sufficient number of input data in one batch. 2) Like visual quality analysis of video, interpretability of motion imagery should be content independent. By keeping the spatial extent of video blocks from being too large, it is less likely that an object completely resides in a video block. In this work, different video block sizes are experimented. Specifically, the values tested of $\{\text{height}(h) \times \text{width}(w) \times \text{frames}(f)\}$ include $\{64 \times 64 \times 16\}$, $\{32 \times 32 \times 16\}$, and $\{64 \times 64 \times 32\}$. In our implementation, AMIIP applies a 3D sliding window approach at the center part of each frame with step sizes Δh, Δw, Δf equal to h, w, and $0.5f$ respectively.

Intuitively, an ideal VB should contain sufficient spatial (in x-y plane, or frame-wise) and temporal (in the z direction) variations. A frame without spatial variation is an indication of lack of foreground in the frame, and a volume without intensity variation along the z-direction which indicates either no object is present, or the object is not moving. For this reason, two VB selection criteria are devised to select VBs of large spatial and temporal variations. In the first criterion, *spatial STD test*, AMIIP first computes the standard variation of pixel intensities for each frame of a VB. Next, AMIIP denotes the median of the STDs of all frames in a VB as $\delta_{spatial}$. Then, a selected VB must satisfy:

$$\delta_{spatial} > Th_{spatial} \tag{2}$$

Likewise, in the second criterion, *temporal STD test*, AMIIP first computes the standard deviation of pixel intensities for each x-y position along z-direction for each VB. Next, AMIIP denotes the 99th percentile of the STDs of all x-y positions in a VB as $\delta_{temporal}$. Then, a selected small volume must satisfy:

$$\delta_{temporal} > Th_{temporal} \tag{3}$$

To test the validity of the two VB selection criteria, experiments are conducted to compare the performances obtained by selecting the VBs that satisfied both criteria and by selecting the VBs that do not satisfy both criteria. In other words, in the latter case, the selected VBs are either homogeneous in each frame or almost no moving objects are contained in them.

4.2 Three-Dimensional CNN Based Video Block Classification

Inspired by the C3D network structure shown in Fig. 2(a), AMIIP is designed by constructing several variants of the C3D based on the size of the input video block. One typical structure is given in Fig. 2(b), which corresponds to input block size of $64 \times 64 \times 32$. In this case, because of the longer input image sequence, conv6 and the subsequent max pooling layers are added to reduce the dimension of the feature vector. In addition, batch normalization, dropout and residual blocks are incorporated into the proposed AMIIP 3D CNN structure. The final feature vector has length 256 and the number of class is 9, which is explained in Sect. 5. For other variants of C3D, for example, when the input video block size is $64 \times 64 \times 16^3$, conv6 related layers such as bn6, relu6, and maxPool6 are removed.

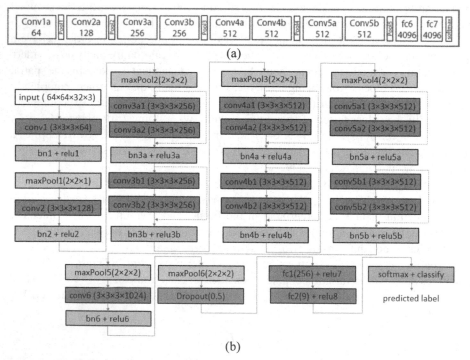

Fig. 2. (a) Basic C3D structure for video of size $112 \times 112 \times 16$. (b) The proposed 3D CNN structure for video block of size $64 \times 64 \times 32$.

---

[3] Different video block sizes are experimented in this paper.

4.3   Video NIIRS Prediction from Label Histogram

Results of the second stage for each test video clip can be represented as a label histogram as illustrated in Fig. 3, where each label in the horizontal axis corresponds to a different VNIIRS level. To obtain the predicted VNIIRS level for the test video clip, AMIIP simply computes the weighted average of the nearest 5 entries surrounding the highest histogram.

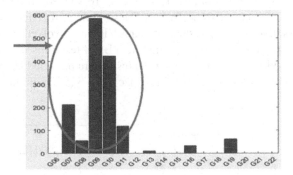

Fig. 3. VNIIRS prediction from label histogram

5   Experiments

As a preliminary study, in this section we report three experimental results using a set of 76 high definition aerial video clips among which 66 clips are used as the training data set and the remaining 10 video clips are adopted as test data set. All clips have been subjectively assigned non-integer VNIIRS levels ranging from 7 to 11 by several image analysts. Some information about the video clips including the duration, frame-size and frame-rate are provided in Table 1. The AMIIP classifiers are implemented in MATLAB. In all experiments, the batch size is 54 with stochastic gradient descent optimization with initial learning rate 0.001 and momentum 0.8.

Table 1. Information of video clips used in the experiments.

Clip length	Frame size (width × height)	Frame rate (fps)
10 s	1920 × 1080	25

5.1   Data Preparation

We first assign each training video clip a group label from G14 to G22 according to its ground truth VNIIRS levels rounded to half-integers. For example, the group G16 includes the training clips whose rounded VNIIRS values are 8. In other words, the ground truth VNIIRS values of the clips in the group G16 are between 7.75 and 8.25. In this way, we divide the 66 training clips into nine groups of different labels.

5.2 Experiment 1: Performance Comparison of Two Spatial Extents

In the experiment to compare *spatial extent*, we evaluate the performances of two different VB sizes, $64 \times 64 \times 16$ and $32 \times 32 \times 16$. AMIIP first generates VBs of size $64 \times 64 \times 16$ and select 22984 VBs by using both the spatial and the temporal STD tests given in Eqs. (2) and (3). Both thresholds are set to be 10. For VBs of size $32 \times 32 \times 16$, in order to use the same 3D CNN structure, AMIIP re-uses the generated VBs of size $64 \times 64 \times 16$ by dividing each VB into four $32 \times 32 \times 16$ VBs followed by up-sampling each $32 \times 32 \times 16$ VB to $64 \times 64 \times 16$ VB. The sampling procedure, as illustrated in Fig. 4, also ensures that exactly the same training VBs are involved in both cases. The same procedure is employed when preparing the VBs of test clips. Figure 5 shows the results of the 10 test video clips. The numerical results are provided in Table 2. Clearly, VBs of size $64 \times 64 \times 16$ outperform VBs of size $32 \times 32 \times 16$ in this experiment.

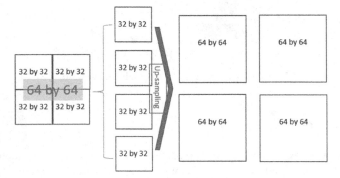

Fig. 4. Video Blocks generation in experiment 1 (spatial extent)

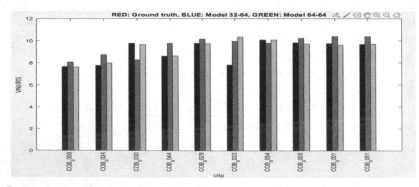

Fig. 5. Result of experiment 1. Blue: VBs of size $32 \times 32 \times 16$; Red: Ground truth; Green: VBs of size $64 \times 64 \times 16$. (Color figure online)

Table 2. Numerical result of experiment 1

Video Block	Total # of VBs	Mean error	STD
64 × 64 × 16	22984	0.67	0.35
32 × 32 × 16	91936 (22984 × 4)	0.86	0.34

5.3 Experiment 2: Performance Comparison of Two Temporal Extents

In the experiment to compare *temporal extent*, we evaluate the performances of two different VB lengths, 64 × 64 × 16 and 64 × 64 × 32. AMIIP first generates VBs of size 64 × 64 × 32 and select 23308 VBs by using both the spatial and the temporal STD tests given in Eqs. (2) and (3). Both thresholds are set to be 10. For VBs of size 64 × 64 × 16, in order to use exactly the same training data, AMIIP re-uses the VBs of size 64 × 64 × 32 by splitting each VB into two 64 × 64 × 16 VBs. This procedure is graphically illustrated in Fig. 6. Due to the different VB lengths, different 3D CNN structures are used as explained in Sect. 4.2. The experiment is repeated three times, resulting in three classifiers for each VB size. In addition, during the test phase, instead of using all VBs, AMIIP randomly selects 40 and 100 VBs per clip in order to speed up the prediction process. The same test VBs are used in all three runs. The results are provided in Fig. 7 and Table 3. From the results, we observe: 1) VBs of size 64 × 64 × 32 outperform VBs of size 64 × 64 × 16; 2) Selecting 100 VBs for each test clip outperforms selecting 40 VBs for each test clip; and 3) even when the same training VBs are used, performances of the three trained classifiers fluctuates. The first observation seems indicate that longer VBs captures motion information better than shorter VBs, while the second observation suggests that an insufficient number of test VBs per video clip deteriorates the performance.

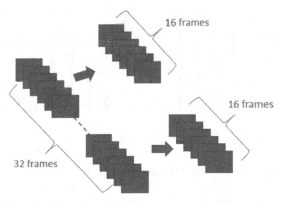

Fig. 6. Video Block generation scheme adopted in experiment 2 (temporal extent)

Table 3. Numerical results of three runs of the second experiment *(temporal extent)*.

VB length	# of VBs	Avg. error (40 VBs)	Avg. STD (40 VBs)	Avg. error (100 VBs)	Avg. STD (100 VBs)
32-1	23308	0.650	0.694	0.509	0.385
32-2	23308	0.560	0.561	0.410	0.260
32-3	23308	0.709	0.720	0.481	0.371
16-1	46616	0.689	0.503	0.538	0.380
16-2	46616	0.649	0.596	0.830	0.731
16-3	46616	0.681	0.477	0.560	0.378

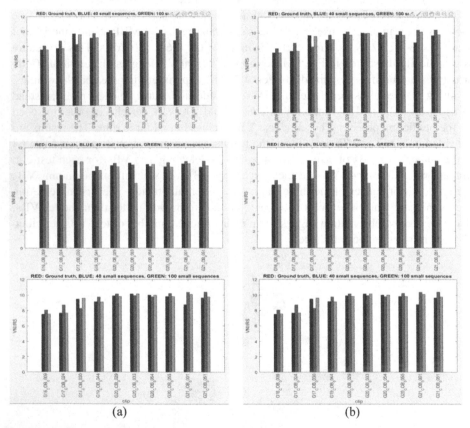

(a)   (b)

Fig. 7. Results of the second experiment (temporal extent). Each row is the results of one run of the experiment. (a) VBs of size $64 \times 64 \times 16$. (b) VBs of size $64 \times 64 \times 32$. Blue: 40 VBs per test clip. Red: Ground truth. Green: 100 VBs per test clip. (Color figure online)

5.4   Experiment 3: Test the Effectiveness of Both VB Selection Criteria

The final experiment tests the effectiveness of the spatial STD test and the temporal STD test for VB selection. Both tests are given in Eqs. (2) and (3). For this experiment, we adopt the setup of Experiment 2 for the case of VBs of size $64 \times 64 \times 32$, but the selected training VBs are those that fail both tests. In addition, we also test the performance of employing more VBs in the test phase. Table 4 and Fig. 8 show the results. In Table 4, the values in the first three rows are taken from the first three rows of Table 3. Surprisingly, although the performance resulting from those training VBs that pass both tests is better, the difference between them is not significant. It indicates that the *VBs that mostly contain homogeneous background and lack of moving objects do capture useful information for VNIIRS prediction*. However, the performances of the resulting classifiers seem not as stable as those resulting from using the classifiers trained by the VBs that pass both criteria.

Table 4. Numerical results of three runs of the third experiment (block selection).

VB selection tests	# of VBs	Avg. error (230 VBs)	Avg. STD (230 VBs)	Avg. error (100 VBs)	Avg. STD (100 VBs)
Pass – 1	23308	n/a	n/a	0.509	0.385
Pass – 2	23308	n/a	n/a	0.410	0.260
Pass – 3	23308	n/a	n/a	0.481	0.371
Fail – 1	18904	0.420	0.340	0.461	0.307
Fail – 2	18904	0.617	0.691	0.897	0.814
Fail – 3	18904	0.423	0.518	0.593	0.561

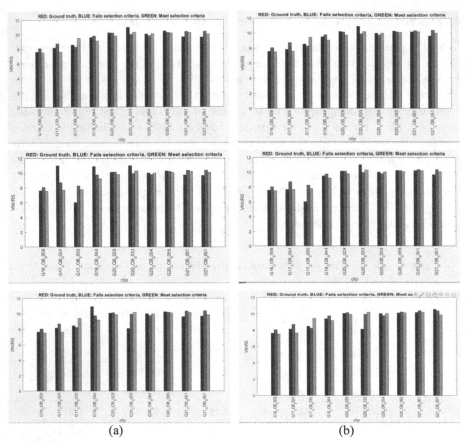

Fig. 8. Results of the third experiment (block selection). Each row is the results of one run of the experiment. (a) 100 test VBs per test clip. (b) 230 test VBs per test clip. Blue: VBs fail to pass both VB selection tests. Red: Ground truth. Green: VBs pass both VB selection tests. (Color figure online)

6 Concluding Remarks

In this paper, a fully automated approach for predicting the interpretability of motion imagery, based on advanced 3D convolutional neural networks is presented. The AMIIP (*automated motion imagery interpretability prediction*) predicts the interpretability of high definition aerial videos with VNIIRS ranging from 7 to 11, by casting it as a video classification problem. Due to the large frame size and the adoption of 3D CNN, AMIIP divides the entire video clip into many small video blocks (VBs) and predicts the VNIIRS level of a test clip based on the labels predicted for all VBs. The AMIIP 3D CNN structure is based on the C3D network that utilizes small 3D convolutional kernels. Using a set of 76 short HD aerial video clips, three preliminary experimental results demonstrate the feasibility of the proposed fully automated VNIIRS prediction.

One surprising observation is that VBs with mostly homogeneous backgrounds still contain information that can be used by the 3D classifier to distinguish clips with different interpretability. However, due to the limited video dataset tested, future work will investigate (1) more video data sets of different lengths, (2) different imagery types, and (3) multimodal analysis. The extent of these variations for robustness is required to consolidate and verify the findings reported in this paper.

References

1. MISB ST 0901.2: Video-National Interpretability Rating Scale, Feb 2014
2. MISB RP 1203.3: Video Interpretability and Quality Measurement and Prediction, Feb 2014
3. ITU-T Recommendation P.912, Subjective Video Quality Assessment Methods for Recognition Tasks, Aug 2008
4. Blasch, E., Kahler, B.: Application of VNIIRS for target tracking. In: Proceedings of SPIE vol. 9473 (2015)
5. Blasch, E., Kahler, B.: V-NIIRS fusion modeling for EO/IR systems. In: IEEE National Aerospace and Electronics Conference (2015)
6. Blasch, E., Chen, H-M., Wang, Z., Jia, B., et al.: Target broker compression for multi-level fusion. In: IEEE National Aerospace and Electronics Conference (2016)
7. Blasch, E., Chen, H-M., Wang, Z., Jia, B., et al.: Compression induced image quality degradation in terms of NIIRS. In: IEEE Applied Imagery Pattern Recognition Workshop (AIPR) (2016)
8. Zheng, Y., Dong, W., et al.: Qualitative and quantitative comparisons of multispectral night vision colorization techniques. Opt. Eng. **51**(8), 08004 (2012)
9. Zheng, Y., Blasch, E., Liu, Z.: Multispectral Image Fusion and Colorization. SPIE Press (2018)
10. Palaniappan, K., et al.: Moving object detection for vehicle tracking in wide area motion imagery using 4D filtering. In: International Conference on Pattern Recognition (ICPR) (2016)
11. Snidaro, L., García, J., Llinas, J., Blasch, E. (eds.): Context-Enhanced Information Fusion. ACVPR, Springer, Cham (2016). https://doi.org/10.1007/978-3-319-28971-7
12. Wu, R., Liu, B., Chen, Y., et al.: A Container-based elastic cloud architecture for pseudo real-time exploitation of wide area motion imagery (WAMI) stream. J. Signal Process. Syst. **88**(2), 219–231 (2017)
13. Al-Shakarji, N.M., Bunyak, F., Seetharaman, G., Palaniappan, K.: Robust multi-object tracking for wide area motion imagery. In: IEEE Applied Imagery Pattern Recognition Workshop (AIPR) (2018)
14. Aktar, R., AliAkbarpour, H., Bunyak, F., Seetharaman, G., Palaniappan, K.: Performance evaluation of feature descriptors for aerial imagery mosaicking. In: IEEE Applied Imagery Pattern Recognition (AIPR) Workshop (2018)
15. Zheng, Y., Chen, G., Wang, Z., et al.: Image quality (IQ) guided multispectral image compression. In: Proceedings of SPIE, vol. 9871 (2016)
16. Blasch, E., et al.: Prediction of compression-induced image interpretability degradation. Opt. Eng. **57**(4), 043108 (2018)
17. Gao, K., Yao, S., AliAkbarpour, H., Agarwal, S., Seetharaman, G., Palaniappan, K.: Sensitivity of multiview 3D point cloud reconstruction to compression quality and image feature detectability. In: IEEE Applied Imagery Pattern Recognition (AIPR) Workshop (2019)
18. Al-Shakarji, N.M., Bunyak, F., AliAkbarpour, H., Seetharaman, G., Palaniappan, K.: Performance evaluation of semantic video compression using multi-cue object detection. In: IEEE Applied Imagery Pattern Recognition (AIPR) Workshop (2019)

19. Prasath, V.B.S., Pelapur, R., Seetharaman, G., Palaniappan, K.: Multiscale structure tensor for improved feature extraction and image regularization. IEEE Trans. Image Process. **28**(12), 6198–6210 (2019)
20. Çetin, M., Stojanović, I., Önhon, N.O., Varshney, K., Samadi, S., et al.: Sparsity-driven synthetic aperture radar imaging: reconstruction, autofocusing, moving targets, and compressed sensing. IEEE Signal Process. Mag. **31**(4), 27–40 (2014)
21. Majumder, U., Blasch, E., Garren, D.: Deep Learning for Radar and Communications Automatic Target Recognition. Artech House, Norwood (2020)
22. Huynh-Thu, Q., Garcia, M.N., Speranza, F., et al.: Study of rating scales for subjective quality assessment of high-definition video. IEEE Trans. Broadcast **57**(1), 1–14 (2011)
23. Zhang, Y., Gao, X., He, L., et al.: Blind video quality assessment with weakly supervised learning and resampling strategy. IEEE Trans. Circuits Sys. Video Tech. **29**(8), 2244–2255 (2018)
24. Li, Y., et al.: No-reference video quality assessment with 3D shearlet transform and convolutional neural networks. IEEE Trans Circuits Sys Video Tech. **26**(6), 1044–1057 (2016)
25. Shahid, M., Rossholm, A., Lövström, B., Zepernick, H.-J.: No-reference image and video quality assessment: a classification and review of recent approaches. EURASIP J. Image Video Process. **2014**(1), 1–32 (2014). https://doi.org/10.1186/1687-5281-2014-40
26. Vega, M.T., Sguazzo, V., Mocanu, D.C., et al.: An experimental survey of no-reference video quality assessment methods. Int. J Pervasive Comp. Comm **12**(1), 66–86 (2016)
27. Xu, L., Lin, W., Kuo, C.C.J.: Visual quality assessment by machine learning. Springer, Berlin (2015)
28. Varga, D.: No-reference video quality assessment based on the temporal pooling of deep features. Neural Process. Lett. **50**(3), 2595–2608 (2019)
29. Ji, S., Xu, W., et al.: 3D convolutional neural networks for human action recognition. IEEE Trans. Pattern Anal. Mach. Intell. **35**(1), 221–231 (2012)
30. Karpathy, A., Toderici, G., et al.: Large-scale video classification with convolutional neural networks. In: IEEE Conference on Computer Vision and Pattern Recognition (2014)
31. Tran, D., Bourdev, L., et al.: Learning spatiotemporal features with 3D convolutional networks. IEEE International Conference on Computer Vision (2015)
32. He, K., Zhang, X., Ren, S., Sun, J.: Deep residual learning for image recognition. In: IEEE Conference on Computer Vision and Pattern Recognition, pp. 770–778 (2016)
33. Blasch, E., Seetharaman, G., et al.: Wide-area motion imagery (WAMI) exploitation tools for enhanced situation awareness. In: IEEE Applied Imagery Pattern Recognition Workshop (2012)

Remote Liveness and Heart Rate Detection from Video

Yunbin Deng[(✉)]

BAE Systems' FAST Labs, Burlington, MA, USA
Yunbin.deng@baesystems.com

Abstract. The remote detection of liveness is critical for senior and baby care, disaster response, the military, and law enforcement. Existing solutions are mostly based on special sensor hardware or the spectral signature of living skin. This paper uses commercial electro-optical and infrared (EO/IR) sensors to capture a very short video for low cost and fast liveness detection. The key components of our system include: tiny human body and face detection from long range and low-resolution video, and remote liveness detection based on micro-motion from a short human body and face video. These micro-motions are caused by breathing and heartbeat. A deep learning architecture is designed for remote body and face detection. A novel algorithm is proposed for adaptive sensor and background noise cancellation. An air platform motion compensation algorithm is tested on video data collected on a drone. The key advantages are: low cost, requires very short video, works with many parts of a human body even when skin is not visible, works on any motion caused by eyes, mouth, heartbeat, breathing, or body parts, and works in all lighting conditions. To the author's best knowledge, this is the first work on video micro-motion based liveness detection on a moving platform and from a long standoff range of 100 m. Once a subject is deemed alive, video-based remote heart rate detection is applied to assess the physiological and psychological state of the subject. This is also the first work on outdoor remote heart rate detection from a long standoff range of 100 m. On a public available indoor COHFACE data evaluation, our heart rate estimation algorithm outperforms all published work on the same dataset.

Keywords: Remote liveness detection · Micro-motion detection · Tiny body and face detection · Remote heart rate detection

1 Introduction

Remote detection of vital signs is necessary for situations where direct measurement of vital signs is infeasible, time consuming, or unsafe. Standoff detection of liveness has many life-saving applications in health care, security, law enforcement, and military, as detailed in Sect. 3. Existing solutions use radar [5], Doppler laser radar [6], and video-based spectral reflection change of the skin [8] to detect the human liveness at a distance. Although there are many computer vision studies on human pose estimation and tracking [4, 7], little attention is given to micro-motion detection on a mostly stationary person,

© Springer Nature Switzerland AG 2021
A. Del Bimbo et al. (Eds.): ICPR 2020 Workshops, LNCS 12668, pp. 89–105, 2021.
https://doi.org/10.1007/978-3-030-68793-9_7

especially for a person lying on the ground, sensing from a very long range, or sensing from a moving platform.

This paper makes use of widely available video sensors, which can be webcams equipped on most laptops, tablets, and smart phones. The video sensor can be common IR cameras for nighttime and military applications. The sensor can also be commonly-used surveillance cameras. This makes the standoff liveness detection low cost, easy to deploy, and widely applicable. In addition, this invention is based on micro-motion introduced by any part of the human body, including micro-motions introduced by breathing and heartbeat. Thus, it is not limited by the amount of skin visible to the camera. In fact, it works even when no skin is visible.

For most civilian application, liveness detection at a few meters can be useful. However, a safe distance of 50+ m are more desirable for most law enforcement and military applications. For time sensitive liveness detection in a large area, un-manned ground vehicles (UGV) and un-manned aerial vehicles (UAV) need to be deployed [21, 22]. The algorithm development needs to consider many practical issues, such as detection of humans and faces at a long distance with very few pixels, environment and sensor noise (i.e. sensor agnostic), and UAV sensor platform motion to detect micro-motions of a human body.

The key contribution of this paper is a proof of concept of video-based liveness detection from a long standoff range and on a moving platform based on human body micro-motion. We propose novel computer vision algorithms to compute local micro-motion heat maps, compensate sensor noise and platform motion, conduct various sensor data collection, and prove the effectiveness through experimentation. We describe the first work on outdoor 100 m range heart rate detection. Our heart rate estimation algorithm outperforms all other algorithms on a public indoor dataset.

This paper is organized as follows: Sect. 2 describes the design of experiment and data collection on a variety of sensors, Section 3 details technology components and experimental studies on liveness detection. We propose computationally - efficient algorithms for low resolution face and body detection (Sect. 3.A), facial micro-motion detection from EO and IR video (Sect. 3.B), solve practical issues of sensor and environment noise cancellation (Sect. 3.C), extend the algorithm to work with micro-motion from other parts of the human body (Sect. 3.D), study the impact of long standoff range and lower image resolution (Sect. 3.E), and propose an approach to moving platforms (Sect. 3.F). Section 4 describes our heart rate detection algorithm and evaluation on outdoor and indoor datasets; Sect. 5 discusses the potential application domains of this technology. Section 6 provides a summary and lists future work.

2 Design of Experiment and Data Collection

To author's best knowledge, there is no publicly-available dataset for remote liveness detection (LD) or remote heart rate detection (HRD). To test the performance of the proposed algorithms in all different application scenarios, we conducted data collection under the settings listed in Table 1. For each sensor, we listed the frame rate (frame per second), subject standoff range (meters), number of subjects, and purpose of study. The corresponding algorithm evaluation subsections of each dataset are listed at the last row in Table 1.

For shorter range indoor sets, a Logitech USB webcam C270 with HD 720p and a FLIR ONE PRO thermal camera are used [23]. The subjects are in sitting and lying postures.

To study the feasibility for long standoff range liveness and heart rate detection a SONY Exmor R 4k camcorder is used. The subjects performed three actions: standing still, walking toward the camera, and walking across the camera. This paper only reports the analysis on the standing still data. Each frame contained 3840 by 2160 pixels. The face in the video contains 95 by 102 pixels. The ground truth heart rates are recorded using a CMS 50-DL Pulse Oximeter. The data was collected at day- time without any dedicated light source. The data was collected in one day. The weather was cloudy with occasional drizzle.

The UAV liveness detection data are collected using an overhead camera on a DJI drone W232A. There subjects are asked to lie still on a soccer field. The data was collected on a very windy day. An example video frame is shown in Fig. 1.

Table 1. Liveness and heart rate detection setups

Environment	Indoor		Outdoor	
Sensors	Logitech Webcam	FLIR ONE	Camera on drone	SONY 4K camcorder
Frame rate	24	8.7	23	29
Range (m)	1, 3	1	21	50/100/150
# of subject	3	2	3	4
Purpose	LD	LD	LD	LD, HRD
Experiment	III.B, C, D	III.B	III.A,F	III.E,IV.A

We took videos of a male and female subject's photo at one meter range as negative examples for indoor liveness detection study. These videos should contain no subject motion. For outdoor liveness detection, we compare the motions from real subjects with the background scene. Our study serves as a proof-of-concept for remote liveness and heart rate detection. To verify the effectiveness the proposed algorithm, we also evaluated it on a publicly-available indoor short-range heart rate detection dataset, called COFACE. The results are reported in Subsect. 4.B.

3 Video-Based Remote Liveness Detection System

The liveness detection system works via the following steps: 1) detection of a person and face from the first image frame. In some extreme long range applications, such as air to ground, the person and face can be tiny and have very low resolution and a very limited number of pixels on the human body. The system first detects these tiny objects, and zooms in, or flies in, to get a better view if necessary. This generates a bounding box for each region of interest (ROI). 2) For each ROI, use the bounding box computed on the first frame to crop the images of all subsequent frames. 3) For each ROI, calculate the mean square error (MSE) between subsequent cropped sub-image and the first cropped sub-image. As we assume moving subjects are alive, the invention focuses on detection of micro-motions caused by breathing and heartbeat, but it works on any motion. 4) Estimate the sensor noise level. For simplicity, we take the MSE between the second frame and first frame as the sensor noise estimate. 5) Adaptive sensor noise cancellation. We subtract the sensor noise from all the MSEs between all subsequent frames and the first frame. 6) Apply a threshold and frequency analysis on the noise removed MSEs to make the liveness decision or plot a heat map of micro-motion for human in the loop detection. The details of each step are described in the following subsections.

A. *Low resolution person and face detection*

For wide area surveillance and air-to-ground applications, the captured video can have a very low resolution. Depending on the standoff range, the number of pixels on a person or face can vary widely. A multi-scale deep neural network (DNN) is trained on a multi-scale human body and face dataset and leverages scene context information. The DNN is then used to perform a multi-scale search for a person and face [3]. This allows robust detection of a person or a partial view of a person when the body image is less than 50 pixels tall. The moving platform can then come close to the target or zoom until the face image is about 20 pixels tall for robust face detection, as shown in Fig. 1. The faces of three people on the ground are all detected, with a bounding box on each face.

Fig. 1. A video frame from a DJI hovering drone shows three people on the ground. A DNN tiny face detection algorithm detected all three low resolution faces.

B. *Facial micro-motion detection from EO/IR video*

Signs of life can be represented in a video in the form of any motion. The bigger movement of body limb are easy to detect by both the naked eye and computer algorithms. This invention focuses on micro-motion introduced by breathing and heartbeat. The pumping of blood from the heart to the head causes the human head to exhibit oscillatory micro-vibrations patterns [1]. These can be captured by oscillatory motion of pixels on the head and face. We take any frame, for example the first frame, as a reference, and compute the Mean Square Error (MSE) between the subsequence frames and the first frame to represent this motion.

Specifically, let X represents a facial Region of Interest (ROI) sub-image, which is a matrix containing r rows and c columns of pixels. This can be a facial area for face-based micro-motion detection. Let $X(n)$, $n = 1, 2,..., M$, represent M consecutive ROI matrixes. We compute the MSE between subsequent ROI to the first ROI and get a new MSE sequences $Y(k)$, $k = 1,2,..., M-1$.

$$Y(k) = MSE\,(X\,(k+1), X\,(1)), \, for\, k = 1, 2, .., M-1,$$

An example of MSE time series of a man sitting still in a chair is shown in Fig. 2. The 30-s video was captured by a Logitech USB webcam. For this facial area EO video with micro-motion induced by breathing and heartbeat, the MSE time series displays an oscillatory behavior. The absolute difference between the first and last frame is shown in Fig. 3 left.

For non-oscillatory movement, such as eye movement or mouth movement, the computed MSE time series show larger values. An example of an MSE time series plot of a man sitting still in a chair but with some eye movement is shown in Fig. 4. Another example of an MSE time series plot of a man lying still sideways on the floor is shown in Fig. 5. All these MSE time series plots are based on about 30 s of EO video on facial area ROI.

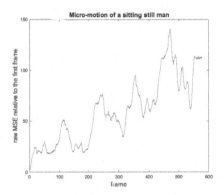

Fig. 2. A webcam MSE time series based on a detected facial region of a man sitting still.

The same algorithm is applied to an IR video. The FLIR ONE PRO IR sensor is connected to an iPhone and the video is captured using FLIR ONE App. An example of MSE time series of a man sitting still in a chair is shown in Fig. 6.

If there are no life signs of breathing or heartbeat, i.e., without any micro-movement in the video, the computed MSE time series only displays very small random fluctuations induced by sensor noise and environmental lighting variation noise. To illustrate this principle, videos of two still photos were taken. These two photos contain a woman's face and a man's face, respectively. Their corresponding MSE time series are similar. One of them is shown in Fig. 7. Compared to Figs. 1, 3, 4, 5, the MSE values are much smaller. As there is no motion in these two videos, the MSE time series only represents the sensor noise and lighting noise. The difference between the first and last frame is

Fig. 3. The difference between the last frame and first frame for Fig. 2 (shown on left) and Fig. 7 (right).

Fig. 4. A webcam MSE time series based on a detected facial region of a man sitting still with some eye movement.

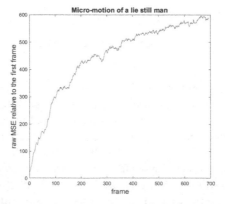

Fig. 5. A webcam MSE time series based on a detected facial region of a man lying still sideway.

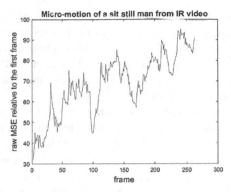

Fig. 6. A FLIR ONE IR MSE time series based on a detected facial region of a man sitting still.

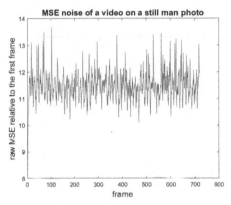

Fig. 7. MSE time series based on a detected facial region of a still photo. It only show sensor noise signal.

shown in Fig. 3 right, which shows no visible change. To perform sensor agnostic and lighting condition robust liveness detection, these noises need to be removed.

C. *Sensor platform motion compensation*

To make the liveness detection algorithm sensor agnostic and environmental condition robust, we need to cancel the noise introduced by the sensor and environmental lighting condition. For videos taken on a still photo, the computed MSEs should be zero for all frames if there were no noise. However, as show in Fig. 6, noise is shown in the computed MSE time series. We assume the lighting noise is low frequency in nature and the sensor introduces noise in each frame. Thus, the MSE between the second frame and the first frame (or the MSE between any two consecutive frames) represents only the sensor noise. This sensor noise can be removed by subtracting the first MSE from the whole MSE time series. Specifically, we define sensor noise normalized MSE as $Y\_norm(k)$, which can be derived from the raw MSE time series $Y(K)$ as follows:

$$Y\_norm(k) = Y(k+1) - Y(0), for\, k = 1, 2, .., M-2,$$

To illustrate the effect of sensor noise cancellation, a couple sensor noise compensated MSE time series are shown in Fig. 8 and Fig. 9. These are corresponding to the raw MSE time series shown in Fig. 3 and Fig. 7. After sensor noise cancellation, video with life sign-introduced micro-motions becomes obvious in the *Y_norm* plot of Fig. 8. The still video with no life signs only shows *Y_norm* with small random environmental lighting introduced noise, as shown in Fig. 9.

In a typical environment, the lighting condition does not change much within a few seconds, or up to 30 s. As shown in these real data, the lighting noise floor is much less compared with the signal presented by the life sign introduced micro-motion. However, for extreme lighting condition variations, the lighting noise may need to be further removed. This can be done by taking many sub-images from a large frame and finding the minimum *Y_norm*. The minimum *Y_norm* corresponding to the lighting noise and can be subtracted from other *Y_norm* time series to represent the sensor and light noise compensated MSE time series.

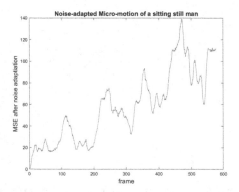

Fig. 8. Sensor noise compensated MSE time series based on a detected facial region of a man sitting still.

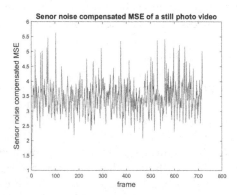

Fig. 9. Sensor noise compensated MSE time series based on a detected facial region of a still photo video. It shows only lighting noise signal.

D. *Effectiveness of micro-motion detection from other parts of human body*

All previously computed MSE time series and plots are based on ROI of a facial region. However, the facial region may not be available in all scenarios. Moreover, due to the limited published literature on this topic, it is not clear whether the face is the best region for micro-motion based video liveness detection. To gain insight, we captured a video of a whole human body lying on the floor. We windowed each frame of the video into grids of 100 by 100 pixels, and with a window shift of 30 pixels, and then computed the MSE time series in each grid. The maximum MSE value in each time series is used to present the motion at that grid. This creates a heat map of micro-motion on the video to illustrate the relative magnitude of micro-motion on various parts of a human body. The first frame of the video is shown in Fig. 10. Only the edge of the image is plotted for privacy concerns. The computed heat map is shown in Fig. 11. This heat map clearly shows the human chest area exhibiting large motion. This is due to breathing. We also notice some false motion at the left upper edge, although that is small compared with the motion at check region.

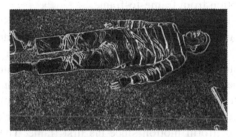

Fig. 10. The full body video of a person lying still and flat on a carpeted floor. Only the edge from the first frame of the video is shown.

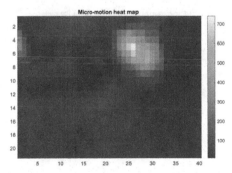

Fig. 11. The maximum of MSE time series of windowed grids on the video, shown as a heat map of micro-motions of the video in Fig. 9.

E.   *The impact of longer standoff range and lower resolution video*

The same face detection, MSE time series computation, and sensor noise compensation algorithms are applied to 100 m range video data. The raw MSE time series plot is shown in Fig. 12, which shows clear micro-motion signals well above lighting variation noise level. To simulate the impact of greater distance and less image resolution, the original video frames are down sampled by a factor of 10. The same algorithm is then applied to the down sampled video frames. The new detected face contains only 10 by 12 pixels. The raw MSE time series plot of this lower resolution video is shown in Fig. 13. Compared with Fig. 12, the impact on MSE time series is fairly small after the pixel is down sampled by a factor of 10.

F.   *Sensor platform motion compensation*

There are applications using a moving platform for sensor data collection, such as mounting an imagery sensor on a UAV. For reliable micro-motion detection from video captured from a moving platform, video stabilization has to be applied to compensate platform-introduced motion from frame-to-frame.

The video stabilization algorithm works via the following steps: 1) apply fast corner detection algorithm to generated salient points in each image frame. 2) for each two consecutive image frames, find the corresponding feature points using Fast Retina Key point (FREAK) descriptor and Hamming distance [19]. 3) Estimate a robust geometric affine transform from these noisy point correspondences using a variant of the RANSAC algorithm, called M-estimator Sample Consensus (MSAC) algorithm [20]. 4) Compute an accumulative scale-rotation-translation transform based on each pair of local transforms to represent the platform motion since the first frame. The video stabilization algorithm achieves real time computation with a frame rate of 12 FPS on a 2.7 GHz CPU laptop.

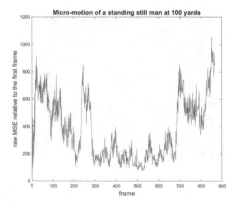

Fig. 12. MSE time series based on a detected facial region of a man standing still at 100 m range.

We apply this algorithm to the DJI drone hovering data shown in Fig. 1. After video stabilization, we compute the full frame heat map, similar to Sect. 3.D. We window each

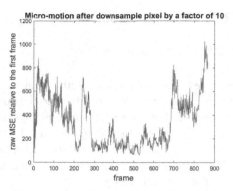

Fig. 13. Same plot as Fig. 12, but the original video resolution was down sampled by a factor of 10. The impact on MSE is very small

frame of the video into grids of 50 by 50 pixels, and with a window shift of 30 pixels, and then compute the maximum MSE at each grid. A Zoom-in view of the drone data micro-motion heat map is shown in Fig. 14. It clearly shows the motion of arms on chest, head and legs of the first person on the left, the motion of head, with arms and legs spread out of the second person in the middle, and the motion of head, arms and legs of the third person on the right. Although three people are lying still on the floor, the heat map clearly shows captured micro-motions of body parts well above the background noise level of the grass movement in a windy day.

Our system first conducted person detection and then performed micro-motion detection in the person region of interest. This way, non-human motion false alarms are all excluded. For all data collections listed in Table 1, 100% liveness detection accuracy is achieved with 1 s of video data. However, when the drone is too far from the subjects (>300 m), due to its lack of zoom function, there are not enough pixels to detect any person on the ground.

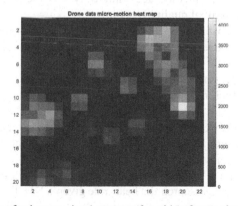

Fig. 14. Zoom-in view of micro-motion heat map for video frame shown in Fig. 1. There are three persons lying still on grass. The heat map captured micro-motion of heads, hands, and legs of three person.

4   Remote Heart Rate Detection from Video

A. *Remote Outdoor Heart Rate Detection from Video*

Once a subject is deemed alive based on the micro-motion analysis, video-based remote heart rate (HR) estimation is applied to assess the physiological or psychological state of the subject. Most existing studies on remote photoplethysmography (rPPG) are conducted indoors with a very limited standoff range of a few feet [9–12].

To study the feasibility of long standoff range outdoor heart rate detection, we use video data recording at 100 m range on four adult subjects standing still. A SONY Exmor R 4k camcorder is used for the video recording.

We designed our standoff heart rate estimation algorithm to balance accuracy and computational complexity. Our rPPG algorithm consists of the following steps:

1. Apply Dlib for 68 face landmarks detection [13]. To reduce the computation, the landmark detection is applied once for every 1 s of data.
2. The facial region, with the exclusion of mouth, eyes, eyebrow, and nose, is then divided into 5 by 5 pixels grids. The average pixel value of green channel is used to represent the signal of interest for each grid. The green channel has shown to give better performance than red and blue channel [14]. A 1-d time series is extracted for each grid with number of sample equal to the frame count. The number of grid is fixed for one video as we assume the subject is in stationary state.
3. A singular value decomposition (SVD) is applied on the high dimensional spatiotemporal time series.
4. A heuristic signal quality metric is defined to select a subset of high quality components in the SVD [15]. We use fast Welch Fourier transform to compute the energy in the frequency bands for real time performance. We then compute the quality of each component as the ratio of heart beat relevant frequency band energy to the overall energy.
5. The top components are merged accumulatively and the same quality metric is measured until the maximal quality is achieved.
6. Short time Fourier transform (STFT) is then applied to constructed signal.
7. The highest energy frequency component of STFT is considered the estimated heart rate at each time step, or
8. Perform dynamic programming to search the 'optimum' smoothed heart rate estimation curve, which is explained below.

Most published work uses the step 7 to compute the instantaneous heart rate from rPPG signal. However, due to the low SNR of the rPPG signal, the heart rate curve estimated this way often shows dramatic heart rate changes at each step. Given the prior that human heart rate typically doesn't change drastically at each time, we can enforce a smoothness constrains when search the heart rate given a STFT vector series. Similar idea was proposed for human gait pace estimation [28]. Our dynamic programming heart rate hypotheses smoothing algorithm works as follows:

1. Initially the heart rate scores at the time step is assigned as the absolute value of STFT at each time step, denoted as energy $E(m, n)$, where m is time steps, and m is the frequency bins of STFT.
2. From time step 2 till m, for each frequency bin, compute a combined scores of all previous time step energy and a weighted penalty term, which is square of frequency difference between previously time step and current time step. Find the maximum combined score and update the energy at current time step and frequency bin as the sum of initial energy and the combined score. Bookkeep the best frequency bin of previous step for each current step and each current frequency bin.
3. At time step m, find the maximum score among all frequency bins and back trace all the best frequency bins till time step 1. This give the 'optimum' smoothed heart rate time series.

This is the first empirical study of rPPG on 100 m standoff range outdoor data. The performance of heart rate estimation on these four subjects is shown in Table 2. Each video is about 30 s long and STFT is updated every 5 s. We take the mean of all STFTs as the estimate. The ground truth is read from the oximeter at the end of each video recording. The rPPG error is the relative percentage difference between the rPPG estimated HR and the Oximeter reading. The table shows even at 100 m range, heart rate can be estimated with a reasonable good accuracy by our algorithm. The table also shows the performance varies among subjects.

Table 2. 100 m Standoff rPPG performance

Subject	rPPG HR	Oximeter HR	rPPG Error
1	84	90	6.6%
2	74.4	93	20%
3	80.6	94	14.3%
4	75	79.5	5.7%
Average	78.5	89.1	11.7%

B. *Remote indoor Heart Rate Detection from Video*

There is no published work on outdoor long standoff range heart rate detection. To provide a comparison basis, we also applied our algorithm to a public available indoor dataset, called COHFACE dataset. The COHFACE data contains a total of 160 one-minute-long videos from 40 subjects, with 12 females and 28 males [16], [17]. The test set contains 64 videos. Videos are recorded with a standard webcam and data are sampled at 20 PFS. The data considers the case of well controlled lighting condition and natural indoor lighting conditions. We use COHFACE in this study as data is publicly available to industry. Many other public rPPG data sets are only shared among universities.

To extract the 'ground truth' heart rate time series from the COFACE data, we designed a peaking detection based method to the Blood-Volume Pulse data. It works slight better than Bio-signal processing in Python (Biosppy) toolkit [24]. We apply linear interpolation on ground truth data to match the time stamps where the rPPG estimates are made.

Our algorithm achieved average Root Mean Square Error (RMSE) of 8.67 beat per minute (BPM) on the test set of COHFACE. Our algorithm outperforms all evaluated algorithms in published work on the COHFACE data [16]. This is summarized in in Table 3. Our algorithm reduced the RMSE of the best published convolutional neural network approach from 10.78 to 8.34, which is 22.6% relative error reduction.

The great performance of our algorithm is mostly due to the exclusion of mouth, eyes, eyebrow, and nose region, the use of green channel, automatic selection of high quality rPPG signal grids for each video, and the novel idea of heart rate smoothing by dynamic programming search. This gives a more reliable and realistic heart rate estimation. This is very important when the natural light conditions is not controlled. This study has shown that our algorithm performs well on both indoor short range and outdoor long range natural lighting conditions.

Table 3. rPPG algorithm performance comparison on public available COHFACE indoor dataset

rPPG algorithm	RMSE (BPM)
2SR [27]	25.84
CHROM [25]	12.45
LiCVPR [26]	25.59
HR-CNN [18]	10.78
Ours without smoothing	9.55
Ours	8.34

5   Application Domains

The video micro-motion based liveness and heart rate detection is widely applicable to the military, homeland security, law enforcement, and civilian applications.

A. *Law enforcement and military application*

This is a low cost, efficient, and critical technology for the military. Similar to law enforcement and combat engagements, military forces need to search bodies of enemy combatants. There is a great risk when approaching the remains of a criminal or an enemy combatant as they may be pretending to be dead. The capability of detecting life or death at a safe distance can thus save lives.

B. *Disaster response*

Immediately following a mass casualty event, for example, a helicopter crash, or the terrorist bombing of a public event, the ability to quickly identify survivors from the dead can be very useful to rescue management. The remote liveness detection capability is extremely useful in disaster response scenarios. For example, the task of searching for survivors among collapsed buildings is hazardous and tedious work. Using an unmanned ground vehicle (i.e. Packbot) or quad-copter type unmanned aircraft system, with a liveness detection enabled sensor, the unmanned system can conduct a more effective search for survivors.

C. *Commercial and health care*

For commercial applications, the most notable are:

- Health monitor during pandemic. Standoff heart rate detection can be done much more efficiently than traditional methods. More importantly, it can be done in a non-invasive manner, without concerns for spreading a contagious virus.
- Baby and child monitoring for daycare and home. The ability of liveness and heart rate detection without placing any sensors on a child can give caregivers and parents solace. Especially when the child is sick, or there are concerns of Sudden Infant Death Syndrome, or the child is struggling to breathe.
- For senior care at nursing homes, seniors living alone, people with high risk of cardiac arrest [2], and general public area remote health monitoring. The video based liveness and heart rate estimation technique can detect such events within seconds to give a timely alert.
- For hospital, prison, depressed people with high risks of suicide, and ill people living alone. The video-based re-mote liveness detection can save these lives as well.
- For airport, border, and other security check point, the standoff detection of abnormal heart rate enables quick identification of potential high-risk suspects warranting further investigation.

6 Summary and Future Work

In Summary, the proposed micro-motion video liveness detection technology has shown effectiveness using various commercial-off-the-shelf EO and IR sensors, at various standoff ranges, and on moving platforms. It offers law enforcement and military personnel the ability to create a safe standoff from potential threats, and the ability to better assess the situation for disaster response. For civilians, this same technology could provide peace of mind to the parents and caretakers of infants, seniors, and people at higher health risk.

The future work of liveness detection should focus on developing a fully functional UGV and UAV system, which can automatically search for liveness in a cluttered environment. In addition, it needs to improve computational speed, system robustness, and performance of field test at longer distances. The future work of rPPG should investigate subjects with free body and head movement while performing daily routines, such as walking and running. This will enable many applications, for example, video surveillance and sports training monitoring.

Acknowledgment. The author of this paper would like to thank the Empower team of BAE Systems, Inc. for funding this project. Volunteers from the Empower team helped with data collection for this research. The author would also like to thank Dr. Stephen DelMarco, Mr. Derek Baker, ICPR and WAAMI reviewers for reviewing this paper.

References

1. Balakrishnan, G., Durand, F., Guttag, J.: Detecting pulse from head motions in video. In: Proceedings of the IEEE Conference on Computer Vision and Pattern Recognition, pp. 3430–3437 (2013)
2. https://www.procpr.org/blog/training/cpr-length
3. Hu, P., Ramanan, D.: Finding tiny faces. In: Proceedings of the IEEE Conference on Computer Vision and Pattern Recognition, pp. 951–959 (2017)
4. Neumann, L., Vedaldi, A.: Tiny people pose. In: Jawahar, C. V., Li, Hongdong, Mori, Greg, Schindler, Konrad (eds.) ACCV 2018. LNCS, vol. 11363, pp. 558–574. Springer, Cham (2019). https://doi.org/10.1007/978-3-030-20893-6_35
5. Polonskiy, L., et al.: U.S. Patent No. 7,417,727. U.S. Patent and Trademark Office, Washington, DC (2008)
6. Rice, R.R., Zediker, M.S.: U.S. Patent No. 5,867,257. U.S. Patent and Trademark Office, Washington, DC (1999)
7. Yazdi, M., Bouwmans, T.: New trends on moving object detection in video images captured by a moving camera: a survey. Comput. Sci. Rev. **28**, 157–177 (2018)
8. Yuen, A., Droitcour, A., Madsen, A.H., Park, B.K., El Hourani, C., Shing, T.: U.S. Patent No. 8,454,528. U.S. Patent and Trademark Office, Washington, DC (2013)
9. Deng, Y., Kumar, A.: Standoff Heart Reate Estimation from Video –A Review, SPIE Defense + Commercial Sensing Expo, April 2020, Online, CA
10. Verkruysse, W., Svaasand, L.O., Nelson, J.S.: Remote plethysmographic imaging using ambient light. Opt. Express **16**(26), 21434–21445 (2008). https://doi.org/10.1364/OE.16.021434
11. Procházka, A., Schätz, M., Vyšata, O., Vališ, M.: Microsoft kinect visual and depth sensors for breathing and heart rate analysis. Sensors **16**(7), 996 (2016)
12. Rouast, P.V., Adam, M.T.P., Chiong, R., Cornforth, D., Lux, E.: Remote heart rate measurement using low-cost RGB face video: a technical literature review. Front. Comput. Sci. **12**(5), 858–872 (2018). https://doi.org/10.1007/s11704-016-6243-6
13. Viola, P., Jones, M.J.: Robust real-time face detection. Int. J. Comput. Vision **57**(2), 137–154 (2004). https://doi.org/10.1023/B:VISI.0000013087.49260.fb
14. Lin, Y.C., Lin, Y.H.: A study of color illumination effect on the SNR of rPPG signals. In: 2017 39th Annual International Conference of the IEEE Engineering in Medicine and Biology Society (EMBC), pp. 4301–4304. IEEE, July 2017
15. Martinez, N., Bertran, M., Sapiro, G., Wu, H.: Non-contact photoplethysmogram and instantaneous heart rate estimation from infrared face video. In: 2019 IEEE International Conference on Image Processing (ICIP), Taipei, Taiwan, pp. 2020–2024 (2019)
16. The COHFACE Dataset made available by the Idiap Research Institute, Martigny, Switzerland. https://www.idiap.ch/dataset/cohface

17. Heusch, G., Anjos, A., Marcel, S.: A reproducible study on remote heart rate measurement. arXiv preprint arXiv:1709.00962 (2017)
18. Špetlík, R., Franc, V., Matas, J.: Visual heart rate estimation with convolutional neural network. In: Proceedings of the British Machine Vision Conference, Newcastle, UK, pp. 3–6, September 2018
19. Alahi, A., Ortiz, R., Vandergheynst, P.: Freak: fast retina keypoint. In: 2012 IEEE Conference on Computer Vision and Pattern Recognition, pp. 510–517. IEEE, June 2012
20. Torr, P.H., Murray, D.W.: The development and comparison of robust methods for estimating the fundamental matrix. Int. J. Comput. Vision 24(3), 271–300 (1997). https://doi.org/10.1023/A:1007927408552
21. Seguin, C., Blaquière, G., Loundou, A., Michelet, P., Markarian, T.: Unmanned aerial vehicles (drones) to prevent drowning. Resuscitation 127, 63–67 (2018)
22. Pensieri, M.G., Garau, M., Barone, P.M.: Drones as an integral part of remote sensing technologies to help missing people. Drones 4(2), 15 (2020)
23. FLIR ONE PRO User Guide, Third Gneration for Android and iOS
24. Carreiras, C., Alves, A.P., Lourenço, A., Canento, F., Silva, H., Fred, A., et al.: BioSPPy - Biosignal Processing in Python (2015)
25. De Haan, G., Jeanne, V.: Robust pulse rate from chrominance-based rPPG. IEEE Trans. Biomed. Eng. 60(10), 2878–2886 (2013)
26. Li, X., Chen, J., Zhao, G., Pietikainen, M.: Remote heart rate measurement from face videos under realistic situations. In: Proceedings of the IEEE Conference on Computer Vision and Pattern Recognition (2014)
27. Wang, W., Stuijk, S., De Haan, G.: A novel algorithm for remote photoplethysmography: spatial subspace rotation. IEEE Trans. Biomed. Eng. 63(9), 1974–1984 (2015)
28. Zhong, Y., Deng, Y., Meltzner, G.: Pace independent mobile gait biometrics. In: 2015 IEEE 7th International Conference on Biometrics Theory, Applications and Systems (BTAS), September 2015

RADARSAT-2 Synthetic-Aperture Radar Land Cover Segmentation Using Deep Convolutional Neural Networks

Mirmohammad Saadati[1]([⊠]), Marco Pedersoli[1], Patrick Cardinal[1], and Peter Oliver[2]

[1] École de Technologie Supérieure, Montreal, QC, Canada
mirmohammad.saadati.1@ens.etsmtl.ca,
{marco.pedersoli,patrick.cardinal}@etsmtl.ca
[2] MDA Corporation, 57 Auriga Dr, Ottawa, ON K2E 8B2, Canada
peter.oliver@mda.space

Abstract. Synthetic Aperture Radar (SAR) imagery captures the physical properties of the Earth by transmitting microwave signals to its surface and analyzing the backscattered signal. It does not depends on sunlight and therefore can be obtained in any condition, such as nighttime and cloudy weather. However, SAR images are noisier than light images and so far it is not clear the level of performance that a modern recognition system could achieve. This work presents an analysis of the performance of deep learning models for the task of land segmentation using SAR images. We present segmentation results on the task of classifying four different land categories (urban, water, vegetation and farm) on six Canadian sites (Montreal, Ottawa, Quebec, Saskatoon, Toronto and Vancouver), with three state-of-the-art deep learning segmentation models. Results show that when enough data and variety on the land appearance are available, deep learning models can achieve an excellent performance despite the high input noise.

Keywords: RADARSAT-2 SAR imagery · Deep convolutional neural network · Land cover classification · Semantic segmentation

1 Introduction

Land use and land cover (LULC) information has many applications in remote sensing [16] both in military and civil fields [4]. Automatic LULC classification plays a significant role in urban planning, natural resource management [10], forest monitoring [9], and understanding the rapid changes on the surface of the Earth [17]. Optical images can be obtained from the Earth's surface using aerial photography or satellite imagery. Another technique in satellite imagery

© Springer Nature Switzerland AG 2021
A. Del Bimbo et al. (Eds.): ICPR 2020 Workshops, LNCS 12668, pp. 106–117, 2021.
https://doi.org/10.1007/978-3-030-68793-9_8

i.e. Synthetic Aperture Radar (SAR) imagery, captures physical properties by transmitting electromagnetic energy (microwave signals), toward the surface of the Earth and measuring the distance between the sensor and the point on the Earth's surface where the signal is backscattered. Unlike optical satellite imagery which depends on natural light, SAR signals can penetrate through clouds and other obstacles e.g. rain and snow, and can be taken during night. Detecting changes in the Earth's surface e.g. changes in habitats, levels of water and moisture, effects of natural or human disturbance, etc. are some applications of SAR imagery [1].

Complex scattering characteristics caused by different wavelengths and incidence angles [7] introduce significant levels of noise in SAR images. The lack of large public labeled SAR datasets along with noisy images and imbalanced land cover categories contribute to the challenging nature of land cover classification using SAR imagery. In this work, a private dataset of multiple SAR images obtained by RADARSAT-2 satellite on major Canadian cities (Montreal, Ottawa, Quebec, Saskatoon, Toronto and Vancouver) is used to train different deep learning models. We compare the performance for pixel-level classification of four different land cover classes: Urban, Water, Vegetation and Farm. Multiple SAR samples obtained at different times over each city are averaged to reduce noise and increase the quality of the SAR image. Using stacked SAR data, three top performing deep semantic segmentation models are trained and evaluated. The proposed networks are proved to have excellent generalization performance. The achieved segmentation performance on unseen data, promises a general robust solution for automatic remote sensing, specifically land cover pixel-level classification.

2   Related Work

The research in remote sensing, specifically land cover classification, is mostly motivated by the lack of large annotated SAR datasets. In [7], a very deep pretrained residual network is fine tuned on natural images for remote sensing and validated on SAR data using transitive learning. A cost-sensitive top-2 smooth loss function is used to reduce the effect of imbalanced dataset with mislabeled training samples. In [15], a new dataset is developed to evaluate the performance of deep residual CNN models on polarimetric SAR scene classification. Using transfer learning, manifold polarimetric decompositions are incorporated into the model without losing the spatial features. In [14], a feature pyramid network (FPN), pretrained on ImageNet, is utilized to develop a model for multi-class segmentation of land cover on satellite imagery collected by DigitalGlobe's satellite. To reduce overfitting, a spatial dropout unit is deployed on the output layer. In [17], the labels of land cover and land use are utilized jointly to train a deep convolutional neural network for land cover classification.

Most of the research in land cover classification focuses on particular tasks over similar regions. Optical imagery is usually incorporated for label generation. More importantly, models are developed for image-level land cover classification.

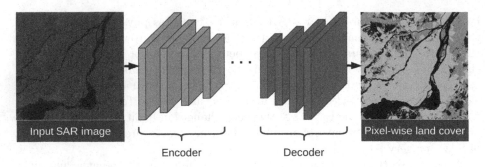

Input SAR image   Encoder   Decoder   Pixel-wise land cover

Fig. 1. Overview of our method. The illustrated CNN model is based on the Encoder-Decoder approach for semantic segmentation.

In this work, we train and validate deep segmentation models using SAR imagery only. Also, rather than image-level, we perform the classification on pixel-level.

3 Proposed Method

In this section, we present the proposed method. Starting by an overview to the method, and then presenting the architecture of deep CNNs used for semantic segmentation, we describe the details of our method.

3.1 Overview

We are given a set of data with land cover annotations, $D = \{I_n, Y_n\}_{n=1}^{N}$ where N is the number of images, I_n is the nth image, and Y_n is the pixel-level annotations. The land cover annotations have the same dimensions as the SAR image with only one channel. The value for each pixel represents the class label of that pixel. The land cover classes are annotated at 30-meter resolution. We aim to learn a CNN-based model in an end-to-end fashion for land cover segmentation by using the training data $X \subset D$.

The overview of our method is given in Fig. 1. Segmentation models that are used in this work, are designed based on two approaches. 1. *Convolutional Encoder-Decoder*, and 2. *Multi-Scale Pyramid Pooling*. In the **encoder-decoder** approach, first, encoder part of the network extracts meaningful features from the SAR image by transforming the image to a multidimensional vector representing features of the image [13]. The represented features are input to the decoder part of the network, where the target segmentation map is reconstructed by predicting pixel-wise class probabilities from extracted patterns [11]. In the **multi-scale pyramid pooling** approach, a residual network [6] works as the feature extractor. Using pyramid pooling, the feature maps are downsampled at multiple scales. Summarized pooled features are upsampled and concatenated with the initial feature maps to reconstruct the segmentation map by generating pixel-wise predictions [18]. The entire network is trained using cross entropy loss.

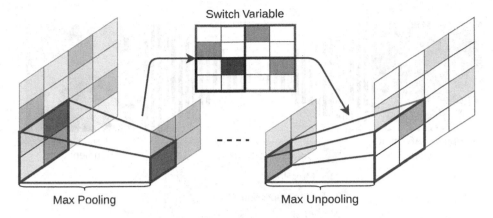

Fig. 2. Illustration of unpooling operation.

Working with extremely large SAR images – over 100 million pixels per image – it is impractical to train deep models without a proper sampling method where samples are smaller overlapping images preserving information around the borders, and only containing valid category labels. We use Deconvnet [13], Segnet [2], and PSPNet [18] for evaluating the performance of deep convolutional segmentation models with SAR images. Now, we provide more details about each model's architecture.

3.2   Encoder-Decoder

Most common deep models for image segmentation are based on the convolutional encoder-decoder architecture. The encoder network takes the input image, e.g. an image of a street full of cars, and extracts different patterns. The decoder network takes the extracted features and reconstructs a map of pixel-wise class probabilities, e.g. segmentation masks of cars, pedestrians, and trees.

Deconvnet. Based on the architecture of VGG 16-layer net, the encoder of Deconvnet consists of five pooling layers following five groups of convolutional layers with {64, 128, 256, 512, 512} channels. Two fully connected layers with 4096 features follow the last pooling layer. The decoder – deconvolution – network is designed by mirroring the encoder, replacing convolutional layers with transposed convolution operation and max pooling layers with max unpool operation. Every weighted layer is followed by batch normalization [8] and rectification [12] layers. The encoder network reduces the size of activations through convolution and pooling layers, and the decoder network enlarges the size of activations through deconvolution and unpooling layers [13]. The last layer of Deconvnet is a 1 × 1 convolution producing the score map for segmentation.

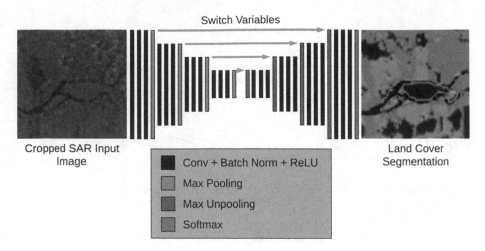

Fig. 3. Illustration of Segnet architecture. Switch variables are saved during downsampling and used to unpool the activations during upsampling.

Unpooling operation is used to reconstruct the spatial structure of input image for segmentation. The indices of selected activations during pooling are stored in a switch variable. The saved indices are then used for placing each activation back to its original pooled index. This operation is illustrated in Fig. 2.

Deconvolution operation is used to associate the sparse enlarged activations obtained by unpooling to a dense activation map using multiple learned filters. These filters learn to reconstruct the shape of input image. While the shape of SAR images are captures by the filters in lower layers of the decoder network, the filters in higher layers tend to learn the details of textures, that is used subsequently to predict the land cover labels for each pixel.

Segnet. The architecture of Segnet is almost identical to Deconvnet. However, Segnet promises better efficiency by removing the two fully-connected layers. Therefore, the pooled activations obtained from the last layer of encoder network are immediate inputs to the first layer of decoder network. One advantage of removing fully connected layers is the significant reduction in number of model parameters – from 134M to 14.7M. This improves generalization performance and reduces computational cost. Also, the feature maps at the deepest layer of decoder network retain higher spatial resolution. This helps the decoder network to reconstruct the segmentation map with finer details. Similar to Deconvnet, Segnet stores the indices of pooled activations in a switch variable used by unpooling layers to reconstruct the shape of segmentation map. The architecture of Segnet is illustrated in Fig. 3.

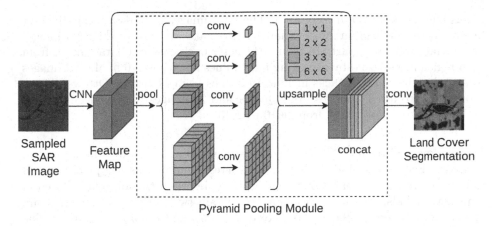

Fig. 4. Illustration of PSPNet architecture. Pyramid pooling is applied at four different resolutions to preserve global context information as well as finer details.

3.3 Pyramid Pooling

Spatial pyramid pooling (SPP) [5] is a pooling mechanism that is usually applied to the activations of the last convolutional layer. Assuming a fix number of bins, the feature maps are spatially divided into bins with sizes proportional to the input image. Using max pooling operation, SSP downsamples feature maps inside each bin individually. This results in an output vector of size $n \times C$, where n and C are the number of bins and the number of channels of input activations respectively. Bins are captured at different pyramid scales. Smaller bins contour fine-grained information; where larger bins include coarse-grained information. Lastly, the pooled features of bins within each scale are concatenated together forming a single feature vector.

PSPNet. Pyramid scene parsing network (PSPNet) proposes an effective global context prior for tackling complex scene parsing problems. Problems related to contextual relationship and global information e.g. mismatched relationship, confusion categories, and inconspicuous classes are addressed by pyramid pooling module in PSPNet. The architecture of PSPNet is illustrated in Fig. 4.

4 Experimental Results

In this section, we evaluate the proposed method. We describe the dataset and evaluation metrics. We also present our final results.

4.1 Dataset

The LCSAR dataset contains 116 high resolution SAR images from regions of Montreal, Ottawa, Quebec, Saskatoon, Toronto and Vancouver with land cover labels annotated at 30-m resolution. The SAR images are taken using different beam modes resulting in more variance in the dataset. Most of the SAR images are obtained 24 days apart. To reduce the noisy backscattered data, images from each region are stacked by averaging pixel values resulting in 6 final SAR images to sample from. These stacks include 19 images from Montreal, Ottawa, Saskatoon and Toronto, 18 images from Quebec and 23 images from Vancouver. The SAR images were obtained from 2010 to 2015.

Land Cover Classes. The land cover segmentation labels are summarized in 4 classes. Each class is identified with an integer number as the pixel value in the ground-truth segmentation image. Table 1 describes the four classes used in land cover labels. The land cover images contain two auxiliary classes that are identified by ID codes -999 and 0 labeled *Unknown* and *Empty* respectively. The unknown class describes that the correct land cover category is not determined; where, the empty class fills the blank area surrounding originally tilted SAR images – due to the angle offsets.

Table 1. Land cover classes. Vegetation class includes natural parks and forests, while Farm class labels include agricultural lands.

ID code	Class description	Color code
21	Urban	Green
31	Water	Water
41	Vegetation	Red
51	Farm	Yellow

Sampling Method. Loading very high resolution, single channel, gray-scale SAR images into GPU memory is not feasible, while experimenting on very deep segmentation models. Therefore, we adapt a sampling approach to reduce the resolution/size of the input image. A set of overlapping crops are generated from each SAR image with a kernel size of $K = (K_h, K_w)$ and a stride of $S = (S_h, S_w)$. In our experiments, square crops are sampled with $K_h = K_w$ and $S_h = S_w$. Discarding crops that contain invalid pixel labels (namely *Unknown* and *Empty*) helps to keep the data clean and inhibits outliers. The empty area surrounding tilted SAR images amounts to a considerable area labeled *(Empty)*, matching pixels where water is present that are captured almost black in SAR imagery. The number of sample crops, $|D|$, generated from an image with dimensions of (H, W) can be found using Eq. 1. This method is illustrated in Fig. 5.

$$|D| = \lfloor \frac{H - K_h}{S_h} + 1 \rfloor \times \lfloor \frac{W - K_w}{S_w} + 1 \rfloor \tag{1}$$

We experiment with the variants defined in Table 2. The size of training and validation sets decreases proportionally to the size of sampling stride.

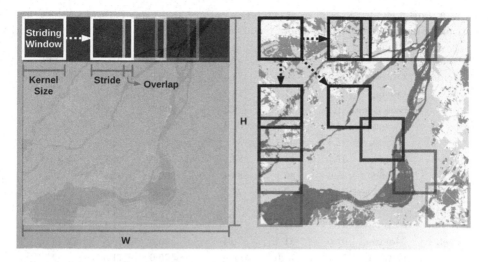

Fig. 5. Illustration of the sampling method. A crop of the SAR image on Montreal is shown on left with its corresponding land cover label on the right.

Therefore, using a smaller stride, we expect to gain generalization performance at the cost of longer training time.

Training and Validation Sets. The initial experiments on every SAR image are performed by fixing sampling size, model architecture, hyperparameters, and random initialization to evaluate the performance of each SAR image both for training and validation. The results of these experiments are reported in Table 3.

The difference in accuracy of each class is caused by two factors. First, the number of pixels of that class in training and validation samples. Second, the difficulty of classifying that class. In order to further investigate the performance of selected segmentation models and evaluate variables such as sampling size, we split the dataset into two fixed training and validation sets. We define the following split for training and validation:

- **Training Set**: SAR (Montreal, Quebec, Saskatoon, Vancouver)
- **Validation Set**: SAR (Ottawa, Toronto)

Table 2. Sampling modes. Larger stride size reduces the number of samples and the amount of overlap per sample.

Mode	Kernel	Stride	Overlap
(**L**)arge	224	112	112
(**M**)edium		152	72
(**S**)mall		192	32

Table 3. Initial results. Summary of validation performance using pairs of SAR stacks for training and validation sets. These results are obtained using SegNet model.

Train	Validation	Urban 21	Water 31	Vegetation 41	Farm 51	Average	Overall
Montreal	Ottawa	83.9	82.9	74.6	89.8	80.4	80.86
	Quebec	91.7	91.1	78.2	78.2	87.1	
	Saskatoon	81.5	0.7	6.3	92.8	75.0	
	Toronto	92.9	97.5	61.8	83.8	89.6	
	Vancouver	92.4	96.1	35.1	64.9	72.2	
Ottawa	Montreal	87.7	88.7	84.8	74.0	83.7	76.3
	Quebec	90.6	89.1	84.4	60.5	84.9	
	Saskatoon	78.3	2.0	24.9	88.0	73.8	
	Toronto	92.6	95.9	59.3	79.3	88.0	
	Vancouver	91.7	91.8	95.4	89.5	51.1	
Quebec	Montreal	91.0	81.4	70.4	65.0	79.8	72.44
	Ottawa	77.3	71.0	66.9	75.6	71.5	
	Saskatoon	84.6	0.7	18.7	64.7	61.8	
	Toronto	92.7	94.4	29.3	70.7	83.9	
	Vancouver	86.4	92.1	25.1	41.2	65.2	
Saskatoon	Montreal	92.6	0.0	0.2	86.4	66.2	52.98
	Ottawa	88.3	0.0	0.2	90.2	38.9	
	Quebec	93.4	0.0	0.2	83.5	63.0	
	Toronto	93.4	0.0	0.3	81.4	69.2	
	Vancouver	79.0	13.7	4.5	82.8	27.6	
Toronto	Montreal	89.9	83.9	68.8	86.9	85.4	76.42
	Ottawa	78.9	70.3	59.3	95.7	71.8	
	Quebec	91.2	85.1	65.8	81.2	84.2	
	Saskatoon	82.5	0.1	9.1	91.3	74.8	
	Vancouver	93.0	95.3	17.3	92.4	65.9	
Vancouver	Montreal	84.9	80.5	88.8	0.1	61.8	60.48
	Ottawa	71.8	66.9	94.8	0.1	69.3	
	Quebec	79.1	85.8	88.6	0.1	70.3	
	Saskatoon	72.7	0.2	94.3	0.5	32.4	
	Toronto	87.3	95.0	82.1	0.2	68.6	

This is used to produce the final results from here on; unless otherwise specified. The first consideration for splitting the dataset is to make sure every region in a SAR image appears only in one set (training or validation). The next consideration is to make sure the total number of pixels per class divides as equally as possible in training and validation sets. Using this split, pixels with class C21 and C31 are divided almost equally; where, pixels with class C41 are divided with 9% error, and pixels with class C51 are divided with 5% error. This is the optimal combination of SAR images given the dataset D. Since Quebec, Saskatoon, and Vancouver SAR images are taken with lower quality beam mode, we select their split as the training set. This ensures more practical evaluation results assuming cheaper SAR images, and leaves Ottawa and Toronto stacks for the validation set.

4.2   Final Results

We implemented our experiments using *PyTorch*. Cross entropy loss is deployed for training pixel level classifier on the task of distinguishing four different land cover classes. The largest possible mini-batch size with respect to GPU memory constrains is 32 which is used for all experiments. The segmentation models are optimized using Stochastic Gradient Descent, with learning rate of 1^{-3}, momentum of 0.9, and weight decay of 5^{-4} as regularization hyperparameter.

Since all the four categories in sample images are important for segmentation, the Union over Intersection (UoI) reduces to average pixel accuracy as the evaluation metric. The accuracy is reported for correctly classified pixels of validation set in percentage, individually per class and in average.

We compare three sampling modes—Large, Medium, Small—with strides of 112, 152, and 192 respectively. The kernel size 224 is fixed for all experiments, mainly because larger input images require more GPU memory than available to us without reducing the mini-batch size considerably. Results using different sampling modes are presented in Table 4. Finally, we compare three deep CNN-based segmentation models using sampling mode **S**. The final results are presented in Table 5.

Table 4. Evaluation of segmentation results using different sampling modes. These results are obtained using SegNet model.

Sampling mode	Urban 21	Water 31	Vegetation 41	Farm 51	Average
(**L**)arge	90.4	94.1	82.0	87.7	88.3
(**M**)edium	90.3	93.4	80.8	87.8	87.8
(**S**)mall	90.6	91.5	78.7	87.8	87.2

Table 5. Final results. Summary of the land cover segmentation performance of our trained deep CNN models on the validation set using LCSAR dataset. These results are obtained by sampling at a stride size of 192.

Model	Urban 21	Water 31	Vegetation 41	Farm 51	Average
DeconvNet	89.4	84.0	72.4	75.5	82.4
SegNet	**90.6**	91.5	78.7	**87.8**	87.2
PSPNet	90.2	**93.3**	**82.3**	86.8	**88.9**

5   Conclusion

In this work, we implemented three models to evaluate the performance of deep convolutional neural networks on land cover pixel-level classification using Synthetic Aperture Radar imagery. To alleviate the inherited noise in SAR imagery, we stacked several SAR images by averaging the pixel values. We also developed a sampling method to build training and validation sets from extremely large SAR images. Achieving near 90% average segmentation accuracy on validation set, our trained models promise a practical and robust solution for applications in automatic remote sensing and land cover classification. Future work can include incorporating image transformations with a smaller dataset to evaluate the efficiency of data augmentation in SAR imagery, experimenting with more complex networks e.g. Dual attention segmentation model [3], and exploring the applications of automatic land cover segmentation in challenging tasks of remote sensing where the accuracy of non-deep learning models is not sufficient.

References

1. What is SAR. https://asf.alaska.edu/information/sar-information/what-is-sar/. Accessed 17 Oct 2020
2. Badrinarayanan, V., Kendall, A., Cipolla, R.: SegNet: a deep convolutional encoder-decoder architecture for image segmentation. CoRR abs/1511.00561 (2015). http://arxiv.org/abs/1511.00561
3. Fu, J., Liu, J., Tian, H., Fang, Z., Lu, H.: Dual attention network for scene segmentation. CoRR abs/1809.02983 (2018). http://arxiv.org/abs/1809.02983
4. Gao, F., Huang, T., Sun, J., Wang, J., Hussain, A., Yang, E.: A new algorithm of SAR image target recognition based on improved deep convolutional neural network. Computation (2018). https://doi.org/10.1007/s12559-018-9563-z
5. He, K., Zhang, X., Ren, S., Sun, J.: Spatial pyramid pooling in deep convolutional networks for visual recognition. CoRR abs/1406.4729 (2014). http://arxiv.org/abs/1406.4729
6. He, K., Zhang, X., Ren, S., Sun, J.: Deep residual learning for image recognition. CoRR abs/1512.03385 (2015). http://arxiv.org/abs/1512.03385
7. Huang, Z., Dumitru, C.O., Pan, Z., Lei, B., Datcu, M.: Classification of large-scale high-resolution SAR images with deep transfer learning. IEEE Geosci. Remote Sens. Lett. 1–5 (2020). https://doi.org/10.1109/LGRS.2020.2965558
8. Ioffe, S., Szegedy, C.: Batch normalization: accelerating deep network training by reducing internal covariate shift. CoRR abs/1502.03167 (2015). http://arxiv.org/abs/1502.03167
9. Lapini, A., Pettinato, S., Santi, E., Paloscia, S., Fontanelli, G., Garzelli, A.: Comparison of machine learning methods applied to SAR images for forest classification in Mediterranean areas. Remote Sens. 12(3), 369 (2020). https://doi.org/10.3390/rs12030369
10. Liu, X., et al.: Classifying urban land use by integrating remote sensing and social media data. Int. J. Geogr. Inf. Sci. 31(8), 1675–1696 (2017). https://doi.org/10.1080/13658816.2017.1324976
11. Minaee, S., Boykov, Y., Porikli, F., Plaza, A., Kehtarnavaz, N., Terzopoulos, D.: Image segmentation using deep learning: a survey (2020)

12. Nair, V., Hinton, G.E.: Rectified linear units improve restricted Boltzmann machines. In: Proceedings of the 27th International Conference on International Conference on Machine Learning, ICML 2010, pp. 807–814. Omnipress, Madison (2010)
13. Noh, H., Hong, S., Han, B.: Learning deconvolution network for semantic segmentation. CoRR abs/1505.04366 (2015). http://arxiv.org/abs/1505.04366
14. Seferbekov, S.S., Iglovikov, V.I., Buslaev, A.V., Shvets, A.A.: Feature pyramid network for multi-class land segmentation. CoRR abs/1806.03510 (2018). http://arxiv.org/abs/1806.03510
15. Wu, W., Li, H., Zhang, L., Li, X., Guo, H.: High-resolution PolSAR scene classification with pretrained deep convnets and manifold polarimetric parameters. IEEE Trans. Geosci. Remote Sens. **56**(10), 6159–6168 (2018)
16. Yumus, D., Ozkazanc, Y.: Land cover classification for synthetic aperture radar imagery by using unsupervised methods. In: 2019 9th International Conference on Recent Advances in Space Technologies (RAST), pp. 435–440 (2019)
17. Zhang, C., et al.: Joint deep learning for land cover and land use classification. Remote Sens. Environ. **221**, 173–187 (2019). https://doi.org/10.1016/j.rse.2018.11.014. http://www.sciencedirect.com/science/article/pii/S0034425718305236
18. Zhao, H., Shi, J., Qi, X., Wang, X., Jia, J.: Pyramid scene parsing network. CoRR abs/1612.01105 (2016). http://arxiv.org/abs/1612.01105

Deep Learning Based Domain Adaptation with Data Fusion for Aerial Image Data Analysis

Jingyang Lu[1], Chenggang Yu[1], Erik Blasch[2], Roman Ilin[2], Hua-mei Chen[1],
Dan Shen[1], Nichole Sullivan[1], Genshe Chen[1(✉)], and Robert Kozma[3]

[1] Intelligent Fusion Technology, Inc., Germantown, MD 20876, USA
gchen@intfusiontech.com
[2] Air Force Research Laboratory, Dayton, OH 45435, USA
[3] The University of Memphis, Memphis, TN 38152, USA

Abstract. Current Artificial Intelligence (AI) machine learning approaches perform well with similar sensors for data collection, training, and testing. The ability to learn and analyze data from multiple sources would enhance capabilities for Artificial Intelligence (AI) systems. This paper presents a deep learning-based multi-source self-correcting approach to fuse data with different modalities. The data-level fusion approach maximizes the capability to detect unanticipated events/targets augmented with machine learning methods. The proposed Domain Adaptation for Efficient Learning Fusion (DAELF) deep neural network adapts to changes of the input distribution allowing for self-correcting of multiple source classification and fusion. When supported by a distributed computing hierarchy, the proposed DAELF scales up in neural network size and out in geographical span. The design of DAELF includes various types of data fusion, including decision-level and feature-level data fusion. The results of DAELF highlight that feature-level fusion outperforms other approaches in terms of classification accuracy for the digit data and the Aerial Image Data analysis.

Keywords: Motion imagery · Domain adaptation · Aerial image analysis

1 Introduction

Deep learning, as an element of machine learning (ML), has revolutionized many traditional data fusion approaches including wavelet fusion [1, 2], manifold fusion [3, 4] and target tracking [5–7]. Data fusion approaches include data-level, feature-level, and decision-level fusion for such applications as audio-video [8], video-text [9], and visual-infrared fusion [10]. The data fusion methods for aerial sensing extend to situation awareness [11] and temporal awareness [12]. The combination of deep learning-based multi-source analysis and data-level fusion provide a self-correcting approach to combine data of different modalities. Cognitively-motivated approaches provide flexibility and robustness of sensory fusion required under partially unknown conditions and in response to unexpected scenarios [4, 14]. Both machine learning and heterogeneous data-level fusion can enhance detection of unanticipated events/targets through the use of

© Springer Nature Switzerland AG 2021
A. Del Bimbo et al. (Eds.): ICPR 2020 Workshops, LNCS 12668, pp. 118–133, 2021.
https://doi.org/10.1007/978-3-030-68793-9_9

domain adaptation, see Fig. 1. The proposed ***Domain Adaptation for Efficient Learning Fusion*** (DAELF) deep neural network approach adapts to changes of the input distribution allowing self-correcting multiple source classification and fusion. When supported by a scalable distributed computing hierarchy, DAELF *scales up* in neural network size, *scales out* in geographical span, and *scales across* modalities.

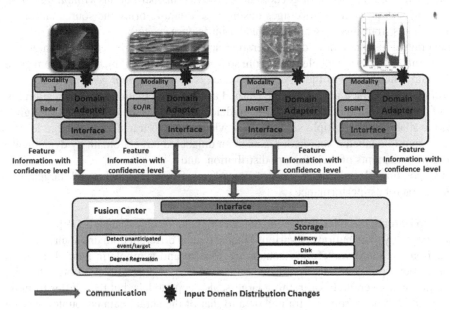

Fig. 1. Machine Learning based Domain Adaptation for Multiple Source Classification and Fusion

Generalizing models learned on one domain to another novel domain has been a major challenge in the quest for universal object recognition, especially for aerial motion imagery [15]. The performance of the learned models degrades significantly when testing on novel domains due to the presence of *domain shift* [16]. In Fig. 1, the proposed Domain Adaptation for Efficient Learning Fusion (DAELF) highlights heterogeneous data fusion for unanticipated event/target detection. The data from different sensing modalities are processed through a ML-based domain adapter, which can leverage unsupervised data to bring the source and target distributions closer in a learned joint feature space. DAELF includes a symbiotic relationship between the learned embedding and a generative adversarial network (GAN). Note, the GAN in DAELF supports joint multimodal analysis as contrasted to traditional GAN methods, which use the adversarial framework for generating realistic data and retraining deep models with such synthetic data [17, 18].

Based on the single source unsupervised domain adaptation (UDA), DAELF is an innovative approach to align multiple source domains with the target domain, which incorporates the moment Matching Component (MC) with GANs into deep neural network (DNN) to train the model in an end-to-end fashion. The key advantages of the DAELF approach include:

- Learning features that combine (i) discriminativeness and (ii) domain-invariance achieved by jointly optimizing the underlying features as well as two discriminative classifiers operating on these features. Namely, (i) the *label predictor* that predicts class labels and is used both during training and at test time and (ii) the *domain classifier* that discriminates between the source and the target domains during training;
- Adapting classifiers to the target domain with different distributions *without retraining* new input data. DAELF leverages unsupervised data to bring the source and target domain distributions closer in a learned joint feature space;
- Leveraging an adversarial data generation approach to directly learn the shared feature embedding using labeled data from source domain and unlabeled data from target domain. The novelty of the DAELF approach is in using a *joint generative discriminative method*: the embeddings are learned using a combination of classification loss and data generation procedure that is modeled using a variant of GANs. Then, given the availability of multiple sources data, which aims to transfer knowledge learned from multiple labeled source domains to an unlabeled target domain by dynamically aligning moments of their feature distribution; and
- Incorporating decision-level and feature-level fusion for enhanced target/event detection robust performance.

Deep learning has been utilized to uncover rich, hierarchical models [19] that represent probability distributions of various labeled data in different domains such as natural aerial images, audio waveforms containing speech, and symbols in natural language corpora. For a problem lacking labeled data, it may be still possible to obtain training sets that are large enough for training large-scale deep models, but they suffer from the *domain shift* in data from the trained data to that of the actual data encountered at the application time.

To account for domain shift, methods are needed to learn features that combine discriminativeness and domain-invariance in order to address environmental changes. While the parameters of the classifier are optimized in order to minimize errors on the training set, the parameters of the underlying deep feature mapping are optimized in order to minimize the loss of the label classifier and to maximize the loss of the domain classifier. The label classifier update works adversarially to the domain classifier, and it encourages domain-invariant features to emerge in the course of the optimization.

The rest of the paper is as follows. Section 2 describes the methods of domain adaptation with adversarial networks. Section 3 provides results using the Aerial Image Data (AID) dataset and Sect. 4 concludes the paper.

2   Methods

For data analysis, consider the tasks where $X = \{x_i\}_{i=1}^{N}$ is the input space and $Y = \{y_i\}_{i=1}^{N}$ is the label space. It is assumed that there exists a source-domain distribution $S(x, y)$ and target-domain distribution $T(x, y)$ over the samples in X. There are three types of *domain adaptation* shown in Table 1.

Table 1. Types of domain adaptation

	Source and Target domain	Source and Target tasks
Inductive Domain Adaptation	Same	Different but related
Transductive Domain Adaptation	Different but related	Same
Unsupervised Domain Adaptation	Different but related	Different but related

For unsupervised domain adaptation, the source distribution using labeled data from X is only accessible for the machine model training. The problem of unsupervised domain adaptation

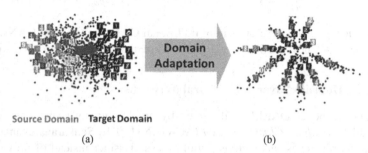

Source Domain   Target Domain

(a)   (b)

Fig. 2. Illustration of Domain Adaptation of samples of the same class from Source and Target Domains that are (a) sep-arated and (b) close to each other.

(Fig. 2) can be stated as learning a predictor that is optimal in the joint distribution space by using labeled source domain data and unlabeled target domain data sampled from X. The objective is to learn an embedding map $F : X \rightarrow \mathbb{R}^d$ and a prediction function $C : \mathbb{R}^d \rightarrow Y$. In DAELF, both F and C are modeled as deep neural networks. The predictor has access to the labels only for the data sampled from source domain and not from the target domain during the training process, so F implicitly learns the domain shift between source domain distribution $S(x, y)$ and target domain distribution $T(x, y)$. Likewise, a GAN-based approach is proposed to bridge the gap between the source and target domains. The target can be accomplished by using both generative and discriminative process which takes as much information as possible to learn the invariant features existing between the source and target domain.

2.1 Generative Adversarial Network

Generative Adversarial Networks (GANs) [1, 18] are utilized in many machine learning methods in domain adaptation. In a traditional GAN, two competing mappings are learned, the discriminator D and the generator G, both of which are modeled as deep neural networks. G and D play minmax the game, where D tries to classify the generated samples as fake and G tries to fool D by producing examples that are as realistic as possible. In order to train a GAN, the following optimization problem is solved in an iterative manner,

$$\min_G \max_D V(D, G) = E_{x \sim p_{data}}\left[\log D(x)\right] + E_{z \sim p_{noise}}\left[\log(1 - D(G(z)))\right] \quad (1)$$

where $D(x)$ represents the probability that x comes from the real data distribution rather than the distribution modeled by the generator $G(z)$, where z are noise variables. As an extension to traditional GANs, *conditional GANs* enable conditioning the generator and discriminator mappings on additional data such as a class label or an embedding. They have been shown to generate data on the class label or the embedding respectively. As in training a traditional GAN, the conditional GAN involves optimizing the following minimax objective, conditioned on the variable y:

$$\min_{G} \max_{D} E_{x \sim p_{data}}(\log(D(x|y))) + E_{z \sim p_{noise}} \log(1 - D(G(z|y))) \tag{2}$$

Building on the development of traditional GANs, conditional GANs, and multi-modal GANs, the next sections highlights a domain adaptation approach using GANs.

2.2 Domain-Adversarial Neural Networks

The proposed DAELF is designed by employing a variant of the conditional GAN called *Auxiliary Classifier GAN* (AC-GAN) [20] by Sankaranarayanan, et al., where the discriminator is modeled as a multi-class classifier instead of providing conditioning information at the input, as shown in Fig. 3.

The AC-GAN set up for the domain adaptation is as follows:

- *Sampling*: Given a real data set x as input to F, the input to the generator network G is $x_g = [F(x), z, l]$, which is a concatenated version of the encoder embedding $F(x)$, a random noise vector $z \in \mathbb{R}^d$ sampled from $N(0, 1)$ and a one-hot encoding of the class label, $l \in \{0, 1\}^{(N_c+1)}$ with N_c real classes and $\{N_c + 1\}$ being the fake class. For all target samples, since the class labels are unknown, l is set as the one-hot encoding of the fake class $\{N_c + 1\}$.
- *Classifier*: The classifier network C that takes as input the embedding generated by F and predicts a multiclass distribution $C(x)$, i.e. the class probability distribution of the input x, which is modeled as a N_c-way classifier.
- *Discriminator*: The discriminator mapping D takes the real input data x or the generated input $G(x_g)$ as input and outputs two distributions: (1) $D_{data}(x)$: the probability of the input being real, which is modeled as a binary classifier, and (2) $D_{cls}(x)$: the class probability distribution of the input x, which is modeled as a N_c-way classifier. To clarify the notation, $D_{cls}(x)_y$ implies the probability assigned by the classifier mapping D_{cls} from input x to y. It should be noted that, for target domain data, since class labels are unknown, only D_{data} is used to backpropagate the gradients. Please refer to [20] for additional details. It is worth mentioning that in order to better improve the training performance, the target domain data is also used to update the generator (G), which is denoted as follows,

$$L_G = \min_{G} E_{x \sim s} - \log\left(D_{cLs}(G(x_g))_y\right) + \log(1 - D_{data}(G(x_g))) + \log(1 - D_{data}(G(h_{gi})))$$
$$\tag{3}$$

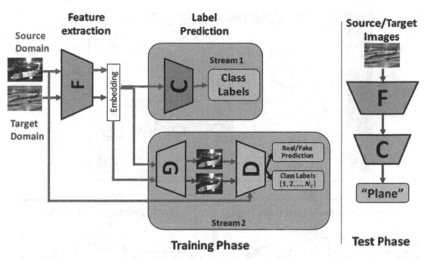

Fig. 3. Illustration of DAELF AC-GAN Approach [adapted from 20] ("F" denotes Feature Extraction Network, "C" denotes Label Prediction Network, "G" denotes Generator Network, and "D" denotes Discriminator Network)

2.3 Fusion Network Model

A fusion network model integrates two sources of input. For clarity, **netF** and **netC** is equivalent to **F** and **C** denoted in Fig. 3. If each sensor has a domain adaptation network (**netF**) followed by a *centralized fusion network* (**netC**) as in Fig. 4. Each **netF** is first trained by a different pair from the source/target

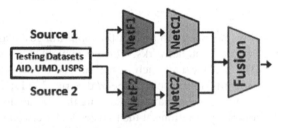

Fig. 4. Decision-Level Fusion for Multiple Sensors as GTA or Source-only fusion network

dataset. See Table 3 in the Results section, where two pair datasets *MNIST → USPS* and *SVHN → JP* are used to demonstrate the validity of the proposed DAELF sensor fusion. The weights of the two netFs are then brought into the centralized fusion network and the netC is trained by using two source datasets. The two networks {**netF** and **netC**} are trained and the whole fusion network is able to predict both target domain inputs.

Two fusion approaches widely used are decision-level fusion (DLF) shown in Fig. 4 and feature-level fusion (FLF) shown in Fig. 5. The FLF consists of two separately trained feature networks (netF1 and netF2) followed by one decision network that takes the concatenation of the outputs of the two feature networks (i.e., two embedding feature vectors) as inputs. The decision network needs to be trained by the two source domain training datasets with matched class labels.

Compared to feature-level fusion (FLF), decision-level fusion (DLF) does not need a second training. DLF consists of the two classification networks, as each was formed by a feature network (netF) and a decision network (netC) that were trained by the ***Generate to Adapt*** (GTA) method [20] with using one pair of source/target domain data. DAELF

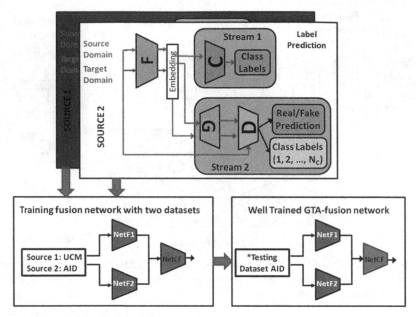

Fig. 5. Feature-level Data Fusion for Multiple Sensors

employs a strategy to predict the input images' class label according to the outputs of the two decision networks, which is explained as follows.

The last layer of each *netCF* has 10 outputs that represent the class labels of 10 digits from 0 to 9. A class label *d* described in Eq. (4) is predicted if the corresponding output value is the maximum among the 10 outputs. In order to make a final prediction *D* from the predictions of the two decision networks, DAELF assesses each prediction's reliability by computing an entropy *H* using Eq. (5), where p_0 through p_9 are 10 output values from one *netCF*. The final prediction would be the one that has a smaller entropy (Eq. (6)).

$$d = argmax(p_i, i = 0, 1, \ldots 9) \tag{4}$$

$$H = - \sum_{i=0}^{9} p_i \log(p_i) \tag{5}$$

$$D = \begin{cases} d_1 & if \ \ H_1 < H_2 \\ d_2 & if \ \ H_2 < H_1 \end{cases} \tag{6}$$

DAELF uses the two separately trained neural networks to form a fusion network to simulate a two-sensor two-modality system (Fig. 5). Because there are two sensors used to detect the same object, then it is required that every two images feeding to the fusion network must have an identical class label, which is also the true output of the network.

The next section demonstrates the DAELF approach for different scenarios.

3 Simulation Results

3.1 Classification of Digits Dataset

Comparing to other standard image datasets, the three DIGITS datasets, USPS (U.S. Postal Service), MNIST (Modified National Institute of Standards and Technology database), and SVHN (Google Street View House Number) are simple, and the domain shift from one to the other is relatively small [16]. The datasets are widely used as the first set of data in the testing of various domain adaptation algorithms. The original algorithm has two ways in training a network to classify images of handwriting digits:

1) **Source-only** that trains a network (formed by netF and netCF) with labeled source training data only;
2) *Generate to Adapt* (GTA) that trains netF and netCF separately. NetF is trained by labeled source training data and unlabeled target training data through a GAN, while netC is trained by source training data only.

A target testing dataset was used to evaluate the performance of the network (netF plus netC) trained by the two different ways. Various datasets exist for comparison: MNIST, USPS, and SVHN. Table 2 compares the classification accuracies obtained to that of the results by using Source-only approach. In all three domain adaptation cases, the network trained by GTA significantly outperformed the network trained by the source-only method. Through inspecting the clustering of embedding features, we found that it is possible to achieve an accuracy as high as 96% if we are able to modify the model selection strategy. This potential improvement by *model selection* is discussed in the next section.

Table 2. Performance Comparison

	MNIST→USPS	USPS→MNIST	SVHN→MNIST
Source only	79.1 ± 0.9	57.1 ± 1.7	60.3 ± 1.5
GTA	95.3 ± 0.7	90.8 ± 1.3	92.4 ± 0.9
DAELF	93.8	97.0	88.9

3.2 Visualization and Potential Improvement of Embedding Features

DAELF employs a *T-distributed Stochastic Neighbor Embedding* (TSNE) method to visualize the embedding features produced by netF. TSNE is a widely-used feature reduction and visualization method that transfers samples in a high-dimensional space to a low-dimensional space while retaining their relative distribution in the original space. Therefore, a cluster of samples on a 2D graph indicates a similar cluster of these samples in their original high dimensional space.

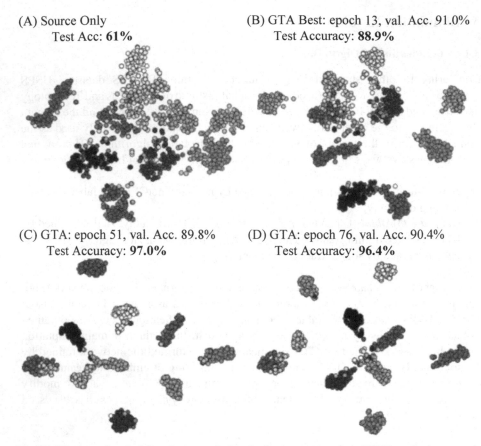

(A) Source Only
    Test Acc: **61%**

(B) GTA Best: epoch 13, val. Acc. 91.0%
    Test Accuracy: **88.9%**

(C) GTA: epoch 51, val. Acc. 89.8%
    Test Accuracy: **97.0%**

(D) GTA: epoch 76, val. Acc. 90.4%
    Test Accuracy: **96.4%**

Fig. 6. 2D view of embedding features of a batch of target testing data. TSNE method was used to map the 128 features generated by **netF** that was trained by (A) source-only mode, (B) GTA mode at when maximal validation accuracy was reached, (C) GTA mode at epoch 51, (D) GTA mode at epoch 76.

By visually inspecting the distribution of target samples' embedding features (128 dimensions) that were mapped onto a 2D graph via the TSNE method, the results are promising. Figure 6 shows the 2D maps of embedding features for MNIST testing data generated by netF that were trained by SVHN as source training data (Fig. 6A, source only), and by SVHN as source and MNIST as target training data (Fig. 6B to Fig. 6D, GTA).

Comparing embedding features obtained through GTA and source-only training, GTA features could better separate testing images of 10 digits into distinct clusters, which led to a significantly improvement of classification accuracy for target testing data from 61% to 88%. Interestingly, DAELF didn't obtain the best performance from the GTA trained netF that was selected when the validation accuracy reached maximum at epoch 13. On the contrary, DAELF obtained significantly higher testing accuracies for netF selected after more training iterations, for example at epoch 51, epoch 76. At these times, the validation accuracy (on source data) was slightly decreased from 91.0% to 89.8% and 90.4%. However, the testing accuracy increased from 88.9% to 97.0% and 96.4%. Correspondingly, the clusters of the testing images of 10 digits are more clearly separated on the 2D graphs by the embedding features from netF selected later at epochs 51 and 76 (Fig. 6C and Fig. 6D).

The results demonstrate that the validation accuracy measured on source domain data may not be the ideal metric for selecting the optional model (netF) to classify target domain data. Since domain adaptation is driven by both source and target domain data during GTA mode training, a model's performance on source domain could be a trade-off to its performance on the target domain. Therefore, the selection of a model solely based on its best performance on the source domain data could be sub-optimal for the target domain data. An optimal model selection strategy should balance the performance on both domains.

A model's performance on target domain cannot be directly estimated without knowing target sample labels. In this case, a *surrogate metric* is needed to indirectly estimate a model's potential performance on the target domain. One of such surrogate metrics could be based on the clustering of target domain data in the embedding feature space as its correlation with target domain performance has been shown in Fig. 6. To achieve correlation without knowing the labels of target samples, it is possible to rely on the labeled source training samples to determine the clustered regions in the embedding feature space and quantify how well the target training samples may fall into those dense regions.

3.3 Data Fusion for Multiple Sensors

Using the four DIGIT datasets simulates two sensor modalities. The four datasets include two datasets (SVHN and USPS) that have been used in previous studies by Taigman, *et al.* [16], and the two new datasets, *MNIST-N (noise)* and MNIST-JP (*Japanese*). MNIST-N consists of images derived from MNIST by adding background *noise*. MNIST-JP consists of is a dataset similar to MNIST but the images of hand writing digits were written by *Japanese*. We used these two new datasets in order to increase learning difficulty so that the performance improvement of the fusion approaches could be observed.

We separated the four datasets into two pairs and applied the GTA algorithm to train two separate neural networks. The first neural network was trained by using SVHN as source domain data and MNIST-JP as target domain data (SVHN → MNIST-JP). The second neural network as trained by using MNIST-N as source domain data and USPS as target domain data (MNIST-N → USPS). The two networks were evaluated by testing data from the target domain, i.e., MNIST-JP and USPS, respectively.

We evaluated the performances of the feature-level and the decision-level fusion approaches and compared them with single GTA-trained networks. Table 3 lists the classification accuracy when each method was used to predict testing datasets, which were not used in any training processes.

The GTA-trained network can effectively improve the classification accuracy for target domain data. DAELF shows improvement here again in each single GTA trained network. The network trained by MNIST-N → USPS achieved 71.9% (Fig. 7) accuracy for USPS testing data and the network trained by SVHN → MNIST-JP achieved 74.37%

(Fig. 8) accuracy for MNIST-JP testing data. However, the two networks don't perform well for new domain data. The former network only achieved 56.89% accuracy for MNIST-JP and the latter network achieved 58.44% accuracy for USPS.

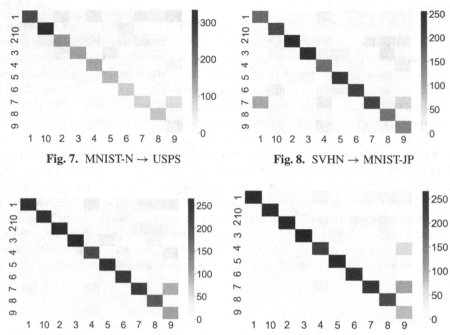

Fig. 7. MNIST-N → USPS

Fig. 8. SVHN → MNIST-JP

Fig. 9. Decision Level Data Fusion for Multiple Sensors

Fig. 10. Feature Level Data Fusion for Multiple Sensors

After incorporating the two networks together, either through feature-level or decision-level fusion, the new system outperformed any single network for every one of the two testing datasets. The two fusion methods achieved 84.28% (Fig. 9) and 86.07% (Fig. 10) accuracy, respectively. This more than 10% increase demonstrates the effectiveness of our proposed fusion approaches.

Table 3. Classification accuracies achieved by single GTA-trained and the fusion networks: Feature-Level Fusion (FLF), Decision-Level Fusion (DLF)

Testing Dataset	Single GTA-trained network		FLF	DLF
	MNIST-M→USPS	SVHN→MNIST-JP		
USPS	**71.90**	*58.44*		
MNIST-JP	*56.89*	**74.37**		
USPS + MNIST-JP			**86.07**	**84.28**

3.4 Classification of Aerial Image Dataset

Aerial imagery analysis provides a good showcase for advances in deep learning [21]. Using the DAELF model, it was modified to enable the classification of aerial images. We chose two datasets: *Aerial Image Dataset* (AID) and the *University of California, Merced* (UCM) dataset as source and target domain datasets, respectively. AID is a new large-scale aerial image dataset that collected images from the Google Earth imagery. The dataset contains 10000 600 × 600-pixel land images that are categorized in 30 scenes. The UCM is a similar land image dataset, which contains 2100 256 × 256-pixel images that are categorized in 21 scenes (100 images per scene). The images were manually extracted from large images from the USGS National Map Urban Area Imagery collection for various urban areas around the country. In order to test the DAELF model, we only used five classes of images from each dataset in the model development. These classes are: baseball field, medium residential area, sparse residential area, beach, and parking lot. We randomly chose 70% of images from AID and UCM to form source and target training datasets and used the remaining images as testing datasets. Figure 11 shows two example images from AID and UCM.

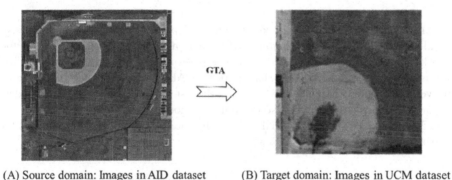

(A) Source domain: Images in AID dataset   (B) Target domain: Images in UCM dataset

Fig. 11. Domain adaptation between AID and UCM datasets.

The DAELF network's architecture for domain adaption was tailored between AID and UCM. In particular, the Resnet-50 network with pre-trained weights was used and the last layer removed as netF, and one linear layer as netC. Figure 12 illustrates the architectures of netF, netC, netG, and netD (replacing those of Fig. 3 with similar constructs of F, C, G, and D). Since the input image size for Resnet-50 is 224 × 224 pixels, both the AID and UCM images were re-sized to 224 × 224 before feeding them to the network.

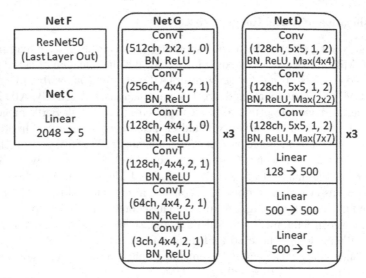

Fig. 12. Architectures for domain adaptation between AID and UCM dataset

DAELF was developed as a method for domain adaptation and data fusion. To achieve optimal performance, different combinations of parameters are explored in training the network. The parameters and the performance of 'source only' and GTA method are listed in Table 4. By choosing parameters properly, DAELF was able to obtain significant improvement for the GTA method when using the last trained model after 1000 epochs. Compared with the corresponding 'source only' method, the GTA accuracy can increase up to 12%. Figure 13 shows the TSNE method for the target domain testing images for the results in Table 4.

Table 4. Effect of parameters for the performance of the GTA method

		1	2	3	4	5
Parameters	Learning Rate	0.0004	0.0004	0.0004	0.0001	0.0004
	Learning Rate decay	0.0002	0.0002	0.0002	0.0010	0.0010
	Alpha	0.05	0.01	0.08	0.05	0.05
	Beta	0.05	0.01	0.08	0.05	0.05
Testing Accuracy	Source Only	69.7	69.7	69.7	69.7	69.7
	Best GTA Method	66.4	**56.2**	66.7	54.7	65.1
	Last GTA Method	**78.7**	48.5	**75.6**	**60.3**	**65.7**

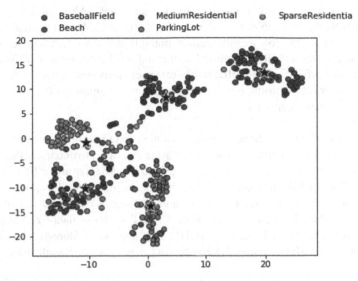

Fig. 13. 2D view of embedding features extracted by the TSNE method for the target domain testing images for Table 4 with accuracy of 78.7%.

4 Discussion and Conclusions

The paper introduces a deep neural network-based method DAELF, which adapts to changes of the input distribution allowing for self-correcting of multiple source classification and fusion. The DAELF results showed that optimum performance can be achieved, which reaches or even exceeds state-of-art approaches in common datasets. The performance of the DAELF depends on various hyper-parameters, each of which must be tuned to achieve optimum. The optimization is a sensitive process, requiring great attention and significant computational efforts. Hence, future results seek to better interpret the selection of the hyper-parameters for different scenarios.

It is known that the training process of GAN models may exhibit oscillations and instabilities, which is called *generator collapse* [18]. There are various methods to address these issues. Two such methods which have been used in our studies as ongoing work:

- *Unrolled GAN*: The original GAN framework is a minimax optimization problem, which is practically unfeasible to solve for optimal parameters of discriminator and generator. Instead, it is solved by iteratively using gradient descent on G and gradient ascent on D. *Unrolled GANs* [22] are simultaneous recurrent networks (SRN), which extend the time horizon of the iterative solution, when the theory of ordered derivatives in *backpropagation through time* (BPTT) is directly applicable [23, 24]. SRNs provide are a natural way to improve the performance of GANs by considering the unfolding iterations over a given time horizon, e.g., 10–20 iterations. The stability and convergence are improved using unrolled GANs.

- *Wasserstein GAN*: WGAN is an alternative to traditional GAN training, by replacing the original Kullback-Leibler (KL)-based distance measure by a new, mathematically justified function [25, 26]. Results demonstrated that Wasserstein loss stabilizes the performance of the DAELF system. The method has been extended to Wasserstein GAN as well. Performance stabilization is extremely important when using GANs for domain transfer applications, as when the data changes, sometimes in an unpredictable way, stability issues can arise.

In conclusion, this paper develops a deep learning-based multi-source self-correcting approach to fuse data with different modalities at the data-level to maximize their capabilities to detect unanticipated events/targets. The Domain Adaptation for Efficient Learning Fusion (DAELF) deep neural network approach adapts to changes of the input distribution allowing self-correcting across multiple source classifications. When supported by a distributed computing hierarchy, DAELF scales in data size, geographical span, and sensor modalities. From the aerial data sets analysis, feature-level fusion (FLF) outperforms decision-level fusion (DLF) approaches in terms of classification accuracy.

Acknowledgements. This material is based on research sponsored by Air Force under contract FA864920P0350. The views and conclusions contained herein are those of the authors and should not be interpreted as necessarily representing the official policies or endorsements, either expressed or implied, of the United States Air Force.

References

1. Zheng, Y., Blasch, E., Liu, Z.: Multispectral Image Fusion and Colorization, SPIE Press, Bellingham (2018)
2. Zhang, R., Bin, J., Liu, Z., et al.: WGGAN: a wavelet-guided generative adversarial network for thermal image translation. In: Naved, M. (ed.), Generative Adversarial Networks for Image-to-Image Translation. Elsevier (2020)
3. Shen, D., et al.: A joint manifold leaning-based framework for heterogeneous upstream data fusion. J. Algorithms Comput. Technol. (JACT) **12**(4), 311–332 (2018)
4. Vakil, A., Liu, J., Zulch, P., et al.: A survey of multimodal sensor fusion for passive RF and EO information integration. In: IEEE Aerospace and Electronics System Magazine (2020)
5. Bunyak, F., Palaniappan, K., Nath, S.K., Seetharaman, G.: Flux tensor constrained geodesic active contours with sensor fusion for persistent object tracking. J. Multimedia **2**(4), 20 (2007)
6. Jia, B., Pham, K.D., et al.: Cooperative space object tracking using space-based optical sensors via consensus-based filters. IEEE Tr. Aerosp. Electron. Syst. **52**(3), 1908–1936 (2016)
7. Shen, D., Sheaff, C., Guo, M., et al.: Enhanced GANs for satellite behavior discovery. In: Proc SPIE, p. 11422 (2020)
8. Nicolaou, M.A., Gunes, H., Pantic, M.: Audio-visual classification and fusion of spontaneous affective data in likelihood space. In: ICPR (2010)
9. Muller, H., Kalpathy–Cramer, J.: The image CLEF medical retrieval task at ICPR 2010 — information fusion to combine visual and textual information. In: ICPR (2010)
10. Li, H., Wu, X.J., Kittler, J.: Infrared and visible image fusion using a deep learning framework. In: ICPR (2018)
11. Blasch, E., Seetharaman, G., Palaniappan, K., Ling, H., Chen, G.: Wide-area motion imagery (WAMI) exploitation tools for enhanced situation awareness. In: IEEE Applied Imagery Pattern Recognition Workshop (2012)

12. Palaniappan, K., et al.: Moving object detection for vehicle tracking in wide area motion imagery using 4D filtering. In: International Conference on Pattern Recognition (ICPR) (2016)
13. Kozma, R.: A cognitively motivated algorithm for rapid response in emergency situations. In: IEEE Conference on Cognitive and Computational Aspects of Situation Management (CogSIMA) (2017)
14. Kozma, R.: Intentional systems: review of neurodynamics, modeling, and robotics implementation. Phys. Life Rev. **5**(1), 1–21 (2008)
15. Majumder, U., Blasch, E., Garren, D.: Deep Learning for Radar and Communications Automatic Target Recognition. Artech House, Norwood (2020)
16. Taigman, Y., Polyak, A., Wolf, L.: Unsupervised cross-domain image generation. arXiv preprint arXiv:1611.02200 (2016)
17. Goodfellow, I.J.: NIPS 2016 tutorial: Generative adversarial networks. arXiv:1701.00160v4 (2016)
18. Goodfellow, I.J., Courville, A., Bengio, Y.: Generative adversarial nets. In: Advances in Neural Information Processing Systems (NIPS), p. 27 (2014)
19. Tzeng, E., Devin, C., Hoffman, J., Finn, C., Abbeel, P.: Adapting deep visuomotor representations with weak pairwise constraints. arXiv, https://arxiv.org/abs/1511.07111 (2015)
20. Sankaranarayanan, S., Balaji, Y., Castillo, C.D.: Generate to adapt: aligning domains using generative adversarial networks. In: IEEE Conference on Computer Vision and Pattern Recognition, pp. 8503–8512 (2018)
21. Savakis, A., Nagananda, N., Kerekes, J.P., et al.: Change detection in satellite imagery with region proposal networks. Defense Syst. Inform. Anal. Center (DSIAC) J. **6**(4), 23–28 Fall (2019)
22. Metz, L., Poole, B., Pfau, D., Sohl-Dickstein, J.: Unrolled generative adversarial networks. arXiv preprint arXiv:1611.02163 (2016)
23. Werbos, P.J.: Backpropagation through time: what it does and how to do it. Proc. IEEE **78**(10), 1550–1560 (1990)
24. Ilin, R., Kozma, R., Werbos, P.J.: Beyond feedforward models trained by backpropagation: a practical training tool for a more efficient universal approximator. IEEE Trans. Neural Netw. **19**(6), 929–937 (2008)
25. Arjovsky, M., Chintala, S., Bottou, L.: Wasserstein GAN. arXiv preprint arXiv:1701.07875 (2017)
26. Gulrajani, F., Ahmed, M., Arjovsky, V., Dumoulin Courville, A.C.: Improved training of Wasserstein GANs. In: Advances in Neural Information Processing Systems, pp. 5767–5777 (2017). https://arxiv.org/pdf/1704.00028.pdf.

WMWB - TC4 Workshop on Mobile and Wearable Biometrics 2020

TC4 Workshop on Mobile and Wearable Biometrics (WMWB)

Workshop Description

Mobile devices are nowadays widely employed by people all over the world, with almost 3 billion users interacting with smartphones or tablets in their daily life. Such devices are not anymore used for personal communication only, but also for a variety of other applications, ranging from accessing the Internet, storing personal data, making payments, and gaining access to restricted services or areas.

With the rise of the Internet of Things, a growth trend similar to the one characterizing mobile devices in the recent past is now observed for wearable devices such as smartwatch and activity trackers, that is, smart electronic devices equipped with micro-controllers which can be incorporated into clothing or worn on the body as implants or accessories.

Most of the services made available through the aforementioned technologies are related to security- and privacy-sensitive tasks, which typically require secure mechanisms for access control, in order to avoid potentially harmful threats related to security and privacy loss.

It is therefore of paramount importance to design workable and effective solutions to implement automatic recognition systems within mobile and wearable devices, and biometric systems certainly represent the most interesting alternative to achieve this goal.

Actually, most of currently available devices are able to capture multiple biometric traits. For example, the cameras, microphones, and gyroscope sensors commonly included in smartphones could be exploited to capture face, voice, or gait biometric data. Several recent models also include sensors dedicated to fingerprint acquisition. Moreover, behavioral traits such as signature and keystoke can be also easily captured. On the other hand, wearable devices are naturally designed to collect biological signals related to the heart rate through techniques such as electrocardiography (ECG) or photoplethysmography (PPG), while also the electrodermal activity (EDA) can be often recorded.

Designing systems able to properly exploit the information made available while collecting the aforementioned biometric traits, with the purpose of implementing secure biometric recognition system, is therefore a relevant and timely challenge. In fact, with respect to the design of standard biometric recognition systems for desktop applications, in the considered scenarios some additional constraints should be taken into account, such as the lower processing power, the reduced power consumption, and the need for novel user interfaces guaranteeing acceptable human-device interaction.

The TC4 Workshop on Mobile and Wearable Biometrics (WMWB) represented a forum for researchers and practitioners working on the evolving areas of pattern recognition techniques for mobile and wearable biometric recognition systems. The workshop also aimed at promoting further collaboration within the researchers working in this research paradigm, bringing together research and industry partners, and stimulating interest for research in practical aspects of mobile and wearable biometrics. Experiences from ongoing H2020 European Projects was also shared.

The first edition of the TC4 Workshop on Mobile and Wearable Biometrics (WMWB) was held virtually, in conjunction with the 25th International Conference on Pattern Recognition (ICPR) 2020. The format of the workshop included a keynote talk, followed by technical presentations.

The first edition of the workshop received 13 submissions for reviews, from authors belonging to 7 distinct countries. After an accurate and thorough single-blind peer-review process, 8 papers were selected for presentation at the workshop. The review process focused on the quality of the papers and their scientific novelty. The acceptance of the papers was the result of the reviewers' discussion and agreement. All the high quality papers were accepted, and the acceptance rate was 61%. The accepted articles presented interesting techniques to solve issues in biometric data processing on devices with limited resources, results from competitions, exploitation of novel biometric traits. The workshop program was completed by the invited talk, regarding recent advances in the use of biometrics on *mobile devices from the H2020* Marie Skłodowska-Curie Innovative Training Network AMBER ("enhAnced Mobile BiomEtRics"), given by Prof. Richard Guest from University of Kent, United Kingdom.

January 2020   Emanuele Maiorana

Organization

General Chair

Emanuele Maiorana   Roma Tre University, Italy

Program Committee

Carmen Bisogni	University of Salerno, Italy
Patrizio Campisi	Roma Tre University, Italy
Maria De Marsico	Sapienza University of Rome, Italy
Farzin Deravi	University of Kent, UK
Jana Dittmann	Otto-von-Guericke-Universität Magdeburg, Germany
Julian Fierrez	Universidad Autonoma de Madrid, Spain
Richard Guest	University of Kent, UK
Leandros Maglaras	De Montfort University, UK
Michele Nappi	University of Salerno, Italy
Fernando Pérez-González	University of Vigo, Spain
Claus Vielhauer	Otto-von-Guericke-Universität Magdeburg, Germany
Hao Wang	Norwegian University of Science and Technology, Gjøvik, Norway

Additional Reviewers

Rig Das	Technical University of Denmark, Denmark
Emanuela Piciucco	Roma Tre University, Italy

SqueezeFacePoseNet: Lightweight Face Verification Across Different Poses for Mobile Platforms

Fernando Alonso-Fernandez[1]([✉]), Javier Barrachina[2], Kevin Hernandez-Diaz[1], and Josef Bigun[1]

[1] School of Information Technology, Halmstad University, Halmstad, Sweden
feralo@hh.se, kevher@hh.se, josef.bigun@hh.se
[2] Facephi Biometria, Av. México 20, Edificio Marsamar, 03008 Alicante, Spain
jbarrachina@facephi.com

Abstract. Ubiquitous and real-time person authentication has become critical after the breakthrough of all kind of services provided via mobile devices. In this context, face technologies can provide reliable and robust user authentication, given the availability of cameras in these devices, as well as their widespread use in everyday applications. The rapid development of deep Convolutional Neural Networks (CNNs) has resulted in many accurate face verification architectures. However, their typical size (hundreds of megabytes) makes them infeasible to be incorporated in downloadable mobile applications where the entire file typically may not exceed 100 Mb. Accordingly, we address the challenge of developing a lightweight face recognition network of just a few megabytes that can operate with sufficient accuracy in comparison to much larger models. The network also should be able to operate under different poses, given the variability naturally observed in uncontrolled environments where mobile devices are typically used. In this paper, we adapt the lightweight SqueezeNet model, of just 4.4 MB, to effectively provide cross-pose face recognition. After trained on the MS-Celeb-1M and VGGFace2 databases, our model achieves an EER of 1.23% on the difficult frontal vs. profile comparison, and 0.54% on profile vs. profile images. Under less extreme variations involving frontal images in any of the enrolment/query images pair, EER is pushed down to <0.3%, and the FRR at FAR = 0.1% to less than 1%. This makes our light model suitable for face recognition where at least acquisition of the enrolment image can be controlled. At the cost of a slight degradation in performance, we also test an even lighter model (of just 2.5 MB) where regular convolutions are replaced with depth-wise separable convolutions.

Keywords: Face recognition · Mobile biometrics · CNNs

1 Introduction

All kind of services are migrating from physical to digital domains. Mobiles have become data hubs, storing sensitive data like payment information,

© Springer Nature Switzerland AG 2021
A. Del Bimbo et al. (Eds.): ICPR 2020 Workshops, LNCS 12668, pp. 139–153, 2021.
https://doi.org/10.1007/978-3-030-68793-9_10

photos, emails or passwords [1]. In this context, biometric technologies hold a great promise to provide reliable and robust user authentication using the sensors embedded in such devices [14]. But in order for algorithms to operate with sufficient accuracy, they need to be adapted to the limited processing resources of mobile devices. Data templates also have to be small if they are to be transmitted. On top of it, mobile environments usually imply little control in the acquisition (e.g. on-the-move or on-the-go), leading to huge variability in data quality.

In this work, we are interested in face technologies in mobile environments. Face verification is increasingly used in applications such as device unlock, mobile payments, login to applications, etc. Recent developments involve deep learning [18]. Given enough data, they generate classifiers with impressive performance in unconstrained scenarios with high variability. However, state-of-the-art solutions are built upon big deep Convolutional Neural Networks (CNNs), e.g. [8], with dozens of millions of parameters and models that typically occupy hundreds of megabytes. Such a big size and the computational resources that such networks require make them unfeasible for embedded mobile applications.

In recent years, lighter CNN architectures have been proposed for common visual tasks, e.g. MobileNet [10], MobileNetV2 [17], ShuffleNet [22] or SqueezeNet [12]. Several works have bench-marked some of these networks for face recognition [4,6,16]. Even if they employ training databases that contain images captured under a wide range of variations, these works have not specifically assessed performance across different poses. In this work, our main contribution is therefore a novel lightweight face recognition network which is tested against a database specifically designed to explore pose variations [3]. We base our developments on SqueezeNet, which is a much lighter architecture than the other networks. To the best of our knowledge, this is the first work testing deep face recognition performance specifically under different poses and in mobile environments. With a database of 11040 images from 368 subjects, our experiments show that the proposed network compares well against two larger benchmark networks having a size >30 times bigger and >20 times more parameters.

2   Related Works

Lightweight CNNs employ different techniques to achieve less parameters and faster processing, such as point-wise convolution, depth-wise separable convolution, and bottleneck layers. Point-wise convolutions consist of 1×1 filters with a depth equal to the number of input channels, and it is used to reduce or augment the number of channels. Depth-wise separable convolution splits convolution in two steps, the first one performing lightweight filtering by using a single convolutional filter per input channel, followed by a 1×1 point-wise convolution that carries out linear combinations of the input channels. For single convolutional filters of 3×3, depth-wise separable convolution achieves a computational reduction of 8–9 times in comparison to standard convolution, with a small cost in accuracy only [10]. Bottleneck layers consist on obtaining a representation of

Table 1. Top: proposed lightweight models in the literature for face recognition. Bottom: networks evaluated in the present paper. (*) Inference times are as reported in the respective papers, so they are not fully comparable. The hardware used in the reported studies includes a Qualcomm Snapdragon 820 mobile CPU @ 2.2 GHz [4], an Intel i7-6850K CPU @ 3.6GHz [6], and an Intel i7-7700HQ CPU @ 2.80 GHz [16]. The latter also carries out a comparison of different devices, including high-end GPUs, with inference times reduced around one order of magnitude. Please refer to the original papers for details. Inference in this paper is done with an Intel i7-8650U CPU @ 1.9GHz.

Network	Input size	Layers	Model size	Parameters	Vector size	Inference time
Existing lightweight CNN architectures for face recognition						
LightCNN [19]	128 × 128	29	n/a	12.6M	256	n/a
MobileFaceNets [4]	112 × 112	50	4 MB	0.99M	256	24 ms (*)
MobiFace [6]	112 × 112	45	11.3 MB	n/a	512	28 ms (*)
ShuffleFaceNet [16]	112 × 112	n/a	10.5 MB	2.6M	128	29.1 ms (*)
SeesawFaceNets [21]	112 × 112	50	n/a	1.3M	512	n/a
Networks evaluated in the present paper						
SqueezeFacePoseNet	113 × 113	18	4.41 MB	1.24M	1000	37.7 ms
+GDC	113 × 113	18	5.01 MB	1.4M	1000	38.7 ms
+DWC	113 × 113	18	2.5 MB	0.69M	1000	36.4 ms
+DWC+GDC	113 × 113	18	3.1 MB	0.86M	1000	36.9 ms
ResNet50ft [3]	224 × 224	50	146 MB	25.6M	2048	0.16 s
SENet50ft [3]	224 × 224	50	155 MB	28.1M	2048	0.21 s

the input with reduced dimensionality before processing it with a larger amount of filters that usually have bigger spatial dimensions as well.

SqueezeNet is one of the early works presenting an architecture with fewer parameters and a smaller size (1.24M parameters, 4.6 MB, and 18 convolutional layers). The authors proposed 1 × 1 point-wise convolutions with squeeze and expand modules that follow the bottleneck concept. Later, MobileNet (4.M parameters) and MobileNetV2 (3.5M parameters, 13 MB, and 53 convolutional layers) were proposed. The former uses faster depth-wise and point-wise convolutions, and the latter uses bottlenecks and inverted residual structures. Inverted residual structures consist of adding a shortcut between bottleneck layers, similar to residual connections [8], that allows to reuse features through the network and to improve the ability of a gradient to propagate across multiple layers. Lastly, ShuffleNet (1.4M parameters, 6.3 MB, and 50 convolutional layers) employs point-wise group convolution and channel shuffle to reduce the computational cost.

Some works have designed light face recognition models based on these or other architectures (Table 1). To carry out biometric verification, they typically use as feature vector the output before the fully-connected part. The authors in [19] presented LightCNN, with 29 convolutional layers and residual connections, which has 12.6M parameters. With a compact vector of 256 elements, they achieved 99.33% verification accuracy on the LFW database. MobileFaceNets [4] is based on MobileNetV2 but with smaller expansion factors on bottleneck layers, obtaining a network of 0.99M parameters and 4 MB. The authors introduced Global Depth-wise Convolution (GDC) to substitute the standard Global Average Pooling (GAP) at the end of the network. The motivation is that GAP treats all pixels of the last channels equally, but in face recognition, the center pixels should not have the same role than corner pixels. They also used PReLU as non-linearity, and fast down-sampling at the beginning of the network. With a vector of 256 element, the reported accuracy on LFW was 99.55%. MobiFace [6] is also based on MobileNetV2. Besides fast down-sampling and PReLU, they change GAP by a fully-connected layer in the last stage of the embedding to allow learning of different weights for each spatial region of the last channels. With a network of 11.3 MB and a vector of 512 elements, the reported accuracy on LFW was 99.73%. ShuffleNet is used as base for ShuffleFaceNet [16]. Here the authors also use PReLU, and replace GAP with GDC. They test a different number of channels in each block, and the network with the best speed-accuracy trade-off has a size of 10.5 MB and 2.6M parameters, with a feature model of 128 elements. The reported accuracy on LFW is of 99.67%. Lastly, the work [21] presented SeesawFaceNets, based on seesaw blocks [20]. Based on inverted residual bottleneck blocks, seesaw blocks replace point-wise convolutions with uneven group convolutions and channel permute/shuffle operations. The author also added Squeeze-and-Excitation (SE) [11], and used Swish as non-linearity. SE blocks explicitly model channel relationships in order to adaptively recalibrate channel-wise feature responses, and they can be integrated with many architectures, improving their representation power. With a network of 1.3M parameters and vectors of 512 elements, the author reported an accuracy on LFW of 99.7%.

3   Network Architecture

As back-bone model, we employ SqueezeNet [12]. This is the smallest architecture among the generic light CNNs mentioned. With only 1.24M parameters and 4.6 MB in its uncompressed version, it matched AlexNet accuracy on ImageNet with 50x fewer parameters. Its building brick, called fire module (Fig. 1), contains two layers: a squeeze layer and an expand layer. The squeeze layer uses 1 × 1 (point-wise) filters as a bottleneck to reduce dimensionality of the feature maps that will be processed in the expand layer with (more costly) 3 × 3 filters. Also, to achieve further parameter reduction, some filters in the expand layer are of 1 × 1 instead of 3 × 3. The squeezing (bottleneck) and expansion behavior is common in CNNs, helping to reduce the amount of parameters while keeping the same feature map size between the input and output [17]. In addition, SqueezeNet uses late downsampling, so many convolution layers have large activation maps. Intuitively, this should lead to a higher accuracy. The architecture of the employed network is shown in Table 2, which mirrors [12] with slight changes.

The network has been modified to employ an input size of 113 × 113 × 3. It starts with a convolutional layer with 64 filters of 3 × 3 × 3 (the original paper uses 96 filters), followed by 8 fire modules. The stride of the first convolutional layer has been changed from 2 to 1, so the rest of the network can remain unchanged. Then, the network ends with a convolutional layer with 1000 filters of $1 \times 1 \times 512$. ReLU is applied after each convolutional layer, and dropout of 50% is applied after the last fire module. All convolutional layers have stride 1, and all max-pooling layers are of 3×3 and stride 2. As it can be observed, the number of filters in each fire module increases gradually. Also, the network uses GAP, which carries out down-sampling by computing the average of each input channel. This reduces the input size to the classification layer. After GAP, we add a fully connected layer that matches as output size the number of classes of the training database. Batch-normalization and dropout at 50% is also added to counteract over-fitting in the fully connected layer due to the high number of training classes (35K and 8.6K). We will refer to this network as SqueezeFacePoseNet. To achieve an even smaller model, we will test the replacement of standard convolution with depth-wise separable convolution in all 3×3 filters, and we will also evaluate the replacement of GAP with GDC. The size and amount of parameters of the different combinations is shown in Table 1, bottom.

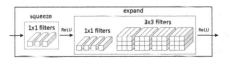

Fig. 1. Internal architecture of a fire module. In this example, the squeeze layer has three 1×1 filters, and the expand layer has four 1×1 and four 3×3 filters. Adapted from [12].

We also evaluate the CNNs used in [3] to assess face recognition performance with the VGGFace2 database. They use ResNet50 [8] and SE-ResNet50 [11] as backbone architectures, both with 50 convolutional layers, and ending with a GAP layer with produces a vector of 2048 elements before the fully connected layer. ResNet networks presented the concept of residual connections to ease the training of CNNs. The models employed in this paper[1] are initialized from scratch, then trained on the MS-Celeb-1M [7] dataset, and further fine-tuned on the VGGFace2 dataset. We will refer to these as ResNet50ft and SENet50ft.

4   Database and Experimental Protocol

We use the VGGFace2 dataset, with 3.31M images of 9131 celebrities, and an average of 363.6 images per person [3]. The images, downloaded from the Internet, show large variations in pose, age, ethnicity, lightning and background. The database is divided into 8631 training classes (3.14M images), and the remaining

---

[1] https://github.com/ox-vgg/vgg_face2.

Table 2. Architecture of the network used. C is the number of training classes.

Layer	Output size	#1 × 1 squeeze	#1 × 1 expand	#3 × 3 expand
input	$113^2 \times 3$	–	–	–
conv1	$113^2 \times 64$	–	–	–
maxpool1	$56^2 \times 64$	–	–	–
fire2	$56^2 \times 128$	16	64	64
fire3	$56^2 \times 128$	16	64	64
fire4	$56^2 \times 256$	32	128	128
maxpool4	$27^2 \times 256$	–	–	–
fire5	$27^2 \times 256$	32	128	128
fire6	$27^2 \times 384$	48	192	192
fire7	$27^2 \times 384$	48	192	192
fire8	$27^2 \times 512$	64	256	256
maxpool8	$13^2 \times 512$	–	–	–
fire9	$13^2 \times 512$	64	256	256
dropout9	$13^2 \times 512$	–	–	–
conv10	$13^2 \times 1000$	–	–	–
averagepool10	$1^2 \times 1000$	–	–	–
batchnorm10	$1^2 \times 1000$	–	–	–
dropout10	$1^2 \times 1000$	–	–	–
fc	$1^2 \times$ C	–	–	–
softmax	$1^2 \times$ C	–	–	–

500 for testing. To enable recognition across different pose, a subset of 368 subjects from the test set is provided (VGGFace2-Pose for short), with 10 images per pose (frontal, three-quarter, and profile), totalling 11040 images.

To further improve recognition performance of our mobile network, we also use the RetinaFace cleaned set of the MS-Celeb-1M database [7] to pre-train our model (MS1M for short). Face images are pre-processed to a size of 112 × 112 by five facial landmarks provided by RetinaFace [5]. In total, there are 5.1M images of 93.4K identities. While MS1M has a larger number of images, its intra-identity variation is limited due to an average of 81 images per person. For this reason, we investigate the benefit of first pre-training on a dataset with a large number of

Table 3. Number of biometric verification scores.

Template	SAME-POSE		CROSS-POSE	
	Genuine	Impostor	Genuine	Impostor
1 image	$368 \times (9+8+...+1) = 16560$	$368 \times 100 = 36800$	$368 \times 10 \times 10 = 36800$	$368 \times 100 = 36800$
5 images	$368 \times 1 = 368$	$368 \times 100 = 36800$	$368 \times 2 \times 2 = 1472$	$368 \times 100 = 36800$

VGGFace2 pose templates from three viewpoints (frontal, three-quarter, and profile, arranged by row). Image from [3].

MS-Celeb-1M from three users (by row) and three profiles (by column: frontal (1-2), three-quarter (3-4), and profile (5)).

VGGFace2 training images with random crop.

Fig. 2. Example images of the databases employed.

images (MS1M), then fine-tune with more intra-class diversity (VGGFace2). This is the protocol in [3], and it has been shown to provide enhanced performance, in comparison to training the models only with VGGFace2. Some example images of these databases are shown in Fig. 2.

Our network is trained for biometric identification using the soft-max function. The network is initialized using ImageNet weights, since it has been shown that such transfer-learning strategy can provide equal or better performance than if initialized from scratch, while converging much faster [15]. For training, the bounding box of VGGFace2 images are resized, so the shorter side has 256 pixels, then a 224×224 region is randomly cropped [3]. To accommodate to the input size of the CNN, images of both databases are scaled to 113×113. SGDM is used as optimizer, with mini-batches of 128. The initial learning rate is 0.01, which is decreased to 0.005, 0.001, and 0.0001 when the validation loss plateaus. Also, the learning rate of newly added layers is multiplied by 10 during the epochs that the global learning rate is 0.01. Two percent of images of each user in the training set are set aside for validation. To speed-up training and reduce parameters of the fully connected layer dedicated to under-represented classes, we remove users from MS1M with less than 70 images, resulting in 35016 users and 3.16M images. This ensures also that at least one image per user is available in the validation set. All experiments have been done in a stationary computer with an i9-9900 processor, 64 Gb RAM, and a NVIDIA RTX 2080 Ti GPU. We carry out training using Matlab r2019a, while the implementations of ResNet50ft and SENet50ft are run using MatConvNet.

We carry out verification experiments with the 368 subjects of VGGFace2-Pose. To enable comparison with state-of-the-art, the test protocol follows the procedure of [3]. A template is defined for each user, consisting of five faces with the same pose, so two templates are available per user and per pose. A template is represented by a single vector, which is computed by averaging the descriptors given by the CNN of the faces in the template set. To test the robustness of the employed networks, we also carry out experiments using only one image as template. During testing, VGGFace2 images are resized, so the shorter side has 256 pixels. A 224×224 crop of the center is then done (instead of a random crop), followed by a resize to 113×113. To extract a face descriptor, the last layers of our network trained in identification mode are removed, and the features are extracted from the GAP layer, having dimensionality 1000. A distance measure (χ^2 in our case) is then used to obtain the similarity between two templates. With ResNet50ft and SENet50ft architectures, we use as descriptor the output of the layer adjacent to the classification layer, with dimensionality 2048. Also, ResNet50ft and SENet50ft employ input images of 224×224, so VGGFace2 images are kept in this size when testing with these two networks.

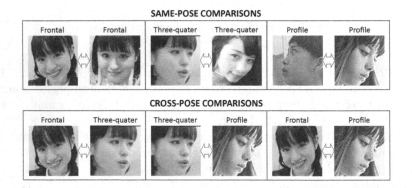

Fig. 3. Evaluation protocols: same-pose (left) and cross-pose comparisons (right).

5   Results

5.1   Same-Pose Comparisons

We first report experiments of same-pose comparisons, i.e. comparing only templates generated with images having the same pose (Fig. 3, left). Genuine trials are done by comparing each template of a user to the remaining templates of the same user, avoiding symmetric comparisons. Concerning impostor experiments, the first template of a user is used as enrolment template, and compared with the second template of the next 100 users. Table 3 (left) shows the total number of scores with this protocol. Recall than when templates are generated using 5 images, there are only two templates available per user and per pose. On the other hand, when templates are generated with only one image, there are ten

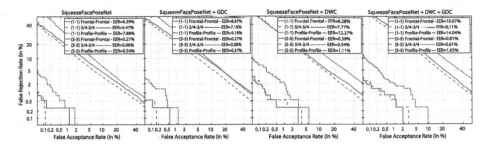

Fig. 4. SqueezeFacePoseNet: Face verification results (same-pose comparisons). Better in colour (Color figure online).

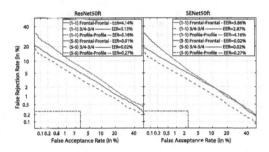

Fig. 5. ResNet50ft and SENet50ft (same-pose comparisons). Better in colour (Color figure online).

templates per user and per pose. Face verification results following this protocol are given in Figs. 4 and 5. Also, Table 4, shows the EER values of the same-pose experiments in the second and fourth sub-columns.

A first observation is that our SqueezeFacePoseNet model provides in general better results without the inclusion of Global Depth-wise Convolution (GDC). This is in contrast to some previous studies where GDC is reported to provide a better performance [4,6]. It should be mention though that the authors of our baseline networks kept the GAP layer in ResNet50ft and SENet50ft models [3]. One possible reason of these results is that in training with VGGFace2, the face region is randomly cropped from the detected bounding box [3], leading to images where faces are not aligned (Fig. 2c). This may serve as an 'augmentation' strategy, making counterproductive the use of GDC to learn different weights for each spatial region, since faces are not spatially aligned during training. The use of depth-wise separable convolution (DWC) in SqueezeFacePoseNet also results in a slight decrease of performance. This is to be expected [10], although it should be taken into account that adding DWC to our network reduces its model size by about 60% (Table 1).

Among all the networks evaluated, SENet50ft clearly stands out, specially when templates are generated with only one image (left part of Table 4), which is a much adverse case than the combination of five images (right part). The

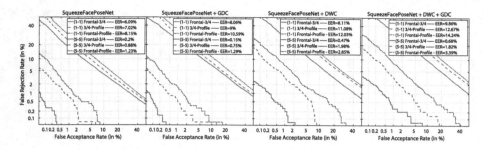

Fig. 6. SqueezeFacePoseNet: Face verification results (cross-pose comparisons). Better in colour (Color figure online).

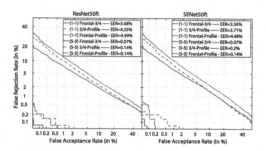

Fig. 7. ResNet50ft and SENet50ft (cross-pose comparisons). Better in colour (color figure online).

superiority of SENet50ft over ResNet50ft for face recognition is also observed in the paper where they were presented [3], due to the inclusion of Squeeze-and-Excitation blocks. Regarding SqueezeFacePoseNet, its performance is comparatively worse. Even in that case, we believe that it obtains meritorious results, considering that it employs images of 113×113 (instead of 224×224), its size is >30 times smaller than ResNet50ft and SENet50ft, and it has >20 times fewer parameters. The good results of SqueezeFacePoseNet are specially evident when using templates of five images, in whose case its EER is <0.55% for any given pose, and with frontal images it is just 0.27%. With the lighter SqueezeFacePoseNet+DWC version, the EER of same-pose comparisons is below 1.1%, and just 0.39% with frontal images.

By looking at the different poses, we observe that performance decreases slightly in profile vs. profile comparisons with all networks. Even in this case, where only half of the face is visible, using templates of five images provides very good performance with any given network (EER < 0.55%). For the other two poses, SqueezeFacePoseNet gives a meritorious EER of 0.27/0.06%, and an order of magnitude less is given by the baseline networks. If templates of one image are used, our network worsens by a factor of ∼1.9 only w.r.t. ResNet50ft/SENet50ft. An interesting phenomena also with all network is that the three-quarter vs. three-quarter case provides better performance than the frontal vs. frontal.

Table 4. Face verification results on the VGGFace2-Pose database (EER%). F = Frontal View. 3/4 = Three-Quarter. P = Profile. The best result of each column is marked in bold.

Recognition network	One face image per template						Five face images per template					
	Same-pose			Cross-pose			Same-pose			Cross-pose		
	F-F	3/4-3/4	P-P	F-3/4	3/4-P	F-P	F-F	3/4-3/4	P-P	F-3/4	3/4-P	F-P
SqueezeFacePoseNet	6.39	5.47	7.88	6.09	7.02	8.15	0.27	0.06	0.54	0.2	0.88	1.23
+GDC	8.67	7.18	9.18	8.06	9	10.59	0.27	0.08	0.37	0.15	0.75	1.29
+DWC	8.28	7.77	12.27	8.11	11.08	12.03	0.39	0.54	1.11	0.47	1.98	2.85
+DWC+GDC	10.07	9.11	14.04	9.86	12.67	14.24	0.81	0.61	1.63	0.68	1.82	3.39
ResNet50ft	4.14	3.13	5.16	3.68	4.25	4.99	**0.01**	**0.02**	0.27	**0.07**	**0.14**	**0.14**
SENet50ft	**3.86**	**2.87**	**4.16**	**3.36**	**3.71**	**4.48**	0.02	**0.02**	**0.27**	**0.07**	0.2	**0.14**

It is also worth noting the substantial improvement observed when five images are used to generate user's templates (right part of Table 4) in comparison to using one (left part). This points out that collecting just five images of a user is sufficient to obtain good performance across different poses with the networks employed. Even in a higher security scenario (e.g. FAR = 0.1%), the FRR of SqueezeFacePoseNet is below 1% in frontal vs. frontal and three-quarter vs. three-quarter cases, and of ∼2% with the lighter SqueezeFacePoseNet+DW (see Fig. 4). It should be considered though that the images of any user are mostly captured in different moments and they contain a very diverse variability, so the model generated when combining them is probably richer than if they were taken consecutively (e.g. from a video). In this sense, it could be expected that the improvement would not be so high if for example we combine several shots taken consecutively, although confirming this would need extra experiments.

5.2   Cross-Pose Comparisons

We now carry out cross-pose verification experiments. Pair-wise comparisons are done between templates generated with images of different poses (Fig. 3, right). We follow the same protocol for scores generation as in Sect. 5.1, resulting in the amount indicated in Table 3 (right). Face verification results of cross-pose experiments are given in Figs. 6 and 7. Also, Table 4 shows the EER values of the cross-pose experiments in the third and fifth sub-columns.

In a similar vein as Sect. 5.1, SqueezeFacePoseNet works better in general without Global Depth-wise Convolution (GDC), and a slight performance decrease is seen when using depth-wise separable convolutions (DWC). Also, SENet50ft stands out. With SqueezeFacePoseNet, results are up to one order of magnitude worse with templates of five images, and only ∼1.9 times worse with templates of one image. Still, the EER of our network for cross-pose experiments is between 0.2–1.23% when richer models of five images per user are employed.

Regarding the different types of poses, the worst performance is seen when there is maximum variation between the templates being compared (frontal vs. profile). This is to be expected, given the higher variability of this combination.

Nevertheless, it should be highlighted the meritorious performance of any of the networks when templates of five images are used, with EER ranging between 0.14–1.23% for this difficult cross-pose situation. The best performance is always observed in the frontal vs. three-quarter case, and the three-quarter vs. profile case stands in the middle of the other two. From these results, it can be concluded that it is not the amount of pose difference between templates that matters, but that the images appear as much frontal as possible. In this sense, if we compare the frontal vs. frontal and frontal vs. three-quarter cases, their performance is not so different (and sometimes the frontal vs. three-quarter case is better). In a similar vein, the frontal vs. profile is sometimes better than the profile vs. profile case. This reinforces our above observation that, in very difficult lateral poses, it is probably better to have frontal images if possible in one of the templates, rather than having all images with the same profile pose.

Similarly as Sect. 5.1, using five images to generate templates is a very effective way to cope with cross-pose situations. Its performance compared to using one image as template is significantly better (left vs. right part of Table 4), with improvements of one order of magnitude or more for any network. In higher security situations (e.g. FAR = 0.1%), ResNet50ft and SENet50ft provide impressive FRRs below 0.5% for any cross-pose combination, while SqueezeFacePoseNet ranks between 0.4–10% depending on the case.

5.3   Effect of Training Database

We now investigate the effect of the training set in our mobile architecture (Table 5), with all networks started from ImageNet pre-training, and trained from biometric identification as described in Sect. 4. In case that only one database is used for training, it can be seen that better results are obtained if the model is trained on a database with more samples per user (VGGFace2), rather than on a database with more samples and more users overall but with less samples per user (MS1M). But the biggest benefit in most cases is when the model is trained first on MS1M, and then fine-tuned on VGGFace2 (row 'both'). This is in line with the results in [3]. The biggest advantage is obtained when only one image is used to generate a user template, with improvements of up to 28% in comparison to training on VGGFace2 only. The effect is more diluted when five images are combined to create a user template, specially in cross-pose experiments. In this case, it is slightly better to train only on VGGFace2. However, it is not always the case that such amount of images are always available to generate a user template, e.g. in forensics [13].

6   Conclusion

We are interested in the development of a lightweight deep network architecture capable of providing accurate cross-pose face recognition under the restrictions of mobile architectures. For this purpose, we have adapted a very light model of

Table 5. Effect of the training database in SqueezeFacePoseNet (EER%). F = Frontal View. 3/4 = Three-Quarter. P = Profile. The best result of each column is marked in bold. Performance variation of the 'both' w.r.t. the 'VGGFace2' row is given in brackets.

Training data	One face image per template						Five face images per template					
	Same-pose			Cross-pose			Same-pose			Cross-pose		
	F-F	3/4-3/4	P-P	F-3/4	3/4-P	F-P	F-F	3/4-3/4	P-P	F-3/4	3/4-P	F-P
MS1M	16.82	16.23	20.24	17.45	21.24	24.19	1.17	2.17	3.25	1.7	5.24	7.01
VGGFace2	8.93	6.97	8.34	8.35	8.16	10.35	**0.27**	0.27	0.64	**0.2**	**0.55**	**1.09**
Both	**6.39** (−28%)	**5.47** (−22%)	**7.88** (−6%)	**6.09** (−27%)	**7.02** (−14%)	**8.15** (−21%)	**0.27** (−)	**0.06** (−78%)	**0.54** (−16%)	**0.2** (−)	0.88 (+60%)	1.23 (+13%)

only 4.41 MB [12] to operate with small face images of 113×113 pixels. Training is done using the large-scale MS-Celeb-1M [7] and VGGFace2 [3] datasets. VGGFace2 (3.31M images, 9.1K identities) is a dataset with a rich variation of imaging conditions. Being a large-scale database, it is designed to have a larger number of images per user as well (364 on average) in comparison to other databases. MS-Celeb-1M contains a larger number of images (3.16M in our experiments), but a larger number of identities as well (35K), so its number of images per identity is smaller. Following recommendations [3], we combine a large database (MS-Celeb-1M) and a database with more intra-class diversity (VGGFace2) to train the recognition network. This has shown to provide increased performance in comparison to using only one of them (Table 5).

To achieve further reductions in model size, we test the replacement of standard convolutions with depth-wise separable convolutions [10], leading to a network of just 2.5 MB. We also test Global Depth-wise Convolution (GDC) in substitution of the standard Global Average Pooling (GAP), since some works report that it provides better face recognition performance [4,6]. The employed architecture is bench-marked against two state-of-the-art architectures [3] with a size >30 times bigger and >20 times more parameters (Table 1). We evaluate two verification scenarios, consisting of using a different number of face images to generate a user template. In one case, a template consists of a combination of five face images with the same pose, following the evaluation protocol of [3]. In the second case, we consider the much more difficult case of employing only one image to generate a user template. Different pose combinations between enrolment and query templates are tested (Fig. 3).

Obviously, the use of five face images to create a user template provides a much more better performance, with improvements of up to two orders of magnitude in some cases. Also, in our experiments, we have not observed better performance by using Global Depth-wise Convolution, but the opposite. We speculate that this may be because training images of the VGGFace2 database are obtained by randomly cropping the face bounding box, so faces are not spatially aligned (Fig. 2c). In this sense, trying to learn different weights for each spatial region may be counterproductive. In addition, as expected [10], the use of depth-wise separable convolution results in a slight decrease of performance.

Even if our light architecture does not outperform the state-of-the-art networks, it obtains meritorious results even under severe pose variations between enrolment and query templates. For example, the comparison of frontal vs. profile images gives an EER of 1.23%. Also, the comparison of profile vs. profile images gives an EER of 0.54%, even if just half of the face is visible in this case. These results are with a template of five face images, which is revealed as a very effective way to improve cross-pose recognition performance. With only one face image per template, the performance of our network goes up to 8.15/7.88% respectively in the two mentioned cases. In less extreme cases of pose variability, performance of our network is even better, for example: 0.88% (three-quarter vs. profile view), 0.2% (frontal vs. three-quarter), or 0.27% (frontal vs. frontal).

A number of combinations to create enrolment and query templates would be of interest, which will be the source of future work. For example, if video is available, a collection of frames could be combined for user template generation, probably selecting those with near to frontal pose as well. How many images per template are necessary to obtain accurate performance is also worth to study. In some scenarios like forensics [13], query data may consist of only one image with an arbitrary pose, but several images per suspect may be available in the enrolment database. Therefore, one-query vs. multiple-enrolment images is also of interest to evaluate. Also, in our protocol, a template is generated using only images of the same pose. Combining images of multiple poses in the same template could be a way to create a richer user model, further improving performance.

To improve the performance of our mobile model, we are also looking into the use of residual connections [8] and pre-activation of convolutional layers inside residual blocks [9]. Giving the current context where face engines are forced to work with images of people wearing masks, we are also evaluating the accuracy of our model when using partial images containing only the ocular regions [2].

Acknowledgment. This work was partly done while F. A.-F. was a visiting researcher at Facephi Biometria, funded by the Sweden's Innovation Agency (Vinnova) under the staff exchange and AI program. Authors F. A.-F., K. H.-D. and J. B. also thank the Swedish Research Council for funding their research. Part of the computations were enabled by resources provided by the Swedish National Infrastructure for Computing (SNIC) at NSC Linköping. We also gratefully acknowledge the support of NVIDIA with the donation of a Titan V GPU used for this research.

References

1. Akhtar, Z., Hadid, A., Nixon, M.S., Tistarelli, M., Dugelay, J., Marcel, S.: Biometrics: in search of identity and security. IEEE Multimedia **25**(3), 22–35 (2018)
2. Alonso-Fernandez, F., Bigun, J.: A survey on periocular biometrics research. Pattern Recogn. Lett. **82**, 92–105 (2016)
3. Cao, Q., Shen, L., Xie, W., Parkhi, O.M., Zisserman, A.: VGGFace2: a dataset for recognising faces across pose and age. In: 13th IEEE International Conference on Automatic Face and Gesture Recognition (FG 2018), pp. 67–74 (2018)

4. Chen, S., Liu, Y., Gao, X., Han, Z.: MobileFaceNets: efficient CNNs for accurate real-time face verification on mobile devices. CoRR abs/1804.07573 (2018). http://arxiv.org/abs/1804.07573

5. Deng, J., Guo, J., Zhou, Y., Yu, J., Kotsia, I., Zafeiriou, S.: RetinaFace: single-stage dense face localisation in the wild. CoRR abs/1905.00641 (2019). http://arxiv.org/abs/1905.00641

6. Duong, C.N., Quach, K.G., Jalata, I.K., Le, N., Luu, K.: MobiFace: a lightweight deep learning face recognition on mobile devices. In: Proceedings BTAS, September 2019

7. Guo, Y., Zhang, L., Hu, Y., He, X., Gao, J.: MS-Celeb-1M: a dataset and benchmark for large-scale face recognition. In: Leibe, B., Matas, J., Sebe, N., Welling, M. (eds.) ECCV 2016. LNCS, vol. 9907, pp. 87–102. Springer, Cham (2016). https://doi.org/10.1007/978-3-319-46487-9_6

8. He, K., Zhang, X., Ren, S., Sun, J.: Deep residual learning for image recognition. In: Proceedings CVPR, pp. 770–778, June 2016

9. He, K., Zhang, X., Ren, S., Sun, J.: Identity mappings in deep residual networks. In: Leibe, B., Matas, J., Sebe, N., Welling, M. (eds.) ECCV 2016. LNCS, vol. 9908, pp. 630–645. Springer, Cham (2016). https://doi.org/10.1007/978-3-319-46493-0_38

10. Howard, A.G., et al.: MobileNets: efficient convolutional neural networks for mobile vision applications. CoRR abs/1704.04861 (2017). http://arxiv.org/abs/1704.04861

11. Hu, J., Shen, L., Sun, G.: Squeeze and-excitation networks. In: IEEE Conference on Computer Vision and Pattern Recognition, CVPR (2018)

12. Iandola, F.N., Moskewicz, M.W., Ashraf, K., Han, S., Dally, W.J., Keutzer, K.: SqueezeNet: AlexNet-level accuracy with 50x fewer parameters and ¡1mb model size. CoRR abs/1602.07360 (2016). http://arxiv.org/abs/1602.07360

13. Jain, A.K., Ross, A.: Bridging the gap: from biometrics to forensics. Phil. Trans. R. Soc. 370, 20140254 (2015)

14. Jain, A., Nandakumar, K., Ross, A.: 50 years of biometric research: accomplishments, challenges, and opportunities. Pattern Recogn. Lett. 79, 80–105 (2016)

15. Kornblith, S., Shlens, J., Le, Q.V.: Do better ImageNet models transfer better? In: Proceedings CVPR, pp. 2656–2666 (2019)

16. Martinez-Díaz, Y., Luevano, L.S., Mendez-Vazquez, H., Nicolas-Diaz, M., Chang, L., Gonzalez-Mendoza, M.: ShuffleFaceNet: a lightweight face architecture for efficient and highly-accurate face recognition. In: Proceedings if ICCVW, pp. 2721–2728 (2019)

17. Sandler, M., Howard, A., Zhu, M., Zhmoginov, A., Chen, L.: MobileNetv 2: inverted residuals and linear bottlenecks. In: Proceedings of CVPR, pp. 4510–4520 (2018)

18. Sundararajan, K., Woodard, D.L.: Deep learning for biometrics: a survey. ACM Comput. Surv. 51(3), 1–34 (2018)

19. Wu, X., He, R., Sun, Z., Tan, T.: A light CNN for deep face representation with noisy labels. IEEE TIFS 13(11), 2884–2896 (2018)

20. Zhang, J.: Seesaw-Net: convolution neural network with uneven group convolution. CoRR abs/1905.03672 (2019). http://arxiv.org/abs/1905.03672

21. Zhang, J.: SeesawFaceNets: sparse and robust face verification model for mobile platform. CoRR abs/1908.09124 (2019), https://arxiv.org/abs/1908.09124

22. Zhang, X., Zhou, X., Lin, M., Sun, J.: ShuffleNet: an extremely efficient convolutional neural network for mobile devices. In: Proceedings of CVPR, pp. 6848–6856 (2018)

Deep Learning-Based Semantic Segmentation for Touchless Fingerprint Recognition

Jannis Priesnitz[1,2(✉)], Christian Rathgeb[1], Nicolas Buchmann[2], and Christoph Busch[1]

[1] da/sec - Biometrics and Internet Security Research Group, Hochschule Darmstadt, Schöfferstraße 8b, 64295 Darmstadt, Germany {jannis.priesnitz,christian.rathgeb,christoph.busch}@h-da.de
[2] Freie Universität Berlin, Takustraße 9, 14195 Berlin, Germany {jannis.priesnitz,nicolas.buchmann}@fu-berlin.de

Abstract. Fingerprint recognition is one of the most popular biometric technologies. Touchless fingerprint systems do not require contact of the finger with the surface of a capture device. For this reason, they provide an increased level of hygiene, usability, and user acceptance compared to touch-based capturing technologies. Most processing steps of the recognition workflow of touchless recognition systems differ in comparison to touch-based biometric techniques. Especially the segmentation of the fingerprint areas in a 2D capturing process is a crucial and more challenging task.

In this work a proposal of a fingertip segmentation using deep learning techniques is presented. The proposed system allows to submit the segmented fingertip areas from a finger image directly to the processing pipeline. To this end, we adapt the deep learning model DeepLabv3+ to the requirements of fingertip segmentation and trained it on the database for hand gesture recognition (HGR) by extending it with a fingertip ground truth. Our system is benchmarked against a well-established color-based baseline approach and shows more accurate hand segmentation results especially on challenging images. Further, the segmentation performance on fingertips is evaluated in detail. The gestures provided in the database are separated into three categories by their relevance for the use case of touchless fingerprint recognition. The segmentation performance in terms of Intersection over Union (IoU) of up to 68.03% on the fingertips (overall: 86.13%) in the most relevant category confirms the soundness of the presented approach.

Keywords: Biometrics · Fingerprint recognition · Touchless fingerprint recognition · Semantic segmentation · Hand segmentation · Fingertip segmentation

A. Del Bimbo et al. (Eds.): ICPR 2020 Workshops, LNCS 12668, pp. 154–168, 2021.
https://doi.org/10.1007/978-3-030-68793-9_11

1   Introduction

Fingerprints, *i.e.* ridge-valley patterns on the tip of a human finger, are one of the most important biometric characteristics due to their known uniqueness and persistence properties [9,16]. Opposed to touch-based systems touchless fingerprint recognition does not suffer from problems like distortions due to pressing the finger on a sensor plate, areas of low contrast caused by dirt, humidity, or latent fingerprints left on the sensor plate [12,17].

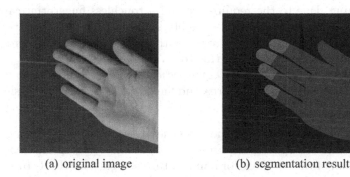

(a) original image   (b) segmentation result

Fig. 1. Example of (a) an input image to the proposed touchless fingerprint segmentation approach and (b) the corresponding segmentation result. Note that the depicted thumb does not contain a fingerprint suitable for recognition purposes.

However, reaching sufficient biometric performance in the preprocessing of touchless fingerprints is a challenging task. Segmenting the fingertip from the background is an essential step during the preprocessing [15]. In this context, the fingertip is defined as only the tip on the underside of the finger where the ridge-valley patterns are located. Figure 1 illustrates the segmentation of the fingertip region from a 2D image by the segmentation approach presented in this work.

State-of-the-art hand and finger segmentation systems employed in touchless fingerprint recognition schemes are mostly based on the analysis of sharpness, color, or shape. First approaches employ simple filter, *e.g.* Sobel operator [13] or Gaussian filter [14], in order to separate the sharp foreground from the background area. Such approaches require a clear gap between sharp and blurred areas and assume that the finger area is focused. Jonietz *et al.* [10] proposed a conjunction of a shape and color-based finger detection using edge pairing. The authors apply machine learning algorithms to estimate the finger shape on color-based segmented images. Several contributions use properties of color models to segment the skin-tone color from the background. Here the YCbCr color model is most prominent [1,8,23,24]. Raghavendra *et al.* [22] used a mean shift segmentation to filter the input image and segment it by fusing the convergence points in homogeneous regions. Multiple approaches utilize Otsu's algorithm to find a proper threshold between hand and background area, *e.g.* Wang *et al.*

[24]. The detection of fingertips is further investigated by Raghavendra *et al.* [22] who aim to find the first finger knuckle based on its darker color. Lee *et al.* [13] present a region growing scheme by analyzing ridge-valley patterns in the frequency domain. Such two-stage schemes of segmenting the hand area and detecting the fingertip is considered error-prone in unconstrained use cases.

Semantic segmentation using deep learning techniques represents an active field of research in recent years. For a comprehensive overview on the topic the interested reader is referred to surveys on this topic [5,6,18]. Especially in challenging environments object detection and segmentation greatly benefit from machine learning. Due to the requirements of a touchless fingerprint capturing process deep learning techniques are highly suitable for segmenting the hand area and the fingertips. To the best of the authors' knowledge no comprehensive research has yet been published on this topic.

This work proposes a fingertip segmentation system based on deep learning which is able to segment the hand area and fingertips in a single processing step. The contributions of this work are:

- An adaptation of the state-of-the-art general purpose deep learning model DeepLabv3+ to the specific requirements of touchless fingerprint recognition.
- The extension of the database for hand gesture recognition (HGR) by fingertip ground truth masks.
- The application of suitable data augmentation to the database to obtain a sufficient amount of training samples.
- A comprehensive evaluation in a tenfold cross-validation on a subject disjoint training and evaluation split including a comparison against a color-based segmentation system (baseline) and a detailed discussion of the segmentation performance.

The rest of this paper is structured as follows: The following Sect. 2 describes the proposed system. Section 3 presents our experimental setup. Section 4 summarizes the results obtained in our experiments. Finally, Sect. 5 concludes.

2   Proposed System

The workflow proposed system consists of two stages (1) data preparation and preprocessing and (2) semantic segmentation of hands and fingertips which is based on the DeepLabv3+ model. Figure 2 gives an overview on key components of the proposed system.

2.1   Preprocessing and Training Data Preparation

For this work, we use all subsets of the database for Hand Gesture Recognition HGR [7,11,19] created at the Silesian University of Technology. The original intent of this database is to provide gestures from the Polish and American sign language. A total number of 53 gestures are represented. Overall, the database provides 1,558 images from 33 subjects along with a skin-based ground truth masks, and a list of feature point positions, *e.g.* fingertips and knuckles.

To make the HGR database suitable for training a semantic hand and fingertip segmentation network, we implemented the following adaptations. First, the ground truth masks are extended by a fingertip class. To this end, the feature points representing fingertips and the first finger knuckle are employed. Precisely, a circular area is defined with the fingertip as center point and the distance between the fingertip and the first knuckle as radius. This circular area is intersected with the hand labeled pixels to consider only hand area pixels as fingertip. This process is illustrated in Fig. 3. During a manual revision, the labels of a few fingertips were manually post-processed in order to increase their accuracy. In particular, fingertips for which the underside of the finger are not visible were discarded.

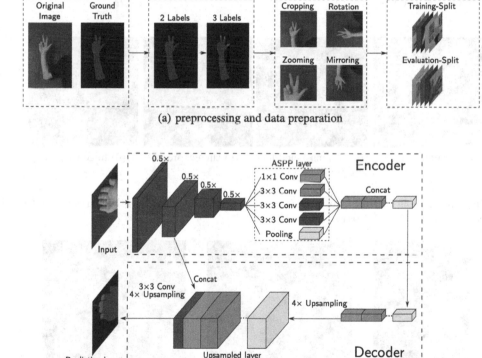

Fig. 2. Overview on the proposed system: (a) in the training stage, the skin-based ground truth of a hand gesture recognition database is extended by incorporating a fingertip class and data augmentation employed; (b) in the evaluation stage a comprehensive evaluation of the semantic segmentation network based on DeepLabv3+ for hand and fingertip segmentation is performed.

The used deep learning model DeepLabv3+ works with square input images and an image size which is a power of two. For this reason, all samples are scaled and cropped to a size of 512 × 512 pixels, *cf.* Fig. 4 (left, middle). Even so a 512 × 512 pixels hand pose image is not suitable for fingerprint extraction the resulting segmentation mask can be utilized for fingerprint extraction on the full size image in a practical application. The model uses feature points to preserve as much hand area and fingertips of the original image as possible.

Second, a data augmentation is applied. The cropped samples are further augmented by a rotation of 90°, −90°, 180°, or a mirroring on the vertical or horizontal axis. Additionally, a combination of rotation by 90° and a vertical mirroring is applied. Further a zooming is implemented to a subset of 1103 samples to emphasize the fingertip region *cf.* Fig. 4 (right). It should be noted that not all samples are suitable for zooming because not every sample contains a fingertip area. The zoomed samples are also augmented by a rotation of 90° or −90° and a mirroring on the vertical or horizontal axis. In total, this results in 15,318 samples.

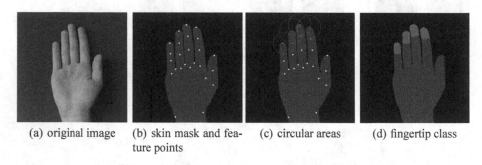

(a) original image   (b) skin mask and feature points   (c) circular areas   (d) fingertip class

Fig. 3. Example of the proposed extension of original ground truth skin mask with feature points by a fingertip class.

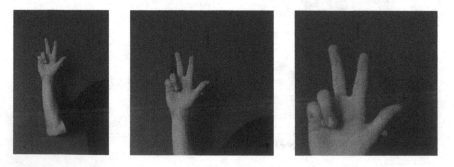

Fig. 4. Examples of an original image (left) of the resulting cropped (middle) and zoomed (left) images used for subsequent data augmentation.

2.2   Semantic Segmentation

As deep learning model, DeepLabv3+ [2,3] is utilized. To this day, DeepLabv3+ is one of the best performing general purpose segmentation networks on the Pascal VOC Challenge [4]. It is based on a encode-decoder structure using Atrous Spatial Pyramid Pooling (ASPP). For more details on DeepLabv3+ the reader is referred to [2,3].

For better segmentation results on small data sets, the DeepLab developers provide pre-trained models. In this research a model is used which was pre-trained on the general-purpose Pascal VOC data set for transfer learning [20]. The number of classes is reduced to three (hand area, fingertips and background)

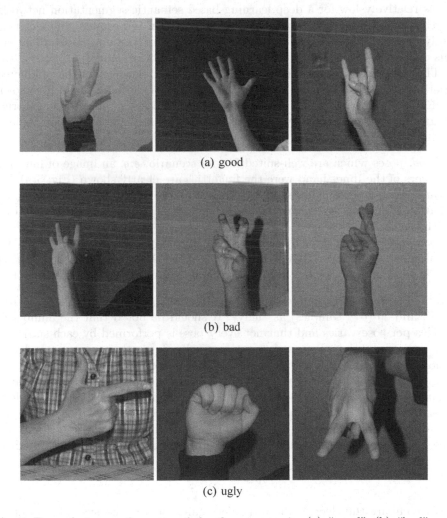

(a) good

(b) bad

(c) ugly

Fig. 5. Example images for poses of the three categories (a) "good", (b) "bad", and (c) "ugly".

in order to fit to the extended HGR database. The neural network is trained over 24 epochs whereas one epoch consists of a run through all images included in the training.

3 Experimental Setup

For a reliable segmentation result, the HGR database is separated into a training set and an evaluation set. The separation is performed subject disjoint to ensure that the model is not evaluated on subjects which it has already seen during the training phase.

Despite the data augmentation the amount of training and evaluation samples is relatively low for a deep learning-based semantic segmentation network. For this reason, a cross-validation is performed. Over ten rounds, different randomly selected distributions of subjects are used for training and evaluation. This ensures a proper assessment of segmentation performance.

The HGR database contains 53 poses of different relevance for the conducted experiment. For example, a pose were four fingers of the inner hand are shown (*cf.* Fig. 1) has much higher relevance for the use case of touchless fingerprint recognition than a pose showing a fist. For this reason, the evaluation is done for three categories of poses:

- *Good:* poses which are well-suited for our scenario, *e.g.* an image of multiple fingers of the inner hand were the fingertips are clearly shown (Fig. 5(a)).
- *Bad:* more challenging poses where fingertips are shown but rotated (Fig. 5b left, middle), or partly covered by other fingers or parts of the hand (Fig. 5(b) right).
- *Ugly:* poses which do not contain a clear fingertip area or the fingertips are only partially visible. This is the case, *e.g.* when the hand is clenched in a fist (Fig. 5(c) middle), or the back of the hand is shown (Fig. 5(c) left, right).

In total 18 poses (470 samples) are categorized as "good", 15 (441 samples) as "bad", and 20 (674 samples) as "ugly". It should be noted that the number of samples per pose varies and that not every pose is performed by each subject.

For the evaluation of our segmentation results we use the very common Intersection over Union (IoU) metric as defined in equation 1. Here G stands for the ground truth whereas S refers to the segmentation result. The IoU is estimated for single classes while the mean IoU (mIoU) is estimated for all classes including background. Additionally, the inter-class IoU is computed. This refers to the erratic intersection between two different classes which should be disjoint and gives us a better understanding how the segmentation errors are distributed.

$$IoU = \frac{G \cap S}{G \cup S} \tag{1}$$

To compare the deep learning model against a baseline system we implemented a well-established color-based segmentation system. Here Otsu's adaptive threshold algorithm is applied to the RGB image. The algorithm segments the hand area from the background which results in a binary image as segmentation mask.

Depending on the brightness distribution of each color channel the hand area in the segmented image is either black or red. Therefore, the IoU is computed on the original segmentation mask and its inverse. A max filter takes the image with the better IoU score. It should be noted that this approach is principally not capable of detecting the fingertip regions.

4   Results

In our experiments, we first compare the segmentation performance in terms of IoU and mIoU between the proposed system and the baseline. Further, a more detailed evaluation of the segmentation results on the hand and fingertips areas is done. All results are generated in the tenfold cross-validation.

4.1   Proposed System vs. Baseline

In a first experiment, we compare the color-based baseline system with the deep learning-based segmentation. This evaluation considers only the overall

Table 1. Comparison of the segmentation performance between the deep learning-based system and the baseline approach.

System	Class	IoU (%)	Std Dev (%)
Proposed	Mean	95.02	2.29
	Hand	89.01	0.93
Baseline	Mean	91.58	20.97
	Hand	85.20	16.44

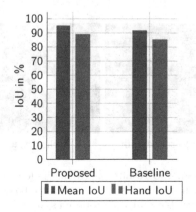

Fig. 6. Comparison on segmentation performance between the baseline and the deep learning system.

segmentation performance and the segmentation performance on the hand area because the baseline system does not feature a fingertip detection.

Both systems show a promising overall segmentation accuracy. The deep learning system shows a slightly better mIoU of 95.02% than the baseline system with 89.01%, as shown in Fig. 6. Consequentially, the IoU of the hand area shows similar results (deep learning: 89.01%, baseline: 85.20%) as summarized in *cf.* Table 1. The good performance of the color-based segmentation is attributed to a homogeneous background and the high contrast between hand and background in most of the images in the database. Figure 7 shows a more challenging sample. Here a background which is of a skin tone-like color leads to an inaccurate segmentation result of the baseline system whereas the deep learning system segments the hand area more accurate. On the one hand, from Fig. 7(c) it can be observed that the baseline system is more vulnerable to segmenting background area as hand area because it features no metric which considers the shape. On the other hand, the deep learning system more thoroughly segments the hand area, as can be seen in Fig. 7(d). The high standard deviation on the baseline system (mean IoU: 20.97%, hand IoU: 16.44%) is also attributed to challenging samples. This illustrates a lack of robustness of the color-based segmentation.

4.2   Segmentation of Hand and Fingertips

In a second experiment, we evaluate the segmentation performance especially on the fingertip class and analyze the kind of errors the deep learning system makes. As discussed, we separate the poses in three categories, "good", "bad", and "ugly". For each category the mean IoU, hand IoU, and fingertip IoU is computed. Obtained results are listed in Table 2 and plotted in Fig. 8. Moreover, we estimate the IoU between the background and the hand, and between the background and the fingertip. Illustratively, this can be seen as the erratic IoU between two classes which should be separated. Corresponding results are summarized in Table 3.

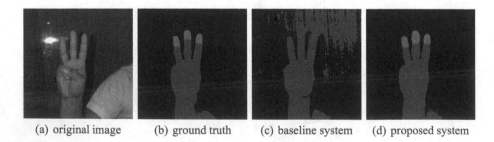

(a) original image   (b) ground truth   (c) baseline system   (d) proposed system

Fig. 7. Comparison between the results on (a) a challenging input image with (b) corresponding ground truth of the (c) the color-based baseline system and (d) our proposed system. It is observable that the proposed system is close to the ground truth whereas the baseline system fails to segment the hand area.

Table 2. Segmentation performance of the proposed system across image categories.

Category	Class	IoU (%)	Std. Dev (%)
Good	Mean	86.13	1.81
	Hand	92.05	0.35
	Fingertip	68.03	3.44
Bad	Mean	82.75	3.68
	Hand	90.63	1.93
	Fingertip	61.10	3.29
Ugly	Mean	72.95	1.38
	Hand	92.06	0.50
	Fingertip	33.12	8.05

In general, deep learning techniques learn color, contrast, and shape properties of every class. In our use case the hand area is well separated from the background by color and contrast. In general, the experimental results of our proposed deep learning system showcase a competitive hand and fingertip segmentation performance on the most relevant category. The fingertip class has naturally no separation from the hand area by color or contrast. Here the learning of shapes is most important. The results show that the learning of fingertip areas was successful in most cases but also highlight some challenges. Figure 9 highlights a collection of good performing samples.

The fingertip segmentation performs competitively on samples categorized as "good" with a fingertip IoU at 68.03%, *cf.* Fig. 8. Samples categorized as "bad" still show a fingertip IoU of 61.10%, whereas the performance of "ugly" samples drops to 33.12%. The reason for better results of the "good" and "bad" categories is that there are one or more fingers raised and the inner hand is

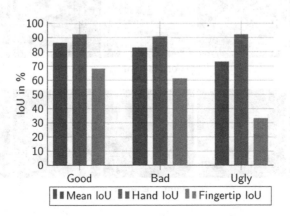

Fig. 8. Overview on segmentation performance in terms of IoU of the different three categories "good", "bad", and "ugly".

Table 3. Segmentation errors (inter-class IoU) of the proposed system across image categories.

Category	Classes	IoU (%)	Std. Dev (%)
Good	Background and fingertip	0.08	0.02
	Background and hand	0.34	0.09
	Hand and fingertip	1.88	0.18
Bad	Background and fingertip	0.12	0.03
	Background and hand	0.48	0.10
	Hand and fingertip	1.95	0.20
Ugly	Background and fingertip	0.06	0.02
	Background and hand	0.49	0.10
	Hand and fingertip	1.85	0.26

presented. The performance drop on the "ugly" category can be explained by the challenging task of estimating if the front or back of the hand is visible. In such cases, the deep learning system often fails by wrongly segmenting fingertips on the back of the hand (*cf.* Fig. 10).

An important aspect of the proposed system is which kind of segmentation errors it makes. For this reason, the inter-class intersections between background, hand, and fingertip are computed. From Table 3 we observe that the IoU between background and fingertip is very low ("good": 0.08%, "bad": 0.12%, "ugly": 0.06%). The IoU between background and hand is respectively ("good": 0.34%, "bad": 0.48%, "ugly": 0.49%). The highest inter-class IoU value can be

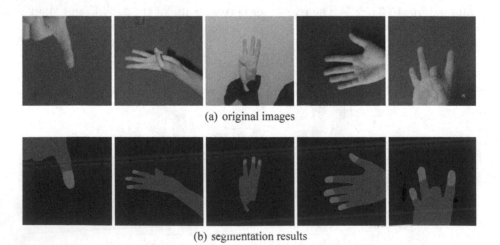

(a) original images

(b) segmentation results

Fig. 9. Examples of correctly segmented fingertips for various poses: all visible fingertips with visible fingerprints are segmented.

observed between the hand and the fingertip ("good": 1.88%, "bad": 1.95%, "ugly": 1.85%). This distribution suggests that the system segments fingertips almost exclusively within the hand area. The high hand to fingertip IoU is caused by segmenting a fingertip area which is too big or a fingertip at the back of the hand. However, such errors might not be considered as critical as the fingerprint will still be contained in the segmented fingertip. Further examples of sub-optimal segmentation results are shown in Fig. 10.

In all three categories the standard deviation on the fingertips is much higher than the standard deviation on the hand area and the background. One hypothesis is that learning solely through shape (fingertip) is more vulnerable to misssegmentation than learning based on color, shape, and contrast (hand). Another important aspect is that in some training-evaluation splits, hand poses with few samples are not shown to the neural network during the training phase but in the evaluation. In these constellations the segmentation performance on these poses is rather low which leads to a higher standard deviations. On "ugly" poses the standard deviation is even higher. Here, the fact that only a few of the "ugly" categorized samples contain a fingertip area further increases the standard deviation.

Some aspects could further improve the segmentation results: a training database which is more suitable for the intended application scenario will most likely lead to a more robust segmentation result. Furthermore, in a guided capturing process, instructions can be given to not present the back of the hand. This lowers the variety of poses which must be estimated and subsequently increases the segmentation accuracy. The proposed system is not able to assess how many fingertips are segmented and of which quality they are. Quality assessment of touchless fingerprint using NFIQ2.0 is investigated in [21]. Hence, multiple

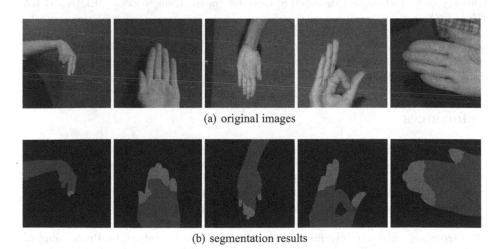

(a) original images

(b) segmentation results

Fig. 10. Examples of inaccurately segmented fingertips: falsely segmented fingertips on the back of the hand, and connected fingertip areas.

fingertips of the inner hand might be segmented as one connected area. Moreover, rotated fingertips, especially the thumb, are segmented, regardless of their rotation angle (*cf.* Fig. 10). Hence, a dedicated postprocessing would be required to extract single fingerprint regions.

5   Conclusion

In this work, we present a feasibility study on direct fingertip segmentation for touchless fingerprint recognition through the use of a deep learning-based semantic segmentation. For this purpose, we adapted a general-purpose segmentation network to fit the use case of fingertip segmentation by extending a hand gesture database with a fingertip class and adding suitable data augmentation. A tenfold cross-validation was conducted and evaluated, including a comparison to a well-established color-based segmentation scheme. The resulting comparison with the color-based baseline system shows superior segmentation results of the hand area and represents a demonstrates the feasibility of direct fingertip segmentation. Compared to traditional contrast-based finger knuckle detection approaches, the presented method is expected to be less error-prone. Especially in unconstrained environments with challenging heterogeneous background and illumination the proposed system is expected to be more robust.

The development of adequate postprocessing to extract single fingerprint images from obtained segmentation results as well as an integration to the processing pipeline of a touchless fingerprint recognition system are subject to future work.

Acknowledgments. The authors acknowledge the financial support by the Federal Ministry of Education and Research of Germany in the framework of MEDIAN (FKZ 13N14798).

This research work has been funded by the German Federal Ministry of Education and Research and the Hessian Ministry of Higher Education, Research, Science and the Arts within their joint support of the National Research Center for Applied Cybersecurity ATHENE.

References

1. Birajadar, P., et al.: Touch-less fingerphoto feature extraction, analysis and matching using monogenic wavelets. In: 2016 International Conference on Signal and Information Processing (IConSIP), pp. 1–6, October 2016
2. Chen, L.C., Papandreou, G., Schroff, F., Adam, H.: Rethinking Atrous convolution for semantic image segmentation. arXiv preprint arXiv:1706.05587 (2017)
3. Chen, L.C., Zhu, Y., Papandreou, G., Schroff, F., Adam, H.: Encoder-decoder with Atrous separable convolution for semantic image segmentation. In: Proceedings of the European Conference on Computer Vision (ECCV), pp. 801–818 (2018)
4. Everingham, M., Eslami, S.A., Van Gool, L., Williams, C.K., Winn, J., Zisserman, A.: The Pascal visual object classes challenge: a retrospective. Int. J. Comput. Vis. **111**(1), 98–136 (2015)

5. Garcia-Garcia, A., Orts-Escolano, S., Oprea, S., Villena-Martinez, V., Martinez-Gonzalez, P., Garcia-Rodriguez, J.: A survey on deep learning techniques for image and video semantic segmentation. Appl. Soft Comput. **70**, 41–65 (2018)
6. Ghosh, S., Das, N., Das, I., Maulik, U.: Understanding deep learning techniques for image segmentation. ACM Comput. Surv. (CSUR) **52**(4), 1–35 (2019)
7. Grzejszczak, T., Kawulok, M., Galuszka, A.: Hand landmarks detection and localization in color images. Multimed. Tools Appl. **75**(23), 16363–16387 (2016)
8. Hiew, B.Y., Teoh, A.B.J., Ngo, D.C.L.: Automatic digital camera based fingerprint image preprocessing. In: International Conference on Computer Graphics, Imaging and Visualisation (CGIV 2006), pp. 182–189, July 2006
9. Jain, A.K., Flynn, P., Ross, A.A.: Handbook of Biometrics. Springer, July 2007. https://doi.org/10.1007/978-0-387-71041-9
10. Jonietz, C., Monari, E., Widak, H., Qu, C.: Towards mobile and touchless fingerprint verification. In: 2015 12th IEEE International Conference on Advanced Video and Signal Based Surveillance (AVSS), pp. 1–6, August 2015
11. Kawulok, M., Kawulok, J., Nalepa, J., Smolka, B.: Self-adaptive algorithm for segmenting skin regions. EURASIP J. Adv. Signal Process. **2014**(170), 1–22 (2014)
12. Khalil, M.S., Wan, F.K.: A review of fingerprint pre-processing using a mobile phone. In: 2012 International Conference on Wavelet Analysis and Pattern Recognition, pp. 152–157. IEEE (2012)
13. Lee, C., Lee, S., Kim, J., Kim, S.-J.: Preprocessing of a fingerprint image captured with a mobile camera. In: Zhang, D., Jain, A.K. (eds.) ICB 2006. LNCS, vol. 3832, pp. 348–355. Springer, Heidelberg (2005). https://doi.org/10.1007/11608288_47
14. Lee, D., Choi, K., Choi, H., Kim, J.: Recognizable-image selection for fingerprint recognition with a mobile-device camera. IEEE Trans. Syst. Man Cybern. Part B (Cybern.) **38**(1), 233–243 (2008)
15. Malhotra, A., Sankaran, A., Mittal, A., Vatsa, M., Singh, R.: Chapter 6 - fingerphoto authentication using smartphone camera captured under varying environmental conditions. In: Human Recognition in Unconstrained Environments, pp. 119–144. Academic Press (2017)
16. Maltoni, D., Maio, D., Jain, A., Prabhakar, S.: Handbook of Fingerprint Recognition, 1st (edn.). Springer-Verlag (2009). https://doi.org/10.1007/978-1-84882-254-2
17. Mil'shtein, S., Pillai, A.: Perspectives and limitations of touchless fingerprints. In: 2017 IEEE International Symposium on Technologies for Homeland Security (HST), pp. 1–6, April 2017
18. Minaee, S., Boykov, Y., Porikli, F., Plaza, A., Kehtarnavaz, N., Terzopoulos, D.: Image segmentation using deep learning: a survey. arXiv preprint arXiv:2001.05566 (2020)
19. Nalepa, J., Kawulok, M.: Fast and accurate hand shape classification. In: Kozielski, S., Mrozek, D., Kasprowski, P., Małysiak-Mrozek, B., Kostrzewa, D. (eds.) BDAS 2014. CCIS, vol. 424, pp. 364–373. Springer, Cham (2014). https://doi.org/10.1007/978-3-319-06932-6_35
20. Pan, S.J., Yang, Q.: A survey on transfer learning. IEEE Trans. Knowl. Data Eng. **22**, 1345–1359 (2010)
21. Priesnitz, J., Rathgeb, C., Buchmann, N., Busch, C.: Touchless Fingerprint Sample Quality: Prerequisites for the Applicability of NFIQ2.0. In: Proceedings of International Conference of the Biometrics Special Interest Group (BIOSIG) (2020)
22. Raghavendra, R., Busch, C., Yang, B.: Scaling-robust fingerprint verification with smartphone camera in real-life scenarios. In: 2013 IEEE Sixth International Conference on Biometrics: Theory, Applications and Systems (BTAS), pp. 1–8, September 2013

23. Sisodia, D.S., Vandana, T., Choudhary, M.: A conglomerate technique for finger print recognition using phone camera captured images. In: 2017 IEEE International Conference on Power, Control, Signals and Instrumentation Engineering (ICPCSI), pp. 2740–2746, September 2017
24. Wang, K., Cui, H., Cao, Y., Xing, X., Zhang, R.: A preprocessing algorithm for touchless fingerprint images. In: You, Z., et al. (eds.) CCBR 2016. LNCS, vol. 9967, pp. 224–234. Springer, Cham (2016). https://doi.org/10.1007/978-3-319-46654-5_25

FaceHop: A Light-Weight Low-Resolution Face Gender Classification Method

Mozhdeh Rouhsedaghat[1(✉)], Yifan Wang[1], Xiou Ge[1], Shuowen Hu[2], Suya You[2], and C.-C. Jay Kuo[1]

[1] University of Southern California, Los Angeles, CA, USA
{rouhseda,wang608,xiouge,jckuo}@usc.edu
[2] Army Research Laboratory, Adelphi, MD, USA
{shuowen.hu.civ,suya.you.civ}@mail.mil

Abstract. A light-weight low-resolution face gender classification method, called FaceHop, is proposed in this research. We have witnessed rapid progress in face gender classification accuracy due to the adoption of deep learning (DL) technology. Yet, DL-based systems are not suitable for resource-constrained environments with limited networking and computing. FaceHop offers an interpretable non-parametric machine learning solution. It has desired characteristics such as a small model size, a small training data amount, low training complexity, and low-resolution input images. FaceHop is developed with the successive subspace learning (SSL) principle and built upon the foundation of PixelHop++. The effectiveness of the FaceHop method is demonstrated by experiments. For gray-scale face images of resolution 32×32 in the LFW and the CMU Multi-PIE datasets, FaceHop achieves correct gender classification rates of 94.63% and 95.12% with model sizes of 16.9K and 17.6K parameters, respectively. It outperforms LeNet-5 in classification accuracy while LeNet-5 has a model size of 75.8K parameters.

Keywords: Gender classification · Light-weight model · Small data · SSL · PixelHop++

1 Introduction

Face attributes classification is an important topic in biometrics. The ancillary information of faces such as gender, age, and ethnicity is referred to as soft biometrics in forensics [1–3]. The face gender classification problem has been extensively studied for more than two decades. Before the resurgence of deep neural networks (DNNs) around 7–8 years ago, the problem was treated using the standard pattern recognition paradigm. It consists of two cascaded modules: 1) unsupervised feature extraction and 2) supervised classification via common machine learning tools such as support vector machine (SVM) and random forest (RF) classifiers.

We have seen fast progress on this topic due to the application of deep learning (DL) technology in recent years. Generally speaking, cloud-based face

© Springer Nature Switzerland AG 2021
A. Del Bimbo et al. (Eds.): ICPR 2020 Workshops, LNCS 12668, pp. 169–183, 2021.
https://doi.org/10.1007/978-3-030-68793-9_12

verification, recognition, and attributes classification technologies have become mature, and they have been used in many real world biometric systems. Convolution neural networks (CNNs) offer high-performance accuracy. Yet, they rely on large learning models consisting of several hundreds of thousands or even millions of model parameters. The superior performance is contributed by factors such as higher input image resolutions, more and more training images, and abundant computational/memory resources.

Edge/mobile computing in a resource-constrained environment cannot meet the above-mentioned conditions. The technology of our interest finds applications in rescue missions and/or field operational settings in remote locations. The accompanying face inference tasks are expected to execute inside a poor computing and communication infrastructure. It is essential to have a smaller learning model size, lower training and inference complexity, and lower input image resolution. The last requirement arises from the need to image individuals at farther standoff distances, which results in faces with fewer pixels.

In this work, we propose a new interpretable non-parametric machine learning solution called the FaceHop method. FaceHop has quite a few desired characteristics, including a small model size, a small training data amount, low training complexity, and low-resolution input images. FaceHop follows the traditional pattern recognition paradigm that decouples the feature extraction module from the decision module. However, FaceHop automatically extracts statistical features instead of handcrafted features. It is developed with the successive subspace learning (SSL) principle [4–6] and built upon the foundation of the PixelHop++ system [7]. The effectiveness of the FaceHop method is demonstrated by experiments on two benchmarking datasets. For gray-scale face images of resolution 32×32 obtained from the LFW and the CMU Multi-PIE datasets, FaceHop achieves gender classification accuracy of 94.63% and 95.12% with model sizes of 16.9K and 17.6K parameters, respectively. FaceHop outperforms LeNet-5 while the LeNet-5 model is significantly larger and contains 75.8K parameters.

There are three main contributions of this work. First, it offers a practical solution to the challenging face biometrics problem in a resource-constrained environment. Second, it is the first effort that applies SSL to face gender classification and demonstrates its superior performance. Third, FaceHop is fully interpretable, non-parametric, and non-DL-based. It offers a brand new path for research and development in biometrics.

The rest of this paper is organized as follows. Related work is reviewed in Sect. 2. The FaceHop method is presented in Sect. 3. Experimental set-up and results are detailed in Sect. 4. Finally, concluding remarks and future extensions are given in Sect. 5.

2   Related Work

2.1   Face Attributes Classification

We can classify face attributes classification research into two categories: non-DL-based and DL-based. DL-based solutions construct an end-to-end parametric model (i.e. a network), define a cost function, and train the network to minimize the cost function with labeled face gender images. The contribution typically arises from a novel network design. Non-DL-based solutions follow the pattern recognition paradigm and their contributions lie in using different classifiers or extracting new features for better performance.

Non-DL-Based Solutions. Researchers have studied different classifiers for gender classification. Gutta *et al.* [8] proposed a face-based gender and ethnic classification method using the ensemble of Radial Basis Functions (RBF) and Decision Trees (DT). SVM [9] and AdaBoost [10] have been studied for face gender classification. Different feature extraction techniques were experimented to improve classification accuracy. A Gabor-kernel partial-least squares discrimination (GKPLSD) method for more effective feature extraction was proposed by Štruc *et al.* [11]. Other handcrafted features were developed for face gender classification based on the local directional patterns (LDP) [12] and shape from shading [13]. Cao *et al.* [14] combined Multi-order Local Binary Patterns (MOLBP) with Localized Multi-Boost Learning (LMBL) for gender classification.

Recent research has focused more on large-scale face image datasets. Li *et al.* [15] proposed a novel binary code learning method for large-scale face image retrieval and facial attribute prediction. Jia *et al.* [16] collected a large dataset of 4 million weakly labeled face in the wild (4MWLFW). They trained the C-Pegasos classifier with Multiscale Local Binary Pattern (LBP) features using the 4MWLFW dataset and achieved the highest test accuracy on the LFW dataset for Non-DL-based methods up to now. Fusion of different feature descriptors and region of interests (ROI) were examined by Castrillón-Santana *et al.* [17].

The mentioned methods either have a weak performance as a result of failing to extract strong features from face images or have a large model size.

DL-Based Solutions. With the rapid advancement of the DL technology, DL-based methods become increasingly popular and achieve unprecedented accuracy in face biometrics [18]. Levi *et al.* [19] proposed a model to estimate age and gender using a small training data. Duan*et al.* [20] introduced a hybrid CNN-ELM structure for age and gender classification which uses CNN for feature extraction from face images and ELM for classifying the features. Taherkhani *et al.* [21] proposed a deep framework which predicts facial attributes and leveraged it as a soft modality to improve face identification performance. Han *et al.* [22] investigated the heterogeneous face attribute estimation problem with a deep multi-task learning approach. Ranjan *et al.* [23] proposed a multi-task learning framework for joint face detection, landmark localization, pose estimation, and gender recognition. Antipov *et al.* [24] investigated the relative importance of various regions of human faces for gender and age classification by blurring different parts of the faces and observing the loss in performance. ResNet50 [24], AlexNet [25], and VGG16 [18] were applied to gender classification of the LFW dataset, and decent performance was observed. However, these models have very large model sizes. Considerable amounts of computation and storage resources are required to implement these solutions.

Light-Weight CNNs. Light-weight networks are significantly smaller in size than regular networks while achieving comparable performance. They find applications in mobile/edge computing. One recent development is the SqueezeNet [26] which achieves comparable accuracy with the AlexNet [27] but uses 50x fewer parameters. It contains 4.8M model parameters. In the area of face recognition, Wu *et al.* [28] proposed a light CNN architecture that learns a compact embedding on a large-scale face dataset with massive noisy labels. Although the mentioned models are relatively small, they still require a large amount of training data.

2.2   Successive Subspace Learning (SSL)

Representation learning plays an important role in many representation learning methods are built upon DL, which is a supervised approach. It is also possible to use an unsupervised approach for representation learning automatically (i.e. not handcrafted). For example, there exist correlations between image pixels and their correlations can be removed using the principal component analysis (PCA). The application of PCA to face images was introduced by Turk and Pentland [29]. The method is called the "Eigenface". One main advantage of converting face images from the spatial domain to the spectral domain is that, when face images are well aligned, the dimension of input face images can be reduced significantly and automatically. Since we attempt to find a powerful subspace for face image representation, it is a subspace learning method.

Chan *et al.* [30] proposed a PCANet that applies the PCA to input images in two stages. Chen *et al.* [31] proposed a PixelHop system that applies cascaded Saab transforms [6] to input images in three stages, where the Saab transform is a variant of the PCA that adds a positive bias term to avoid the sign confusion problem [4]. The main difference between Eigenface, PCANet and PixelHop is to conduct the PCA transform in one, two, or multiple stages. If we apply one-stage PCA, the face is a pure spatial- and spectral-domain representations before and after the transform, respectively. Since the spatial representation is local, it cannot offer the global contour and shape information easily. On the contrary, the spectral representation is global, it fails to differentiate local variations. It is desired to get multiple hybrid spatial/spectral representations. This can be achieved by multi-stage transforms. Kuo *et al.* developed two multi-stage transforms, called the Saak transform [32] and the Saab transform [6], respectively. Recently, the channel-wise (c/w) Saab transform was proposed in [7] to enhance the efficiency of the Saab transform.

Inspired by the function of convolutional layers of CNNs [6], the PixelHop system [31] and the PixelHop++ system [7] were developed to serve the same function but derived based on a completely different principle. The weights of convolutional filters in CNNs are obtained by end-to-end optimization through backpropagation. In contrast, the convolutional kernels used in PixelHop and PixelHop++ are the Saab filters. They are derived by exploiting statistical correlations of neighboring pixels. As a result, both PixelHop and PixelHop++ are

Fig. 1. An overview of the proposed FaceHop method.

fully unsupervised. Neither label nor backpropagation is needed in filter weights computation.

The PixelHop++ system [7] is an enhanced version of the PixelHop system [31]. The main difference between PixelHop and PixelHop++ is that the former uses the Saab transform while the latter adopts the c/w Saab transform. The c/w Saab transform requires fewer model parameters than the Saab transform since channels are decoupled in the c/w Saab transform.

3   Proposed FaceHop Method

An overview of the proposed FaceHop system is shown in Fig. 1. It consists of four modules: 1) Preprocessing, 2) PixelHop++, 3) Feature extraction, and 4) Classification. Since PixelHop++ is the most unique module in our proposed solution for face gender classification, it is called the FaceHop system. The functionality of each module will be explained below in detail.

3.1   Preprocessing

Face images have to be well aligned in the preprocessing module to facilitate their processing in the following pipeline. In this work, we first use the dlib [33] tool for facial landmarks localization. Based on detected landmarks, we apply a proper 2D rotation to each face image to reduce the effect of pose variation. Then, all face images are centered and cropped to remove the background. Afterwards, we apply histogram equalization to each image to reduce the effect of different illumination conditions. Finally, all images are resized to a low resolution one of 32×32 pixels.

3.2   PixelHop++

Both PixelHop and PixelHop++ are used to describe local neighborhoods of a pixel efficiently and successively. The size of a neighborhood is characterized by the hop number. One-hop neighborhood is the neighborhood of the smallest size. Its actual size depends on the filter size. For example, if we use a convolutional filter of size 5×5, then the hop-1 neighborhood is of size 5×5. The Saab filter weights are obtained by performing dimension reduction on the neighborhood of a target pixel using PCA. The Saab filters in PixelHop and PixelHop++ serve as an equivalent role of convolutional filters in CNNs. For example, a neighborhood of size 5×5 has a dimension of 25 in the spatial domain. We can use the Saab transform to reduce its original dimension to a significantly lower one. We should

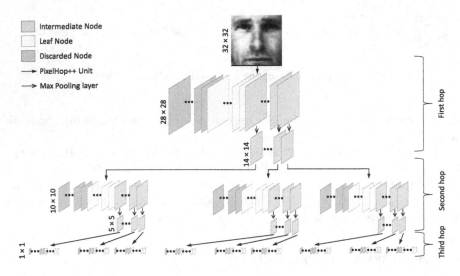

Fig. 2. Illustration of the proposed 3-hop FaceHop system as a tree-decomposed representation with its depth equal to three, where each depth layer corresponds to one hop. (Color figure online)

mention that the neighborhood concept is analogous to the receptive field of a certain layer of CNNs. As we go to deeper layers, the receptive field becomes larger in CNNs. In the SSL context, we say that the neighborhood size becomes larger as the hop number increases.

The proposed 3-hop PixelHop++ system is shown in Fig. 2, which is a slight modification of [7] so as to tailor to our problem. The input is a gray-scale face image of size 32×32. Each hop consists of a PixelHop++ unit followed by a (2×2)-to-(1×1) max-pooling operation. A PixelHop++ system has three ingredients: 1) successive neighborhood construction, 2) channel-wise Saab transform, and 3) tree-decomposed feature representation. They are elaborated below.

1) Successive Neighborhood Construction. We need to specify two parameters to build the neighborhood of the center pixel at each hop. There are the window-size and the stride. We use a window size of 5×5 and stride of 1 in all three hops in Fig. 2. The neighborhood size grows bigger as the hop number becomes larger due to the max-pooling operation. The first, second, and third hops characterize the information of the short-, mid-, and long-range neighborhoods of the center pixel. Apparently, each neighborhood has a degree of freedom of 25 in the spatial domain. By collecting these neighborhood samples from different spatial locations, we can study their statistical correlations via a covariance matrix of dimension 25×25. Then, we conduct the eigenvector/eigenvalue analysis to the covariance matrix to find a more economical representation. That is, we can convert pixel values from the spatial domain to the spectral domain, which leads to the PCA transform, for dimension reduction.

2) Channel-wise (c/w) Saab Transform. The PCA transform has both positive and negative responses. We encounter a sign-confusion problem [4] when a convolutional operation in the $(i+1)$th stage has the sum of two terms: 1) a positive response in the ith stage multiplied by a positive outgoing link and 2) a negative response in the ith stage multiplied by a negative outgoing link. Both terms contribute positive values to the output while their input patterns are out of phase. Similarly, there will be another sign-confusion when the convolutional operation in the $(i+1)$th stage has the sum of a positive response multiplied by a negative filter weight as well as a negative response multiplied by a positive filter weight. They both contribute to negative values.

To resolve such confusion cases, a constant bias term is added to make all responses positive. This is called the Saab (subspace approximation via adjusted bias) transform [6]. Typically, the input of the next pixelhop unit is a 3D tensor of dimension $N_x \times N_y \times k$, where $N_x = N_y = 5$ are spatial dimensions of a filter and k is the number of kept spectral components. The Saab transform is used in PixelHop.

Since channel responses can be decorrelated by the eigen analysis, we are able to treat each channel individually. This results in channel-wise (c/w) Saab transform [7]. The main difference between the standard Saab and the c/w Saab transforms is that one 3D tensor of dimension $N_x \times N_y \times k$ can be decomposed into k 2D tensors of dimension $N_x \times N_y$ in the latter. Furthermore, responses in higher frequency channels are spatially uncorrelated so that they do not have to go to the next hop. The c/w Saab transform is used in PixelHop++. It can reduce the model size significantly as compared with the Saab transform while preserving the same performance.

3) Tree-Decomposed Representation. Without loss of generality, we use the first hop to explain the c/w Saab transform design. The neighborhood of a center pixel contains 25 pixels. In the spectral domain, we first decompose it into the direct sum of two orthogonal subspaces - the DC (direct current) subspace and the AC (alternating current) subspace. Then, we apply the PCA to the AC subspace to derive Saab filters. After the first-stage Saab transform, we obtain one DC coefficient and 24 AC coefficients in a grid of size 28×28. We classify AC coefficients into three groups based on their associated eigenvalues: low-, mid-, and high-frequency AC coefficients.

When the eigenvalues are extremely small, we can discard responses in these channels without affecting the quality of the input face image. This is similar to the eigenface approach in spirit. For mid-frequency AC coefficients, the spatial correlation of their responses is too weak to offer a significant response in hop-2. Thus, we can terminate its further transform. For low-frequency AC coefficients, the spatial correlation of their responses is strong enough to offer a significant response in hop-2. Then, we conduct max-pooling and construct the hop-2 neighborhood of these frequency channels in a grid of size 14×14. It is easy to show these hop-by-hop operations using a tree. Then, each channel corresponds to a node. We use the green, yellow and pink colors to denote low-, mid- and high-frequency AC channels in Fig. 2. Where the DC channel is also colored in green.

They are called the intermediate, leaf, and discard nodes in a hierarchical tree of depth equal to three.

To determine which node belongs to which group, we use the energy of each node as the criterion. The energy of the root node is normalized to one. The energy of each node in the tree can be computed and normalized against the energy value of the root node. Then, we can choose two thresholds (in terms of energy percentages) at each hop to partition nodes into three types. These energy thresholds are hyperparameters of the PixelHop++ model.

3.3   Feature Extraction

Responses at each of the three hops of the FaceHop system have different characteristics. As shown in Fig. 2, Hop-1 has a response map of size 28×28, Hop-2 has a response map of size 10×10 and Hop-3 has a response map of size 1×1. Hop-1 responses give a spatially detailed representation of the input. Yet, it is difficult for them to offer regional and full views of the entire face unless the dimension of hop-1 responses becomes extremely large. This is expensive and unnecessary. Hop-2 responses give a coarser view of the entire face so that a small set of them can cover a larger spatial region. Yet, they do not have face details as given by Hop-1 responses. Finally, Hop-3 responses lose all spatial details but provide a single value at each frequency channel that covers the full face. The eigenface approach can only capture responses of the full face and cannot obtain the information offered by hop-1 and hop-2 responses in the FaceHop system. We will extract features based on responses in all three hops.

We group pixel responses in hop-1 and hop-2 to form region responses as shown in Fig. 3.

- **Hop-1.** We collect pixel responses in hop-1 to form four regions as shown in Fig. 3(a). They cover the left eye, the right eye, the nose, and the mouth regions. Their spatial dimensions (height versus width) are 10×12, 10×12, 12×10 and 8×18, respectively. There are spatial correlations for responses of the same channel. Thus, we can apply another PCA to responses of the same hop/region for dimension reduction. Usually, we can reduce the dimension to the range between 15 and 20. Afterwards, we concatenate the reduced dimension vector of each region across all hop-1 channels (including both leaf and intermediate nodes) to create a hop/region feature vector and feed it to a classifier. There are four hop-1 regions, and we have four feature vectors that contain both spatial and spectral information of a face image. The dimension of hop-1 feature vectors in four regions will be given in Table 2.
- **Hop-2.** We collect pixel responses in hop-2 to form three regions as shown in Fig. 3(b). They are: one horizontal stripe of dimension 3×10 covering two eyes, another horizontal stripe of dimension 4×10 covering the mouth, and one vertical stripe of dimension 10×4 covering the nose as well as the central 40% region. Similarly, we can perform dimension reduction via PCA and concatenate the spatially reduced dimension of each region across all

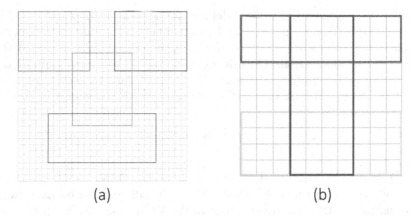

Fig. 3. Collection of regional responses in hop-1 and hop-2 response maps as features in the FaceHop system: (a) four regions in hop-1 and (b) three regions in hop-2.

hop-2 channels to train three classifiers. The dimension of hop-2 feature vectors in the three regions will be summarized in Table 2.

– **Hop-3.** We use all responses of hop-3 as one feature vector to train a classifier.

It is worthwhile to point out that, although some information of intermediate nodes will be forwarded to the next hop, different hops capture different information contents due to varying spatial resolutions. For this reason, we include responses in both intermediate and leaf nodes at hop-1 and hop-2 as features.

3.4   Classifiers

As described in Sect. 3.3, we train four classifiers in hop 1, another three classifiers in hop 2, and one classifier in hop 3. Each classifier takes a long feature vector as the input and makes a soft decision, which is the probability for the face to be a male or a female. Since the two probabilities add to unity, we only need to record one of them. Then, at the next stage, we feed these eight probabilities into a meta classifier for the final decision. The choice of classifiers can be the Random Forest (RF), the Support Vector Machine (SVM), and the Logistic Regression (LR). Although the SVM and the RF classifiers often give higher accuracy, they have a larger number of model parameters. Since our interest lies in a smaller model size, we adopt the LR classifier in our experiments only.

4   Experiments

In this section, we evaluate the proposed FaceHop gender classification method. We compare the FaceHop solution with a variant of LeNet-5 in model sizes and verification performance. The reason for choosing the LeNet-5 for performance benchmarking is that it is a small model which is demonstrated to have a relatively high classification accuracy on gray-scale 32×32 images. The neuron numbers of the modified LeNet-5 model are changed to 16 (1st Conv), 40 (2nd Conv), 140 (1st FC), 60 (2nd FC) and 2 (output). The modification is needed since human faces are more complicated than handwritten digits in the MNIST dataset. For fair comparison, we train both models on the same training data which is achieved by applying the preprocessing and data augmentation to the original face images. We use only logistic regression (LR) classifiers in FaceHop due to its small model size.

Datasets. We adopt the following two face image datasets in our experiments.

- **LFW dataset** [34]
  The LFW dataset consists of 13,233 face images of 5,749 individuals, which were collected from the web. There are 1,680 individuals who have two or more images. A 3D aligned version of LFW [35] is used in our experiments.
- **CMU Multi-PIE dataset** [36]
  The CMU Multi-PIE face dataset contains more than 750,000 images of 337 subjects recorded in four sessions. We select a subset of the 01 session that contains frontal and slightly non-frontal face images (camera views 05_0, 05_1, and 14_0) with all the available expressions and illumination conditions in our experiments.

Data Augmentation. Since both datasets have significantly fewer female images, we use two techniques to increase the number of female faces.

- Flipping the face images horizontally.
- Averaging a female face image with its nearest neighbor in the reduced dimension space to generate a new female face image. To find the nearest neighbor, we project all female images to a reduced dimension space, which is obtained by applying PCA and keeping the highest energy components with 90% of the total energy. Dimension reduction is conducted to eliminate noise and high-frequency components. The quality of augmented female images is checked to ensure that they are visually pleasant.

After augmentation, the number of male images is still slightly more than the number of female images.

Configuration of PixelHop++. The configurations of the PixelHop++ module for LFW and CMU Multi-PIE datasets are shown in Table 1. We list the numbers of intermediate nodes, leaf nodes and discarded nodes at each hop (see Fig. 2) in the experiments. In our design, we partition channels into two groups (instead of three) only at each hop. That is, they are either discarded or all forwarded to the next hop. As a result, there are no leaf nodes at hop-1 and hop-2.

Table 1. Configurations of PixelHop++ for LFW and CMU Multi-PIE.

Hop index	LFW			CMU Multi-PIE		
	Interm node no.	Leaf node no.	Discarded node no.	Interm node no.	Leaf node no.	Discarded node no.
Hop-1	18	0	7	18	0	7
Hop-2	122	0	328	117	0	333
Hop-3	0	233	2,817	0	186	2,739

Feature Vector Dimensions of Varying Hop/Region Combinations. The dimensions of feature vectors of varying hop/region combinations are summarized in Table 2. As discussed earlier, hop-1 has 4 spatial regions, hop-2 has three spatial regions and all nodes of hop-3 form one feature vector. Thus, there are eight hop/region combinations in total. Since there are spatial correlations in regions given in Fig. 3, we apply PCA to regional responses collected from all channels and keep leading components for dimension reduction. We keep 15 components for the LFW dataset and 20 components for the CMU Multi-PIE datasets, respectively. Then, the dimension of each feature vector at hop-1 and hop-2 is the product of 15 (or 20) and the sum of intermediate and leaf nodes at the associated hop for the LFW (or CMU Multi-PIE) dataset.

Table 2. Feature vector dimensions for LFW and CMU Multi-PIE.

Hop/Region	LFW	MPIE	Hop/Region	LFW	MPIE
Hop-1 (left eye)	270	360	Hop-2 (upper stripe)	1,830	2,340
Hop-1 (right eye)	270	360	Hop-2 (lower stripe)	1,830	2,340
Hop-1 (nose)	270	360	Hop-2 (vertical strip)	1,830	2,340
Hop-1 (mouth)	270	360	Hop-3		233	186

Performance and Model Size Comparison for LFW. We randomly partition male and original plus augmented female images in the LFW dataset into 80% (for training) and 20% (for testing) two sets individually. Then, they are mixed again to form the desired training and testing datasets. This is done to ensure the same gender percentages in training and testing. We train eight individual hop/region LR classifiers and one meta LR classifier for ensembles. Then, we apply them to the test data to find out their performance. We repeat the same process four times to get the mean testing accuracy and the standard deviation value, and report the testing performance of each individual hop/region in Table 3.

The mean testing accuracy ranges from 82.90% (hop-1/nose) to 92.42% (hop-2/vertical stripe). The standard deviation is relatively small. Furthermore, we see that hop-2 and hop-3 classifiers perform better than hop-1 classifiers. Based on

Table 3. Performance comparison of each individual hop/region classifier for LFW.

Classifier	Accuracy (%)	Classifier	Accuracy (%)
Hop-1 (left eye)	86.70 ± 0.65	Hop-2 (upper stripe)	92.25 ± 0.22
Hop-1 (right eye)	86.14 ± 0.66	Hop-2 (lower stripe)	89.70 ± 0.73
Hop-1 (nose)	82.90 ± 0.61	Hop-2 (vertical strip)	92.42 ± 0.56
Hop-1 (mouth)	83.42 ± 0.74	Hop-3	91.22 ± 0.46

this observation, we consider two ensemble methods. In the first scheme, called FaceHop I, we fuse soft decisions of all eight hop/region classifiers with a meta classifier. In the second scheme, called FaceHop II, we only fuse soft decisions of four hop/region classifiers from hop-2 and hop-3 only. The testing accuracy and the model sizes of LeNet-5, FaceHop I and FaceHop II are compared in Table 4. FaceHop I and FaceHop II outperform LeNet-5 in terms of classification accuracy by 0.70% and 0.86%, respectively, where their model sizes are only about 33.7% and 22.2% of LeNet-5. Clearly, FaceHop II is the favored choice among the three for its highest testing accuracy and smallest model size.

Table 4. Performance comparison of LeNet-5, FaceHop I and FaceHop II in accuracy rates and model sizes for LFW.

Method	Accuracy (%)	Model size
LeNet-5	93.77 ± 0.43	75,846
FaceHop I (all three hops)	94.47 ± 0.54	25,543
FaceHop II (hop-2 & hop-3 only)	94.63 ± 0.47	16,895

Performance and Model Size Comparison for CMU Multi-PIE. Next, we show the classification accuracy of each individual hop/region classifier for the CMU Multi-PIE dataset in Table 5. Their accuracy values range from 63.02% (hop-1/mouth) to 91.95% (hop-2/upper stripe). It appears that CMU Multi-PIE is more challenging than LFW if we focus on the performance of each individual classifier by comparing Tables 3 and 5.

Table 5. Performance comparison of each individual hop/region classifier for CMU Multi-PIE.

Classifier	Accuracy (%)	Classifier	Accuracy (%)
Hop-1 (left eye)	79.33 ± 0.33	Hop-2 (upper stripe)	91.95 ± 0.18
Hop-1 (right eye)	78.64 ± 0.25	Hop-2 (lower stripe)	87.00 ± 0.15
Hop-1 (nose)	65.19 ± 0.36	Hop-2 (vertical strip)	91.34 ± 0.22
Hop-1 (mouth)	63.02 ± 0.41	Hop-3	84.55 ± 0.77

We consider two ensemble schemes as done before. FaceHop I uses all eight soft decisions while FaceHop II takes only four soft decisions from hop-2 and hop-3. The mean accuracy performance of LeNet-5, FaceHop I and FaceHop II are compared in Table 6. It is interesting to see that FaceHop I and II have slightly better ensemble results of CMU Multi-PIE than of LFW, respectively. The performance of LeNet-5 also increases from 93.77% (LFW) to 95.08% (CMU Multi-PIE). As far as the model size is concerned, the model sizes of FaceHop I and FaceHop II are about 38.4% and 23.2% of LeNet-5, respectively. Again, FaceHop II is the most favored solution among the three for its highest testing accuracy and smallest model size.

Table 6. Performance comparison of LeNet-5, FaceHop I and FaceHop II in accuracy rates and model sizes for CMU Multi-PIE.

Method	Accuracy (%)	Model size
LeNet-5	95.08	75,846
FaceHop I (all three hops)	95.09 ± 0.24	29,156
FaceHop II (hop-2 and hop-3 only)	95.12 ± 0.26	17,628

5   Conclusion and Future Work

A light-weight low-resolution face gender classification method, called FaceHop, was proposed. This solution finds applications in resource-constrained environments with limited networking and computing. FaceHop has several desired characteristics, including a small model size, a small training data amount, low training complexity, and low-resolution input images. The effectiveness of the FaceHop method for gender classification was demonstrated by experiments on two benchmarking datasets.

In this paper, we demonstrated the potential of the SSL principle for effective feature extraction from face images. As to future work, we would like to test more datasets for gender classification and also extend the SSL principle for identifying heterogeneous and correlated face attributes such as gender, age, and race. It is particularly interesting to develop a multi-task learning approach. Furthermore, it will be desired to work on high-resolution face images and see whether we can get significant performance improvement using the SSL principle in classification accuracy, computational complexity, and memory usage.

References

1. Jain, A.K., Dass, S.C., Nandakumar, K.: Soft biometric traits for personal recognition systems. In: Zhang, D., Jain, A.K. (eds.) ICBA 2004. LNCS, vol. 3072, pp. 731–738. Springer, Heidelberg (2004). https://doi.org/10.1007/978-3-540-25948-0_99

2. Riccio, D., Tortora, G., De Marsico, M., Wechsler, H.: EGA-ethnicity, gender and age, a pre-annotated face database. In: IEEE Workshop on Biometric Measurements and Systems for Security and Medical Applications (BIOMS) Proceedings. IEEE, vol. 2012, pp. 1–8 (2012)
3. Gonzalez-Sosa, E., Fierrez, J., Vera-Rodriguez, R., Alonso-Fernandez, F.: Facial soft biometrics for recognition in the wild: recent works, annotation, and cots evaluation. IEEE Trans. Inf. Forensics Secur. **13**(8), 2001–2014 (2018)
4. Kuo, C.-C.J.: Understanding convolutional neural networks with a mathematical model. J. Vis. Commun. Image Represent. **41**, 406–413 (2016)
5. Kuo, C.-C.J.: The CNN as a guided multilayer RECOS transform [lecture notes]. IEEE Sign. Process. Mag. **34**(3), 81–89 (2017)
6. Kuo, C.-C.J., Zhang, M., Li, S., Duan, J., Chen, Y.: Interpretable convolutional neural networks via feedforward design. J. Vis. Commun. Image Represent. **60**, 346–359 (2019)
7. Chen, Y., Rouhsedaghat, M., You, S., Rao, R., Kuo, C.-C.J.: PixelHop++: a small successive-subspace-learning-based (SSL-based) model for image classification. arXiv preprint arXiv:2002.03141 (2020)
8. Gutta, S., Wechsler, H., Phillips, P.J.: Gender and ethnic classification of face images. In: Proceedings Third IEEE International Conference on Automatic Face and Gesture Recognition. IEEE, pp. 194–199 (1998)
9. Moghaddam, B., Yang, M.-H.: Learning gender with support faces. IEEE Trans. Pattern Anal. Mach. Intell. **24**(5), 707–711 (2002)
10. Baluja, S., Rowley, H.A.: Boosting sex identification performance. Int. J. Comput. Vis. **71**(1), 111–119 (2007)
11. Štruc, V., Pavešić, N.: Gabor-based Kernel partial-least-squares discrimination features for face recognition. Informatica **20**(1), 115–138 (2009)
12. Jabid, T., Kabir, M.H., Chae, O.: Gender classification using local directional pattern (LDP). In: 2010 20th International Conference on Pattern Recognition, pp. 2162–2165. IEEE (2010)
13. Wu, J., Smith, W.A., Hancock, E.R.: Facial gender classification using shape-from-shading. Image Vis. Comput. **28**(6), 1039–1048 (2010)
14. Cao, D., He, R., Zhang, M., Sun, Z., Tan, T.: Real-world gender recognition using multi-order LBP and localized multi-boost learning. In: IEEE International Conference on Identity, Security and Behavior Analysis, pp. 1–6. IEEE (2015)
15. Li, Y., Wang, R., Liu, H., Jiang, H., Shan, S., Chen, X.: Two birds, one stone: jointly learning binary code for large-scale face image retrieval and attributes prediction. In: Proceedings of the IEEE International Conference on Computer Vision, pp. 3819–3827 (2015)
16. Jia, S., Cristianini, N.: Learning to classify gender from four million images. Pattern Recogn. Lett. **58**, 35–41 (2015)
17. Castrillón-Santana, M., Lorenzo-Navarro, J., Ramón-Balmaseda, E.: Descriptors and regions of interest fusion for in-and cross-database gender classification in the wild. Image Vis. Comput. **57**, 15–24 (2017)
18. Lee, B., Gilani, S.Z., Hassan, G.M., Mian, A.: Facial gender classification-analysis using convolutional neural networks. Digital Image Comput. Tech. Appl. (DICTA) **2019**, 1–8 (2019)
19. Levi, G., Hassner, T.: Age and gender classification using convolutional neural networks. In: Proceedings of the IEEE Conference on Computer Vision and Pattern Recognition Workshops, pp. 34–42 (2015)
20. Duan, M., Li, K., Yang, C., Li, K.: A hybrid deep learning CNN-ELM for age and gender classification. Neurocomputing **275**, 448–461 (2018)

21. Taherkhani, F., Nasrabadi, N.M., Dawson, J.: A deep face identification network enhanced by facial attributes prediction. In: The IEEE Conference on Computer Vision and Pattern Recognition (CVPR) Workshops, June 2018

22. Han, H., Jain, A.K., Wang, F., Shan, S., Chen, X.: Heterogeneous face attribute estimation: a deep multi-task learning approach. IEEE Trans. Pattern Anal. Mach. Intell. 40(11), 2597–2609 (2017)

23. Ranjan, R., Patel, V.M., Chellappa, R.: HyperFace: a deep multi-task learning framework for face detection, landmark localization, pose estimation, and gender recognition. IEEE Trans. Pattern Anal. Mach. Intell. 41(1), 121–135 (2017)

24. Antipov, G., Baccouche, M., Berrani, S.-A., Dugelay, J.-L.: Effective training of convolutional neural networks for face-based gender and age prediction. Pattern Recogn. 72, 15–26 (2017)

25. Cheng, J., Li, Y., Wang, J., Yu, L., Wang, S.: Exploiting effective facial patches for robust gender recognition. Tsinghua Sci. Technol. 24(3), 333–345 (2019)

26. Iandola, F.N., Han, S., Moskewicz, M.W., Ashraf, K., Dally, W.J., Keutzer, K.: SqueezeNet: AlexNet-level accuracy with 50x fewer parameters and ¡ 0.5 MB model size." arXiv preprint arXiv:1602.07360 (2016)

27. Krizhevsky, A., Sutskever, I., Hinton, G.E.: ImageNet classification with deep convolutional neural networks. In: Advances in Neural Information Processing Systems, pp. 1097–1105 (2012)

28. Wu, X., He, R., Sun, Z., Tan, T.: A light CNN for deep face representation with noisy labels. IEEE Trans. Inf. Forensics Secur. 13(11), 2884–2896 (2018)

29. Turk, M., Pentland, A.: Face recognition using Eigenfaces. In: Proceedings 1991 IEEE Computer Society Conference on Computer Vision and Pattern Recognition, pp. 586–587 (1991)

30. Chan, T.-H., Jia, K., Gao, S., Lu, J., Zeng, Z., Ma, Y.: PCANET: a simple deep learning baseline for image classification? IEEE Trans. Image Process. 24(12), 5017–5032 (2015)

31. Chen, Y., Kuo, C.-C.J.: PixelHop: a successive subspace learning (SSL) method for object recognition. J. Vis. Commun. Image Represent. 70, 102749 (2020)

32. Kuo, C.-C.J., Chen, Y.: On data-driven Saak transform. J. Vis. Commun. Image Represent. 50, 237–246 (2018)

33. King, D.E.: Dlib-ml: a machine learning toolkit. J. Mach. Learn. Res. 10, 1755–1758 (2009)

34. Huang, G.B., Ramesh, M., Berg, T., Learned-Miller, E.: Labeled faces in the wild: a database for studying face recognition in unconstrained environments. Technical report University of Massachusetts, Amherst, pp. 7–49, October 2007

35. Ferrari, C., Lisanti, G., Berretti, S., Del Bimbo, A.: Effective 3D based frontalization for unconstrained face recognition. In: 2016 23rd International Conference on Pattern Recognition (ICPR), pp. 1047–1052. IEEE (2016)

36. Gross, R., Matthews, I., Cohn, J., Kanade, T., Baker, S.: Multi-PIE. Image Vis. Comput. 28(5), 807–813 (2010)

Advanced Temporal Dilated Convolutional Neural Network for a Robust Car Driver Identification

Francesco Rundo[1(✉)], Francesca Trenta[2], Roberto Leotta[2],
Concetto Spampinato[3], Vincenzo Piuri[4], Sabrina Conoci[5],
Ruggero Donida Labati[4], Fabio Scotti[4], and Sebastiano Battiato[2]

[1] STMicroelectronics, ADG Central R&D, Catania, Italy
francesco.rundo@st.com
[2] IPLAB Group, University of Catania, Catania, Italy
francesca.trenta@unict.it, leotta.rob@gmail.com, battiato@dmi.unict.it
[3] PerCeiVe Lab, University of Catania, Catania, Italy
cspampin@dieei.unict.it
[4] Computer Science Department, University of Milan, Milan, Italy
{vincenzo.piuri,ruggero.donida,fabio.scotti}@unimi.it
[5] University of Messina, Messina, Italy
sconoci@unime.it

Abstract. The latest generation cars are often equipped with advanced driver assistance systems, usually known as ADAS (*Advanced Driver Assistance Systems*). These systems are able to assist the car driver by leveraging several levels of automation. Therefore, it is essential to adapt the ADAS technology to the car driver's identity to personalize the provided assistance services. For these reasons, such car driver profiling algorithms have been developed by the scientific community. The algorithm herein proposed is able to recognize the driver's identity with an accuracy close to 99% thanks to ad-hoc specific analysis of the driver's PhotoPlethysmoGraphic (PPG) signal. In order to rightly identify the driver profile, the proposed approach uses a 1D Dilated Temporal Convolutional Neural Network architecture to learn the features of the collected driver's PPG signal. The proposed deep architecture is able to correlate the specific PPG features with subject identity enabling the car ADAS services associated with the recognized identity. Extensive validation and testing of the developed pipeline confirmed its reliability and effectiveness.

Keywords: ADAS · Deep learning · Automotive

1 Introduction

The automotive industry is continually evolving to improve the reliability and safety of the latest technology inside the cars. To meet this high demand for efficient and safe automotive systems, the technology is becoming increasingly

© Springer Nature Switzerland AG 2021
A. Del Bimbo et al. (Eds.): ICPR 2020 Workshops, LNCS 12668, pp. 184–199, 2021.
https://doi.org/10.1007/978-3-030-68793-9_13

sophisticated and the products currently on the market include intelligent solutions in the ADAS field [4,17]. The ADAS systems, an acronym of *Advanced Driver Assistance Systems*, are becoming a very useful resource for the design of latest generation cars in order to increase the overall safety driving as well as to address classical automotive issues related to a drop of driver attention [2,16]. Anyway, it is clear that the driving assistance systems must be customized to the driver and his driving dynamics. For this reason, it is necessary to profiling the driver or the recognition of his identity both before and during driving in order to enable the most appropriate ADAS assistance services. The present contribution is composed as follows. In the next section, an examination of the prior art in relation to the driver profiling methods is presented. In the "Methods and Materials" section, the proposed methodology will be illustrated in detail. Therefore in the "Results" section, some performance indices of the proposed method will be shown, which will be commented on and discussed in the last section, "Discussion and Conclusion".

2 Related Works

In [6], the authors analyzed several Android smartphone embedded sensors and classification pipelines in order to characterize the car driver behavior. The authors proposed a driver profiling approach by means of such Machine Learning based algorithms. More in detail, in the aforementioned survey [6] the authors have investigated several promising solutions based on the usage of Support Vector Machines (SVM), Random Forest (RF), Bayesian Network (BN) and Artificial Neural Networks (ANN). The final results confirmed that accelerometer and gyroscope represent the most appropriate sensors to monitor the driving behaviour (also showing that the use of all sensor axes accomplish the task better than using a single one). In terms of machine learning architectures, they proved that the RF is the best performing pipeline, followed by ANN even if the performance of both is satisfactory and equivalent, varying from 0.980 to 0.999 mean AUC values [6].

In [5] the authors proposed an interesting approach for profiling the car driver behaviour including identity recognition. In particular, trough a simulator they were able to analyse the key-pressed dynamics of the analyzed subject. Through the analysis of the so collected key-pressed patterns, the authors were able to discriminate the identity of a specific driver with acceptable accuracy. In [9] a system named *Driver Adaptive Vehicle Interaction System* was implemented and analyzed. The main modules of the aforementioned method are the follows: the *Profile Management Module*, the *Driver Management Module* and the *Interaction Management Module*. In particular, the first module is able to handle the car driver identity and correlated driver's driving characteristics. Through this collected data for each subject, the authors were able to provide a custom user-adaptive interaction system suitable to profile the driving dynamic. In [11] the authors performed a proper investigation about a model of human driving behaviour, and its correlated main issues. They described an interesting discussion about the principal human factors that might have an impact on driving:

age, gender, personality, anger, mental stress, distraction, and so on. The authors
have implemented and analyzed different pipelines with very interesting results.
More details in [11]. In [3] the authors designed a pipeline named "Sense Fleet"
based on the output analysis of such specific smartphone's sensors in order to
identify and profile the subject who is driving. The method performs well but it
suffers from the limitations of similar methods that use devices external to the
car, therefore problems of invasiveness and compatibility with the automotive
systems of the car. In [13] the author proposed an interesting car driver identity
recognition based on the usage of combined approach which includes machine
learning and dynamic time warping methodology. Through the analysis of such
physiological signals of the car driver (collected from specific bio-sensor embedded on the car systems) the author was able to recognize the driver identity
with high accuracy. The pipeline herein proposed is an improvement of the one
described in [13]. Specifically, the authors propose an approach for the car driver
identity recognition based on the analysis of the "physiological imprinting" of
the subject [14]. The following section introduce and describe with more detail
the proposed pipeline.

3   Methods and Materials

In this section the overall proposed pipeline for the car driver identity recognition will be described. The whole implemented pipeline is based on the use of
an innovative analysis of the "physiological imprinting" of the driver that the
authors characterize through the photoplethysmographic signal (PPG) of the
subject [14,20]. The PPG signal represents a non-invasive physiological track of
the subject's cardiovascular system correlated to the heart pulse-rate dynamic.
This physiological signal, can be used to monitoring the heart pulse and respiratory rate of a subject [15]. Furthermore, the PPG signal may be also used to
obtain a non-invasive measure the blood volume dynamic for several cardiovascular assessments [1,15]. A brief description of the PPG signal features is reported.
A classical PPG waveform collected from a bio-sensor placed in contact with the
skin of the examined subject contains a pulsatile ('AC') physiological waveform
which is related to the cardiac-synchronous changes in the blood volume super-
posed with a slowly varying ('DC') component that contains the lower frequency
information correlated to respiration, thermo-regulation [14]. The arteries and
arterioles in the subcutaneous tissue of the analyzed subject's skin are stretched
by the pressure of the blood pumped by the heart into the periphery, with a specific pressure, in each cardiac cycle (systolic phase). This dynamic tends to be
reduced in the diastolic phase of cardiac activity [1,15]. Through ad-hoc designed
bio-sensor it will be possible to capture the mentioned blood dynamics regulated
by cardiac activity in order to reconstruct a signal that is strongly correlated
with the aforementioned cardiac phases and therefore with the changes in blood
flow. More in detail a small secondary peak, observed by a pressure pulse from
the venous plexus, can be detected through a sensing device made-up by a light-
emitter and photo-detector placed over the skin. The blood dynamic changes,

will be detected by illuminating the skin and then by measuring the amount of light either transmitted or back-scattered to the coupled photo-detector. This is exactly the operating principle with which the PPG signal is constructed from a bio-sensor consisting of a light emitter and a photo-detector that captures the transmitted or back-scattered light. More detail in [1,14,15,20]. Therefore, the PPG signal can effectively be considered as a subject's "physiological imprint" or "cardiac imprint". The PPG waveform can be used as a fingerprint or bio-marker of a car driver; this implies that the features extracted from PPG signal can be properly used to recognize the subject from which the PPG is sampled [13]. In the Fig. 1 the implemented PPG bio-sensor is reported.

SiPM Probe Device

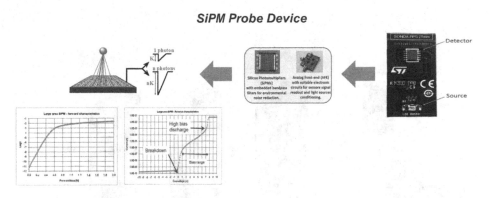

Fig. 1. The implemented PPG signal sensing probe.

The sensing device reported in Fig. 1 and employed by the authors for implementing the PPG sampling in the pipeline herein described consists of two main components: a Silicon PhotoMultipliers (SiPMs) detector and two sources LED emitters. The SiPM photo-detector used in our system is produced by STMicro-electronics (Catania, Italy) [10,23]. The SiPM device has a total area of 4.0×4.5 mm^2 and 4871 square microcells with 60μm of pitch. It has a geometrical fill factor of 67.4% wrapped in a surface mount housing (SMD) of 5.1×5.1 mm^2 total area [10,22,23]. A Pixelteq dichroic bandpass filter (Bryan Dairy Rd, Largo, FL, USA) centered at 542 nm (Full Width at Half Maximum (FWHM) of 70nm and optical transmission higher than 90% in the passband range) was glued on the SMD package by using 352TM adhesive (Loctite®, Milan, Italy). With the described setup, considering the driving range $0 - 3V$, the device has a maximum Photon Detection Efficiency (PDE) of about 29.4% at 565 nm and of about 27.4% at 540 nm (central wavelength in the filter pass band). Moreover, a dichroic filter has been included in order to reduce the absorption of environmental light of more than 60% in the linear operation range. The emitter that has been used as optical light source is composed of two LT M673 LEDs (OSRAM, Milan, Italy). In particular, both LEDs are based on InGaN technology (in SMD package) emitting at 873 nm, they also have an area of 2.3×1.5 mm^2 viewing angle of 120 and typical power emission of a few mW in the standard operation range. More details in [15–17].

In Fig. 1, the implemented sensing device is shown in which the part containing the SiPM photo-detector (Detector in Fig. 1) is highlighted, whose characteristic curves are shown. In addition, the part showing the LEDs (Source in Fig. 1) which in this case emit, as indicated, at a wavelength of 873 nm, is highlighted. Introduced the bio-sensor to reconstruct the PPG signal, we now describe the implemented pipeline for the recognition of the driver's identity based on the processing of the physiological signals of the subject. An overall outline of the implemented car driver identity recognition pipeline is shown in Fig. 2. Each block of designed pipeline will be described in the following subsections.

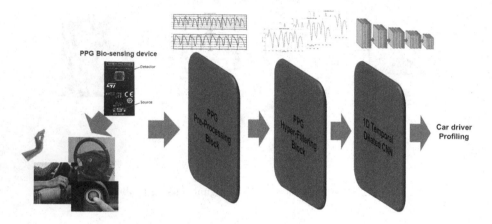

Fig. 2. Car driver identity recognition pipeline.

3.1   The PPG Pre-processing Block

This block takes care of acquiring, filtering, stabilizing and pre-processing the PPG signal sampled from the driver. In order to be able to sample the so called physiological imprint of whom is driving the vehicle, the PPG sensing device will be embedded into different part of the car dashboard, specifically, in the car steering, in the start button or in the gear shift. Each time the driver places the hand on the start button or on the steering or over the gear lever, the PPG signal will be sampled from the palm of the hand by means of the bio-sensing probes embedded in these parts of the car. In this way the PPG driver's signal will be persistently collected. The sensing devices so designed produce a raw PPG signal from the hand of the car driver. A micro-controller device detects the first raw PPG signal sampled by one of the bio-sensors placed in the various points of the car mentioned above and therefore selects the latter for the subsequent processing steps to recognize the driver's identity. To increase the robustness of the PPG sampling pipeline we have distributed several PPG sensors in the car's steering equidistant from each other as well as in the start button or in the gear shift.

In the case where the driver will not put any hands on a PPG sensor placed in the car, the last identification setup will be considered. If no identity has been acquired when the vehicle is turned on, the system will asked to the driver to place the hand in one of the PPG sensors embedded in the steering wheel in order to proceed with identification. However, a recovery system based on innovative motion magnification algorithms (preliminary introduced in [21]) is ongoing to be implemented for covering the issue related to the case in which the PPG signal is no longer available. More detail in the conclusion section of this paper. About the sampled raw PPG signal, as introduced, it is originally an optical signal which require to be converted before to be used in our pipeline. For this purpose, we used a 24-bits Analog to Digital Converters embedded in a board we designed for collecting and pre-processing the raw PPG signal. The Fig. 3, shows an instance of the designed motherboard which is integrated into the vehicle control unit. More detail on the hardware setup implemented can be found in [10,22,23]. The PPG sensing devices located on the car's steering wheel/gear shift or start button have been plugged-in to the USB connectors of the developed motherboard. The so sampled raw PPG signal was managed by such algorithms running as firmware in a 32-bits Micontrollers (STA1295 Accordo5 MCU) and SPCx Chorus MCU series[1,2]. The so gathered raw PPG signal will be afterwards post-processed by the Hyper-Filtering block as described in the next section. The described hardware setup is reported in Fig. 3.

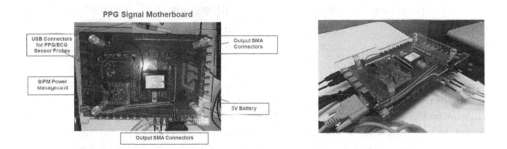

Fig. 3. The designed PPG signal pre-processing motherboard

---

[1] STMicroelectronics SPC5 MCUs: https://www.st.com/en/automotive-microcontrollers/spc5-32-bit-automotive-mcus.html.

[2] STMicroelectronics ACCORDO 5 Automotive Microcontroller: https://www.st.com/en/automotive-infotainment-and-telematics/automotive-infotainment-socs.html?icmp=tt4379_gl_pron_nov2016.

3.2   The PPG Hyper-Filtering Block

To properly work with the PPG signal a frequency filter is needed since the raw format embeds several components useless for our goal. This particular detail have been carried out by the authors in [1,10,17,22,23]. Furthermore, taking into account of a real driving scenario which includes motion artifacts, noises, car engine vibrations and so on, ad-hoc filtering or stabilization task is needed. Expressly, a classical approach for PPG filtering and stabilization is based on the usage of a set of FIR (Finite Impulse Response) block designed to work band-pass filter in the range 0.5–10 Hz. A classical FIR filter used for both low frequencies (low pass) and high frequencies (high pass) carry out a classic processing formalized by the following classic discrete-time equation:

$$y_{PPG}[n] = \sum_{i=0}^{N_0} \delta_i \cdot x[n-i], \tag{1}$$

where N_0 represents the order of the used filter, while the δ_i define the filter coefficients and n the number of samples of the source raw PPG signal $x[k]$. Evidently, the signal $y_{PPG}[n]$ shows the filtered PPG waveforms. In the following Table 1 the FIR setup usually applied for PPG filtering is reported [14].

Table 1. Low-pass and high-pass filter design for the photoplethysmgraphic (PPG) raw signal.

Type	Frequency pass (Hz)	Frequency stop (Hz)	Passband attenuation (dB)	Stoband attenuation (dB)
Low-pass	3.8	7.21	0.001	100
High-pass	1	0.3	0.01	40

In this contribution, the authors intend to propose a different solution in relation to the filtering of the raw PPG signal. This idea will be better described in the following paragraphs. In the pipeline described herein, we replace the above introduced classical FIR filters setup with another set of properly configured hyper-filtering layers. The idea that we intend to propose in this work is inspired from the well known hyper-spectral method applied to 2D imaging [17]. Hyperspectral imaging, like other spectral imaging, collects visual information from across the whole electromagnetic spectrum. The goal of hyperspectral imaging methodology is to retrieve the so-called "frequency spectrum of each pixel" in order to address the classical image processing issues such as objects recognition, materials identification, and so on [17]. With the aim to emulate the same approach, the authors investigated the effectiveness of applying the same approach to the study and analysis of 1D PPG signals. Specifically, the authors investigated whether, by collecting the information deriving from a "hyper-filtering" processing of the original 1D signal (PPG, in this case), we could obtain useful information to characterize the "frequency spectrum of each signal sample", that is, the information useful to address the problem for which the signal is analyzed in our case, the detection of the driver identity. For this reason, instead of applying a single filter set (low pass and high pass) we analyzed the source PPG signal over a range of frequencies that would allow us to better characterize the value of the single signal-sample. Considering that the useful frequency range, which allows to obtain an information component of the PPG signal, is included in the 0.5–10 Hz range, we have investigated the scenario of properly splitting this frequency range in sub-bands to be applied to simulate the phenomenon of hyper-filtering. Considering that, in the case of the PPG signal, it is necessary to apply both a low-pass and a high-pass filtering (therefore, a band-pass filter is required), we opted for two layers of hyper-filtering, i.e. one that varied the frequencies in the low-pass band maintaining instead the cut-off frequency of the high-pass filter (hyper low-pass filtering layer) and, vice versa, one that varied the cut-off frequencies of the high-pass filter while maintaining constant the frequency of the low pass filter (hyper high-pass filtering layer). Furthermore, considering the need to have filters that do not create distortions in the PPG bandwidth, we decided to adopt the Butterworth filters in both layers of hyper-filtering [17]. As known, Butterworth filters are the simplest electronic filters usable for signal processing applications [1,10,22,23]. The first and most important part of the proposed method was related to the selection of the sub-bands intervals of the range 0.5–10 Hz and the relative cut-off frequencies. To address this issue, we have used a classical "trial and error" approach that would first search for the best number of sub-intervals in the 0.5–10 Hz frequency range. Specifically, after a series of heuristic tests, we selected a value equal to 11 sub-bands as the best trade-off between computational load and discriminative ability. Practically, in our experiments, we found that when using a smaller number of frequency sub-bands (< 11), the detection performance driver identity decreased a lot. Meanwhile, increasing the number of sub-bands (> 11), the performances remained almost stable, although the computational load of the whole algorithm obviously increased. Therefore, in order to find a correct trade-off between performance and computational load, we established that 11 sub-bands were enough to properly discriminate the driver identity. Therefore, for each hyper-filtering layer, we proceeded to split the range of applicable frequency in 11 specific sub-bands. Once the number of sub-bands was set, we put together a reinforcement learning algorithm structured as follows:

- We defined an action a_t as the sub-band frequency value between 0.5 Hz and cut-off frequency according to the type of filtering (low-pass or high-pass);
- We defined an Agent select the action a_t;
- We defined a next state S_{t+1} as a set of pre-processed signals obtained collecting the value of each input PPG samples (in a windows of 5 sec sampling at 1 KHz as sampling frequency) of the filtered PPG raw signal at specific sub-band frequency of the action a_t;
- We defined an environment Reward as $R(.|s_t, a_t)$, that is, a measure of drowsiness of the car driver. We defined as $R(.|s_t, a_t)$ the distance of the output of

ad-hoc machine learning system (regression layer plus SoftMax classification) with respect to the actual driver identity;

We are interested to determine the optimal policy P_o that minimizes the cumulative discount reward:

$$P_o = argmax_{P_o} \ E[\sum_{t \geq 0} \gamma^t R(.|s_t, a_t)|P_o], \tag{2}$$

where γ is a proper discounted coefficient in $(0, 1)$. In order to evaluate the goodness of a state s_t and the goodness of a state-action couple (s_t, a_t), we defined the value function and the Q-value function, respectively, as follows:

$$V^{P_o}(s_t) = E[\sum_{t \geq 0} \gamma^t R(.|s_t)|P_o] \tag{3}$$

$$Q^{P_o}(s_t, a_t) = E[\sum_{t \geq 0} \gamma^t R(.|s_t, a_t)|P_o]. \tag{4}$$

By solving the above models through classical Q-learning algorithms [17], we found the following set of sub-band frequency for each hyper-filtering layer. Once we have identified the optimal frequency setup using the described RL algorithm, the latter system will be disconnected from the main pipeline as it is no longer needed for the operation of the proposed approach concerning the discrimination of the driver identity. Therefore, the RL algorithm is needed simply as "one-shot" optimization algorithm to be used only in the initial setup of the filtering frequency framework, and thus it will no longer needed for achieving the target of the proposed solution. Once the frequency sets of the two hyper-filtering filter sub-systems have been identified, the sampled raw PPG signal will be processed accordingly. Formally, if we set with $x(k)$ the sampled raw PPG signal, for each frequency setup, we obtain the following hyper-filtered time series:

$$\varphi^i_{H_{LP}}(k) = F_{Butterworth}(f^i_L, f_H, x(k)) i = 1, 2, \ldots 11; k = 1, 2, \ldots . n, \tag{5}$$

$$\varphi^i_{H_{HP}}(k) = F_{Butterworth}(f_L, f^i_H, x(k)) \ \ i = 1, 2, \ldots 11 ; k = 1, 2, \ldots n, \tag{6}$$

where $\varphi^i_{H_{HP}}(k)$ and $\varphi^i_{H_{LP}}(k)$ represent the set of hyper-filtered time series coming from hyper-filtering high-pass and low-pass processing, respectively. The function $\mathbf{F}_{Butterworth}$ represents the filter processing performed by the so configured Butterworth filter, while f_L, f_H represent the fixed cut-off frequencies and f^i_H, f^i_L the variable frequency (fc-pass-x) as per Tables 2 and 3. Now, for each sample of the single so hyper-filtered PPG signals, a dataset of further signals will be created, each having a temporal dynamics represented by the intensity value of the single sample of the so filtered PPG signal.

Formally, if we indicate with $W^i_{PPG}(t_k)$ the single segmented waveform of each hyper-filtered PPG time series, we proceed computing for each sample $s(tk)$ of the waveform $W^i_{PPG}(t_k)$ a signal-pattern depending on how that sample $s(tk)$ varies in intensity in the various hyper-filtered PPG signals $\varphi^i_{H_{HP}}(k)$ and

Table 2. Hyper low-pass filtering setup (in Hz)

F	Fc-pass-1	Fc-pass-2	Fc-pass-3	Fc-pass-4	Fc-pass-5	Fc-pass-6	Fc-pass-7	Fc-pass-8	Fc-pass-9	Fc-pass-10	Fc-pass-11
HP	0.5	/	/	/	/	/	/	/	/	/	/
LP	1.00	1.34	2.09	2.231	3.09	3.44	4.2	4.23	5.2	5.52	6.87

Table 3. Hyper high-pass filtering setup (in Hz)

F	Fc-pass-1	Fc-pass-2	Fc-pass-3	Fc-pass-4	Fc-pass-5	Fc-pass-6	Fc-pass-7	Fc-pass-8	Fc-pass-9	Fc-pass-10	Fc-pass-11
HP	0.5	1.5	2.2	2.75	3.12	3.65	4.1	4.48	5.23	5.3	6.11
LP	7	/	/	/	/	/	/	/	/	/	/

$\varphi^i_{H_{LP}}(k)$ for $i = 1, 2, ..., 11$. In this way, we will obtain a fairly large dataset of signals whose length will thus be equal exactly to the number of filtering frequencies, that is, 11 in this application setup. The following equations show how we obtain the signal-patterns $\zeta^k_{HP}(s(t_k))$ and $\zeta^k_{LP}(s(t_k))$ for each sample of the acquired PPG waveforms:

$$\zeta^k_{HP}(s(t_k)) = [\varphi^1_{H_{HP}}(t_k), \varphi^2_{H_{HP}}(t_k), ... \varphi^{11}_{H_{HP}}(t_k)] \ k = 1, 2, ...n, \quad (7)$$

$$\zeta^k_{LP}(s(t_k)) = [\varphi^1_{H_{LP}}(t_k), \varphi^2_{H_{LP}}(t_k), ... \varphi^{11}_{H_{LP}}(t_k)] \ k = 1, 2, ...n. \quad (8)$$

Figure 4 shows some instances of the hyper-filtering PPG time series $\varphi^i_{H_{HP}}(k)$ and $\varphi^i_{H_{LP}}(k)$, as well as related generated signal patterns $\zeta^k_{HP}(s(t_k))$ and $\zeta^k_{LP}(s(t_k))$. As for the classic hyper-spectral method, by means of the hyper-filtering approach herein described we are able to highlight multiple features of the PPG source signal as the frequency setup varies so as to significantly increase the discriminating features relating to the source sampled PPG signal of each subject. The dynamic of the signal-patterns $\zeta^k_{HP}(s(t_k))$ and $\zeta^k_{LP}(s(t_k))$ shows how the single sample of the acquired PPG time series varies according to the applied frequency filter setup. We collected several signal-patterns as we performed the analysis of each sample of the hyper-filtered PPG time series in a proper timing window after the car-driver put the hand over the steering wheel or in other part in which we have embedded the PPG sensor probe. The generated signal-patterns will be fed as input of the designed deep classifier block, as described in the following sub-section.

3.3 The 1D Temporal Dilated Deep Classifier

Ad-hoc 1D Temporal Dilated Convolutional Neural Network (1D-CNN) has been designed for classifying the collected hyper-filtered PPG signal patterns [19]. The following Fig. 5 report the overall scheme of the proposed 1D deep classifier. Our proposed network takes as input the signal-patterns $s(t_k)$ generated from each PPG hyper-filtered signals, specifically the proposed architecture requires at least 6 seconds of sampled PPG signal (at 1KHz) in order to proper identify a subject. The main novelty of the proposed architecture is the introduction of dilated causal convolution layers. The term "causal" denotes that the activation

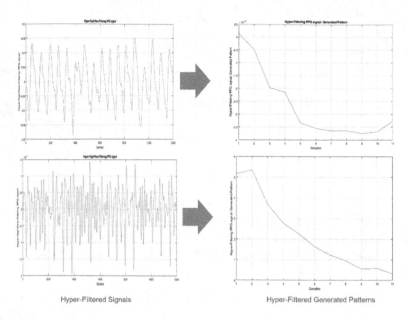

Hyper-Filtered Signals   Hyper-Filtered Generated Patterns

Fig. 4. In the left column some instances of the hyper-filtered high-pass PPG time series $\varphi^i_{H_{HP}}(k)$; In the right column an instance of the corresponding generated signal-patterns: $\zeta^k_{HP}(s(t_k))$; (c), (d) $\zeta^k_{LP}(s(t_k))$.

at time t depend on the activation computed at time $t-1$. The proposed 1D-CNN includes such multiple residual blocks. Specifically, the proposed deep network consists of a sequence of 16 residual blocks stacked together. Each block consists of a dilated convolution layer, batch normalization, ReLU and a spatial dropout. A dilated layer includes a 3×3 convolution operation. The dilation factor is set to 2 increasing for each block up to the eighth block. After that no dilation was applied. A downstream softmax layer completes the proposed pipeline. The output of the designed 1D-CNN predicts the driver identity from source hyper-filtered PPG generated signal-patterns. Specifically, the output of the 1D-CNN, thus, is able to predict the specific driver profile or identity which turns out to be the most likely profile among those on which it has been earlier trained by means of a system calibration phase. Consequently, the profiles of users who are allowed to obtain specific services enabled by the car control unit. In fact, a preliminary calibration-training phase of the algorithm allows this to be trained on specific profiles related to very exact identities of drivers. For each of the recruited drivers for the training phase, the PPG signal is acquired through the described pipeline and then the hyper-filtering block is applied in order to obtain the features to train the deep classifier so that it associates the retrieved features with the driver identity from which the PPG signal is sampled. So, as soon as a subject start to drive the car and the related PPG signal is sampled by the bio-sensors placed in the car's passenger compartment, according to the so sampled PPG signal and

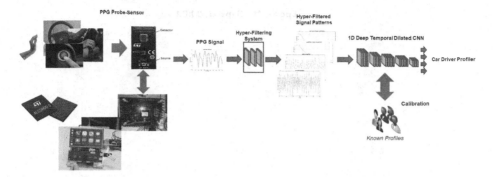

Fig. 5. The 1D deep classifier based pipeline for a robust car driver physiological identification

its related patterns obtained from the Hyper-filtering system, the classifier will be able to output a confidence level for each profile previously learned in the training-calibration phase. The above-mentioned confidence level, in our case, represents the percentage of belonging of the patterns to the previously learned driver profiles. If a new driver is driving whose identity does not match to any learned profiles in the calibration phase, a low probability (under 50%) will output by the classifier for each confidence level. The results, detailed in the next section, confirms that the implemented Deep Learning framework is able to identify the right car driver profile with high accuracy. The implemented 1D Deep CNN backbone is ongoing to be ported over the STA1295 Accordo5 embedded MCU platform with Linux YOCTO as Operating System (See footnote 1 and 2). Figure 6 shows a loss dynamic of the 1D-CNN properly trained.

4   Results

In order to validate the proposed pipeline, the authors asked for support from a team of physiologists they are with were collected several PPG measurements of different subjects. In order to have a complete mapping of the PPG signal dynamic of each recruited subject, the physiologists stimulated several physiological states (inattentive, enthusiastic, stressed, and so on) monitoring the subject through the ElectroEncephaloGraphic (EEG). Experiments were performed on 75 mixed healthy subjects: 35 men and 40 women aged between 20 and 79 years; none of the participants were using drugs suitable of changing cortical excitability. Volunteers authorised informed consent to the procedures approved by the *Ethical Committee Catania 1 (authorization n.113/2018/PO)* in according to the *Declaration of Helsinki*. Participation criteria encompassed the possession of a valid driving licence for motor vehicles. Our team have collected 10 min of PPG signal with the bio-sensing device described in previous sections and based on coupled LED-SiPM technology with sampling frequency of 1kHz. A car has been equipped with six LED-SiPM coupled sensing device placed equidistant from each other in order to cover the most common driving

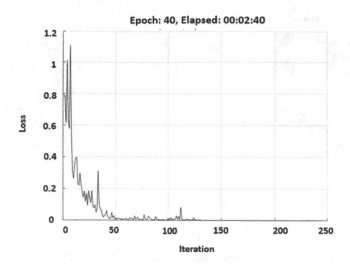

Fig. 6. The loss dynamic of the 1D-CNN.

styles of a subject. The implemented pipeline was hosted by the following setup: MATLAB full toolboxes vers. 2019b running in a server having an Intel 16-Cores and NVIDIA GeForce RTX 2080 GPU. We have configured a scenario of 4 known car driver profiles to be identified by proposed pipeline. The scenario included two young and two aged people from opposite sex. The subjects were chosen from the dataset described above and there was not any relationship between them. All other subjects are recognised as unknown profiles (which were not used in the training session). To be able to test the designed pipeline, the acquired PPG data for the selected known profiles have been divided as follow: 70% has been used for training and validation while the remaining 30% for testing. In order to verify both in the training phase and in the testing phase if the algorithm was able to recognise the identity of the drivers, the authors have constructed artificial PPGs composed of subset of waveforms coming from various recruited subjects (both from the selected four known subjects as well as the remaining unknown subjects). The overall testing accuracy stands at 98.7487%, thus, confirming the robustness of the pipeline proposed in this contribution. The previous pipeline [13] was tested on a subset of the herein used dataset, showing a discrimination performance of 97.12% significantly lower than the method proposed here. Although it is a matter of a few percentage points of difference between the two pipelines, in the case of automotive applications, the accuracy must be as high as possible. The proposed method shows higher performance with respect to the previous pipeline [13] regarding to the speed of recognition of the subject (as it requires fewer samples to perform a robust recognition) as well as a greater ability in the discrimination of more drivers.

5 Discussion and Conclusion

The aforementioned experimental results confirm the ability of the proposed pipeline to recognise the car driver identity by analysing some physiological features of related PPG signal. The suggested approach has introduced the concept of "cardiac imprinting or "physiological imprinting" as a valuable replacement of the classic fingerprint to outline and correctly identify a subject. Specifically, through the designed contribution the embedded ADAS system will be able to consistently monitor the driver's identity, steadily knowing whom is driving. Conducted analysis revealed that a better understanding of personal driving factors would allow automotive manufacturers to take account of them in the development of road safety technologies and procedures, possibly leading to a greater effectiveness in reducing road traffic incidents. Moreover, by recognition of the driver identity, the mentioned approach will be able to offer congruous information to the car control unit for enabling the services and ad-hoc configurations for the recognized identity, providing a tailor-made ADAS systems. In addition, detecting the driver's identity could lead to a proper investigation regarding drowsiness accidents caused by personal attributes (e.g., eye blinks, ongoing driving behaviour, etc.), identifying what personality factors appear to be related to vigilance performance. The performance accuracy confirmed the effectiveness of the proposed approach. As future works of the presented work, the authors are researching the integration of vision algorithms able to analyze also the anxiety and stress level of the driver, in order to improve the driving safety and assistance systems. In conclusion, preparatory and encouraging results are being found by examining the driver's identity recognition within the fusion of data coming from both (PPG) physiological signals. A promising results were obtained by integrating some statistical analyzes (Markov models) of the integrated driver's PPG signal with some visual features extracted from the viewer's face acquired from a camera located on the dashboard [7,18,19]. Future scientific contributions will show these results which also integrate the use of Deep Long Short Term Memory and further Reinforcement Learning model for the characterization of discriminating features [8,12].

References

1. Banna, G.L., et al.: Oral metronomic vinorelbine in advanced non-small cell lung cancer patients unfit for chemotherapy. Anticancer Res. 38(6), 3689–3697 (2018)
2. Caber, N., Langdon, P.M., Clarkson, P.J.: Intelligent driver profiling system for cars – a basic concept. In: Antona, M., Stephanidis, C. (eds.) UAHCI 2018. LNCS, vol. 10908, pp. 201–213. Springer, Cham (2018). https://doi.org/10.1007/978-3-319-92052-8_16
3. Castignani, G., Frank, R.: SenseFleet: a smartphone-based driver profiling platform. In: 2014 Eleventh Annual IEEE International Conference on Sensing, Communication, and Networking (SECON), pp. 144–145. IEEE (2014)

4. Conoci, S., Rundo, F., Fallica, G., Lena, D., Buraioli, I., Demarchi, D.: Live demonstration of portable systems based on silicon sensors for the monitoring of physiological parameters of driver drowsiness and pulse wave velocity. In: 2018 IEEE Biomedical Circuits and Systems Conference (BioCAS), pp. 1–3. IEEE (2018)
5. Dangra, B.S., Rajput, D., Bedekar, M., Panicker, S.S.: Profiling of automobile drivers using car games. In: 2015 International Conference on Pervasive Computing (ICPC), pp. 1–5. IEEE (2015)
6. Ferreira, J., Carvalho, E., Ferreira, B.V., de Souza, C., Suhara, Y., Pentland, A., Pessin, G.: Driver behavior profiling: an investigation with different smartphone sensors and machine learning. PLoS ONE **12**(4), e0174959 (2017)
7. Grasso, G., Perconti, P., Plebe, A.: Assessing social driving behavior. In: Karwowski, W., Ahram, T. (eds.) IHSI 2019. AISC, vol. 903, pp. 111–115. Springer, Cham (2019). https://doi.org/10.1007/978-3-030-11051-2_17
8. Grasso, G.M., Lucifora, C., Perconti, P., Plebe, A.: Evaluating mentalization during driving. In: VEHITS, pp. 536–541 (2019)
9. Kim, K., Choi, H., Jang, B.: Design of the driver-adaptive vehicle interaction system. In: 2018 International Conference on Information and Communication Technology Convergence (ICTC), pp. 297–299. IEEE (2018)
10. Mazzillo, M., et al.: Characterization of SiPMs with NIR long-pass interferential and plastic filters. IEEE Photonics J. **10**(3), 1–12 (2018)
11. Mubasher, M.M., Jaffry, S.W., Jahangir, R.: Modeling of individual differences in car-following behaviour of drivers. In: 2017 International Multi-topic Conference (INMIC), pp. 1–7. IEEE (2017)
12. Rundo, F.: Deep LSTM with reinforcement learning layer for financial trend prediction in FX high frequency trading systems. Appl. Sci. **9**(20), 4460 (2019)
13. Rundo, F.: Deep LSTM with dynamic time warping processing framework: a novel advanced algorithm with biosensor system for an efficient car-driver recognition. Electronics **9**(4), 616 (2020)
14. Rundo, F., Conoci, S., Ortis, A., Battiato, S.: An advanced bio-inspired photoplethysmography (PPG) and ECG pattern recognition system for medical assessment. Sensors **18**(2), 405 (2018)
15. Rundo, F., Petralia, S., Fallica, G., Conoci, S.: A nonlinear pattern recognition pipeline for PPG/ECG medical assessments. In: Andò, B., et al. (eds.) CNS 2018. LNEE, vol. 539, pp. 473–480. Springer, Cham (2019). https://doi.org/10.1007/978-3-030-04324-7_57
16. Rundo, F., et al.: An innovative deep learning algorithm for drowsiness detection from EEG signal. Computation **7**(1), 13 (2019)
17. Rundo, F., Spampinato, C., Conoci, S.: Ad-hoc shallow neural network to learn hyper filtered photoplethysmographic (PPG) signal for efficient car-driver drowsiness monitoring. Electronics **8**(8), 890 (2019)
18. Rundo, F., Trenta, F., Di Stallo, A.L., Battiato, S.: Advanced Markov-based machine learning framework for making adaptive trading system. Computation **7**(1), 4 (2019)
19. Rundo, F., Trenta, F., di Stallo, A.L., Battiato, S.: Grid trading system robot (GTSbot): a novel mathematical algorithm for trading FX market. Appl. Sci. **9**(9), 1796 (2019)
20. Taeihagh, A., Lim, H.S.M.: Governing autonomous vehicles: emerging responses for safety, liability, privacy, cybersecurity, and industry risks. Transp. Rev. **39**(1), 103–128 (2019)

21. Trenta, F., Conoci, S., Rundo, F., Battiato, S.: Advanced motion-tracking system with multi-layers deep learning framework for innovative car-driver drowsiness monitoring. In: 2019 14th IEEE International Conference on Automatic Face & Gesture Recognition (FG 2019), pp. 1–5. IEEE (2019)
22. Vinciguerra, V., et al.: Progresses towards a processing pipeline in photoplethysmogram (PPG) based on SiPMs. In: 2017 European Conference on Circuit Theory and Design (ECCTD), pp. 1–5. IEEE (2017)
23. Vinciguerra, V., et al.: PPG/ECG Multisite Combo System Based on SiPM Technology. In: Andò, B., et al. (eds.) CNS 2018. LNEE, vol. 539, pp. 353–360. Springer, Cham (2019). https://doi.org/10.1007/978-3-030-04324-7_44

VISOB 2.0 - The Second International Competition on Mobile Ocular Biometric Recognition

Hoang (Mark) Nguyen[1(✉)], Narsi Reddy[1], Ajita Rattani[2], and Reza Derakhshani[1]

[1] Department of Computer Science and Electrical Engineering, University of Missouri at Kansas City, Kansas City, USA
hdnf39@umsystem.edu
[2] Department of Electrical Engineering and Computer Science, Wichita State University, Wichita, USA
ajita.rattani@wichita.edu

Abstract. Following the success of VISOB 1.0 visible light ocular biometrics competition at IEEE ICIP 2016, we organized VISOB 2.0 competition at IEEE WCCI 2020. The aim of VISOB 2.0 competition was to evaluate and compare the performance of ocular biometrics recognition approaches in visible light using (a) stacks of five images captured in burst mode and (b) subject-independent evaluation, where subjects do not overlap between training and testing set. We received three submissions in which the authors developed various deep learning based and texture-analysis based methods. The best results were obtained by a team from Federal University of Parana (Curitiba, Brazil), achieving an Equal Error Rate (EER) of 5.25% in a subject-independent evaluation setting.

1 Introduction

Biometric user verification in mobile devices has all but won the top spot as the user access control method of choice [8,13]. Biometrics has brought convenience and enhanced security to a wide range of applications such as user login, payments[1], and eCommerce in general[2]. The use of biometrics in mobile devices is termed as mobile biometrics [13].

Thanks to deep learning and advanced camera technologies, mobile face biometrics has come a long way in terms of robustness, accuracy, and user experience. However, given the recent privacy concerns, especially amid the COVID-19 pandemic, and the resulting face-covering mandates, there is an intensified desire for alternate solutions to face recognition [1,2]. According to a recent 2020 NIST

---

[1] https://www.aitrends.com/financial-services/facial-recognition-making-its-way-in-banking/.
[2] https://www.ft.com/content/5d8100b6-ca6e-11e9-af46-b09e8bfe60c0.

© Springer Nature Switzerland AG 2021
A. Del Bimbo et al. (Eds.): ICPR 2020 Workshops, LNCS 12668, pp. 200–208, 2021.
https://doi.org/10.1007/978-3-030-68793-9_14

study [9], the presence of face masks could cause face recognition systems to fail up to 50%. Ocular biometrics offers a viable alternative to mobile face recognition given that similar to face, the ocular band can be acquired using the front-facing RGB camera of the mobile device. Ocular biometrics in and of itself has attracted exceeding attention from the research community thanks to its accuracy, security, and robustness against many facial expressions [12, 16]. The ocular regions that have been studied for their biometric utility include the iris [5], conjunctival and episcleral vasculature [4], and the periocular region [7]. Several datasets have been published capturing ocular images in the visible spectrum under various conditions, including UBIRIS [11] (241 subjects), MICHE-I [3] (92 subjects), and VISOB [10]. The last one offers the largest number of subjects (550) captured in mobile environment. Part of this dataset was used for VISOB 1.0 ICIP 2016 ocular biometric recognition competition.

Following the success of our previous VISOB ICIP 2016 competition [14], we organized VISOB 2.0 competition [10] as a part of the IEEE WCCI 2020 conference using a different subset of the VISOB database. The differences between VISOB dataset used in WCCI 2020 compared to ICIP 2016 version are given in Table 1. In VISOB 2.0 competition, we extended the region of interest from the tight eye crop (mainly iris, conjunctival, and episcleral vasculature) to larger periocular (a region encompassing the eye and the surrounding skin). The evaluation protocol for VISOB 2.0 is subject-independent (akin to open-set for identification), in which the subjects in the training and testing set do not overlap. This is compared to the less challenging subject-dependent evaluation used in ICIP VISOB 1.0 competition. More specifically, in VISOB 1.0 the 150 subjects in the testing set overlapped with the 550 identities in the training set; while there are no such overlapping identities between training and testing sets in VISOB 2.0. Further, instead of single frame eye captures of VISOB 1.0, VISOB 2.0 samples are comprised of stacks of five images captured in rapid succession (burst mode), opening the door for multi-frame enhancements.

Table 1. Differences between VISOB 1.0 and VISOB 2.0 competition.

	VISOB 1.0	VISOB 2.0
Devices	iPhone, OPPO, Note 4	OPPO, Note 4
ROI	Tight eye crops	Larger periocular region
Data type	Single frame image	Stack of five images
Train-test identities	Overlapping	Independent
Training set	550 subjects in Visit 1	150 subjects in Visit 1 and 2
Testing set	290 subjects in Visit 2	100 subjects in Visit 1 and 2

We note that *multi-frame* ocular biometrics in the visible spectrum has not attracted much attention in the research community [15], which could be in part due to a lack of public multi-frame datasets, something that VISOB 2.0 strives

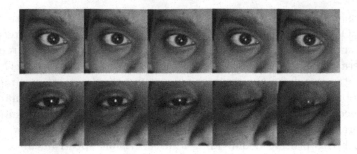

Fig. 1. Example eye images from VISOB 2.0, WCCI 2020 competition edition.

to overcome. Single-frame mobile captures from the front-facing "selfie" camera may unexpectedly introduce degradation due to illumination variations, noise, blur, and user to camera distance; all adversely affecting matching performance. One way to mitigate this problem is by capturing multiple frames of the eye in burst-mode, followed by multi-frame image enhancement. Frames may be fused at the input level (e.g., using multi-frame image enhancement and super-resolution techniques) or at the feature or score level for enhanced matching performance (e.g. a multi-match system) (Fig. 1).

2   VISOB 2.0 Dataset and Protocol

VISOB 2.0 Dataset: WCCI 2020 VISOB 2.0 competition VISOB Dataset is publicly available[3], and consists of stacks of eye images captured using the burst mode by two mobile devices: Samsung Note 4 and Oppo N1. During the data collection, the volunteers were asked to take their selfie images in two visits, 2 to 4 weeks apart from each other. The selfie-like images were captured with the participant holding the phone naturally, using front-facing camera of the mobile devices under three lighting conditions: daylight, indoor (office) lighting, and dim indoors in two sessions (about 10 to 15 min apart). The ocular burst stacks were cropped from full face frames. The burst sequences were selected if correlation coefficient between the center frame and the remaining four images was greater than 90% (i.e. no excessive motion). We detected the face and eye landmarks using Dlib library [6]. The eye crops were generated such that the width and height of the crop is 2.5× that of the eye's corner to corner width.

Protocol: VISOB 2.0, WCCI 2020 edition, consists of captures from 150 identities. Both left and right eyes from two visits were provided to the participants. Data characteristics is given in Table 2. Also, we provided images from visit 1 and visit 2 (2–4 weeks apart) under earlier mentioned three lighting conditions in order to keep the focus on the long-term verification and cross-illumination

---

[3] https://sce.umkc.edu/research-sites/cibit/dataset.html/.

Table 2. Number of VISOB 2.0 training images provided to the challenge participants.

Device	Lighting condition	Visit 1	Visit 2
Note 4	Office light	4,542	6,138
	Dim indoors	4,788	6,158
	Daylight	4,868	6,148
OPPO	Office light	7,848	10,546
	Dim indoors	5,138	7,076
	Daylight	5,314	6,864

comparisons. No image enhancement was applied to the data so that the participants could perform end-to-end learning to obtain the best fusion of biometrics information and multi-frame image enhancement from the burst of input images. In order to evaluate the submissions according to real-life scenarios, we set up this competition in a subject independent environment. For the competition, the participants were simply asked to submit a model that generates the match score from a pair of images (simple reference-probe comparison). Table 3 shows 18 experiments with 3.6M comparisons across different lighting conditions at the evaluation stage. We used Equal Error Rate (EER), ROC Area Under the Curve (AUC), and Genuine Match Rates (GMR) at 10^{-2}, 10^{-3}, and 10^{-4} False Match Rates (FMR) to evaluate accuracies.

3   Summary of Participants' Algorithms

Department of Informatics, Federal University of Parana (UFPR), Curitiba, PR, Brazil: Zanlorensi et al.'s submitted model is an ensemble of five ResNet-50 models pre-trained on the VGG-Face dataset proposed in [17]. Each ResNet-50 was fine-tuned using a softmax loss through 30 epochs on the periocular images from VISOB 2.0 training subset. The last fully connected layer from the original architecture was removed and replaced by two fully connected layers. The first layer is the feature layer containing 256 neurons, and the last one is the prediction layer consisting of 300 neurons as the number of classes in the training set (left and right eyes from 150 subjects). Eventually, the prediction layer was removed, and the output of the feature layer was taken as the deep feature vector for each input image. For each stack of five images, the five ResNet-50 ensemble generates a combined feature vector of length 1280 (5×256). The authors used cosine distance similarity to generate a match score and compare template-test ocular image pairs.

Bennett University, India: Ritesh Vyas' submission employed hand-crafted features, namely directional threshold local binary patterns (DTLBP) and a wavelet transform for feature extraction. This was the only non-deep learning approach submitted to the competition. The authors used Daubechies, an orthogonal

Table 3. Data distribution for the 18 experiments performed on the test set, as used by the organizers to evaluate the submitted methods.

Device	Experiment number	Enrollment	Verification	# of Comparison
Note 4	1	Dim	Dim	82,322
	2	Dim	Daylight	116,028
	3	Dim	Office	123,168
	4	Daylight	Dim	105,614
	5	Daylight	Daylight	153,416
	6	Daylight	Office	184,512
	7	Office	Dim	99,684
	8	Office	Daylight	143,716
	9	Office	Office	169,890
OPPO	10	Dim	Dim	184,360
	11	Dim	Daylight	190,444
	12	Dim	Office	303,686
	13	Daylight	Dim	178,418
	14	Daylight	Daylight	184,438
	15	Daylight	Office	294,356
	16	Office	Dim	290,082
	17	Office	Daylight	332,696
	18	Office	Office	494,492
			Total	3,631,322

Table 4. Details of the algorithm submitted to the IEEE WCCI VISOB 2.0 competition.

Participant	Feature extraction	Matcher/Classifier
Team 1	ResNet-50	Cosine
Team 2	DTLBP	Cosine
Team 3	GoogleNet	Euclidean distance + LSTM

wavelet, to facilitates the multi-resolution analysis. The local texture representation operator captures the unique intensity variations of the periocular image. DTLBP is more robust to noise and is able to extract more distinctive feature representation than the local binary pattern (LBP). Chi-square distance was utilized to compare features from two stacks of images, followed by score normalization.

Anonymous Participant: The authors used a GoogleNet pre-trained on the ImageNet dataset to extract the representation features. Euclidean distance was employed to calculate the similarity between pairs of periocular images.

Following the distance calculation, the scores were used to train Long Short Term Memory (LSTM) model to predict if the pair of images belong to the same individual.

4 Result and Discussion

Table 4 shows the details of the three algorithms submitted to the competition. Experiments were setup as subject independent (open-set-like). All the algorithms consisted of a feature extractor and a similarity-based matcher. The former extracts the feature representation of the image, and the latter computes the match score between two data samples (enrollment and verification). Two out of the three submissions employed deep learning based approaches.

Table 5 shows the EER and AUC of the competition's 18 experiments using Note4 and OPPO N1 challenge data for the three submitted algorithms (note that OPPO N1 has a better camera). Figure 2 shows the average GMRs at different FMRs in 18 experiments. These values are calculated by taking the average of GMRs from the 18 experiments. It can be easily seen that team 1 outperformed the other two teams by a large margin. The best result obtained by team 1 for Note 4 is 5.256% EER and 0.988 AUC for the 9th experiment (office versus office), shown in the result table. For OPPO N1, team 1 achieved the highest performance for dim light versus dim light condition with 6.394% EER and 0.984 AUC. Three experiments with enrollment and verification under the same lighting condition (experiment 10, 14, and 18) generally obtained slightly better performance than the other experiments. This implies cross illumination comparison degrades the performance of the model submitted by team 1.

As shown in Table 5, team 2 achieved the 2nd best place in our competition. Using a similar cosine matcher as team 1, team 2 utilized a non-deep learning based textural feature extractor, DTLBP. The lowest EER for team 2 was 27.05% for Note 4 and 26.208% for OPPO N1 device in the office versus office lighting

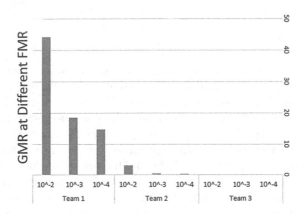

Fig. 2. GMR% at 10^{-2}, 10^{-3}, and 10^{-4} FMR of the three submissions.

Table 5. EER and AUC of the 9 experiments for three submissions, Note 4 device.

	Team 1		Team 2		Team 3	
	AUC	EER (%)	AUC	EER (%)	AUC	EER (%)
1	0.98	7.462	0.715	35.014	0.597	42.074
2	0.952	10.025	0.625	40.468	0.57	44.688
3	0.978	6.659	0.614	42.153	0.583	43.435
4	0.955	11.456	0.615	41.499	0.568	44.41
5	0.971	7.763	0.767	30.679	0.604	40.685
6	0.985	6.722	0.716	34.403	0.585	42.514
7	0.951	12.102	0.605	43.651	0.557	46.085
8	0.968	8.063	0.722	34.309	0.582	42.686
9	0.988	5.256	0.804	27.05	0.629	39.772
10	0.984	6.394	0.732	34.334	0.61	40.301
11	0.961	9.397	0.628	40.362	0.549	44.943
12	0.974	8.082	0.622	40.898	0.568	43.705
13	0.971	8.282	0.623	41.993	0.551	45.411
14	0.965	8.112	0.776	29.697	0.573	42.46
15	0.979	6.672	0.745	31.911	0.548	45.137
16	0.959	9.757	0.603	42.945	0.535	46.679
17	0.961	8.654	0.746	31.785	0.541	45.698
18	0.978	6.487	0.819	26.208	0.581	42.047

setting. However, the model performance degraded significantly for other experiments with EER fluctuating from 30% to 43%. It appears that the non-deep learning features from DTLBP are not as robust against changes in illumination. Team 3's model did not obtain satisfactory results for any of the experiments.

5   Conclusion

Ocular biometric is becoming an attractive alternative to face recognition in the mobile environment, especially due to occlusion caused by masks worn during the COVID-19 pandemic. We organized the VISOB 2.0 competition at IEEE WCCI 2020 conference to further advance the state-of-the-art in such ocular recognition methods, with a focus on multi-frame captures. We performed a thorough evaluation of three ocular recognition algorithms submitted to our VISOB 2.0 Challenge Competition. VISOB 2.0 dataset consists of stacks of five ocular images captured in burst mode using the front-facing camera from two different smartphones. From the obtained test results, it is obvious that the deep learning approach could obtain better results in our more challenging subject-independent evaluation settings. The comparison across different illumination settings showed adverse effects on the performance of all three submissions. These results can serve as a reference for future research and development in multi-frame RGB ocular recognition.

Acknowledgement. This work was funded in part by a gift from EyeVerify, Inc. (dba ZOLOZ) an affiliate of Ant Group Co., Ltd., and its affiliates. Dr. Derakhshani is also a consultant for ZOLOZ.

References

1. Carlaw, S.: Impact on biometrics of covid-19. Biometric Technol. Today **2020**(4), 8–9 (2020)
2. Damer, N., Grebe, J.H., Chen, C., Boutros, F., Kirchbuchner, F., Kuijper, A.: The effect of wearing a mask on face recognition performance: an exploratory study. arXiv preprint arXiv:2007.13521 (2020)
3. De Marsico, M., Nappi, M., Riccio, D., Wechsler, H.: Mobile iris challenge evaluation (miche)-i, biometric iris dataset and protocols. Pattern Recogn. Lett **57**, 17–23 (2015)
4. Derakhshani, R., Ross, A., Crihalmeanu, S.: A new biometric modality based on conjunctival vasculature. In: Proceedings of Artificial Neural Networks in Engineering, pp. 1–8 (2006)
5. Gangwar, A., Joshi, A.: Deepirisnet: deep iris representation with applications in iris recognition and cross-sensor iris recognition. In: 2016 IEEE International Conference on Image Processing (ICIP), pp. 2301–2305. IEEE (2016)
6. King, D.E.: Dlib-ml: a machine learning toolkit. J. Mach. Learn. Res. **10**, 1755–1758 (2009). http://dl.acm.org/citation.cfm?id=1577069.1755843
7. Kumari, P., Seeja, K.: Periocular biometrics: a survey. J. King Saud Univ.-Comput. Inf. Sci. **38**, 945–951 (2019)
8. Lovisotto, G., Malik, R., Sluganovic, I., Roeschlin, M., Trueman, P., Martinovic, I.: Mobile biometrics in financial services: A five factor framework. University of Oxford, Oxford, UK (2017)
9. Ngan, M.L., Grother, P.J., Hanaoka, K.K.: Ongoing face recognition vendor test (frvt) part 6a: Face recognition accuracy with masks using pre-covid-19 algorithms (2020)
10. Nguyen, H., Reddy, N., Rattani, A., Derakhshani, R.: Visob dataset wcci2020 challenge version (2020). https://sce.umkc.edu/research-sites/cibit/dataset.html#visob-data-descrip
11. Proença, H., Alexandre, L.A.: UBIRIS: a noisy iris image database. In: Roli, F., Vitulano, S. (eds.) ICIAP 2005. LNCS, vol. 3617, pp. 970–977. Springer, Heidelberg (2005). https://doi.org/10.1007/11553595_119
12. Rattani, A., Derakhshani, R.: Ocular biometrics in the visible spectrum: a survey. Image Vis. Comput. **59**, 1–16 (2017)
13. Rattani, A., Derakhshani, R., Ross, A. (eds.): Selfie Biometrics. ACVPR. Springer, Cham (2019). https://doi.org/10.1007/978-3-030-26972-2
14. Rattani, A., Derakhshani, R., Saripalle, S.K., Gottemukkula, V.: Icip 2016 competition on mobile ocular biometric recognition. In: 2016 IEEE International Conference on Image Processing (ICIP), pp. 320–324. IEEE (2016)
15. Reddy, N., Fahim Noor, D., Li, Z., Derakhshani, R.: Multi-frame super resolution for ocular biometrics. In: Proceedings of the IEEE Conference on Computer Vision and Pattern Recognition (CVPR) Workshops (2018)

16. Reddy, N., Rattani, A., Derakhshani, R.: Generalizable deep features for ocular biometrics. Image Vis. Comput. **103**, 103996 (2020)
17. Zanlorensi, L.A., Lucio, D.R., Junior, A.D.S.B., Proença, H., Menotti, D.: Deep representations for cross-spectral ocular biometrics. IET Biometrics **9**(2), 68–77 (2019)

Adapting to Movement Patterns for Face Recognition on Mobile Devices

Matthew Boakes$^{(\boxtimes)}$ ⓘ, Richard Guest ⓘ, and Farzin Deravi ⓘ

University of Kent, Canterbury, Kent CT2 7NZ, England
{mjb228,r.m.guest,f.deravi}@kent.ac.uk

Abstract. Facial recognition is becoming an increasingly popular way to authenticate users, helped by the increased use of biometric technology within mobile devices, such as smartphones and tablets. Biometric systems use thresholds to identify whether a user is genuine or an impostor. Traditional biometric systems are static (such as eGates at airports), which allow the operators and developers to create an environment most suited for the successful operation of the biometric technology by using a fixed threshold value to determine the authenticity of the user. However, with a mobile device and scenario, the operational conditions are beyond the control of the developers and operators.

In this paper, we propose a novel approach to mobile biometric authentication within a mobile scenario, by offering an adaptive threshold to authenticate users based on the environment, situations and conditions in which they are operating the device. Utilising smartphone sensors, we demonstrate the creation of a successful scenario classification. Using this, we propose our idea of an extendable framework to allow multiple scenario thresholds. Furthermore, we test the concept with data collected from a smartphone device. Results show that using an adaptive scenario threshold approach can improve the biometric performance, and hence could allow manufacturers to produce algorithms that perform consistently in multiple scenarios without compromising security, allowing an increase in public trust towards the use of the technology.

Keywords: Mobile · Face · Adaptive · Threshold · Motion · Scenario · Classification

1 Introduction

Biometric facial recognition is a useful security tool, allowing a method of authentication with little interaction from the users' perspective since images can be captured from a distance and while in motion merely requiring the use of a camera. The technology has gained prevalence in recent years with its incorporation into mobile devices.

Facial recognition has its share of criticism as campaigners claim the current technology is inaccurate, intrusive and infringes on an individual's right to privacy [1]. Recently, several locales have implemented or are considering

© Springer Nature Switzerland AG 2021
A. Del Bimbo et al. (Eds.): ICPR 2020 Workshops, LNCS 12668, pp. 209–228, 2021.
https://doi.org/10.1007/978-3-030-68793-9_15

implementing a ban of fixed system facial recognition technology, including San Francisco [16] and the European Union [1]. In order to support broad adoption of the technology, we must assure to certify that it is 'fit for purpose' and one method to achieve this would be to ensure consistently high recognition accuracy across a range of scenarios.

With a camera now installed on the majority of smartphone devices, it is becoming increasingly convenient to take a self-portrait image ('selfie') intended for facial recognition. Service providers are increasingly asking for users to submit an ID document photo alongside a selfie, captured on a mobile device, to authenticate their claimed identity as part of Electronic Identity Verification (eIDV) services [8]. Furthermore, smartphones now increasingly incorporate facial technology allowing users to verify themselves as well as access services and resources within the device and beyond.

Static biometric systems, fixed in position, such as airport eGates, have been in use for a while. In these scenarios, the operators have great control over the environment to help optimise recognition performance. The same is not valid with mainstream mobile biometrics, where the operator has no control over the operational environment. It, therefore, stands to reason that mobile biometrics would require a more adaptive approach for handling the authentication system.

In this paper, we describe a proof-of-concept adaptive model for mobile devices which has the potential to outperform a static threshold applied to all environments and usage conditions. Section 2 introduces related work and our inspiration for this. Sections 3–4 introduces our data collection and discuses how movement scenario impact recognition performance. Section 5 introduces our theory behind an adaptive framework to better deal with changing movement patterns. Section 6 discuses our approach to a scenario detection algorithm Sections 7–8 shows our experimental work and results in testing the adaptive threshold algorithm and Sect. 9 draws conclusions and suggests future work.

2   Related Work

The concept of adaptive biometrics systems is not new as Pisani *et al.* [23] has provided a comprehensive review of adaptive biometrics systems. However, the majority of approaches work by updating the biometric reference over time usually to account for template ageing. Pisani *et al.* note how "there is still a limited number of studies that evaluate adaptive biometric systems on mobile devices" and how researchers "should also acquire data from the sensors on these devices over time". Here we take a condition-sensitive (and quality index) adaptation criterion approach based on Pisani *et al.* taxonomy.

Our method intends not to alter either the sample or the probe but to utilise the mobile device's sensor information to determine the operation scenario and set thresholds accordingly. Techniques utilising the sensors embedded into smartphones and combining them with the biometric authentication process are present in the literature. Including the creation of behavioural biometric data to assess unique traits to identify individuals either independently or as part of a multimodal system with another physical or behavioural biometric trait to produce accurate biometric systems, commonly for continuous authentication purposes [15,21,25]. Another involvement of smartphone sensor data is in liveness detection [17] and defending against presentation attacks, Chen et al. [5] demonstrated a presentation attack detection approach to use the motion sensors to defend against 2D media attacks and virtual camera attacks.

The need for a more adaptive recognition framework is present in the literature as aspects like movement and portability of the device can vary between enrolment and recognition phases [24]. We previously [2] highlighted the potential factors that can affect a mobile biometric system and highlighted 'Scenarios' as one of these factors by categorising them under 'Stationary' and 'Motion'. Gutta et al. [12] have filed patents that suggest work and ideas relating to an adaptive biometric threshold, including the use of a light intensity sensor to assist in adjusting the threshold value in a facial recognition system. Similarly, Brumback et al. [3] (Fitbit Inc) has also filed patents for continuous authentication purposes on wearable technologies such as smartwatches and fitness trackers. However, they provide no practical examples of the proposals for mobile systems. Castilllo-Guerra et al. [4] proposed an adaptive threshold estimation for voice verification systems allowing the threshold to adapt to specific speakers. Similarly, Mhenni et al. [20] proposed to use an adaptive strategy specific to each category of users while investigating using Doddington's Zoo classification of user's keystroke dynamics.

Lunerti et al. [18] showed that for face verification in a mobile environment "it can be possible to ensure good sample quality and high biometric performance by applying an appropriate threshold that will regulate the amplitude on variations of the smartphone movements during facial image capture". This paper aims to contribute in showing how an adaptive approach can be the answer to having an "appropriate threshold" and begin to explore the gap in mobile biometric adaptive systems by exploring the potential impact of motion scenarios on recognition performance. We aim to answer the following question: can we improve mobile biometric recognition performance and security by using an adaptive approach to the decision component using knowledge of the operating scenario?

3   Data Collection

To trial this approach, we conducted a data collection. This paper will focus on the results achieved using the Android-based Samsung Galaxy S9 smartphone device. We developed a custom application to collect and capture data from this device in an attempt to mimic a biometric authentication. Using the Samsung Galaxy S9, we were able to collect data including a 'selfie' image taken by the participant in the scenarios and background metadata obtained from the multitude of sensors (including accelerometer, gyro sensor and geomagnetic sensor) within the device. The device features an 8 megapixel (1.22 μm, f/1.7) front-facing camera. However, the default front picture size captures images at 5.2 megapixels meaning for the study we had images of resolution 2640x1980.

We had a total of 25 participants who completed this part of the study during one session visit. We tasked participants with operating the device in a variety of scenarios, the order of which was:

1. Sitting - Participant sat down in a chair.
2. Standing - Participant standing.
3. Treadmill - Participant walking at a steady speed on a treadmill (speed set by the participant).
4. Corridor - Participant walking at a steady speed down a corridor.

The aim was to mimic likely scenarios for smartphone use, the exception being treadmill, where the aim was to create a controlled walking scenario. We wanted to ensure the tasks were not too strenuous owing to the repetitive nature of repeat biometric transactions. The theory is to test the approach on indoor scenarios in typical biometric authentication environments (room lighting), allowing us to focus specifically on motion and movement. However, we would like to see the approach adapted to other scenarios and factors in the future.

In each of the scenarios, the participant held the device with their own hands as they usually would when operating a smartphone device. The participants were pre-enrolled at the start of the session using the device's biometric system while in the seated position. For each scenario, we asked the participant to take a 'selfie' image. We deliberately did not make any recommendations on how to position the face within the image; the only requirement was that the face was within the image, as an additional part of the experiment was to see the impact on the device's facial recognition system.

Once the participant had captured the image, they remained in the same position, including the handling of the device. They were then presented with the device's in-built Android BiometricPrompt [10] to perform an authentication. While this was happening, we simultaneously collected the metadata (sensors, including Gyroscope, Linear Acceleration, Magnetic Field, Orientation) from the moment the device's face authentication started until the process had finished utilising the abilities of Android SensorManager [9]. As the face recognition authentication can be over within a second, we wanted to make sure we collected as much sensor data as possible. Therefore we set the sensor delay to 0.005s; however, we should note as stated in the documentation "this is only a hint to the system. Events may be received faster or slower than the specified rate".

Figure 1 shows examples of one captured 'selfie' image from each tested scenario, taken by a single participant in our study. Table 1 displays the number of images we collected from each scenario and within how many of those the facial recognition algorithm we used was able to detect a face. The work in this paper uses the images where the algorithm detected a face. Table 2 shows the breakdown of our participant ages. We can see that 76% of our participants who used the Samsung Galaxy S9 were under the age of 30, as we are capturing within a student population. Our participants had a gender split of 52% Female to 48% Male.

4   Scenario Performance

To test whether our adaptive framework has the potential to outperform a traditional system, we needed to create a prototype. Commercial off-the-shelf smartphone devices have the biometric components tightly locked down for security and privacy concerns. Therefore, we decided to use open-source software to help create a prototype of how a potential adaptive system could perform and function. We used the open-source 'face-recognition' python library (version 1.3.0) by Geitgey [6,7] as the face recognition algorithm for our prototype. This library utilises the machine learning library 'Dlib'.

(a) Sitting   (b) Standing   (c) Treadmill   (d) Corridor

Fig. 1. One example image from each scenario obtained from one participant during the first session

Table 1. Amount of images collected from each scenario

Scenario	Images	Face detected	No face detected
Sitting	139	139	0
Standing	124	123	1
Treadmill	121	116	5
Corridor	122	120	2

Table 2. Participant age ranges

Age ranges	# of Subjects
19–21	3
22–24	8
25–29	8
30–39	4
40–49	2
Total	25

For each user, we took their first sitting attempt as the enrolment reference, to act as the base-case scenario, and used the remaining images from all the scenarios as verification probes. Meaning we had a total of 114 verification probes for the sitting scenario, 123 for the standing scenario, 116 for the treadmill scenario and finally 120 for the corridor scenario. The 'face-recognition' library calculated and returned the dissimilarity distance scores (between 0 and 1) of a given enrolled sample and a new verification probe. Here, a high score indicates that two images are unlikely to be of the same person (no match), and a low score indicates that the two images are likely to be of the same person (match). The library recommends a decision threshold of 0.6, meaning, we consider all comparisons that score 0.6 or below to be the same person, and anything above is different people.

We previously [2] showed how scenarios could impact the false reject rate of the Samsung Galaxy S9 and showed the performance results from the device, although also noted how additional factors could have caused this impact. As an exploratory investigation, we used the dissimilarity score information provided by this library, and investigated if a need existed for having a different threshold for each scenario by examining the performance observed within each. We can see this by exploring how the dissimilarity scores from the genuine transactions vary in each scenario. Table 3 shows this information along with the standard deviation and informs us that our average dissimilarity score for the stationary scenarios was $0.21(\pm0.08)$, whereas the average score for our in-motion scenarios was $0.30(\pm0.06)$. It is indicating a 43% score increase from a user being in a stationary scenario to them being in a motion scenario. The unpaired two-tailed t-test gives a t-score equal to 13.84 with an associated p-value of less than 0.00001 demonstrating a statistically significant difference between the genuine distance scores in stationary and motion scenarios. Similar statistical tests proved that the difference between the impostor distance scores in this instance was not statistically significant. We can also see that the baseline recognition performance varies across scenarios.

Here we used a total of four impostors for each genuine user as discussed in Sect. 7.1, and the largest FAR occurs in the same scenario as used for the enrolment. However, this is also the scenario which has a mean dissimilarity score significantly lower than the baseline threshold of 0.6, highlighting the problem and affect that using impostor probes taken in the same scenario has on the false accept rate. We believe that an adaptive threshold could provide greater security by restricting these passive impostor attacks. These findings highlight reasons for the introduction of unique thresholds into biometric algorithms.

Table 3. Performance variations for each tested scenario

	Genuine mean dissimilarity score	Baseline recognition performance
Sitting	0.16 (±0.07)	FRR: 0.00 FAR: 11.30
Standing	0.25 (±0.06)	FRR: 0.00 FAR: 9.04
Treadmill	0.31 (±0.07)	FRR: 0.00 FAR: 8.70
Corridor	0.29 (±0.05)	FRR: 0.00 FAR: 9.41

5   The Adaptive Scenario Threshold

A traditional biometric system can be seen in Fig. 2 from the International Organization for Standardization (ISO) based on prior work from Mansfield et al. [19]. The component we are interested in here is the 'Decision' ('Matcher') component of the system. In a traditional static system, this component is relatively straightforward. We compare our stored enrolment reference to an additionally provided probe and receive a match score from the system that can determine how similar or dissimilar the two are. Having received this match score, we can use a threshold pre-defined to allow our genuine users to access the system while keeping as many impostors from accessing the system as possible. The aim is to set a threshold to keep the False Reject Rate (FRR), the percentage of genuine people rejected by the system, and False Accept Rate (FAR), the percentage of impostors accepted by the system, as low as possible. The equal error rate (EER) is the value where the FRR and FAR are identical with a low equal error rate indicating a high accuracy for the biometric system. Figure 3 shows an example of the 'Decision' component of a static system.

Our method addresses whether we can achieve an improvement in overall biometric performance, by adjusting the threshold adaptively, based on what we can find out from the authentication environment. When using a traditional (static) biometric system, we can create an appropriate environment and provide directions to users to help ensure optimal usage, giving the best chance of successful authentication. However, with the unpredictability of the environments, scenarios and conditions in which mobile devices are operated within, and hence where the biometric authentication can occur, can we alter the decision threshold instead to allow for optimal performance? We present a sample of how this framework could function in Fig. 4. Here we illustrate that instead of having a single threshold to cover the entire spectrum of environments and scenarios as depicted in Fig. 3; we can have a separate limit set for specified situations, such as in this example using 'Stationary' and 'Motion'. To the best of our knowledge, this is the first work to utilise smartphone sensor data to classify scenarios in an

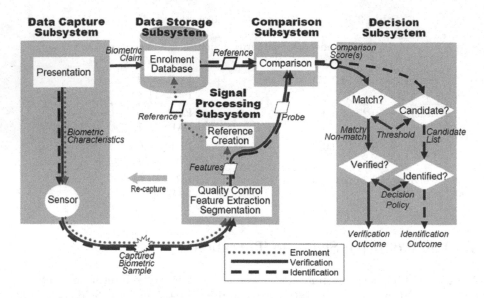

Fig. 2. Components of a general biometric system [14]

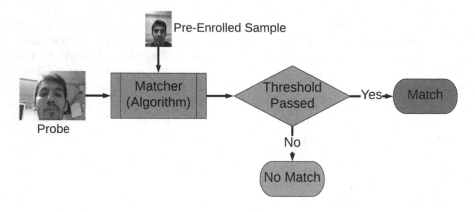

Fig. 3. A traditional matcher/decision of a biometric system

attempt to create an adaptive biometric system for mobile devices by adjusting the threshold accordingly.

In using an adaptive threshold, we expect that we will be able to tailor the authentication experience to better deal with changing movement patterns and allow for enhanced security and user satisfaction. Our primary driver is to allow genuine users unobstructed access while keeping out passive impostors. We, therefore, considered it vital to use appropriate impostors while designing and testing the framework. This is discussed further in Sect. 7.1.

6 Automatic Scenario Detection

To achieve this adaptive threshold, we need a methodology to allow us to know in what scenario the user of the device was performing the authentication within. The first step is to distinguish between our 'Stationary' and 'Motion' scenarios.

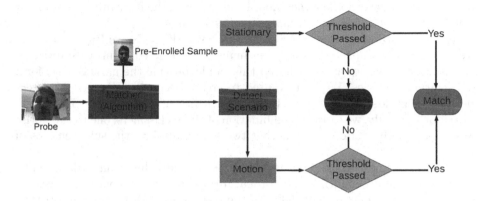

Fig. 4. An example framework for a simplified adaptive threshold decision for a biometric system

We used a total of five features for our classifiers, including four of the in-build mobile sensors, two motion-based sensors, two position-based sensors and a facial image quality assessment. The motion sensors were Gyroscope and Linear Acceleration. The position sensors were Magnetometer (Magnetic Field) and phone Orientation. All of these sensors operate on an x, y, and z axis system, and the data from each channel was collected. We began collecting the sensor data from the moment the participant started the authentication until the transaction was complete (successful authentication, timeout, attempt limit exceeded). Because we collected the sensor data during the authentication process alone, we used the entire sample for analyses purposes. The participant was already and remained within the scenario when the authentication process began, meaning, we do not expect outliers in the data from the participants preparing themselves.

Our fifth and final feature was the quality assessment of the 'selfie' image. This information came from an open-source library known as 'FaceQnet' and which uses a Convolutional Neural Network to "predict the suitability of a specific input image for face recognition purposes" [13]. FaceQnet provides a score for an input image between 0 and 1 where 0 means the worst quality, 1 means the best quality. FaceQnet recommends cropping images to the facial region first before assessing them. By using the open-source Multi-task Cascaded Convolutional Neural Networks (MTCNN) library based on the work provided by Zhang *et al.* [26], we were able to achieve this. In the rare occasion that the

MTCNN algorithm was unable to produce a cropped version of the image (usually because the facial region was already over the frames of the images), we used the original un-cropped image instead.

We processed the data in the feature set to allow us to achieve reasonable accuracy. The magnitude ($\sqrt{x^2 + y^2 + z^2}$) of the gyroscope, linear acceleration and magnetometer were calculated for each data point obtained for each authentication attempt. Figure 5 shows a sample of plotted Gyroscope data from one random sitting scenario. For the orientation, we used the median value from our captured data as our feature from each transaction.

We tested standard classifier algorithms (SVM, kNN, Naive Bayes, Decision Tree) to see the impact on the performance. We started from a 'Stationary' and 'Motion' classifier as we believed this would provide the most generic form of scenario categories. We then wanted to create a classifier that could detect the four scenarios that we are interested in ('Sitting', 'Standing', 'Treadmill', 'Corridor'). Finally, we tested a combination of three classifiers; one to categorise 'Stationary' and 'Motion' and another two to classify into the sub-scenarios of each.

At this point, we grouped our features into the individual transactions, and a transaction contains multiple rows of features as the sensors continue to release information. We removed half (50%) of the transactions for training and testing the classifiers. The reason for doing this was to simulated having unseen data for

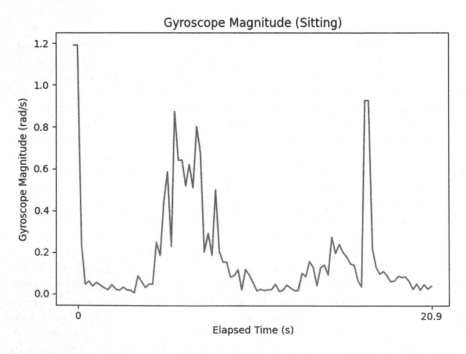

Fig. 5. A sample of gyroscope plot recorded from one transaction during the sitting scenario

testing the adaptive framework in its entirety later. We repeated this five times, selecting a different 50% each time to see the impact of classification accuracy.

To produce a classifier, we used Python's Scikit Learn library [22]. We split our features into a training (66%) and testing set (33%). We estimated the accuracy using k-fold cross-validation with a fold value of five and reported the F1-score. We found that with our features the k-nearest neighbour algorithm, with a k-value of three, performed the best. Table 4 shows the accuracy results for tested classifiers when classifying our four scenarios.

Table 4. Classification accuracy for standard classifiers

Classifier	Cross-Val (F1-score)	Training	Testing
Support Vector Machine	0.57 (± 0.03)	0.57	0.57
Decision Tree	0.81 (± 0.04)	0.83	0.83
Random Forest	0.80 (± 0.02)	0.79	0.81
Naive Bayes	0.57 (± 0.09)	0.59	0.60
Quadratic Discriminant	0.58 (± 0.09)	0.60	0.62

The kNN classifier with a k-value of three was capable of classifying all four of our scenarios with a testing accuracy of **97%**. Table 5 shows the accuracy results for each of our scenario detection classifiers using the k-nearest neighbour algorithm for each attempt. The random split of data from attempt five provided the most accurate classifier according to the F1 scores, and this is the one we use for the remaining work in this paper. Table 6 gives the corresponding confusion matrix for the 'Four Scenarios' classifier when testing with the kNN classifier in attempt five. We can bin the vast majority of errors under 'Stationary' and 'Motion' where scenarios within each category are getting misclassified with each other.

Table 5. Scenario classification results (kNN)

Scenario classifications	Accuracy	1	2	3	4	5
Stationary vs Motion	Cross-Val (F1-score)	0.99 (±0.01)	0.98 (±0.01)	0.98 (±0.01)	0.98 (±0.00)	0.99 (±0.01)
	Training	0.99	1.00	1.00	0.99	1.00
	Testing	0.99	0.99	0.99	0.99	0.99
Four Scenarios	Cross-Val (F1-score)	0.95 (±0.01)	0.96 (±0.01)	0.96 (±0.01)	0.96 (±0.01)	0.97 (±0.01)
	Training	0.98	0.99	0.99	0.98	0.99
	Testing	0.95	0.97	0.97	0.97	0.97
Stationary	Cross-Validation (F1-score)	0.95 (±0.02)	0.96 (±0.03)	0.98 (±0.01)	0.97 (±0.01)	0.98 (±0.01)
	Training	0.98	0.98	0.99	0.99	0.99
	Testing	0.96	0.96	0.98	0.97	0.97
Motion	Cross-Val (F1-score)	0.96 (±0.02)	0.98 (±0.01)	0.97 (±0.01)	0.98 (±0.02)	0.97 (±0.01)
	Training	0.99	1.00	0.99	0.99	0.99
	Testing	0.97	0.99	0.98	0.98	0.99

Using the kNN classifier to classify all four of our scenarios provided a testing accuracy of **97%** and **99%** when classifying between stationary and motion scenarios. In all our classifiers we have been able to achieve a testing accuracy of above 90%.

Table 6. 'Four scenarios' confusion matrix

		Predicted			
		Sitting	Standing	Treadmill	Corridor
True	Sitting	775	14	5	4
	Standing	24	570	3	4
	Treadmill	1	2	494	11
	Corridor	6	5	3	563

7   Testing the Framework

We tested our framework by using the metadata (features) with our classifier(s) and the 'selfie' image with the 'face-recognition' python library [6, 7]. However, in theory, we would like to see the approach incorporated into commercial devices and working in real-time by integrating it into the biometric authentication process. The approach for this would be similar to our off-line approach, the main difference being the real-time collection of the data. The device would collect the sensor information relating to motion and position as the biometric process was happening and continuously turn this information into a feature set similar to ours. This feature set would be continuously passed to a classifier to assign a scenario, whereby a majority vote method, where the operational scenario with the highest number of occurrences, would be used to assign the overall scenario classification. The overall scenario classification will be the one used to assign an adaptive decision threshold. For our prototype, we took the same approach off-line by using our pre-collected data.

We achieved this with a custom Python program which works by excepting two facial images. All our image files had unique names to allow us to locate the data associated with each one. The first image was an enrolment template (taken as the first sitting attempt for each user) and the second was the verification probe. The authentication sensor data captured for the supplied probe image was retrieved, and each feature row of data was processed by the classifier to predict a scenario, and a majority vote method assigned the final scenario classification. Once the predicted scenario was known, the program set the decision threshold appropriately. The program then marks the probe image as either being a 'match' or a 'no match' decision based on the dissimilarity score and the set threshold. We could then use this information to produce the performance results and begin to validate our approach.

7.1   Choosing the Impostors

To assess the effectiveness of the proposed adaptive framework, we need to test the potential to keep out passive impostors and evaluate the false accept rate of the system. For each enrolled participant, we wanted to find the most suitable (tailored) participants to act as impostors. The set theory below represents our algorithm for achieving this.

- Amount of Impostors Required: x
- Current User: c
- Set of Users: U where $c \in U$
- Set of Impostors: $I \subset U = c \notin U$
- An Impostor: i where $i \in I$
- Gender Subset: $G \subseteq I \ \forall \ c$.Gender $== i$.Gender
- Age Group Subset: $A \subseteq I \ \forall \ c$.AgeGroup $== i$.AgeGroup
- Ethnicity Subset: $E \subseteq I \ \forall \ c$.Ethnicity $== i$.Ethnicity
- Nationality Subset: $N \subseteq I \ \forall \ c$.Nationality $== i$.Nationality
- Subset of Tailored Impostors: $T = G \cap A \cap E \cap N \subseteq I$
- if $|T| >= x$ {Randomly select x elements from set}
- while $|T| < x$
  - Randomly select from $G \cap A \cap E \cap N$ until $|T| == x$ is reached
  - if $G \cap A \cap E \cap N$ becomes $\emptyset$ {Randomly select from $G \cap A \cap E$ until $|T| == x$ is reached}
  - if $G \cap A \cap E$ becomes $\emptyset$ {Randomly select from $G \cap A$ until $|T| == x$ is reached}
  - if $G \cap A$ becomes $\emptyset$ {Randomly select from G until $|T| == x$ is reached}

For our purposes, we define our 'AgeGroup' as the ranges specified in Table 2 and our 'Ethnicity' under the five broad ethnic groupings specified by the UK Government [11]. This algorithm should result in a set of x tailored impostors for each participant who most resembles that of the participant. We expected our impostor set to provide the most likely cases to cause a false accept to occur. We experimented adjusting the number of tailored impostors to provide meaningful results because when using our algorithm, the more impostors we add, the less tailored they will be resulting in dilution of the results. For our data, we found using a total of four impostors per genuine user (2015 impostor comparisons) seemed to provide a fair balance before our impostors became less tailored. We discuss this more in Sect. 8 and Fig. 6.

7.2   Examining the Threshold

The recommended threshold from the python 'face-recognition' library [6,7] is 0.6. When using our data, this gives us a false reject rate of 0.00%, a false accept rate of 10.22% and an equal error rate of approximately 0.64%. It seems the library is recommending a practical threshold value for the majority of cases. To test our adaptive theory, we would like to devise a scenario whereby security is of great concern. Therefore, we require a low (<1%) false accept rate by setting tighter, more restrictive thresholds.

We identified in Sect. 4 that the match score varies across scenarios and that we should be setting other thresholds for each. We took several approaches to set appropriate threshold values, and in our case, we wanted to consider trialling multiple thresholds for our scenarios. The trials allowed us to see how varying thresholds could affect overall system performance. For example, we could use the maximum distance score obtained from our data. We experimented with using the 95th percentile, maximum distance, and the EER threshold value from our scenario data as the threshold values. Our theory is that this will allow for the majority of genuine cases without causing extremes and outliers in our data to be accepted.

Similarly to how we handled the creation of the scenario classifier, we used a random 75% sample from our dissimilarity score data (75% from genuine and 75% from impostors) to create the thresholds. The impostor scores used for this were the ones created using our tailored impostors. We repeated this five times, picking a new random set each time to see the impact as shown in Table 7.

8   Results

Bringing the framework together, we can use the classifiers produced as discussed in Sect. 6, along with the thresholds found in Sect. 7.2 and chosen tailored impostors as based on Sect. 7.1. Using the open-source 'face-recognition' library [6,7] and our pre-collected data, we can examine how our adaptive framework could perform.

Figure 6 shows how the false accept rate changes as we used our algorithm to alter the number of impostors used (the algorithm was rerun for each iteration). We randomly selected a total of 450 comparisons, to provide a reasonable sample, from the impostor comparisons pool with x number of impostors per genuine user, we repeated this three times and took an average to produce the graph. We can see that the baseline's FAR declines as the impostors become less tailored; however, our adaptive approach outperforms the baseline with the most tailored impostors and continues to do so even when we include less tailored impostors.

We tested our more generic classifier that can classify the authentication metadata into a 'Stationary' and 'Motion' category. We followed this with a test of the classier that could distinguish between the four scenarios that we were experimenting with: 'Sitting', 'Standing', 'Treadmill', 'Corridor'. Finally, we trialled a combination of the two classifiers, where the data would first classify into 'Stationary' and 'Motion' and then into separate classifiers for the scenario that belonged to either category. Trialling both using '95th', 'Max' and 'EER' thresholds, we can achieve recognition results as shown in Table 7.

We know previously from our classifier accuracy that we are not classifying all the scenarios correctly every time. Meaning there is a risk of an incorrect classification to a scenario that has an alternative acceptance threshold. This

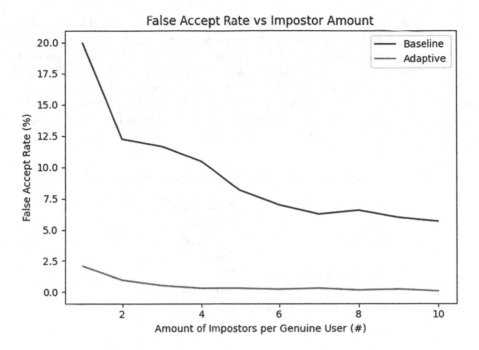

Fig. 6. Changes to false accept rate with varying impostor amounts

Table 7. Recognition performance results when trialing the adaptive threshold

Classifier	Threshold	1	2	3	4	5
Stationary vs Motion	95th	FRR: 5.29 FAR: 0.00	FRR: 4.65 FAR: 0.00	FRR: 6.98 FAR: 0.00	FRR: 5.07 FAR: 0.00	FRR: 6.13 FAR: 0.00
	Max	FRR: 0.00 FAR: 2.53	FRR: 0.00 FAR: 2.53	FRR: 0.00 FAR: 2.53	FRR: 0.00 FAR: 2.53	FRR: 0.63 FAR: 0.35
	EER	FRR: 0.42 FAR: 0.35	FRR: 0.42 FAR: 0.69	FRR: 0.42 FAR: 0.50	FRR: 0.42 FAR: 0.50	FRR: 0.85 FAR: 0.25
Four Scenarios	95th	FRR: 6.13 FAR: 0.05	FRR: 7.19 FAR: 0.10	FRR: 7.40 FAR: 0.00	FRR: 5.92 FAR: 0.10	FRR: 6.98 FAR: 0.00
	Max	FRR: 0.85 FAR: 1.39	FRR: 1.06 FAR: 1.39	FRR: 0.00 FAR: 2.53	FRR: 0.00 FAR: 2.53	FRR: 1.48 FAR: 0.25
	EER	FRR: 0.85 FAR: 1.39	FRR: 1.27 FAR: 0.89	FRR: 1.06 FAR: 0.50	FRR: 1.06 FAR: 0.55	FRR: 1.48 FAR: 0.25
Stationary/Motion + Scenarios	95th	FRR: 6.13 FAR: 0.05	FRR: 7.19 FAR: 0.10	FRR: 7.40 FAR: 0.00	FRR: 5.92 FAR: 0.10	FRR: 6.98 FAR: 0.00
	Max	FRR: 0.85 FAR: 1.39	FRR: 1.06 FAR: 1.39	FRR: 0.85 FAR: 1.39	FRR: 0.00 FAR: 2.53	FRR: 1.48 FAR: 0.25
	EER	FRR: 1.06 FAR: 0.55	FRR: 1.27 FAR: 0.89	FRR: 1.06 FAR: 0.50	FRR: 1.06 FAR: 0.55	FRR: 1.48 FAR: 0.25

misclassification poses a risk for impostors to be accepted by the system. Further work to improve the classifier accuracy will result in improved recognition performance.

Our results show that using an adaptive approach can be capable of producing reliable recognition accuracy, particularly with maintaining and improving a low false accept rate above a traditional fixed value. Table 8 highlights this comparison when using our four scenario classifier and EER (number 3 in Table 7) thresholds, to the baseline and a perfect classifier. A perfect classifier would be able to accurately categories our scenarios 100% of the time. Our most significant success in using our adaptive approach has been in reducing the false accept rate by approximately 95% from baseline performance.

Table 8. Comparing recommended baseline performance to our adaptive approach

	Recognition performance
Baseline	FRR: 0.00 FAR: 10.22
Adaptive Threshold	FRR: 1.06 FAR: 0.50
Perfect Scenario Classifier	FRR: 0.42 FAR: 0.60

8.1   Verification

Having had success testing our scenario adaptive threshold method on the Samsung Galaxy S9, we wanted to test the same concept on another device to see if the approach was interoperable. We experimented with another Android-based device the Google Pixel 2. However, Google Pixel 2 does not allow developer access to its 'Trusted Face' feature meaning that we cannot collect background sensor data during the authentication process. To counter for this, we had the device collect the sensor features while the participant was operating the in-built device's camera and taking a 'selfie' in an attempt to simulate the authentication process. The side effect of this means there was a lot more sensor data collected as operating and using the camera on average takes more time than the usual biometric authentication prompt to complete.

We collected the data under the same scenario conditions. We had an additional 100 genuine 'sitting' transactions, 116 'standing' transactions, 124 'treadmill' and 141 'corridor' from around 30 different individuals of a similar student demographic which operated the Samsung Galaxy S9. When running the 'selfie' data collected from the Google Pixel 2 through the 'face-recognition' Python library with baseline threshold (0.6), we receive the performance results of FRR: 0.00% and FAR: 9.50%.

We took the same approach as before by removing half of the transactions before attempting to classify. As devices are unique with different sensors, we cannot rely on using the same classifier as before, and unique ones will need producing for each device/model. The classifier evaluation results were promising with the 'four scenarios' classifier reporting results of cross-validation accuracy being 1.00 (±0.00) along with both the training and testing accuracy being 1.00%. We also use 75% of the dissimilarity score data to set appropriate thresholds. As a trial, we generated three sets of EER thresholds by altering the 75% of the data used. For the three trials, our results were again showing improvements over the baseline case and beginning to prove that the adaptive threshold is interoperable:

- FRR: 1.25% and FAR: 0.00%
- FRR: 2.91% and FAR: 0.00%
- FRR: 1.66% and FAR: 0.00%

9   Conclusion

In this paper, we presented a novel adaptive approach to biometric authentication for a mobile device, an area of research currently lacking in the literature, as noted by Pisani *et al.* [23]. We proposed the creation of an extendable 'Adaptive Framework', whereby we set a unique threshold value for specified scenarios. The theoretical advantage to this approach is to allow for stricter control over access, by not having to specify a one-off static threshold value to account for the vast amount of conditions where a biometric authentication may occur.

Our approach utilised the sensors readily available on the vast majority of modern smartphones (and wearables) with developer access. It showed the transformation into potential features for building a classifier that could recognise simple scenario categories. Our classifier for detecting our four simple scenarios had a testing accuracy of **97%**. The framework relies on having the ability to identify the scenario reliably, and our results suggest that this ability is a significant factor in the overall function of the adaptive framework to perform optimally. The paper focuses on using an adaptive approach for face recognition, but we see no significant obstacles for using the same technique for other physical and behavioural biometric modalities. We intend to continue this work into mobile scenario detection to investigate the impact features have on classification accuracy.

We demonstrated using collected data from a commercial device, and an open-source face recognition algorithm that this method has potential merit. By imagining a scenario where security and privacy are of grave concern, and hence a low false accept rate may be considered more important than the false reject rate, we tested our method against a static, fixed threshold. With this in mind, we produced an algorithm to help us identify the best impostors to use for each participant to help stress-test the approach. We demonstrated the impact of tailoring in Fig. 6, which proved that our algorithm was working.

We then performed off-line testing using Python's 'face recognition' library [6, 7], which recommends a threshold of around 0.6. We saw when using our collected data; this threshold gave a false reject rate of 0.00% and a false accept rate of 10.22%. By taking our adaptive approach, we found that one of our best methods was using the classifier to detect between stationary and motion scenarios along with the EER threshold value. In doing so, we were able to achieve a result that gave a false reject rate of **0.42%** and a false accept rate of **0.35%**, a reduction of 95% over the algorithm's baseline threshold. We also showed the interoperability of the approach by replicating it using another device with similarly successful results. Our relatively simple adaptive method was able to produce an improvement on recognition performance, which could outperform an algorithm using a single static threshold value.

We acknowledge that this has been one relatively simple example to demonstrate the practicalities and proof-of-concept of using this adaptive approach. Further testing will be required to prove the competency of the method thoroughly, including a greater variety of scenarios and environmental lighting and weather conditions. Testing should include an approach to adapt presentation attack detection (PAD) methods for individual scenarios and mitigate malicious actors in exploiting weaknesses in the adaptive approach. We hope that others will take the work we have started to produce and further investigate the effectiveness of the method. As well as allow developers and manufacturers to incorporate a scenario-based threshold adaptive approach into future algorithms in mobile biometric systems, to allow for higher security without jeopardising performance.

References

1. BBC News: Facial recognition: Eu considers ban of up to five years, January 2020. https://www.bbc.co.uk/news/technology-51148501, https://www.bbc.co.uk/news/technology-51148501, Accessed 29 Mar 20
2. Boakes, M., Guest, R., Deravi, F., Corsetti, B.: Exploring mobile biometric performance through identification of core factors and relationships. IEEE Trans. Biometrics Behavior Identity Sci. **1**(4), 278–291 (2019)
3. Brumback, C.B., Knight, D.W., Messenger, J.D.M., Hong, J.O.: Biometric sensing device having adaptive data threshold, a performance goal, and a goal celebration display, 27 May 2014, uS Patent 8,734,296
4. Castilllo-Guerra, E., Diaz-Amador, R., Julian, C.B.L.: Adaptive threshold estimation for speaker verification systems. J. Acoust. Soc. Am. **123**(5), 3877 (2008)
5. Chen, S., Pande, A., Mohapatra, P.: Sensor-assisted facial recognition: an enhanced biometric authentication system for smartphones. In: Proceedings of the 12th Annual International Conference on Mobile Systems, Applications, and Services, pp. 109–122 (2014)
6. Geitgey, A.: face-recognition. https://pypi.org/project/face-recognition/, March 2013. https://pypi.org/project/face-recognition/. Accessed 29 Mar 20
7. Geitgey, A.: Machine learning is fun! part 4: Modern face recognition with deep learning. https://medium.com/@ageitgey/machine-learning-is-fun-part-4-modern-face-recognition-with-deep-learning-c3cffc121d78, July 2016. https://medium.com/@ageitgey/machine-learning-is-fun-part-4-modern-face-recognition-with-deep-learning-c3cffc121d78. Accessed 29 Mar 20
8. Goode, A.: Digital identity: solving the problem of trust. Biometric Technol. Today **2019**(10), 5–8 (2019)

9. Google: SensorManager—Android Developers (2016). https://developer.android. com/reference/android/hardware/SensorManager. Accessed 16 Oct 20
10. Google: Show a biometric authentication dialog—Android Developers (2020). https://developer.android.com/training/sign-in/biometric-auth. Accessed 16 Oct 20
11. GOV.UK: List of ethnic groups. https://www.ethnicity-facts-figures.service. gov.uk/ethnic-groups, https://www.ethnicity-facts-figures.service.gov.uk/ethnic-groups. Accessed 04 June 20
12. Gutta, S., Trajkovic, M., Philomin, V.: System and method for adaptively setting biometric measurement thresholds, 4 Jan 2007, uS Patent App. 10/574,138
13. Hernandez-Ortega, J., Galbally, J., Fierrez, J., Haraksim, R., Beslay, L.: Faceqnet: Quality assessment for face recognition based on deep learning. arXiv preprint arXiv:1904.01740 (2019)
14. ISO: Text of standing document 11 (sd 11), part 1 overview standards harmonization document. Standard, International Organization for Standardization, August 2010
15. Kumar, R., Phoha, V.V., Serwadda, A.: Continuous authentication of smartphone users by fusing typing, swiping, and phone movement patterns. In: 2016 IEEE 8th International Conference on Biometrics Theory, Applications and Systems (BTAS), pp. 1–8. IEEE (2016)
16. Lee, D.: San francisco is first us city to ban facial recognition. https://www. bbc.co.uk/news/technology-48276660, May 2019, https://www.bbc.co.uk/news/ technology-48276660. Accessed 29 Mar 20
17. Li, Y., Li, Y., Yan, Q., Kong, H., Deng, R.H.: Seeing your face is not enough: an inertial sensor-based liveness detection for face authentication. In: Proceedings of the 22nd ACM SIGSAC Conference on Computer and Communications Security, pp. 1558–1569 (2015)
18. Lunerti, C., Guest, R., Baker, J., Fernandez-Lopez, P., Sanchez-Reillo, R.: Sensing movement on smartphone devices to assess user interaction for face verification. In: 2018 International Carnahan Conference on Security Technology (ICCST), pp. 1–5. IEEE (2018)
19. Mansfield, A.J., Wayman, J.L.: Best practices in testing and reporting performance of biometric devices. Centre for Mathematics and Scientific Computing, National Physical Laboratory (2002)
20. Mhenni, A., Cherrier, E., Rosenberger, C., Amara, N.E.B.: Adaptive biometric strategy using doddington zoo classification of user's keystroke dynamics. In: 2018 14th International Wireless Communications & Mobile Computing Conference (IWCMC), pp. 488–493. IEEE (2018)
21. Patel, V.M., Chellappa, R., Chandra, D., Barbello, B.: Continuous user authentication on mobile devices: recent progress and remaining challenges. IEEE Signal Process. Mag. **33**(4), 49–61 (2016)
22. Pedregosa, F., et al.: Scikit-learn: machine learning in python. J. Mach. Learning Res. **12**, 2825–2830 (2011)
23. Pisani, P.H., et al.: Adaptive biometric systems: review and perspectives. ACM Comput. Surv. (CSUR) **52**(5), 1–38 (2019)
24. Poh, N., Wong, R., Kittler, J., Roli, F.: Challenges and research directions for adaptive biometric recognition systems. In: Tistarelli, M., Nixon, M.S. (eds.) ICB 2009. LNCS, vol. 5558, pp. 753–764. Springer, Heidelberg (2009). https://doi.org/ 10.1007/978-3-642-01793-3_77

25. Vasiete, E., et al.: Toward a non-intrusive, physio-behavioral biometric for smart-phones. In: Proceedings of the 16th International Conference on Human-Computer Interaction with Mobile Devices & Services, pp. 501–506 (2014)
26. Zhang, K., Zhang, Z., Li, Z., Qiao, Y.: Joint face detection and alignment using multitask cascaded convolutional networks. IEEE Signal Process. Lett. **23**(10), 1499–1503 (2016)

Probing Fairness of Mobile Ocular Biometrics Methods Across Gender on VISOB 2.0 Dataset

Anoop Krishnan, Ali Almadan, and Ajita Rattani[✉]

Department of Electrical Engineering and Computer Science,
Wichita State University, Wichita, USA
{axupendrannair,aaalmadan}@shockers.wichita.edu,
ajita.rattani@wichita.edu

Abstract. Recent research has questioned the fairness of face-based recognition and attribute classification methods (such as gender and race) for dark-skinned people and women. Ocular biometrics in the visible spectrum is an alternate solution over face biometrics, thanks to its accuracy, security, robustness against facial expression, and ease of use in mobile devices. With the recent COVID-19 crisis, ocular biometrics has a further advantage over face biometrics in the presence of a mask. However, fairness of ocular biometrics has not been studied till now. This first study aims to explore the fairness of ocular-based authentication and gender classification methods across males and females. To this aim, VISOB 2.0 dataset, along with its gender annotations, is used for the fairness analysis of ocular biometrics methods based on ResNet-50, MobileNet-V2 and lightCNN-29 models. Experimental results suggest the equivalent performance of males and females for ocular-based mobile user-authentication in terms of genuine match rate (GMR) at lower false match rates (FMRs) and an overall Area Under Curve (AUC). For instance, an AUC of 0.96 for females and 0.95 for males was obtained for lightCNN-29 on an average. However, males significantly outperformed females in deep learning based gender classification models based on ocular-region.

Keywords: Fairness and Bias in AI · Mobile ocular biometrics · Deep learning

1 Introduction

With AI and computer vision reaching an inflection point, face biometrics is widely adopted for recognizing identities, surveillance, border control, and mobile user authentication with Apple introducing Face ID moniker in iPhone X[1].

---

[1] https://www.apple.com/iphone/.

A. Krishnan and A. Almadan—Contributed equally.

© Springer Nature Switzerland AG 2021
A. Del Bimbo et al. (Eds.): ICPR 2020 Workshops, LNCS 12668, pp. 229–243, 2021.
https://doi.org/10.1007/978-3-030-68793-9_16

The wide-scale integration of biometrics technology in mobile devices facilitate enhanced security in a user login, payment transaction, and eCommerce. Over the last few years, *fairness of these automated face-based* recognition [1,5,12,23] and gender classification methods have been questioned [4,11,14] across demographic variations. *Fairness* is defined as the absence of any prejudice or favoritism toward a group based on their inherent or acquired characteristics. Specifically, the majority of these studies raise the concern of higher error rates of face-based recognition and gender[2] classification methods[3] for darker-skinned people like African-American, and **for women**.

Speculated causes of the difference in the accuracy rates are skin-tone, make-up, facial expression change rate, pose, and illumination variations for face biometrics. Further, there has been a recent push for alternate solutions for face biometrics due to a significant drop in its performance in the presence of occlusion, such as mask amid COVID-19 [6]. Recent 2020 NIST study [15] suggests the presence of a mask could cause a face recognition system to fail up to 50%.

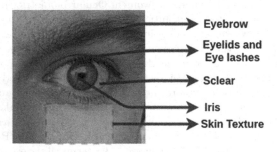

Fig. 1. An ocular image labeled with vasculature pattern, eyebrow, eyelids, eyelashes, and periocular skin texture.

Ocular biometrics in the visible spectrum offers a perfect alternate solution over the face and can be acquired using the front-facing RGB camera already installed in the mobile device [17,19,20]. It comprises of scanning regions in the eye and those around it, i.e., iris, conjunctival and episcleral vasculature and periocular region for person authentication. Figure 1 shows an ocular image labeled with vasculature pattern, eyebrow, eyelids, eyelashes, and periocular skin texture. It has obtained significant attention from the research community due to its accuracy, security, robustness against facial expressions, and ease of use in mobile device. The use of ocular biometrics technology in the mobile device is termed as *mobile ocular biometrics* [13,19].

With advances in deep learning, deeply coupled autoencoders and convolutional neural networks (CNNs) have been trained from scratch and re-purposed

---

[2] The term "sex" would be more appropriate, but in consistency with the existing studies, the term "gender" is used in this paper.

[3] The term "methods", "algorithms" and "models" are used interchangeably.

for mobile ocular recognition[4] [19,21]. Thorough evaluation of fine-tuned CNNs suggests efficacy of ResNet-50, LightCNN and MobileNet in mobile ocular recognition [21]. Datasets such as MICHE-I [7] (92 subjects) and VISOB 1.0 [16] (550 subjects) have been assembled for ocular recognition in mobile devices. VISOB 1.0 dataset was used in the IEEE 2016 ICIP international competition for mobile ocular biometrics. Studies in [3,18,19] also suggested the efficacy of deep learning-based methods for gender classification from the ocular region in the visible spectrum acquired using a mobile device. The reported results obtained from fine-tuned CNNs suggest that equivalent performance could be obtained in gender classification (with an accuracy of about 85%) from the ocular region over face biometrics.

Recent interest has been in using subject-independent evaluation of these ocular recognition methods where subjects *do not* overlap between the training and testing set to simulate realistic scenarios. To this front, VISOB 2.0 competition [16] in IEEE WCCI 2020 conference has been organized using VISOB 2.0 database. VISOB 2.0 [16] is a new version of the VISOB 1.0 dataset where the region of interest is extended from the eye (iris, conjunctival, and episcleral vasculature) to periocular (a region encompassing the eye). Further, the evaluation protocol followed is subject-independent, over subject-dependent evaluation in IEEE ICIP VISOB 1.0 competition [20]. Furthermore, instead of a single frame eye image in VISOB 1.0 [20], the data sample consists of a stack of five images captured in burst mode to facilitate multi-frame analysis.

However, to date, *the fairness of these deep learning based mobile ocular biometrics analysis models (such as ResNet-50, LightCNN and MobileNet) has not been evaluated.* It is not known whether ocular biometrics also have an advantage over face biometrics in terms of performance across demographic variations. The aim of this paper is to evaluate the fairness of ocular-based recognition and gender classification models across males and females from images acquired using mobile devices. In the context of this study, *fairness* is defined as equivalent error rates (or accuracy rates) for user authentication and gender classification across males and females. *To the best of our knowledge, this is the first study of its kind.* To this aim, the contributions of this paper are as follows:

- Evaluation of the fairness of deep learning-based methods for mobile ocular-based user authentication across males and females. To this front, performance of the fine-tuned version of ResNet-50 [8] and lightCNN-29 [24] have been evaluated using Softmax and cosine loss functions (ArcFace, CosFace, SphereFace, and AdaCos [2]) in three lighting conditions (office, dark and daylight condition).
- Evaluation of the fairness of gender classification methods based on ocular region across males and females. The performance of fine-tuned ResNet-50 [8], MobileNet-V2 [9,22] and their ensemble have been evaluated in three lighting conditions across gender.

---

[4] The term "recognition" and "user authentication" are used interchangeably.

All the experiments are conducted on VISOB 2.0 dataset [16], which facilitates subject-independent evaluation across three lighting conditions; office, daylight, and dark light. This paper is organized as follows: Sect. 2 details deep learning architectures used in this study for ocular analysis. Section 3 discusses the VISOB 2.0 training and testing dataset. Sections 4 and 5 discuss implementation details, and the obtained results on the fairness of the mobile ocular-based user authentication and gender classification methods, respectively, across males and females. Conclusions are drawn in Sect. 6.

2   Convolutional Neural Networks (CNN) Models Used

We used the popular ResNet [8], mobile friendly lightCNN [24] and MobileNet [22] based ocular analysis models for our evaluation. Efficacy of these models have already been established for mobile user recognition [21] and gender classification from ocular region [3,18,19]. Experimental results are reported for only two best models for user authentication and gender classification for the sake of space. These models (networks) are described below as follows:

- **ResNet**: ResNet [8] is a short form of residual network based on the idea of "identity shortcut connection" where input features may skip certain layers. The residual or shortcut connections introduced in ResNet allow for identity mappings to propagate around multiple nonlinear layers, preconditioning the optimization and alleviating the vanishing gradient problem. In this study, we used ResNet-50 model, which has 23.5M parameters.
- **LightCNN**: This model extensively uses the Max-Feature-Map (MFM) operation instead of ReLu activation, which acts as a feature filter after each convolutional layer [24]. The operation takes two feature maps, eliminates the element-wise minimums, and returns element-wise maximums. By doing so across feature channels, only 50% of the information-bearing nodes from each layer reach the next layer. Consequently, during training, each layer is forced to preserve only compact feature maps. Therefore, model parameters and the extracted features are significantly reduced. We used the lightCNN-29 model consisting of 12K parameters in this study.
- **MobileNet**: MobileNet [9,22] is one of the most popular mobile-centric deep learning architectures, which is not only small in size but also computationally efficient while achieving high performance. The main idea of MobileNet is that instead of using regular 3×3 convolution filters, the operation is split into depth-wise separable 3×3 convolution filters followed by 1×1 convolutions. While achieving the same filtering and combination process as a regular convolution, the new architecture requires less number of operations and parameters. In this study, we used MobileNet-V2 [22] which consist of 3.4M parameters.

3   VISOB 2.0 Dataset

In this section, we discuss VISOB 2.0 dataset along with the experimental protocol.

VISOB 2.0 [16] is the 2nd version of VISOB 1.0 dataset used in IEEE WCCI competition 2020. This publicly available dataset consists of a stack of eye images captured using the burst mode via two mobile devices: Samsung Note 4 and Oppo N1. During the data collection, the volunteers were asked to take their selfie images in two visits, 2 to 4 weeks apart from each other. At each visit, the selfie-like images were captured using the front-facing camera of the mobile devices under three lighting conditions (daylight, office light, and dark light) and two sessions (about 10 to 15 min apart). The stack consisting of five consecutive eye images were extracted from the stack of full-face frames selected such that the correlation coefficient between the center frame and the remaining four images is greater than 90%. The face and eye landmarks are detected using the Dlib library [10]. The eye crops were generated such that the width and height of the crop are 2.5× that of eye width.

Training and Testing Subset: The subset of the VISOB 2.0 dataset consisting of 150 subjects each for left and right eye (ocular regions) from two visits are used as the training set. This set was provided to the participants at the IEEE WCCI competition 2020. All the images from visit 1 and visit 2 (2–4 weeks apart) under three lighting conditions are included in this training set.

In order to evaluate the submission for real-life scenarios, 100 subjects each for left and right eye images are used as the testing set. All the stack of five images per sample from two visits across three lighting conditions is available in this set as well. We used a gender-balanced subset of the dataset for training and testing the models for user-authentication and gender classification (detailed in Sects. 4 and 5). This is in order to mitigate the impact of training and testing set imbalance on the fairness of the models.

4 Fairness of Mobile Ocular Recognition Methods Across Gender

In this section, we discuss the implementation of the models (networks) for ocular-based user authentication evaluated across males and females. All the implementations are done using Pytorch library (https://pytorch.org/).

4.1 Network Training and Implementation Details

ResNet-50 [8] and lightCNN-29 [24] are fine-tuned on the training subset of the VISOB 2.0 dataset [16] using five different loss functions; Softmax and cosine-based (ArcFace, CosFace, SphereFace, and AdaCos [2]) for the first time for ocular recognition. For ResNet-50 based on cosine loss functions (ArcFace, CosFace, SphereFace, and AdaCos [2]), batch normalization, drop-out, and fully connected layers of 2048 and 512 are added after the last convolutional layer. This is followed by the final output layer. In case of lightCNN-29, the layers added after the last pooling layer: batch normalization, drop-out, and a fully connected layer of $128 \times 128 \times 8$ and 512, and followed by the output layer. The angular margins are set to 0.50, 0.40, and 4.0 for ArcFace, CosFace, and SphereFace. AdaCos adjusts its scale parameter automatically. SphereFace obtained equivalent performance with AdaCos and results are not included due to space constraints. The ResNet-50 network is trained using Adam optimizer with a batch size of 128 for 15 iterations, and lightCNN-29 using stochastic gradient decent optimizer with a batch size of 64 and the same number of iterations as ResNet-50. The learning rate was set to 0.001.

We used a gender-balanced subset of the training set of these models. Following IEEE WCCI competition protocol, left and right eye images are treated as different identities. To this aim, 288 subjects consisting of left and right eye individually (with 50% male and 50% female distribution) are randomly chosen. The training set consists of 64K ocular images from all the lighting conditions and the two visits. In particular, the number of samples from visit 1 is around 32K and 40K from visit 2 where each subject has 500 images. The models are trained and validated on a split of 80/20 using samples from both the visits and across all the lighting conditions for left and right eyes[5] are used for training the models.

The trained models are evaluated using a subject-independent testing set of VISOB 2.0. For the purpose of this study, we used a gender-balanced version of the test set as well. This results in a total of 21K ocular images for each gender for Oppo device, and 15K images for Note-4 from 86 subjects for all the three lighting conditions. The deep features of size $512 - D$ are extracted from the fully connected layers of these trained models for the evaluation. The deep features from the samples in visit 1 and visit 2 are chosen as the template and query pairs, respectively. The scores are computed in a pairwise fashion over a stack of images and are averaged per template-query pair. Cosine similarity is used to compute scores between deep features from a pair of template-query pair.

4.2   Experimental Results

In this section, we compare the verification performance of the ResNet-50 and lightCNN-29 models trained using multiple loss functions on the gender-balanced subset. Both models are evaluated in the same lighting conditions for both left and right eye regions. Table 1 and 2 compare the Equal Error Rate (EER) and Genuine Match Rate (GMR) across males and females at 1^{-4}, 1^{-3}, and 1^{-2} FMRs.

Tables 1 and 2 shows Equal Error Rates (EER) and Genuine Match Rates (GMR) at three different False Match Rates (FMR). In general, both models performed better for females than males. For instance, lightCNN-29 obtained an average EER of 9.94 for females and 11.16 for males, respectively. ResNet-50 obtained higher EER of 17.47 for females and 20.15 for males over ResNet-50. However, both the genders obtained similar Genuine Match Rate (GMR) averaged over both the models. For instance, lightCNN-29 obtained 36.94 and

---

[5] The term "eye" and "ocular region" are used interchangeably.

Table 1. EER(%), GMR@1^{-4}FMR, GMR@1^{-3}FMR, and GMR@1^{-2}FMR for lightCNN-29 model (trained on gender balanced subset of VISOB 2.0) for five loss functions and evaluated in different light conditions for males (M) and females (F) for mobile user authentication. Gender-balanced training and testing subset of VISOB 2.0 are used.

Loss function	Light condition	Eye	EER(%)		GMR(/%)@1−4FMR		GMR(%)@1−3FMR		GMR(%)@1−2FMR	
			lightCNN-29 - Note-4							
			M	F	M	F	M	F	M	F
AdaCos	Office	L	7.73	3.43	29.04	50.33	46.25	58.89	72.06	87.02
		R	4.26	4.15	67.25	56.76	76.56	69.48	87.53	87.15
	Daylight	L	4.93	3.19	55.96	65.42	71.90	78.39	84.29	92.42
		R	4.66	2.84	76.40	64.79	81.69	80.12	90.37	93.84
	Dark	L	6.39	2.20	38.99	53.36	56.43	65.61	78.93	93.15
		R	5.54	2.61	72.22	79.85	77.82	86.75	85.79	95.38
ArcFace	Office	L	17.21	14.25	11.84	12.85	25.65	28.52	49.17	44.60
		R	13.12	11.04	39.15	11.71	48.30	29.85	64.64	54.08
	Daylight	L	9.01	5.34	39.38	31.49	59.12	39.00	78.93	82.15
		R	4.53	6.16	64.48	55.82	71.27	68.27	90.21	79.52
	Dark	L	11.10	7.87	17.25	21.84	38.26	40.77	63.39	76.76
		R	6.37	9.63	53.03	39.94	60.28	65.16	77.98	77.05
CosFace	Office	L	10.37	11.53	49.17	34.02	61.38	46.30	74.95	68.42
		R	9.36	7.93	60.18	54.58	70.92	73.75	82.39	82.53
	Daylight	L	11.38	8.81	51.65	34.30	58.26	40.49	72.75	74.79
		R	6.16	8.22	60.37	58.73	71.10	65.82	86.97	85.46
	Dark	L	22.93	19.96	8.35	17.53	14.40	25.40	30.09	42.92
		R	17.71	16.45	25.96	10.01	33.49	25.21	51.93	48.91
Softmax	Office	L	11.93	9.56	31.56	13.03	44.13	34.68	64.31	68.98
		R	11.38	10.57	45.87	39.66	60.64	57.88	74.50	76.96
	Daylight	L	5.95	9.27	47.19	30.96	62.45	44.35	78.35	75.54
		R	6.49	3.92	64.61	64.26	71.54	71.00	90.37	87.38
	Dark	L	3.14	5.02	72.29	45.10	81.71	60.51	91.77	82.27
		R	4.44	2.60	73.16	78.29	81.28	84.56	90.58	93.42
	Dark	L	8.69	8.01	34.96	33.36	43.51	54.97	77.06	77.56
		R	3.35	6.90	73.16	61.76	79.11	70.53	90.37	81.66
			lightCNN-29 - Oppo							
AdaCos	Office	L	9.68	10.46	28.31	27.10	36.20	47.07	63.16	71.48
		R	14.32	11.08	17.99	28.10	27.04	43.57	51.96	70.02
	Daylight	L	12.42	10.71	23.82	21.04	41.44	42.17	60.02	69.51
		R	15.51	11.87	21.20	35.32	30.35	43.68	46.90	63.21
	Dark	L	16.10	10.98	28.58	20.04	38.90	39.62	52.30	70.83
		R	13.39	12.22	25.80	22.41	35.37	36.65	60.39	60.71
ArcFace	Office	L	21.24	18.72	12.53	12.12	18.91	26.17	30.09	43.13
		R	20.42	19.70	9.36	10.22	17.68	22.25	32.01	44.22
	Daylight	L	16.42	14.05	19.83	18.14	29.12	31.44	49.43	54.34
		R	16.71	13.57	11.74	17.09	19.23	28.63	32.57	49.23
	Dark	L	11.93	7.97	21.36	32.26	37.21	56.92	59.98	78.64
		R	12.03	8.48	39.81	33.17	49.35	57.27	65.31	79.59
CosFace	Office	L	13.29	9.39	22.23	55.53	39.81	66.19	61.53	79.11
		R	12.25	7.67	49.53	40.47	62.43	50.93	71.69	74.08
	Daylight	L	14.12	10.55	30.37	45.86	41.93	58.66	60.99	77.61
		R	11.64	10.99	53.57	44.15	60.95	55.69	71.76	70.83
	Dark	L	20.21	15.50	15.09	8.28	19.09	26.20	34.40	53.23
		R	15.22	13.08	19.20	22.24	26.59	32.46	47.98	54.82
Softmax	Office	L	18.14	15.58	27.70	47.25	39.63	58.34	52.27	71.30
		R	12.90	9.31	41.43	43.56	50.86	53.47	64.48	70.31
	Daylight	L	9.93	8.56	34.41	29.67	47.85	41.97	73.88	70.33
		R	10.48	7.24	32.50	42.84	46.94	52.25	61.07	74.98
	Dark	L	6.38	8.84	20.69	44.46	42.74	60.23	77.51	74.45
		R	8.13	9.17	40.44	39.50	53.73	57.20	77.10	76.55

Table 2. EER(%), GMR@1^{-4}FMR, GMR@1^{-3}FMR, and GMR@1^{-2}FMR for ResNet-50 model using five loss functions and evaluated in different light conditions across males (M) and females (F) for mobile user authentication. Gender-balanced training and testing subset of VISOB 2.0 are used.

Loss function	Light condition	Eye	EER(%)		GMR(/%)@1−4FMR		GMR(%)@1−3FMR		GMR(%)@1−2FMR	
			M	F	M	F	M	F	M	F
			ResNet-50 - Note-4							
AdaCos	Office	L	19.65	12.38	0.00	4.48	4.74	12.38	27.86	41.63
		R	10.45	8.45	9.87	1.00	28.57	15.66	58.41	59.84
	Daylight	L	24.80	16.24	0.28	16.49	3.67	24.27	19.08	48.55
		R	19.36	13.69	5.41	0.00	18.35	2.27	41.93	31.35
	Dark	L	17.54	13.61	4.65	5.24	7.36	14.88	19.05	40.39
		R	18.29	14.65	5.19	8.54	17.97	17.87	51.62	46.87
ArcFace	Office	L	25.36	18.71	1.10	2.24	5.21	7.18	22.65	25.76
		R	19.02	11.24	12.23	3.15	18.94	26.97	38.12	61.18
	Daylight	L	21.83	15.87	1.10	6.00	6.33	13.50	34.59	45.36
		R	18.94	16.52	0.18	6.70	7.16	27.10	30.83	50.90
	Dark	L	21.64	17.35	5.41	4.64	10.17	11.52	29.55	30.59
		R	15.27	11.99	4.55	5.02	20.89	19.20	46.43	48.12
CosFace	Office	L	19.42	11.73	2.68	8.83	5.84	15.68	19.10	49.47
		R	12.31	12.38	0.95	20.62	14.44	31.79	55.56	56.43
	Daylight	L	24.60	17.06	3.76	10.31	9.27	18.93	26.61	44.89
		R	21.96	19.64	1.19	3.78	2.75	9.92	26.97	38.05
	Dark	L	15.58	19.45	0.65	0.90	4.44	3.89	27.38	19.00
		R	15.19	16.22	10.82	6.97	18.40	21.00	48.70	41.85
Softmax	Office	L	20.44	7.97	8.13	13.11	20.36	32.54	43.96	62.12
		R	10.90	9.24	15.63	7.70	31.49	20.88	59.19	60.84
	Daylight	L	15.59	18.27	11.28	21.37	18.90	29.80	45.50	47.80
		R	12.66	13.31	33.21	26.63	38.81	38.81	55.87	65.72
	Dark	L	16.12	10.11	19.16	4.94	28.68	19.37	44.70	52.88
		R	8.66	10.97	20.02	20.92	33.87	32.84	65.48	58.86
			ResNet-50 - Oppo							
AdaCos	Office	L	22.00	20.65	1.46	8.31	11.78	18.39	32.52	36.09
		R	27.25	19.59	6.10	3.00	10.91	14.86	23.32	38.69
	Daylight	L	28.76	22.31	0.68	3.25	1.66	12.05	19.31	28.97
		R	23.05	25.29	1.62	2.73	10.59	12.45	30.08	35.16
	Dark	L	18.43	17.48	4.11	3.87	14.19	9.82	43.14	42.42
		R	17.70	17.14	0.56	3.42	13.73	5.11	32.62	32.18
ArcFace	Office	L	24.21	23.91	7.29	4.20	19.61	15.42	36.36	33.72
		R	25.24	20.93	13.19	3.11	18.56	12.66	30.92	36.41
	Daylight	L	27.61	28.74	1.19	1.39	7.89	8.20	21.90	26.28
		R	23.27	24.49	3.46	4.40	10.66	16.45	32.13	34.68
	Dark	L	22.50	18.66	6.10	3.83	13.32	11.49	27.31	31.50
		R	21.39	16.46	7.86	2.41	14.09	9.01	29.64	37.05
CosFace	Office	L	22.99	24.08	0.81	0.02	1.24	0.70	29.07	16.79
		R	24.21	22.34	7.91	0.72	12.51	2.42	26.99	34.56
	Daylight	L	31.41	23.50	2.09	2.54	9.55	9.75	24.03	28.38
		R	25.50	26.40	2.92	1.55	15.13	4.44	31.81	32.58
	Dark	L	19.62	20.92	5.98	3.71	15.43	23.96	36.04	43.56
		R	22.40	20.55	0.36	2.37	7.38	14.92	27.82	35.96
Softmax	Office	L	21.40	17.24	8.81	9.01	17.61	18.81	38.74	41.59
		R	23.69	17.95	6.98	9.20	10.96	20.09	25.59	44.10
	Daylight	L	20.10	16.01	8.29	13.48	21.65	26.91	40.85	48.55
		R	20.82	16.80	7.78	8.13	18.88	18.31	42.76	42.73
	Dark	L	11.56	12.80	13.04	14.87	26.36	27.55	49.72	50.00
		R	17.30	10.92	10.71	18.10	22.10	33.39	43.49	53.70

37.69 for females and males at GMR@1^{-4}FMR, respectively. At the same FMR, ResNet-50 obtained GMR of 6.43 and about 5.44 for females and males, respectively. However, females tends to outperform males remarkably at GMR@1^{-2}FMR. This can be noticed for lightCNN-29, which obtained an average of 71.00 GMR on females compared to 66.87 on males. Similarly, a difference of about 7% was obtained for ResNet-50 across females and males.

Across lighting conditions, females obtained equivalent EERs across dark and office lighting conditions. For lightCNN model, females obtained an average EER of 9.94 for dark and 9.43 for office light, respectively. For ResNet-50, EER of 16.04 and 16.54 for dark and office light, respectively. On the other hand, males performed the best in dark conditions for both models compared to other lighting conditions. This can be observed as the EERs increased by about 4.5% for daylight and 3% for office light compared to dark lighting condition.

The performance across gender for different loss functions varied depending on the lighting conditions and the CNN model. AdaCos loss function results in lower EER for females than males for both the models and across all the lighting conditions. For instance, in dark condition, an overall increase in EER of 0.964 for lightCNN-29 and 2.27 for ResNet-50 was observed. ArcFace also performed better for females than males except in the case of lightCNN-29 in dark conditions where the EER of females increased by 0.88. For other lighting conditions, males obtained an average increase of 2.67 in EER over females. At GMR@1^{-2}FMR, females obtained higher performance across many loss functions and lighting conditions, yet the performance for females dropped uniquely across all loss functions in the dark conditions for lightCNN-29, except for Ada-Cos. The average drop at GMR@1^{-2}FMR was about 2.79% for ArcFace, Cos-Face, SphereFace, and Softmax where AdaCos declined for males by only 1.14%. In daylight and office light conditions, a constant increase in GMR@1^{-2}FMR for females was noticed.

Generally, the average AUC of both genders were equivalent for lightCNN-29 (**0.96** for females and **0.95** for males). In the case of ResNet-50, the average AUC for females was **0.90**, whereas males obtained an AUC of **0.87**.

5   Fairness of Mobile Ocular-Based Gender Classification Methods

In this section, we evaluate the fairness of the gender classification models based on the ocular region. Following the studies in [3,18,19], we fine-tuned ResNet-50, MobileNet-v2 and their ensemble for gender classification. Next, we discuss the implementation details and the obtained results.

5.1   Network Training and Implementation Details

ResNet-50 and MobileNet-V2 CNN models are fine-tuned on training subset of VISOB 2.0 dataset. We also evaluated ensemble of ResNet-50 and MobileNet-V2 models.

Table 3. Almost gender-balanced subset of VISOB 2.0 dataset subset used for training gender classification models.

Lighting condition	Left eye		Right eye	
	M	F	M	F
Dark	35,917	31,023	35,917	31,023
Daylight	36,095	30,742	36,095	30,742
Office	44,669	38,424	44,669	38,424

Table 4. Gender-balanced subject independent testing subset of VISOB 2.0 dataset used for gender classification model evaluation.

Lighting condition	NOTE4				Oppo			
	Left eye		Right eye		Left eye		Right eye	
	M	F	M	F	M	F	M	F
Dark	1019	1020	1020	1020	1525	1525	1525	1525
Daylight	1300	1300	1300	1300	1590	1590	1590	1590
Office	1485	1485	1485	1485	2515	2515	2515	2515

For fine-tuning ResNet-50 and MobileNet-V2, fully connected layers of 512 and 512 were added after the last convolutional layer, followed by the final output layer. Ensemble of ResNet-50 and MobileNet-V2 was obtained by concatenating their first fully connected layers (of size 1024), followed by the final output layer. The above models were trained using an Adamax optimizer[6] on a batch size of 128 for 100 epochs using an early stopping mechanism on the validation set (80-20 split of training and validation). The learning rate was set equal to $1e-4$ and decay of $5e-4$. In order to mitigate the impact of imbalanced training and evaluation set on the fairness of the models. We used an almost gender balanced subset of the VISOB 2.0 training set (shown in Table 3) for these models training. Samples across both the visits (1 and 2) and all three lighting conditions are used all together to train the models for left and right eye, individually. Validation accuracy of about 90% was obtained for most of the cases. The trained models are evaluated on a subject independent gender-balanced testing subset of the VISOB 2.0 dataset shown in Table 4. Results are reported in terms of accuracy values across gender and lighting conditions for the left and right eye, individually. Further, false positive rate (FPR), indicating females misclassified as males, and false negative rate (FNR), indicating males misclassified as females, are also reported for further insight.

5.2   Experimental Results

In this section, we report the gender classification accuracy of the ocular-based models across males and females.

---

[6] https://pytorch.org/docs/stable/optim.html.

Tables 5, 6, 7, 8 shows the accuracy of the fine-tuned ResNet-50, MobileNet-V2, and their ensemble across gender and lighting conditions for left and right ocular images acquired using Note-4 and Oppo, individually. FPR and FNR are also reported in these tables.

Table 5. Gender classification accuracy rates of ResNet-50, MobileNet-V2 and their ensemble across males (M) and females (F) in different lighting conditions, when trained and test on left eye images acquired using Note-4.

	ResNet-50			MobileNet-V2			Ensemble		
	M	F	Overall Acc.	M	F	Overall Acc.	M	F	Overall Acc.
Dark	98	59	78.71	83	79	80.88	93	74.5	83.93
Daylight	90.2	69	80.76	91.7	63	78.56	89.6	71.7	81.12
Office	94	64.6	79.69	93.5	76.6	85.43	94.2	78.9	87.01
	FPR	FNR		FPR	FNR		FPR	FNR	
Dark	29.4	3.2		20.3	17.8		21.4	8	
Daylight	25.6	12.4		28.9	11.7		24	12.6	
Office	27.3	8.5		20	7.8		18.2	6.8	

Table 6. Gender classification accuracy rates of ResNet-50, MobileNet-V2 and their ensemble across males (M) and females (F) in different lighting conditions, when trained and tested on left eye images acquired using Oppo.

	ResNet-50			MobileNet-V2			Ensemble		
	M	F	Overall Acc.	M	F	Overall Acc.	M	F	Overall Acc.
Dark	96.26	66.67	81.6	95.74	63.34	79.64	96.6	70	83.4
Daylight	91.76	60.75	77.31	93.2	58.05	76.71	92.07	62.45	77.41
Office	95.6	61.07	78.61	97.25	56.18	77.11	97.23	62.94	80.47
	FPR	FNR		FPR	FNR		FPR	FNR	
Dark	25.7	5.3		27.69	6.3		23.72	4.64	
Daylight	29.96	11.9		31.0 3	0.104		28.96	11.26	
Office	28.94	6.7		31.05	4.65		27.58	4.11	

For Note-4, the average gender classification accuracy across lighting conditions is 79.72%, 81.62%, and 84.02% for ResNet-50, MobileNet-V2 and their ensemble, respectively, when trained and tested on the left ocular region (as can be seen from Table 5). Similarly, for the right ocular region, Resnet-50 has the highest average accuracy of 83.98%, followed by ensemble with an accuracy of 82.46% and MobileNet-v2 with an average accuracy of 81.02% (as can be seen from Table 7).

Across gender for left ocular region acquired using Note4; males obtained the highest average accuracy of 94.07% and the lowest of 89.4% for ResNet-50 and

Table 7. Gender classification accuracy rates of ResNet-50, MobileNet-V2 and their ensemble across males (M) and females (F) in different lighting conditions, when trained and tested on right eye images acquired using Note-4.

	ResNet-50			MobileNet-V2			Ensemble		
	M	F	Overall Acc.	M	F	Overall Acc.	M	F	Overall Acc.
Dark	91.3	70.3	80.83	80.5	81.6	81.02	89.7	76.2	82.94
Daylight	95	57	77.59	92	74	84.03	95.5	61.7	79.32
Office	98.4	70.2	84.64	95.3	78.2	86.89	98.2	71	85.12
	FPR	FNR		FPR	FNR		FPR	FNR	
Dark	24.6	11		18.6	19.3		21	12	
Daylight	31.3	8.55		21.9	9.6		28.6	6.7	
Office	23.2	2.2		18.6	5.7		22.8	2.5	

MobileNet-V2, respectively. However, females obtained the highest of 75.03% and the lowest of 64.2% for Ensemble and ResNet-50, respectively, averaged over three different lighting conditions (Table 5). Similarly, for the right ocular region, males obtained the highest average accuracy of 94.9% and the lowest of 89.27% for ResNet-50 and Ensemble, respectively. However, females obtained the highest of 77.93% and the lowest of 65.83% for MobileNet-v2 and ResNet-50, respectively (see Table 7).

Table 8. Gender classification accuracy rates of ResNet-50, MobileNet-V2 and their ensemble across males (M) and females (F) in different lighting conditions, when trained and tested on right eye images acquired using Oppo.

	ResNet-50			MobileNet-V2			Ensemble		
	M	F	Overall Acc.	M	F	Overall Acc.	M	F	Overall Acc.
Dark	92.45	67.47	80.04	81.97	90.82	86.33	90.36	77.9	84.19
Daylight	91.26	66.3	79.22	85.03	81.44	83.7	89.94	72.96	81.49
Office	95.86	67.91	82.21	92.36	76.38	84.63	95.6	71	83.59
	FPR	FNR		FPR	FNR		FPR	FNR	
Dark	26.02	10.05		10.07	16.57		19.65	11.01	
Daylight	26.97	11.65		17.91	15.52		23.11	12.12	
Office	25.07	5.74		20.34	9.086		23.3	5.85	

Average difference in the accuracy between males and females is 21.21% for left ocular images acquired using Note-4. The average difference in the accuracy between males and females is 21.75% for right ocular images acquired using Note-4.

For Oppo, the average gender classification across different lighting conditions is 79.17%, 77.8%, and 80.42% for ResNet-50, MobileNet-V2 and their ensemble, respectively, when trained and tested on left ocular region (as can be seen from

Table 6). Similarly for right ocular region, ResNet-50, MobileNet-v2 and their ensemble obtained 80.49%, 84.89% and 83.09%, respectively (see Table 8).

Across gender for left ocular region acquired using Oppo; males obtained the highest average accuracy of 95.4% and the lowest of 94.54% for MobileNet-V2 and ResNet-50, respectively. However, females obtained the highest of 65.13% and the lowest of 59.19% for Ensemble and MobileNet-V2, respectively, averaged over three different lighting conditions (refer Table 6). Similarly, for the right ocular region, males obtained the highest average accuracy of 93.19% and the lowest of 86.45% for ResNet-50 and MobileNet-v2, respectively. However, females obtained the highest of 86.38% and the lowest of 67.23% for MobileNet-v2 and ResNet-50, respectively (see Table 8). Better classification accuracy for Oppo device is due to the higher resolution images of better quality compared to Note-4. Also, in general, higher accuracy rates are obtained for samples acquired in controlled lighting conditions, i.e., office light.

Average difference in the accuracy between males and females is 32.7% for left ocular images acquired using Oppo. The average difference in the accuracy between males and females is 14.68% for right ocular images for Oppo. Lowest FPR (15.49%) and FNR (13.78%) are obtained for left ocular images under dark lighting conditions acquired using Oppo. The lowest FPR (18.2%) and FNR (6.8%) are obtained for left ocular images under office lighting conditions for Note-4. Our results are in contrary to those obtained in [3] where females outperformed males in gender classification based on ocular region. However, in this study [3] ocular regions are cropped from Labeled Faces in the Wild dataset.

Further, based on manual inspection, we observed that *covariates such as eye-gazing, eyeglasses, obstructions, the presence of hair, and low lighting to be the major factors contributing to the error rate of the gender classifier especially*

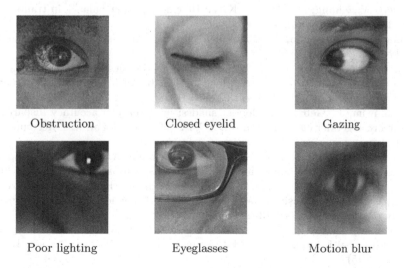

| Obstruction | Closed eyelid | Gazing |
| Poor lighting | Eyeglasses | Motion blur |

Fig. 2. Example of covariates in ocular images of females, commonly available in mobile environment, and attributing to the error rate of the gender classifiers.

for females. Figure 2 shows some of the female sample eye images misclassified by the gender classification models.

6   Conclusion

This paper evaluates the fairness of the mobile user authentication and gender classification algorithms based on ocular region across males and females. In contrary to the existing studies on face recognition, we obtained equivalent authentication performance for males and females based on the ocular region at lower FMR points (1^{-4}) and an overall Area Under Curve (AUC). The reason could be the robustness of the subject-specific templates of ocular region to facial expression change, make-up, and facial morphological differences over face biometrics. However, males outperformed females by a significant difference of 22.58% in gender classification. This error rate was mainly due to the presence of covariates such as hair, eyeglasses, motion blur, and eye gazing. As a part of future work, experiments will be extended on other ocular biometric datasets captured in the near-infrared and visible spectrum across gender, race and age. The impact of the covariates and multi-frame fusion in unequal accuracy rates of the ocular-based gender classifiers will be quantified.

Acknowledgment. Rattani is the co-organizer of the IEEE ICIP 2016 VISOB 1.0 and IEEE WCCI 2020 VISOB 2.0 mobile ocular biometric competitions. Authors would like to thank Narsi Reddy and Mark Nguyen for their assistance in dataset processing.

References

1. Albiero, V., Zhang, K., Bowyer, K.W.: How does gender balance in training data affect face recognition accuracy? (2020)
2. Almadan, A., Krishnan, A., Rattani, A.: Bwcface: open-set face recognition using body-worn camera (2020)
3. Alonso-Fernandez, F., Diaz, K.H., Ramis, S., Perales, F.J., Bigun, J.: Soft-biometrics estimation in the era of facial masks. In: 2020 International Conference of the Biometrics Special Interest Group (BIOSIG), pp. 1–6 (2020)
4. Buolamwini, J., Gebru, T.: Gender shades: intersectional accuracy disparities in commercial gender classification. In: ACM Conference on Fairness, Accountability, and Transparency, pp. 77–91 (2018)
5. Cavazos, J.G., Phillips, P.J., Castillo, C.D., O'Toole, A.J.: Accuracy comparison across face recognition algorithms: where are we on measuring race bias? (2019)
6. Damer, N., Grebe, J.H., Chen, C., Boutros, F., Kirchbuchner, F., Kuijper, A.: The effect of wearing a mask on face recognition performance: an exploratory study. arXiv preprint arXiv:2007.13521 (2020)
7. De Marsico, M., Nappi, M., Riccio, D., Wechsler, H.: Mobile iris challenge evaluation (miche)-i, biometric iris dataset and protocols. Pattern Recogn. Lett **57**, 17–23 (2015)
8. He, K., Zhang, X., Ren, S., Sun, J.: Deep residual learning for image recognition (2015)

9. Howard, A.G., et al.: Mobilenets: efficient convolutional neural networks for mobile vision applications. arXiv preprint arXiv:1704.04861 (2017)
10. King, D.E.: Dlib-ml: a machine learning toolkit. J. Mach. Learn. Res. **10**, 1755–1758 (2009). http://dl.acm.org/citation.cfm?id=1577069.1755843
11. Krishnan, A., Almadan, A., Rattani, A.: Understanding fairness of gender classification algorithms across gender-race groups. In: 19th IEEE International Conference on Machine Learning and Applications, pp. 1–8. IEEE, Miami (2020)
12. Krishnapriya, K.S., Albiero, V., Vangara, K., King, M.C., Bowyer, K.W.: Issues related to face recognition accuracy varying based on race and skin tone. IEEE Trans. Technol. Soc. **1**(1), 8–20 (2020)
13. Lovisotto, G., Malik, R., Sluganovic, I., Roeschlin, M., Trueman, P., Martinovic, I.: Mobile Biometrics in Financial Services: A Five Factor Framework. University of Oxford, Oxford (2017)
14. Muthukumar, V.: Color-theoretic experiments to understand unequal gender classification accuracy from face image. In: Conference on Computer Vision and Pattern Recognition Workshops (CVPRW (2019)
15. Ngan, M.L., Grother, P.J., Hanaoka, K.K.: Ongoing face recognition vendor test (frvt) part 6a: face recognition accuracy with masks using pre-covid-19 algorithms (2020)
16. Nguyen, H., Reddy, N., Rattani, A., Derakhshani, R.: VISOB 2.0 - second international competition on mobile ocular biometric recognition. In: IAPR International Conference on Pattern Recognition, Rome, Italy, pp. 1–8 (2020)
17. Raja, K., Ramachandra, R., Busch, C.: Collaborative representation of blur invariant deep sparse features for periocular recognition from smartphones. Image Vision Comput. **101**, 103979 (2020)
18. Rattani, A., Reddy, N., Derakhshani, R.: Convolutional neural networks for gender prediction from smartphone-based ocular images. IET Biometrics **7**(5), 423–430 (2018)
19. Rattani, A., Derakhshani, R., Ross, A. (eds.): Selfie Biometrics. ACVPR. Springer, Cham (2019). https://doi.org/10.1007/978-3-030-26972-2
20. Rattani, A., Derakhshani, R., Saripalle, S.K., Gottemukkula, V.: ICIP 2016 competition on mobile ocular biometric recognition. In: 2016 IEEE International Conference on Image Processing (ICIP), pp. 320–324. IEEE (2016)
21. Reddy, N., Rattani, A., Derakhshani, R.: Comparison of deep learning models for biometric-based mobile user authentication. In: 2018 IEEE 9th International Conference on Biometrics Theory, Applications and Systems (BTAS), pp. 1–6 (2018)
22. Sandler, M., Howard, A., Zhu, M., Zhmoginov, A., Chen, L.: Mobilenetv 2: inverted residuals and linear bottlenecks. In: IEEE Conference on Computer Vision and Pattern Recognition, pp. 4510–4520 (2018)
23. Singh, R., Agarwal, A., Singh, M., Nagpal, S., Vatsa, M.: On the robustness of face recognition algorithms against attacks and bias (2020)
24. Wu, X., He, R., Sun, Z., Tan, T.: A light CNN for deep face representation with noisy labels. IEEE Trans. Inf. Forensics Secur. **13**(11), 2884–2896 (2018)

Biometric Recognition of PPG Cardiac Signals Using Transformed Spectrogram Images

Ruggero Donida Labati[1]([✉])(iD), Vincenzo Piuri[1], Francesco Rundo[2],
Fabio Scotti[1], and Concetto Spampinato[3]

[1] Department of Computer Science, Università degli Studi di Milano,
20133 Milan, Italy
{ruggero.donida,vincenzo.piuri,fabio.scotti}@unimi.it
[2] STMicroelectronics, ADG, Central R&D, 95121 Catania, Italy
francesco.rundo@st.com
[3] Department of Electrical, Electronic and Computer Engineering,
Università degli Studi di Catania, 95125 Catania, Italy
concetto.spampinato@dieei.unict.it

Abstract. Nowadays, the number of mobile, wearable, and embedded devices integrating sensors for acquiring cardiac signals is constantly increasing. In particular, plethysmographic (PPG) sensors are widely diffused thanks to their small form factor and limited cost. For example, PPG sensors are used for monitoring cardiac activities in automotive applications and in wearable devices as smartwatches, activity trackers, and wristbands. Recent studies focused on using PPG signals to secure mobile devices by performing biometric recognitions. Although their results are promising, all of these methods process PPG acquisitions as one-dimensional signals. In the literature, feature extraction techniques based on transformations of the spectrogram have been successfully used to increase the accuracy of signal processing techniques designed for other application scenarios. This paper presents a preliminary study on a biometric recognition approach that extracts features from different transformations of the spectrogram of PPG signals and classifies the obtained feature representations using machine learning techniques. To the best of our knowledge, this is the first study in the literature on biometric systems that extracts features from the spectrogram of PPG signals. Furthermore, with respect to most of the state-of-the-art biometric recognition techniques, the proposed approach presents the advantage of not requiring the search of fiducial points, thus reducing the computational complexity and increasing the robustness of the signal preprocessing step. We performed tests using a dataset of samples collected from 42 individuals, obtaining an average classification accuracy of 99.16% for identity verification (FMR of 0.56% at FNMR of 13.50%), and a rank-1 identification error of 7.24% for identification. The results obtained for the considered dataset are better or comparable with respect to the ones of the best-performing methods in the literature.

Keywords: Biometrics · PPG · Spectrogram

© Springer Nature Switzerland AG 2021
A. Del Bimbo et al. (Eds.): ICPR 2020 Workshops, LNCS 12668, pp. 244–257, 2021.
https://doi.org/10.1007/978-3-030-68793-9_17

1   Introduction

The wide diffusion of mobile, wearable, and embedded systems introduced the need of novel mechanisms to protect the access to their data using user friendly recognition technologies. Therefore, biometrics are playing a primary role in this scenario thanks to their capability of recognizing people from physiological or behavioral characteristics. As an example, most of the current mobile devices and smartphones integrate biometric recognition sensors for face or fingerprint recognition. Anyway, the wide availability of heterogeneous sensors integrated in consumer technologies allowed the study of additional biometric recognition methods usable in conjunction or in different scenarios with respect to face and fingerprint recognition [7,27]. In this context, cardiac signals present important advantages with respect to other biometric traits [8]: i) they are more difficult to counterfeit with respect to biometric characteristics that can be acquired using cameras; ii) they can be acquired only from living individuals; iii) they present additional information that can be used for supplementary applications (e.g., health monitoring [30] or stress level estimation [6]); they can be collected continuously for long periods of time without requiring any activity from the users since they can be acquired using wearable sensors.

Most of the studies on biometric recognition systems based on cardiac signals focus on electrocardiographic (ECG) sensors. This is due to the fact that ECG signals are widely used for clinical applications and to the availability of different public datasets of ECGs [28]. However, PPG sensors are nowadays more diffused in mobile, wearable and embedded systems with respect to ECG sensors thanks to their smaller size and inferior cost. Therefore, recent studies in the literature analyzed and proved the discriminability of PPG signals as biometric traits. Furthermore, empirical evaluations proved that PPG has sufficient stability for short periods of time [13].

The state-of-the-art methods for biometric recognition based on PPG signals can use algorithmic approaches [2,10,31,32,35], machine learning techniques based on hand-crafted features [5,14,18,19,22–25,29,33,36,37], or deep neural networks (DNNs) [1,9,13,17,26]. To the best of our knowledge, all the methods in the literature process PPG signals using features directly extracted from one-dimensional representations of the signals. Furthermore, most of these methods need to extract fiducial points from the samples to compute distinctive features from PPG signals, thus performing an error-prone and computationally expensive task.

Motivated by the successful application of feature extraction techniques based on transformations of the spectrogram of other types of cardiac signals [3,4], in this paper, we propose a preliminary study on a biometric recognition approach able to extract features from transformed spectrograms of PPG signals. The main advantage of using the proposed representation of one-dimensional signals consists of obtaining pseudo-images analyzable by a human observer, who can easily understand similitudes between genuine comparisons and differences between impostor comparisons. Another advantage of the proposed feature representation consists of the simple preprocessing method, which is more com-

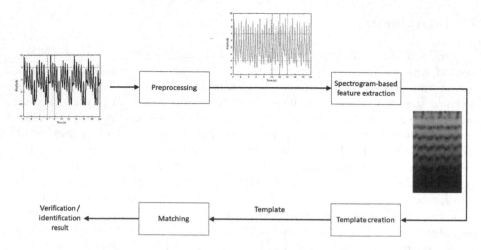

Fig. 1. Schema of the proposed approach for biometric recognition based on PPG signals. The approach uses a simpler preprocessing with respect to most of the state-of-the-art techniques, which need to detect fiducial points.

putationally efficient and less prone to errors with respect to the algorithms commonly used to detect fiducials points.

Our proposed approach first performs a simple signal preprocessing to normalize the PPG signal. Second, it computes a specific pseudo image from the signal. Third, it extracts a template using a dimensionality reduction strategy based on the Principal Component Analysis (PCA). Finally, our approach performs an identity verification or identification using dedicated matching strategies, which are based on k-Nearest Neighbors (k-NN) and ensembles of Support Vector Machines (SVM). Figure 1 shows the schema of the proposed approach.

We validated the proposed approach using the publicly available dataset CapnoBase PRRB [20,21], including signals collected from 42 individuals. We achieved an average classification accuracy of 99.16% (FMR of 0.56% at FNMR of 13.50%) for identity verification, and a rank-1 identification error of 7.24% for identification. The results obtained for this dataset are better or comparable with respect to the ones of the best performing methods in the literature.

The paper is organized as follows. Section 2 reviews the related works on PPG-based biometric recognition. Section 3 describes the proposed approach. Section 4 presents the performed experiments and the achieved results. Section 5 concludes the work and discusses future research directions.

2   Related Works

Most of the studies in the literature on biometric recognition techniques based on PPG signals consider data acquired for clinical purposes. With the increasing diffusion of mobile devices, the number of studies on PPG biometrics using signals captured from mobile devices is also increasing. For example, the method described in [25] considers the finger placed on top of the smartphone camera to capture PPG signals. Similarly, the method proposed in [37] exploits wrist-bands to perform continuous biometric authentications. In the context of mobile devices, the combination of PPG signals with different biometric traits has also been investigated. As an example, the approach described in [33] combines PPG with face biometrics to ensure a more accurate liveness detection for smart-phones.

It is possible to divide the methods for PPG-based biometric recognition into three categories [13]: i) methods based on algoritmic approaches [2,10,31,32,35]; ii) methods based on handcrafted features and machine learning classifiers [5, 14,18,19,22,25,29,33,36,37]; iii) methods based on DNNs [1,9,13,17,24,26].

Methods based on algoritmic approaches usually perform a preprocessing step to enhance the PPG signal, compute a template by extracting a set of features corresponding to the distinctive characteristics of the signal, and use a correlation-based matcher to compare the templates [2]. There are also algorithmic approaches applicable to PPGs in conjunction to other cardiac signals [10]. To investigate the stability of PPG signals for biometric recognition applications, the approaches presented in [31,32] use a correlation-based methodology to compare the performance of several feature extractors and matchers for PPG signals acquired after several days. Other methods in the literature consider correlation-based algorithms as a feature extractors, such as the method presented in [35], which uses auto-correlation and derivatives to extract a feature vector, then apply a distance-based classifier to compare templates.

Methods based on handcrafted features and machine learning usually process the PPG signal to extract a set of discriminant features, then apply a classifier based on machine learning to perform the biometric recognition. In the literature, there are several methods which differ one to each other according to the extracted features and to the used classifier. For example, the method described in [14] considers acceleration-based features computed using the derivative of the PPG signal, then applies a Bayes Network and a k-NN classifier. Similarly, the method proposed in [5] extracts features related to the derivative and frequency of the PPG signal, then applies a Linear Discriminant Analysis for classification. To investigate which features and classifiers could improve the recognition accuracy using PPG signals, the method described in [29] performs statistical analyses to extract a redundant set of features, then applies a forward feature selection algorithm. The classification is performed by comparing several methods such as k-NN, Fuzzy k-NN, and Gaussian Mixture Model. Similarly, a comparison with k-NN and other classifiers such as decision trees and SVM is also presented in [22].

Methods based on DNNs can take advantage of the capability of Convolutional Neural Networks (CNN) to automatically learn data representations. As an example, the method described in [26] proposes an end-to-end architecture for biometric recognition based on PPG signals, which uses a CNN to directly extract a discriminant representation from the raw signals and to perform the classification. Similarly, a combination of CNNs with DNNs based on Long Short-Term Memory (LSTM) is proposed in [1,9] to process and classify PPG signals

Table 1. State-of-the-art methods based on deep neural networks

Work	Method	Datasets	Performance
[13]	CNN + LSTM + individual classifiers	Biosec 1 (2 sessions for 15 individuals)	AVG ACC = 87.0%
		Biosec 2 (3 signals for 100 individuals)	AVG ACC = 87.1%
		PRRB (single session, 24 individuals)	1 ch.: AVG ACC = 99% 2 ch.: AVG ACC = 100%
[1,9]	CNN + LSTM	TROIKA (22 signals, 12 individuals, sport)	AVG ACC = 96%
[17]	DBN + RBM	TROIKA (22 signals, 12 individuals, sport)	ACC = 96.1%
[26]	CNN with end-to-end biomarker learning	PulseID (5 signals for 43 individuals)	AUC = 78.2%
		TROIKA (22 signals, 12 individuals, sport)	AUC = 83,2%
[24]	GAN for cross-domain adaption	in-house (multiple sessions, 10 individuals)	ACC = 95.68%
		TROIKA (22 signals, 12 individuals, sport)	ACC = 89.35%

Notes: AVG ACC = avarage accuracy, ACC = accuracy, AUC = area under the curve, ch. = channel.

captured from wrist sensors. The same CNN and LSTM combination is used in [13] to analyze the stability of PPG-based biometric information over time. Different DNNs models can also be succesfully used. As an example, the method presented in [17] is based on Deep Belief Networks (DBN) and Restricted Boltzman Machines (RBM). To address the accuracy reduction due to different acquisition sources, the method presented in [24] uses a Generative Adversarial Network (GAN).

Currently, methods based on DNNs and machine learning classifiers are achieving the best performance in terms of biometric recognition accuracy. To provide examples of the achieved accuracy, Table 1 summarizes the results achieved by recent methods based on DNNs.

While the majority of the methods in the literature use fiducial points to extract features, the approach described in [18, 19] propose non-fiducial features based on wavelet transforms, then applies FeedForward Neural Networks and SVM for classification. With a similar computational strategy, the method proposed in [36] investigates the accuracy of wavelet-based non-fiducial features in the case of PPG signals captured in different mental states.

3   Proposed Approach

Our proposed approach can be applied for identity verification as well as for identification. It takes in input a PPG signal s of fixed time duration of t seconds. Our method extracts features from different transformations of the spectrogram of PPG signals, performs biometric recognitions without needing to extract fiducial points, and computes the matching phase by using machine learning classiers. Figure 1 shows the schema of the method, which can be divided into the following steps:

1. signal preprocessing,
2. spectrogram-based feature extraction,
3. template creation,
4. matching.

3.1   Signal Preprocessing

The proposed approach uses a simple preprocessing technique, by only applying a bandpass filter to the signal s, as performed by most of the state-of-the-art algorithms for processing PPG signals. Specifically, it applies a second order high-pass Butterworth filter and a sixth order low-pass Butterworth filter, with cutoff frequencies f_h and f_l, respectively.

3.2   Spectrogram-Based Feature Extraction

In this subsection, we describe the proposed algorithm for extracting features from different transformations of the spectrogram of PPG signals. Our approach computes the spectrogram of the filtered signal x to obtain a specific single-channel image I showing distinctive characteristics of the individuals in the frequency and time domain.

A spectrogram is a visual representation of the spectrum of frequencies of a signal as it varies with time. The spectrogram can be defined as an intensity plot of the squared magnitude of the Short-Time Fourier Transform (STFT) magnitude [34]. The STFT is a sequence of FFTs of windowed data segments, where the windows are usually allowed to overlap in time. More formally, given a signal x of duration N, consecutive segments of x of length m (where $m \ll N$). Let $X \in \mathbb{R}^{m \times (N-m+1)}$. As an example, $[x(0), x(1), \ldots, x(m-1)]^T$ is the first column, while $[x(1), x(2), \ldots, x(m)]^T$ is the second column. The rows as well as the columns of X are indexed by time. Hence, the STFT of the input signal $\hat{X}$ is defined as:

$$\hat{X} = \bar{F}X, \tag{1}$$

$$X = (1/m)F\hat{X}, \tag{2}$$

where $\bar{F}$ is the complex conjugate of F, and F is the Fourier matrix. In our case, we use slinding windows of size m and overlap o_m.

The STFT of the input signal x is composed of complex numbers. Therefore, a common way to obtain a two dimensional image to be further processed consists of computing a gray-scale representation as the logarithm of the power spectral density. However, this representation of PPG signals is not producing the highest accuracy if directly applied for biometric recognition approaches. In the proposed approach, taking as example specific methods used to plot spectrograms using pseudo images in audio processing applications, we create three different channels from the spectrogram. In order to improve the final accuracy, we compute a pseudo image I_p composed of three channels (A, B, C) as follows.

For each row r of $\hat{X}$, we compute $A(i)$ as follows:

$$A(i) = f/f_{max}, \tag{3}$$

where f represents the cyclical frequencies, and f_{max} is the maximum value of f.

We compute the chanel B as follows:

$$B = L/L_{max}, \tag{4}$$

$$L = \log_{10}\left(1 + 10 \times (P'_s)\right), \tag{5}$$

$$P' = (P - P_{min})/(P_{max} - P_{min}), \tag{6}$$

where P is power spectral density or the power spectrum of each segment, P_{min} is the minimum value of P, P_{max} is the maximum value of P, and L_{max} is the maximum value of L.

We compute the channel C as follows:

$$C = [(P - P_{min})/(P_{max} - P_{min})]^{0.2}. \tag{7}$$

To further improve the final accuracy, a second transformation can be profitable. Therefore, we evaluated different channel transformations, obtaining the best results by computing a pseudo image I_s representing I_p after converting it from the HSV color space to the RGB color space. Figure 2 shows examples of images I_s obtained from samples acquired from two individuals. It is possible to observe that the patterns of the images obtained from samples of the same individual are similar one to each other, while images computed from samples of different individuals present local differences one to each other.

With the aims of improving the final recognition accuracy and of reducing the dimensionality of the final feature vectors, we explored the possibility of reducing the number of channels. We obtained the best results using the first channel of I_s. Therefore, in the following, we will refer to the first channel of I_s as the single channel image I, and we use this image as the input of the subsequent step of the proposed method.

| Individual A | Individual A | Individual B | Individual B |
| Sample 1 | Sample 2 | Sample 1 | Sample 2 |

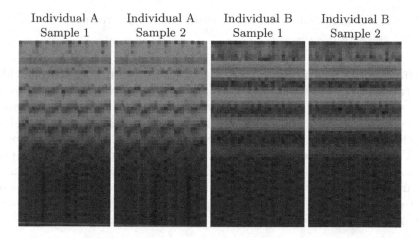

Fig. 2. Examples of images I_s obtained from samples acquired from two individuals. It is possible to observe that the patterns of the images obtained from samples of the same individual are similar one to each other, while images computed from samples of different individuals present local differences one to each other.

3.3   Template Creation

Our approach computes a vector V composed of n_f floating point numbers representing the biometric template. In particular, from the image I, the proposed method computes V as the vector of scores obtained from the first n_c coefficients of a PCA processed from the vector of intensity values of the image I. The PCA coefficients are computed using all the samples of a training set. The samples of every enrolled individual are therefore used to compute PCA coefficients to be used for every fresh sample. In this preliminary study, the PCA coefficients should therefore be updated for each new user enrollment.

3.4   Matching

Our approach use different strategies for identity verification and identification.

Identity Verification. The identity verification strategy aims at confirming or denying the identity declared by the user from the analysis of a template V. To this purpose, we use a binary classifier for each individual enrolled in the gallery. The output of every classifier is equal to 0 and 1 for impostor and genuine comparisons, respectively. Then, for each identity verification attempt, the user declares that her identity corresponds to the enrolled individual i and then only the classifier c_i is used to check if the template V corresponds to the declared identity. We use SVMs since they can provide relatively robust classification results when applied to imbalanced data sets [12]. The proposed approach can perform open set identity verifications since it does not assume that fresh samples correspond to any identity enrolled in the gallery database.

However, in this preliminary study, a classifier should be created and trained for each new user enrollment.

Identification. The identification strategy aims at searching the enrolled identity corresponding to the template V using only the knowledge-base of the biometric system. Therefore, having a set of n_i identities enrolled in the gallery, we consider the identification task as a classification problem with n_i classes. From the wide set of machine learning classifiers in the literature, we chose to adopt kNN and ensembles of SVMs due to their capability of dealing with problems characterized by high numbers of classes. In particular, we use ensembles of binary SVM classifiers with a voting strategy based on the error-correcting output codes model [11]. In this preliminary study, the SVM classifiers should be created and trained for each new user enrollment.

4   Experimental Results

We experimentally evaluated the performance of the proposed approach for identity verification as well for identification scenarios, comparing the obtained results with that of recent state-of-the-art biometric recognition techniques.

We evaluated the performance of the proposed approach using a publicly available dataset, CapnoBase PRRB [20,21]. This dataset has been collected in a single session and is composed of PPG signals acquired from 42 subjects (29 children and 13 adults). The acquisitions have been performed by physicians in monitored conditions. The sampling rate is equal to 300 Hz and the duration of every acquisition is 8 minutes. We considered only the first PPG channel.

Our approach uses fixed length signals of t seconds as input. We estimated that $t = 20$ is a good tradeoff between the system usability and the amount of information usable to compute discriminative features. Therefore, we divided the CapnoBase PRRB dataset into non-overlapping samples of 20 s, obtaining 24 signals per individual, for a total of 1008 samples.

We used different figures of merit to evaluate the accuracy of the proposed method for identity verification and identification. Specifically, for the identity verification scenario we used figures of merit typically adopted to evaluated the performance of biometric recognition systems, as False Match Rate (FMR), and False Non Match Rate (FNMR) [15]. Width the aim of simplifying the comparison of the achieved performance with that of recent methods in the literate based on DNNs [1,9,13,17,24], we also computed the average classification accuracy. For the identification scenario, we used the rank-1 error [16].

For identity verification, as well as for identification, we validated the performance of the proposed approach using a k-fold cross-validation technique performing the selection of the test set by considering samples contiguous in time. Having a dataset composed of n_i samples per individual, for each iteration i, we create a testing set composed of n_i/k samples contiguous in time by starting from the $(i - 1) \times (n_i/k) + 1$ th sample. For each fold i, we computed the

PCA coefficients and trained the proposed matchers by using the i th training set. We considered $k = 2$ and $k = 8$.

We implemented all the methods using Matlab 2020b. The operating system was Windows 10 professional 64 bit.

We set the parameters of the Butterworth pass-band filter used for the signal preprocessing as $f_h = 50$ Hz and $f_l = 90$ Hz. This configuration is used by many state-of-the-art methods for processing PPG signals.

We analyzed the performance of the proposed approach by varying the parameters m and o_m used to compute the spectrograms. The values considered for m are 150, 300, 450, 600, 750, and 900. The values considered for o_m are 50, 100, 150, 200, 250, 300, 350, 400, 450, and 500. We achieved the best results using $m = 600$ and $o_m = 400$. Similarly, we evaluated the performance of the proposed approach by varying the number of PCA coefficients used to compute the templates, achieving the best results with $n_c = 10$.

4.1   Identity Verification Accuracy

We computed the accuracy of the proposed identity verification strategy for the CapnoBase PRRB dataset by performing a 2-fold cross-validation and a 8-fold cross-validation. Table 2 resumes the achieved results.

Table 2 shows that the obtained FMR is particularly low, thus showing a great robustness of the biometric recognition method to impostor attacks. The achieved FNMR, however could imply multiple authentication attempts from the users, but can be considered as satisfactory for a wide set of applications. Furthermore, the results show that the performance achieved using the 2-fold cross-validation and 8-fold cross-validation are comparable, thus proving the capability of the proposed identity verification approach of learning from a limited number of training samples.

As a reference, we computed the performance of the correlation-based method presented in [2] for the same dataset and by using the same time partitioning strategy. The method presented in [2] obtaining an Equal Error Rate [15] of 14.7% and FMR at FNMR = 1% equal to 93.62%. Our proposed method clearly outperforms the compared algorithm.

As a further comparison, the method based on deep learning presented in [13] reports an average classification accuracy of 99% for the CapnoBase PRRB dataset. It should be considered that the method proposed in [13] used a different time division of the signals and a different validation protocol with respect to the ones adopted in this work. Anyway, the obtained results prove that the proposed approach can achieve better or comparable accuracy with respect to the best performing state-of-the-art methods for the considered dataset.

4.2   Identification Accuracy

We computed the accuracy of the proposed identity verification strategy for the CapnoBase PRRB dataset by performing a 2-fold cross-validation and a 8-fold cross-validation. Table 3 resumes the achieved results.

Table 2. Identity verification accuracy

Validation strategy	Average accuracy (%)	FMR (%)	FNMR (%)
2-fold cross-validation	99.03	0,73	12.87
8-fold cross-validation	99.16	0.56	13.50

Table 3. Identification accuracy

Validation strategy	Classifier	Rank-1 (%)
2-fold cross-validation	k-NN (1-NN)	11.11
2-fold cross-validation	SVM	10.32
8-fold cross-validation	k-NN (1-NN)	8.93
8-fold cross-validation	SVM	7.24

Table 3 shows that the identification accuracy of the proposed approach can be sufficient for heterogenous applications, with the best rank-1 error equal to 7.24%. Furthermore, the ensembles of SVMs achieved better performance with respect to k-NN classifiers. However, the performance achieved for the 8-fold cross-validation test are better than the ones achieved for the 2-fold cross-validation test, proving the need for a greater number of samples for training the proposed identification method to further improve its accuracy.

5   Conclusions

This paper presented a preliminary study on extracting features from different transformations of the spectrogram of PPG signals for biometric recognition. The proposed biometric recognition method classifies the obtained feature representations using machine learning techniques. To the best of our knowledge, this is the first study in the literature proposing the use of two-dimensional representations for biometric recognition systems based on PPG signals. Furthermore, with respect to most of the state-of-the-art techniques, the proposed approach presents the advantage of not needing to extract fiducial points. We validated our method for a dataset of 42 individuals acquired for 8 minutes, and tested it in k-fold cross-validation. Our approach achieved average classification accuracy of 99.16% for identity verification (FMR of 0.56% at FNMR of 13.50%), and rank-1 error of 7.24%. The results achieved for the considered dataset are better or comparable with respect to the ones of the best performing state-of-the-art techniques. Further studies should consist of designing more robust classification strategies and evaluating the performance in heterogeneous conditions. Since in this preliminary study we only considered a single session dataset acquired in controlled physical conditions, future work should also consider bigger datasets acquired in challenging and less-constrained conditions.

References

1. Biswas, D., et al.: CorNET: deep learning framework for PPG-based heart rate estimation and biometric identification in ambulant environment. IEEE Trans. Biomed. Circuits Syst. **13**(2), 282–291 (2019)
2. Bonissi, A., Donida Labati, R., Perico, L., Sassi, R., Scotti, F., Sparagino, L.: A preliminary study on continuous authentication methods for photoplethysmographic biometrics. In: Proceedings of the 2013 IEEE Workshop on Biometric Measurements and Systems for Security and Medical Applications (BioMS), pp. 28–33 (2013)
3. Byeon, Y., Pan, S., Kwak, K.: Ensemble deep learning models for ECG-based biometrics. In: Proceedings of the 2020 Cybernetics Informatics (K I), pp. 1–5 (2020)
4. Byeon, Y.H., Kwak, K.C.: Pre-configured deep convolutional neural networks with various time-frequency representations for biometrics from ECG signals (2019)
5. Chakraborty, S., Pal, S.: Photoplethysmogram signal based biometric recognition using linear discriminant classifier. In: Proceedings of the 2016 2nd International Conference on Control, Instrumentation, Energy Communication (CIEC) pp. 183–187 (2016)
6. Chauhan, U., Reithinger, N., Mackey, J.R.: Real-time stress assessment through PPG sensor for VR biofeedback. In: Proceedings of the 20th International Conference on Multimodal Interaction: Adjunct (2018)
7. Donida Labati, R., Genovese, A., Piuri, V., Scotti, F.: A scheme for fingerphoto recognition in smartphones. In: Rattani, A., Derakhshani, R., Ross, A. (eds.) Selfie Biometrics. ACVPR, pp. 49–66, Springer, Cham (2019). https://doi.org/10.1007/978-3-030-26972-2_3
8. Donida Labati, R., Muñoz, E., Piuri, V., Sassi, R., Scotti, F.: Deep-ECG: convolutional neural networks for ECG biometric recognition. Pattern Recogn. Lett. **126**, 78–85 (2019)
9. Everson, L., et al.: BiometricNet: deep learning based biometric identification using wrist-worn PPG. In: Proceedings of the 2018 IEEE International Symposium on Circuits and Systems (ISCAS), pp. 1–5 (2018)
10. Faragó, P., Groza, R., Ivanciu, L., Hintea, S.: A correlation-based biometric identification technique for ECG, PPG and EMG. In: Proceedings of the 2019 42nd International Conference on Telecommunications and Signal Processing (TSP), pp. 716–719 (2019)
11. Fürnkranz, J.: Round robin classification. J. Mach. Learn. Res. **2**, 721–747 (2002)
12. He, H., Garcia, E.A.: Learning from imbalanced data. IEEE Trans. Knowl. Data Eng. **21**(9), 1263–1284 (2009)
13. Hwang, D.Y., Taha, B., Lee, D.S., Hatzinakos, D.: Evaluation of the time stability and uniqueness in PPG-based biometric system. IEEE Trans. Inf. Forensics Secur. **16**, 116–130 (2021)
14. Jaafar, N.A.L., Sidek, K.A., Mohd Azam, S.N.A.: Acceleration plethysmogram based biometric identification. In: Proceedings of the 2015 International Conference on BioSignal Analysis, Processing and Systems (ICBAPS), pp. 16–21 (2015)
15. Jain, A.K., Flynn, P., Ross, A.A.: Handbook of Biometrics, 1st edn. Springer Publishing Company, Incorporated (2010)
16. Jang, J., Kim, H.: Performance Measures, pp. 1062–1068. Springer, US, Boston, MA (2009)

17. Jindal, V., Birjandtalab, J., Pouyan, M.B., Nourani, M.: An adaptive deep learning approach for PPG-based identification. In: Proceedings of the 2016 38th Annual International Conference of the IEEE Engineering in Medicine and Biology Society (EMBC), pp. 6401–6404 (2016)
18. Karimian, N., Guo, Z., Tehranipoor, M., Forte, D.: Human recognition from photoplethys mography (PPG) based on non-fiducial features. In: Proceedings of the 2017 IEEE International Conference on Acoustics, Speech and Signal Processing (ICASSP), pp. 4636–4640 (2017)
19. Karimian, N., Tehranipoor, M., Forte, D.: Non-fiducial PPG-based authentication for healthcare application. In: Proceedings of the 2017 IEEE EMBS International Conference on Biomedical Health Informatics (BHI), pp. 429–432 (2017)
20. Karlen, W., Raman, S., Ansermino, J.M., Dumont, G.A.: Multiparameter respiratory rate estimation from the photoplethysmogram. IEEE Trans. Bio-Med. Eng. **60**(7), 1946–53 (2013)
21. Karlen, W., Turner, M., Cooke, E., Dumont, G., Ansermino, J.M.: CapnoBase: signal database and tools to collect, share and annotate respiratory signals. In: Annual Meeting of the Society for Technology in Anesthesia (STA). West Palm Beach (2010)
22. Khan, M.U., Aziz, S., Hassan Naqvi, S.Z., Zaib, A., Maqsood, A.: Pattern analysis towards human verification using photoplethysmograph signals. In: Proceedings of the 2020 International Conference on Emerging Trends in Smart Technologies (ICETST), pp. 1–6 (2020)
23. Lee, A., Kim, Y.: Photoplethysmography as a form of biometric authentication. In: Proceedings of the 2015 IEEE SENSORS, pp. 1–2 (2015)
24. Lee, E., Ho, A., Wang, Y., Huang, C., Lee, C.: Cross-domain adaptation for biometric identification using photoplethysmogram. In: Proceedings of the 2020 IEEE International Conference on Acoustics, Speech and Signal Processing (ICASSP), pp. 1289–1293 (2020)
25. Lovisotto, G., Turner, H., Eberz, S., Martinovic, I.: Seeing red: PPG biometrics using smartphone cameras. In: Proceedings of the 2020 IEEE/CVF Conference on Computer Vision and Pattern Recognition Workshops (CVPRW), pp. 3565–3574 (2020)
26. Luque, J., Cortès, G., Segura, C., Maravilla, A., Esteban, J., Fabregat, J.: END-to-END Photopleth YsmographY (PPG) based biometric authentication by using Convolutional Neural Networks. In: Proceedings of the 2018 26th European Signal Processing Conference (EUSIPCO), pp. 538–542 (2018)
27. Maiorana, E., Campisi, P., Gonzalez-Carballo, N., Neri, A.: Keystroke dynamics authentication for mobile phones. In: Proceedings of the 2011 ACM Symposium on Applied Computing, pp. 21–26 (2011)
28. Merone, M., Soda, P., Sansone, M., Sansone, C.: ECG databases for biometric systems: a systematic review. Expert Syst. Appl. **67**, 189–202 (2017)
29. Namini, S.P.M., Rashidi, S.: Implementation of artificial features in improvement of biometrics based PPG. In: Proceedings of the 2016 6th International Conference on Computer and Knowledge Engineering (ICCKE), pp. 342–346 (2016)
30. Rundo, F., Conoci, S., Ortis, A., Battiato, S.: An advanced bio-inspired photoplethysmography (PPG) and ECG pattern recognition system for medical assessment. Sensors **18**(2), (2018)
31. Sancho, J., Alesanco, A., Garca, J.: Photoplethysmographic authentication in long-term scenarios: a preliminary assessment. EMBEC/NBC -2017. IP, vol. 65, pp. 1085–1088. Springer, Singapore (2018). https://doi.org/10.1007/978-981-10-5122-7_271

32. Sancho, J., Iglesias, Á.A., García, J.: Biometric authentication using the PPG: a long-term feasibility study. Sensors **18**(5), 1525 (2018)
33. Spooren, J., Preuveneers, D., Joosen, W.: PPG2Live: using dual PPG for active authentication and liveness detection. In: Proceedings of the 2019 International Conference on Biometrics (ICB), pp. 1–6 (2019)
34. Tan, L., Jiang, J.: Digital Signal Processing: Fundamentals and Applications. Elsevier Science (2018)
35. Walia, A., Kaul, A.: Human recognition via PPG signal using temporal correlation. In: Proceedings of the 2019 5th International Conference on Signal Processing, Computing and Control (ISPCC), pp. 144–147 (2019)
36. Yadav, U., Abbas, S.N., Hatzinakos, D.: Evaluation of PPG biometrics for authentication in different states. In: Proceedings of the 2018 International Conference on Biometrics (ICB), pp. 277–282 (2018)
37. Zhao, T., Wang, Y., Liu, J., Chen, Y., Cheng, J., Yu, J.: TrueHeart: continuous authentication on wrist-worn wearables using PPG-based biometrics. In: Proceedings of the IEEE Conference on Computer Communications (INFOCOM), pp. 30–39 (2020)

EndoTect: A Competition on Automatic Disease Detection in the Gastrointestinal Tract

EndoTect: A Competition on Automatic Disease Detection in the Gastrointestinal Tract

Workshop Description

EndoTect is a challenge focused on improving the current state of gastroenterology using multimodal data and predictive models to automatically find different findings in the gastrointestinal (GI) tract. The human digestive system is one of the most diverse and complex organ systems in the human body, with its primary purpose being to break down food into nutrients so that the body can absorb it. Starting at the mouth and ending at the anus, the gastrointestinal tract carries many possibilities for disease and other abnormalities that range from minor annoyances to severely lethal. Among the most deadly is colorectal cancer (CRC), which, despite being among the most preventable cancers, also causes the third-most cancer-related deaths worldwide. In most cases, if the precursors of CRC are detected early enough, it can be treated with a high chance of full recovery. Therefore, all abnormalities must be identified and reported during a routine investigation of the gastrointestinal tract. The gold standard in performing these investigations is through video endoscopies, a procedure involving a small camera attached to a tube inserted either orally or rectally. However, this procedure is highly reliant on the skill and experience of the person operating the endoscope, with the consequence being variable performance between operators. We see this as an opportunity to introduce a "third eye" in the form of automatic detection algorithms to raise the bar for all endoscopists to lessen the performance gap between operators.

The challenge consists of three tasks, each targeting a different requirement for in-clinic use. The first task involves classifying images from the GI tract into 23 distinct classes. The second task focuses on efficient classification measured by the amount of time it takes to classify each image. The last task relates to automatically segmenting polyps using pixel-level binary segmentation masks. To complete these tasks, we provide a large dataset consisting of over 10, 000 labeled images belonging to 23 different classes, over 100, 000 unlabeled images, and 1, 000 segmented images. We hope that this challenge inspires other researchers in the pattern recognition community to use their knowledge to help solve this difficult problem, which affects thousands of lives each year.

In total, we received six submissions for review, of which all were selected to be presented at the workshop. The accepted articles focus on using deep learning to solve the aforementioned tasks and do so with good results. The organization committee evaluated the results, and the scripts used to calculate the quantitative metrics are available online. Next year, we plan to hold the challenge again, but this time with an extended evaluation dataset and an additional task for efficient segmentation.

Organization

EndoTect Organizers

Steven A. Hicks   SimulaMet, Oslo, Norway
Debesh Jha   SimulaMet, Oslo, Norway
Vajira Thambawita   SimulaMet, Oslo, Norway
Hugo Hammer   OsloMet, Oslo, Norway
Pål Halvorsen   SimulaMet, Oslo, Norway
Michael A. Riegler   SimulaMet, Oslo, Norway

The EndoTect 2020 Challenge: Evaluation and Comparison of Classification, Segmentation and Inference Time for Endoscopy

Steven A. Hicks[1,2]([✉]), Debesh Jha[1,3], Vajira Thambawita[1,2], Pål Halvorsen[1,2], Hugo L. Hammer[1,2], and Michael A. Riegler[1]

[1] SimulaMet, Oslo, Norway
steven@simula.no
[2] Oslo Metropolitan University, Oslo, Norway
[3] UIT The Arctic University of Norway, Tromsø, Norway

Abstract. The EndoTect challenge at the International Conference on Pattern Recognition 2020 aims to motivate the development of algorithms that aid medical experts in finding anomalies that commonly occur in the gastrointestinal tract. Using HyperKvasir, a large dataset containing images taken from several endoscopies, the participants competed in three tasks. Each task focuses on a specific requirement for making it useful in a real-world medical scenario. The tasks are (i) high classification performance in terms of prediction accuracy, (ii) efficient classification measured by the number of images classified per second, and (iii) pixel-level segmentation of specific anomalies. Hopefully, this can motivate different computer science researchers to help benchmark a crucial component of a future computer-aided diagnosis system, which in turn, could potentially save human lives.

Keywords: GI endoscopy · Anomaly detection · Segmentation · Accuracy · Efficient processing · Challenge

1 Introduction

The human digestive system is prone to suffer from many different diseases and abnormalities throughout a human lifetime. Some of these may be life-threatening and pose a severe risk to a patient's health and well-being. In most cases, if the detection of lethal disease is done early enough, it can be treated with a high chance of being fully healed. Therefore, it is important that all lesions are identified and reported during a routine investigation of the gastrointestinal (GI) tract. Currently, the gold-standard in performing these investigations is through video endoscopies, which is a procedure involving a small camera attached to a tube that is inserted either orally or rectally. However, there is one major downside to this procedure. The method is highly dependent on the skills and

© Springer Nature Switzerland AG 2021
A. Del Bimbo et al. (Eds.): ICPR 2020 Workshops, LNCS 12668, pp. 263–274, 2021.
https://doi.org/10.1007/978-3-030-68793-9_18

experience of the person operating the endoscope, which in turn results in a high operator variation and performance [18,28,47]. This is one of the reasons for high miss-rates when measuring polyp detection performance, with some miss-rates being as high as 20% [25]. Polyps are small mushroom-like growths that appear on the inner-lining of the GI wall and are the leading cause to colorectal cancer.

Automated detection of GI anomalies has been a research topic for at least two decades, and in the last few years, there have been various AI-based solutions have been proposed using both hand-crafted features and representation learning methods (such as neural networks). However, even though there are many approaches for detecting [1,4,7,13,32,33,35,37,42,44,45,48] and segmenting [14,23,24] GI findings, even some targeting real-time analysis [2,39,40], there is room for improvement. One popular way of benchmarking and improving the state-of-the-art in machine learning is through publicly hosted challenges that motivate researchers to contribute to a use-case they otherwise would not work on. For GI automatic image and video analysis, there have been several such challenges hosted the last few years [3,19,38,41], with each bringing new insights into the current state of the field.

This year, we present three different tasks for participants to complete. The tasks are as follows: (i) The *detection* task which aims for high classification accuracy among 23 different classes, (ii) the *efficient detection* task which targets real-time performance for the same 23 classes of the *detection* task, and (iii) the *segmentation* task that aims to segment polyps in GI images. To participate, the teams had to solve at least one of the provided tasks. Overall, six teams participated, where all participants, in one way or another, utilize deep neural networks to solve the provided tasks. The results vary between teams, but most are able to achieve satisfactory scores in terms of what is suitable for use in clinics [36].

We see this as an opportunity to aid medical doctors by helping them detect lesions through automatic frame analysis done live during endoscopy examinations. The pattern recognition community has a lot of knowledge that could assist in this task, making this challenge a perfect fit for the International Conference on Pattern Recognition (ICPR). The work done in this competition, detecting and segmenting medical findings in the GI tract, has the potential of making a real societal impact, as it directly affects the quality of care that healthcare professionals can provide.

2   Dataset Details

For this challenge, we provided the participants with a development dataset that was to be used to train their algorithms. This year, we provided HyperKvasir [6], which is a large GI dataset consisting of labeled and unlabeled images taken from several different GI endoscopies. The dataset is split into four distinct parts; Labeled image data, unlabeled image data, segmented image data, and annotated video data. In total, the dataset contains 110, 079 images (see Fig. 1 for examples) and 374 videos where it captures anatomical landmarks, pathological

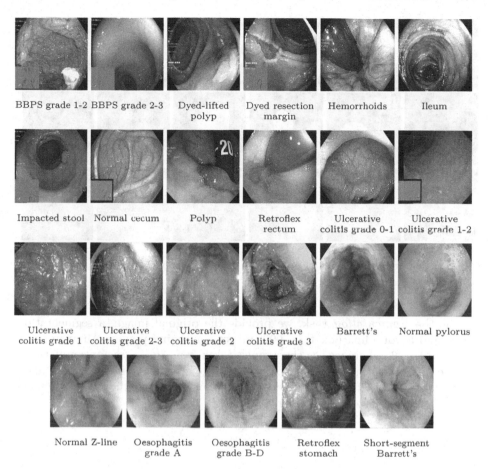

BBPS grade 1-2   BBPS grade 2-3   Dyed-lifted   Dyed resection   Hemorrhoids   Ileum
                                  polyp   margin

Impacted stool   Normal cecum   Polyp   Retroflex   Ulcerative   Ulcerative
                                                   rectum   colitis grade 0-1 colitis grade 1-2

Ulcerative   Ulcerative   Ulcerative   Ulcerative   Barrett's   Normal pylorus
colitis grade 1 colitis grade 2-3 colitis grade 2 colitis grade 3

Normal Z-line   Oesophagitis   Oesophagitis   Retroflex   Short-segment
                 grade A   grade B-D   stomach   Barrett's

Fig. 1. One example taken from each of the classes contained within the development dataset.

findings, and normal findings. The result is more than one million images and video frames altogether.

For the *detection* and *efficient detection* tasks, participants used the 23 classes provided in the labeled part of the dataset to develop their algorithms. The number of images per class is not balanced, which is a general challenge in the medical field due to the fact that some findings occur more often than others. This adds an additional challenge for researchers since methods applied to the data should also be able to learn from a small amount of training data. The participants could also use the unlabeled part of the dataset to further improve their algorithm by using, for example, a student-teacher approach or the pseudo labels provided in the HyperKvasir GitHub repository[1].

---

[1] https://github.com/simula/hyper-kvasir.

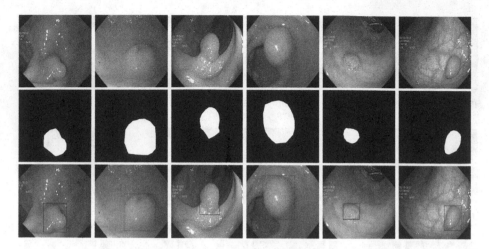

Fig. 2. Some example images of polyps and their corresponding masks and bounding boxes.

For the *segmentation* task, we provide the original image, a segmentation mask, and a bounding box for 1,000 images containing polyps. An example is shown in Fig. 2, where we see six samples taken from the segmentation dataset. For the image masks, the white pixels depict the area of the image containing a polyp, while the black background pixels do not. The bounding box is defined as the outermost pixels of the found polyp.

3   Tasks

With the end-goal of helping medical experts detect more lesions, we present three different tasks that each target a different requirement for in-clinic use. In the following, we give a detailed description of each task and describe how each was evaluated using the appropriate metrics. The script used to evaluate each task is on GitHub[2].

3.1   Detection Task

The detection task stems from the requirement of the high detection accuracy needed to be viable for use in a clinical setting. Participants are asked to develop algorithms that achieve high classification scores on the 23 different classes present in the labeled part of the development dataset (further described in Sect. 2). Submissions to this task was a comma-separated values (CSV) file, where each line contained the filename of the predicted image in the test dataset, the predicted label, and a confidence score ranging from 0 to 1 for the predicted label.

---

[2] https://github.com/simula/endotect-2020-submission-evaluation.

For this detection task, we use several standard metrics commonly used to evaluate classification tasks. We collect all true and false positives and negatives, and we then calculate metrics such as precision, recall/sensitivity, specificity, F1, and Matthews correlation coefficient (MCC) for multi-classification (also called R_k statistic for multiclass classification). The officially reported metric for evaluating this task is the MCC, which will also be the metric used to rank the submissions.

3.2   Efficient Detection Task

The efficient detection task focuses on the real-time analysis needed to deliver instant feedback to doctors performing endoscopies. To satisfy this requirement, the algorithm must achieve good classification scores while also being able to classify images as fast as they are put on screen, which is approximately 30 frames per second. For the efficient detection task, we asked participants to submit a Docker [31] image so that we can evaluate the speed and efficiency of the proposed algorithm on the same hardware. The Docker image was set up to produce a submission file similar to the one described for the detection task, but in addition to the aforementioned value entries, the classification processing time was also appended to the end of each row. All submissions submitted to this task were run on what could be considered consumer-grade hardware, that is, a computer running Arch Linux with an Intel Core i9-10900K processor, an Nvidia GeForce 1080 Ti graphics processing unit (GPU), and 32 gigabytes of RAM.

As one could generally achieve higher processing speeds with an algorithm with lower prediction accuracy, the evaluation used a combination of the MCC classification score and the number of frames processed per second. The focus here is on the "speed" aspect of the algorithm, so the only requirement from a classification standpoint is that it exceeds a set MCC threshold so that it is still viable for in-clinic use. We set the threshold of 85% as it is considered standard for automatic detection systems for colonoscopies [36].

3.3   Segmentation Task

In the segmentation task, we asked participants to use the segmented images provided in the dataset to generate segmentation masks of polyps automatically. Polyps are clumps of cells that form on the mucosal wall of the GI tract and come in a variety of shapes and sizes. Polyps are among the most critical findings in an endoscopy procedure as they are a precursor to different cancer types, including colorectal cancer, which is one of the most lethal cancer types worldwide [22]. The motivation behind this task is rooted in the requirement for not only detecting that a frame contains a polyp, but also showing where it is so that it can be properly removed. A typical example of a segmented polyp is shown in Fig. 2.

For the evaluation of this task, we use the standard metrics commonly used to evaluate segmentation tasks. This includes precision, recall, the Dice coefficient, and the Intersection over Union (IoU, also known as the Jaccard index). The metric which will be used to rank submissions will be the IoU. To calculate the metrics, we use the implementation provided by the Python library scikit-learn [34].

4   Participants

This year, we received 26 registrations, of which six submitted results. Each participating team was allowed to submit as many runs to each task as they wished. In the following, we give a short summary of each participant's approach. A more detailed description of each approach can be found in the teams' corresponding challenge papers.

4.1   Team DeepBlueAI

Team *DeepBlueAI* participated in the detection and segmentation tasks. For the detection task, they trained a series of (CNNs), of which the best performing approach is an ensemble network consisting of a ResNet-50 [15] with batch normalization and an EfficientNet B7 [43]. For the segmentation task, they used two different approaches, namely instance and semantic segmentation. The instance segmentation approach used the Mask Scoring R-CNN [21] with ResNeXt-101 [49] as the backbone. As for the semantic segmentation, they used DeepLab V3 plus [9] with multi-scale training. More information on the specific implementation for both tasks can be found in [30].

4.2   Team Spearheads

Team *Spearheads* participated in all three tasks, where two runs were submitted to the detection and efficient detection tasks, and one run to the segmentation task. For the detection and efficient detection task, they used a Tiny Darknet model[3], which was trained using an augmented version of the provided development dataset. For the segmentation task, they used a standard UNet architecture trained on the provided segmentation dataset, which was expanded using augmentation by Augmentor [5]. More information about team *Spearheads* approach can be found in [11].

4.3   Team NKT

Team *NKT* participated in the segmentation task, where they submitted one run. Their approach used a novel CNN-based architecture, which they named Dual Decoder Attention Network (DDANet). The architecture uses a single encoder network together with multiple decoders that use a combination of residual learning [16] and squeeze and excitation networks [20]. A more detailed explanation of the approach can be found in [46].

---

[3] https://pjreddie.com/darknet/tiny-darknet/.

4.4 Team aggcmab

Team *aggcmab* participated in the detection and segmentation tasks, for which they submitted one run to each. For the detection task, *aggcmab* used a ResNet-50x1 with a BiT-M [27] backbone trained with a hierarchical loss function. For the segmentation task, they use a double encoder-decoder network with a dual path network [10] for the encoders and a Feature-Pyramid [29] for the decoders. More information on the specifics of team *aggcmab's* approach can be found in [12].

Table 1. Results for the best runs from the **detection** task. The table entries are ordered after the best MCC score.

Team name	Macro average			Micro average			MCC (R_K)
	Precision	Recall	F1-score	Precision	Recall	F1-score	
howard	0.683	0.646	0.659	0.913	0.913	0.913	0.903
DeepBlueAI	0.629	0.568	0.590	0.874	0.874	0.874	0.860
aggcmab	0.598	0.533	0.558	0.870	0.870	0.870	0.856
FAST-NU-DS	0.453	0.431	0.413	0.603	0.603	0.603	0.568
Spearheads	0.333	0.220	0.223	0.440	0.440	0.440	0.388

Table 2. Results for the best runs from the **efficient detection** task. Please note that FPS signifies the average FPS calculated over the provided test dataset.

Team name	Macro average			Micro average			MCC (R_K)	FPS
	Precision	Recall	F1-score	Precision	Recall	F1-score		
howard	0.528	0.496	0.503	0.785	0.785	0.785	0.765	129.748
Spearheads	0.333	0.220	0.223	0.440	0.440	0.440	0.388	49.132

Table 3. Results for the best runs from the **segmentation** task. The table entries are ordered after according to the best IoU score.

Team name	Precision	Recall	F1-score/Dice	IoU
aggcmab	0.928	0.937	0.920	0.871
DeepBlueAI	0.907	0.947	0.915	0.861
howard	0.915	0.882	0.879	0.822
NKT	0.858	0.799	0.787	0.701
Spearheads	0.801	0.801	0.754	0.656

4.5 Team FAST-NU-DS

Team *FAST-NU-DS* participated in the detection task, where they submitted three runs. Their approach used bagging with 11 DenseNet169 models, where the final classification was made through hard majority voting. More information on the method can be found in [26].

4.6   Team howard

Team *howard* participated in all three tasks, where they submitted one run to each. For the detection and efficient detection task, they used a CNN based on the ResNet152 [15] architecture trained with a hybrid loss. During training, they also applied some data augmentation, namely, contrast augmentation, color shift, brightness augmentation, flipping, perspective transformation, and blur. For the segmentation task, their solution is based on Cascade Mask R-CNN [8]. More information about their solution can be found in [17].

5   Results and Discussion

Tables 1, 2, and 3 show the results for all tasks in the challenge. Looking at the results for the *detection* task (Table 1), we see that team *howard* achieved the best result with their use of ResNet-152 together with a custom hybrid loss. They achieved an MCC score of 0.903, 0.043 ahead of *DeepBlueAI*, who came in second place. For the *efficient detection* task (Table 2), only two teams participated, but also here, team *howard* achieved the best average frames per second (FPS) while also keeping the classification performance high. None of the teams reached the target MCC threshold of 85%, but team *howard* achieved an MCC of 0.765 at an FPS of 129, far above the real-time requirement. Thus, maybe some speed can be traded for a more complex model, achieving a slightly higher MCC while still reaching a real-time speed of 30 FPS. A common trend in this task was using neural networks with less parameters, like MobileNet or Tiny Darknet, to achieve a higher FPS. For the *segmentation* task (Table 3), team *aggcmab* achieved the highest IoU with their double encoder-decoder network approach. They reached an IoU score of 0.871, which is quite close to the runner up score of 0.861 submitted by team *DeepBlueAI*. Overall, the results prove that deep learning works well for analyzing GI image data and confirms the potential of computer-assisted detection and segmentation of GI anomalies, but they also suggest that there is still some room for improvement.

From an organizational perspective, the challenge went smoothly, without any significant hiccups or sudden difficulties. Docker submissions seem to work well, but may require some extra effort from the participants, which may explain why we only got two submissions to the *efficient detection* task. The difficulty level of the tasks appears to be quite balanced as the different teams achieved a variety of scores. Next year, we plan to hold the challenge again, but this time with an extended evaluation dataset and an additional task for efficient segmentation.

6   Conclusion

This paper described the EndoTect 2020 challenge, which asked participants to build algorithms that automatically detect different findings commonly found in the GI tract. The challenge consisted of three distinct tasks, where participants were given a large open dataset composed of videos from real endoscopies. We believe that computer scientists can make a real impact on the field of medicine, and the results presented in this paper show that we are at the point where machine learning algorithms have much potential in helping doctors detect more diseases.

References

1. Alammari, A., Islam, A.R., Oh, J., Tavanapong, W., Wong, J., De Groen, P.C.: Classification of ulcerative colitis severity in colonoscopy videos using CNN. In: Proceedings of the ACM International Conference on Information Management and Engineering (ACM ICIME), pp. 139–144 (2017). https://doi.org/10.1145/3149572.3149613
2. Angermann, Q., et al.: Towards real-time polyp detection in colonoscopy videos: adapting still frame-based methodologies for video sequences analysis. In: Cardoso, M.J., et al. (eds.) CARE/CLIP -2017. LNCS, vol. 10550, pp. 29–41. Springer, Cham (2017). https://doi.org/10.1007/978-3-319-67543-5_3
3. Bernal, J., Aymeric, H.: MICCAI endoscopic vision challenge polyp detection and segmentation (2017). https://endovissub2017-giana.grand-challenge.org/home/. Accessed 11 Dec 2017
4. Bernal, J., et al.: Polyp detection benchmark in colonoscopy videos using GTCreator: a novel fully configurable tool for easy and fast annotation of image databases. In: Proceedings of Computer Assisted Radiology and Surgery (CARS) (2018). https://hal.archives-ouvertes.fr/hal-01846141
5. Bloice, M.D., Roth, P.M., Holzinger, A.: Biomedical image augmentation using Augmentor. Bioinformatics (Oxford Engl.) **35**(21), 4522–4524 (2019). https://doi.org/10.1093/bioinformatics/btz259
6. Borgli, H., et al.: HyperKvasir, a comprehensive multi-class image and video dataset for gastrointestinal endoscopy. Sci. Data **7** (2020). https://doi.org/10.1038/s41597-020-00622-y. Article no. 283
7. Bychkov, D., et al.: Deep learning based tissue analysis predicts outcome in colorectal cancer. Sci. Rep. **8**(1), 3395 (2018). https://doi.org/10.1038/s41598-018-21758-3
8. Cai, Z., Vasconcelos, N.: Cascade R-CNN: high quality object detection and instance segmentation. IEEE Trans. Pattern Anal. Mach. Intell. (2019)
9. Chen, L.C., Zhu, Y., Papandreou, G., Schroff, F., Adam, H.: Encoder-decoder with atrous separable convolution for semantic image segmentation. arXiv:1802.02611 (2018)
10. Chen, Y., Li, J., Xiao, H., Jin, X., Yan, S., Feng, J.: Dual path networks. In: Proceedings of the Annual Conference on Advances in Neural Information Processing Systems (NeurIPS), pp. 4467–4475 (2017)
11. Dutta, A., Bhattacharjee, R.K., Barbhuiya, F.A.: Efficient detection of lesions during endoscopy. In: Proceedings of the ICPR 2020 Workshops and Challenges. LNCS. Springer (2020)
12. Galdran, A., Carneiro, G., Ballester, M.A.G.: A hierarchical multi-task approach to gastrointestinal image analysis. In: Proceedings of the ICPR 2020 Workshops and Challenges. LNCS. Springer (2020)
13. Ghatwary, N.M., Ye, X., Zolgharni, M.: Esophageal abnormality detection using DenseNet based faster R-CNN with gabor features. IEEE Access **7**, 84374–84385 (2019). https://doi.org/10.1109/ACCESS.2019.2925585

14. Guo, Y., Bernal, J., Matuszewski, B.J.: Polyp segmentation with fully convolutional deep neural networks–extended evaluation study. J. Imaging **6**(7), 69 (2020)
15. He, K., Zhang, X., Ren, S., Sun, J.: Deep residual learning for image recognition. In: Proceedings of the IEEE Conference on Computer Vision and Pattern Recognition (CVPR), pp. 770–778 (2016). https://doi.org/10.1109/CVPR.2016.90
16. He, K., Zhang, X., Ren, S., Sun, J.: Deep residual learning for image recognition. In: Proceedings of the IEEE Conference on Computer Vision and Pattern Recognition (CVPR), pp. 770–778 (2016)
17. He, Q., Bano, S., Stoyanov, D., Zuo1, S.: Hybrid loss with network trimming for disease recognition in digestive endoscopy. In: Proceedings of the ICPR 2020 Workshops and Challenges. LNCS. Springer (2020)
18. Hewett, D.G., Kahi, C.J., Rex, D.K.: Efficacy and effectiveness of colonoscopy: how do we bridge the gap? Gastrointest. Endosc. Clin. **20**(4), 673–684 (2010). https://doi.org/10.1016/j.giec.2010.07.011
19. Hicks, S., et al.: ACM multimedia BioMedia 2019 grand challenge overview. In: Proceedings of the ACM International Conference on Multimedia (ACM MM), pp. 2563–2567 (2019). https://doi.org/10.1145/3343031.3356058
20. Hu, J., Shen, L., Sun, G.: Squeeze-and-excitation networks. In: Proceedings of the IEEE/CVF Conference on Computer Vision and Pattern Recognition (CVPR), pp. 7132–7141 (2018). https://doi.org/10.1109/CVPR.2018.00745
21. Huang, Z., Huang, L., Gong, Y., Huang, C., Wang, X.: Mask scoring R-CNN. In: Proceedings of the IEEE/CVF Conference on Computer Vision and Pattern Recognition (CVPR), pp. 6402–6411 (2019). https://doi.org/10.1109/CVPR.2019.00657
22. International Agency for Research on Cancer - WHO: Cancer fact sheets (2019). https://gco.iarc.fr/today/fact-sheets-cancers. Accessed 16 Dec 2019
23. Jha, D., Riegler, M., Johansen, D., Halvorsen, P., Johansen, H.: DoubleU-Net: a deep convolutional neural network for medical image segmentation. In: Proceeding of the International Symposium on Computer Based Medical Systems (CBMS) (2020)
24. Jha, D., et al.: ResUNet++: an advanced architecture for medical image segmentation. In: Proceedings of the International Symposium on Multimedia (ISM), pp. 225–230 (2019). https://doi.org/10.1109/ISM46123.2019.00049
25. Kaminski, M.F., et al.: Quality indicators for colonoscopy and the risk of interval cancer. N. Engl. J. Med. **362**(19), 1795–1803 (2010). https://doi.org/10.1056/NEJMoa0907667
26. Khan, Z., Tahir, M.A., Memon, S.: Medical diagnostic by data bagging for various instances of neural network. In: Proceedings of the ICPR 2020 Workshops and Challenges. LNCS. Springer (2020)
27. Kolesnikov, A., et al.: Big Transfer (BiT): general visual representation learning. arXiv preprint arXiv:1912.11370, June 2019
28. Lee, S.H., et al.: Endoscopic experience improves interobserver agreement in the grading of esophagitis by Los Angeles classification: conventional endoscopy and optimal band image system. Gut Liver **8**(2), 154 (2014). https://doi.org/10.5009/gnl.2014.8.2.154
29. Lin, T.Y., Dollár, P., Girshick, R., He, K., Hariharan, B., Belongie, S.: Feature pyramid networks for object detection. In: Proceedings of the IEEE Conference on Computer Vision and Pattern Recognition (CVPR), pp. 2117–2125 (2017)
30. Luo, Z., Che, L., He, J.: A hierarchical multi-task approach to gastrointestinal image analysis. In: Proceedings of the ICPR 2020 Workshops and Challenges. LNCS. Springer (2020)

31. Merkel, D.: Docker: lightweight Linux containers for consistent development and deployment. Linux J. **2014**(239) (2014)
32. Min, M., Su, S., He, W., Bi, Y., Ma, Z., Liu, Y.: Computer-aided diagnosis of colorectal polyps using linked color imaging colonoscopy to predict histology. Sci. Rep. **9**(1), 2881 (2019). https://doi.org/10.1038/s41598-019-39416-7
33. Mori, Y., et al.: Real-time use of artificial intelligence in identification of diminutive polyps during colonoscopy: a prospective study. Ann. Intern. Med. **169**(6), 357–366 (2018). https://doi.org/10.7326/M18-0249
34. Pedregosa, F., et al.: Scikit-learn: machine learning in Python. J. Mach. Learn. Res. **12**, 2825–2830 (2011)
35. Pogorelov, K., et al.: A holistic multimedia system for gastrointestinal tract disease detection. In: Proceedings of the ACM on Multimedia Systems Conference (MMSYS), pp. 112–123 (2017). https://doi.org/10.1145/3193740
36. Pogorelov, K., et al.: Deep learning and hand-crafted feature based approaches for polyp detection in medical videos. In: Proceedings of the IEEE International Symposium on Computer-Based Medical Systems (CBMS). IEEE (2018)
37. Pogorelov, K., et al.: Efficient disease detection in gastrointestinal videos-global features versus neural networks. Multimedia Tools Appl. **76**(21), 22493–22525 (2017). https://doi.org/10.1007/s11042-017-4989-y
38. Pogorelov, K., et al.: Medico multimedia task at mediaeval 2018. In: Proceeding of the MediaEval Benchmarking Initiative for Multimedia Evaluation Workshop (MediaEval) (2018)
39. Pogorelov, K., et al.: GPU-accelerated real-time gastrointestinal diseases detection. In: Proceedings of the International Symposium on Computer-Based Medical Systems (CBMS), pp. 185–190. IEEE (2016). https://doi.org/10.1109/CBMS.2016.63
40. Riegler, M., et al.: EIR - efficient computer aided diagnosis framework for gastrointestinal endoscopies. In: Proceedings of the IEEE International Workshop on Content-Based Multimedia Indexing (CBMI), pp. 1–6 (2016). https://doi.org/10.1109/CBMI.2016.7500257
41. Riegler, M., et al.: Multimedia for medicine: the medico task at MediaEval 2017. In: Proceeding of the MediaEval Benchmarking Initiative for Multimedia Evaluation Workshop (MediaEval) (2017)
42. Silva, J., Histace, A., Romain, O., Dray, X., Granado, B.: Toward embedded detection of polyps in WCE images for early diagnosis of colorectal cancer. Int. J. Comput. Assist. Radiol. Surg. **9**(2), 283–293 (2014). https://doi.org/10.1007/s11548-013-0926-3
43. Tan, M., Le, Q.V.: EfficientNet: rethinking model scaling for convolutional neural networks. In: Proceedings of the International Conference on Machine Learning, pp. 6105–6114 (2019)
44. Thambawita, V., et al.: The medico-task 2018: disease detection in the gastrointestinal tract using global features and deep learning. In: Proceeding of the MediaEval Benchmarking Initiative for Multimedia Evaluation Workshop (MediaEval) (2018)
45. Thambawita, V.L., et al.: An extensive study on cross-dataset bias and evaluation metrics interpretation for machine learning applied to gastrointestinal tract abnormality classification. ACM Trans. Comput. Healthcare **1** (2020)
46. Tomar, N.K., Jha, D., Ali, S., Johansen, H.D.J.D., Riegler, M.A., Halvorsen, P.: DDANet: dual decoder attention network for automatic polyp segmentation. In: Proceedings of the ICPR 2020 Workshops and Challenges. LNCS. Springer (2020)

47. Van Doorn, S.C., et al.: Polyp morphology: an interobserver evaluation for the Paris classification among international experts. Am. J. Gastroenterol. **110**(1), 180–187 (2015). https://doi.org/10.1038/ajg.2014.326
48. Wang, Y., Tavanapong, W., Wong, J., Oh, J.H., De Groen, P.C.: Polyp-Alert: near real-time feedback during colonoscopy. Comput. Methods Programs Biomed. **120**(3), 164–179 (2015). https://doi.org/10.1016/j.cmpb.2015.04.002
49. Xie, S., Girshick, R., Dollár, P., Tu, Z., He, K.: Aggregated residual transformations for deep neural networks. arXiv preprint arXiv:1611.05431 (2016)

A Hierarchical Multi-task Approach to Gastrointestinal Image Analysis

Adrian Galdran[1]([✉]), Gustavo Carneiro[2], and Miguel A. González Ballester[3,4]

[1] Department of Computing and Informatics, Bournemouth University, Poole, UK
agaldran@bournemouth.ac.uk
[2] Australian Institute for Machine Learning, University of Adelaide,
Adelaide, Australia
[3] BCN Medtech, Department of Information and Communication Technologies,
Universitat Pompeu Fabra, Barcelona, Spain
[4] ICREA, Barcelona, Spain

Abstract. A large number of different lesions and pathologies can affect the human digestive system, resulting in life-threatening situations. Early detection plays a relevant role in the successful treatment and the increase of current survival rates to, *e.g.*, colorectal cancer. The standard procedure enabling detection, endoscopic video analysis, generates large quantities of visual data that need to be carefully analyzed by an specialist. Due to the wide range of color, shape, and general visual appearance of pathologies, as well as highly varying image quality, such process is greatly dependent on the human operator experience and skill. In this work, we detail our solution to the task of multi-category classification of images from the gastrointestinal (GI) human tract within the 2020 Endotect Challenge. Our approach is based on a Convolutional Neural Network minimizing a hierarchical error function that takes into account not only the finding category, but also its location within the GI tract (lower/upper tract), and the type of finding (pathological finding/therapeutic intervention/anatomical landmark/mucosal views' quality). We also describe in this paper our solution for the challenge task of polyp segmentation in colonoscopies, which was addressed with a pretrained double encoder-decoder network. Our internal cross-validation results show an average performance of 91.25 Mathews Correlation Coefficient (MCC) and 91.82 Micro-F1 score for the classification task, and a 92.30 F1 score for the polyp segmentation task. The organization provided feedback on the performance in a hidden test set for both tasks, which resulted in 85.61 MCC and 86.96 F1 score for classification, and 91.97 F1 score for polyp segmentation. At the time of writing no public ranking for this challenge had been released.

Keywords: Colonoscopy image classification · Polyp segmentation

1 Introduction

The human gastrointestinal tract can be affected by a variety of pathological abnormalities that may indicate different kind of diseases, ranging from

A. Del Bimbo et al. (Eds.): ICPR 2020 Workshops, LNCS 12668, pp. 275–282, 2021.
https://doi.org/10.1007/978-3-030-68793-9_19

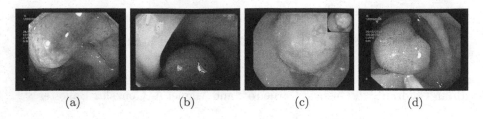

(a)   (b)   (c)   (d)

Fig. 1. Polyp appearance is widely variable in terms of shape, size, and color. Four different polyps extracted from the Kvasir-Seg database [10].

moderately concerning to potentially life-threatening. minor annoyances to highly lethal diseases. For example, Colorectal Cancer (CRC) is the second most common cancer type in women and third most common for men [8]. Among other pathological findings of interest, gastro-intestinal polyps are known to be early precursors of this class of cancer [15], presenting themselves in half of the patients over 50 undergoing screening endoscopies [14]. This kind of pathologies show a wide range of shapes and visual appearances, as shown in Fig. 1, and its identification and segmentation represents a challenging problem for both computational techniques and human specialists.

During colonoscopy screenings, a flexible tube with a light camera mounted on it is inserted into the human body through the rectum to analyze it and look for polyps or other pathologies. Early detection of CRC substantially increases survival rates, with screening programs enabling even pre-symptomatic treatment [14]. However, it is estimated that around 6–27% of polyps are not found during a colonoscopic examination [1], and it has been recently proven in [13] that up to 80% of missed lesions could be detected with effective real-time computer-aided colonoscopic image analysis systems. Therefore, computational approaches to endoscopic image analysis have been intensely researched as a tool for enhancing colonoscopic procedures and enhance detection rates, enabling early treatment, and increasing survival rates.

The most relevant computer-aided tasks associated with in computational endoscopic image analysis are: 1. Pathology Detection: Deciding if certain findings/lesions appear in an endoscopic frame [2]. 2. Pathology Classification: Assigning the frame to one among a range of categories, or predict a pathologies' degree of malignancy [4]. 3. Pathology Localization: finding the position (often in terms of a bounding box) of lesions within a frame [17]. 4. Pathology Segmentation: delineating the exact lesion contour in a given endoscopic frame [16].

In this paper we approach the task of pathology classification and pathology segmentation. In the following pages we describe our solution for these two tracks of the 2020 Endotect challenge [9] consisting of a 23-class endoscopic image classification and a polyp segmentation task.

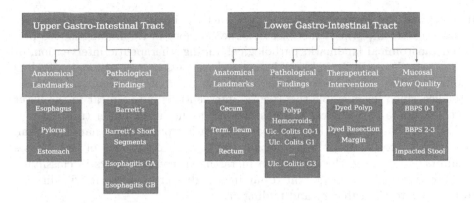

Fig. 2. Label structure for the endoscopic image classification task of the Endotect Challenge. Blue blocks correspond to Gastro-Intestinal Tract (Lower/Upper), green blocks represent the nature of the finding, and brown blocks the finding. In this work we follow this hierarchy to define a multi-task loss function that minimizes inconsistencies in predictions. (Color figure online)

2   Methodology

2.1   Endoscopic Image Classification

In this section we describe our approach to multi-class endoscopic frame classification. We first detail the CNN architecture of choice for this work, and then introduce a hierarchical error function that we minimize for obtaining our solution.

Convolutional Neural Network - BiT. When working with deep neural networks for image classification, it is common to employ weights from previously optimized models to favor training and reach higher performances with the need of less annotated data. For RGB images like endoscopic frames, this is a particularly efficient approach, since they share common low-level features with natural imagery. The standard approach in this case is to start the training from weights learned from the Imagenet database, which contains 1.3M images. Instead, in this work we leverage the recent work of Big Transfer (BiT, [11]), and start our training from a model pre-trained on the ImageNet-21k extension, which contains 14M images. The architecture of choice in this paper corresponds with ResNet-50x1/BiT-M in [11].

Hierarchical Loss Function. The data used for multi-category classification on endoscopic images for the Endotect challenge was labeled with a rich structure, as illustrated in Fig. 2. In this work, we leverage such structure by introducing a hierarchical loss function that reflects the different ways in which the same image is labeled. For this, an input image x is classified in a three-fold manner: first the network predicts which tract the image belongs to, *e.g.* upper or lower gastro-intestinal tract; second, the category of the finding is also predicted (anatomical landmark, pathological finding, therapeutic intervention, or mucosal view's quality), and last the network outputs the corresponding finding among the 23 different classes. The aim of this approach is to minimize inconsistencies, since for example therapeutic interventions only appear in the lower tract, and some pathological findings are only found in the upper tract.

Each of the aforementioned three classification problems is handled by an independent cross-entropy loss function $\mathcal{L}_{\text{tract}}$, $\mathcal{L}_{\text{cat}}$, $\mathcal{L}_{\text{find}}$; each of these losses attempts to minimize the errors in a hierarchical manner: errors in classifying the tract for a given image will result in a higher error, since it will directly propagate into the category and finding error.

In order to balance the contribution of each of these losses, we consider the amount of classes n and the cross-entropy error that a random prediction would produce in each sub-task, $\log(1/n)$, as follows:

$$\begin{aligned} \mathcal{L}_{\text{overall}}(U(x), y) = {} & \log(n_{\text{tract}}) \cdot \mathcal{L}_{\text{tract}}(U(x), y_{\text{tract}}) \\ & + \log(n_{\text{cat}}) \cdot \mathcal{L}_{\text{cat}}(U(x), y_{\text{cat}}) \\ & + \log(n_{\text{find}}) \cdot \mathcal{L}_{\text{find}}(U(x), y_{\text{find}}) \end{aligned} \tag{1}$$

In the above equation, there is a slight abuse of notation: while the network's output is the probability of belonging to each of the 23 different findings, probabilities of higher hierarchical levels (category and tract) are computed by suitably aggregating probabilities of the lower hierarchical levels. For example, in order to compute $U(x)$ in the $\mathcal{L}_{\text{tract}}$ case, we would add all the probabilities corresponding to findings that are known to appear only in the lower or upper GI tracts.

2.2   Gastrointestinal Polyp Segmentation

In the following lines we describe our solution to the polyp segmentation task of the Endotect Challenge.

Double Autoencoders. For the segmentation of polyps we adopt the solution presented in [7], which is based on a double encoder-decoder network introduced in [6]. Double encoder-encoders are a straightforward extension of encoder-decoder architectures in which two encoder-decoder networks are sequentially combined, as shown in Fig. 3. Being x the input RGB image, $E^{(1)}$ the first CNN, and $E^{(2)}$ the second CNN, a double encoder-decoder feeds the output $E^{(1)}(x)$ of the first network to the second network together with x, which effectively acts as an attention map allowing $E^{(2)}$ to focus on the most relevant areas of the image x:

$$E(x) = E^{(2)}(x, E^{(1)}(x)), \tag{2}$$

where x and $E^{(1)}(x)$ are stacked so that the input to $E^{(2)}$ has four channels instead of the three channels corresponding to the RGB components of x. Differently from [7], we employ a Dual Path Networks DPN92 [5] as our encoder

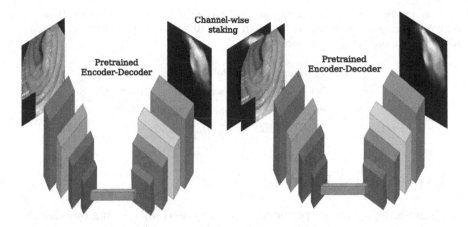

Fig. 3. Pre-trained double encoder-decoder network for polyp segmentation. The second network receives as input a stack of four channels: the original image together with the prediction of the first network; this facilitates the task of the second network, which can focus on interesting or error-prone areas of the image, enhancing its segmentation capability.

for both networks, and Feature-Pyramid decoders [12]. Supervision is applied at the output of both networks by means of a standard cross-entropy loss.

2.3   Training Details

For both classification and segmentation tasks we followed a similar training procedure. Both networks were optimized using standard Stochastic Gradient Descent by minimizing the loss in Eq. (1) for classification, and the pixel-wise cross-entropy loss for segmentation, with a learning rate of $l = 0.01$ and a batch-size of 8 and 4 respectively. The learning rate was decayed following a cosine law from its initial value to $l = 1e - 8$ during n epochs, which defines a training cycle. In the classification case, $n = 10$ whereas in the segmentation case $n = 50$. We then repeated this process for 5 cycles in the classification scenario and 20 cycles in the segmentation case, restarting the learning back at the beginning of each cycle. Images were re-scaled to 640×512, which respects the predominant rectangular aspect ratio of the original data, and were augmented with standard techniques (random rotations, vertical/horizontal flipping, contrast/saturation/brightness changes) during training. The mean Dice score is monitored on a separate validation set and the best performing model is kept for testing purposes. For testing, we generate four different versions of each image by horizontal/vertical flipping, predict on each of them, and average the results.

Table 1. Performance of our solution to the classification and segmentation tasks. First row: average performance on five-fold cross validation. Second row: results on the hidden test set provided by the organizers.

	Finding Classif.		Polyp segmentation			
	MCC	F1-micro	Jaccard	F1	Precision	Recall
5-fold CV (Avg.)	85.61	86.96	88.03	92.30	93.19	94.14
Hidden test set	91.25	91.82	87.10	91.97	92.82	93.73

3   Experimental Results

The Hyper-Kvasir dataset, provided in [3], was used for training our classification model, whereas the Kvasir-seg dataset [10] was used for polyp segmentation training purposes. In the first case, 10,662 labeled images containing one of the 23 different findings is available, but the frequency of these categories is highly imbalanced. We choose to compensate for this by simple oversampling of minority classes. In the second case, 1,000 images containing manually delineated polyps are provided by the organization. For both the classification and segmentation tasks we carry out a five-fold cross-validation training; the average result is shown in the first row of Table 1. The five models, which are trained on different subsets of the training dataset, are then employed to generate ensembled predictions on two hidden tests set that are submitted to the organization for performance ranking. The resulting performance on the test set is also shown in the second row of Table 1. At the time of writing no public leaderboard has been released yet by the organizers.

4   Discussion and Conclusion

In this work we have described our solution to the 2020 Endotect challenge, classification and segmentation sub-challenges. Our approach to endoscopic image classification relied on a CNN trained so as to minimize in a multi-task manner a hierarchical set of three loss functions that penalize inconsistencies not only in the final finding classification but also in higher levels of classification like the section of the gastrointestinal tract the image comes from or the kind of finding it contains. For the segmentation sub-challenge, we leveraged our recent work on polyp segmentation [7]: a double decoder-encoder network with a DPN92 encoder and a FP-Net decoder was trained to accurately delineate polyp boundaries.

Although at the time of writing the organizers have not released a public ranking yet, performance in internal cross-validation analysis was promising. Certain overfitting is observed in the classification sub-challenge, but segmentation performance scores on the hidden test set of the challenge seem well-aligned with our average cross-validation indicators.

References

1. Ahn, S.B., Han, D.S., Bae, J.H., Byun, T.J., Kim, J.P., Eun, C.S.: The miss rate for colorectal adenoma determined by quality-adjusted, back-to-back colonoscopies. Gut Liver **6**(1), 64–70 (2012)
2. Bernal, J., et al.: Comparative validation of polyp detection methods in video colonoscopy: results from the MICCAI 2015 endoscopic vision challenge. IEEE Trans. Med. Imaging **36**(6), 1231–1249 (2017)
3. Borgli, H., et al.: HyperKvasir, a comprehensive multi-class image and video dataset for gastrointestinal endoscopy. Sci. Data **7**(1), 283 (2020)
4. Carneiro, G., Pu, Z.C.T.L., Singh, R., Burt, A.: Deep learning uncertainty and confidence calibration for the five-class polyp classification from colonoscopy. Med. Image Anal. **62**, 101653 (2020)
5. Chen, Y., Li, J., Xiao, H., Jin, X., Yan, S., Feng, J.: Dual path networks. In: Proceedings of the 31st International Conference on Neural Information Processing Systems, NIPS 2017, pp. 4470–4478. Curran Associates Inc., Red Hook, December 2017
6. Galdran, A., Anjos, A., Dolz, J., Chakor, H., Lombaert, H., Ayed, I.B.: The little w-net that could: state-of-the-art retinal vessel segmentation with minimalistic models. arXiv:2009.01907, September 2020
7. Galdran, A., González Ballester, M.A., Carneiro, G.: Double encoder-decoder networks for gastrointestinal polyp segmentation. In: ICPR Workshop on Artificial Intelligence for Healthcare Applications (2020)
8. Haggar, F.A., Boushey, R.P.: Colorectal cancer epidemiology: incidence, mortality, survival, and risk factors. Clin. Colon Rectal Surg. **22**(4), 191–197 (2009)
9. Hicks, S., Jha, D., Thambawita, V., Halvorsen, P., Hammer, H.L., Riegler, M.: The EndoTect 2020 challenge: evaluation and comparison of classification, segmentation and inference time for endoscopy. In: ICPR (2020)
10. Jha, D., et al.: Kvasir-SEG: a segmented polyp dataset. In: Ro, Y.M., et al. (eds.) MMM 2020. LNCS, vol. 11962, pp. 451–462. Springer, Cham (2020). https://doi.org/10.1007/978-3-030-37734-2_37
11. Kolesnikov, A., et al.: Big Transfer (BiT): general visual representation learning. In: Vedaldi, A., Bischof, H., Brox, T., Frahm, J.-M. (eds.) ECCV 2020. LNCS, vol. 12350, pp. 491–507. Springer, Cham (2020). https://doi.org/10.1007/978-3-030-58558-7_29
12. Lin, T.Y., Dollár, P., Girshick, R., He, K., Hariharan, B., Belongie, S.: Feature pyramid networks for object detection. In: 2017 IEEE Conference on Computer Vision and Pattern Recognition (CVPR), pp. 936–944, July 2017. ISSN 1063–6919
13. Lui, T.K., et al.: New insights on missed colonic lesions during colonoscopy through artificial intelligence-assisted real-time detection (with video). Gastrointest. Endosc. **93**, 193–200.e1 (2020)
14. Sánchez-Peralta, L.F., Bote-Curiel, L., Picón, A., Sánchez-Margallo, F.M., Pagador, J.B.: Deep learning to find colorectal polyps in colonoscopy: a systematic literature review. Artif. Intell. Med. **108**, 101923 (2020)
15. Vázquez, D., et al.: A benchmark for endoluminal scene segmentation of colonoscopy images. J. Healthcare Eng. **2017**, 4037190 (2017)

16. Wickstrøm, K., Kampffmeyer, M., Jenssen, R.: Uncertainty and interpretability in convolutional neural networks for semantic segmentation of colorectal polyps. Med. Image Anal. **60**, 101619 (2020)
17. Zhang, R., Zheng, Y., Poon, C.C.Y., Shen, D., Lau, J.Y.W.: Polyp detection during colonoscopy using a regression-based convolutional neural network with a tracker. Pattern Recogn. **83**, 209–219 (2018)

Delving into High Quality Endoscopic Diagnoses

Zhipeng Luo[✉], Lixuan Che[✉], and Jianye He[✉]

DeepBlue Technology (Shanghai) Co. Ltd., Shanghai, China
{luozp,chelx,hejianye}@deepblueai.com

Abstract. This paper introduces the solution to the Detection Task and Segmentation Task of ICPR 2020 EndoTect Challenge [7] from the Deep-BlueAI Team. The Detection Task is essentially a classification problem whose target is to distinguish between 23 types of digestive system diseases. For this task, we try different data augmentation methods and feature representation networks. Ensemble learning is also adopted to improve classification performance. For the Segmentation Task, we implement it in both semantic segmentation manner and instance segmentation manner. In comparison, semantic segmentation gets a relatively better result.

Keywords: Classification · Semantic segmentation · Instance segmentation

1 Introduction

Computer vision technologies can play an assisting role in the diagnosis of digestive system diseases. The ICPR 2020 EndoTect Challenge [7] consists of three tasks. The first task is to distinguish between 23 types of digestive system diseases, namely Detection Task, which is essentially a classification problem. The first task focuses on classification accuracy, while the second task is more about speed. The target of the third task is to segment polyps, namely Segmentation Task. We participant in the Detection Task and Segmentation Task. The organizers provide four distinct parts of the data set [2], including labeled images, unlabeled images, segmented images, and annotated videos. For the Detection Task, we use the labeled images for training, and the unlabeled images are used to generate pseudo labels to augment training data. For the Segmentation task, the segmented images are used.

1.1 Detection Task

There are 10662 labeled images representing 23 different classes of digestive system diseases. The distribution of these categories is incredibly unbalanced, as shown in Table 1, which brings a great challenge to this task. Besides, the differences between some categories are not very clear, such as ulcerative-colitis-0-1,

© Springer Nature Switzerland AG 2021
A. Del Bimbo et al. (Eds.): ICPR 2020 Workshops, LNCS 12668, pp. 283–290, 2021.
https://doi.org/10.1007/978-3-030-68793-9_20

ulcerative-colitis-1-2, and ulcerative-colitis-2-3. In a word, we need to solve the following two problems to get a good result:
(a) Unbalanced data distribution;
(b) Classification of similar pictures belonging to different categories, as illustrated in Fig. 1.

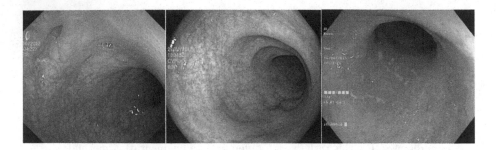

Fig. 1. Three similar images above belong to different categories: ulcerative-colitis-0-1(left), ulcerative-colitis-grade-1(middle), and ulcerative-colitis-1-2(right).

Table 1. Distribution of 23 categories.

Category name	Number	Category name	Number
Barretts	41	Oesophagitis-b-d	260
Bbps-0-1	646	Polyp	1028
Bbps-2-3	1148	Retroflex-rectum	391
Dyed-lifted-polyps	1002	Retroflex-stomach	764
Dyed-resection-margins	989	Short-segment-barretts	53
Hemorrhoids	6	Ulcerative-colitis-0-1	35
Ileum	9	Ulcerative-colitis-1-2	11
Impacted-stool	131	Ulcerative-colitis-2-3	28
Normal-cecum	1009	Ulcerative-colitis-grade-1	201
Normal-pylorus	999	Ulcerative-colitis-grade-2	443
Normal-z-line	932	Ulcerative-colitis-grade-3	133
Oesophagitis-a	403		

1.2 Segmentation Task

The Segmentation Task only focuses on polyps, an essential item in endoscopy, as it is the precursor of some types of cancer. The challenge organizers provide 1000 polyps mask images and 1071 bounding boxes. The target of this task is to generate the segmentation of polyps automatically. Polyps vary greatly in size and have irregular shapes, which is the difficulty of this task. As shown in Fig. 2, each red box contains a polyp. There are dense small polyps in the left image, a large polyp in the middle, and a polyp with an irregular shape in the right.

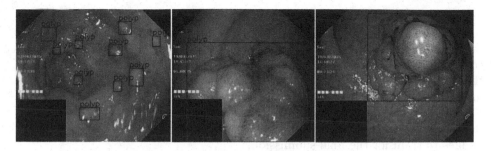

Fig. 2. Polyps with different sizes and shapes.

2 Methods

2.1 Detection Task

We divide the labeled images into two parts in this task, 80% of each category for training and 20% for validation. We take ResNet-50 [6] as the baseline model. If not specified, our experiments' classification loss is the cross-entropy loss, and Adam [10] is adopted as the optimizer. Each mini-batch has 60 images per GPU. We train on 3 GPUs for 40 epochs, with an initial learning rate of 0.001. The learning rate decays tenfold if the accuracy of the prediction on the validation set is still not improved after four epochs.

Using more capable models, such as efficientnet-b7 [15], and larger input image size gets better results on the validation set. We follow BNNeck [12], adding a BN layer without the bias before the network's last linear layer. Multi-scale training and multi-scale testing can also bring a boost to performance.

To alleviate the unbalanced problem, we try to draw frames from the labeled videos to expand the Barretts and hemorrhoids data. However, the prediction results on the validation set are not satisfactory. We also generate pseudo-labels to balance the number of images in each category. Specifically, we use labeled images to train a baseline model and predict on the unlabeled images. Add the images whose confidence over 0.99 to the training data set for the less-labeled categories. Retrain the model with new training data, and predict the unlabeled images again. Repeat these steps three times. However, the predicted results on the validation set are not satisfactory, neither.

Furthermore, some methods to deal with long-tailed recognition are also tried for the unbalanced distribution. Apart from the conventional re-sample and re-weight methods, we try to decouple the representation from the classification by training the classifier using class-balanced data after freezing the backbone got from the instance-balanced data [9]. Nevertheless, they fail to bring a positive impact because of the limited classes, perhaps.

2.2 Segmentation Task

The target of this task is to segment polyps automatically. As the shape of polyps is irregular, if two polyps are too close to each other, it is hard to tell them apart. This task only segments one category, and some small polyps are difficult to distinguish from the background. With this in mind, if there is a confidence score for each segmentation, we can easily remove the segmentation with lower confidence and improve the performance. Considering these above, we realize the segmentation in semantic segmentation manner and instance segmentation manner separately.

The challenge organizers provide 1000 polyps images with the mask. We randomly sample 800 for training and 200 for validation while utilizing all the images to train for the final submission.

Semantic Segmentation. We try some popular semantic segmentation algorithms, such as UNet [13], PSPNet [20], OCRNet [17] and DeepLab series. Overall, the performance of these algorithms does not differ much, and we get the best result in the validation data set through DeepLab V3 plus [4] algorithm. In the training phase, apart from cross-entropy loss, Dice loss, Lovasz loss [1] and their combinations are tried. We reach no better result evaluated by the Dice coefficient, and cross-entropy loss is optimal. In general, a larger batch size in training will lead to a better performance in segmentation for a more stable batch normalization operation. However, it seems the opposite when it applies to polyps. The optimal batch-size is 8 per GPU in our experiments, and we attribute it to the simple foreground and background. Among augmentation methods, rotation significantly boosts the performance, considering the perspective diversity of endoscopy. We test multi-scale images in the test phase, which improves the boundary and depress the outliers.

Instance Segmentation. Our baseline and hyper-parameters follow Mask R-CNN [5], with ResNet-50 as the backbone. An example of instance segmentation is shown in Fig. 3. From the raw polyp image, the folds in the intestine are similar to polyps. It is easy to predict folds in the intestine as polyps, but usually with low confidence. We can improve the performance by removing the segmentation whose confidence below a certain threshold. We try ResNet and ResNeXt [16] as the backbone. As expected, increasing the depth and width of the feature extraction network will improve the performance. We try Cascade R-CNN [3], but the improvement is slight. Furthermore, we follow Mask Scoring R-CNN [8] to couple the Mask R-CNN network with a MaskIou Head. MaskIoU Head is aimed to regress the IoU between the ground truth mask and predicted segmentation, which improves the performance of segmentation. We randomly resize the input images for the data augmentation while keeping the ratio the same and randomly flip the input images. In the test phase, we perform the model ensemble by voting for each pixel, but the segmentation edges obtained are not smooth.

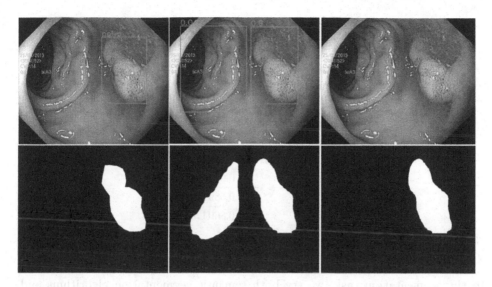

Fig. 3. An example of instance segmentation. The ground truth bounding box and mask(left column), predicted results(middle column), and the input image coupled with the final result after removing less confident ones(right column).

Table 2. Ablation experiments.

Model	MCC	Accuracy	F1 score
Resnet50(baseline)	0.904867	0.912289	0.620710
Resnet50 + cutmix [18]	0.900880	0.908537	0.615830
Resnet50 + mixup [19]	0.900493	0.908068	0.613842
Resnet50 + label smoothing [14]	0.904860	0.912289	0.622744
Resnet50 + focalloss [11]	0.897882	0.905767	0.623911
Efficientnet-b7	0.910260	0.913525	0.632279

3 Experiment

3.1 Detection Task

If not specified, the input images are resized to 480 * 480. The initial learning rate is 0.001. The ablation experiment results on the validation set are shown in Table 2. For the final submission, we retrain the resnet50 and efficientnet-b7 using all data sets (both training and validation) with an ensemble of two models followed. Our results on the test set are shown in Table 3. The macro average precision and recall are not high, which is consistent with the validation phase. It mainly attributes to too little data on some categories, like hemorrhoids and ileum. It is too hard for models to master their representation while the performance on the categories with adequate data is favourable.

Table 3. Results on the test set

Metric	Value
True-positives	630
True-negatives	15771
False-positives	91
False-negatives	91
Precision	0.628856829
Recall/sensitivity	0.5678750063
Specificity	0.9940994382
F1	0.5897401386
Mcc	0.8604281862

3.2 Segmentation Task

In the segmentation task, we try both semantic segmentation algorithms and instance segmentation algorithms. If not specified, the input image size is $320 * 240$ for semantic segmentation. The input size is multiplied by a ratio from $[0.75, 1.0, 1.25, 1.5]$ for multi-scale testing. The best result on the test set is obtained from Deeplab v3 plus with the multi-scale training strategy, as shown in Table 4.

Table 4. Results of Deeplab v3 plus on the test set.

Metric	Value
Jaccard	0.86104518
F1	0.91507558
Recall	0.947264645
Precision	0.906951733

For instance segmentation, the input image size is $1333 * 800$. The shorter side of images can be any value between 800 and 2000 for multi-scale training while keeping the ratio of the image the same. The best result on the test data is obtained from Mask Scoring R-CNN with ResNeXt-101 as the backbone. The results on the test set are shown in Table 5.

Table 5. Results of Mask Scoring R-CNN on the test set.

Metric	Value
Jaccard	0.858222295
F1	0.914602588
Recall	0.945745467
Precision	0.902458603

4   Conclusion

For task 1 and task 3 of the EndoTect challenge, we design different schemes. For the detection task, we focus on the unbalanced distribution problem of data and the representation network's effectiveness. We try to deal with the segmentation problem both in semantic and instance manners. A better result is reached by the semantic algorithm. Some custom tricks, such as multi-scale training, multi-scale testing, and ensemble learning, show their value in both these two tasks.

References

1. Berman, M., Rannen Triki, A., Blaschko, M.B.: The lovász-softmax loss: a tractable surrogate for the optimization of the intersection-over-union measure in neural networks. In: Proceedings of the IEEE Conference on Computer Vision and Pattern Recognition, pp. 4413–4421 (2018)
2. Borgli, H., et al.: HyperKvasir, a comprehensive multi-class image and video dataset for gastrointestinal endoscopy. Sci. Data **7**(1), 283 (2020). https://doi.org/10.1038/s41597-020-00622-y
3. Cai, Z., Vasconcelos, N.: Cascade r-cnn: delving into high quality object detection. In: Proceedings of the IEEE Conference on Computer Vision and Pattern Recognition, pp. 6154–6162 (2018)
4. Chen, L.C., Zhu, Y., Papandreou, G., Schroff, F., Adam, H.: Encoder-decoder with atrous separable convolution for semantic image segmentation. In: Proceedings of the European Conference on Computer Vision (ECCV), pp. 801–818 (2018)
5. He, K., Gkioxari, G., Dollár, P., Girshick, R.: Mask r-cnn. In: Proceedings of the IEEE International Conference on Computer Vision, pp. 2961–2969 (2017)
6. He, K., Zhang, X., Ren, S., Sun, J.: Deep residual learning for image recognition. In: Proceedings of the IEEE Conference on Computer Vision and Pattern Recognition, pp. 770–778 (2016)
7. Hicks, S.A., Jha, D., Thambawita, V., Halvorsen, P., Hammer, H., Riegler, M.A.: The EndoTect 2020 challenge: evaluation and comparison of classification, segmentation and inference time for endoscopy. In: ICPR 2020 Workshops and Challenges. LNCS, Springer (2020)
8. Huang, Z., Huang, L., Gong, Y., Huang, C., Wang, X.: Mask scoring r-cnn. In: Proceedings of the IEEE Conference on Computer Vision and Pattern Recognition, pp. 6409–6418 (2019)
9. Kang, B., et al.: Decoupling representation and classifier for long-tailed recognition. arXiv preprint arXiv:1910.09217 (2019)
10. Kingma, D.P., Ba, J.: Adam: a method for stochastic optimization. arXiv preprint arXiv:1412.6980 (2014)
11. Lin, T.Y., Goyal, P., Girshick, R., He, K., Dollár, P.: Focal loss for dense object detection. In: Proceedings of the IEEE International Conference on Computer Vision, pp. 2980–2988 (2017)
12. Luo, H., Gu, Y., Liao, X., Lai, S., Jiang, W.: Bag of tricks and a strong baseline for deep person re-identification. In: Proceedings of the IEEE Conference on Computer Vision and Pattern Recognition Workshops, pp. 0–0 (2019)
13. Ronneberger, O., Fischer, P., Brox, T.: U-Net: convolutional networks for biomedical image segmentation. In: Navab, N., Hornegger, J., Wells, W.M., Frangi, A.F. (eds.) MICCAI 2015. LNCS, vol. 9351, pp. 234–241. Springer, Cham (2015). https://doi.org/10.1007/978-3-319-24574-4_28

14. Szegedy, C., Vanhoucke, V., Ioffe, S., Shlens, J., Wojna, Z.: Rethinking the inception architecture for computer vision. In: Proceedings of the IEEE Conference on Computer Vision and Pattern Recognition, pp. 2818–2826 (2016)
15. Tan, M., Le, Q.V.: Efficientnet: Rethinking model scaling for convolutional neural networks. arXiv preprint arXiv:1905.11946 (2019)
16. Xie, S., Girshick, R., Dollár, P., Tu, Z., He, K.: Aggregated residual transformations for deep neural networks. In: Proceedings of the IEEE Conference on Computer Vision and Pattern Recognition, pp. 1492–1500 (2017)
17. Yuan, Y., Chen, X., Wang, J.: Object-contextual representations for semantic segmentation. arXiv preprint arXiv:1909.11065 (2019)
18. Yun, S., Han, D., Oh, S.J., Chun, S., Choe, J., Yoo, Y.: Cutmix: regularization strategy to train strong classifiers with localizable features. In: Proceedings of the IEEE International Conference on Computer Vision, pp. 6023–6032 (2019)
19. Zhang, H., Cisse, M., Dauphin, Y.N., Lopez-Paz, D.: mixup: Beyond empirical risk minimization. arXiv preprint arXiv:1710.09412 (2017)
20. Zhao, H., Shi, J., Qi, X., Wang, X., Jia, J.: Pyramid scene parsing network. In: Proceedings of the IEEE Conference on Computer Vision and Pattern Recognition, pp. 2881–2890 (2017)

Medical Diagnostic by Data Bagging for Various Instances of Neural Network

Zeshan Khan[1(✉)], Muhammad Usman Tariq Alvi[1], Muhammad Atif Tahir[1], and Shahbaz Memon[2]

[1] National University of Computer and Emerging Sciences, Karachi, Pakistan
{zeshan.khan,k173042,atif.tahir}@nu.edu.pk
[2] Jülich Supercomputing Centre, Forschungszentrum Jülich GmbH, Leo-Brandt Straße, 52428 Jülich, Germany
m.memon@fz-juelich.de

Abstract. Computer-aided diagnostics is helping the medical experts for fast diagnostics, using machine learning and representation learning techniques. Various types of diagnostics are using the assistance of machine learning approaches including endoscopy. In this paper, a transfer learning based bagging approach is investigated for endoscopy images analysis. Bagging is used to fine-tune several instances of the deep learning model with 70% of data in each bag. These all models of deep learning are combined to generate a single prediction using majority voting and neural-network-based decision approach. The best approach resulted in an F1-score of 0.60 on the EndoTech 2020 dataset having 23 abnormalities in the GI-Tract.

Keywords: Endoscopy analysis · Medical image classification · Deep learning · Bagging

1 Introduction

The computational power is increasing and led to advancements in disease detection using machine learning. There are several systems developed for disease detection using machine learning approaches [16,27]. Machine learning based diagnostics solved several medical problems including Genetic Diseases, XRay, ECG Analysis, GI-Tract abnormalities detection [5,8]. There are several datasets [2,25,26] and systems for the detection of GI-Tract abnormalities.

There are several systems using visual features [11,21] for the classification of abnormalities. The features set used by these systems are Haralick features [7], Local Binary Patterns [22] and LiRE [19] features. The detection speed of such systems is very high as the computation of such features and the application of some classifiers is faster. There is another set of classification techniques using deep learning and transfer learning for abnormalities detection in GI-Tract. These systems are using pre-trained neural networks on some image classification datasets, for example ImageNet [4] or MS-COCO [17], instead of random

A. Del Bimbo et al. (Eds.): ICPR 2020 Workshops, LNCS 12668, pp. 291–298, 2021.
https://doi.org/10.1007/978-3-030-68793-9_21

weights. The datasets for GI-Track abnormalities are limited and fine-tuning of the deep neural networks provided a good classification accuracy.

The approach in this paper is using bagging of the data to fine-tune multiple instances of the deep neural networks for classification. These instances of the neural network were used as a feature extractor. The features extracted from these neural networks were combined by using two different techniques namely majority voting and neural network based approach. The main contributions of the work, to solve the EndoTech challenge [8], is the bagging with neural-network, majority voting of the bagging results, and the neural-network-based decision on bagging outputs.

2   Datasets

There are several data-sets available for GI-Tract disease detection. The datasets have been gathered from various hospitals and then labeled by the medical experts. Most of the data-sets were build with the consideration of the abnormality classes. The comparable number of patients and images for each abnormality class. The dataset used in this research is the ICPR EndoTech 2020 dataset [2].

Hyper Kvasir, which is used for the challenge, is a dataset of GI-tract images annotated by various medical domain experts [2]. The dataset consists of 110,800 JPEG images of the GI-Track abnormalities varying image sizes and class distribution. The image dataset was divided into 10,662 labeled images (training) of 23 classes, 99,417 unlabeled images, and 721 images for the test set. The image sizes are varying from $352 \times 332 \times 3$ to $1079 \times 1920 \times 3$. The dataset is highly class imbalance with a minimum of 6 images in class hemorrhoids and a maximum of 1148 images in class bbps-2-3. Some of the images from ICPR EndoTech 2020 are shown in Fig. 1. The classes are belonging to the categories including anatomical landmarks, pathological and normal findings, and endoscopic procedures.

3   Literature Review

There is significant work available on GI-Tract abnormalities detection, using different techniques including state of the art feature extraction and classifications techniques and the representation learning techniques. Various features were extracted, including global features [19], Haralick features [7], local binary patterns [22] and local ternary patterns [29] for image classification. The set of extracted features were used for the various classification algorithms for the abnormalities detection [6,15,20,33,35]. The systems built on texture features were tested on various datasets for accuracy and speed detection. The detection of these systems was real-time with an accuracy of 0.90 to 0.95 with the F1-score of 0.91 to 0.94.

There are some approaches using texture features with the alteration of basic classification approaches. One such approach is applied to the Kvasir Version 1 dataset [26] and resulted in the accuracy and F1-score of 0.94 and 0.48 respectively [13].

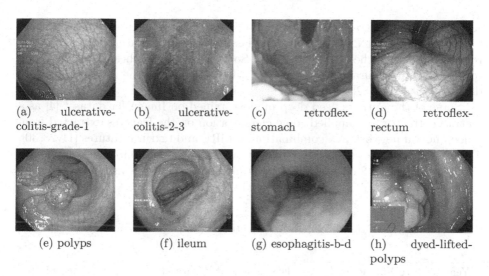

(a) ulcerative-colitis-grade-1   (b) ulcerative-colitis-2-3   (c) retroflex-stomach   (d) retroflex-rectum

(e) polyps   (f) ileum   (g) esophagitis-b-d   (h) dyed-lifted-polyps

Fig. 1. Images from ICPR 2020 dataset [2] with some of the classes

The higher amount of data availability in the domain of image classification enhanced the usage of deep learning in image classification [14]. The GI-Tract images are RGB and similar to the camera images in many aspects that enable the usage of transfer learning using the weights of the networks obtained by training on image classification datasets like ImageNet [4] and MS-COCO [17]. There is a sound contribution in the domain of transfer learning or the usage of deep models as feature extractors [11,21,29,34] for image classification. The deep models used in the domain of GI-Tract abnormalities detection are DenseNet, ResNet and VGG, Inception V3, Google LeNet, etc. The features extracted from these deep learning models were used by various classifiers and the combinations of those classifiers.

The abnormalities in the GI-Tract were detected by fine-tuning of the neural networks of ResNet, DenseNet, VGG, and Inception V3 [1,24,31]. These approaches applied to the Kvasir Version 1 dataset for the abnormalities detection and resulted in the F1-score of 0.92 with the accuracy of 0.95. The accuracy of the neural network based approaches increased to the 0.961 and F1-score of 0.847 by using LIRE features [19] with deep features [21]. The most used LIRE features were Tamura, JCD, AutoColor Correlation, Color Layout, PHOG, and Edge Histogram.

There are some alterations in the neural network proposed for the classification. The most common approach is using convolutions and max-pooling in parallel at starting stages and in the later stages, convolutions and pooling in series [23]. This approach, when applied to the Kvasir Version 1 dataset [26] resulted in an accuracy of 0.93 with an F1-score of 0.75. Another alteration of the deep learning approach is using the stacking of the networks [10,18]. An approach using RCNN at the end of RNN101 for the detection is applied to the

Kvasir Version 2 dataset [10]. The RCNN is a detector for the instances where the confidence of RNN is low for any class. The empirical accuracy of the approach is 0.99 with the F1-score of 0.95. Some other approaches of deep learning resulted in an accuracy of above 0.95 when applied on the Kvasir Version 2 dataset [5,9,12,25,32]

Some of the authors used deep models trained on ImageNet dataset [4] as a feature extractor and applied some classification on the features extracted from a deep neural network in a combination of LIRE and texture features [11,28,30]. These methodologies resulted in an accuracy of more than 0.97 when applied to the Kvasir Version 2 dataset [25]. A detailed analysis of the various approaches on Kvasir datasets [25,26] are available in the Table 1.

Table 1. Analysis of the abnormalities detection approaches on Kvasir datasets [25,26]

Year	Technique used	Features used	Dataset	Acc.	F1
2017 [1]	Inception V3, VGG16, SVM	Deep Features, LIRE Features	Kvasir Version 1 [26]	0.96	0.85
2017 [24]	Inception V3, ResNet50, Logistic Model Tree	Deep Features	Kvasir Version 1 [26]	0.96	0.83
2018 [10]	RNN and RCNN	Deep Features	Kvasir Version 2 [25]	0.99	0.95
2018 [9]	DenseNet169	Deep Features	Kvasir Version 2 [25]	0.99	0.94
2018 [12]	Inception ResNet V2	Deep Features	Kvasir Version 2 [25]	0.99	0.92
2018 [5]	ResNet	Deep Features	Kvasir Version 2 [25]	0.99	0.86
2018 [11]	Majority Voting	LIRE Features	Kvasir Version 2 [25]	0.98	0.76
2018 [31]	Deep Neural Networks	Deep Features	Kvasir Version 2 [25]	0.95	0.94

4   Approach

Bagging is a method of generating multiple versions of the data with or without repetition to get multiple predictions. The aggregation of these predictions can be helpful to generate an unbiased prediction [3]. The prediction in the bagging can be expressed by Eq. 1, where $C(X|D)$ is the prediction of class X by the classifier C at input D. The $P(C(X, D) == j)$ represents the probability of class j at input X using classifier C and with a data version of D.

$$Y(j|X) = \sum_{D \in Data-Versions} P(C(X, D) == j) \qquad (1)$$

The methodology used in this research is based on bagging and neural network fine-tuning, for the prediction of abnormality in a GI-Tract image. In this research, eleven data chunks or bags of the data were generated randomly with repetition using 70% of the data in each bag. The data bags were random so there may also exist the class imbalanced (which reflects reality in medical settings) problem in the data bags. A 169 layer DenseNet was taken as a deep neural network with its ImageNet weights. The last fully connected dense layer of the DenseNet169 was replaced with a new set of dense layers with 1024, 512, and 23 output neurons with an activation function of softmax. Eleven instances of the DenseNet169 were fine-tuned for 500 epochs each on a different bag (70% chunk) of the dataset. The fine-tuning of the DenseNet169 returned new weights for each instance called a separate instance of DenseNet169.

The training and testing dataset was provided to these eleven instances of the DenseNet169 and extracted a vector of size 23 for each image as a class probability. These eleven 23-dimensional vectors were concatenated to generate a single 253-dimensional vector which was used as a feature vector. The 253-dimensional feature vector was taken for the classification using two different approaches. These two approaches are as follows:

4.1   Hard Majority Voting

The hard majority-voting is applied to the probabilities extracted from all eleven models. The majority class of all the models was selected and then the maximum repetition class label from eleven retrieved labels was selected as the final class.

4.2   Neural Network for Class Prediction

A neural network of five fully connected layers built with the activation function Relu, Sigmoid, and Softmax. The neural network was trained for 500 epochs on the 253-dimensional input vector to provide an output of class probability for 23 classes. The trained network was used for the detection of the class with the highest class probability.

5   Experimental Setup and Results

A set of Eleven bags, with repetition, of the data were extracted from each dataset with the 70% data usage. These bags were used for the fine-tuning of the DenseNet169. The network's output at the Global Average Pooling Layer named avg_pool is provided to three fully connected dense layers of 1024, 512, and 23 (Number of Classes in the dataset) neurons. The fine-tuning is done for 500 epochs with a batch size of 25 for all the layers. The Eleven fine-tuned instances were used to extract the features of the size 23. There was no constant layer, the layer with unchanged weights. The fine-tuning was done for the layers starting from the first layer of DenseNet to the last dense layer of 23 neurons. The parameters of the bagging are as follows:

- Repetition: **with repetition**
- Data size of the bag: **70%**

- Neural Networks used: **DenseNet169**
- Constant/Excluded from fine-tuning Layers: **0**
- Network output Layer Name: **avg_pool**
- Network output Layer Type: **Global Average Pooling**
- Layers added at end of DenseNet169: **Three Dense Layers**
- Fine-tuning epochs: **500**
- Batch size: **25**
- Feature/Output classes size: **23**

The features extracted from all the bags are combined using majority voting and neural network based approach for the aggregated output classes of test data.

5.1 Results and Analysis

The methodology discussed in Sect. 4 was applied to the dataset by using 70% as training and 30% as testing. The f1-scores, on the training data, by applying majority voting and neural network approach were 0.88 and 0.92 respectively. The combination approach resulted in an accuracy of more than 0.92. The F1-score of classes hemorrhoids, barretts, barretts-short-segment, and ileum was 0.0, 0.53, 0.58, and 0.5 respectively. The F1-score for the rest of the classes was more than 0.80. The TP of the training data (30%) was 2969.

The same approach is applied to the test data provided by the competition organizers resulted in the F1-score of 0.60 with an MCC of 0.57 on the best run. Various accuracy measures computed on the test data are TP = 435, TN = 15576, FP = 286, FN = 286, Precision = 0.60, Recall = 0.60, Specificity = 0.98.

The accuracy measure showing that there are some of the classes with a good detection rate while the rest with low. The reason of low accuracy is the highly class imbalance data. The training samples for some of the classes are very few i.e. 6 images for training that led to the low detection rate (0) for such classes.

6   Conclusion and Future Work

Bagging of the neural network is applied for the abnormalities detection in GI-Tract. The dataset of the GI-Tract abnormalities was the set of images taken from endoscopic procedures. The usage of different bags for training different instances of neural network reduced the business due to class imbalance. The bagging approach with hard majority voting resulted in an F1-score of 0.92 on the training data and 0.60 on the test data.

In the future, data-augmentation will be explored and used for the classes with very few training samples. The classes with a higher miss-classification rate will be further explored and analyzed. Some state of the art features will be added with the deep learning approaches for a better understanding of the images.

References

1. Agrawal, T., Gupta, R., Sahu, S., Espy-Wilson, C.Y.: Scl-umd at the medico task-mediaeval 2017: transfer learning based classification of medical images. In: MediaEval (2017)
2. Borgli, H., et al.: HyperKvasir, a comprehensive multi-class image and video dataset for gastrointestinal endoscopy. Sci. Data **7**(1), 283 (2020)
3. Breiman, L.: Bagging predictors. Mach. Learn. **24**(2), 123–140 (1996)
4. Deng, J., Dong, W., Socher, R., Li, L.J., Li, K., Fei-Fei, L.: Imagenet: a large-scale hierarchical image database. In: 2009 IEEE Conference on Computer Vision and Pattern Recognition, pp. 248–255. IEEE (2009)
5. Dias, D., Dias, U.: Transfer learning with CNN architectures for classifying gastrointestinal diseases and anatomical landmarks. In: MediaEval (2018)
6. Esgiar, A.N., Naguib, R.N., Sharif, B.S., Bennett, M.K., Murray, A.: Microscopic image analysis for quantitative measurement and feature identification of normal and cancerous colonic mucosa. IEEE Trans. Inform. Technol. Biomed. **2**(3), 197–203 (1998)
7. Haralick, R.M., Shanmugam, K., et al.: Textural features for image classification. IEEE Trans. Syst. Man Cybern. **6**, 610–621 (1973)
8. Hicks, S.A., Jha, D., Thambawita, V., Halvorsen, P., Hammer, H., Riegler, M.A.: The EndoTect 2020 challenge: evaluation and comparison of classification, segmentation and inference time for endoscopy. In: ICPR 2020 Workshops and Challenges. LNCS, Springer (2020)
9. Hicks, S.A., Smedsrud, P.H., Halvorsen, P., Riegler, M.: Deep learning based disease detection using domain specific transfer learning. In: MediaEval (2018)
10. Hoang, T.H., Nguyen, H.D., Nguyen, T.A., Nguyen, V.T., Tran, M.T.: An application of residual network and faster-RCNN for medico: multimedia task at mediaeval 2018. In: MediaEval (2018)
11. Khan, Z., Tahir, M.A.: Majority voting of heterogeneous classifiers for finding abnormalities in the gastro-intestinal tract. In: MediaEval (2018)
12. Kirkerød, M., Thambawita, V., Riegler, M., Halvorsen, P.: Using preprocessing as a tool in medical image detection. In: MediaEval (2018)
13. Ko, T.H., Gu, Z., Liu, Y.: Weighted discriminant embedding: discriminant subspace learning for imbalanced medical data classification. In: MediaEval (2018)
14. Krizhevsky, A., Sutskever, I., Hinton, G.E.: Imagenet classification with deep convolutional neural networks. In: Advances in Neural Information Processing Systems, pp. 1097–1105 (2012)
15. Kumar, A., Kim, J., Lyndon, D., Fulham, M., Feng, D.: An ensemble of fine-tuned convolutional neural networks for medical image classification. IEEE J. Biomed. Health Inform. **21**(1), 31–40 (2016)
16. Kumar, V.B., Kumar, S.S., Saboo, V.: Dermatological disease detection using image processing and machine learning. In: 2016 Third International Conference on Artificial Intelligence and Pattern Recognition (AIPR), pp. 1–6. IEEE (2016)
17. Lin, T.-Y., et al.: Microsoft COCO: common objects in context. In: Fleet, D., Pajdla, T., Schiele, B., Tuytelaars, T. (eds.) ECCV 2014. LNCS, vol. 8693, pp. 740–755. Springer, Cham (2014). https://doi.org/10.1007/978-3-319-10602-1_48
18. Liu, Y., Gu, Z., Cheung, W.K.: Hkbu at mediaeval 2017 medico: medical multimedia task (2017)
19. Lux, M., Chatzichristofis, S.A.: Lire: lucene image retrieval: an extensible java cbir library. In: Proceedings of the 16th ACM International Conference on Multimedia, pp. 1085–1088. ACM (2008)

20. Maroulis, D.E., Iakovidis, D.K., Karkanis, S.A., Karras, D.A.: Cold: a versatile detection system for colorectal lesions in endoscopy video-frames. Comput. Methods Programs Biomed. **70**(2), 151–166 (2003)

21. Naqvi, S.S.A., Nadeem, S., Zaid, M., Tahir, M.A.: Ensemble of texture features for finding abnormalities in the gastro-intestinal tract. In: MediaEval (2017)

22. Ojala, T., Pietikäinen, M., Harwood, D.: A comparative study of texture measures with classification based on featured distributions. Pattern Recogn. **29**(1), 51–59 (1996)

23. Petscharnig, S., Schöffmann, K., Lux, M.: An inception-like CNN architecture for gi disease and anatomical landmark classification. In: MediaEval (2017)

24. Pogorelov, K., et al.: A comparison of deep learning with global features for gastrointestinal disease detection (2017)

25. Pogorelov, K., et al.: Medico multimedia task at mediaeval 2018. In: CEUR Workshop Proceedings (2018)

26. Riegler, M., et al.: Multimedia for medicine: the medico task at mediaeval **2017** (2017)

27. Saad, A.E., Elsayed, A.R., Mahmoud, S.E., Elkheshen, Y.M.: Breast cancer detection using machine learning (2020)

28. Steiner, M., Lux, M., Halvorsen, P.: The 2018 medico multimedia task submission of team noat using neural network features and search-based classification. In: MediaEval (2018)

29. Tan, X., Triggs, W.: Enhanced local texture feature sets for face recognition under difficult lighting conditions. IEEE Trans. Image Process. **19**(6), 1635–1650 (2010)

30. Taschwer, M., Primus, M.J., Schoeffmann, K., Marques, O.: Early and late fusion of classifiers for the mediaeval medico task. In: MediaEval (2018)

31. Thambawita, V., et al.: The medico-task 2018: disease detection in the gastrointestinal tract using global features and deep learning. CoRR abs/1810.13278 (2018)

32. Thambawita, V., et al.: The medico-task 2018: disease detection in the gastrointestinal tract using global features and deep learning. arXiv preprint arXiv:1810.13278 (2018)

33. Tjoa, M.P., Krishnan, S.M.: Feature extraction for the analysis of colon status from the endoscopic images. BioMed. Eng. OnLine **2**(1), 9 (2003)

34. Waqas, M., Khan, Z., Anjum, S., Tahir, M.A.: Lung-wise tuberculosis analysis and automatic ct report generation with hybrid feature and ensemble learning. In: CLEF2020 Working Notes. CEUR Workshop Proceedings, Thessaloniki, Greece, CEUR-WS. org¡ http://ceur-ws. org¿(September 22-25 2020)

35. Zheng, M., Krishnan, S., Tjoa, M.P.: A fusion-based clinical decision support for disease diagnosis from endoscopic images. Comput. Biol. Med. **35**(3), 259–274 (2005)

Hybrid Loss with Network Trimming for Disease Recognition in Gastrointestinal Endoscopy

Qi He[1(⊠)], Sophia Bano[2], Danail Stoyanov[2], and Siyang Zuo[1]

[1] Key Laboratory of Mechanism Theory and Equipment Design of Ministry of
Education, Tianjin University, Tianjin, China
howard@tju.edu.cn

[2] Wellcome/EPSRC Centre for Interventional and Surgical Sciences (WEISS),
University College London, London, UK

Abstract. *EndoTect Challenge 2020*, which aims at the detection of gastrointestinal diseases and abnormalities, consists of three tasks including Detection, Efficient Detection and Segmentation in endoscopic images. Although pathologies belonging to different classes can be manually separated by experienced experts, however, existing classification models struggle to discriminate them due to low inter-class variability. As a result, the models' convergence deteriorates. To this end, we propose a hybrid loss function to stabilise model training. For the detection and efficient detection tasks, we utilise *ResNet-152* and *MobileNetV3* architectures, respectively, along with the hybrid loss function. For the segmentation task, *Cascade Mask R-CNN* is investigated. In this paper, we report the architecture of our detection and segmentation models and the performance of our methods on *HyperKvasir* and *EndoTect* test dataset.

Keywords: Endoscopy · Object detection · Polyp segmentation ·
Computer-assisted intervention

1 Introduction

The gastrointestinal endoscopy is a routine examination process via natural cavity for digestive disease detection. It is the most efficient procedure for gastrointestinal disease detection. Although biopsy is the only gold standard for recognising pathology, previous studies on endoscopic imaging reported the potential capability of endoscopy for lesion classification [10,15]. In these reports, the micro-vascular pattern and micro-surface pattern of the mucosa under the view of endoscopy provided strong evidence for the preliminary diagnosis of gastrointestinal lesion [16]. Well-trained practitioners and experienced endoscopists can detect benign polyps and malignant tumours and tag these lesion with different labels through the micro-anatomical findings visualised by the endoscope. However, these critical clues are unintelligible for a novice practitioner due to

© Springer Nature Switzerland AG 2021
A. Del Bimbo et al. (Eds.): ICPR 2020 Workshops, LNCS 12668, pp. 299–306, 2021.
https://doi.org/10.1007/978-3-030-68793-9_22

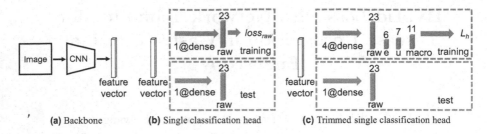

Fig. 1. Proposed hybrid loss with trimming for improving model stability during training. The baseline models are trained using backbone (a) and single classification head (b). $loss_{raw}$ denotes $CE(y_{raw}, \hat{y}_{raw})$. The proposed method with hybrid loss are trained with backbone (a) and multiple classification heads and trimmed to single head during inference (c).

their seemly similar appearances. To improve the quality of endoscopy examination, several guidelines have been proposed aiming at quantifying the anatomical sites to diminish the blind points [1,15]. The recent studies on smart quality control methods based on these guidelines also show their efficiency for endoscopic quality control [7,14]. These computer-assisted lesion detection and anatomical site detection methods showed great potential towards automating the digestive disease diagnosis and endoscopic quality control.

Towards this end, *EndoTect Challenge 2020 (EndoTect)* called for recognising digestive disease through computer vision methods [8]. The challenge consists of three tasks, namely, detection, efficient detection and segmentation. In this paper, we propose the hybrid loss-based methods utilising *ResNet-152* [6] and *MobileNetV3* [9] for the detection and efficient detection tasks, respectively. The proposed hybrid loss helped in improving the model convergence. For the polyp segmentation task, we use the *Cascade Mask R-CNN* [3] method. Our methods are evaluated on the *HyperKvasir* dataset [2] and the test data of *EndoTect*.

2 Methodology

2.1 Detection and Efficient Detection

Baseline Methods. *ResNet-152* [6] and *MobileNetV3-large* [9] are the backbone Convolutional Neural Network (CNN) models that we utilise for the detection and efficient detection tasks, respectively. These models are pre-trained on the *ImageNet* [5] dataset. For fine-tuning, the last fully connected layers are replaced by new dense layers with output units equal to the number of disease classes.

Hybrid Loss Function. We propose a hybrid loss function (L_h) in which the disease labels are rearranged into raw, macro, oesophagus (e) and ulcer (u).

$$L_h = CE(y_{raw}, \hat{y}_{raw}) + CE(y_{macro}, \hat{y}_{macro}) + CE(y_e, \hat{y}_e) + CE(y_u, \hat{y}_u), \quad (1)$$

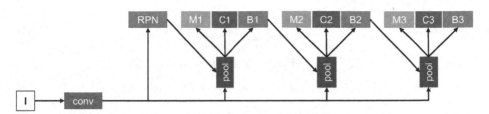

Fig. 2. *Cascade Mask R-CNN.* "I" is input image, "conv" backbone convolution, "RPN" region proposal network, "pool" region-wise feature extraction, "B" bounding box, "C" classification and "M" mask.

where CE is the cross-entropy loss. L_h is implemented by adding multiple classification heads after the backbone model as shown in Fig. 1. Corresponding labels of y_{raw}, y_{macro}, y_e and y_u for training multiple classification heads are listed in Sect. 2.3. Our models are trained using the proposed hybrid loss function made up of four cross-entropy loss functions as shown in Fig. 1(b).

Model Trimming. The multiple classification heads derived from single classification head have a dense layer for the detection task with 23 output units as defined in *EndoTect* and three more dense layers for the extra tasks. This addition of extra units is discussed in more detail in Sect. 4. Though these extra layers improved our model stability during training, they are redundant for inference. Therefore, after training, the multiple classification heads model is trimmed into the single classification head model as shown in Fig. 1(b). This change makes the model lighter and faster during inference.

For brevity, "⟨*model*⟩" denotes backbone, such as *ResNet-152*, "⟨*model*⟩ *w.*" denotes the model trained with hybrid loss, and "⟨*model*⟩ *w.* ⟨*head*⟩" denotes the classification head, such as *raw*, from model trained with hybrid loss.

2.2 Segmentation Model

Our solution is based on *Cascade Mask R-CNN* [3] as shown in Fig. 2, which is implemented using the MMDetection toolbox [4]. The pipeline is formulated as:

$$
\begin{aligned}
m_t &= M_t(P(x, b_{t-1})), \\
c_t &= C_t(P(x, b_{t-1})), \\
b_t &= B_t(P(x, b_{t-1})).
\end{aligned}
\tag{2}
$$

where x indicate the CNN features of backbone network, $P(.)$ is a pooling operator, e.g., Region of Interest (RoI) Align or RoI pooling, M_t, C_t and B_t denote the mask, class and box head at the tth stage, m_t, c_t and b_t represent the corresponding mask predictions, class predictions and box predictions, respectively. The overall loss function (L_{seg}) takes the form of a multi-task learning:

$$L_{seg} = \sum_{t=1}^{T} (L_{mask}^t + L_{bbox}^t), \tag{3}$$

$$L_{mask}^t(m_t, \hat{m}_t) = BCE(m_t, \hat{m}_t), \tag{4}$$

$$L_{bbox}^t(c_t, b_t, \hat{c}_t, \hat{b}_t) = L_{cls}(c_t, \hat{c}_t) + L_{reg}(b_t, \hat{b}_t). \tag{5}$$

Here, L_{mask}^t is the loss of mask predictions at stage t, which adopts the binary cross-entropy loss. L_{bbox}^t is the loss of the bounding box predictions at stage t, which combines two terms $L_{cls}(c_t, \hat{c}_t)$ and $L_{reg}(b_t, \hat{b}_t)$, respectively for classification and bounding box regression.

2.3   Data Augmentation and Training Details

Data Augmentation. Training augmentation for detection and efficient detection consists of contrast augmentation, colour shift, brightness augmentation, flipping, perspective transformation and blur. Different from detection, flipping, cutout, colour shift, JPEG compression and affine transform augmentations are applied at random for training the segmentation model.

Labels of Hybrid Loss. The hybrid loss takes label from four categories:

- Raw labels are the original 23 classes provided for *EndoTect*.
- Macro labels consist of 11 classes, namely, 'other', 'bbps-0-1', 'bbps-2-3', 'dyed-lifted-polyps', 'dyed-resection-margins', 'impacted-stool', 'normal-cecum', 'normal-pylorus', 'polyp', 'retroflex-rectum' and 'retroflex-stomach'.
- Oesophagus labels consist of 6 classes, namely, 'other', 'barretts', 'normal-z-line', 'oesophagitis-a', 'oesophagitis-b-d' and 'short-segment-barretts'.
- Ulcer labels consist of 7 classes, namely, 'other', 'ulcerative-colitis-grade-0-1', 'ulcerative-colitis-grade-1-2', 'ulcerative-colitis-grade-2-3', 'ulcerative-colitis-grade-1', 'ulcerative-colitis-grade-2', 'ulcerative-colitis-grade-3'.

Implementation Details. The detection and efficient detection models are re-implemented with PyTorch [13]. We fine-tuned the models with single GPU for 40 epochs by SGD optimiser with an initial learning rate of 0.003 and momentum of 0.9, and decrease it by 0.1 after 10th, 20th and 30th epochs. The batch sizes for *ResNet-152* and *MobileNetV3* are set to 32 and 128, respectively.

The segmentation model is re-implemented using the MMDetection [4] open-source toolbox based on PyTorch. The model is pre-trained from COCO dataset [12]. Then we fine-tuned it with 2 GPUs for 20 epochs with an initial learning rate of 0.004 and decrease it by 0.1 after 10th and 18th epochs, respectively. The batch size is set to 2 for each GPU. Image data is resized to 1024×1024 pixel resolution for training and inference. For inference, we adjusted the thresholds of the detector. The Non-Maximum Suppression (NMS) threshold of Region Proposal Network (RPN), score threshold of R-CNN, NMS threshold of R-CNN and mask threshold of R-CNN are set to 0.7, 0.5, 0.3 and 0.45, respectively.

Table 1. Average results for detection and efficient detection models

Method	Dataset	Macro average			Micro average			
		PREC	REC	F1	PREC	REC	F1	MCC
ResNet-152 raw	HyperKvasir	0.588	0.584	0.584	0.901	0.901	0.901	0.892
ResNet-152 w. raw	HyperKvasir	0.598	0.601	0.596	0.904	0.904	0.904	0.895
ResNet-152 w. raw	EndoTect	0.683	0.646	0.659	0.913	0.913	0.913	0.903
MobileNetV3 raw	HyperKvasir	0.513	0.556	0.504	0.845	0.845	0.845	0.833
MobileNetV3 w. raw	HyperKvasir	0.519	0.557	0.505	0.851	0.851	0.851	0.840
MobileNetV3 w. raw	EndoTect	0.528	0.496	0.503	0.785	0.785	0.785	0.765

3 Results

3.1 Detection and Efficient Detection

Evaluation metrics consist of precision (PREC), recall (REC), f1-score (F1) and Matthews correlation coefficient (MCC). We trained and validated *ResNet-152* (*ResNet-152 raw*), *ResNet-152* with hybrid loss (*ResNet-152 w. raw*), *MobileNetV3* (*MobileNetV3 raw*) and *MobileNetV3* with hybrid loss (*MobileNetV3 w. raw*) on *HyperKvasir* dataset following the 2-fold cross validation on the official splits [2]. For *EndoTect*, the models with hybrid loss are trained on *HyperKvasir* and evaluated on the test data provided by *EndoTect*. The models with hybrid loss have an improved performance on *HyperKvasir* than the baseline as shown in Table 1. The *ResNet-152 w. raw* has a superior performance on the images from macro labels than oesophagus labels and ulcer labels, which is demonstrated by the confusion matrix of detection models on *HyperKvasir* as shown in Fig. 3.

MobileNetV3 w. is susceptible to the extra black border on the test dataset due to its lighter structure. This is supported by the performance drop of the *MobileNetV3 w. raw* on the test data as shown in Table 1. The test data included dark border regions that were not present in the training data, which made the test data distribution to be slightly different than the training data. These dark borders made the scale of the colour image region on the test data smaller than training data. Though there is some performance drop on it, *MobileNetV3 w. raw* has a great advantage on speed since it has much fewer parameters than *ResNet-152 w. raw*. The speed of *MobileNetV3 w. raw* is evaluated using average time, minimum time, max time, average FPS, minimum FPS and maximum FPS, which are found to be 7.7 ms, 7.6 ms, 22.2 ms, 129.7, 45.0 and 132.0, respectively.

3.2 Polyp Segmentation

The segmentation model is evaluated using 2-fold cross validation on *HyperKvasir* dataset. For submission, the model are trained on *HyperKvasir* dataset and evaluated on *EndoTect* test dataset. The evaluation results are shown in Table 2,

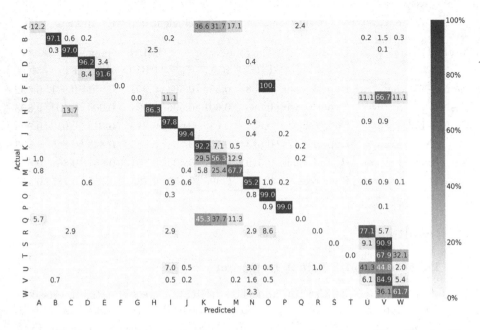

Fig. 3. Confusion matrix of *ResNet-152 w. raw* evaluated on *HyperKvasir*. The labelling of the classes follows [2].

Table 2. Evaluation of segmentation model

Method	Dataset	Jaccard	F1-score	Recall	Precision
Cascade Mask R-CNN	HyperKvasir	0.792	0.850	0.904	0.846
Cascade Mask R-CNN	EndoTect	0.822	0.879	0.882	0.915

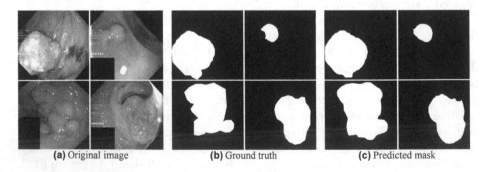

(a) Original image   (b) Ground truth   (c) Predicted mask

Fig. 4. Qualitative evaluation of the segmentation model

and the qualitative evaluation is shown in Fig. 4. F1-score and Jaccard of 0.879 and 0.822 on the EndoTect test dataset which shows promising performance of our trained model.

4   Discussion

We proposed a hybrid loss to stabilise convergence of model, which slightly improved the performance of *ResNet-152* and *MobileNetV3* on *HyperKvasir* as shown in Table 1. This change is motivated by an observation, that the CNN model is likely to wrongly classify oesophagus and ulcer images. Such misclassification would last during the whole training process. To narrow the range of misclassification, we filtered these indiscriminate labels through the confusion matrix of *ResNet-152* on *HyperKvasir* and redesign the labels based on the connected component from the confusion matrix. Though focal loss [11] has been demonstrated to achieve a better performance than CE loss in the object detection task, CE loss was found to be experimentally better than the focal loss in this task. Therefore, we designed this hybrid loss (presented in Sect. 2) using the rearrange labels and CE loss for detection and efficient detection tasks.

Beside the redesigning of labels, we also focused on improving the performance of models via strong image augmentation. After we experimented with various combinations of data augmentation, we found the blur in image augmentation to be detrimental for training segmentation model, because blurring makes it hard to distinguish the features representing boundary and minuscule texture.

5   Conclusion

We addressed the problems of disease detection, efficient disease detection and polyp segmentation for the EndoTect2020 Challenge. We introduced the hybrid loss and model trimming for improving the gastrointestinal disease detection in endoscopic images. The hybrid loss and model trimming is shown to stabilise model training, improve classification of indiscriminate classes and make the model lighter and faster during inference. We utilised Cascade Mask R-CNN with heavy data augmentation for polyp segmentation. We observed that heavy data augmentation helped in better generalising the model for unseen dataset. This was evident from our model superior performance on the EndoTect challenge test dataset compared to the HyperKvasir dataset. The proposed methods are experimentally demonstrated efficient for gastrointestinal image classification and polyp segmentation. In future work, we plan to further improve the multiple classification heads of the hybrid loss for further improving the model performance.

Acknowledgements. This work is supported by the Key Technologies Research and Development Program of China (2019YFB1311501), National Natural Science Foundation of China (61773280), Engineering and Physical Sciences Research Council (EP/P027938/1, EP/R004080/1) and Wellcome/EPSRC Centre for Interventional and Surgical Sciences (WEISS) at UCL (203145Z/16/Z).

References

1. Beg, S., et al.: Quality standards in upper gastrointestinal endoscopy: a position statement of the British Society of Gastroenterology (BSG) and Association of Upper Gastrointestinal Surgeons of Great Britain and Ireland (AUGIS). Gut **66**(11), 1886–1899 (2017)
2. Borgli, H., et al.: HyperKvasir, a comprehensive multi-class image and video dataset for gastrointestinal endoscopy. Sci. Data **7**(1), 283 (2020)
3. Cai, Z., Vasconcelos, N.: Cascade R-CNN: high quality object detection and instance segmentation. arXiv:1906.09756 [cs] (2019)
4. Chen, K., et al.: MMDetection: open MMLab detection toolbox and benchmark. arXiv:1906.07155 [cs] (2019)
5. Deng, J., Dong, W., Socher, R., Li, L., Li, K., Fei-Fei, L.: ImageNet: a large-scale hierarchical image database. In: 2009 IEEE Conference on Computer Vision and Pattern Recognition, pp. 248–255 (2009)
6. He, K., Zhang, X., Ren, S., Sun, J.: Deep residual learning for image recognition. In: Proceedings of the IEEE Conference on Computer Vision and Pattern Recognition, pp. 770–778 (2016)
7. He, Q., et al.: Deep learning-based anatomical site classification for upper gastrointestinal endoscopy. Int. J. Comput. Assist. Radiol. Surg. **15**(7), 1085–1094 (2020). https://doi.org/10.1007/s11548-020-02148-5
8. Hicks, S.A., Jha, D., Thambawita, V., Halvorsen, P., Hammer, H., Riegler, M.A.: The EndoTect 2020 challenge: evaluation and comparison of classification, segmentation and inference time for endoscopy. In: ICPR 2020 Workshops and Challenges. LNCS, Springer (2020)
9. Howard, A., et al.: Searching for MobileNetV3. In: Proceedings of the IEEE International Conference on Computer Vision, pp. 1314–1324 (2019)
10. Kaise, M., et al.: Magnifying endoscopy combined with narrow-band imaging for differential diagnosis of superficial depressed gastric lesions. Endoscopy **41**(04), 310–315 (2009)
11. Lin, T.Y., Goyal, P., Girshick, R., He, K., Dollár, P.: Focal loss for dense object detection. arXiv:1708.02002 [cs] (2018)
12. Lin, T.Y., et al.: Microsoft COCO: common objects in context. arXiv:1405.0312 [cs] (2015)
13. Paszke, A., et al.: PyTorch: an imperative style, high-performance deep learning library. In: Advances in Neural Information Processing Systems 32, pp. 8026–8037 (2019)
14. Wu, L., et al.: Randomised controlled trial of WISENSE, a real-time quality improving system for monitoring blind spots during esophagogastroduodenoscopy. Gut **68**(12), 2161–2169 (2019)
15. Yao, K.: The endoscopic diagnosis of early gastric cancer. Ann. Gastroenterol. Q. Publ. Hellenic Soc. Gastroenterol. **26**(1), 11 (2013)
16. Yao, K.: Zoom Gastroscopy: Magnifying Endoscopy in the Stomach. Springer, Tokyo (2014). https://doi.org/10.1007/978-4-431-54207-0

DDANet: Dual Decoder Attention Network for Automatic Polyp Segmentation

Nikhil Kumar Tomar[1], Debesh Jha[1,3(✉)], Sharib Ali[4,5], Håvard D. Johansen[3], Dag Johansen[3], Michael A. Riegler[1], and Pål Halvorsen[1,2]

[1] SimulaMet, Oslo, Norway
debesh@simula.no
[2] Oslo Metropolitan University, Oslo, Norway
[3] UIT The Arctic University of Norway, Tromsø, Norway
[4] Department of Engineering Science, University of Oxford, Oxford, UK
[5] Oxford NIHR Biomedical Research Centre, Oxford, UK

Abstract. Colonoscopy is the gold standard for examination and detection of colorectal polyps. Localization and delineation of polyps can play a vital role in treatment (e.g., surgical planning) and prognostic decision making. Polyp segmentation can provide detailed boundary information for clinical analysis. Convolutional neural networks have improved the performance in colonoscopy. However, polyps usually possess various challenges, such as intra-and inter-class variation and noise. While manual labeling for polyp assessment requires time from experts and is prone to human error (e.g., missed lesions), an automated, accurate, and fast segmentation can improve the quality of delineated lesion boundaries and reduce missed rate. The Endotect challenge provides an opportunity to benchmark computer vision methods by training on the publicly available Hyperkvasir and testing on a separate unseen dataset. In this paper, we propose a novel architecture called "DDANet" based on a dual decoder attention network. Our experiments demonstrate that the model trained on the Kvasir-SEG dataset and tested on an unseen dataset achieves a dice coefficient of 0.7874, mIoU of 0.7010, recall of 0.7987, and a precision of 0.8577, demonstrating the generalization ability of our model.

Keywords: Polyp segmentation · Deep learning · Convolutional neural network · Benchmarking

1 Introduction

Colorectal cancer is one of the leading causes of cancer. Colonoscopy is a standard medical procedure for the surveillance examination and treatment. Regular screening and removal of pre-cancerous lesions through colonoscopy is essential for early cancer detection and prevention. Studies suggest that the miss-rate of adenoma is between 6 to 27% [1].

© Springer Nature Switzerland AG 2021
A. Del Bimbo et al. (Eds.): ICPR 2020 Workshops, LNCS 12668, pp. 307–314, 2021.
https://doi.org/10.1007/978-3-030-68793-9_23

The automatic segmentation of the suspected areas with lesions in colonoscopy images can play a crucial role, and identifying each colon pixel can significantly impact clinical settings. With the increase of publicly available datasets, dominant methodology such as convolutional neural network, improved hardware, and collaboration between computational and clinical communities to tackle the problems in endoscopic imaging through computer vision tasks is gaining momentum than ever before. An automatic polyp detection or surveillance system can help to achieve low-cost design solutions and save time of clinicians allowing them to use their time to look into more severe cases.

In this respect, the Endotect challenge [8] offers three tasks, namely, detection of Gastrointestinal (GI) tract images, efficient detection on the same images, and automatic polyp segmentation. The detection and efficient detection task are based on the HyperKvasir dataset [5], and the segmentation is based on the Kvasir-SEG dataset [12]. Out of these three tasks, we participated in the "segmentation task", where the goal was to generate an automatic segmentation of the polyps for the unseen dataset.

In this paper, we propose a novel deep learning architecture, called Dual Decoder Attention Network (DDANet), for automatic polyp segmentation. It follows an encoder-decoder scheme and incorporates a single encoder that is shared by two parallel decoders, where the first decoder acts as a segmentation network and the second decoder acts as an autoencoder network. The autoencoder network helps to strengthen the feature maps in the encoder network. It is used as an auxiliary task training, which is used to generate an attention map. This attention map is used in each decoder to improve the semantic representation of the feature maps. This, in turn, helps to improve the performance of the entire network. The proposed DDANet is fed with an RGB input image, where it predicts the segmentation mask and the reconstructed grayscale image. The architecture is efficient in terms of Frame per Second (FPS) and also has a decent evaluation score. These metrics are the requirement for the real-world settings toward developing a Computer Aided Diagnosis (CADx) system.

2   Related Work

Automatic polyp segmentation task is a well-defined computer vision problem. Recently, there have been several competitions [2–4,10] and individual efforts [6,7,9,11,13] toward building a CADx system for the polyp segmentation. With these competitions and individual efforts, polyp segmentation is becoming more and more mature. However, comparing models and results of the many individual approaches is difficult due to the use of diverse (often publicly non-available) datasets and different hardware. In this respect, competitions provide an opportunity to benchmark and compare the designed methods with other competitors' on the same dataset. Moreover, the evaluation metrics are independently calculated by the organizers, including the ranking decision of each team.

The competitions can help us to define the strengths and weaknesses of each method. It also provides us with an opportunity to disseminate methods and

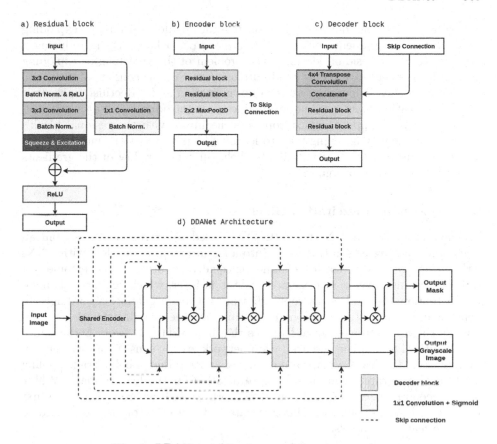

Fig. 1. DDANet architecture and its components.

discuss the results collectively in the same space. Through this year's Endotect challenge, we provide a novel solution to develop more efficient algorithms that can be useful to build an automatic polyp segmentation system. Our architecture is composed of an autoencoder branch in addition to the segmentation branch, which is different from other encoder-decoder based network (for example, UNet [14], ResUNet++ [13], DoubleUNet [11]). The benefit of incorporating autoencoder in the network can be seen from the quantitative and qualitative results.

3   DDANet

In this section, we will first describe each component of our DDANet and then detail the overall proposed DDANet architecture.

3.1   Residual Block

As the network depth increases, the performance also increases to a certain limit as the gradients can be effectively calculated. However, after a certain depth, the performance of the model may be impacted due to the vanishing or exploding gradients as the gradients become either zero or too large. By introducing a skip-connection in residual learning, the problem of the vanishing or exploding gradients has been solved. Our residual block (see Fig. 1a) consists of two 3×3 convolutions, each followed by a batch normalization and a Rectified linear unit (ReLU) activation function. The residual learning introduces a shortcut connection or identity mapping, which connects the input with the residual block's output. The identity mapping tries to learn an identity function since the input is directly passed to the output. It also helps in a better flow of the gradients during the backpropagation.

3.2   Squeeze and Excitation Block

A Convolutional Neural Network (CNN) is used to extract features from an image and then transform the image into a feature map. A problem with CNNs is that they treat every feature channel as equally important. To overcome this problem, we introduce a squeeze and excitation layer, which acts as a channel-wise attention mechanism. It re-weights every feature channel accordingly to create a more accurate feature map. In this way, the overall network becomes more sensitive towards essential features that improve the network performance significantly. The squeeze and excitation network mainly consists of two steps. In the first step, the feature maps are compressed using the global average pooling function to generate a compressed representation for the feature maps. While, in the second step, a 2-layered neural network is used, where features are first reduced and then expanded. This generates a feature vector, which is used to scale the feature channels.

3.3   The DDANet Architecture

The proposed architecture named DDANet follows an encoder-decoder design similar to ResUNet++ [13]. The DDANet combines the strength of the residual learning and the squeeze and excitation network. The proposed DDANet is a fully convolutional network that consists of a single encoder shared by dual decoders. The encoder network consists of a 4 encoder block, whereas each decoder network also consists of 4 decoder block (see Fig. 1d).

The RGB input image is first fed into the encoder network (see Fig. 1b), which encodes it into an abstract feature representation while gradually downsampling it. The output of the encoder network is fed to both decoders (see Fig. 1c), where it is followed by a 4×4 transpose convolution that doubles its spatial dimensions. After that, the image is concatenated with an appropriate feature maps from the encoder network using the skip connection. These skip connections fetch the features from earlier layers at their original resolution, which increases their feature representation strength. The skip connections also act as an alternative path for the gradient flow and are often beneficial for model convergence.

Two residual blocks are then used to learn the necessary feature required by the network during back-propagation. The output of the second decoder block (autoencoder branch) follows a 1×1 convolution and a sigmoid activation function to generates an attention map. This attention map is multiplied by the output of the first decoder block (segmentation branch), which acts as an input for the next decoder block in the segmentation branch. The final decoder block's output is passed through a 1×1 convolution and a sigmoid activation function, where the first decoder outputs a segmentation mask, and the second outputs the reconstructed grayscale image.

4 Experimental Setup

In this section, we present the implementation details and datasets used in this work.

4.1 Implementation Details

The proposed DDANet architecture is implemented in the PyTorch 1.6 framework[1]. For training the DDANet, we used an NVIDIA DGX-2 machine that uses an Nvidia V100 Tensor Core GPUs.During training, we have used an input image resolution of 512×512. We use a combination of binary cross-entropy and dice loss for calculating the loss between the predicted masks and the ground-truth masks. We have used binary cross-entropy in the case of predicting the grayscale image. An Adam optimizer was used with a learning rate of $1e^{-4}$. The models were trained for 200 epochs.

4.2 Datasets

The Kvasir-SEG [12] dataset was used for training the model. We have used 88% of the dataset for training and the remaining 12% images for development-test-set. Kvasir-SEG consists of 1000 polyp images, ground truth segmentation masks, and bounding boxes. A separate test dataset with 200 images was provided for prediction. However, the ground truth for this dataset was not provided by the organizers. The exact number of images used for the training and testing can also be found in our GitHub repository. More details about the dataset and the baseline results on it can be found in [12].

5 Results

Table 1 shows the results of the DDANet trained and validated on Kvasir-SEG. Additionally, evaluation scores on the test dataset can also be found here. The evaluation metrics for the challenge was Dice Coefficient (DSC). However, we have also calculated other commonly used metrics such as mean Intersection over Union (mIoU), recall, precision, and FPS. The DDANet obtained a DSC of 0.8576, a mIoU of 0.7800, a recall of 0.8880, and a precision of 0.8643. All

---

[1] https://github.com/nikhilroxtomar/DDANet.

Table 1. Quantitative results on Kvasir-SEG and unseen (Challenge) dataset.

Dataset	Method	DSC	mIOU	Recall	Precision	FPS
Kvasir-SEG	DDANet	0.8576	0.7800	0.8880	0.8643	69.59
Unseen (**Challenge**)	DDANet	0.7874	0.7010	0.7987	0.8577	70.23

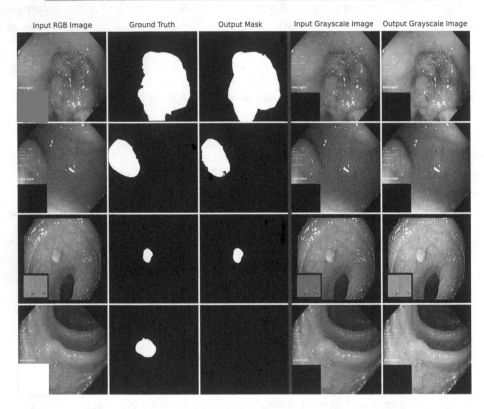

Fig. 2. Qualitative results of the DDANet on the Kvasir-SEG test dataset. The blue line divides the segmentation and the reconstruction part. Columns 4 and 5 show the reconstruction part that was used in the DDANet as an auxiliary task. (Color figure online)

the metrics suggest that our method performs quite well on the Kvasir-SEG dataset. When we compare the results with our previous results [12,13], where the DSC values were 0.8133, and 0.7877, DDANet achieves a higher DSC of 0.8576. However, we can not compare directly with this work with our previous works as a different train-test split of the dataset is used.

Figure 2 shows the qualitative results of the DDANet on Kvasir-SEG. The figure shows that the proposed DDANet is able to segment both larger and smaller polyps. However, the figure also shows the challenges in identifying the flat polyps, which is one of the open issues in the field of development of

CADx systems for colonoscopy. From the quantitative results on development and unseen test dataset, we can say that the proposed method is comprehensive in producing reliable segmentation output.

6   Discussion

The qualitative results (see Fig. 2) show that the proposed model was able to segment polyps ranging from large to small (Fig. 2), but still, challenges remain within some polyps (for example, flat or sessile). We can also see a nearly perfect reconstruction of the grayscale image. In the future, we would like to use image super-resolution instead of just a grayscale image reconstruction.

From all the results, we can see that our method achieves high precision and recall evaluation scores on both the Kvasir-SEG validation dataset and on the unseen test dataset (see Table 1). Additionally, we also achieved a DSC of 0.7874 on the unseen dataset. Thus, high DSC, recall, and precision results validate our proposed method. Moreover, our approach is quite fast with an average FPS of 70.23. Thus, the results show that our method can identify polyps in real-time.

7   Conclusion

The Endotect challenge [8] aims to benchmark various computer-vision approaches on the HyperKvasir dataset containing GI images and videos. Here, we have proposed the DDANet architecture for automatic polyp segmentation, and the proposed architecture provides good results in the segmentation task. We have obtained a high precision, recall, DSC, mIoU, and FPS. However, there are large rooms for improvements. We intend to further improve the architecture by applying post-processing and analyzing the optimal parameters in the future.

Acknowledgements. This work is funded in part by the Research Council of Norway, project number 263248 (Privaton) and project number 282315 (AutoCap). We performed all computations in this paper on equipment provided by the Experimental Infrastructure for Exploration of Exascale Computing (eX^3), which is financially supported by the Research Council of Norway under contract 270053.

References

1. Ahn, S.B., Han, D.S., Bae, J.H., Byun, T.J., Kim, J.P., Eun, C.S.: The miss rate for colorectal adenoma determined by quality-adjusted, back-to-back colonoscopies. Gut Liver **6**(1), 64 (2012)
2. Ali, S., et al.: A translational pathway of deep learning methods in gastrointestinal endoscopy. arXiv preprint arXiv:2010.06034 (2020)
3. Ali, S., et al.: An objective comparison of detection and segmentation algorithms for artefacts in clinical endoscopy. Sci. Rep. **10**(1), 1–15 (2020)
4. Bernal, J., et al.: Comparative validation of polyp detection methods in video colonoscopy: results from the MICCAI 2015 endoscopic vision challenge. IEEE Trans. Med. Imaging **36**(6), 1231–1249 (2017)

5. Borgli, H., et al.: HyperKvasir, a comprehensive multi-class image and video dataset for gastrointestinal endoscopy. Sci. Data **7**, Article no. 283 (2020). https://doi.org/10.1038/s41597-020-00622-y
6. Guo, Y.B., Matuszewski, B.: Giana polyp segmentation with fully convolutional dilation neural networks. In: Proceedings of the International Joint Conference on Computer Vision, Imaging and Computer Graphics Theory and Applications, pp. 632–641 (2019)
7. Guo, Y., Bernal, J., Matuszewski, B.J.: Polyp segmentation with fully convolutional deep neural networks-extended evaluation study. J. Imaging **6**(7), 69 (2020)
8. Hicks, S.A., Jha, D., Thambawita, V., Halvorsen, P., Hammer, H., Riegler, M.A.: The EndoTect 2020 challenge: evaluation and comparison of classification, segmentation and inference time for endoscopy. In: Del Bimbo, A., et al. (eds.) ICPR 2021 Workshops. LNCS, vol. 12668, pp. 263–274. Springer, Cham (2021). https://doi.org/10.1007/978-3-030-68793-9_18
9. Jha, D., et al.: Real-time polyp detection, localisation and segmentation in colonoscopy using deep learning. arXiv preprint arXiv:2006.11392 (2020)
10. Jha, D., et al.: Medico multimedia task at MediaEval 2020: automatic polyp segmentation. In: Proceedings of MediaEval CEUR Workshop (2020)
11. Jha, D., Riegler, M., Johansen, D., Halvorsen, P., Johansen, H.: DoubleU-Net: a deep convolutional neural network for medical image segmentation. In: Proceedings of the International Symposium on Computer Based Medical Systems (CBMS) (2020)
12. Jha, D., et al.: Kvasir-SEG: a segmented polyp dataset. In: Ro, Y.M., et al. (eds.) MMM 2020. LNCS, vol. 11962, pp. 451–462. Springer, Cham (2020). https://doi.org/10.1007/978-3-030-37734-2_37
13. Jha, D., et al.: ResUNet++: an advanced architecture for medical image segmentation. In: Proceedings of the International Symposium on Multimedia (ISM), pp. 225–230 (2019)
14. Ronneberger, O., Fischer, P., Brox, T.: U-Net: convolutional networks for biomedical image segmentation. In: Navab, N., Hornegger, J., Wells, W.M., Frangi, A.F. (eds.) MICCAI 2015. LNCS, vol. 9351, pp. 234–241. Springer, Cham (2015). https://doi.org/10.1007/978-3-319-24574-4_28

Efficient Detection of Lesions During Endoscopy

Amartya Dutta[1]([⊠]), Rajat Kanti Bhattacharjee[2],
and Ferdous Ahmed Barbhuiya[1]

[1] Indian Institute of Information Technology, Guwahati, India
amartyad7@gmail.com, ferdousa@gmail.com
[2] Typito, Guwahati, India
rajatk.dev@gmail.com

Abstract. Endoscopy is a very important procedure in the medical field. It is used to detect almost any diseases associated with the gastrointestinal (GI) tract. Hence, the current work attempts to use Machine learning methods such that such medical procedures can be automated and used in real-time to ensure the proper diagnosis of patients. The current work implements the Tiny Darknet model with an attempt to efficiently classify the various medical conditions specified in the dataset used. Eventually, the Tiny Darknet succeeds in achieving a high classification speed, achieving up to a maximum speed of about *60* fps.

Keywords: GI tract · Tiny Darknet · Hyper-Kvasir

1 Introduction

Machine learning and its applications in the field of healthcare has come to play an integral role in recent times. The main motivation for that is to ensure that human errors can be taken care of by a machine learning model. One such application is detecting medical conditions and other lesions in the GI tract. Endoscopy is a very important process that is used to detect almost any disorder related to the GI tract. However, detection of these conditions depends highly upon the experience and the skill of the doctor performing it. Therefore, it may often result in high miss rates, averaging at about 20% [2].

It is following the same motivation, that in this work attempts have been made to implement such models to not just accurately but also efficiently classify the images of the GI tract into known medical conditions.

2 Related Works

Borgli et al. [2] introduced a dataset which is a high quality and the largest yet dataset of the human GI tract. With the dataset, they provided a baseline where they trained several states of the art CNN models on the labelled dataset and

© Springer Nature Switzerland AG 2021
A. Del Bimbo et al. (Eds.): ICPR 2020 Workshops, LNCS 12668, pp. 315–322, 2021.
https://doi.org/10.1007/978-3-030-68793-9_24

achieved a maximum Matthews Correlation Coefficient (MCC) score of 0.902. However, according to their work, there is still a lot of improvement potential, in terms of accuracy and especially in terms of the speed of classification. Tong et al. [8] used semi-supervised learning so that they could also use unlabelled data for training their model. However, that method could not be applied since the unlabelled data also includes classes of data that are not of interest to the task and will lead to poor models if not handled properly. Kang et al. [4] attempted to use image processing methods such that the defects in the endocrine system can be detected in real-time. The main aim of their work was not to classify the conditions at real-time, rather make it properly visible to the physician so that it doesn't go unnoticed. Therefore Hicks et al. [3] provided an opportunity to use the Hyper-Kvaisr dataset to encourage more research on this field of work.

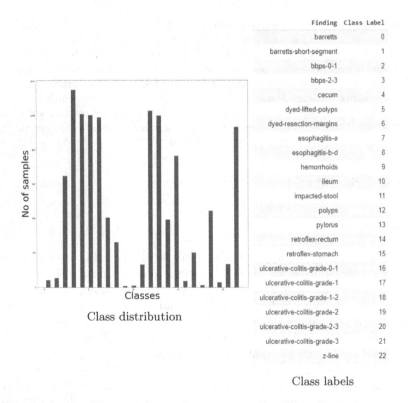

Finding	Class Label
barretts	0
barretts-short-segment	1
bbps-0-1	2
bbps-2-3	3
cecum	4
dyed-lifted-polyps	5
dyed-resection-margins	6
esophagitis-a	7
esophagitis-b-d	8
hemorrhoids	9
ileum	10
impacted-stool	11
polyps	12
pylorus	13
retroflex-rectum	14
retroflex-stomach	15
ulcerative-colitis-grade-0-1	16
ulcerative-colitis-grade-1	17
ulcerative-colitis-grade-1-2	18
ulcerative-colitis-grade-2	19
ulcerative-colitis-grade-2-3	20
ulcerative-colitis-grade-3	21
z-line	22

Class distribution

Class labels

Fig. 1. Distribution of samples across the 23 classes

3   Dataset

One of the major disadvantages researchers faces while working on medical data is the lack of properly labelled data, especially when it comes to images related to the GI tract. Most of the datasets available have very few such images, ones that are not sufficient enough to be exploited to the best possible extent. Hence, we were provided with the Hyper-Kvasir dataset. This is the largest dataset of the human GI tract available to date. It consists of ≈ 10k labelled images and ≈ 99k unlabelled images and 373 labelled videos. The labelled images are classified across 23 such medical conditions along with an existing class imbalance. Figure 1 shows the distribution across the 23 classes and also the class names.

4   Methodology

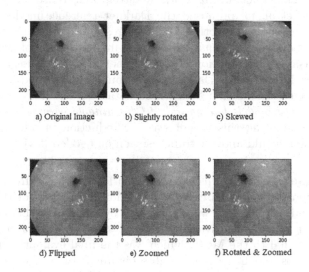

Fig. 2. Augmented images

4.1   Data Preprocessing

The Hyper-Kvasir dataset contains ≈10k labelled images and ≈99k unlabelled images, which if exploited and labelled properly can provide an additional large amount of labelled data. However, classes that are not of interest to task could exist among the unlabelled images [2]. Hence, the current work avoids using unlabelled images. The dataset contained only about 10k labelled images. A test set was created separately from the existing 10k images. This was done so that the model could finally predict on images it had never seen. Furthermore, the test set was created such that it contained at least *1* sample from each class. Finally, the images that were to be used for training were increased in number by augmenting them. Augmentations for each image involves images that were zoomed in, skewed, flipped, rotated or a combination of one of these, which was done using the Augmentor proposed by Bloice et al. [1], which was specifically meant for biomedical images. Each image was augmented an equal number of times to not disturb the class distribution. The images in the test set were left undisturbed. Once the images were augmented, the labelled images dataset was expanded to about ≈70k images. Figure 2 shows the original image along with its augmentations.

4.2 Tiny Darknet

One important thing to keep in mind while classifying medical images is that besides being accurate, one also needs to be fast such that it can be implemented in real-time. Thus, in this work, we attempted to use the *Tiny Darknet*, model. Redmon et al. [5] proposed the Darknet reference model which has a smaller model size than most other architectures and reduces the total number of floating-point operations, thus reducing the inference time of the model. The Tiny Darknet is a reduced version of the Darknet model which is not just about 7 times smaller the size of the Darknet model but also has good accuracy scores on popular image classification benchmark datasets. The Tiny Darknet model is only a *23 layered models having only 913k trainable parameter*. The primary motivation behind using this model was the reduction in inference time and smaller size which would allow it to be used on embedded devices as well.

Training Phase. The model used for this work was trained from scratch. Initially, $1/6^{th}$ images from each class were randomly selected for the generation of the initial seed. Initial seeds were generated by comparing the results of both *Adam optimizer* and *SGD optimizer*. The *F1 score* was monitored since it is directly proportional to the MCC, which was the final evaluation metric. SGD gave better results and hence the weights obtained using it were chosen. The weights obtained after this process was used for initialising the new model. SGD along with *weighted categorical cross entropy* was eventually used to train the model. After this, the new dataset that included the image augmentations was split accordingly into train and validation data. Both the training and the validation sets included the augmented images. The validation and training set were split according to a *1:10* ratio and was run for about *8k epochs*. The final training for the model was carried out by comparing the following two approaches.

SGD + Momentum. The first method followed was SGD optimizer along with a *momentum value of 0.002*. It was observed that this model, in particular, showed positive learning every time it was preceded by a spike in loss or a dip in the F1 score. This was especially observed while training the model from scratch and can be useful for anyone intending to reproduce the same results. Figure 3 shows the F1 score monitored for a few thousand epochs.

CyclicLR. Smith [7] introduced the concept of cyclic learning rates where the learning could be varied within a base and maximum value. This work exploits

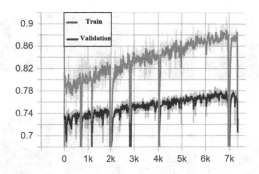

Fig. 3. F1 score of Train vs Validation in SGD + Momentum

the concept of CyclicLR because it varies the *learning rate* after a set of steps such that the model can leave saddle points and can reach the optimal point at some point of time. Few dips, that are representative that the model is about to have positive growth in terms of learning was also observed in this. Figure 4 shows the F1 score monitored for a few thousand epochs.

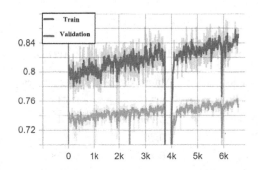

Fig. 4. F1 score of Train vs Validation in CyclicLR

4.3   UNet

The work done also predicts the segmentation masks of images of class *polyps*, which is an important class of medical findings in the human GI system. Ronneberger et al. [6] proposed the *UNet model* for the purpose of semantic segmentation. Since the current work aims to do the same, it has been done using the *UNet model*. The number of images and their masks in the dataset were about 1,000. Hence, each image along with their masks was augmented using Augmentor [1] and thus the dataset was expanded to about 5k. A Test data was created using some of the original images. Finally the remaining data was split into train and validation sets in a *8:2 ratio* and then run for about *2k epochs*. Figure 5 shows a few augmentations of the mask images.

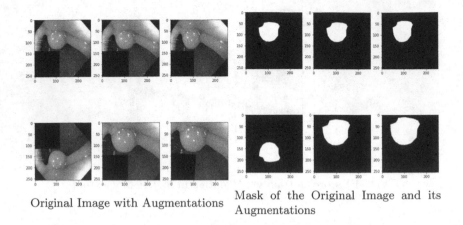

Original Image with Augmentations

Mask of the Original Image and its Augmentations

Fig. 5. Augmented images for segmentation Task

5 Analysis

5.1 Classification

Table 1. Classification results on test data

Metric	Macro average	Micro average
Precision	0.712	0.74
Recall	0.708	0.74
F1	0.708	0.74
MCC	0.758	0.758
Average FPS	49.354	49.354
Maximum FPS	57.695	57.695

The training on the Tiny Darknet model using *SGD + Momentum* was found to give relatively better results than *CyclicLR* and hence the weights obtained from it were chosen for the final predictions. The final model was used to predict the classes of images one at a time and using the time recorded, the speed of the model was recorded in terms of *fps*. The results obtained using the Tiny Darknet model on the Test data are shown in Table 1 while the ones obtained on the Evaluation Data are as shown in Table 2. The *F1 score, Precision and Recall* in both the cases were greater in case of *Micro* than in *Macro*. This is expected because Macro does not take into consideration the class imbalance whereas Micro does. The Tiny Darknet model achieved a good score on the

Evaluation data, for the *efficient detection task*, achieving up to *60* fps. However, as observed, there is a significant difference between the classification results between the Test and the Evaluation data. One plausible reason could be that the model is under-parameterized for the task. Therefore, chances are that it could overfit easily and thus fail on the evaluation data. Added the fact that the model was trained from scratch, further training for longer duration may be required for bringing in better performance.

Table 2. Classification results on evaluation data

Metric	Macro average	Micro average
Precision	0.3328	0.4396
Recall	0.2198	0.4396
F1	0.2228	0.4396
MCC	0.3879	0.3879
Average FPS	49.13	49.13
Maximum FPS	58.27	58.27

5.2 Segmentation

Once the UNet model was trained, the model was used for evaluation. The average evaluation metrics for UNet generated on the Test and Evaluation data are as given in Table 3 and Table 4. The UNet model achieved a moderate score on the Segmentation task in terms of the Jaccard distance. Even though the difference between the results generated on the Test set and Evaluation set is not much. Yet the difference could exist because of lack of sufficient training. Furthermore, the masks generated by prediction needed some amount of post-processing. Improvements in that could perhaps give better results.

Table 3. Segmentation results on test data

Metric	Metric value
Precision	0.821
Recall	0.832
F1	0.802
Jaccard distance	0.853

Table 4. Segmentation results on evaluation data

Metric	Metric value
Precision	0.8005
Recall	0.8012
F1	0.7536
Jaccard distance	0.6559

6   Conclusion and Future Works

After performing this work, several observations had been made. The accuracy achieved by the classification model still needs to be improved upon. One of the most important observations that was made from this work was the *speed* and *size* of the model. The model had a size of only about **3.5 MB**. Having achieved the high classification speed, if the accuracy of the model can also be improved, it will immensely benefit the medical processes. Even though quite an additional amount of work needs to be done, some of the results obtained show good potential for successful future implementation.

References

1. Bloice, M.D., Roth, P.M., Holzinger, A.: Biomedical image augmentation using Augmentor. Bioinformatics **35**(21), 4522–4524 (2019)
2. Borgli, H., et al.: HyperKvasir, a comprehensive multi-class image and video dataset for gastrointestinal endoscopy. Sci. Data **7**(1), 283 (2020). https://doi.org/10.1038/s41597-020-00622-y
3. Hicks, S.A., Jha, D., Thambawita, V., Halvorsen, P., Hammer, H., Riegler, M.A.: The EndoTect 2020 challenge: evaluation and comparison of classification, segmentation and inference time for endoscopy. In: ICPR 2020 Workshops and Challenges. LNCS. Springer, Heidelberg (2020)
4. Kang, J., Doraiswami, R.: Real-time image processing system for endoscopic applications. In: CCECE 2003-Canadian Conference on Electrical and Computer Engineering. Toward a Caring and Humane Technology (Cat. No. 03CH37436). vol. 3, pp. 1469–1472. IEEE (2003)
5. Redmon, J., Farhadi, A.: YOLOv3: an incremental improvement. arXiv (2018)
6. Ronneberger, O., Fischer, P., Brox, T.: U-Net: convolutional networks for biomedical image segmentation. In: Navab, N., Hornegger, J., Wells, W.M., Frangi, A.F. (eds.) MICCAI 2015. LNCS, vol. 9351, pp. 234–241. Springer, Cham (2015). https://doi.org/10.1007/978-3-319-24574-4_28
7. Smith, L.N.: Cyclical learning rates for training neural networks. In: 2017 IEEE Winter Conference on Applications of Computer Vision (WACV), pp. 464–472. IEEE (2017)
8. Tong, L., Wu, H., Wang, M.D.: CAESNet: convolutional autoencoder based semi-supervised network for improving multiclass classification of endomicroscopic images. J. Am. Med. Inf. Assoc. **26**(11), 1286–1296 (2019)

The 2nd Grand Challenge of 106-Point Facial Landmark Localization

Preface

Facial landmark localization is a crucial step in numerous face related applications. For example, it is utilized for face alignment and face manipulation. It is a very challenging task due to the large variations in facial identity, head pose, facial expression and occlusion. In order to promote the development of this technology, we hosted the 1st 106-Point Facial landmark Localization Grand Challenge in conjunction with IEEE International Conference on Multimedia and Expo (ICME) 2019. However, it only pays attention on accuracy, without considering on efficiency, which is very important for the deployment on mobile devices. Therefore, in this year, we host the 2nd 106-Point Lightweight Facial Landmark Localization Grand Challenge. We extend the JD-landmark dataset in the first challenge with thousands of in-the-wild facial images. The upgraded JD-landmark-v2 dataset contains more than 24,000 images. Each of them is manually annotated with 106-point facial landmarks. Strict limits of model size ($\leq$ 20M) and computational complexity ($\leq$ 1G Flops) are employed for computational efficiency. The purpose is to make effort to benchmark lightweight facial landmark localization technologies.

The competition has received much attention from academia and industry. More than 70 teams registered in the competition. 15 teams participated in the validation phase and 9 teams participated in the test phase. The submissions were ranked according to the Area-Under-the-Curve (AUC) from the Cumulative Errors Distribution (CED) curves and the top three were awarded prizes. The organizers provide a summary of the competition, including the introduction of the competition and the methods of the winners.

November 2020

Yinglu Liu
Hailin Shi

Organization

General Chairs

Hailin Shi   JD Cloud & AI, China
Zhenan Sun   Institute of Automation, Chinese Academy
of Sciences, China

Program Committee Chair

Yinglu Liu   JD Cloud & AI, China

Program Committee

Peipei Li   JD Cloud & AI, China
Yinglu Liu   JD Cloud & AI, China
Xin Tong   JD Cloud & AI, China
Hailin Shi   JD Cloud & AI, China
Zhenan Sun   Institute of Automation, Chinese Academy
of Sciences, China

Xiangyu Zhu   Institute of Automation, Chinese Academy
of Sciences, China

The 2nd 106-Point Lightweight Facial Landmark Localization Grand Challenge

Yinglu Liu[1], Peipei Li[1], Xin Tong[1], Hailin Shi[1(✉)], Xiangyu Zhu[2],
Zhenan Sun[2], Zhen Xu[3], Huaibo Liu[3], Xuefeng Su[3], Wei Chen[3], Han Huang[4],
Duomin Wang[4], Xunqiang Tao[4], Yandong Guo[4], Ziye Tong[5], Shenqi Lai[5],
and Zhenhua Chai[5]

[1] JD AI Research, Beijing, China
{liuyinglu1,lipeipei32,tongxin,shihailin}@jd.com
[2] Institute of Automation, Chinese Academy of Sciences, Beijing, China
{xiangyu.zhu,znsun}@nlpr.ia.ac.cn
[3] SogouAI, Beijing, China
{xuzhen216234,liuhuaibiao,SuXueFeng,chenweibj8871}@sogou-inc.com
[4] OPPO Research Institute, Beijing, China
huangh92@gmail.com, wangduomin@gmail.com, taoxunqiang@gmail.com,
yandong.guo@live.com
[5] Vision Intelligence Center, Meituan, Beijing, China
{tongziye,laishenqi, chaizhenhua}@meituan.com

Abstract. Facial landmark localization has been applied to numerous face related applications, such as face recognition and face image synthesis. It is a very crucial step for achieving high performance in these applications. We host the 2nd 106-point lightweight facial landmark localization grand challenge in conjunction with ICPR 2020. The purpose is to make effort towards benchmarking lightweight facial landmark localization, which enables efficient system deployment. Compared with the 1st grand challenge (https://facial-landmarks-localization-challenge.github.io/), the JD-landmark-v2 dataset contains more than 24,000 images with larger variations in identity, pose, expression and occlusion. Besides, strict limits of model size ($\leq$20M) and computational complexity ($\leq$1G Flops) are employed for computational efficiency. The challenge has attracted attention from academia and industrial practitioners. More than 70 teams participate in the competition, and nine of them involve in the final evaluation. We give a detailed introduction of the competition and the solution by the winners in this paper.

Keywords: Facial landmark localization · Lightweight · Challenge

1 Overview

Facial landmark localization, also known as facial landmark detection, is to locate a set of predefined facial fiducial points on facial images. It has been successfully

© Springer Nature Switzerland AG 2021
A. Del Bimbo et al. (Eds.): ICPR 2020 Workshops, LNCS 12668, pp. 327–338, 2021.
https://doi.org/10.1007/978-3-030-68793-9_25

applied to many face related applications. For example, facial landmarks are usually employed to implement face alignment for the recognition tasks including face identity recognition, facial expression recognition, facial attribute recognition, *etc.* The landmark-based alignment is crucial for the high recognition performance. Besides, facial landmarks are also taken as features for face manipulation such as face aging, face swapping, face cartoonization and face attribute editing. Furthermore, the methods of facial landmark localization can also be applied on other fields such as pose estimation [10,23]. Recent years, with the popularity of the internet and smart phones, more and more face-related applications are implemented on the mobile device, thus the lightweight models are required to enable efficient system deployment. However, the prior competitions of facial landmark localization (*i.e.,* 300-W [1,24], Menpo [2,34], 300-VW [3,26] and JD-landmark [4,20]) focus only on accuracy, without consideration on the efficiency. To push the frontier of the lightweight facial landmark localization algorithm, we host the 2nd 106-point lightweight **F**acial **L**andmark **L**ocalization **C**hallenge (FLLC[1]) in conjunction with the 25th International Conference on Pattern Recognition (ICPR2020). We extend the JD-landmark dataset in the 1st challenge with thousands of in-the-wild facial images. The upgraded JD-landmark-v2 dataset contains more than 24,000 images. Figure 2 shows some examples in this dataset. The challenge has attracted much attention from both academia and industrial practitioners. We will introduce the details of the challenge along with the methods of the winner teams in this paper (Fig. 1).

Fig. 1. Example images of the grand challenge dataset.

2   Related Work

In order to provide a fair comparison between the different methods of automatic facial landmark localization, the Intelligent Behaviour Understanding Group (I·BUG[2]) from Imperial College London held a series of competitions, including

---

[1] https://fllc-icpr2020.github.io/home/.
[2] https://ibug.doc.ic.ac.uk/home.

2D/3D facial landmark localization in static imagery and 2D/3D facial landmark tracking in videos. The annotated data has been used by the academia and industrial community for training and testing facial landmark localization models. Before presenting FLLC, we outline the previous competitions along with the related datasets.

2.1 Competitions

300-W Challenge. The first Automatic Facial Landmark Detection in-the-Wild Challenge (300-W Challenge [1,24]) is held in conjunction with ICCV 2013 in Sydney, Australia. It was the first event to benchmark the efforts in the facial landmark localization field. The competition provides 4,350 "in-the-wid" images with around 5,000 faces. All the faces are annotated using a 68-landmark frontal face mark-up scheme as Multi-PIE [5].

300-VW Challenge. In conjunction with ICCV 2015, Zafeiriou *et al.* held the 300 Videos in the Wild (300-VW [3,26]) challenge. The purpose is to develop a comprehensive benchmark for evaluating in-the-wild facial landmark tracking algorithms. The competition collects a large number of long face videos recorded in the wild. Each video has a duration of about 1 min. (at 25–30 FPS). In total, the 300-VW benchmark consists of 114 videos and 218,595 frames. All frames have been annotated with regards to the same 68 points mark-up used in the 300-W competition.

Menpo Challenge. The 300-W and 300-VW challenges have two limitations: 1) lack of faces in extreme poses; 2) limited test images (around 600). To address these issues, the Menpo [2,34] challenge is held in conjunction with CVPR 2017. It consists of 5,658 semi-frontal and 1,906 profile facial images in the training set, and 5,335 frontal and 1,946 profile facial images in the test set. Besides, the 68-point mark-up scheme is used for frontal faces while a 39 points mark-up scheme is adopted for profiles.

3D Menpo Challenge. The I·BUG held the 3D Menpo Challenge [6,33] in conjunction with ICCV 2017 to develop a comprehensive benchmark for evaluating 3D facial landmark localization algorithms in the wild in arbitrary poses. They fitted all the 2D faces provided by the 300-W and Menpo challenges with the state-of-the-art 3D facial morphable models. They also provided 3D facial landmarks for all the videos of 300-VW competition.

106-Point Facial Landmark Localization Challenge. As mentioned above, many efforts have been made for the 68-point facial landmark localization. However, the 68-point landmarks are incompetent to depict the detailed structure of facial components. For example, the lower boundary of eyebrows and the wing of nose are out of the definition in 68-point landmarks, while they are important in some cases such as face parsing [21]. To overcome this problem, a challenging dataset (named as JD-landmark) is constructed and employed for the competition [4,20] of 106-point facial landmark localization in conjunction with ICME 2019.

2.2 Datasets

Large amount of annotated data are important for training the high performance landmark localization model, especially for the deep learning based methods. We summary the commonly used 2D facial landmark datasets in static images as follows.

LFPW. The Labeled Face Parts in the Wild (LFPW [7,11]) dataset consists of 1,432 face images downloaded from the internet using simple text queries on sites such as google.com, flickr.com, and yahoo.com. Each image was labeled by three MTurk workers with 29 fiducial points.

HELEN. The HELEN [8,19] dataset collected images from the Flickr. It contains 2,330 images of high resolution. Each image is annotated with 194 points. It is also extended to a face parsing benchmark [27].

AFW. The Annotated Face in-the-Wild (AFW [35]) dataset is also built using Flickr images. It includes 205 images with 473 labeled faces. For each image, six landmarks along with the pose angles and a rectangular bounding box are provided.

AFLW. The Annotated Facial Landmarks in the Wild (AFLW [9]) dataset provides a large-scale collection of images gathered from Flickr. It consists of 25,993 faces in 21,997 real-world images, each of them is annotated with up to 21 landmarks.

300-W. The training images of the 300-W dataset [1] consists of the LPFW, AFW, Helen and XM2VTS datasets. Each image is re-annotated using the 68-point markup as the landmark configuration of MultiPIE. Besides, a new dataset (IBUG), which includes 135 images with large variations in expression, illumination conditions and pose, are released as part of 300W dataset. The test set consists of 300 images captured indoors and 300 images captured outdoors.

Menpo. The training set of Menpo dataset [2] consists of 5,658 semi-frontal and 1,906 profile facial images. The test set contains 5,335 frontal and 1,946 profile facial images. The frontal/semi-frontal images employ the same landmark configuration of 300W with 68 points, while the profile facial images are annotated with a 39 profile landmark scheme. All the images are taken from LFW and FDDB datasets.

WFLW. The Wider Facial Landmarks in-the-wild (WFLW [32]) contains 10,000 faces (7,500 for training and 2,500 for testing) with 98 fully manual annotated landmarks. Apart from the landmark annotation, this dataset provides several attribute annotations, *i.e.,* occlusion, pose, make-up, illumination, blur and expression for comprehensive analysis of existing algorithms.

JD-landmark. The JD-landmark dataset [4] is an incremental dataset based on 300W, composed of LFPW, AFW, Helen and IBUG, and re-annotated with the 106-point mark-up. The dataset contains 11,393 face images for training. Besides, 2,000/2,000 facial images are collected from the open-source face dataset Megaface as validation/test set. The JD-landmark covers a large variation of pose, illumination and expression.

Fig. 2. Example images of the 2D facial landmark localization datasets. (a) LFPW; (b) HELEN; (c) AFW; (d) AFLW; (e) 300-W; (f) Menpo; (g) WFLW; (h) JD-landmark.

3   Introduction of Competition

3.1   Datasets

Compared with the first version of JD-landmark dataset, we expand it by about 9,000 in-the-wild facial images, which are collected from the Megaface dataset [15]. Each sample is annotated with 106-point landmarks. Expect for the facial images in extreme poses and expressions, many low quality (low resolution) images are added to increase the difficulty of the competition. In total, the second version, *i.e.* JD-landmark-v2 dataset consists of 20,386 images for training, 2,000 images for validation and 2,000 images for testing. Each image is provided with the 106-point landmarks along with the referenced bounding box.

3.2   Evaluation Criteria

The submissions are ranked according to the Area-Under-the-Curve (AUC) from the Cumulative Errors Distribution (CED) curves. Furthermore, the statistics from the CED curves such as the failure rate and average Normalized Mean Error (NME) are also taken into account. The CED curve reflects the proportion of the test images with regard to the NME less than a threshold α. The AUC is the area under the CED curve calculated up to the threshold, then divided by the threshold α. In this competition, we set the value of α to 0.08. Similarly, we regard each image with a NME larger than α as a failure case. NME is computed as:

$$NME = \frac{1}{N} \sum_{k=1}^{N} \frac{\|y_k - \hat{y}_k\|_2}{d} \tag{1}$$

where k refers to the index of landmarks. y and $\hat{y}$ denotes the ground truth and the prediction of landmarks for a given facial image, respectively. In order to alleviate the bias in profile faces caused by the small interocular distance, we employ the square-root of the ground truth bounding box as the normalization factor d, computed as $d = \sqrt{w_{bbox} \times h_{bbox}}$. Here w_{bbox} and h_{bbox} are the width and height of the enclosing rectangle of the ground truth landmarks, respectively. If no face is detected, the NME will be set to infinite.

3.3   Detailed Requirements

The upper bound of computational complexity is set to 1G Flops, and the upper bound of model size is set to 20 MB. For the training/validation/testing images, we provide the bounding boxes obtained by an off-the-shelf face detector. Nevertheless, the participants are allowed to employ their own face detector. Except for the face detectors, any external datasets and models are not allowed. Any test augmentation or multi-model ensemble strategy is not allowed, either.

The 2nd 106-point Lightweight Facial Landmark Localization (FLLC) grand challenge began by July 13, 2020. During the validation phase (from July 27 to October 08), the participants were allowed to evaluate their models on the validation set, and the leaderboard on the validation set was updated every day with respect to the submissions. The test images were released on October 09. To prevent cheating on the test set, each team was given an 24-h window to submit their predicted test results (Fig. 3).

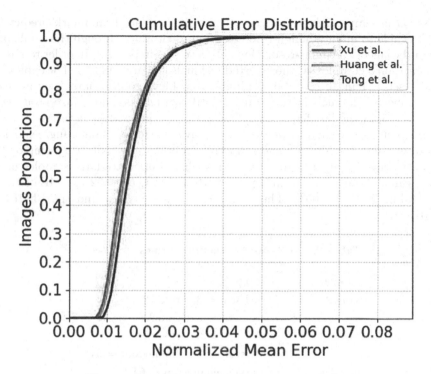

Fig. 3. The CED curve of the top three teams.

4   Summary of Participants

The competition has attracted much attention from both academia and industry. There are more than 70 teams registered in the competition. 15 teams participate in the validation phase, and 9 of them enter in the final test phase.

As shown in Table 1, the champion of the competition is Xu *et al.* from SogouAI. Huang *et al.* from OPPO Research Institute achieve the second place. The third place goes to Tong *et al.* from the Vision Intelligence Center of Meituan. Next, we will give a brief algorithm introduction of the top three winners.

Table 1. Leaderboard of the 2nd 106-point Lightweight Facial Landmark Localization Competition. The top three teams are ranked according to the AUC of the CED curve.

Rank	AUC (%)	Failure rate (%)	NME (%)	Model size (M)	Flops (M)
1	80.52	0.05	1.58	12	887.073
2	79.92	0.05	1.63	17	995.922
3	78.88	0.05	1.71	16	996.190

Xu *et al.* employ the advanced HRNet [14] for facial landmark prediction, which is able to maintain high-resolution representations through the whole process and connect the multi-resolution sub-networks in parallel. In order to reduce computational complexity, the inverted residuals [25] are adopted. The expansion ratio is set to 1 in all inverted residuals. To achieve good results, they increase the number of channels in the branch of HRNet blocks, and utilize group convolution [16] in the last few layers. The settings of network structure is given in Table 2. During the training phase, they apply some forms of data augmentation, including randomly rotating and randomly cropping. Specially, they employ the PDB strategy [12] against pose variations which duplicates large samples many times. Finally, they won the first place with the AUC of 80.52%, NME of 1.58% and Failure rate of 0.05%. The model size is about 12M and the FLOPS is 887.073M.

Table 2. The network structure settings of Xu *et al.*

Operator	Settings
conv2d	kernel_size = 3, stride=2
	channel_in = 3, channel_out = 32
conv2d	kernel_size = 3, stride=2
	channel_in = 32, channel_out = 64
bottleneck	stride =1, channel_in = 64
	channel_out = 64
HRNet_block	number_blocks = 4, 4
	number_channels = 24, 48
HRNet_block	number_block = 4, 4, 4
	number_channels = 24, 48, 96
HRNet_block	number_block = 4, 4, 4, 4
	number_channels = 24, 48, 96, 192
conv2d	kernel_size = 1, stride = 1
	channel_in = 360, channel_out = 360
conv2d	kernel_size = 1, stride = 1
	channel_in = 360, channel_out = 106

Huang *et al.* propose a multi-level supervision strategy to train the facial landmark localization models. They take ResNet-18 [13] as the backbone and reduce the channel size of the last two residual blocks from 256/512 to 192/256 due to the limits of computational complexity. Instance Normalization [31] is adopted instead of Batch Normalization, which further improves the details of individual differences without increasing computational overhead. As shown in Fig. 4, apart from the main branch, an additional branch from feature map of the 3rd blocks is introduced for the contour landmarks prediction. Finally, mean aggregation is used for the final output. The AUC, NME and Failure rate are 79.92%, 1.63% and 0.05%, respectively. The model size is 17M while FLOPS is 995.922M. Huang *et al.* gain the second place in the competition.

Tong *et al.* take the improved HRNet [28] structure as the backbone, in which the bottleneck block [13] and group convolution [29] are used to replace the standard residual block in the original HRNet. In order to prevent the accuracy loss by the coordinates quantization, they use a mapping function named Dual Soft Argmax (DSA [18]) to map the heatmap response to final coordinates, which overcomes the problem of weight imbalance problem of Soft Argmax (SA [22]). The Normalized Mean Error (NME) loss [17] is taken as the training loss. Besides, inspired by [30], they propose a Similarity-FeatureMap knowledge distillation model. As Figure 5 shows, it guides the training of a student network by keeping the feature maps' similarity of input pairs according to the teacher network. Specifically, similarity matrices are derived from the feature maps and a distillation loss is computed on the matrices produced by the student network and the teacher network. Finally, the submitted model achieves 78.88%, 1.71%, 0.05% of the AUC, NME, and Failure rate, respectively. The model size is about 16M and the FLOPS is 996.190M. Tong *et al.* won the third place.

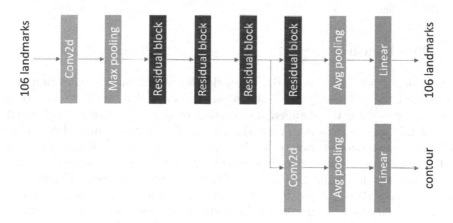

Fig. 4. The network structure of Huang *et al.*

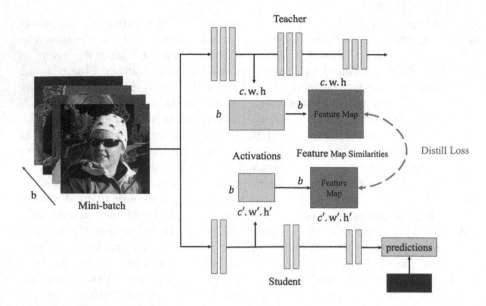

Fig. 5. Similarity-FeatureMap knowledge distillation guides the training of a student network such that input pairs that produce similar (dissimilar) feature maps in the pre-trained teacher network produce similar (dissimilar) feature maps in the student network. Given an input mini-batch of b images, we derive similarity matrices from the feature maps, and compute a distillation loss on the matrices produced by the student and the teacher.

5   Conclusion

In this paper, we first summarize the prior facial landmark localization challenges and the commonly used 2D facial landmark datasets in recent years. Then we introduce the detailed information of the 2nd 106-point lightweight facial landmark localization grand challenge. We construct and release a new facial landmark dataset, named JD-landmark-v2. Compared with the previous challenges, our work pays attention on the lightweight facial landmark localization model, which is important for the efficient system deployment. Finally, there are more than 70 teams participate in the competition and 9 teams involve in the final evaluation. We introduce the methods together with the performance of top three teams in this paper. We hope this work could push the frontier of the lightweight facial landmark localization algorithm.

Acknowledgment. This work was supported by the National Key R&D Program of China under Grant No. 2020AAA0103800.

References

1. https://ibug.doc.ic.ac.uk/resources/300-W/

2. https://ibug.doc.ic.ac.uk/resources/2nd-facial-landmark-tracking-competition-menpo-ben/
3. https://ibug.doc.ic.ac.uk/resources/300-VW/
4. https://facial-landmarks-localization-challenge.github.io/
5. http://www.cs.cmu.edu/afs/cs/project/PIE/MultiPie/Multi-Pie/Home.html
6. https://ibug.doc.ic.ac.uk/resources/1st-3d-face-tracking-wild-competition/
7. https://neerajkumar.org/databases/lfpw/
8. http://www.ifp.illinois.edu/~vuongle2/helen/
9. https://www.tugraz.at/institute/icg/research/team-bischof/lrs/downloads/aflw/
10. Bao, Q., Liu, W., Hong, J., Duan, L., Mei, T.: Pose-native network architecture search for multi-person human pose estimation. In: Proceedings of the 28th ACM International Conference on Multimedia, pp. 592–600 (2020)
11. Belhumeur, P.N., Jacobs, D.W., Kriegman, D.J., Kumar, N.: Localizing parts of faces using a consensus of exemplars. IEEE Trans. Pattern Anal. Mach. Intell. **35**(12), 2930–2940 (2013)
12. Feng, Z.H., Kittler, J., Awais, M., Huber, P., Wu, X.J.: Wing loss for robust facial landmark localisation with convolutional neural networks. In: Proceedings of the IEEE Conference on Computer Vision and Pattern Recognition, pp. 2235–2245 (2018)
13. He, K., Zhang, X., Ren, S., Sun, J.: Deep residual learning for image recognition. In: Proceedings of the IEEE Conference on Computer Vision and Pattern Recognition, pp. 770–778 (2016)
14. Huang, J., Zhu, Z., Huang, G.: Multi-stage HRNet: multiple stage high-resolution network for human pose estimation. arXiv preprint arXiv:1910.05901 (2019)
15. Kemelmacher-Shlizerman, I., Seitz, S.M., Miller, D., Brossard, E.: The megaface benchmark: 1 million faces for recognition at scale. In: Proceedings of the IEEE Conference on Computer Vision and Pattern Recognition, pp. 4873–4882 (2016)
16. Krizhevsky, A., Sutskever, I., Hinton, G.E.: ImageNet classification with deep convolutional neural networks. In: Advances in Neural Information Processing Systems, pp. 1097–1105 (2012)
17. Lai, S., Chai, Z., Li, S., Meng, H., Yang, M., Wei, X.: Enhanced normalized mean error loss for robust facial landmark detection. In: British Machine Vision Conference, p. 111 (2019)
18. Lai, S., Chai, Z., Wei, X.: Improved hourglass structure for high performance facial landmark detection. In: Proceedings of IEEE International Conference on Multimedia & Expo Workshops, pp. 669–672. IEEE (2019)
19. Le, V., Brandt, J., Lin, Z., Bourdev, L., Huang, T.S.: Interactive facial feature localization. In: Fitzgibbon, A., Lazebnik, S., Perona, P., Sato, Y., Schmid, C. (eds.) ECCV 2012. LNCS, vol. 7574, pp. 679–692. Springer, Heidelberg (2012). https://doi.org/10.1007/978-3-642-33712-3_49
20. Liu, Y., et al.: Grand challenge of 106-point facial landmark localization. In: IEEE International Conference on Multimedia & Expo Workshops (ICMEW), pp. 613–616. IEEE (2019)
21. Liu, Y., Shi, H., Shen, H., Si, Y., Wang, X., Mei, T.: A new dataset and boundary-attention semantic segmentation for face parsing. In: Association for the Advancement of Artificial Intelligence, pp. 11637–11644 (2020)
22. Nibali, A., He, Z., Morgan, S., Prendergast, L.: Numerical coordinate regression with convolutional neural networks. arXiv preprint arXiv:1801.07372 (2018)
23. Ruan, W., Liu, W., Bao, Q., Chen, J., Cheng, Y., Mei, T.: POINet: pose-guided ovonic insight network for multi-person pose tracking. In: Proceedings of the 27th ACM International Conference on Multimedia, pp. 284–292 (2019)

24. Sagonas, C., Tzimiropoulos, G., Zafeiriou, S., Pantic, M.: 300 faces in-the-wild challenge: the first facial landmark localization challenge. In: Proceedings of the IEEE International Conference on Computer Vision Workshops, pp. 397–403 (2013)

25. Sandler, M., Howard, A., Zhu, M., Zhmoginov, A., Chen, L.C.: MobileNetV2: inverted residuals and linear bottlenecks. In: Proceedings of the IEEE Conference on Computer Vision and Pattern Recognition, pp. 4510–4520 (2018)

26. Shen, J., Zafeiriou, S., Chrysos, G.G., Kossaifi, J., Tzimiropoulos, G., Pantic, M.: The first facial landmark tracking in-the-wild challenge: benchmark and results. In: Proceedings of the IEEE International Conference on Computer Vision Workshops, pp. 50–58 (2015)

27. Smith, B.M., Zhang, L., Brandt, J., Lin, Z., Yang, J.: Exemplar-based face parsing. In: Proceedings of the IEEE Conference on Computer Vision and Pattern Recognition, pp. 3484–3491 (2013)

28. Sun, K., Xiao, B., Liu, D., Wang, J.: Deep high-resolution representation learning for human pose estimation. In: Proceedings of the IEEE Conference on Computer Vision and Pattern Recognition, pp. 5693–5703 (2019)

29. Ting, Z., Guo-Jun, Q., Bin, X., Jingdong, W.: Interleaved group convolutions for deep neural networks. In: Proceedings of the IEEE International Conference on Computer Vision (2017)

30. Tung, F., Mori, G.: Similarity-preserving knowledge distillation. In: Proceedings of the IEEE International Conference on Computer Vision, pp. 1365–1374 (2019)

31. Ulyanov, D., Vedaldi, A., Lempitsky, V.: Instance normalization: the missing ingredient for fast stylization. arXiv preprint arXiv:1607.08022 (2016)

32. Wu, W., Qian, C., Yang, S., Wang, Q., Cai, Y., Zhou, Q.: Look at boundary: a boundary-aware face alignment algorithm. In: Proceedings of the IEEE Conference on Computer Vision and Pattern Recognition (2018)

33. Zafeiriou, S., Chrysos, G.G., Roussos, A., Ververas, E., Deng, J., Trigeorgis, G.: The 3D Menpo facial landmark tracking challenge. In: Proceedings of the IEEE International Conference on Computer Vision Workshops, pp. 2503–2511 (2017)

34. Zafeiriou, S., Trigeorgis, G., Chrysos, G., Deng, J., Shen, J.: The Menpo facial landmark localisation challenge: a step towards the solution. In: Proceedings of the IEEE Conference on Computer Vision and Pattern Recognition Workshops, pp. 170–179 (2017)

35. Zhu, X., Ramanan, D.: Face detection, pose estimation, and landmark localization in the wild. In: Proceedings of IEEE Conference on Computer Vision and Pattern Recognition, pp. 2879–2886. IEEE (2012)

ICPR2020 Competition on Text Detection and Recognition in Arabic News Video Frames

ICPR2020 Competition on Text Detection and Recognition in Arabic News Video Frames – AcTiVComp

Challenge Description

The present competition represents a part of the AcTiVComp series that have been organized respectively within the ICPR'16 and ICDAR'17 international con-ferences, using AcTiV dataset as a benchmark. The main goal is to evaluate the performance of participants' systems to locate and recognize embedded textlines in Arabic news video frames. A direct application of such competition is to au-tomate the interpretation of graphically-embedded Arabic texts, which has a broad range of benefits, e.g., content-based multimedia retrieval and automatic broadcast annotation.

This edition of AcTiVComp has attracted four teams for participating with five systems. All the submitted systems have followed a CRNN-based architec-ture, which is now the de facto choice for text detection and OCR problems. The achieved results are very interesting, showing a significant improvement from the state-of-the-art per-formances on this field of research.

This work has been organized in a joint collaboration between the ICoSys in-stitute from the HES-SO//Fribourg, LATIS lab. from the National Engineering School of Sousse and DIVA group from the University of Fribourg.

November 2020

Organization

ActivCom Chairs

Oussama Zayene	HES-SO//Fribourg, Switzerland
Rolf Ingold	University of Fribourg, Switzerland
Najoua Essoukri BenAmara	University of Sousse, Tunisia
Jean Hennebert	HES-SO//Fribourg, Switzerland

Program Committee

Bastian Laasch	University of Rostock, Germany
Fouad Slimane	University of Fribourg, Switzerland

ICPR2020 Competition on Text Detection and Recognition in Arabic News Video Frames

Oussama Zayene[1]([✉])(ID), Rolf Ingold[2](ID), Najoua Essoukri BenAmara[3](ID), and Jean Hennebert[1](ID)

[1] Institute of Complex Systems, HES-SO, Fribourg, Switzerland
{oussama.zayene,jean.hennebert}@hefr.ch
[2] DIVA Group, Department of Informatics, University of Fribourg, Fribourg, Switzerland
rolf.ingold@unifr.ch
[3] LATIS Laboratory, National Engineering School of Sousse, University of Sousse, Sousse, Tunisia
najoua.benamara@eniso.rnu.tn

Abstract. After the success of the two first editions of the "Arabic Text in Videos Competition—AcTiVComp", we are proposing to organize a new edition in conjunction with the 25th International Conference on Pattern Recognition (ICPR'20). The main objective is to contribute in the research field of text detection and recognition in multimedia documents, with a focus on Arabic text in video frames. The former editions were held in the framework of ICPR'16 and ICDAR'17 conferences. The obtained results on the AcTiV dataset have shown that there is still room for improvement in both text detection and recognition tasks. Four groups with five systems are participating to this edition of AcTiVComp (three for the detection task and two for the recognition task). All the submitted systems have followed a CRNN-based architecture, which is now the de facto choice for text detection and OCR problems. The achieved results are very interesting, showing a significant improvement from the state-of-the-art performances on this field of research.

Keywords: Text detection · Text recognition · Arabic news indexing · AcTiVComp · ICPR competition

1 Introduction

Among the pattern recognition fields, automatic text recognition, known as OCR, has been widely studied for its prominent position in our everyday life. OCR has a long history of research that started from isolated character recognition and evolved to printed/handwriting document recognition. Over the last decade, embedded texts in videos and natural scenes have received increasing attention as they often give crucial information about the media content [9]. Nevertheless, extracting text from such content is a non-trivial task due to many

© Springer Nature Switzerland AG 2021
A. Del Bimbo et al. (Eds.): ICPR 2020 Workshops, LNCS 12668, pp. 343–356, 2021.
https://doi.org/10.1007/978-3-030-68793-9_26

challenges like low resolution, background complexity and text variability in terms of size, color and font. All these challenges may give rise to failures in video text detection and recognition tasks.

Over the last decade, interest in this area of research has led to a plethora of text detection and recognition methods. So far, these methods have focused only on Latin and Chinese characters. For a language like Arabic, which is used by more than one billion people around the world, the literature concerning video text analysis is limited to few studies [2,5,10]. In contrast to non Arabic text where most of the methods have been tested and compared in the context of international competitions, e.g., ICDAR Robust Reading Competition (RRC) [1], most of the existing methods for Arabic video text detection/recognition were tested on private datasets with non-uniform evaluation protocols. This makes direct comparison and scientific benchmarking rather impractical.

The present competition[2] aims to fill the aforementioned gap by encouraging Arabic Video OCR researchers to develop and test their systems on a standard dataset and using the same evaluation metrics.

This contest represents a part of the AcTiVComp series that have been organized respectively within the ICPR'16 [19] and ICDAR'17 [20] conferences. Actually, the former editions have attracted seven groups for participating and have received ten systems in total. The best achieved F-score for the channel-free detection protocol was 0.85 (more details about the protocols are explained in Sect. 3). For the recognition task, the best results in the channel-free protocol have not exceeded 0.76 in terms of Line Recognition Rate (LRR). Furthermore, the obtained results on the recently added subset (SD 480 × 360) were quite low for almost all the participating systems. For this reason, we are organizing a new edition so as to improve these results, especially for the channel-free evaluation protocols.

AcTiVComp has been organized by ICoSys Institute[3] from the University of Applied Sciences and Arts, Western Switzerland and LATIS Lab[4] from the National Engineering School of Sousse, Tunisia, in collaboration with DIVA Group[5], from the University of Fribourg, Switzerland.

The participants to this third edition of AcTiVComp had roughly five months to train their systems before the test data was released. After two additional weeks the teams had to submit their results.

In the following, we first present the used datasets in Sect. 2. Section 3 is dedicated to the competition tasks. We describe the participating systems in Sect. 4. The results are discussed in Sect. 5 and Sect. 6 draws the conclusions.

---

[1] https://rrc.cvc.uab.es/.
[2] https://diuf.unifr.ch/main/diva/AcTiVComp/.
[3] https://icosys.ch.
[4] http://www.latis-eniso.org.
[5] https://www3.unifr.ch/inf/diva/en/.

2   Competition Datasets

AcTiV is a real-content database where video clips are recorded from four Arabic news channels, TunisiaNat1, France24 Arabic, Russia Today Arabic and AljazeeraHD, using a DBS system and then transcoded and segmented into frames. It was presented in the ICDAR 2015 conference [21] and then in the Journal of Imaging 2018 [23] as the first publicly accessible annotated dataset designed to assess the performance of different Arabic Video OCR systems. The two main challenges addressed by this dataset are the following:

- The variability of text patterns, e.g. text colors, fonts, sizes and position.
- the presence of complex backgrounds with various text-like objects. It is currently used by more than 40 research groups around the world.

AcTiV includes two appropriate datasets, namely AcTiV-D and AcTiV-R, for detection and recognition tasks. These datasets were used as a benchmark in the two first editions of AcTiVComp.

Fig. 1. Typical video frames from AcTiV-D dataset. From left to right: Examples of RussiaToday Arabic, France24 Arabe, TunisiaNat1 and AljazeeraHD

Table 1. Detection dataset and evaluation protocols

Protocol	TV channel	Training set	Test set	Closed-test set
		#Frames	#Frames	#Frames
1	AljazeeraHD	337	87	103
4	France24 arabe	331	80	104
	RussiaToday arabic	323	79	100
	TunisiaNat1	492	116	106
	All SD channels	1,146	275	310
4bis	TunisiaNat YouTube	–	150	149
7	All channels	1,483	362	413

2.1   AcTiV-D

AcTiV-D represents a dataset of non-redundant frames used to build and evaluate text detection methods. It contains a total of 2,557 news video frames that
have been hand-selected with a particular attention to achieve a high diversity in
text regions. Figure 1 states some examples from AcTiV-D for typical problems
in video text detection. ActiV-D frames are distributed over four sets (one set per
TV channel). Every set includes three sub-sets: training set, test set and closed-
test set (used for competitions only). The statistics are presented in Table 1.
ActiV-D includes some frames that do not contain any text and some others
that contain the same text regions but with different backgrounds. The detection ground-truth is provided at the line level for each frame. Figure 2a depicts a
part of the ground-truth XML file of protocol4.3 (TunisiaNat TV channel). One
bounding box is described by the element *rectangle*, which contains the rectangle
attributes: (x, y) upper-left coordinates, width and height.

```xml
<?xml version="1.0" encoding="UTF-8"?>
- <Protocol4 channel="TunisiaNat1">
    - <frame id="7" source="vd01">
        <rectangle id="1" x="506" y="464" width="61" height="14"/>
        <rectangle id="2" x="66" y="499" width="491" height="32"/>
      </frame>
    - <frame id="16" source="vd01">
        <rectangle id="1" x="441" y="464" width="127" height="18"/>
        <rectangle id="2" x="373" y="499" width="184" height="27"/>
      </frame>
    - <frame id="64" source="vd01">
        <rectangle id="1" x="429" y="462" width="138" height="24"/>
      </frame>
```

(a)

جبل الشعانبي

```xml
<?xml version="1.0" encoding="UTF-8" standalone="true"?>
- <Image id="TunisiaNat1_vd07_frame_131-4">
    <ArabicTranscription>جبل الشعانبي</ArabicTranscription>
    <LatinTranscription> Jiim_B Baa_M Laam_E Space Alif_I Laam_B Shiin_M
      Ayn_M Alif_E Nuun_B Baa_M Yaa_E </LatinTranscription>
  </Image>
```

(b)

Fig. 2. (a) Part of detection XML file of TunisiaNat1 TV channel. (b) Recognition
ground-truth file and its corresponding textline image.

2.2   AcTiV-R

AcTiV-R is a dataset of textline images used to build and evaluate Arabic text
recognition systems. Different fonts, sizes, backgrounds and colors are represented in the dataset. Figure 3 illustrates typical examples from AcTiV-R. The

Fig. 3. Example of text images from AcTiV-R dataset depicting typical characteristics of video text images

Table 2. Recognition dataset and evaluation protocols. *Lns, Wds, Chars* and *YT* respectively denote *Lines, Words, Characters* and *YouTube*.

Protocol	TV channel	Training set			Test set			Closed-test set		
		Lns	Wds	Chars	Lns	Wds	Chars	Lns	Wds	Chars
3	AlJazeeraHD	1,909	8,110	46,563	196	766	4,343	262	1,082	6,283
6	France24 arabe	1,906	5,683	32,085	179	667	3,835	191	734	4,600
	RussiaToday	2,127	13,462	78,936	250	1,483	8,749	256	1,598	9,305
	TunisiaNat1	2,001	9,338	54,809	189	706	4,087	221	954	5,597
	All SD channels	6,034	28,483	165,830	618	2,856	16,671	668	3,286	19,502
6bis	TunisiaNat1 YT	–	–	–	320	1,487	8,726	311	1,148	6,645
9	All channels	7,943	36,593	212,393	814	3,622	21,014	930	4,368	25,785

collected text images cover a broad range of characteristics that distinguish video frames from scanned documents. AcTiV-R consists of 10,415 textline images, 44,583 words and 259,192 characters. The recognition ground-truth is provided at the line level for each text image. Figure 2b depicts an example of a ground-truth XML file and its corresponding textline image. The file is composed of two principal markup sections: ArabicTranscription and LatinTranscription. To have an easily accessible representation of Arabic text, it is transformed into a set of Latin labels with a suffix that refers to the letter's position in the word, i.e. B: Begin, M: Middle, E: End and I: Isolate. During the annotation process, 164 character shapes were considered, including 10 digits and 12 punctuation marks. The statistics are presented in Table 2.

3   Competition Tasks

AcTiVComp20 includes three main tasks: i) Text detection, ii) text recognition and iii) end-to-end text recognition in Arabic news video frames. Each of these tasks may include one or more evaluation protocols. Only the two first tasks are described in what follows, as the third one has not received any submission. Please refer to the competition website[6] for more details about this task.

---

[6] https://diuf.unifr.ch/main/diva/AcTiVComp/.

3.1   Task 1: Text Detection

The objective of this task is to obtain an estimation of text regions in a video frame in terms of bounding boxes (x, y, width and height). In the following paragraphs we present details about the used evaluation protocols and metrics for this task.

Evaluation Protocols:

– **Protocol 1** aims to measure the performance of text detection methods in HD frames.

– **Protocol 4** is similar to protocol 1, varying only in channel resolution. All SD (720 × 576) channels in AcTiV dataset are targeted by this protocol, which is split in four sub-protocols: three *channel-dependent* protocols (p4.1, p4.2 and p4.3) and one *channel-free* protocol (p4.4).

– **Protocol 4bis** is dedicated to the last added resolution (480 × 360). The main idea of this protocol is to train a given system with SD (720 × 576) data, i.e. Protocol 4.3, and test it with different data resolution and quality.

– **Protocol 7** is the generic version of protocols 1 and 4 where text detection is evaluated regardless of data quality.

Table 1 summarizes the detection protocols.

Metrics: Following the evaluation metrics of AcTiVComp's previous editions and those of ICDAR RRC series, the text detection task of AcTiVComp20 is evaluated in terms of Precision, Recall and F-measure that are calculated as

$$Precision = \frac{\sum_i match_D(D_i, G, t_r, t_p)}{|D|} \tag{1}$$

$$Recall = \frac{\sum_j match_G(G_j, D, t_r, t_p)}{|G|} \tag{2}$$

$$Fmeasure = 2 \times \frac{Precision \times Recall}{Precision + Recall} \tag{3}$$

where D is the list of detected rectangles, G is the list of ground-truth rectangles, $match_D$ and $match_G$ are the matching functions, and t_r and t_p are two quality constraints on area recall and area precision respectively. In the experiments, t_r is fixed to 0.8 and t_p is fixed to 0.4[7]. These measures are calculated using the evaluation tool presented in [22], which takes into account all types of matching cases between G and D bounding boxes, i.e. one-to-one, one-to-many and many-to-one matching.

---

[7] This choice is motivated by the fact that a detection result which cuts parts of the text rectangle is more disturbing than a detection which results in a too large rectangle.

3.2   Task 2: Text Recognition

Taking a textline image as input, the objective of this task is to generate the corresponding text transcriptions. The used evaluation protocols and metrics are presented below.

Evaluation Protocols:

- **Protocol 3** is dedicated to evaluate the performance of OCR systems to recognize text in HD frames.

- **Protocol 6** is similar to protocol 3, differing only in the channel resolution. All SD (720 × 576) channels in AcTiV dataset are targeted by this protocol, which is split in four sub-protocols: three *channel-dependent* protocols (p6.1, p6.2 and p6.3) and one *channel-free* protocol (p6.4).

- **Protocol 6bis** is dedicated to last added resolution (480 × 360) for TunisiaNat1 TV. The idea behind is to train a given system with SD (720 × 576) data and test it with different data resolution and quality.

- **Protocol 9** is the generic version of the previous protocols where text recognition is assessed without considering data quality.

Table 2 presents these protocols in more details.

Metrics: The performance measure for the recognition task is based on the Line Recognition Rate (LRR), and on the computation of Insertion (I), Deletion (Dl) and Substitution (S) errors at the level of Character Recognition Rate (CRR). CRR and LRR are calculated as

$$CRR = \frac{\#characters - I - S - Dl}{\#characters} \tag{4}$$

$$LRR = \frac{\#lines\_correctly\_recognized}{\#lines} \tag{5}$$

4   Submitted Methods

Overall, 5 methods from 4 different teams were submitted for the two first tasks of AcTiVComp challenge. All the methods followed a CNN-based architecture, which is now the de facto choice for text detection and recognition problems.

4.1   Text-Fcos

The Text-Fcos method is submitted for the detection task by Michael Jungo, Beat Wolf and Andreas Fischer from the School of Engineering and Architecture of Fribourg (HEIA-Fr), Switzerland.

The used model is based on FCOS [15], a one-stage anchor-free object detector. EfficientNet [14] is used as a backbone with two key changes: i) Group Normalization [17] instead of Batch Normalization. ii) Every point-wise convolution (i.e. 1×1 convolution) has been replaced by Ghost Convolutions [3] with $ghost\_factor = 2$, where $\frac{1}{2}$ of the features are generated by a 1×1 convolution and the remaining $\frac{1}{2}$ are created from the resulting features by applying a 3×3 depth-wise convolution to them.

For the training phase, the Adaptive Training Sample Selection (ATSS) [24] has been employed with $k = 9$, which selects the 9 best candidates per Feature Pyramid Network (FPN) level for each ground-truth bounding box. Regarding the loss functions, the Focal Loss [8] was used for the classification, the Generalized Intersection over Union Loss (GIoU) [12] was used for the bounding box regression and the binary cross-entropy loss for the centerness. Only the provided AcTiV-D train dataset has been used for training, but for each image, 10 additional images have been generated by applying random augmentations to that image, resulting in 13,768 images. All images have been resized such that the larger side is 768 pixels while preserving the aspect ratio, regardless of the image resolution. The training was performed on two Titan RTX with mixed-precision. For the B4 model (EfficientNet-B4 as backbone), a batch size of 12 per GPU was used and one epoch took roughly 12 min 30 s. It was trained for a little over 70 epochs, with a total of 15 h.

During inference, only bounding boxes with a classification probability over 5% are considered, but this can result int false-positives. In order to alleviate this problem, a dynamic threshold is calculated based on the mean and standard deviation of the possible bounding box locations. This threshold removes a lot of low quality bounding boxes, which many times do not contain any text, but that also removes some of the bounding boxes containing actual text, simply having a low confidence.

4.2   EffDB-UNet

The EffDB-UNet text detection system is submitted for the detection task by Lokesh Nandanwar and Shivakumara Palaiahnakote which are members of Multimedia Lab, Faculty of Computer Science and Information Technology at the University of Malaya, Malaysia; Ramachandra Raghavendra from NTNU, Norway and Umapada Pal from CVPR Unit, ISI Kolkata, India.

The submitted system contains mainly two stages, namely Deep CNN model and post-processing step. For the first stage, the normalized input frame is passed through the EffDB-UNet model. This model is based on the combination of three major components: EfficientNet Backbone (B4) [14] as Encoder, UNet as Decoder [13] and differentiable binarization (DB) as a head. Inspired by [7], the adaptive thresholding and the DB of output mask are then applied to get the desired output. The EffDB-UNet model takes 3 channel input and gives 2 channel output consisting of segmentation mask and border mask of the same size as the input. In the second stage, the label is generated for the outputs, inspired by the Progressive Scale Expansion Network (PSENet) [16], the threshold segmentation and border mask are used to generate quadrilateral of text regions described by a set of segments with a threshold of 0.6. The model is completely trained on SynthText dataset and ICDAR19-MLT Scene Text dataset [11], and finally finetuned on the competition training dataset along with non-text data collected from ICDAR2015 scene text dataset [6]. While training the model augmentation techniques such as East Random Cropping, Random Flipping, and Random Rotation are used.

4.3   THDL-Det

The THDL-Det system is submitted for the detection task by Shanyu Xiao, Ruijie Yan, Gang Yao, Haodong Shi and Liangrui Peng from the Department of Electronic Engineering, Tsinghua University, Beijing, China.

The system is an end-to-end text spotter based on the Mask R-CNN instance segmentation framework [4], and the text detection process can be divided into two stages. At the first stage, a CNN extracts high-level feature maps from an input image, and the region proposal network (RPN) classifies positive/negative anchors and makes regression to achieve precise location. Guided by the classification and regression objective functions in the training process, the RPN generates a set of rectangle proposal boxes for text regions. At the second stage, a varying-size RoIAlign layer is proposed to extract features for region proposals with different aspect ratios. Then two fully-connected sub-networks filter non-text regions and make more precise location predictions. A fully-convolutional network is used to predict an instance mask for each text region, and a smallest enclosing quadrilateral is constructed from the mask. The hyper-parameters in Mask R-CNN, including anchor aspect ratios, different schemes and parameters of non-maximum suppression are fine-tuned. The ResNeXt-101 [18] is used as the backbone, and the multiscale training strategy is adopted. The system is pre-trained on the SynthText dataset and the ICDAR 2019 MLT dataset [11], and fine-tuned on the AcTiVComp20 training set of text detection. The system is implemented using the PyTorch framework. Detection results of different TV channels in the AcTiVComp20 dataset are generated by a single model.

4.4   THDL-Rec

The THDL-Rec system is submitted for the recognition task by Ruijie Yan, Shanyu Xiao, Gang Yao and Liangrui Peng from the Department of Electronic Engineering, Tsinghua University, Beijing, China.

The system adopts a CNN-LSTM-CTC framework to recognize Arabic text lines in videos. For feature extraction, a modified EfficientNet-B5 [14] with a U-shaped structure is used. The original EfficientNet-B5 has seven convolutional blocks. To construct the U-shaped structure, the output of the seventh convolutional block is up-sampled and summed up with the output of the fifth convolutional block, and further up-sampled and summed up with the output of the third convolutional block. Feature maps output by the U-shaped CNN has a size of $512 \times 8 \times w$, where 512 is the number of channels and 8 is the height of the feature maps. w is the width of the feature maps, which is proportional to the width of the input image. Five additional convolutional layers and a max-pooling layer are then used to transform feature maps into a feature sequence with size $w \times 512$. Finally, the feature sequence is processed by a two-layer bidirectional LSTM network followed by a CTC decoding layer for text transcription. The system is pre-trained on about 3 million synthetic text line images and fine-tuned on the AcTiVComp20 training set of text recognition. The synthetic text line images were generated by using the ANT Corpus [1] as text contents. The system is implemented by using the PyTorch framework on a single NVIDIA Tesla V100 GPU. Recognition results of different TV channels in the AcTiVComp20 dataset are generated by a single model. By evaluating on the whole competition test set with batch size = 1 and beam size = 5, the average recognition time on a single image is 12,8 ms.

4.5   ArabOCR

The ArabOCR system is submitted for the recognition task by Abdul Rehman from the School of Electrical Engineering and Computer Science, NUST, Islamabad, Pakistan, Adnan Ul-Hasan and Faisal Shafait from the Deep Learning Laboratory, National Center of Artificial Intelligence (NCAI), Islamabad, Pakistan.

This system is based on a CRNN architecture, which consists of three parts: i) First a CNN block is used to extract features from the input text image. Each convolution layer of this block is activated with a Leaky Rectifier Linear Units (LeakyReLU) layer. Batch Normalization is also used in all convolutional layers to normalize the inputs of non-linear activation functions. ii) After the CNN stage, 2 Bi-directional GRU recurrent layers (with 256 cells per layer) are applied. BatchNorm and LeakyReLU are again used here. iii) The last part contains a single convolution layer with kernel size of 1, followed by a LogSoftmax layer. Finally the CTC layer is used to decode the output.

The original images are converted into grayscale and resized to have a fixed height of 64 while keeping the aspect ratio. During training, input images have been randomly augmented. A total of 8 augmentations were (3 shape-based and 5 color-based) applied per image. The system was implemented using Pytorch Framework. The training was performed on a single Nvidia GeForce GTX1080 Ti GPU. The model took approximately 8 h to be trained.

5   Results and Analysis

This section presents results of the submitted methods under each task along with their analysis. Final results at the end of the competition period are pro-

Table 3. Results of Task 1 (Text detection). R, P and F respectively denote Recall, Precision and F-measure.

Protocol/System		P1	P4.1	P4.2	P4.3	P4.3bis	P4.4	P7
Text-Fcos	R	0.83	0.88	0.91	0.91	**0.87 (1)**	0.89	0.88
	P	0.85	0.87	0.91	0.91	0.87	0.89	0.88
	F	0.84 (3)	0.88 (2)	0.91 (2)	0.91 (2)	**0.87**	0.89 (2)	0.88 (2)
THDL-Det	R	0.92	0.90	0.92	0.92	0.79	0.91	0.91
	P	0.90	0.90	0.92	0.92	0.79	0.91	0.91
	F	**0.91 (1)**	**0.90 (1)**	**0.92 (1)**	**0.92 (1)**	0.79	**0.91 (1)**	**0.91 (1)**
EffDB-UNet	R	0.89	0.83	0.76	0.77	0.86	0.79	0.79
	P	0.89	0.83	0.76	0.77	**0.88 (1)**	0.79	0.79
	F	0.89 (2)	0.83 (3)	0.76 (3)	0.77 (3)	**0.87**	0.79 (3)	0.79 (3)

Table 4. Results of Task 2 (Text recognition)

Protocol/System		P3	P6.1	P6.2	P6.3	P6.3bis	P6.4	P9
THDL-Rec	CRR	99.83	99.34	99.48	99.43	–	99.43	99.53
(1)	LRR	**95.80**	**87.43**	**85.94**	**85.07**	–	**85.63**	**88.71**
ArabOCR	CRR	99.49	98.31	98.72	99.07	–	98.75	98.94
(2)	LRR	90.84	72.77	71.48	77.83	–	74.10	79.03

vided in Table 3 and Table 4. All participants in Task 1 have employed semantic segmentation methods to accurately localize text instances. THDL-Det adopted a two-stage anchor-based strategy following the Mask R-CNN framework, and used ResNeXt as backbone. EffDB-UNet adopted a two-stage anchor-free strategy that combines EfficientNet with UNet followed by PSENet as a refinement step. While Text-Fcos was built on one-stage anchor-free detector (FCOS). EfficientNet was also used here as a backbone.

The THDL-Det team achieves the best score in F-measure, precision and recall for almost all protocols. The system provides an effective F-measure of 0.91 for the global (channel-free) protocol 7, which implies its generalization ability in detecting text regions regardless the resolution. Yet, this score has decreased by 11% in the protocol 4.3bis (SD 480 × 360, YouTube quality). This can be explained by the fact that such object detectors i.e., Mask R-CNN, rely heavily on predefined anchors, which are sensitive to hyper-parameters (e.g., input size, aspect ratio, scales). The Text-Fcos team takes the second place with a small difference from the winner in terms of F-measure (ranging from 1 to 3%) for all protocols except two: Protocol p1 where THDL-Det is ahead by 7% and protocol p4.3bis where Text-Fcos is ahead by 8%. EffDB-UNet team achieves good results for all protocols and gets the first place in protocol p4.3bis with Text-Fcos, and outperformed him by 5% in protocol p1.

The best result of the recognition challenge is marked in bold in Table 4. THDL-Rec system shows a superiority in all the evaluation protocols with a gain ranging from 5% to 14% compared to the ArabOCR system. It is worth to note that both systems have used a CRNN architecture in a different manner.

The best achieved results on the global protocol 9, which are around 88% in terms of line recognition rate, represent a significant improvement in the Arabic Video OCR field.

Yet, working on text detection and text recognition separately is considered less challenging than working on the end-to-end recognition where all textlines in a given input frame should be correctly localized and recognized in a single step. We are hoping to receive more submissions in the next edition of AcTiVComp, especially for the end-to-end task.

6   Conclusions

The third edition of AcTiVComp has attracted four teams for participating in the two tasks of text detection and text recognition. As seen in the results and analysis section, the rates of the winning systems, from the THDL team, are very interesting, showing a significant improvement from the state-of-the-art performances on this research problem [20], e.g., compared to the highest rates of the previous editions of AcTiVComp, the new achieved detection F-score has increased by 6% on the global protocol p7, and for the recognition task, the new results are higher with gains of respectively 13% and 14% on the global protocols p6.4 (SD TV channels) and p9 (All TV channels). The obtained results can be further improved. Hence, we look forward to have more participants in the future editions of AcTiVComp and more researchers joining the Arabic video text detection and recognition research topic.

References

1. Chouigui, A., Khiroun, O.B., Elayeb, B.: Ant corpus: an arabic news text collection for textual classification. In: IEEE/ACS 14th International Conference on Computer Systems and Applications (AICCSA), pp. 135–142. IEEE (2017)
2. Hamroun, M., Lajmi, S., Nicolas, H., Amous, I.: Arabic text-based video indexing and retrieval system enhanced by semantic content and relevance feedback. In: IEEE/ACS 16th International Conference on Computer Systems and Applications (AICCSA), pp. 1–8. IEEE (2019)
3. Han, K., Wang, Y., Tian, Q., Guo, J., Xu, C., Xu, C.: GhostNet: more features from cheap operations. In: Proceedings of the IEEE/CVF Conference on Computer Vision and Pattern Recognition, pp. 1580–1589 (2020)
4. He, K., Gkioxari, G., Dollár, P., Girshick, R.: Mask R-CNN. In: Proceedings of the IEEE International Conference on Computer Vision, pp. 2961–2969 (2017)
5. Jain, M., Mathew, M., Jawahar, C.: Unconstrained scene text and video text recognition for arabic script. In: 1st International Workshop on Arabic Script Analysis and Recognition (ASAR), pp. 26–30. IEEE (2017)
6. Karatzas, D., et al.: ICDAR 2015 competition on robust reading. In: 13th International Conference on Document Analysis and Recognition (ICDAR), pp. 1156–1160. IEEE (2015)
7. Liao, M., Wan, Z., Yao, C., Chen, K., Bai, X.: Real-time scene text detection with differentiable binarization. In: AAAI, pp. 11474–11481 (2020)

8. Lin, T.Y., Goyal, P., Girshick, R., He, K., Dollár, P.: Focal loss for dense object detection. In: Proceedings of the IEEE International Conference on Computer Vision, pp. 2980–2988 (2017)
9. Lu, T., Palaiahnakote, S., Tan, C.L., Liu, W.: Video Text Detection. ACVPR. Springer, London (2014). https://doi.org/10.1007/978-1-4471-6515-6
10. Mirza, A., Zeshan, O., Atif, M., Siddiqi, I.: Detection and recognition of cursive text from video frames. EURASIP J. Image Video Process. **2020**(1), 1–19 (2020). https://doi.org/10.1186/s13640-020-00523-5
11. Nayef, N., et al.: ICDAR 2019 robust reading challenge on multi-lingual scene text detection and recognition–RRC-MLT-2019. In: International Conference on Document Analysis and Recognition (ICDAR), pp. 1582–1587. IEEE (2019)
12. Rezatofighi, H., Tsoi, N., Gwak, J., Sadeghian, A., Reid, I., Savarese, S.: Generalized intersection over union: a metric and a loss for bounding box regression. In: Proceedings of the IEEE Conference on Computer Vision and Pattern Recognition, pp. 658–666 (2019)
13. Ronneberger, O., Fischer, P., Brox, T.: U-Net: convolutional networks for biomedical image segmentation. In: Navab, N., Hornegger, J., Wells, W.M., Frangi, A.F. (eds.) MICCAI 2015. LNCS, vol. 9351, pp. 234–241. Springer, Cham (2015). https://doi.org/10.1007/978-3-319-24574-4_28
14. Tan, M., Le, Q.V.: EfficientNet: rethinking model scaling for convolutional neural networks. arXiv e-prints arXiv:1905.11946 (2019)
15. Tian, Z., Shen, C., Chen, H., He, T.: FCOS: fully convolutional one-stage object detection. In: Proceedings of the IEEE International Conference on Computer Vision, pp. 9627–9636 (2019)
16. Wang, W., et al.: Shape robust text detection with progressive scale expansion network. In: Proceedings of the IEEE Conference on Computer Vision and Pattern Recognition, pp. 9336–9345 (2019)
17. Wu, Y., He, K.: Group normalization. In: Ferrari, V., Hebert, M., Sminchisescu, C., Weiss, Y. (eds.) ECCV 2018. LNCS, vol. 11217, pp. 3–19. Springer, Cham (2018). https://doi.org/10.1007/978-3-030-01261-8_1
18. Xie, S., Girshick, R., Dollár, P., Tu, Z., He, K.: Aggregated residual transformations for deep neural networks. In: Proceedings of the IEEE Conference on Computer Vision and Pattern Recognition, pp. 1492–1500 (2017)
19. Zayene, O., et al.: ICPR 2016 contest on arabic text detection and recognition in video frames-AcTiVComp. In: 23rd International Conference on Pattern Recognition (ICPR), pp. 187–191. IEEE (2016)
20. Zayene, O., Hennebert, J., Ingold, R., Amara, N.E.B.: ICDAR 2017 competition on arabic text detection and recognition in multi-resolution video frames. In: 2017 International Conference on Document Analysis and Recognition, pp. 1460–1465. IEEE (2017)
21. Zayene, O., Hennebert, J., Touj, S.M., Ingold, R., Amara, N.E.B.: A dataset for arabic text detection, tracking and recognition in news videos-activ. In: 13th International Conference on Document Analysis and Recognition (ICDAR), pp. 996–1000. IEEE (2015)
22. Zayene, O., Touj, S.M., Hennebert, J., Ingold, R., Amara, N.E.B.: Data, protocol and algorithms for performance evaluation of text detection in arabic news video. In: 2nd International Conference on Advanced Technologies for Signal and Image Processing (ATSIP), pp. 258–263. IEEE (2016)

23. Zayene, O., Touj, S.M., Hennebert, J., Ingold, R., Amara, N.E.B.: Open datasets and tools for arabic text detection and recognition in news video frames. J. Imaging 4(2), 32 (2018)
24. Zhang, S., Chi, C., Yao, Y., Lei, Z., Li, S.Z.: Bridging the gap between anchor-based and anchor-free detection via adaptive training sample selection. In: Proceedings of the IEEE/CVF Conference on Computer Vision and Pattern Recognition, pp. 9759–9768 (2020)

Competition on HArvesting Raw Tables from Infographics

Preface

This volume contains the proceedings of the 2nd Competition on HArvesting Raw Tables from Infographics (CHART), which was organized in conjunction with the International Conference on Pattern Recognition (ICPR) 2020. The main item of the volume is the competition report written by the competition organizers that gives an overview of all submissions as well as the competition results. Analyzing chart images is an outstanding problem in pattern recognition, and the results of this competition show that there is much potential for improvement.

Out of the 27 teams that registered for participation in the competition, 7 teams submitted results for at least some of the 7 tasks that were defined. Participants had the option to submit results on one or both datasets that were provided for a total of 14 competition tracks, from which the overall competition winner was derived. More details can be found in this volume or the competition website https://chartinfo.github.io/.

We invited the participants to submit their own papers describing the details of their systems. Two participants chose to submit their papers for peer review by the organizing committee. Reviewing was not blind because the competition organizers are public information and participants had to identify themselves in order to register for the competition. Both submitted papers were accepted by the competition organizing committee for publication in this volume.

November 2020

Chris Tensmeyer
Kenny Davila

Organization

Organizing Committee

Kenny Davila   University at Buffalo
Chris Tensmeyer   Adobe Research
Sumit Shekhar   Adobe Research
Hrituraj Singh   Adobe Research
Srirangaraj Setlur   University at Buffalo
Venu Govindaraju   University at Buffalo

ICPR 2020 - Competition on Harvesting Raw Tables from Infographics

Kenny Davila[1]([✉])[iD], Chris Tensmeyer[2][iD], Sumit Shekhar[2][iD],
Hrituraj Singh[2][iD], Srirangaraj Setlur[1][iD], and Venu Govindaraju[1][iD]

[1] Department of Computer Science and Engineering, University at Buffalo,
Buffalo, NY, USA
{kennydav,setlur,govind}@buffalo.edu
[2] Adobe Research, San Jose, USA
{tensmeye,sushekha,hrisingh}@adobe.com

Abstract. This work summarizes the results of the second Competition on Harvesting Raw Tables from Infographics (ICPR 2020 CHART-Infographics). Chart Recognition is difficult and multifaceted, so for this competition we divide the process into the following tasks: Chart Image Classification (Task 1), Text Detection and Recognition (Task 2), Text Role Classification (Task 3), Axis Analysis (Task 4), Legend Analysis (Task 5), Plot Element Detection and Classification (Task 6.a), Data Extraction (Task 6.b), and End-to-End Data Extraction (Task 7). We provided two sets of datasets for training and evaluation of the participant submissions. The first set is based on synthetic charts (Adobe Synth) generated from real data sources using matplotlib. The second one is based on manually annotated charts extracted from the Open Access section of the PubMed Central (UB PMC). More than 25 teams registered out of which 7 submitted results for different tasks of the competition. While results on synthetic data are near perfect at times, the same models still have room to improve when it comes to data extraction from real charts. The data, annotation tools, and evaluation scripts have been publicly released for academic use.

Keywords: Chart recognition · Competition · Chart dataset

1 Introduction

Visualizations can be helpful tools for the communication of complex ideas. Among these, we find statistical charts which are used to display data in a way that facilitates the observation of patterns that are otherwise much harder to perceive using tables. In many cases, charts are also the main source used to share raw data that is not made publicly available in any other formats.

Electronic supplementary material The online version of this chapter (https://doi.org/10.1007/978-3-030-68793-9_27) contains supplementary material, which is available to authorized users.

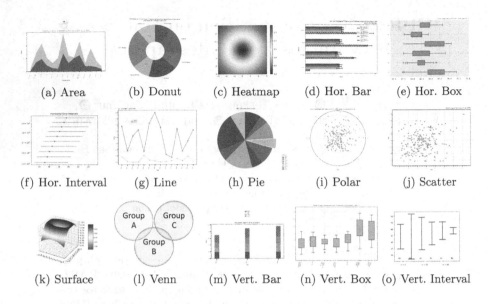

Fig. 1. A sample of 15 types of charts used in the competition.

This is just one out of many reasons that have motivated past works in the field of Chart Recognition [1,7,19]. Despite significant work in this field, not many have used standardized comparisons against previous methods. This is in part due to the lack of large scale benchmarks which can be used for this purpose. This began to change with the first edition of the Competition on Harvesting Raw Tables from Infographics (ICDAR 2019 CHART-Infographics) [8], which provided both data and tools for the chart recognition community. This paper describe the continuation of this effort through the second edition of the CHART-Infographics competition at the International Conference on Pattern Recognition (ICPR) 2020 (Fig. 1).

In the second edition, we provided two pairs of datasets for training and evaluation of chart recognition systems (Sect. 2). The first pair of datasets, *Adobe Synth*, is based on synthetic charts generated from real data using matplotlib. The second pair of datasets, *UB PMC*, is based on manually annotated charts from PubMed Central[1], a free full-text archive of biomedical and life sciences journal literature at the U.S. National Institutes of Health's National Library of Medicine. We divide the Chart Recognition challenge into a pipeline of 6 tasks, and we also consider a seventh task to evaluate end-to-end systems (Sect. 3). We evaluate these tasks using revised versions of the metrics that were proposed in the first edition of the competition [8]. Many teams registered for this edition (Sect. 4), out of which 7 submitted results for different tasks (Sect. 5). We analyzed these results and the methods that generated them to provide our

---

[1] https://www.ncbi.nlm.nih.gov/pmc/.

Table 1. Distribution of chart types on the competition training and testing sets.

Chart Type	Adobe Synth.		UB PMC	
	Train	Test	Train	Test
Area	1,200	250	120	52
Line	1,200	250	7,401	3,155
Manhattan	0	0	123	53
Scatter	1,200	250	875	475
Scatter-line	0	0	1,260	558
Polar	1,200	250	0	0
Donut	1,200	250	0	0
Pie	1,200	250	170	72
Horizontal box	1,200	249	0	0
Vertical box	1,200	250	316	447
Horizontal bar (grouped)	1,200	250	429	358
Horizontal bar (stacked)	1,200	250		
Vertical bar (grouped)	1,200	250	3,818	1,636
Vertical bar (stacked)	1,200	250		
Horizontal interval	0	0	109	47
Vertical interval	0	0	342	147
Map	0	0	373	160
Heatmap	0	0	138	59
Surface	0	0	110	45
Venn	0	0	52	23
Total	14,400	2,999	15,636	7,287

conclusions (Sect. 6) based on this competition. The data, annotation tools, and evaluation scripts have been publicly released for academic use[2].

2   Data

We constructed two types of datasets for this competition: synthetic and real. For each type, we have provided both a training set that was released to participants upon registration and a corresponding testing set that was released to all participants at the same time. Participants were given one week to run their systems on the test data and return their results for evaluation by the organizers. There is a large overlap in terms of the classes covered by both types of datasets, but some classes are only included in one type (see Table 1). Both types are described in this section.

---

[2] https://chartinfo.github.io/.

2.1   Synthetic Chart Dataset

We constructed the synthetic chart dataset using data from several public sources - (a) World Development Indicators[3], (b) Gender Statistics (World Bank)[4], (c) Government of India Open Data[5], (d) Commodity Trade Statistics[6], (e) US Census Data (for 2000 and 2010)[7], (f) Price Volume Data for Stocks and ETFs[8].

Chart Generation: Multiple charts of different categories were created using the Matplotlib library[9]. The tabular data was first cleansed and converted into a common format. From each table, different sets of columns and randomized rows were selected to create the charts. To emulate features of real-world charts, we introduced variations in chart component such as: (1) positioning of titles, legends, and different stackings of legend entries (vertical/horizontal); (2) font families and sizes for different elements; (3) background/foreground text colors, color and/or width of lines, borders, grids, and markers; (4) bar widths and inner/outer radii of pies, exploded pies; and the (5) elements like plot text, minor/major axis ticks, tick direction, axis label variations. The statistics of different types of charts is shown in Table 1.

Chart Annotations: The required annotations for charts were obtained using functions provided by Matplotlib API including tight bounding boxes for text regions, axes, legends, and data elements (e.g. bars, lines, scatter plot markers, box plot elements and pies). For pie charts, tight masks were produced covering each pie region.

2.2   PubMedCentral Chart Dataset

A sample of real charts was extracted from the PubMed Central. The Open Access Section has more than 1.8 million papers, out of which we extracted more than 40,000 papers from different journals in fields such as epidemiology, public health, pathology, and genetics which typically contain many charts. This is the same sample of papers described in the first edition [8].

Data Sampling. We started with the 4242 chart images that were labeled for the first edition of this competition [8]. Using this as a seed, we trained a convolutional neural network using Triplet loss to learn an embedding for different types of charts. This network allowed us to sample images from regions

---

[3] www.datacatalog.worldbank.org/dataset/world-development-indicators.
[4] www.datacatalog.worldbank.org/dataset/gender-statistics.
[5] www.visualize.data.gov.in.
[6] www.kaggle.com/unitednations/global-commodity-trade-statistics/data.
[7] www.kaggle.com/muonneutrino/us-census-demographic-data/data.
[8] www.kaggle.com/borismarjanovic/price-volume-data-for-all-us-stocks-etfs.
[9] www.matplotlib.org/.

Table 2. Distribution of charts in the testing set. All available charts on each dataset were split into 5 sets used to evaluate different tasks. Note that all pairs of splits need to be disjoint except the first and the last one where no ground truth is provided to the participants.

Split	Adobe Synth	UB PMC	Tasks
Split 1	1,240	5103	Task 1
Split 2	352	732	Task 2
Split 3	528	726	Tasks 3, 4, 5
Split 4	527	726	Tasks 6a, 6b
Split 5	352	726	Task 7
Total	2,999	7,287	

of the embedded space that were not covered by the original sample. The newly sampled images were manually labeled first as either chart or non chart, and single-panel or multi-panel (4 possible combinations). We then chose the single panel chart images and sub-classified them into chart types. Using the newly annotated images and the original sample, we then retrained the embedding network and repeated this sampling process until we collected more than 65,000 images, out of which more than 22,500 were single panel charts. For some under-represented classes (e.g. vertical box charts and horizontal bar charts), we further found multi-panel image charts which contained them and manually labeled the panels to split them into single panel chart images. These charts were further split into training and testing datasets as shown in Table 1. The testing set was further split into 5 disjoint sets used to evaluate different tasks each as shown in Table 2. This is necessary due to the fact that some tasks require inputs from the previous task.

Data Annotation. We further extended and improved our existing tools for the annotation of charts. We started with images which were already divided by chart types. We further split them into small batches (around 60 charts each) for further annotation. A small team of annotators was trained to use the tools that we created to produce a variety of annotations on the chart images.

First, they annotated the text regions on the chart by providing the location, transcription and role of each text region. Unlike the previous competition, this time we allowed text regions to be represented by quadrilaterals to handle rotated text properly. Annotators were only required to provide a rough but valid boundary for the text region and the tool included an option which further refined these text regions by fitting them to the text they contained using connected component analysis. The text itself was annotated in a semi-automatic fashion by first using the Tesseract OCR [23] to transcribe most of the selected text regions, and further manual error corrections when required. For special symbols and formulas, the annotators were required to provide LATEXstrings.

The next step was legend and axes annotations. For legends, they had to mark tight boxes around the corresponding data marks for each legend entry. For axes, they had to provide a bounding box of the plot region which defines the position of the x and y axes. They also had to annotate the titles of each axes, tick labels, axis types (categorical vs numeric), and axis scales if they were numeric (linear, logarithmic, other). In addition, they had to provide the tick mark locations, types of tick marks (markers or separators), and associations between tick labels and tick marks. Finally, they had to annotate the data on specific types of charts (Line, Scatter, Horizontal/Vertical Box and Horizontal/Vertical Bar). For each type of chart, the tool was modified to provide different options which made the annotation process faster, allowing us to greatly upscale our datasets. The tool also now includes multiple options for quality control which basically attempts to parse the chart based on the annotations provided and automatically finds and notifies the user of existing inconsistencies in the annotation. After that, all charts were again manually inspected to find and correct additional errors which might not have been captured by the automatic checks.

3   Tasks and Metrics

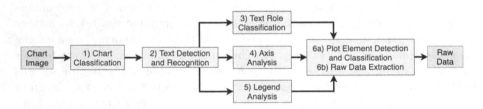

Fig. 2. The process of extracting data from chart images. The output from initial tasks can be used to inform later tasks.

Extracting data from chart images is a complex task. To allow the development of algorithms for specific parts of the process, we have broken it down into smaller tasks (Fig. 2): 1) chart classification, 2) text detection and recognition, 3) text role classification, 4) axis analysis, 5) legend analysis, 6) data extraction, and 7) end-to-end data extraction. In this section, we describe each task and the metrics used for evaluation. For each task, we provide the ground truth output from previous tasks in order to analyze the performance of systems independently of errors made in previous tasks. Note that the implementations of all metrics are publicly available[10].

As mentioned in Sect. 2, we have two datasets with very different properties. We consider individual leaderboards per task per dataset for a total of 14 leaderboards. In order to select the competition winners, we use a point-based system

---

[10] https://chartinfo.github.io/.

where the method that obtains the top-1 rank on each task on each dataset is awarded 4 points, the top-2 rank gets 3 points, the top-3 rank gets 2 points and the remaining teams with a submission get 1 point for participation, while the rest who did not participate on that task or dataset get 0. We then add up all points across the leaderboards to create the overall ranking of participants.

3.1   Task 1. Chart Classification

In this task, chart images are classified into different types as described in Table 1. Note that some classes are only represented in the synthetic dataset and others are only represented in the UB PMC dataset. Most of these classes are only considered for this task. For each class, we compute the precision and recall, and then take the harmonic mean (F-measure). We use the average of these values as the final score.

3.2   Task 2. Text Detection and Recognition

The input for the task is the chart image and its correct chart class. Then, text detection and recognition is performed at the logical element level. This means some multi-word and even multi-line elements such as titles and axis tick labels are treated as a single element. Previously, we used bounding boxes for text regions [8]. In this edition, we now use polygons, specifically quadrilaterals, to represent text regions.

During evaluation, the predicted text regions are compared to the ground truth quadrilaterals and they are considered a match if their intersection over union (IOU) exceeded 0.5. For many to one and one to many matches, the pair with the highest overlap is chosen and the remaining regions are counted as false negatives or false positives. Matched pairs are scored by Normalized Character Recognition Rate (NCRR) for recognition using $\max(1 - NCER, 0)$ as well as IOU for detection. Normalized Character Error Rate (NCER) is measured as the edit distance between ground truth string and predicted string normalized with respect to ground truth string length. Some regions include special symbols and even mathematical expressions which are all labeled using LaTeX. At the moment we simply convert these annotations back to unicode strings which might not be ideal for some complex expression as well as symbols having both super and sub indices.

For each image, the maximum between ground truth text regions and predicted text regions is used to normalize the detection scores. For recognition scores, we simply use the number of ground truth boxes. The harmonic mean of detection and recognition scores is used as the final score per image, and the average of this metric is computed for the entire test as the final score for the task.

3.3   Task 3. Text Role Classification

In this task, participants are provided with the GT chart type and the correct text region-transcripts pairs, and their target is to classify each region based on their semantic roles. The classes considered are: *chart title, axis title, legend title, legend label, mark label, tick label, tick grouping, value label* and *other*. Submissions were evaluated using the average per-class F-measure (same as Task 1).

3.4   Task 4. Axis Analysis

In Task 4, systems must associate tick labels with pixel coordinates. This is a necessary step in order to convert the coordinates of chart data point geometries from pixel space to the chart space represented by the axes. Similar to Task 3, the inputs are the chart image, its class and the text regions with transcriptions, but participants do not know which text regions are the tick labels. Then, for each axis the output is a list of text regions (tick labels), each paired with a (x, y) point representing the tick location in the image.

The evaluation is based on a weighted F-measure, where each tick mark can get a score between 0 and 1 based on location accuracy. Extra elements incorrectly predicted as ticks receive a score of 0. There are two thresholds used ($a = 1.0\%$ and $b = 2.0\%$) which are proportional to the chart image diagonal. With these, we score predictions located at a distance d from the GT tick location using:

$$s(d, a, b) = \left\{ \begin{array}{ll} 1, & \text{for } d \leq a \\ \frac{b-d}{b-a}, & \text{for } a \leq d \leq b \\ 0, & \text{for } d \geq b \end{array} \right\} \tag{1}$$

Recall is computed as the sum of the scores divided by the number of GT ticks, and precision is the sum of scores divided by the number of predicted ticks.

3.5   Task 5. Legend Analysis

The goal of legend analysis is to pair textual legend labels with their corresponding graphical markers. Similar to Task 4, participants must produce a list of text regions, each paired with a bounding box that surrounds its corresponding legend marker. The input is same as Task 4 which means that all text regions are given without knowing which ones belong to the legend. The final score is a normalized IOU score, where true positive predictions must have the text element and a partial score is determined by either the recall or the IOU of the legend marker bounding box. Normalization is done by dividing the sum by the largest between the number of expected legend boxes and the number of predicted boxes, thus punishing for false positives as well. Previously, we only reported the IOU-based metric [8], but this time we are also reporting the Recall-based version.

3.6   Task 6. Data Extraction

Charts are often used to convey numerical data, and the main goal of this competition is to get an approximation of the original data (e.g. data points) used to generate the chart. We further divide this task into two sub-tasks where the inputs are the ideal outputs from all previous tasks.

Task 6.a Plot Element Detection and Classification. All visual elements representing data must be localized in the chart. This includes bars, lines, points and boxes (with whiskers). For bar charts, the expected output is a set of bounding boxes representing each bar. For scatter plots, the output is a set of (x, y) points. For line plots, the output is a set of lines, where each line is represented as an ordered sequence of points. For box plots, the output is a set of boxes, where each box is represented by a tuple with 5 elements corresponding to the min, third quartile, median, first quartile, and max values. We currently ignore outlier marks and assume the ends of the whiskers to be the min and max values.

For all chart types considered here, the metric involves a set of predicted objects that need to be aligned with a set of ground truth objects. We use a difference distance function for each chart type to define a matching score between a predicted object and the ground truth object. For predicted objects $P = \{p_i\}$ and GT objects $G = \{g_i\}$, we construct the $K \times K$ ($K = \max(|P|, |G|)$) cost matrix $\mathbf{C}$ where C_{ij} encodes the cost of matching p_i with g_j. When $i > |P|$ or $j > |G|$, $C_{ij} := 1$ to denote that unmatched objects incur maximum cost. We then use the Hungarian algorithm [16] to solve the assignment problem defined by this cost matrix, which yields the optimal pairing of predicted and GT objects and c, the total cost of this pairing.

The final score (higher is better) for each image is $1 - \frac{c}{K}$. We then average each chart image's score across the entire test set. Further details on the distance functions per chart element are available in our competition website including the scripts used to compute these metrics.

Task 6.b Raw Data Extraction. The output of this task is the data that was used to render the chart image. In the case of box plots, we only require the summary statistics (i.e., min, 1st, 2nd, 3rd quartiles, and max) as those are sufficient to re-create the plot. The output of this task is a set of data series objects, where a data series consists of a name (string) and a sequence of (x, y) values (order only matters for line plots). If the x-axis has a discrete domain, then we represent each x value as a string, otherwise it is a real value. All y values are real numbers. The name of a data series corresponds to the textual label found in the legend or mark. If there is no legend in the chart, then we check for mark labels and if these are also absent then the GT name for the data series is ignored for evaluation purposes.

To compare a set of predicted data series with a set of GT data series, we find the optimal pairing using the Hungarian algorithm [16] of data series under a data series distance function that compares both data series names and sets of points. Specifically, the distance D between data series is

$$D(n_1, d_1, n_2, d_2) = (1 - \beta_1)L(n_1, n_2)^\alpha + \beta_1 M(d_1, d_2) \qquad (2)$$

where n_1 and n_2 are the names of the data series, L is the normalized Levenshtein Edit Distance, M is a distance function appropriate for the chart type, and d_1 and d_2 are the two sets of points. The hyperparameters $\alpha = 1$ and $\beta_1 = 0.75$ control the relative contribution of the point set comparison and the name comparison.

Each evaluation of M may also contain an assignment problem to find the optimal pairing of (x, y) points between d_1 and d_2 (as in Task 6a). When x is discrete, we use the normalized string edit distance, L. For continuous values, we use the Mahalanobis distance to normalize the dataset scales across images. For line plots with continuous x values, instead of pairing points, we approximate the integral of the difference between the predicted and GT line, using linear interpolation to account for differences in the predicted and GT x values. For further details, please see the online supplementary materials and scripts to compute this metric.

3.7   Task 7. Raw Data Extraction

The desired output of this challenging task is the same as task 6b, except that the only input is the chart image (i.e., this is the entire pipeline end-to-end). In this case, idealized outputs of tasks 1–5 are not provided, so the method must perform all of these steps in series, which allows for errors to cascade. This task reflects real-world performance of systems and is scored using the same metric as 6b.

4   Participants

A total of 27 teams registered for the competition, out of which 7 finally submitted results for different subsets of tasks each. In this section, we briefly describe each team who made a submission to the competition.

1) DeepBlueAI: Zhipeng Luo, Zhiguang Zhang, Ge Li, Lixuan Che, Jianye He, and Zhenyu Xu from DeepBlue Technology and Peking University. *Task 1:* Employed a ResNet50 classifier [11] trained with a cross-entropy loss and label smoothing. *Task 2:* The detection model is a Cascade R-CNN model [2] with a ResNext-101 backbone [24], Deformable Convolution layers [5], and GCBlocks [3]. For text recognition, a CRNN model [22] trained with CTC loss [10] and data augmentation is applied to the detected text boxes after rotating them to make the text horizontal. *Task 3:* To classify text role, Random Forest and LightGBM [15] classifiers consume features derived from bounding box geometry, textual content, alignment with other text boxes, and position relative to the detected legend (if present). *Task 4:* A CenterNet [9] with a DLA-34 [26] backbone is used to detect tick locations via heatmap prediction. One branch of the network predicts the offset to the associated text label and matching is performed by L1 distance. *Task 5:* A CenterNet model is used to detect both legend graphics and legend pairs of graphics and legend text blocks. Then the Hungarian algorithm is used to assign graphics to text blocks. *Task 6:* CenterNet is used to detect rectangular elements and point elements are detected by a separate heatmap prediction model. To match chart elements with legend entries, they use similarity between HOG [6] features extracted from the chart elements and the legend entries. For charts without legends, K-means clustering is performed on HOG features to group chart elements.

2) Magic: Wang Chen, Cui Kaixu and Zhang Suya from XinHuaZhiYunInc. and State Key Laboratory of Media Convergence. *Task 1:* A ResNet50 [11] was used for the Synthetic data and an ensemble of 10 ResNet152 models was used for the PMC data. *Task 2:* They detect blocks of text using a Mask RCNN network [12] with a ResNeXt-152-FPN [17] backbone, deformable convolutions [5], and network cascades [2]. An attentional sequence to sequence model [20] composed of BLSTM layers and trained with numerous public datasets is used for text recognition. *Task 3:* They employed fusion approach of an object detector for 5 text classes and LayoutLM [25] for all text classes. *Task 5:* First the legend area was detected using a model similar to that of Task 2. Then the cropped legend image was fed to a Cascade RCNN [2] to find legend markers.

3) Lenovo-SCUT-Intsig: Hui Li, Yuhao Huang, Bangdong Chen, Luyan Wang, Kai Ding, Sihang Wu, Canyu Xie, June Lv, Wei Fei, Yan Li, Qianying Liao, Guozhi Tang, Jiapeng Wang, XinFeng Chang, and Hongliang Li from SCUT, Lenovo, and IntSig. *Task 1:* An ensemble composed of 5 DenseNet-121 [13] models, a ResNet-152 [11], and a ResNet-152 with pyramid convolutions is trained using class-balancing techniques. *Task 2:* They use Cascade R-CNN for the Synthetic dataset and Cascade Mask R-CNN for PMC text block detection. Text blocks are split into lines before inputting them to a CRNN+CTC [10,22] and attention model ensemble. *Task 3:* A weighted ensemble of 3 models that use text semantics, visual features, text features, chart type, and location features is trained with data augmentation.

4) IntSig-SCUT-Lenovo: Hesuo Zhang, Shuang Yan, Weihong Ma Guangsun Yao, Adam Wu, Lianwen Jin from SCUT, Lenovo, and IntSig. *Task 5:* A Cascade Mask R-CNN [2] detects both legend marks and mark-text pairs and the pairing is performed using IoU of the detections. *Task 6:* A modified Pyramid Mask Text Detector [18] is used to detect bar boxes in bar charts, and a Gaussian heatmap regression model [4] is used to detect points in other charts. For task6b, they match the detected elements with legend entries and assign values by interpolation from the tick marks detected locations.

5) SCUT-IntSig-Lenovo: Weihong Ma, Hesuo Zhang, Guozhi Tang, Jiapeng Wang, Sihang Wu, Yuhao Huang, Hui Li, Canyu Xie, Kai Ding, Adam Wu, Qianying Liao, Ptolemy Zhang, and Yichao Huang from SCUT, Lenovo, and IngSig. *Task 4:* Tick detection is performed by Gaussian heatmap regression using a ResNet18 backbone with a deconvolution prediction layer. Heuristics are used to pair detected tick marks with tick labels. *Task 7:* A DenseNet-121 is first used to classify the chart type, and a Cascade RCNN [2] is used for text detection. For text line recognition, the C-RNN model [22] is trained with CTC loss [10]. Tick detection is performed the same as Task 4. Cascade RCNN is used to detect the legend box, the legend marks, and mark-text pairs. Then they detect and classify individual chart elements in the plot area. To associate chart elements with legend entries, they use K-means and RGB histogram features. Finally, real values are created by interpolating between detected tick marks.

6) IPSA: Mandhatya Singh and Puneet Goyal from Indian Institute of Technology Ropar. *Task 1:* DenseNet-121 [13] with an additional set of dense layers, batch normalization [14], and dropout layers have been used. *Task 2:* EAST [27] based text detection (with preprocessing) is used for detecting text boxes.

7) PY: Pengyu Yan from University of Buffalo. *Task 2:* Faster-RCNN [21] is used to detect text regions which are then recognized using the open source Tesseract OCR library. *Task 3:* Faster-RCNN is used to detect plot area, x-axis, y-axis, and legend area, and this information is used to classify text role. *Task 4:* Faster-RCNN is used to detect axis areas after which corner detection is used to localize tick marks. Pairing is performed with nearest bipartition rules.

5   Competition Results

5.1   Task 1. Chart Classification Results

Table 3. Task 1 results: Average F-measure across all predicted chart classes.

Team	Adobe Synth	UB PMC
Lenovo-SCUT-Intsig	**1.00**	**0.928**
DeepBlueAI	**1.00**	0.904
IPSA	0.992	0.863
Magic	0.994	0.905

Table 3 shows the average F-measure of each chart type prediction. For Adobe Synth, all participants achieved near perfect accuracy. The only confusions were among sub-categories of bar-charts. We consider DeepBlueAI and Lenovo-SCUT-Intsig tied for 1st with IPSA and Magic tied for 3rd since their performance difference is not statistically significant.

However, this task is not solved for the real world charts with all 4 systems achieving around 90% average F-measure across the classes. Lenovo-SCUT-Intsig is the clear winner for this dataset, while DeepBlueAI and Magic are tied for the second place.

5.2   Task 2. Text Detection and Recognition Results

Table 4. Task 2 results: Intersection over Union (IoU) for Text Detection; Normalized Character Recognition Rate NCRR for Text Recognition; Combined score is the harmonic mean of IoU and NCRR.

Team	Adobe Synth			UB PMC		
	IoU	NCRR	Combined	IoU	NCRR	Combined
Lenovo-SCUT-Intsig	**0.943**	**0.973**	**0.958**	**0.741**	**0.765**	**0.752**
Magic	0.929	0.922	0.926	0.722	0.735	0.729
DeepBlueAI	0.441	0.702	0.542	0.737	0.584	0.652
Py	–	–	–	0.676	0.606	0.639
IPSA	0.135	0.209	0.164	0.275	0.320	0.296

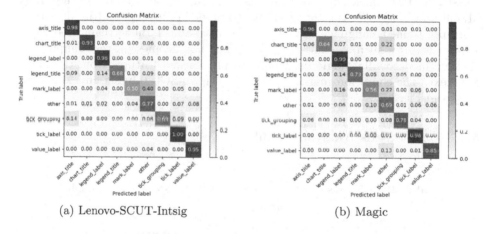

(a) Lenovo-SCUT-Intsig   (b) Magic

Fig. 3. Confusion matrices for Task 3 for the top-2 participants.

Table 4 shows the detection IoU and the NCRR for each submission for both datasets. The top 2 performers, Lenovo-SCUT-Intsig and Magic, used similar techniques, employing Cascade Mask RCNN models [2,12], to achieve similar detection scores. DeepBlueAI also used a similar model and is competitive with the top performer on the UB dataset. The Py submission employed a Faster R-CNN [21], which is shown to not be as effective as the Cascade models at detecting small objects like text.

There was a bigger gap between the top-2 in text recognition with Lenovo-SCUT-Intsig using an ensemble of 2 models (CTC [10] and attention-based), and Magic using a seq-2-seq approach. Tesseract, which is not specifically designed for chart OCR, was used by Py and achieved a lower result, which may suggest that tuning models to perform OCR for charts is necessary for optimal performance.

5.3   Task 3. Text Role Classification Results

Table 5. Task 3 results: Average F-measure across all predicted text role classes.

Team	Adobe Synth	UB PMC
Lenovo-SCUT-Intsig	**1.00**	**0.859**
Magic	**0.999**	0.817
DeepBlueAI	**0.999**	0.772
Py	–	0.654

Table 5 shows the average F-measure for the classification of all text blocks in the charts. There is sufficient regularity in the text placement and style in the synthetic data that 3 participants were able to perfectly or near-perfectly classify all text blocks. In the PMC data, there is much greater variety. Both Magic and Lenovo-SCUT-Intsig employed ensemble models and used features from pre-trained Language Models. The Lenovo-SCUT-Intsig team used hand-crafted features such as chart type, bounding box geometry, etc. as input to a shallow model while Magic used only deeply learned features from the image and text. The confusion matrices for both Lenovo-SCUT-Intsig and Magic are shown in Fig. 3.

5.4   Task 4. Axis Analysis Results

Table 6. Task 4 results: Localization of tick marks for each tick label.

Team	Adobe Synth	UB PMC
DeepBlueAI	**0.999**	**0.813**
SCUT-IntSig-Lenovo	**0.998**	0.801
Py	–	0.588

Table 6 shows the results of Task 4 where tick labels are associated with the pixel location of the corresponding tick mark. We again observe near perfect accuracy on the synthetic data, which is not surprising given that all tick marks in the dataset are rendered using the same pattern of pixels. For the PMC data, DeepBlueAI performed best by a narrow margin over SCUT-IntSig-Lenovo, though both teams used deep models to regress Gaussian heatmaps around tick locations.

Accurate localization of tick marks is critical for performing the later task 6b correctly, since if the ticks are not pixel precise, mapping pixel locations of visual elements onto the axis values will be imprecise. The only exceptions are charts with categorical axes for which the actual tick marks might not be visually aligned with the actual tick values. Charts with this condition are common in the UB PMC dataset and logical tick marks were used to mark the best position within each axis to which the tick values need to be associated. Currently, the best result is 81% and no penalty was given for predictions within 1% (in terms of the image diagonal) of the target location, meaning that at least 19% of the predicted ticks were more than 1% away from the target. Since this task directly impacts the extracted data values, current methods are likely insufficient for real world applications of Chart Recognition and further work is needed on axis analysis.

5.5   Task 5. Legend Analysis Results

Table 7 shows results for legend analysis. We can see that in terms of the recall-based metric both IntSig-SCUT-Lenovo and Magic obtained near perfect scores, and they have a larger gap on the UB PMC dataset. However, in terms of the IOU-based metric, Magic achieved the highest scores on both datasets, including a near perfect score of 99% on the Synthetic dataset. Note that both methods are based on Cascade RCNNs, but the method from Magic first cropped the legend region thus simplifying the recognition problem given that the legend region is correctly detected.

Table 7. Task 5 results: Legend Analysis. We report both normalized Recall-based and normalized IOU-based scores.

	Adobe Synth		UB PMC	
Team	Recall	IoU	Recall	IoU
DeepBlueAI	0.928	0.919	0.864	0.818
IntSig-SCUT-Lenovo	**0.997**	0.950	**0.932**	0.849
Magic	0.993	**0.990**	0.920	**0.860**

5.6   Task 6. Data Extraction Results

We break down and analyze the results for Task 6 by Subtasks 6a and 6b.

Task 6.a Plot Element Detection and Classification Results. Table 8 shows the results of Task 6a which received 2 submissions. DeepBlueAI used a CenterNet for detecting all elements, which outperformed the Pyramid Mask Text Detector [18] used by IntSig-SCUT-Lenovo on all but one bar chart category. However, the Gaussian regression model used by IntSig-SCUT-Lenovo on all other chart types was superior on non-bar charts. This was especially true on scatter plots, which had the lowest performance of all chart types.

Table 8. Task 6a results: Detection of visual elements. Note that the PMC dataset did not differentiate between stacked and grouped bar charts, so results are presented only at the horizontal and vertical bar chart level.

	Adobe Synth		UB PMC	
Chart type	DeepBlueAI	IntSig-SCUT-Lenovo	DeepBlueAI	IntSig-SCUT-Lenovo
Stacked Horz. bar	0.962	0.957	0.929	0.870
Grouped Horz. bar	0.963	0.917		
Stacked Vert. bar	0.963	0.941	0.942	0.932
Grouped Vert. bar	0.927	0.941		
Horz. box	0.804	1.000	–	–
Vert. box	0.832	1.000	0.977	0.989
Scatter	0.799	0.874	0.654	0.793
Line	0.976	0.992	0.842	0.847
All	0.907	**0.954**	0.870	**0.882**

Task 6.b Raw Data Extraction Results. Table 9 shows the results of Task 6b, which with few exceptions are lower than that of Task 6a. This makes sense since solving task 6b entails taking the detections from Task 6a, associating them with legend entries (or inferring clusters if no legend is present), and then mapping the pixel-based detections to the value-space of the axes. It is interesting that IntSig-SCUT-Lenovo scores for bar charts actually increased w.r.t. Task 6a, which may be explained by the fact that Task 6a is scored based on bar bounding box IoU, but perhaps this can be explained because the width of vertical bars (and height of horizontal bars) is irrelevant for data extraction. This suggests that a better metric for Task 6a might only score bar bounding boxes based

Table 9. Task 6b results: Extraction of Data Series. Here we show the combined name and point set scores as described in Sect. 3.6 for each chart type, and show the average name score and data score for all charts. Note that the PMC dataset did not differentiate between stacked and grouped bar charts, so results are presented only at the horizontal and vertical bar chart level.

	Adobe Synth		UB PMC	
Chart type	DeepBlueAI	IntSig-SCUT-Lenovo	DeepBlueAI	IntSig-SCUT-Lenovo
Stacked Horz. bar	0.783	0.987	0.752	0.877
Grouped Horz. bar	0.905	0.980		
Stacked Vert. bar	0.261	0.981	0.649	0.913
Grouped Vert. bar	0.882	0.981		
Horz. box	0.934	0.992	–	–
Vert. box	0.977	0.979	0.599	0.863
Scatter	0.419	0.867	0.232	0.710
Line	0.926	0.987	0.679	0.698
All	0.764	**0.971**	0.610	**0.800**
All-name-score	0.948	**0.999**	0.785	**0.904**
All-data-score	0.703	**0.962**	0.552	**0.765**

Table 10. Task 7 results for SCUT-IntSig-Lenovo, which submitted the only entry for this task. Scores are decomposed by chart type and by name-score and data-score.

Chart type	Adobe Synth			UB PMC		
	Combined	Name	Data	Combined	Name	Data
Stacked Horz. bar	0.960	0.978	0.954	0.742	0.796	0.724
Grouped Horz. bar	0.912	0.965	0.894			
Stacked Vert. bar	0.975	0.995	0.968	0.881	0.951	0.857
Grouped Vert. bar	0.952	0.974	0.945			
Horz. box	0.949	0.926	0.957	–	–	–
Vert. box	0.969	0.948	0.976	0.660	0.662	0.660
Scatter	0.855	1.00	0.806	0.558	0.814	0.472
Line	0.960	0.975	0.955	0.660	0.762	0.626
Average	0.941	0.970	0.932	0.723	0.821	0.691

on the longer dimension rather than requiring precise localization of the shorter dimension.

For this task, the systems were furnished with the GT axes and legend information, which alleviates some of the difficulty, but still leaves some room for error. We see that systems degraded most on scatter plots, which is reasonable, given that overlapping scatter points are difficult to segment and properly associate with legend symbols.

It is indeed impressive that IntSig-SCUT-Lenovo was able to achieve a data score of 96.2% and a near perfect name score on Adobe Synth. However, the same system applied to real world data only achieved a data score of 76.5%, suggesting that a large difficulty gap still exists between the synthetic and real data and that training a chart recognition system on purely homogeneous synthetic data may not work well on real chart images. Interesting future work would examine the learning curve of the systems to gain a better understanding of how much further improvement could be made if more real data were to be annotated.

5.7 Task 7. Raw Data Extraction Results

Table 10 shows the results for the only submission, by SCUT-IntSig-Lenovo, for the end-to-end Task 7. Overall, the scores for bar charts are much higher than those of box, scatter, and line plots. For both datasets, scatter plots had the lowest data-scores, but were among the highest name-scores.

Surprisingly, the overall scores are not much lower than the best scores of Task 6b systems on UB PMC, which systems have the advantage of GT information for the output of Tasks 1–5. Given that other systems were able to get perfect results on Tasks 1 and 3–5 for Adobe Synth, it is reasonable for an end-to-end system to not degrade too much (e.g. 2%) w.r.t. Task 6b results. However, for UB PMC, the Task 1–5 results for other systems were much lower than for Adobe

Synth, and generally in pipeline architectures such as the one designed for this competition (see Fig. 2), errors made on previous tasks tend to cascade and cause even more errors on downstream modules that rely on accurate inputs. We observe only an 8% decrease overall. Further analysis of the performance of the SCUT-IntSig-Lenovo system on Tasks 1–6 could help explain this finding; however, we only have their results for Task 4.

5.8 Final Ranking

The overall ranking for our competition is presented in Table 11. This table applies the scoring scheme described in Sect. 3, where winners of each task per dataset get 4 points, other teams can get at least 1 point for participation or 0 if they did not submit an entry for the task and dataset. Using this method, the overall winner of this competition is DeepBlueAI with an overall score of 35, Magic is second with 27 points, and third is Lenovo-SCUT-Intsig with 24 points. The ties over near perfect scores on Adobe Synth allowed multiple teams to get the 4 points on a few selected tasks. Meanwhile, the differences on the UB PMC were much larger allowing only one team to get the 4 points on each task.

Table 11. Overall Ranking: Total points scored per team across all tasks.

Team	UB PMC							Adobe Synth							Score
	1	2	3	4	5	6	7	1	2	3	4	5	6	7	
DeepBlueAI	3	2	2	4	2	3	0	4	2	4	4	2	3	0	**35**
Magic	3	3	3	0	4	0	0	3	3	4	0	4	0	0	**27**
Lenovo-SCUT-Intsig	4	4	4	0	0	0	0	4	4	4	0	0	0	0	**24**
SCUT-IntSig-Lenovo	0	0	0	3	0	0	4	0	0	0	4	0	0	4	15
IntSig-SCUT-Lenovo	0	0	0	0	3	4	0	0	0	0	0	3	4	0	14
IPSA	2	1	0	0	0	0	0	3	1	0	0	0	0	0	7
PY	0	1	1	2	0	0	0	0	0	0	0	0	0	0	4

6   Conclusion

In this paper, we have presented a summary of all activities of the second Competition on HArvesting Raw Tables from Infographics (CHART-Infographics). Compared to the previous edition [8], this year we provided upscaled datasets including a brand new training set based on real charts from the PubMed Central, and we also had participants for all tasks including task 6 and 7 which did not get any submissions in the previous edition. Consistent with the first version of the competition, we observed higher scores for the synthetic dataset including many near perfect ones, while the new testing dataset based on real charts remained the most challenging. The one submission we received for Task

7 scored fairly well in comparison with submissions for Task 6 which had access to additional ground truth data. We chose a brand new scoring scheme to rank participants across all tasks, and the overall winner this year is Team Deep-BlueAI.

This year we also observed multiple methods for different tasks which were on average, far more complex than the ones we evaluated in the previous edition. However, despite the increased complexity of these methods, there are tasks where results are still far from ideal for large-scale applications. It might be possible that some of these methods will perform better in the future as more data becomes available. We hope that all data and tools and data that were produced during this competition will be valuable assets for future research in the field of chart recognition.

Acknowledgment. This material is based upon work partially supported by the National Science Foundation under Grant No. OAC/DMR 1640867.

References

1. Böschen, F., Beck, T., Scherp, A.: Survey and empirical comparison of different approaches for text extraction from scholarly figures. Multimedia Tools Appl. **77**(22), 29475–29505 (2018). https://doi.org/10.1007/s11042-018-6162-7
2. Cai, Z., Vasconcelos, N.: Cascade R-CNN: delving into high quality object detection. In: Proceedings of the IEEE Conference on Computer Vision and Pattern Recognition, pp. 6154–6162 (2018)
3. Cao, Y., Xu, J., Lin, S., Wei, F., Hu, H.. GCNet: non local networks meet squeeze excitation networks and beyond. In: Proceedings of the IEEE International Conference on Computer Vision Workshops (2019)
4. Cheng, B., Xiao, B., Wang, J., Shi, H., Huang, T.S., Zhang, L.: HigherHRNet: scale-aware representation learning for bottom-up human pose estimation. arXiv preprint arXiv:1908.10357 (2019)
5. Dai, J., et al.: Deformable convolutional networks. In: Proceedings of the IEEE International Conference on Computer Vision, pp. 764–773 (2017)
6. Dalal, N., Triggs, B.: Histograms of oriented gradients for human detection. In: 2005 IEEE Computer Society Conference on Computer Vision and Pattern Recognition (CVPR 2005), vol. 1, pp. 886–893. IEEE (2005)
7. Davila, K., Setlur, S., Doermann, D., Bhargava, U.K., Govindaraju, V.: Chart mining: a survey of methods for automated chart analysis. IEEE Trans. Pattern Anal. Mach. Intell. 1 (2020). https://doi.org/10.1109/TPAMI.2020.2992028
8. Davila, K., et al.: ICDAR 2019 competition on harvesting raw tables from infographics (chart-infographics). In: 2019 International Conference on Document Analysis and Recognition (ICDAR), pp. 1594–1599. IEEE (2019)
9. Duan, K., Bai, S., Xie, L., Qi, H., Huang, Q., Tian, Q.: CenterNet: keypoint triplets for object detection. In: Proceedings of the IEEE International Conference on Computer Vision, pp. 6569–6578 (2019)
10. Graves, A., Fernández, S., Gomez, F., Schmidhuber, J.: Connectionist temporal classification: labelling unsegmented sequence data with recurrent neural networks. In: Proceedings of the 23rd International Conference on Machine Learning, pp. 369–376 (2006)

11. He, K., Zhang, X., Ren, S., Sun, J.: Deep residual learning for image recognition. In: Proceedings of the IEEE Conference on Computer Vision and Pattern Recognition, pp. 770–778 (2016)
12. He, T., Tian, Z., Huang, W., Shen, C., Qiao, Y., Sun, C.: An end-to-end TextSpotter with explicit alignment and attention. In: Proceedings of the IEEE Conference on Computer Vision and Pattern Recognition, pp. 5020–5029 (2018)
13. Huang, G., Liu, Z., Van Der Maaten, L., Weinberger, K.Q.: Densely connected convolutional networks. In: Proceedings of the IEEE Conference on Computer Vision and Pattern Recognition, pp. 4700–4708 (2017)
14. Ioffe, S., Szegedy, C.: Batch normalization: accelerating deep network training by reducing internal covariate shift. arXiv preprint arXiv:1502.03167 (2015)
15. Ke, G., et al.: LightGBM: a highly efficient gradient boosting decision tree. In: Advances in Neural Information Processing Systems, pp. 3146–3154 (2017)
16. Kuhn, H.W.: The Hungarian method for the assignment problem. Nav. Res. Logist. Q. **2**(1–2), 83–97 (1955)
17. Lin, T.Y., Dollár, P., Girshick, R., He, K., Hariharan, B., Belongie, S.: Feature pyramid networks for object detection. In: Proceedings of the IEEE Conference on Computer Vision and Pattern Recognition, pp. 2117–2125 (2017)
18. Liu, J., Liu, X., Sheng, J., Liang, D., Li, X., Liu, Q.: Pyramid mask text detector. arXiv preprint arXiv:1903.11800 (2019)
19. Liu, Y., Lu, X., Qin, Y., Tang, Z., Xu, J.: Review of chart recognition in document images. In: Visualization and Data Analysis, p. 865410 (2013)
20. Mnih, V., Heess, N., Graves, A., et al.: Recurrent models of visual attention. In: Advances in Neural Information Processing Systems, pp. 2204–2212 (2014)
21. Ren, S., He, K., Girshick, R., Sun, J.: Faster R-CNN: towards real-time object detection with region proposal networks. In: Advances in Neural Information Processing Systems, pp. 91–99 (2015)
22. Shi, B., Bai, X., Yao, C.: An end-to-end trainable neural network for image-based sequence recognition and its application to scene text recognition. IEEE Trans. Pattern Anal. Mach. Intell. **39**(11), 2298–2304 (2016)
23. Smith, R.: An overview of the Tesseract OCR engine. In: International Conference on Document Analysis and Recognition, vol. 2, pp. 629–633. IEEE (2007)
24. Xie, S., Girshick, R., Dollár, P., Tu, Z., He, K.: Aggregated residual transformations for deep neural networks. In: Proceedings of the IEEE Conference on Computer Vision and Pattern Recognition, pp. 1492–1500 (2017)
25. Xu, Y., Li, M., Cui, L., Huang, S., Wei, F., Zhou, M.: LayoutLM: pre-training of text and layout for document image understanding. In: Proceedings of the 26th ACM SIGKDD International Conference on Knowledge Discovery & Data Mining, pp. 1192–1200 (2020)
26. Yu, F., Wang, D., Shelhamer, E., Darrell, T.: Deep layer aggregation. In: Proceedings of the IEEE Conference on Computer Vision and Pattern Recognition, pp. 2403–2412 (2018)
27. Zhou, X., et al.: EAST: an efficient and accurate scene text detector. In: Proceedings of the IEEE Conference on Computer Vision and Pattern Recognition, pp. 5551–5560 (2017)

Visual and Textual Information Fusion Method for Chart Recognition

Chen Wang[1,2(✉)], Kaixu Cui[1,2], Suya Zhang[3], and Changliang Xu[1,2]

[1] XinHua ZhiYun Inc., Hangzhou, China
18046522054@163.com
[2] State Key Laboratory of Media Convergence Production Technology and Systems,
Beijing, China
[3] State Key Laboratory of Media Convergence and Communication, Communication University
of China, Beijing, China

Abstract. In this report, we present our method in the ICPR 2020 Competition on Harvesting Raw Tables from Infographics, which is composed of Chart Classification, Text Detection/Recognition, Text Role Classification, Axis Analysis, Legend Analysis, Plot Element Detection/Classification and CSV Extraction. The image classification models of ResNet are adopt in Chart Classification. We adopted a two-stage based pipeline for end-to-end recognition, considering detection and recognition as two modules in Text Detection/Recognition. An ensemble model with LayoutLM and object detection model is adopted in Text Role Classification. A two-stage pipeline with two detection model is adopt in Legend Analysis. The final results are discussed.

Keyword: Chart recognition

1 Introduction

Charts are an effective data visualization tool often used to supplement textual content. They communicate information more efficiently and are common in the media, business documents, and scientific publications [1]. The goal of the ICPR 2020 Competition on Harvesting Raw Tables from Infographics is to provide common benchmarks and tools for the chart recognition community. This competition is composed of a series of sub-tasks (shown in Table 1) for chart data extraction, which when put together as a pipeline go from an input chart image to a CSV file representing the data used to create the chart. Two sets of datasets (Adobe Synth, UB PMC) are provided. The Synthetic Dataset is based on a large number of synthetic chart images (created with mat-plot-lib) with corresponding automatically derived annotations. The UB PMC Dataset is based on a smaller number of chart images extracted from Open-Access publications found in the PubMedCentral (PMC) [2].

In this report we present our solutions on task1, task2, task3 and task5. In the task1, an image classification model is adopted. In the task2, a two-stage based pipeline for

S. Zang—Intern at XinHua ZhiYun Inc.

A. Del Bimbo et al. (Eds.): ICPR 2020 Workshops, LNCS 12668, pp. 381–389, 2021.
https://doi.org/10.1007/978-3-030-68793-9_28

Table 1. Tasks in Competition on harvesting raw tables from infographics

Taks num	Task name
1	Chart classification
2	Text detection/Recognition
3	Text role classification
4	Axis analysis
5	Legend analysis
6	a Plot element detection/Classification
	b CSV extraction
7	End-to-End data extraction

end-to-end recognition is adopted. In the task3, Multi-modal technology is adopted. In the task5, a method based on object detection is adopted.

2   Tasks and Methods

In this section, we present our solutions for chart image classification, text detection and recognition, text role classification and legend analysis. The train datasets of these tasks are divided into train set (90%) and validation (10%). The models with best performance in validations are chosen and the final models fin-tune with both train and validation sets.

2.1   Task1. Chart Image Classification

In this task, model of ResNet [3] with different backbones were valid. According the validation results, the ResNet-50 was used for Synthetic dataset and ResNet152 was used for UB PMC dataset. Additionally, the ensemble learning was adopted for UB PMC dataset to enhance the generalization of the model. In training phase, ten ResNet-152 models were trained with different sub dataset of the whole train dataset. In inference phase, Average voting was used to ensemble the results from the ten models.

The models of ResNet-50 and ResNet-152 were the pre-trained model with ImageNet1000 dataset [4], and were fine-tune by the UB PMC and Synthetic datasets. The parameters of solver were shown as Table 2.

2.2   Task2. Text Detection and Recognition

For this task, we adopted a two-stage based pipeline for end-to-end recognition, considering detection and recognition as two modules. Our team adopted the Mask RCNN [6] based method to detect the line block of text (text with multiple lines considering one text block) in chart images and used the ResNeXt-152-FPN as the backbone network. Deformable convolutions [7] were used in the last three stages to enhance features. Cascade architecture [8] was used in the model to achieve higher detection accuracies. The

Table 2. Parameters of solver.

Parameters	Value
Max epoch	20
Batch size	128
Optimization	Momentum SGD momentum = 0.9 [5]
Learning rate	0.01
Normalization	*L2 regularization Weight = 3e5* .

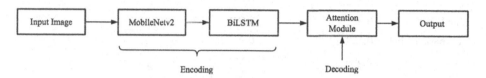

Fig. 1. Structure of recognition network

training dataset were UB PMC Dataset and Synthetic Dataset. For the recognition part, CNN and RNN with attention was adopted shown as follows (Fig. 1).

According to results of the first stage, the cropped images were achieved as input of the recognition model. The encoder first extracted a feature map from the input image with a stack of convolutional layers to enlarge the feature context, we employed a Bidirectional LSTM (BLSTM) network [9] over the feature sequence. The BLSTM network analyzed the feature sequence bidirectionally, capturing long-range dependencies in both directions. The attentional sequence-to-sequence module [10] was built to translate the feature sequence into a character sequence. In the training phase, firstly, the recognition model was train by training data including the publicly available datasets, i.e., ICDAR 2019-LSVT, ICDAR 2013 [11], ICDAR 2015, IIIT5K, ICDAR 2017, ICDAR 2017-MLT [12] English + Chinese, ICDAR 2017 RCTW-17 [13], ICPR 2018-MTWI, and synthetic images [14]. Then the final model fine-tuned with the UB PMC and Synthetic Datasets.

2.3 Task3. Text Role Classification

The text semantic roles of charts were related with both the visual and textual information. Therefore, only applying with object detection or text classification technology could not achieve good results. BERT-like models became the state-of-the-art techniques on several challenging NLP tasks, they usually leveraged text information only for any kind of inputs. The LayoutLM [15] was a new BERT-like pre-trained model, which both text and layout information were jointly learned in a single framework. However, it was not enough for some roles, i.e., Tick grouping, Legend Title, Legend Label, Data Marker Label, and Others.

The results were shown as Table 3. The LayoutLM produced perfect scores for the Synthetic Dataset but very poor scores for some roles in UB PMC Dataset. Therefore,

Table 3. Results of UB PMC and synthetic validation datasets.

Roles	F1 score in UB PMC		F1 score in synthetic
	LayoutLM	LayoutLM + Detection	
Chart title	0.746	0.815	1.0
Axis title	0.976	0.983	1.0
Tick label	0.984	0.992	1.0
Tick grouping	0.558	0.961	–
Legend title	0.214	0.889	1.0
Legend label	0.842	0.976	–
Value label	0.961	0.946	–
Data marker label	0.299	0.918	–
Other	0.594	0.866	–

we adopted object detection to enhance the results of UB PMC Dataset. The detection model was as same as the model for task2. According the results in Table 3 we chose 5 classes (Tick grouping, Legend Title, Legend Label, Data Marker Label, and Others) which reply more on visual information. The final flow chart was shown as follows (Fig. 2):

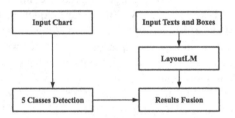

Fig. 2. Flow chart of task3

In the inference phase, we fused the results from the two models. The predicted role class from LayoutLM was changed to the predicted role class from detection model if the Intersection Over Union (IOU) between the predicted bounding box of detection model and the GT bounding box was over 0.5. The merging results were shown in Table 2. It was shown that the visual information made a great improvement on the task3. The confusion matrix of UB PMC validation dataset is shown as Fig. 3. In particular, legend title and mark label texts were more easily misclassified as text roles named other. The reason may be that the mark label and legend title text only appear on a few charts and the presented model was over-fit on these classes. The text roles named other were misclassified as tick label and value label texts. This may be due to the serious imbalance of category. In train dataset, the number of value label and tick label were much more than the other class, which makes model predict more value label and tick label. Some

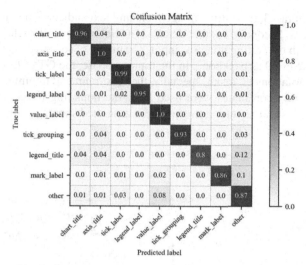

Fig. 3. Confusion matrix of UB PMC validation dataset

tricks for category imbalance (e.g. focal loss, positive sample) were adopted and only a small improvement achieved. It seems the key to obtain higher performance was to add more chart contains legend tile, mark label and other.

2.4 Task5. Legend Analysis

The sizes of Legend markers were mainly from 4 * 4 to 32 * 32, which were not suited for common object detection method. Increasing input image size was one way to address the small object detection, but in this task the sizes of legend markers were so small and increasing image size had little effect. Therefore, we adopted a two steps method to solve the issue, which was shown as follows (Fig. 4):

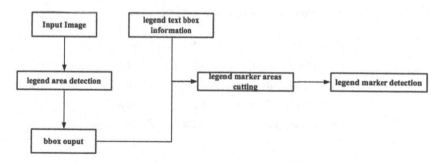

Fig. 4. Flow chart of task5

Firstly, the legend areas including all legend texts and markers were detected by a detection model whose config file was as same as detection model in task2. According with the results of task3, the cutting image including text and corresponding marker can be easily figure out. Secondly, another detection model was apply to detect the bounding box of marker with the cutting image as input. The model of second detection is Cascade RCNN with ResNet-50 as backbone. In the training phase, the GT of legend areas were generated by annotations of Task5, specially, the maximum and minimum of the legend texts' and markers' coordinates were used to be the bounding boxes. For the second detection task of task5, the cutting images were generated shown as Fig. 5.

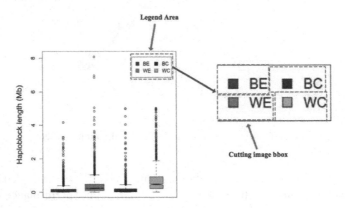

Fig. 5. Legend area and cutting images

We combining the UB PMC and Synthetic datasets for pre-training. Secondly, fine-tune the model on the corresponding dataset.

2.5   Final Results and Discussion

The Final results of the above tasks were shown as follow table (Table 4).

Table 4. Final results of the four tasks.

Task name	UB PMC	Synthetic
Chart classification	90.48%	99.44%
Text detection/Recognition	72.85%	92.56%
Text role classification	81.71%	99.93%
Legend analysis	92.00%	99.30%

The results show that the performance of the above method is very high on the Synthetic Dataset, but the scores of UB PMC left room for considerable improvement. Considering the much complex layout of real charts, our methods on the UB PMC dataset are also good solutions.

The confusion matrix of Chart Classification in UB PMC test dataset is shown as Fig. 6. In particular, area, scatter-line and vertical interval charts were more easily misclassified as line charts. One possible reason is that above misclassified charts have similar linear structure with line charts and the errors were magnified by category imbalance. A special classification model and data augmentation for the above classes may make sense.

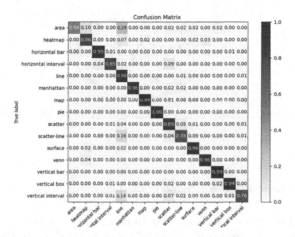

Fig. 6. Confusion matrix of chart classification in UB PMC test dataset

The confusion matrix of Text Role Classification in UB PMC test dataset is shown as Fig. 7. There is a few difference from the validation dataset. The scores of test dataset is obviously lower than the validation, especially for chart title, mark label and other. Chart title, mark label and value label texts were more easily misclassified as the class named other, the legend title and mark label were often misclassified as legend label. The reason may be that the presented models were over-fit on train dataset. A effective data augment and a larger train dataset may make sense.

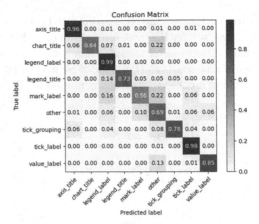

Fig. 7. Confusion matrix of text role classification in UB PMC test dataset

3 Conclusion

In this report we present the solutions on the four tasks (Chart Classification, Text Detection/Recognition, Text Role Classification, Legend Analysis). Our works show that the presented methods achieve good performance at both Synthetic and UB PMC datasets. Additionally, we discuss the drawbacks of the methods in UB PMC test datasets.

References

1. Davila, K., Kota, B.U., Setlur, S., et al.: ICDAR 2019 competition on harvesting raw tables from infographics (CHART-Infographics). In: 2019 International Conference on Document Analysis and Recognition (ICDAR), pp. 1594–1599. IEEE (2019)
2. PMC Homepage. https://www.ncbi.nlm.nih.gov/pmc/
3. He, K., Zhang, X., Ren, S., et al.: Deep residual learning for image recognition. In: Proceedings of the IEEE Conference on Computer Vision and Pattern Recognition, pp. 770–778 (2016)
4. Deng, J., Dong, W., Socher, R., et al.: Imagenet: a large-scale hierarchical image database. In: 2009 IEEE Conference on Computer Vision and Pattern Recognition, pp. 248–255. IEEE (2009)
5. Ruder, S.: An overview of gradient descent optimization algorithms. arXiv preprint arXiv: 1609.04747 (2016)
6. He, T., Tian, Z., Huang, W., Shen, C., Qiao, Y., Sun, C.: An end-to-end textspotter with explicit alignment and attention. In: Proceedings of the IEEE Conference on Computer Vision and Pattern Recognition, pp. 5020–5029 (2018)
7. Dai, J., et al.: Deformable convolutional networks. In: Proceedings of the IEEE International Conference on Computer Vision, pp. 764–773 (2017)
8. Cai, Z., Vasconcelos, N.: Cascade r-cnn: delving into high quality object detection. In: Proceedings of the IEEE Conference on Computer Vision and Pattern Recognition, pp. 6154–6162 (2018)
9. Graves, A., Liwicki, M., Fernandez, S., Bertolami, R., Bunke, H., Schmidhuber, J.: A novel connectionist system for unconstrained handwriting recognition. IEEE Trans. Pattern Anal. Mach. Intell. **31**(5), 855–868 (2009)

10. Mnih, V., Heess, N., Graves, A.: Recurrent models of visual attention. In: Advances in Neural Information Processing Systems, pp. 2204–2212 (2014)
11. Karatzas, D., et al.: ICDAR 2013 robust reading competition. In: Proceedings of ICDAR, pp. 1484–1493. IEEE (2013)
12. ICDAR 2017 competition on multilingual scene text detection and script identifification. https://rrc.cvc.uab.es/?ch=8&com=introduction, Accessed 16 Nov 2018
13. Shi, B., et al.: ICDAR2017 competition on reading chinese text in the wild (RCTW-17). In: 2017 14th IAPR International Conference on Document Analysis and Recognition (ICDAR), vol. 1, pp. 1429–1434.11. IEEE (2017)
14. Gupta, A., Vedaldi, A., Zisserman, A.: Synthetic data for text localisation in natural images. In: IEEE Conference on Computer Vision and Pattern Recognition (2016)
15. Xu, Y., Li, M., Cui, L., et al.: Layoutlm: pre-training of text and layout for document image understanding. In: Proceedings of the 26th ACM SIGKDD International Conference on Knowledge Discovery & Data Mining, pp. 1192–1200 (2020)

A Benchmark for Analyzing Chart Images

Zhipeng Luo$^{(\boxtimes)}$, Zhiguang Zhang$^{(\boxtimes)}$, Ge Li$^{(\boxtimes)}$, Lixuan Che$^{(\boxtimes)}$, Jianye He$^{(\boxtimes)}$, and Zhenyu Xu$^{(\boxtimes)}$

DeepBlue Technology (Shanghai) Co., Ltd, Shanghai, China
{luozp,zhangzhg,lige,chelx,hejianye,xuzy}@deepblueai.com

Abstract. Charts are a compact method of displaying and comparing data. Automatically extracting data from charts is a key step in understanding the intent behind a chart which could lead to a better understanding of the document itself. To promote the development of automatically decompose and understand these visualizations. The CHART-Infographics organizers holds the Competition on Harvesting Raw Tables from Infographics. In this paper, based on machine learning, image recognition, object detection, keypoint estimation, OCR, and others, we explored and proposed our methods for almost all tasks and achieved relatively good performance.

Keywords: Image recognition · Document analysis · Text recognition and classification · Graphics recognition

1 Introduction

It is an efficient direction to get a structured description by inputting images, an excellent medium for data representation and interpretation. An effective chart summarization could help data analysts, business analysts, or journalists better prepare reports from data. However, understanding and getting insights from charts can be difficult and time-consuming. To get a better chart analysis algorithm, the CHART-Infographics Organizers holds the Competition on Harvesting Raw Tables from Infographics. The complex process of automatic chart recognition is divided into multiple tasks for this competition, including Chart Image Classification (Task 1), Text Detection and Recognition (Task 2), Text Role Classification (Task 3), Axis Analysis (Task 4), Legend Analysis (Task 5), Plot Element Detection and Classification (Task 6.a), Data Extraction (Task 6.b), and End-to-End Data Extraction (Task 7).

In this paper, we proposed our methods for the task1-6. Due to the difference between different tasks, we explored and proposed different methods. For task 1 and task 3, one is chart image classification another is text role classification task. So we based on Deep Convolutional Neural Network to complete task1 and Machine learning-based method for task3. For task2, which need to detect text blocks and Recognition the text, different from task 4, which need to detect tick point and associate with the corresponding value (a string). We based on

© Springer Nature Switzerland AG 2021
A. Del Bimbo et al. (Eds.): ICPR 2020 Workshops, LNCS 12668, pp. 390–400, 2021.
https://doi.org/10.1007/978-3-030-68793-9_29

object detection algorithm and OCR to complete task 2, see task4 as a standard keypoint estimation problem. Task 5, which need to detect and match legend with the data series name, we use an object detection based algorithm to solve it. For task 6, a relatively complex task needs to detect and classify each element in the plot area and output the raw data used to generate the chart image. We can only detect different elements separately, then classify them based on image features. Furthermore, deal with each class independently to transform the image coordinate system's element position to the raw data. Finally, based on our method, we achieved relatively good performance on almost all tasks.

2   Method

2.1   Task 1

The first sub-task target is to classify chart images by type both in Synthetic Dataset and UB PMC Dataset. These two independent sets of chart images have a different number of classes. For each type of Adobe Synthetic Dataset, we use 1000 for training and 200 for validation. Our baseline model is resnet-50 [1], and an ensemble of models from 5-fold cross-validation is used.

For UB PMC Dataset, a satisfactory performance can not be reached by the former method. We use grad-cam [2] to visualize the attention of the network to inspire the direction of improvement. Some different losses are tried, such as Arc-Face [3], focal loss [22]. We choose Cross Entropy loss with Label-smoothing [6] finally.

We follow the BNNeck [7], adding a BN layer without the bias before the last linear layer of the network. Some methods to deal with long-tailed recognition are also tried for the unbalanced distribution. Apart from the conventional re-sample and re-weight methods, we try to decouple the representation from the classification by training the classifier using class-balanced data after freezing the backbone got from the instance-balanced data [8]. However, they fail to bring a positive impact because of the limited classes, perhaps.

2.2   Task 2

This sub-task concentrates on detecting and recognizing the text within the chart image. Based on the two-stages Object Detection model (Cascade R-CNN [9]), detect text boxes. In our results, the text box is easy to detect. The task's difficulty is recognizing the text from the rotated text. This task is to identify the text box with distinctive features, besides the foreground-background is clear, so the mask can easily extract the text block. We can get the mask and horizontal angle through the mask's minimum outer matrix and then make the text box horizontal box by an affine transformation.

As for the recognition algorithm, we adopt CRNN [10] and CTC Loss [11] as our pipeline. So that a better result can be achieved. In this task, we still focus on detecting the text box, and after trying some detection models, we adopted the current method for Object Detection. Because the detection target is simple, the model's proposal score is relatively high, and there are obvious errors in the proposal with a low score. We change the IOU threshold from 0.5, 0.6, 0.7 to 0.6, 0.7, and 0.8 to avoid learning samples with low quality. We also adjusted the anchor's scale and stride to fit the characteristics of this task. According to the above settings, localization performance improved through cascading refine boxes and suitable anchor parameters.

What's more, we explore the performance of different backbones such as ResNext [12], HRNet [13], GCNet [14].

2.3   Task 3

This sub-task focuses on identifying the role of each text block in a chart image, and text bounding boxes and transcripts are provided as input. Our technique includes two steps: feature extracting and classification using classifiers. The properties of the texts are used to define feature vectors [15]. The classifiers we use are Random Forest [16] and LightGBM [17].

The features are composed of the properties of the bounding boxes and the text content. These features are grouped into three categories. The first category contains the aspect ratio of the box, whether the text is numeric, whether the text is multi-line, angle of text, length of text, and the chart type. The second category includes three kinds of relative position information, which are the positions relative to the global bounding box for all elements, origin (The bottom left corner of the graph) and legend. The third category contains the number of horizontally/vertically aligned text boxes and horizontal/vertical range of the aligned text boxes. When judging whether the boxes are aligned, the centre points of the boxes, the upper left corners and the lower right corners are used, respectively.

The positions of the graph and legend mentioned above are obtained by a detection model. We train a CenterNet [18] with the backbone DLA-34 [19]. The two categories are graph and legend, and the input size is 512*512.

Random Forest and LightGBM are used to classify the roles of texts. One of the advantages of random forest is that it still has good performance when there are missing features. LightGBM has the advantages of high training efficiency and high accuracy. When training the models, each class is assigned a weight inversely proportional to its frequency in the input data.

Considering that there are cases where legends are not predicted by the model, two classification models are trained, using and not using legend location information respectively. In the inference stage, which model is selected for prediction depends on whether the legend is detected.

2.4   Task 4

In this task, we need to output the location and value of each tick mark on both the X-axis and Y-axis. Tick locations are represented as points and must be

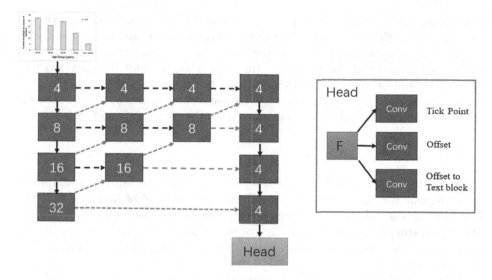

Fig. 1. The pipeline of our model. Dla34 as backbone and augment the skip connections with deformable convolution from lower layers to the head module. In the head module, has three output branches.

associated with the corresponding value (a string). To complete task 4, we split the task into two subtasks: tick point detection and matching.

Model. In the tick point detection task, we see the task as a standard keypoint estimation problem. We refer to CenterNet, use DLA-34 as backbone and add more skip connections from the bottom layers and upgrade every convolutional layer in upsampling stages to deformable convolutional layer [21], finally get output features with size 1/4 of the input and feed the features to head module. In the head module, there include three branches. First is tick point detection branch. Peaks in the heatmaps predict by this branch correspond to tick points and classify points to X-axis or Y-axis by two different heatmaps. To recover the discretization error caused by the output stride, we additionally predict a local offset acts on tick points locations in the offset branch. In the 3rd branch, we additionally predict an offset from tick points to the centre of corresponding text blocks(OTB), which only used in the training stage (see Fig. 1).

Loss Function. To train the tick point detection branch, we use focal loss as loss function to do pixel-wise logistic regression. To train the local offset prediction branch, we use Wing Loss [23] which is proposed in Facial Landmark Localisation task and designed to improve the deep neural network training capability for small and medium-range errors. To train the OTB branch, we simply use Smooth L1 [24] as loss function.

Matching. After getting the detection tick points to be classified into the X-axis or Y-axis, then use linear distribution check to filter out outlier points. To match tick points with text blocks, firstly, we use CenterNet trained by plot box to get the position of the plot box, then based on the plot box position and linear distribution check to further improve the classification accuracy of tick label text blocks. Finally, based on the L1 distance of X-axis or Y-axis between tick point and tick label text blocks, we match the tick points and text blocks.

2.5   Task 5

Task 5 is to associate each legend label text with the corresponding graphical style element within the legend area. We adopt a method of first detecting the legend elements and then matching the legend elements and the legend labels. In order to further improve the accuracy of matching, the legend pairs and legend elements are detected at the same time. The results of legend pairs are used to assist in matching.

Our method for Task5 is divided into three steps:

Firstly, the same method as Task 3 is used to classify the text boxes. And then the text boxes of the legend label category are filtered out.

Secondly, CenterNet is used to detect two categories of legend element and legend pair. The legend pair is obtained by merging the borders of legend elements and the corresponding texts.

Finally, legend elements and legend labels are matched. For each legend label, if there is a legend element in the same pair box, the element is matched. Then the Hungarian Algorithm is used to match the remaining legend elements detected and the legend labels. In order to reduce the impact of the classification error of task 3 on the results of task 5, post-processing is done. For the images without legend labels in the results of task 3, if the legend elements and legend pairs are detected at the same time, the legend elements are matched with all text boxes.

2.6   Task 6

For task 6, the goal is to detect and classify each element in the plot area and output the raw data that was used to generate the chart image. The representation of the element varies, but mainly contains two types of labels: box and point.

Task 6a. In this task, we detect elements by box-based detection algorithm and point-based detection algorithm separately. To detect box representation element like Grouped horizontal bar, Stacked horizontal bar, Grouped vertical bar, Stacked vertical bar, we use CenterNet, which is an anchor free object detection algorithm. To detect point representation element, we use the same point detection algorithm as Task4 and remove OTB branch. Moreover, based on the difference between the different type of chart, we predict different number of channels of heatmaps in tick point detection branch. Like Horizontal box and Vertical box, which have five points in each box, that can predict heatmaps with five channels to complete detection and classification. However, for Line, Scatter, it can only see all element as one class.

In this task some types of chart are need to group elements. For Horizontal box and Vertical box, we can group the five categories of points by L1 distance of X-axis or Y-axis. But for Line and Scatter, it is more complicated. For pictures with legends, the elements of lines and scatters are grouped according to legend elements. We extract the colour histogram features and Hog features [25] of the legend elements and points, respectively. Then each element is divided into a group corresponding to the legend based on the distance between the features. For pictures without legends, after extract the colour histogram features and Hog features of each point respectively, then use K-means to group them.

Task 6b. For task 6b, in the task 6a, we have got position representation in the image coordinate system of each element, the problem is to get position representation in the axis coordinate system. After analysis, we divided UB PMC dataset into five categories and Adobe Synth dataset into eight categories, then deal with each class independently. For data sequence, if the x values are numerical values, we computed x-axis values by interpolation. If the x values are string values, we use L1 distance to find the nearest character content. Moreover, do targeted treatment for different particular situations. For images containing bar and boxplot elements that need to group, the same method based on colour histogram features and Hog features are used like task 6a.

3   Experiments

3.1   Task 1

For Adobe Synthetic Dataset, average the output vector of the fully connected layer of each model in the 5-fold cross-validation. The maximum value of the averaged vector corresponds to the category of the prediction. The accuracy of our randomly divided validation set can reach 100%.

For UB PMC Dataset, some augmentation methods like cutmix [4] and mixup [5] are used in the training phrase, and TenCrop is adopted in the test phrase. The ablation experiment results on the validation set are shown in Table 1. Our results on the two test sets are shown in Table 2.

3.2   Task 2

Data-Augmentation. Because some of the text is slanted, we rotate the text lines to the horizontal position by projection, and our work involved applying an effective data augmentation strategy that included transformations informed specifically by the domain of the data(PMC dataset and Adobe Synth dataset)

Table 1. Ablation experiments for PMC.

Model	Accuracy	F1 score
resnet50(**baseline**)	0.947873	0.922636
resnet50 + cutmix	0.947251	0.924866
resnet50 + mixup	0.948833	0.0.923047
resnet50 + focal loss	0.949153	0.928227
resnet50 + ArcFace	0.948833	0.926474
resnet50 + Label Smoothing	**0.952350**	**0.931243**

Table 2. Task1 results on different datasets.

Dataset	Average Per-Class F-Measure
UB PMC Dataset	90.43%
Adobe Synth Dataset	100%

Training. We followed the training methodology they used and trained with the SGD optimizer using all of the default parameter values, including the base learning rate of 0.01. Also, as in both and, we exponentially decayed the base learning rate. For our experiments, which trained for 20 epochs, we applied an exponential decay rate of 0.99 per epoch, clamped to a minimum of $1e-6$.

Results. Our results are shown in Table 3, we got 99.98 AP_{50} on the local validation dataset, there is a big gap between online and offline results probably due to the lack of extra training data.

Table 3. Results on different datasets.

Dataset	IOU score	OCR score
UB PMC Dataset	**0.44**	0.70
Adobe Synth Dataset	**0.74**	0.58

3.3   Task 3

The two data sets are trained and inferred separately. For Random Forest and LightGBM, the number of trees is 1000. In order to improve accuracy, we use five-fold cross-validation and ensemble learning. The method of ensemble learning we use is weighted average strategy. Specifically, in the inference stage, for Random Forest and LightGBM, we predict the test images with 5 models trained with datasets generated by five-fold cross-validation. We average the output proba-bility of 10(2*5) prediction results to get the final results. The final results on

PMC and Adobe Synthetic datasets are shown in Table 4. The confusion matrix on PMC dataset is shown as Fig. 2.

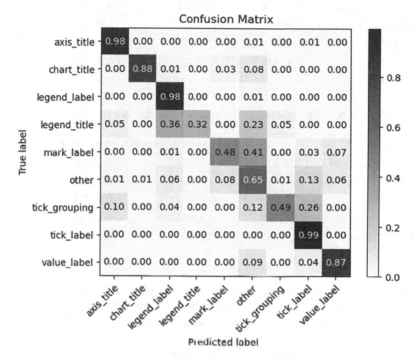

Fig. 2. The confusion matrix on PMC dataset.

Table 4. Results for tasks 3.

Dataset	Synthetic	PMC
Average Per-Class F-measure	99.92%	77.19%

3.4 Task 4

In our experiment, we firstly split the training dataset to Train: Val: Test by 7:2:1. Fix the input resolution to 1024 1024 while training. Keep the original image size while verifying and testing. For data augmentation, we use random scale, blur, channel shuffle, hue saturation, invert, grayscale and so on. And, training the model use or not pre-trained model weight. In particular, during training, we exchange X-axis and Y-axis label of some types of charts like Horizontal bar, Grouped horizontal bar, Stacked horizontal bar, Horizontal box.

Table 5. Performance on the custom test dataset of Adobe Synth.

	Average recall	Average precision	Average F-measure
With pretrained	0.98913	0.99027	0.98970
Without pretrained	0.99594	0.99643	0.99619
+ OTB	0.99611	0.99651	0.99631
Ensemble	0.99826	0.99853	0.99839
Test challenge	–	–	0.9990

Table 6. Performance on the custom test dataset of UB PMC.

	Average recall	Average precision	Average F-measure
With pretrained	0.92032	0.93234	0.92629
Without pretrained	0.93460	0.94606	0.94029
+ OTB	0.94220	0.94434	0.94327
Ensemble	0.95642	0.95861	0.95751
Test challenge	0.81560	0.81000	0.81280

Furthermore, to get better performance, we split datasets into 5-folds for k-fold cross-validation, and ensemble results by Adaptive threshold point NMS algorithm. Finally, on the test challenge stage, we re-split the dataset by 10:2 as Train and Val set, and ensemble results of each type of chart by the performance on the Val set. As summarized in Tables 5 and 6.

3.5 Task 5

CenterNet with the backbone DLA-34 is used to detect legend element and legend pair. We use random flip, cropping, color jittering, and randomly shuffling RGB channels as data augmentation. The input resolution of the network is 1024*1024. The network is trained with Adam [20] for 200 epochs with the initial learning rate being 3.75e-4 and a batchsize of 32 (on 4 GPUs). The learning rate is reduced by a factor of 10 at 150 and 170 epochs, respectively. The final results on PMC and Adobe Synthetic datasets are shown in Table 7.

Table 7. Results for tasks 5.

Dataset	Synthetic	PMC
Average BBox Recall	92.82%	86.43%
Average BBox IOU	91.88%	81.78%

3.6 Task 6

Our experiment split the training dataset to Train: Val 10:2 and used the same method in task 4 to train the model. For the box representation element, point representation element with five channels output or one channel output, we train three models independently, finally, with the methods mentioned in task 6. We get our result on the Test set without k-fold cross-validation and ensemble, As summarized in Table 8.

Table 8. Performance on the test dataset of Task 6.

	Adobe synthetic	UB PMC
Average Visual Element Detection Score	90.67%	87.00%
Average Name Score	94.84%	78.54%
Average Data Score	70.30%	55.40%
Average Metric Score	76.43%	61.18%

4   Conclusion

Chart-info is a task to test the comprehensive ability, including machine learning, image recognition, object detection, keypoint detection, OCR, and other tasks. In every task, we explored and proposed our methods and achieved relatively good performance. However, it is still hard work to understand and get insights from charts, and we need to do more work.

References

1. He, K., Zhang, X., Ren, S., Sun, J.: Deep residual learning for image recognition. In: Proceedings of the IEEE Conference on Computer Vision and Pattern Recognition, pp. 770–778 (2016)
2. Selvaraju, R.R., Cogswell, M., Das, A., Vedantam, R., Parikh, D., Batra, D.: Grad-cam: visual explanations from deep networks via gradient-based localization. In Proceedings of the IEEE International Conference on Computer Vision, pp. 618–626 (2017)
3. Deng, J., Guo, J., Niannan, X., Zafeiriou, S.: Arcface: additive angular margin loss for deep face recognition. In: CVPR (2019). 6
4. Yun, S., Han, D., Oh, S.J., Chun, S., Choe, J., Yoo, Y.: Cutmix: regularization strategy to train strong classifiers with localizable features. arXiv preprint arXiv:1905.04899 (2019)
5. Zhang, H., Cisse, M., Dauphin, Y.N., Lopez-Paz, D.: mixup: beyond empirical risk minimization. CoRR, abs/1710.09412 (2017). 7
6. Szegedy, C., Vanhoucke, V., Ioffe, S., Shlens, J., Wojna, Z.: Rethinking the inception architecture for computer vision. In: Proceedings of the IEEE Conference on Computer Vision and Pattern Recognition, pp. 2818–2826 (2016)

7. Luo, H., Gu, Y., Liao, X., Lai, S., Jiang, W.: Bag of tricks and a strong baseline for deep person re-identification. In: CVPR (2019)
8. Kang, B., et al.: Decoupling representation and classifier for long-tailed recognition. In ICLR (2020)
9. Cai, Z., Vasconcelos, N.: Cascade R-CNN: delving into high quality object detection. In: Proceedings of the IEEE Conference on Computer Vision and Pattern Recognition, pp. 6154–6162 (2018)
10. Shi, B., Bai, X., Yao, C.: An end-to-end trainable neural network for image-based sequence recognition and its application to scene text recognition[J]. IEEE Trans. Pattern Anal. Mach. Intell. **39**(11), 2298–2304 (2016)
11. Graves, A., Fernández, S., Gomez, F., et al.: Connectionist temporal classification: labelling unsegmented sequence data with recurrent neural networks. In: Proceedings of the 23rd International Conference on Machine Learning, pp. 369–376 (2006)
12. Xie, S., Girshick, R., Dollár, P., et al.: Aggregated residual transformations for deep neural networks. In: Proceedings of the IEEE Conference on Computer Vision and Pattern Recognition, pp. 1492–1500 (2017)
13. Sun, K., Xiao, B., Liu, D., et al.: Deep high-resolution representation learning for human pose estimation. In: Proceedings of the IEEE Conference on Computer Vision and Pattern Recognition, pp. 5693–5703 (2019)
14. Cao, Y., Xu, J., Lin, S., et al.: Gcnet: non-local networks meet squeeze-excitation networks and beyond. In: Proceedings of the IEEE International Conference on Computer Vision Workshops (2019)
15. Poco , J., Heer, J.: Reverse-engineering visualizations: recovering visual encodings from chart images. In: Computer Graphics Forum, vol. 36, no. 3. Wiley Online Library, pp. 353–363 (2017)
16. Breiman, L.: Random forests. Mach. Learn. **45**(1), 5–32 (2001)
17. Ke, G., Meng, Q., Finley T., et al.: Lightgbm: a highly efficient gradient boosting decision tree. In: Advances in Neural Information Processing Systems, pp. 3146–3154 (2017)
18. Zhou, X., Wang, D., Krähenbähl, P.: Objects as points. arXiv preprint arXiv:1904.07850 (2019)
19. Yu, F., Wang, D., Shelhamer, E., et al.: Deep layer aggregation. In: Proceedings of the IEEE Conference on Computer Vision and Pattern Recognition, pp. 2403–2412 (2018)
20. Kingma, D.P., Ba, J.: Adam: a method for stochastic optimization. ICLR (2014)
21. Dai, J.: Deformable Convolutional Networks (2017)
22. Lin, T.-Y., Goyal, P., Girshick, R., He, K., Doll'ar, P.: Focal loss for dense object detection. In: ICCV (2017)
23. Feng, Z.H., Kittler, J., Awais, M., et al.: Wing loss for robust facial landmark localisation with convolutional neural networks. In: 2018 IEEE/CVF Conference on Computer Vision and Pattern Recognition. IEEE (2018)
24. Rashid, M., Gu, X., Jae Lee, Y.: Interspecies knowledge transfer for facial keypoint detection. In: IEEE Conference on Computer Vision and Pattern Recognition (CVPR) (2017)
25. Surhone, L.M., Tennoe, M.T., Henssonow, S.F., et al.: Histogram of Oriented Gradients. Betascript Publishing **12**(4), 1368–1371 (2016)

ICPR 2020 Competition on Text Block Segmentation on a NewsEye Dataset

ICPR 2020 Competition on Text Block Segmentation on a NewsEye Dataset (TB-Seg)

Competition Description

TB-Seg was a competition that focused on text block segmentation within the framework of the International Conference on Pattern Recognition (ICPR) 2020. The main goal of this competition was to automatically analyse the structure of historical newspaper pages. In contrast to many existing segmentation methods, instead of working on pixels, the study had a focus on clustering baselines/text lines into text blocks. Working on baseline level addresses directly the application scenario where for a given image the contained text should be extracted in blocks for further investigations.

We received three final submissions and all were accepted for the competition. Their systems represent an interesting mix of ruled-based approaches and different machine learning methods. The competition paper composed by the organizers was reviewed by two independent researchers.

This work was supported by the European Union's Horizon 2020 research and innovation programme under grant agreement No770299 (NewsEye). We would like to thank the Austrian National Library who contributed the historical dataset. We would also like to thank the competitors for their participation, the TB-Seg Program Committee for their review process, as well as the ICPR 2020 Challenge Chairs for their valuable help and support.

Organization

TB-Seg Chairs

Johannes Michael   University of Rostock, Germany
Max Weidemann   University of Rostock, Germany
Bastian Laasch   University of Rostock, Germany
Roger Labahn   University of Rostock, Germany

Program Committee

Oussama Zayene   Haute École d'Ingénierie et d'Architecture de
                          Fribourg, Switzerland
Mickaël Coustaty   La Rochelle Université, France

ICPR 2020 Competition on Text Block Segmentation on a NewsEye Dataset

Johannes Michael[(✉)] [iD], Max Weidemann[iD], Bastian Laasch[iD], and Roger Labahn

Institute of Mathematics, CITlab, University of Rostock, 18057 Rostock, Germany
{johannes.michael,max.weidemann,bastian.laasch,
roger.labahn}@uni-rostock.de

Abstract. We present a competition on text block segmentation within the framework of the International Conference on Pattern Recognition (ICPR) 2020. The main goal of this competition is to automatically analyse the structure of historical newspaper pages with a subsequent evaluation of the participants' algorithms performance. In contrast to many existing segmentation methods, instead of working on pixels, the present study has a focus on clustering baselines/text lines into text blocks. Therefore, we introduce a new measure based on a baseline detection evaluation scheme. But also common pixel-based approaches could participate without restrictions. Working on baseline level addresses directly the application scenario where for a given image the contained text should be extracted in blocks for further investigations. We present the results of three submissions. The experiments have shown that text blocks can be reliably detected both on pages with a simple layout and on pages with a complex layout.

Keywords: Document image analysis · Historical documents · Layout analysis · Text block segmentation · Baseline detection

1 Background and Impact

This competition was held as part of the European Union's Horizon 2020 research and innovation programme NewsEye - A Digital Investigator for Historical Newspapers[1] and was organised by the research group CITlab[2] being part of the NewsEye consortium.

The purpose of the NewsEye project is to enable historians and humanities scholars to investigate a great amount of historical newspaper collections provided by libraries. To ensure an efficient work, the data processing steps should be as automatic as possible.

---

[1] https://www.newseye.eu/.
[2] https://www.mathematik.uni-rostock.de/forschung/projekte/citlab/.

Supported by the European Union's Horizon 2020 research and innovation programme under grant agreement No770299 (NewsEye).

A. Del Bimbo et al. (Eds.): ICPR 2020 Workshops, LNCS 12668, pp. 405–418, 2021.
https://doi.org/10.1007/978-3-030-68793-9_30

To this end, an automatic digitisation of scanned newspaper pages has to be done. This includes especially the detection of the baselines present in the image, the recognition of the corresponding text and finally, the goal of this competition, merging the single lines into text blocks. Afterwards, these blocks can be analysed by humanists or can be used for other document analysis tasks like named entity recognition or topic modelling. A baseline is described by a polygonal chain, i.e., a list of a finite number of ordered two dimensional points.

In the past similar competitions have been organized, like the ICDAR Competition on Recognition of Documents with Complex Layouts[3]. The main difference is that we work on baseline level instead on pixel level. This implies also the need for a new evaluation measure (see Sect. 4). In the following, we first give a brief overview to related work in document image analysis in Sect. 2. In Sect. 3 we will describe the competition in detail. The participating teams and their methods are presented in Sect. 5 and the results are evaluated in Sect. 6.

2   Related Work

In general, if you want to extract the content of a newspaper page, you usually start with an analysis of its logical parts. This includes the recognition of headings, headers, footers, images, tables and related text lines that form text blocks. To extract the mentioned building blocks, various methods can be used that rely on visual features, textual features or both. There are algorithms, relying on specific rules that hold for pages with a certain layout [17,19]. However, models like this do not generalise well and will fail to make good predictions for pages with complex layout. Furthermore, specifically for page segmentation, traditional layout analysis methods like connected components, recursive XY cut, docstrum or voronoi diagrams were used in the past [1,14]. Nonetheless, the best performing algorithms rely on machine learning algorithms from the fields of semantic segmentation [4,15], object detection [24] and instance segmentation [27].

In most cases, CNNs are used to extract the visual features from the input page in a first step. Subsequently, these are used by other neural network modules or combined with other features, e.g.., textual ones. Algorithms using textual information, like [5] for document classification, use word or paragraph embeddings created by deep learning frameworks like BERT [9]. BERT stands for "Bidirectional Encoder Representations from Transformers" which is a transformer-based model used for NLP tasks. Finally, following recent advances in object detection, models like YOLO [22] or Faster R-CNN [23] and its successor Mask R-CNN [16] have been used in document image analysis [27].

The recognition of page objects respectively the segmentation of a document in its logical components was also the topic of recent competitions, in the following just naming a few. At the ICDAR2015/2017/2019 Competition on Recognition of Documents with Complex Layouts [3,7,8], the participants had to segment scanned pages from contemporary magazines and technical articles, classify the resulting regions and to apply text recognition as a bonus challenge.

---

[3] https://www.primaresearch.org/RDCL2019/.

Furthermore, the ICDAR2017 Competition on Page Object Detection [12] was organized, defining the task of detecting page objects like tables, mathematical equations, graphics, figures, etc. from document images. And finally, at the ICDAR2019 Competition on Table Detection and Recognition, the objective was to detect tables in an image on the one hand and to extract the table structure on the other hand.

3   Competition Details

3.1   Data

The data have been collected from the NewsEye project and consists of historical newspaper pages (partially binarised) ranging from the 19th to 20th century provided by the Austrian National Library[4], i.e., especially containing newspapers in German language. The newspapers made available for this competition comprise the titles "Arbeiter Zeitung", "Illustrierte Kronen Zeitung", "Innsbrucker Nachrichten" and "Neue Freie Presse". The data can be downloaded from the competition website[5].

The **training data** contains a set of scanned pages. Furthermore, for every image we provided the coordinates of the baselines, the corresponding text of the lines and the text regions marking the text blocks in the well-established PAGE XML format (see [21]). Additionally, baselines lying within the same block have a unique ID in the so-called "custom tag" (see Figs. 1(a) and 2(a) for marked baselines and Figs. 1(b) and 2(b) for marked text blocks).

Please note that a text block captures a whole paragraph and the block outlines enclose the text very closely. Headlines are marked separately and blocks are not across columns. Furthermore, images can be ignored since they (usually) do not contain baselines and occurring tables and framed advertisements are handled as single text blocks (see Fig. 2(b)).

The following represents a snippet of a PAGE XML file where the baseline with ID "tl_223" forms a block together with all other lines with the block ID "a7"

```
<TextLine id="tl_223" primaryLanguage="German"
custom="readingOrder {index:5;} structure {id:a7; type:article;}">.
```

The type description "article" in the custom tag is a result of the NewsEye project. In connection with this competition an article means simply a text block.

For each sample in the **test data** there is an image of the scanned newspaper page with its corresponding PAGE XML file containing the baselines (without any block IDs), the text and only a single text region surrounding the whole page. The single region should be ignored but is necessary because the PAGE XML

---

[4] https://www.onb.ac.at/en/.

[5] https://www.mathematik.uni-rostock.de/forschung/projekte/citlab/projects/text-block-segmentation-competition-icpr2020/.

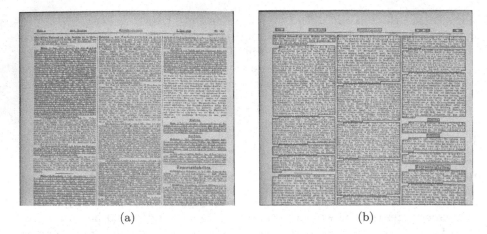

(a)   (b)

Fig. 1. (a) Upper part of a simple newspaper page with marked baselines (baselines belonging to the same block have the same colour). (b) Upper part of a simple newspaper page with marked text blocks. (Color figure online)

format requires that every line is assigned to a region. The ground truth (GT) data, in which the baselines have again the block IDs, is, of course, confidential. GT means, in our context, the ideal of a system's output generated by humans.

3.2   Tasks

The objective of the tasks is to assign baselines belonging to the same detected text block with the same block ID in the custom tag. All given lines have to be assigned where it is possible that a single line forms a block, i.e., it has its own ID.

The competition was split into two tasks where each participant was free to choose one of them or both. A **simple track** with newspaper pages only with continuous text (40 pages training data, 10 pages test data, see Fig. 1) and a **complex track** with pages including additional tables, images or advertisements (40 pages training data, 10 pages test data, see Fig. 2).

When doing page or image segmentation in general this is usually done on pixel level, but in the context of text extraction we are rather interested in text lines. This motivates the introduction of a new measure (see Sect. 4) evaluating the quality of a text block segmentation system at baseline level. Hence, for the evaluation measure only the block IDs of the lines are crucial.

Please note that pixel-based approaches where also invited to participate without restrictions, since the training data contains GT regions for corresponding methods. Afterwards, lines lying within the same detected region could

(a)   (b)

Fig. 2. (a) Upper part of a complex newspaper page with marked baselines (baselines belonging to the same block have the same colour). (b) Upper part of a complex newspaper page with marked text blocks (red blocks indicate images, blue blocks indicate advertisements, violet blocks indicate tables). (Color figure online)

simply be assigned with the same block ID in the custom tag. For entering such tags in PAGE XML files we referred to tools available in our GitHub repository[6].

The training data was published as soon as the competition became open. The participants had roughly five months to train their systems before the test data was released. After two additional weeks the teams had to submit their results.

4 Evaluation Measure

Our final goal is the extraction of text from images for further analysis. Therefore, in terms of segmentation it is sufficient to merge the lines into blocks and not to detect regions on pixel level. Thus, leading to the introduction of a new evaluation measure (available in our GitHub repository[7]).

4.1 Notation

Since we have to get more technical in this section, we want to define some notations. As already mentioned in Sect. 1 a baseline is described by a polygonal chain, i.e., a list of a finite number of ordered two dimensional points (= vertices of the chain), so it is to be understood as a vector. Furthermore, to evaluate the quality of the participating systems, we have to compare the results of the text block segmentation algorithm (i.e., the hypotheses (HY)) with the GT data. Per page we define:

---

[6] https://github.com/CITlabRostock/citlab-python-util/tree/master/citlab_python_util/parser/xml/page.

[7] https://github.com/CITlabRostock/citlab-article-separation-measure.

- $\mathbf{g}_k$ is the GT baseline with index k given by human annotators, $k \in \{1, \ldots, K\}$, where K is the number of all GT baselines of the page.
- $\mathbf{h}_l$ is the HY baseline with index l computed by a baseline detection system, $l \in \{1, \ldots, L\}$, where L is the number of all HY baselines of the page.
- $G_i = \left\{ \mathbf{g}_{i_1}, \ldots, \mathbf{g}_{i_{m_i}} \right\}$ is the GT text block with index i as a set of m_i GT baselines, $i \in \{1, \ldots, M\}$, where M is the number of all GT blocks of the page.
- $H_j = \left\{ \mathbf{h}_{j_1}, \ldots, \mathbf{h}_{j_{n_j}} \right\}$ is the HY text block with index j as a set of n_j HY baselines, $j \in \{1, \ldots, N\}$, where N is the number of all HY blocks of the page.

Remark 1. The measure is developed for an end-to-end system detecting the lines in a first step and the text blocks afterwards. In connection with this competition the baseline detection is not needed since the baselines are given, i.e., the set of HY baselines is equal to the set of GT baselines. For the sake of completeness, however, we would like to present the entire measure.

4.2   R and P Matrices

In the following we want to compare the given M GT text blocks with the generated N HY blocks. To this end, we compute two different types of evaluation scores between every GT block and every HY block. Hence, we get two matrices of dimension $M \times N$.

At this point the baseline detection measure presented in [13] is used, which is composed of the so called R and P values, which are derived from the Precision and Recall values, helping us to study the equality between two sets of baselines. This measure was employed successfully in the recent ICDAR 2017/2019 competitions on baseline detection (see [11] and [10]).

- The **R value** $\in [0, 1]$ (see [13], Sect. 3) indicates, loosely spoken, how well a set of GT baselines is covered by a set of HY baselines. Hence, this score has similar properties to the well-known recall value.
  $\Rightarrow$ Segmentation errors, e.g.., a baseline is split into two lines or two lines are merged into one, are not penalised, because we measure how reliable the text is detected (ignoring layout issues).
- The **P value** $\in [0, 1]$ (see [13], Sect. 3) indicates, loosely spoken, how well a set of HY baselines is covered by a set of GT baselines. Hence, this score has similar properties to the well-known precision value.
  $\Rightarrow$ Segmentation errors are penalised, because we measure how reliable the structure of the baselines (layout) of the page is detected. So, this score gives us information about the over- and under-segmentation of lines.

Definition 1 (R matrix). *The R matrix $\mathcal{R}\left(\{G_1,\ldots,G_M\},\{H_1,\ldots,H_N\}\right)$ between the GT blocks $G_i, i \in \{1,\ldots,M\}$, and the HY blocks $H_j, j \in \{1,\ldots,N\}$, is defined as*

$$
\begin{array}{c}
\begin{array}{ccc} H_1 \cdots & H_j & \cdots H_N \end{array} \\
\begin{array}{c} G_1 \\ \vdots \\ G_i \\ \vdots \\ G_M \end{array}
\left[\quad\quad \widetilde{R}\left(G_i, H_j, \mathcal{T}_i\right) \quad\quad \right]
\end{array}
$$

in which $\widetilde{R}\left(G_i, H_j, \mathcal{T}_i\right)$ is the in [13] defined R value. The set $\mathcal{T}_i$ contains tolerance values for each GT baseline included by G_i effecting that minor deviations in the baseline detection are not penalised.

The value $\widetilde{R}$ indicates for what fraction of the given GT baselines there are corresponding detected HY baselines within a certain tolerance area.

Definition 2 (P matrix). *The P matrix $\mathcal{P}\left(\{G_1,\ldots,G_M\},\{H_1,\ldots,H_N\}\right)$ between the GT blocks $G_i, i \in \{1,\ldots,M\}$, and the HY blocks $H_j, j \in \{1,\ldots,N\}$, is defined as*

$$
\begin{array}{c}
\begin{array}{ccc} H_1 \cdots & H_j & \cdots H_N \end{array} \\
\begin{array}{c} G_1 \\ \vdots \\ G_i \\ \vdots \\ G_M \end{array}
\left[\quad\quad P\left(G_i, H_j, \mathcal{T}_i\right) \quad\quad \right]
\end{array}
$$

in which $\widetilde{P}\left(G_i, H_j, \mathcal{T}_i\right)$ is the in [13] defined P value. The set $\mathcal{T}_i$ contains tolerance values for each GT baseline included by G_i effecting that minor deviations in the baseline detection are not penalised.

The value $\widetilde{P}$ indicates for what fraction of the detected HY baselines there are corresponding given GT baselines within a certain tolerance area.

4.3 R, P and F Values for Text Block Segmentation

After the calculation of the R and P matrix based on an evaluation scheme for baseline detection, we determine the maximum entries in these matrices in a greedy manner.

Remark 2. "Greedy manner" means, in this context, that one by one the maximal values of a given matrix are chosen with following deletion of the corresponding rows and columns. Afterwards, the resulting values are summed up (see Algorithm 1).

Algorithm 1. Greedy Function

1: **procedure** GREEDY(A) with $A \in \mathbb{R}^{M \times N}$
2:     Sum $\leftarrow 0$
3:     $A' \leftarrow A$
4:     **while** A' is not empty **do**
5:         $a \leftarrow$ one of the maximal elements of A'
6:         Sum $\leftarrow$ Sum $+ a$
7:         $A' \leftarrow$ take A' and delete corresponding row/column of the element a
8:     **end while**
9:     **return** Sum
10: **end procedure**

Furthermore, it seems to make sense to create a monotony between the baseline detection and the proposed text block segmentation measure that holds

$$\text{proposed text block segmentation measure} \leq \text{baseline detection measure.} \quad (1)$$

The equality holds if and only if the blocks have been found perfectly. Later, this relation is useful to realise in which step in an end-to-end scenario the mistakes happened (in the baseline detection or in the text block segmentation step). Please note again that in the proposed competition the baselines are given and hence, the baseline detection measure is always 1.

To ensure (1), each row of the R matrix is weighted by the percentage of the GT block (compared to all GT blocks) corresponding to this row (analogous, each column of the P matrix is weighted by the percentage of the HY block (compared to all HY blocks) corresponding to this column).

For example, we consider a page with three given GT blocks G_1, G_2, G_3 and two detected HY blocks H_1, H_2. Hence, the R matrix has the dimension 3×2. The set G_1 has 10 baselines and the sets G_2 and G_3 contain together 30 baselines. Therefore, the first row in the R matrix (this row corresponds to the GT block G_1) is multiplied by 1/4, since the block G_1 includes 25% of all GT baselines assigned to blocks.

After the explained multiplication/weighting step, the above described Greedy Function is applied on the resulting matrices. We want to express this process with

$$\text{GREEDY}_{weighted}(\mathcal{R}) \quad \text{or} \quad \text{GREEDY}_{weighted}(\mathcal{P}).$$

Definition 3 (R, P and F value for Text Block Segmentation). *The R and P value $\in [0,1]$ for the generated HY blocks are defined as*

$$R(\{G_1, \ldots, G_M\}, \{H_1, \ldots, H_N\}) := GREEDY_{weighted}(\mathcal{R}),$$
$$P(\{G_1, \ldots, G_M\}, \{H_1, \ldots, H_N\}) := GREEDY_{weighted}(\mathcal{P}).$$

Thus, we obtain the F value $\in [0,1]$ for text block segmentation, i.e., the harmonic mean of the R and P value,

$$F\left(\{G_1, \ldots, G_M\}, \{H_1, \ldots, H_N\}\right) := \frac{2 \cdot R \cdot P}{R + P}.$$

The target value is 1 in all three cases.

These three values give us an appropriate tool to evaluate the result of an algorithm merging a given set of detected baselines into text blocks. The R and P values ensure that HY blocks with too many or too few baselines in comparison with the corresponding GT blocks are penalised with a lower evaluation score. To identify the winner of the proposed tasks of the competition, the F values were averaged over all test samples.

5   Description of the Systems

Three research teams excluding the organisers followed the competition:

- Cinnamon AI & Ho Chi Minh City University of Technology (HCMC)
- École des hautes études commerciales de Montréal (HEC)
- Lenovo Research & South China University of Technology (SCUT)

The first team used a rule-based approach whereas the other two used machine learning methods to extract the text blocks from the newspaper pages. Note that the former team only took part in the simple track and the other two in both tracks.

5.1   Cinnamon AI and Ho Chi Minh City University of Technology (HCMC)

This subsection is based on [20]. HCMC used spatial baseline analysis which led to splitting and merging the baselines gradually. Also, textual features were utilised for the post-processing. First, polygons around the baselines were observed and interpreted as rectangles which have the attributes xmin, ymin, xmax, ymax. They used the third quartile (Q3) of the vertical distance between nearest baselines as an initial threshold, denoted by vertical_distance_q3. Finally, their workflow is described in the following steps.

In a first step baselines having a horizontal overlap (horizontal_iou) larger than 0.95 and a vertical distance less than vertical_distance_q3 * 1.2 got merged. If there are any top-lines these got merged to the paragraphs constructed in the first step. A top-line is the first line of a paragraph having an indentation. To determine the top-lines, the vertical distance should be less than vertical_distance_q3 * 1.2 and the difference of the top-line's xmin to the below nearest group of baselines xmin should be less than vertical_distance_q3 * 0.5 and larger than 0. For the bottom-lines, if there were any, the same procedure was applied and for cases, where paragraphs only consisted of two lines the same analysis was used. The last case included headings and titles which have two continuous lines having a center alignment. To determine the center alignment, consider the difference between the horizontal centers of the baselines. The absolute value should be less than `vertical_distance_q3 * 0.5`. For hard cases, an additional post-processing was applied. As a last step, a unique integer tag was given to each group of baselines in the custom tag of the PAGE XML file.

5.2   École des hautes études commerciales de Montréal (HEC)

This subsection is based on [26]. HEC used deep neural networks for detecting regions of different text blocks. Specifically, Mask R-CNN [16], a neural network used for instance segmentation was applied using the provided training datasets independently for the simple and the complex track. To this end, the workflow presented in the "Torchvision Object Detection Finetuning Tutorial"[8] was adapted to the text block detection task and is summarised in the following.

First, all regions in the training sets were converted to alpha mask images, in order to make them compatible for the intended deep learning architecture[9]. To avoid overfitting, data augmentation was applied to the images and masks without distorting their colour coding using the fastai library[10].

After the model was trained, the predicted masks (arrays of the same size as the input image with values of 1's for the recognised text blocks and 0's elsewhere) for the test sets were used to determine for each baseline which mask contains the largest number of the baseline points. Note that a baseline is described by a list of ordered points as mentioned in Sect. 4.1. All the baseline points matching a specific mask received the block ID of that mask. The IDs were named arbitrarily while remaining unique. The points, that did not fall into any mask received their unique block ID each. This procedure ensures that a single baseline point will not fall into two categories at the same time. The ID that occurred most frequently under the single points of a baseline was finally the block ID for the whole baseline.

For the full implementation of the algorithm see the GitHub page of the participant[11].

5.3   Lenovo Research and South China University of Technology (SCUT)

This subsection is based on [6]. SCUT also used, among other modules, an instance segmentation model for both tracks and describe their algorithm in the following steps.

First, data augmentation was applied to the training data, including resizing, cropping, swapping, erasing, etc. Afterwards, a contour-based instance segmentation model computed the segmentation information. As input, the digitised

---

[8] https://pytorch.org/tutorials/intermediate/torchvision_tutorial.html.
[9] https://github.com/davoodwadi/ICPR2020-TextBlockSegment/blob/master/ extracting_masks-complex.ipynb.
[10] https://fastai1.fast.ai/vision.transform.html.
[11] https://github.com/davoodwadi/ICPR2020-TextBlockSegment.

image was used and instance contours of the text blocks were outputted by the model. Then, for every baseline the corresponding instance contour was determined. In parallel, a separate model for obtaining the link relationships of text lines was used. It contains a Feature Pyramid Network [18] as a backbone to extract image features, and a BLSTM model to extract textual features. Afterwards, a feature vector containing the image and text information was generated and send to a Graph Attention Network (GAT) [25] model. The output of the GAT was then inputted to a fully connected layer to classify whether a current line and an adjacent line belong to the same block. Finally, a fusion mechanism was used to combine the results of the instance segmentation and the GAT model to generate the final result.

6 Results

The results of the competition are presented in Table 1. The F values are averaged over the 10 pages of the corresponding test sets.

Table 1. Results of the participants (including CITlab baseline method) in terms of the in Sect. 4 presented F value on the test sets.

	F value simple track	F value complex track
CITlab	0.934	0.768
HCMC	**0.999**	–
HEC	0.995	0.887
SCUT	0.997	**0.954**

As organisers, we also provide a baseline method which is out of the competition. The CITlab text block detection system[12] is a rule-based method using the idea of the DBSCAN cluster algorithm (see [2]). The single baselines are interpreted as points and we define with their interline distance and their horizontal overlap a distance concept used by DBSCAN to cluster the points. The resulting clusters are our blocks. The advantage of the DBSCAN method is that the algorithm itself determines the number of clusters, i.e., the number of text blocks, in contrast to other cluster algorithms like K-Means. Since we do not know a priori how many blocks there are on a page, this is a crucial point.

As expected, the simple track did not pose a great challenge for the participants. Hence, the results are close together. HCMC wins the simple track, since they fine tuned their rule-based method on the specific training set which is very similar to the test set (an example output is given in Fig. 3(a)). However, the other two machine learning based methods are only marginally worse than the rule-based approach.

---

[12] https://github.com/CITlabRostock/citlab-article-separation.

The complex test pages with their images, advertisements and tables are much more challenging to process by a text block detection system. Therefore, there is a great gap between CITlabs baseline method and the machine learning algorithms from HEC and SCUT. The instance segmentation using a Mask R-CNN of HEC performs pretty well. On the other hand, the SCUT team computed in addition to instance segmentation features also GAT results based on image and text information. The combination of the segmentation features and the GAT output clearly outperforms the pure instance segmentation model of HEC, i.e., SCUT wins the complex track (an example output is given in Fig. 3(b)).

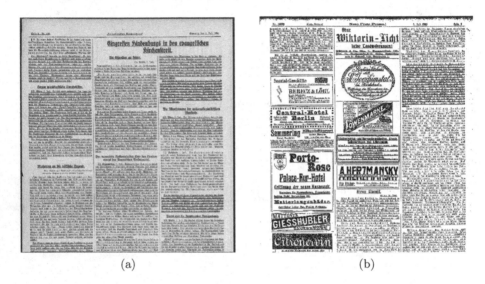

(a)   (b)

Fig. 3. (a) Upper part of a simple newspaper page with baselines marked by the block detection system of HCMC. (b) Upper part of a complex newspaper page with baselines marked by the block detection system of SCUT.

7   Conclusion

This paper described the task, systems and results of the ICPR 2020 Competition on Text Block Segmentation on a NewsEye dataset. The task was to detect text blocks for given historical newspaper pages by grouping baselines belonging to the same block together. The participants could choose between a simple and a complex competition track.

There were three participants who submitted results, one team only took part in the simple track and the other two teams in both tracks. It turned out that the different methods (rule-based and machine learning based) process simple pages similarly and very reliably. Furthermore, it is also possible to develop precisely performing machine learning based systems to detect text blocks on complex pages with only a slightly lower evaluation score in comparison with the score on simple pages.

References

1. Agrawal, M., Doermann, D.: Voronoi++: a dynamic page segmentation approach based on voronoi and docstrum features. In: 2009 10th International Conference on Document Analysis and Recognition, pp. 1011–1015. IEEE (2009)
2. Andrade, G., Ramos, G., Madeira, D., Sachetto, R., Ferreira, R., Rocha, L.: G-dbscan: a GPU accelerated algorithm for density-based clustering. Procedia Comput. Sci. **18**, 369–378 (2013)
3. Antonacopoulos, A., Clausner, C., Papadopoulos, C., Pletschacher, S.: ICDAR 2015 competition on recognition of documents with complex layouts - RDCL2015. In: 2015 13th International Conference on Document Analysis and Recognition (ICDAR), pp. 1151–1155 (2015). https://doi.org/10.1109/ICDAR.2015.7333941
4. Augusto Borges Oliveira, D., Palhares Viana, M.: Fast CNN-based document layout analysis. In: Proceedings of the IEEE International Conference on Computer Vision Workshops, pp. 1173–1180 (2017)
5. Bakkali, S., Ming, Z., Coustaty, M., Rusinol, M.: Visual and textual deep feature fusion for document image classification. In: Proceedings of the IEEE/CVF Conference on Computer Vision and Pattern Recognition Workshops, pp. 562–563 (2020)
6. Chan, X., Wang, L., Li, H., Wu, A., Jin, L.: Method description. private communication, Lenovo Research and South China University of Technology (2020)
7. Clausner, C., Antonacopoulos, A., Pletschacher, S.: ICDAR 2017 competition on recognition of documents with complex layouts - RDCL2017. In: 2017 14th IAPR International Conference on Document Analysis and Recognition (ICDAR), vol. 01, pp. 1404–1410 (2017). https://doi.org/10.1109/ICDAR.2017.229
8. Clausner, C., Antonacopoulos, A., Pletschacher, S.: ICDAR 2019 competition on recognition of documents with complex layouts - RDCL2019. In: 2019 International Conference on Document Analysis and Recognition (ICDAR), pp. 1521–1526 (2019). https://doi.org/10.1109/ICDAR.2019.00245
9. Devlin, J., Chang, M.W., Lee, K., Toutanova, K.: Bert: pre-training of deep bidirectional transformers for language understanding. arXiv preprint arXiv:1810.04805 (2018)
10. Diem, M., Kleber, F., Sablatnig, R., Gatos, B.: cbad: Icdar 2019 competition on baseline detection. In: 2019 International Conference on Document Analysis and Recognition (ICDAR), pp. 1494–1498. IEEE Computer Society, Los Alamitos, CA, USA, September 2019. https://doi.org/10.1109/ICDAR.2019.00240
11. Diem, M., Kleber, F., Fiel, S., Grüning, T., Gatos, B.: cbad: Icdar 2017 competition on baseline detection. In: 2017 14th IAPR International Conference on Document Analysis and Recognition (ICDAR), vol. 1, pp. 1355–1360. IEEE (2017)
12. Gao, L., Yi, X., Jiang, Z., Hao, L., Tang, Z.: Icdar 2017 competition on page object detection. In: 2017 14th IAPR International Conference on Document Analysis and Recognition (ICDAR), vol. 01, pp. 1417–1422 (2017). https://doi.org/10.1109/ICDAR.2017.231
13. Grüning, T., Labahn, R., Diem, M., Kleber, F., Fiel, S.: Read-bad: A new dataset and evaluation scheme for baseline detection in archival documents. In: 2018 13th IAPR International Workshop on Document Analysis Systems (DAS), pp. 351–356. IEEE (2018)

14. Ha, J., Haralick, R.M., Phillips, I.T.: Recursive XY cut using bounding boxes of connected components. In: Proceedings of 3rd International Conference on Document Analysis and Recognition, vol. 2, pp. 952–955. IEEE (1995)
15. He, D., Cohen, S., Price, B., Kifer, D., Giles, C.L.: Multi-scale multi-task FCN for semantic page segmentation and table detection. In: 2017 14th IAPR International Conference on Document Analysis and Recognition (ICDAR), vol. 1, pp. 254–261. IEEE (2017)
16. He, K., Gkioxari, G., Dollár, P., Girshick, R.: Mask R-CNN. In: Proceedings of the IEEE International Conference on Computer Vision, pp. 2961–2969 (2017)
17. Klink, S., Kieninger, T.: Rule-based document structure understanding with a fuzzy combination of layout and textual features. Int. J. Doc. Anal. Recogn. **4**(1), 18–26 (2001)
18. Lin, T.Y., Dollár, P., Girshick, R., He, K., Hariharan, B., Belongie, S.: Feature pyramid networks for object detection. In: Proceedings of the IEEE Conference on Computer Vision and Pattern Recognition, pp. 2117–2125 (2017)
19. Namboodiri, A.M., Jain, A.K.: Document structure and layout analysis. In: Chaudhuri, B.B. (ed.) Digital Document Processing, pp. 29–48. Springer, London (2007). https://doi.org/10.1007/978-1-84628-726-8_2
20. Pham, L., Tran, T.A.: Method description. private communication, Cinnamon AI and Ho Chi Minh City University of Technology (2020)
21. Pletschacher, S., Antonacopoulos, A.: The page (page analysis and ground-truth elements) format framework. In: 2010 20th International Conference on Pattern Recognition, pp. 257–260. IEEE (2010)
22. Redmon, J., Divvala, S., Girshick, R., Farhadi, A.: You only look once: unified, real-time object detection. In: Proceedings of the IEEE Conference on Computer Vision and Pattern Recognition, pp. 779–788 (2016)
23. Ren, S., He, K., Girshick, R., Sun, J.: Faster R-CNN: towards real-time object detection with region proposal networks. In: Advances in Neural Information Processing Systems, pp. 91–99 (2015)
24. Saha, R., Mondal, A., Jawahar, C.: Graphical object detection in document images. In: 2019 International Conference on Document Analysis and Recognition (ICDAR), pp. 51–58. IEEE (2019)
25. Veličković, P., Cucurull, G., Casanova, A., Romero, A., Lio, P., Bengio, Y.: Graph attention networks. arXiv preprint arXiv:1710.10903 (2017)
26. Wadi, D.: Method description. private communication, École des hautes études commerciales de Montréal (2020)
27. Zhong, X., Tang, J., Yepes, A.J.: Publaynet: largest dataset ever for document layout analysis. In: 2019 International Conference on Document Analysis and Recognition (ICDAR), pp. 1015–1022. IEEE (2019)

The 2020 CORSMAL Challenge: Multimodal Fusion and Learning for Robotics

The 2020 CORSMAL Challenge: Multi-modal Fusion and Learning for Robotics

Challenge Description

The 2020 CORSMAL Challenge "Multi-Modal Fusion and Learning for Robotics", organized in conjunction with the International Conference on Pattern Recognition 2020, aimed to stimulate research in the accurate and robust prediction of the physical properties of objects prior to a human-to-robot handover. This estimation is based on sound and vision sensing.

The challenge consists in predicting the properties of previously unseen containers (cups, glasses, mugs, bottles, food boxes), whose physical properties, such as material, stiffness, texture, transparency and shape, vary and must be inferred on-the-fly prior to a handover, along with the different fillings within the container. These predictions enable a robotic arm to apply the correct force when grasping the container, thus avoiding slippage, crashing the container or spilling its content.

Participants were challenged to solve three independent tasks, namely the estimation of the container capacity as well as the classification of the type and level of the content, if any, while the container is manipulated by a human. Tasks were performed on a public and private testing sets from a novel, large dataset (http://corsmal.eecs. qmul.ac.uk/containers_manip.html), released by the CORSMAL project (http:// corsmal.eecs.qmul.ac.uk), and whose containers and fillings were not known in advance, except for a set of object categories (glasses, cups, food boxes) and a set of filling types (water, pasta, rice).

The results from each task were then used to compute the filling mass as overall score of a private testing set of the challenge and for ranking the solutions proposed by the participants.

Five teams participated in the Challenge and three teams produced a paper that describes their solution to the Challenge. A single-blind review process involved 3 reviewers per paper, selected among the experts in the field. Updates on the CORSMAL Challenge can be found here: http://corsmal.eecs.qmul.ac.uk/ ICPR2020challenge.html.

We want to thank the ICPR Challenge Chairs, and the CHIST-ERA program to support the event, through the project CORSMAL, under UK EPSRC grant EP/S031715/1, Swiss NSF grant 20CH21_180444, and French ANR grant 18-CHR3-0006.

Organization

Challenge Organizers

Kaspar Althoefer   Queen Mary University of London, UK

Aude Billard   École polytechnique fédérale de Lausanne, Switzerland

Andrea Cavallaro   Queen Mary University of London, UK

Konstantinos Chatzilygeroudis   École polytechnique fédérale de Lausanne, Switzerland

Nuno Ferreira Duarte   École polytechnique fédérale de Lausanne, Switzerland

Pascal Frossard   École polytechnique fédérale de Lausanne, Switzerland

Dounia Kitouni   Sorbonne Université, France

Ricardo Sanchez-Matilla   Queen Mary University of London, UK

Riccardo Mazzon   Queen Mary University of London, UK

Apostolos Modas   École polytechnique fédérale de Lausanne, Switzerland

Véronique Perdereau   Sorbonne Université, France

Alessio Xompero   Queen Mary University of London, UK

Top-1 CORSMAL Challenge 2020 Submission: Filling Mass Estimation Using Multi-modal Observations of Human-Robot Handovers

Vladimir Iashin[1]([⊠])(iD), Francesca Palermo[2](iD), Gökhan Solak[2](iD), and Claudio Coppola[2](iD)

[1] Computer Vision Group, Information Technology and Communication Sciences, Tampere University, 33720 Tampere, Finland
`vladimir.iashin@tuni.fi`
[2] ARQ (Advanced Robotics at Queen Mary), School of Electronic Engineering and Computer Science, Queen Mary University of London, London E14NS, UK
`{f.palermo,g.solak,c.coppola}@qmul.ac.uk`

Abstract. Human-robot object handover is a key skill for the future of human-robot collaboration. CORSMAL 2020 Challenge focuses on the perception part of this problem: the robot needs to estimate the filling mass of a container held by a human. Although there are powerful methods in image processing and audio processing individually, answering such a problem requires processing data from multiple sensors together. The appearance of the container, the sound of the filling, and the depth data provide essential information. We propose a multi-modal method to predict three key indicators of the filling mass: filling type, filling level, and container capacity. These indicators are then combined to estimate the filling mass of a container. Our method obtained Top-1 overall performance among all submissions to CORSMAL 2020 Challenge on both public and private subsets while showing no evidence of overfitting. Our source code is publicly available: github.com/v-iashin/CORSMAL.

Keywords: Multi-modal · Audio · RGB · Depth · IR · CORSMAL

1 Introduction

In the past, the usage of robots has been confined to heavy industry (e.g. automotive) where the manipulation tasks could be performed in constrained environments with limited human presence. Although this technology was very successful in this setting, it is inadequate for some of the growing areas, such as the light manufacturing industries (e.g., food, consumer electronics) and domestic robotics (e.g., home assistants and companions).

V. Iashin, F. Palermo, G. Solak and C. Coppola—Equally contributed.

© Springer Nature Switzerland AG 2021
A. Del Bimbo et al. (Eds.): ICPR 2020 Workshops, LNCS 12668, pp. 423–436, 2021.
https://doi.org/10.1007/978-3-030-68793-9_31

In order to create robots capable of living and operating in the same space with humans, robots have to be able to interact and co-operate with them. Manipulating objects of daily living scenarios is an easy cognitive task for humans, who are capable to generalise their grasping and manipulation skills to a wide spectra of materials and shapes. This creates the necessity of developing robots that can cope with such object diversity while performing handover and manipulation tasks. This becomes even more challenging when dealing with previously unseen objects as their dimensions, mass and material are unknown. While it is relatively simple for humans to estimate the physical properties (such as mass, stiffness) of the object using vision and other sensing modalities (e.g. tactile, force feedback), it still is an open problem in robotics.

In recent decades, the capabilities of computer vision algorithms have increased significantly due to increased availability in labeled vision data and more performing vision algorithms, based on learnt visual features (such as [8]). Computer Vision researchers have put efforts into developing solutions that support robotic manipulation. However, they rely mostly on pre-selected sets of object models (e.g. [22,28,31]). For real robotic scenarios, it is important to maintain a certain level of flexibility, reducing the prior knowledge required to deal with the wide spectra of situations required for the collaboration between a human and a robot. Furthermore, while vision is very effective in localising and estimating the physical properties of solid objects [6,16,23,24,29,30], it is much harder to estimate the filling properties of container objects with different possible types of filling, unless the container is transparent [21]. Previous works, such as [17,18] and [5], have proved that sound and haptics can be used to estimate the quantity and quality of the filling in a container. Thus, combining different types of modalities can improve to estimate relevant object features that can support safe and accurate handovers.

In this work, we introduce an approach to estimate the filling mass of a container object using audio and multi-view RGB-D sensing modalities. In particular, we split the problem of estimating the filling mass of an object (container) into 3 tasks. We rely on the CORSMAL Container Manipulation Dataset [33] which is designed for this problem.

T_1 **Filling Type.** In this task, we predict the type of content present in the container object, if it is not empty. Thus, the possible types of content are: empty, pasta, rice, or water (for drinking glasses and cups). The classification of the filling level is performed combining 2 audio-based classifiers: the first one uses "classical" audio features (MFCCs, chromagram, energy, spread, etc.) [4] in a random forest classifier, while the second one uses VGGish features [9] in a GRU [3] model.

T_2 **Filling Level.** In this task, we estimate the percentage of the container that is filled with the filling items. The percentage values are discretised into 3 classes: 0, 50, and 90%. The classification of this task combines three models: an RGB-based and two audio-based classifiers. The audio-based models are similar to the T_1 while the RGB-based classifier uses the R(2+1)d features and a GRU model.

T_3 **Container capacity**. In this task, we estimate the volume of the container object. Different from the previous tasks, the target value is a real number. For this task, RGB-D + IR data is used to localise the object and estimate its dimensions [32]. The volume is then computed using a cylindrical approximation.

Finally, once estimated the filling type (T_1), filling level (T_2), and container capacity (T_3), we can calculate the mass of the object easily, assuming a pre-estimated average mass density for each filling type. The solution that we present resulted the top-ranking one for overall performance among the participants of the CORSMAL Challenge 2020 [25].

The main contributions of this article are the following:

1. We present an approach to estimate the container's filling mass based on several different modalities (audio, RGB, IR, and depth) which is formulated as the combination of three sub-tasks: estimation of the filling level of an object, the filling type, and its capacity.
2. An experiment is performed on a public dataset provided in the context of the CORSMAL Challenge 2020 [25]. Our model achieves state-of-the-art performance on both public and private test subsets proving generalization capabilities on previously unseen objects.

Please note that this work is conducted in the context of a competition and some decisions are taken under time limitation.

The paper is organized as follows. Section 2 describes our approach to the estimation of the container filling mass and each of the sub-tasks individually as well as the implementation details. The experimentation is presented in Sect. 3, which includes dataset description, metrics, and results. Section 4 concludes.

2 Our Approach

The task of container mass estimation requires solving three individual sub-tasks: container's filling type and filling level as well as container's capacity estimation. The first two are classification tasks and the latter one is 3D localization. We solve each of the three sub-tasks individually and using the obtained predictions to calculate the mass of a container. We summarize the approach in Fig. 1.

2.1 Filling Level and Filling Type Estimation

The first two sub-tasks require to estimate the filling level and filling type of the container. We formulate both sub-tasks as classification problems. We combine the details for both sub-tasks in one section as we are using a similar approach which differs only in the number of output classes. The approach to these two sub-tasks could be roughly divided into three parts: feature extraction, a classification model, and how the predictions are combined if several classifiers were used.

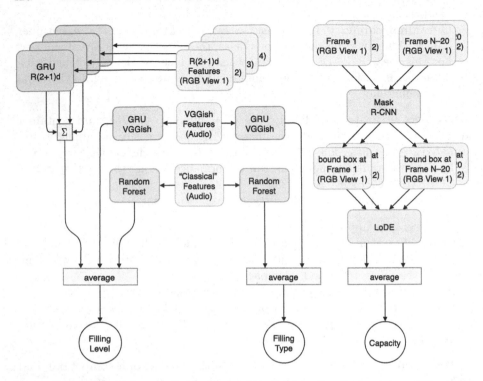

Fig. 1. The design of an individual model for each sub-task: container filling level (left), filling type (middle) classification, and container capacity estimation (right). For the **filling level** estimation we rely on both modalities: RGB (R(2+1)d features) and audio ("classical" and VGGish features). In particular, we encode streams from each camera placed at different view points with the individual GRU models. Next, we sum up the logits and apply softmax at the output. Next, we process VGGish featured extracted from the audio stream and process it with another GRU model which outputs the class probabilities. Then, the "classical" features are classified with the random forest algorithm. Finally, the probabilities from all three models are averaged to produce the final prediction for the filling level. The procedure for **filling type** classification resembles the one for the filling level except for the absence of RGB stream. The **capacity estimation** pipeline starts with the extraction of two frames from two camera views (C1 and C2): the 1st and the 20th frames to the end. The frames are passed through the Mask R-CNN to detect a container. The detected bounding boxes are used to crop both frames. The crops are sent to the LoDE model which outputs the estimation of the container capacity. If an object was not detected on either of the frames, we use the training prior.

Feature Extraction. Being some of the containers not transparent, it would be difficult to rely on vision to recognise the filling type. Thus, it can be assumed that a model designed for *filling type* classification should mostly benefit from audio input as a human, if blinded, could distinguish what is being poured by relying on the sound (e. g. rice vs. water). Similarly, for the *filling level*, the audio might provide information if the container was empty or almost full. However, it might also be useful to let a model utilize some information from the vision as some of the containers are transparent and the current *filling level* could be guessed from the visual information. However, for the opaque containers, vision is not informative. Therefore, we rely on audio in both and additionally employ visual modality for the *filling level* task.

To extract audio features for the filling type classification, we rely on both "classical" audio features and features from a pre-trained deep learning model (VGGish [9]). The "classical" features are extracted in two phases. In the first phase, we extract short-term features for each 50 ms window of the audio. These features include the MFCCs, energy, spectral characteristics, zero crossing rate, chroma vector and deviation [4]. Then, these short-term features are used to derive long-term features that are fed to the classifier. Long-term features summarize a larger portion of the audio. These contain the means and standard deviations of multiple short-term features. There are 136-dimensions of features in the final model.

The features are extracted from every 0.96 s of the original one-channel audio and represented as a 128-d vector obtained from the output of the pre-classification layer. The features form a tensor of size $\mathbf{R}^{T_{vgg} \times 128}$ for each event where $T_{vgg} = floor(T_{sec}/0.96)$, T_{sec} is the duration of the audio in seconds.

For the filling level estimation sub-task we also utilize visual information, which was encoded with a pre-trained model for action recognition (R(2+1)d RGB-only [27]). The R(2+1)d features are a 512-d vector extracted from the pre-classification layer which spans about 0.5 s of the original video (16 RGB frames @ 30 fps). Therefore, for each RGB stream obtained from a camera, we extract $\mathbf{R}^{T_{r21d} \times 512}$ tensor where $T_{r21d} = floor(T_f/16)$ with T_f being the total number of frames in a video. These specific feature extractors (VGGish and R(2+1)d) as they show promising results not only on the tasks they are trained to solve (sound and action classification) but also when applied for other tasks [12,13,20]. Adding these extra features are also motivated with the fact that it is useful to have more diverse individual "opinions" (predictions) for a stronger combined prediction [2,14].

Classification Models. We applied the "classica" audio features to both SVM and random forest classifiers [26]. We selected the random forest as it performed better on the validation set. The random forest fits a set of decision tree classifiers on random subsets of observations from the dataset as well as the random subset of features.

Considering that the VGGish and R(2+1)d features are sequence and the expected output of our model is the class label for filling type and filling level this problem can be treated as "many-to-one" type. For these types of problems, an RNN is usually considered as a natural candidate. In this work, we tried both LSTM [10] and GRU [3] but the latter one was preferred due to both efficiency and accuracy.

The last hidden state at the top layer of GRU is used for classification. Specifically, we pass it through one fully-connected layer which maps the hidden state space into the space of labels (for instance, 3 logits for the filling level and 4 for the filling type tasks). Since we may have several RGB sequences (an event is recorded from several cameras) we may aggregate predictions by summing the individual logits obtained from each RGB sequence, e. g. R(2+1)d features. Note that we do not take into consideration the fact that if the container is a food box, the filling type could not be liquid.

Post-processing. We aggregate the predictions from the models: random forest on "classical" audio features, GRU on VGGish features, and, for the filling level, also the GRU output aggregated from multiple cameras on R(2+1)d features. In our work, we use the simple average of probabilities ("opinions") from each model to form the final prediction for the sub-tasks.

2.2   Container Capacity Estimation

This task requires the estimation of the capacity of the container. Since the shape and size of a container can vary significantly and the model could be tested in different scenarios, it is a challenging task to tackle. Our approach builds on the Localisation and Object Dimensions Estimator (LoDE) algorithm [32]. LoDE is a method based on Mask R-CNN [7] to simultaneously localise objects used as a container and estimate their dimensions. It makes use of RGB frames extracted from the two calibrated RGB cameras positioned on the left and right corners of the room. The depth and infrared data are also used to improve robustness.

A mask of the object is created using a Mask R-CNN ResNet-50-Feature Pyramid Network (FPN) [11] pre-trained on Common Objects in Context (COCO) dataset [19]. The two 2D centroids (x^1 and x^2) are estimated in the segmented images from the left and right camera. To estimate the 3D centroid (X) of an object, a triangulation with the two 2D centroids is performed. The shape of the object is then predicted by initialising a cylindrical model around the estimated 3D object centroid which iteratively fits the object shape. The complete algorithm is given in [32]. Figure 2 [32] shows the above-mentioned method. If the algorithm fails to detect the container, we employ the prior from the training dataset as our prediction.

After the algorithm predicts the width and height of the object, we determine the capacity with the following equation which we designed for the task:

$$C = \bar{r}^2 \cdot h \cdot \pi \qquad (1)$$

where C is the estimated capacity, $\bar{r}$ the average of the radius of the calculated cylindrical shape and h the estimated height of the object.

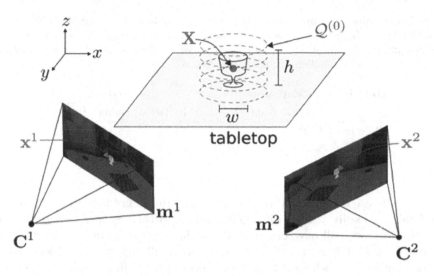

Fig. 2. Two frames m^1 and m^2 extracted from cameras C^1 and C^2 from two different viewpoints (left and right angulation). The 2D centroids, x^1 and x^2, are used to triangulate the 3D centroid X of the object. Image published in [32].

2.3 Implementation Details

We rely on `pyAudioAnalysis` library[1] to extract the "classical" features from the audio and tune the hyper-parameters of the random forest model [4]. VGGish and R(2+1)d features are extracted using `video_features`[2] script. To estimate the capacity of the containers, a modified version of the official LoDE codebase[3] was used.

We tune only the *number of trees* parameter of the random forest classifier. The other parameters are kept as the default values. We retrain the model with different values of this parameter and choose the value that achieves the highest accuracy in the validation set. To train the GRU models we employ batching of size 64 while padding the shorter sequences in a batch to the length of the longest sequence. The sizes of the hidden states are 512. The GRU has 5 layers for VGGish features and 3 layers for R(2+1)d features. We train the GRU models for up to 30 epochs with Adam optimizer [15] with learning rate $3 \cdot 10^{-4}$ and cross-entropy loss. These hyper-parameters are selected on the 3-fold cross-validation which is described next.

Since there is uncertainty about the objects which will occur during the inference, a model requires to be capable to generalize its predictions to unexpected forms and sound feedback of containers. To prevent our model from overfitting, we employ 3-fold cross-validation.

---

[1] github.com/tyiannak/pyAudioAnalysis.
[2] github.com/v-iashin/video_features.
[3] github.com/CORSMAL/LoDE.

Table 1. Performance of individual classification models for the container's filling level and filling type sub-tasks. The results are shown using the average F1-measure obtained by averaging the scores obtained with 3-fold cross-validation and the values obtained from the CORSMAL Challenge 2020 leader board.

Sub-task	Validation set			Test set	
	"class." feats.	VGGish	R(2+1)d	Public	Private
Filling level	69.9	75.5	74.7	78.14	81.16
Filling type	93.3	91.3	–	93.83	94.70

The splits are constructed following the distribution of the hold-out test set. Specifically, we split "train" objects according to their type 2:1 such that the validation dataset will have one object and the other two are used for training. Therefore, we had 3 train: validation splits with 6:3 objects (if 9 objects are in the training set) in each such that each object appears in a validation set once.

Running the training and evaluation scripts are executed on one 1080Ti and takes about 8 h with R(2+1)d feature extraction allocates more than half of the execution time. This time can be significantly reduced by increasing the number of GPUs. We provide the `Docker`[4] image to reproduce the results and the source code[5].

3   Experiments

3.1   Dataset

We train our model on the official training set of the challenging audio-visual-inertial CORSMAL dataset [33]. The CORSMAL dataset is a collection of human interaction with different containers recorded with multi-sensor devices: 8-element circular microphone and 4 cameras from different viewpoints recording RGB, IR, depth, IMU streams.

The dataset consists of three parts: public train, public test, and private test. The public train holds 9 containers: 3 plastic drinking cups, 3 drinking glasses, and 3 cardboard food boxes (e. g. cereal); 1 cup, 1 glass, and 1 food box is reserved for the public test set. The private test is hidden and known to have 3 more containers. The difference between the public and private test sets is in the absence of information about the input.

A container can be filled with rice, pasta, or water (only glasses and cups) and at 3 different levels: 0, 50, and 90 % with respect to the capacity of the container. All combinations of containers are executed by 12 different subjects for 2 different backgrounds and 2 different illumination conditions. In total, there are 1140 different combinations.

---

[4] hub.docker.com/r/iashin/corsmal.
[5] github.com/v-iashin/CORSMAL.

Table 2. The results from the CORSMAL Challenge 2020 leader board by November 23rd 2020. The performance is shown using the modified absolute error between the estimated filling mass and the ground truth.

Sub-task	Test set	
	Public	Private
Filling level	78.14	81.16
Filling type	93.83	94.70
Container capacity	60.56	60.58
Overall performance	64.98	65.15

3.2 Metrics

To track the performance of our classification algorithms, we employ the F1-score which favors a balance between precision and recall. The metric is weighted to account for the class imbalance. While the modified absolute error was used in evaluating container capacity. For a more detailed explanation of how the metrics are calculated on the public and private subsets of CORSMAL, we refer a reader to the technical document provided by CORSMAL Challenge 2020.

3.3 Results

Container Filling Level Classification. We compare the performance of the container's filling level between each classification model individually. Table 1 (first row) shows the results of the classification models averaged among three validation folds on the F1 metric. According to the results, the performance of the VGGish-based GRU model (audio) performs on par with the GRU model which is based on R(2+1)d (visual) features (75.5 and 74.7) while the random forest-based on "classical" features performs the worst (69.9), yet adding it to the final combination improves the overall performance.

The results of the combination of three classification models show the importance of aggregation of the individual predictions as the results on both public and private sets are higher than of the individual models. We also highlight the fact that according to the difference between private and public scores our model has not shown any sign of over-fitting but rather a strong generalization capability.

Container Filling Type Classification. Similar to the filling level sub-task, the classification results of filling type models are compared individually (see Table 1, the second row). The results show the importance of audio modality and "classical" features, in particular. The random forest classifier achieves 93.3 F1 score which slightly higher than VGGish-based GRU with 91.3 F1 score.[6]

---

[6] We also trained the GRU model on R(2+1)d features, yet it reached only F1 = 67.3.

For this sub-task, we also observe the improvement from combining the predictions. Yet, fewer gains are obtained in performance possibly because we rely on only one modality (audio). Nevertheless, the model also preserves the generalization capabilities and absence of over-fitting.

Container Capacity Estimation. For the prediction of the container capacity, a modified version of the LoDE method is implemented. The original LoDE algorithm was developed for calculating the capacity of transparent objects and was tested on a supervised environment with no occluded objects. For the CORSMAL challenge, the objects were manipulated by humans with multiple occlusions and additional items in the camera view.

The three target objects for the public set of the challenge are a beer cup, a cocktail glass, and a pasta box. Since the original Mask R-CNNs were pre-trained on the COCO dataset, there was no label to recognise a pasta box or other similar boxes. To alleviate this, an additional label was introduced. The label is equal to the book (present in the COCO dataset), considering the similarity of its shape to a box. For the future, transfer learning will be considered to better adjust the final weight of the fully connected layer of the Mask R-CNN and better segment the objects.

In the dataset, some videos start with an empty room (no object or person in it). To avoid having a frame with no object to detect, two frames were extracted from the videos: the first and the 20th to last frame. An average of the capacities detected in the two frames was then used for final validation.

Figure 3 shows two examples of the resulting capacity estimation through LoDE estimation. For the beer cup (object 10), occlusion by the human hand breaks the mask into two. Thus, predicting a smaller capacity for the container than the real one. For the pasta box (object 12), the model correctly identifies the container object, although not trained for it. The calculated capacity, similarly to the beer cup, is smaller than the ground-truth, because of the occlusion by the manipulator's hands. Nevertheless, the model achieves an accuracy of 60.56% when tested on the public dataset and 60.58% on the private dataset, for an overall of 60.58%, which is higher than the average (see Table 2).

Container Filling Mass Estimation (the Overall Task). Table 2 (bottom row) shows the results of the container filling mass estimation which takes into consideration the performance of all three sub-tasks together. Since the overall performance metric favours the least "performing" sub-task in the final score we believe it could be further improved by exploring the container capacity estimation sub-task. Our approach outperforms all other submissions to CORSMAL Challenge 2020 leaving us on the top of the leader board (see Fig. 4).

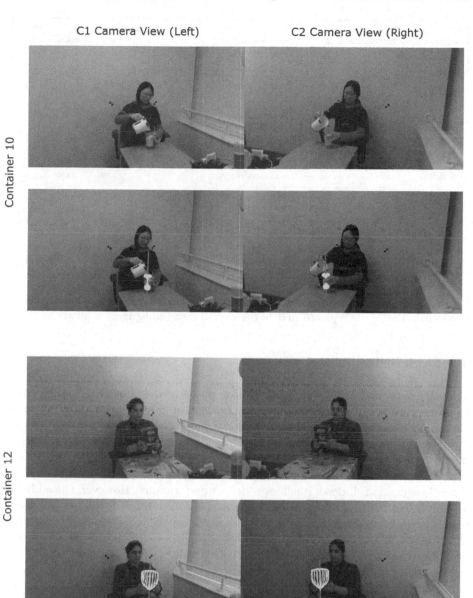

Fig. 3. Examples showing the limitations of the capacity estimation of two of the objects (10 and 12) of the CORSMAL Challenge. The object 10 is occluded by the hand and the object 12 is predicted to be the wrong object, because the training set did not contain boxes.

Team	Description	Task 1	Task 2	Task 3	Public	Private	Overall
Because It's Tactile	GRU+ Random Forest for filling properties estimation. LoDE with RGB-D-IR data from selected frames in a video for volume estimation.	✓	✓	✓	64.98	65.15	65.06
HVRL	Log-Mel spectrogram-based audio features as input to VGG-based CNN and LSTM for filling properties estimation. Container volume from the shape approximation as cuboid of the 3D point cloud obtained with RGB-D data and object detection with Mask R-CNN.	✓	✓	✓	63.32	61.01	62.16
Concatenation	Multi-modal learning with audio features and prior of container categories through object detection for inferring container capacity and fluid properties.	✓	✓	✓	52.80	54.14	53.47
NTNU-ERC	MFCC features in a 20s-window + neural network to classify filling type. Object detection and selection of the closest contours (up to 700 mm) in the depth data + regression with a CNN for container capacity.		✓	✓	38.56	39.80	39.18
Random	Baseline with random estimations for each task.	✓	✓	✓	38.47	31.65	35.06
Challengers	Sound-based classification of filling type and level with STFT and 5-layers fully connected neural network.	✓	✓		29.25	23.21	26.23
SCC-Net	Sound-based hierarchical ensemble of DNNs to jointly classify filling type and level.	✓	✓		28.02	22.92	25.47

Fig. 4. The state of the leader board on 22th of November 2020 showing our team ("Because It's Tactile") placed first in the overall task (filling mass estimation) [1].

4   Conclusion

Complex real-world sensing tasks as those posed in the CORSMAL 2020 Challenge require analysis of multiple data modalities. The amount of information gained by a modality is dependent on the nature of the task and it may be predicted by human intuition. However, a modality may still improve the combined performance, despite having poor performance alone. We observed this in our experiments. We predicted audio modality to be informative in filling level and type classification. Indeed, it achieves decent performance. However, the addition of visual features improves overall accuracy. Besides different modalities, using multiple models that follow different paradigms on the same modality increased the accuracy of our predictions. Achieving the highest score in this challenge was possible thanks to the variety in both the modalities and the algorithms.

In future works, other modalities such as IMU and tactile sensing can be explored. Also, the capacity estimation algorithm will be further improved by training the model for the Mask-RCNN which will permit to recognize objects more reliably. In addition, the LoDE model will be ulterior improved by developing optimal capacity evaluation calculations based on the label of the recognised object.

References

1. The 2020 CORSMAL Challenge. Multi-modal fusion and learning for robotics. https://corsmal.eecs.qmul.ac.uk/ICPR2020challenge.html. Accessed 22 Nov 2020

2. Breiman, L.: Bagging predictors. Mach. Learn. **24**(2), 123–140 (1996). https://doi.org/10.1007/BF00058655
3. Chung, J., Gulcehre, C., Cho, K., Bengio, Y.: Empirical evaluation of gated recurrent neural networks on sequence modeling. In: NIPS 2014 Workshop on Deep Learning, Dec 2014 (2014)
4. Giannakopoulos, T.: pyAudioAnalysis: an open-source python library for audio signal analysis. PLoS One **10**(12), e0144610 (2015)
5. Griffith, S., Sukhoy, V., Wegter, T., Stoytchev, A.: Object categorization in the sink: learning behavior-grounded object categories with water. In: Proceedings of the 2012 ICRA Workshop on Semantic Perception, Mapping and Exploration. Citeseer (2012)
6. Hampali, S., Rad, M., Oberweger, M., Lepetit, V.: Honnotate: a method for 3D annotation of hand and object poses. In: Proceedings of the IEEE/CVF Conference on Computer Vision and Pattern Recognition, pp. 3196–3206 (2020)
7. He, K., Gkioxari, G., Dollár, P., Girshick, R.: Mask R-CNN. In: Proceedings of the IEEE International Conference on Computer Vision, pp. 2961–2969 (2017)
8. He, K., Zhang, X., Ren, S., Sun, J.: Deep residual learning for image recognition. In: Proceedings of the IEEE Conference on Computer Vision and Pattern Recognition, pp. 770–778 (2016)
9. Hershey, S., et al.: CNN architectures for large-scale audio classification. In: 2017 IEEE International Conference on Acoustics, Speech and Signal Processing (ICASSP), pp. 131–135 (2017). https://doi.org/10.1109/ICASSP.2017.7952132
10. Hochreiter, S., Schmidhuber, J.: Long short-term memory. Neural Comput. **9**(8), 1735–1780 (1997)
11. Huang, J., et al.: Speed/accuracy trade-offs for modern convolutional object detectors. In: Proceedings of the IEEE Conference on Computer Vision and Pattern Recognition, pp. 7310–7311 (2017)
12. Iashin, V., Rahtu, E.: A better use of audio-visual cues: dense video captioning with bi-modal transformer. In: British Machine Vision Conference (BMVC) (2020)
13. Iashin, V., Rahtu, E.: Multi-modal dense video captioning. In: The IEEE/CVF Conference on Computer Vision and Pattern Recognition (CVPR) Workshops, pp. 958–959 (2020)
14. King, R.D., et al.: Is it better to combine predictions? Protein Eng. **13**(1), 15–19 (2000)
15. Kingma, D.P., Ba, J.: Adam: a method for stochastic optimization. In: Bengio, Y., LeCun, Y. (eds.) 3rd International Conference on Learning Representations, ICLR 2015, San Diego, CA, USA, 7–9 May 2015, Conference Track Proceedings (2015)
16. Kokic, M., Kragic, D., Bohg, J.: Learning to estimate pose and shape of hand-held objects from RGB images. In: 2019 IEEE/RSJ International Conference on Intelligent Robots and Systems (IROS), pp. 3980–3987. IEEE (2019)
17. Liang, H., et al.: Making sense of audio vibration for liquid height estimation in robotic pouring. In: 2019 IEEE/RSJ International Conference on Intelligent Robots and Systems (IROS), pp. 5333–5339 (2019). https://doi.org/10.1109/IROS40897.2019.8968303
18. Liang, H., et al.: Robust robotic pouring using audition and haptics. arXiv preprint arXiv:2003.00342 (2020)
19. Lin, T.-Y., et al.: Microsoft COCO: common objects in context. In: Fleet, D., Pajdla, T., Schiele, B., Tuytelaars, T. (eds.) ECCV 2014, Part V. LNCS, vol. 8693, pp. 740–755. Springer, Cham (2014). https://doi.org/10.1007/978-3-319-10602-1_48

20. Liu, Y., Albanie, S., Nagrani, A., Zisserman, A.: Use what you have: video retrieval using representations from collaborative experts. In: British Machine Vision Conference (2019)
21. Mottaghi, R., Schenck, C., Fox, D., Farhadi, A.: See the glass half full: reasoning about liquid containers, their volume and content. In: Proceedings of the IEEE International Conference on Computer Vision, pp. 1871–1880 (2017)
22. Peng, S., Liu, Y., Huang, Q., Zhou, X., Bao, H.: PVNet: pixel-wise voting network for 6DoF pose estimation. In: Proceedings of the IEEE Conference on Computer Vision and Pattern Recognition, pp. 4561–4570 (2019)
23. Phillips, C.J., Lecce, M., Daniilidis, K.: Seeing glassware: from edge detection to pose estimation and shape recovery. In: Robotics: Science and Systems, vol. 3 (2016)
24. Sajjan, S., et al.: Clear grasp: 3D shape estimation of transparent objects for manipulation. In: 2020 IEEE International Conference on Robotics and Automation (ICRA), pp. 3634–3642. IEEE (2020)
25. Sanchez-Matilla, R., et al.: Benchmark for human-to-robot handovers of unseen containers with unknown filling. IEEE Robot. Autom. Lett. **5**(2), 1642–1649 (2020). https://doi.org/10.1109/LRA.2020.2969200
26. Statistics, L.B., Breiman, L.: Random forests. Mach. Learn. **45**, 5–32 (2001)
27. Tran, D., Wang, H., Torresani, L., Ray, J., LeCun, Y., Paluri, M.: A closer look at spatiotemporal convolutions for action recognition. In: Proceedings of the IEEE Conference on Computer Vision and Pattern Recognition, pp. 6450–6459 (2018)
28. Wang, C., et al.: Densefusion: 6D object pose estimation by iterative dense fusion. In: Proceedings of the IEEE Conference on Computer Vision and Pattern Recognition, pp. 3343–3352 (2019)
29. Wang, H., Sridhar, S., Huang, J., Valentin, J., Song, S., Guibas, L.J.: Normalized object coordinate space for category-level 6D object pose and size estimation. In: Proceedings of the IEEE/CVF Conference on Computer Vision and Pattern Recognition (CVPR) (June 2019)
30. Wang, Q., Zhang, L., Bertinetto, L., Hu, W., Torr, P.H.: Fast online object tracking and segmentation: a unifying approach. In: Proceedings of the IEEE Conference on Computer Vision and Pattern Recognition, pp. 1328–1338 (2019)
31. Xiang, Y., Schmidt, T., Narayanan, V., Fox, D.: PoseCNN: a convolutional neural network for 6D object pose estimation in cluttered scenes (2018)
32. Xompero, A., Sanchez-Matilla, R., Modas, A., Frossard, P., Cavallaro, A.: Multi-view shape estimation of transparent containers. In: ICASSP 2020–2020 IEEE International Conference on Acoustics, Speech and Signal Processing (ICASSP), pp. 2363–2367 (2020). https://doi.org/10.1109/ICASSP40776.2020.9054112
33. Xompero, A., Sanchez-Matilla, R., Mazzon, R., Cavallaro, A.: CORSMAL containers manipulation (2020). https://doi.org/10.17636/101CORSMAL1, http://corsmal.eecs.qmul.ac.uk/containers_manip.html

Audio-Visual Hybrid Approach for Filling Mass Estimation

Reina Ishikawa$^{(\boxtimes)}$, Yuichi Nagao , Ryo Hachiuma , and Hideo Saito

Keio University, Yokohama, Japan
{reina-ishikawa,soccerbass03,ryo-hachiuma,hs}@keio.jp

Abstract. Object handover is a fundamental and essential capability for robots interacting with humans in many applications such as household chores. In this challenge, we estimate the physical properties of a variety of containers with different fillings such as container capacity and the type and percentage of the content to achieve collaborative physical handover between humans and robots. We introduce multi-modal prediction models using audio-visual-datasets of people interacting with containers distributed by CORSMAL.

Keywords: Audio classification · Log-Mel spectrogram · Mass estimation

1 Introduction

Collaborative Object Recognition Shared Manipulation and Learning (CORSMAL) is aiming to build a framework for robots to recognize physical objects and interact with humans by taking advantage of multi-modal sensory data. This challenge[1] is aiming at working on one of the most difficult challenges in robotics: predicting the properties (*e.g.,* mass, type, the percentage of the content) of previously unseen containers.

The main goal of this challenge is estimating the capacity and mass of containers to achieve smooth hand-over task from a human to a robot, and the organizers proposed three procedures to reach this goal as three tasks at this challenge: filling level classification (Task1), filling type classification (Task2), and container capacity estimation (Task3). The participants in this challenge are required to utilize the CORSMAL Containers Manipulation dataset that has various audio-visual data of 15 different types of containers, and only nine out of those are contained in the training dataset for validating the robustness against unseen containers.

In this paper, we present the three methods for filling level classification, filling type classification, and container capacity estimation. As for filling level

---

[1] http://corsmal.eecs.qmul.ac.uk/ICPR2020challenge.html

R. Ishikawa and Y. Nagao—Equal contribution.

A. Del Bimbo et al. (Eds.): ICPR 2020 Workshops, LNCS 12668, pp. 437–450, 2021.
https://doi.org/10.1007/978-3-030-68793-9_32

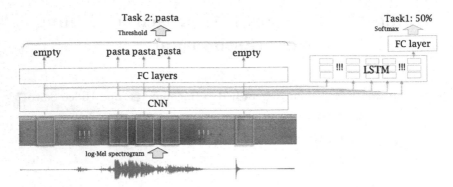

Fig. 1. Overview of our framework for Task1 and Task2. First, the raw audio signal is converted into a log-Mel spectrogram. As for Task2, each cropped frame from the spectrogram is passed through Convolutional Neural Network (CNN) with a VGG backbone [10] to predict the category of the content. Then we count the number of frames of each class(*i.e.,* empty, pasta, rice, and water) in the sequence, and we estimate the overall filling type of the audio clip using threshold over the output. As for Task1, we extract intermediate features of size 1024 of the CNN which is trained for Task2, and the features are passed through Long Short Term Memory (LSTM) [3] networks and fully-connected layers. Then the features are classified into three filling level classes: 0%, 50%, and 90%.

classification and filling type classification tasks, we developed a framework with neural network models for audio data, and as for Task3, we adopted more traditional and geometrical solutions using visual data. Our source code is available from the github repository[2] (Fig. 1).

2   Methodology

In this section, we first introduce our additional annotations, and then we explain our solutions to Task1, Task2, and Task3 in Sect. 2.2, Sect. 2.1, and Sect. 2.3 respectively. As for Task1 and Task2, a neural network-based prediction model is implemented using audio data, and as for Task3, a geometrical approach using visual data is taken.

Additional Annotations. In addition to the original annotations, we added annotations to improve the accuracy of the results of Task1 and Task2. The original annotations include the container capacity (mL) for each container in the training dataset, and they also contain the mass of container (g) and the mass of filling (g) of every combination of containers, filling types (*i.e.,* empty, pasta, rice, and water), and filling levels (*i.e.,* 0%, 50%, and 90%).

The annotations we added are the time when the subject starts to pour the fillings or shake the box and the time when the subject finished pouring

---

[2] https://github.com/YuichiNAGAO/ICPRchallenge2020.

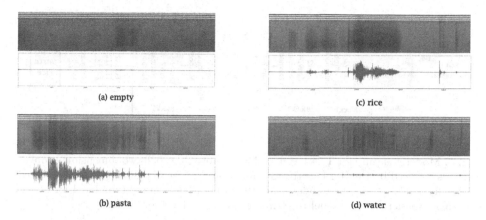

Fig. 2. Comparison of raw wave and log-Mel spectrogram. There are four classes for the filling type: (a) empty, (b) pasta, (c) rice, and (d) water. For each filling content type, the lower figure represents the raw wave, and the upper image is a log-Mel spectrogram converted from the raw waveform.

or shaking in each video clip. In the original dataset, the filling content type is annotated to each video. However, to predict the filling type from the audio data, the irrelevant frames are included, such as before pouring or after pouring. We assume that these irrelevant frames disturb the training of the model. These irrelevant frames are annotated as "empty" for filling type and 0% for the filling level.

2.1 Filling Type Classification (Task2)

Log-Mel Spectrogram. To learn the informative features from the audio data efficiently, we used the log-Mel spectrogram of audio data and inputted the spectrogram to the CNN. In general, humans can identify the filling type being poured or shaken (*i.e.*, in this challenge, water, rice, or pasta) only using sound information. Therefore, we assume some feature extraction methods that mimic human ear acts are effective in this task. Mel-frequency cepstral coefficients (MFCCs) [7] is one of the commonly used feature representations and are inspired by the human hearing perception that weighs the low-frequency region. Example comparison between raw signal data and log-Mel spectrograms of audio clips of different filling types are shown in Fig. 2.

Architecture of the Proposed Network. After the processing of converting into a log-Mel spectrogram, we obtained two-dimensional data for each video clip of different sizes. As the fixed-sized feature should be inputted to a CNN, we cropped the output into 64×64 with 75% overlapping in the time axis direction. The extracted log Mel spectrogram features are passed through a CNN with a VGG backbone as shown in Fig. 3 and finally classified into four classes using

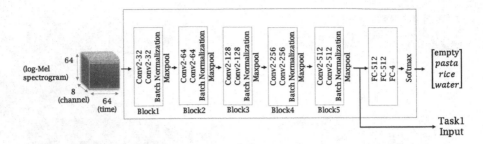

Fig. 3. Model structure for Task1 and Task2. We note that each two-dimensional convolution is followed by the ReLU activation function proposed in [8] which is abbreviated in this figure. We train this model using the ground-truth filling type label for Task2 and then transferred the model to estimate the filling level for Task1.

Softmax activation function: empty, pasta, rice, and water. In detail, the CNN is composed of five times repeat of the set of twice two-dimensional convolution, batch normalization, and two-dimensional max-pooling, and it is followed by three fully connected layers.

Implementation Details. First, we crop the audio clip into small frames with a frame size of 0.025 s and a frame stride of 0.01 s. Second, each audio frame is classified into four classes using the proposed model. Third, the number of frames that were classified by class are counted. Here, we define the number of frames in each class as n_i^{empy}, n_i^{pasta}, n_i^{rice}, and n_i^{water}, where i indicates i-th audio clip. Finally, the overall audio clip which is concerned is classified; if any of n_i^{pasta}, n_i^{rice}, or n_i^{water} is larger than the threshold value, five, we classify the i-th audio clip into the class that has the largest number among the three (*i.e.*, *pasta, rice, or water*), and otherwise classify into the *empty* class.

We employ Adam [4] with a learning rate of $1e^{-5}$, a minibatch size of 32, and train for 200 epochs. To calculate losses, we adopted the CrossEntropyLoss function in PyTorch [9].

2.2   Filling Level Estimation (Task1)

LSTM Network. Long Short-Term Memory (LSTM) is first proposed by Hochreiter *et al.* [3] in 1997. LSTM that integrated *input gate, output gate,* and *forget gate* solved vanishing or exploding gradient problems, that is to say, back-flow problems and enabled the network to learn long-term time-series information. In this challenge, we adopted this LSTM model in PyTorch, considering to transform part of the model for Task1.

Details of Our Prediction Model. Since the filling level is strongly related to the filling type, we decided to reuse the model in Task 2 (filling type estimation). Because taking final four-class output is too compressed to learn the filling level, we decided to extract the intermediate feature after the final Maxpooling appearing in Fig. 3, and flatten them in each time dimension.

There is one problem that individual audio clips have different lengths. Therefore, we pad audio clips that have less than 100 frames, and we truncate those that have more than 100 in the ending. Then the padded or truncated data is input into a one-to-many LSTM model. To classify into 3 classes (0%, 50%, *and* 100%), we added a fully connected layer and the Softmax activation function to the final feature output of the LSTM model.

Implementation Details. We use Adam optimizer with a learning rate of $1e{-}4$, a minibatch size of 16, and train for 400 epochs. We employed the CrossEntropyLoss function in PyTorch. Our many-to-one LSTM model is composed of 3 layers with a dropout probability of 0.2 and hidden cells with a size of 256.

2.3   Container Capacity Estimation (Task3)

We propose a non-deep-learning approach for estimating the capacities of containers using a calibrated RGB camera and depth information.

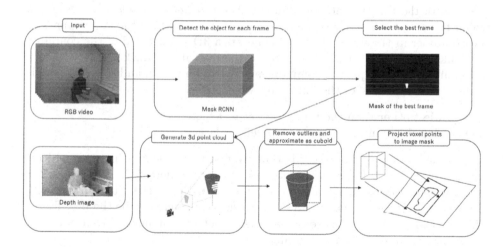

Fig. 4. Overview of our solution for Task3

As shown in Fig. 4, our method for Task3 consists of three components. Firstly, we use Mask R-CNN [1] to extract the silhouette of the target object. Next, we select the most appropriate frame for generating a 3D point cloud. Finally, we create a 3D point cloud, thereby calculating the volume of the container by approximating the cloud shape to a cuboid.

Silhouette Extraction of the Object. First, we apply pre-trained Mask R-CNN with ResNet-50 backbone [2] to each frame of the video and extract the object's silhouette at each frame to generate a 3D model of the target container from that object area. Extracting the silhouette of the target object from the RGB video enables us to simply create a 3D point cloud where unnecessary parts such as person and background are eliminated. Mask R-CNN which is pre-trained on MS-COCO [5] dataset can detect and segment 90 categories of objects. Therefore, it also detects irrelevant classes for the container capacity estimation task, such as *person*, so that these irrelevant classes should be excluded from the instance segmentation result. Our pre-experiments revealed that all target objects in the provided dataset, can be classified as one of the *bottle*, *wine glass*, *cup*, and *vase*, so we set the Mask R-CNN to detect only that four classes. As for food boxes (Container 7, 8, and 9), they are less likely to be detected than the other containers, but they can be detected as the four classes mentioned above.

The Frame Selection Algorithm for the 3D Point Cloud Generation. To estimate the capacity of the container, the 3D point cloud of the container has to be reconstructed. However, during the pouring, the subject's hand is covering the target container or the target container cannot be seen from the camera. As the area of the target container differs between frames, we select one frame in which the target container is the most visible (i.e., in which the largest mask of the container in the video clip) and generate a 3D point cloud of the container only once for the video clip. To achieve this, we apply Mask R-CNN to each frame in the video sequence, compare each detection result, and select the single frame that most satisfies the following two conditions:

1. No object other than the target object is detected.
2. The size of the mask (number of pixels) is large.

The detail of this processing is that we first focus most on how few objects are detected, and if the same number of objects are detected, we consider the frame with the larger mask as the best frame. In Fig. 5, the fourth frame with the fewest detected objects and a large mask is considered to be the best frame. This operation allows us to select one frame out of a number of frames having an accurate silhouette of the container.

Container Capacity Estimation. The depth information of the selected frame and the camera calibrations are then used to reconstruct a 3D point cloud of the container. Among the three environment RGB-D cameras, we use only a single camera for generating the 3D point cloud. As the boundary of the target container mask generated by Mask R-CNN is not accurate, the 3D point cloud of the target container includes some outlier points of the background. These points are removed using the Isolation Forest algorithm [6]. Then, the point cloud is approximated into the cuboid by calculating the minimum and maximum value for each x, y, z coordinate. At last, we re-project all points of the cuboid to the

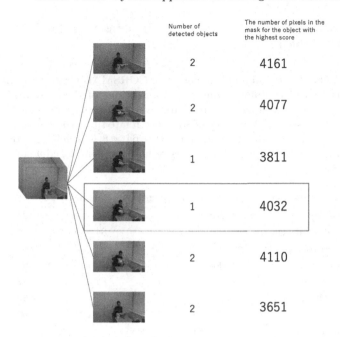

Fig. 5. Detection by Mask R-CNN for frames of a video extracted with a certain step. Two or more objects may be detected in the same frame

original image, and the volume is calculated with the following equation:

$$V = (X_{max} - X_{min})(Y_{max} - Y_{min})(Z_{max} - Z_{min})\frac{B}{A}, \tag{1}$$

where X_{max}, X_{min}, Y_{max}, Y_{min}, Z_{max} and Z_{min} are the maximum and the minimum values of 3D point cloud for the x-axis, the y-axis, and the z-axis in three dimensional space, respectively. A denotes the number of voxels in the cuboid, B denotes the number of voxels projected onto the mask.

This cuboid approximation is a very rough approximation that does not take into account the shape of the objects. It is thought to be better to approximate cups and glasses with cones than with cuboids. However, since we generate a 3D point cloud using only one point of view camera, the representation of the generated point cloud is insufficient to approximate with a cone. Therefore, we use a simple method, the cuboid approximation, to obtain the volume roughly.

3   Experiments

3.1   Dataset

The CORSMAL Containers Manipulation dataset [12] consists of 1140 audio-visual-inertial recordings of people interacting with 15 types of containers, using 4 calibrated cameras (RGB, depth, and infrared) and an 8-element circular microphone array. The details of the training dataset for Task1 and Task2 are summarized in Table 1.

Table 1. Details of the training dataset. The CORSMAL Containers Manipulation dataset consists of 15 containers, and 9 containers out of them are assigned to the training dataset. The container capacities are given by the organizers of this challenge. *# audio clips* represents the number of wav files related to each container. *# log-Mel frames* indicates that the total number of $64 \times 64 \times 8$ log-Mel spectrogram frames associated with each container. The details of how cropping lof-Mel spectrogram are explained in Sect. 2.1

ID	Type	container name	Container capacity[mL]	#audio clips	# log-Mel frames
1	Cup	Red cup	520	84	6134
2		Small white cup	185	84	4534
3		Small transparent cup	202	84	4386
4	Glass	Green glass	296	84	3994
5		Wine glass	363	84	4342
6		Champagne flute glass	128	84	5382
7	Box	Cereal box	3209.397	60	1100
8		Biscuit box	1239.84	60	1017
9		Tea box	471.6	60	923

3.2   Cross-Validation for Task1 and Task2

Since the ground-truth labels of the public and private test dataset are not available for challengers, we trained and fine-tuned the prediction models for Task1 and Task2 via cross-validation. Note that this cross-validation is only conducted for the paper. We used all of the training datasets for the leaderboard submission. As the aim of this challenge is to test the robustness against the unseen container, we employ *Leave-one-container-out* scheme for the cross-validation—that is to say, eight containers are used as the training data and verify the accuracy of the model with the remaining unseen container.

3.3   Evaluation Metrics

Evaluation for Task1 and Task2. In this paper, we evaluate the results of Task1 and Task2 in terms of accuracy (ACC), weighted-F1 scores (WAF), and inference time. WAF is the official evaluation method in this challenge and is applied to the public and private test dataset evaluations. ACC is defined as below:

$$ACC = \frac{N_T}{N}, \tag{2}$$

where N denotes the total number of the test data, and N_T indicates the number of test data that was correctly predicted.

Table 2. The distribution of train dataset by ground-truth filling type. *#audio clips* denotes the number of wav files, and *#log-Mel frames* indicates the number of frames that were cropped from the log-Mel spectrograms with a size of 64 × 64 × 8.

Type	Filling type	#audio clips	#log-Mel frames
Cup	Empty	36	7792
	Pasta	72	2713
	Rice	72	3327
	water	72	1222
Glass	Empty	36	6679
	Pasta	72	2118
	Rice	72	3297
	water	72	1624
Box	Empty	36	1824
	Pasta	72	580
	Rice	72	636
	water	0	0
Total	Empty	108	16295
	Pasta	216	5411
	Rice	216	7260
	water	144	2846

Table 3. The distribution of train dataset by ground-truth filling type. *#audio clips* indicates the number of wav files.

Filling level [%]	Cup			Glass			Box			Total		
	0	50	90	0	50	90	0	50	90	0	50	90
# audio clips	36	108	108	36	108	108	36	72	72	108	228	228

WAF is calculated based on the F1-score of individual classes, $c \in C$, that is defined as:

$$F_c = \frac{2P_c R_c}{P_c + R_c},\tag{3}$$

where P_c represents *Precisions*, which is the number of samples that are correctly classified as the class c over the total number of samples that truly belongs to the class c; R_c means *Recalls*, which is the number of positive samples that should be classified as the class c over the number of correctly classified samples. The F1-score is defined as the harmonic mean of *Precisions* and *Recalls*, and the F_c values range from 0 to 1 (Tables 2 and 3).

Table 4. Computational resources for each task.

Task1, Task2	GPU	GeForce RTX 2080 Ti
	CPU	Intel(R) Core(TM) i7-6950X CPU @3.00 GHz
	RAM	48 GB
Task3	GPU	GeForce RTX 2080 Ti
	CPU	Intel(R) Core(TM) i7-10700 CPU @2.90 GHz
	RAM	64 GB

Table 5. Scores for the public and private datasets. The scores are calculated by the organizers of the CORSMAL challenge

	Public	Private	Overall
Task1	82.63	74.43	78.56
Task2	97.83	96.08	96.95
Task3	57.19	52.38	54.79
Overall task (Mass estimation)	63.32	61.01	62.16

WAF is calculated by means of weighing the F1-score by the number of data in each class as the following:

$$WAF = \frac{\sum\limits_{c \in C} S_c F_c}{\sum\limits_{c \in C} S_c}, \tag{4}$$

where S_c is the number of data that belongs to class c.

Evaluation for Task3. As for Task3, we compute the relative absolute error ε_j^c between the estimated capacity $\hat{x}_j^c$, and the ground-truth capacity x_j^c, for each configuration j of container c as the following equation:

$$\varepsilon_j^c = \frac{\left| \hat{x}_j^c - x_j^c \right|}{x_j^c}. \tag{5}$$

We then compute the Average Capacity Score (ACS), that is the average score across all the configurations S and all the containers. The evaluation metric is calculated as follows:

$$ACS = \frac{1}{S} \sum_{c=1}^{C} \sum_{j=1}^{S_c} \exp\left(-\varepsilon_j^c\right). \tag{6}$$

3.4 Computational Resources

All of the experiments are conducted by the computers shown in Table 4.

4   Results

The final scores for the public and private dataset were reported by the organizers of this challenge, as shown in Table 5.

4.1   Filling Level Estimation (Task2) and Filling Type Classification (Task1)

As the ground-truth labels of both public and private testing datasets are not provided to the challengers, we evaluated the effectiveness of our prediction models using *Leave-one-Container-out* cross-validation scheme. That is to say, the validation is conducted against an unseen container. The results of Task1 and task2 for each container are shown in Table 6, and example confusion matrices are shown in Fig. 6.

Table 6. The quantitative results of Task1 and Task2. Each task is evaluated with accuracy, weighted F1-score, and inference time. The inference time in this table is the average time of inferring both Task1 and Task2 for one audio sequence.

Container	Task2		Task1		Inference time [sec]
	ACC [%]	WAFs [%]	ACC [%]	WAFs [%]	
Red cup	98.80	98.80	48.80	35.23	0.6135
Small white cup	88.09	88.27	75.00	73.16	0.4488
Small transparent cup	97.61	97.65	78.57	78.05	0.4327
Green glass	96.42	96.38	64.28	58.93	0.3942
Wine glass	100.00	100.00	55.95	41.97	0.4334
Champagne flute glass	100.00	100.00	82.14	82.05	0.5256
Cereal box	95.00	95.11	56.66	55.58	0.1749
Biscuit box	98.33	98.34	53.33	44.16	0.2284
Tea box	95.00	95.11	61.66	52.59	0.1505

According to these figures, our proposed model resulted in more than 95% in terms of accuracy and WAFs for filling type classification (Task2). Especially, filling types are 100% correctly classified for *Wine glass* or *Champagne flute glass*. Therefore, our model successfully predicts the filling type for unseen containers. However, the results of filling level classification (Task1) are lower than Task2. We suppose that this is caused by the difference in the capacity and less number of training samples. The prediction model for Task2 is trained on log-Mel frames, but the prediction model for Task1 is trained on overall audio clips that are more than ten times less than Task1. From Table 6 and the confusion matrix of Task1, it can be seen that the prediction accuracy against box-like container objects, such as tea box and cereal box are relatively low on average. One reason for this result can be considered is the lack of training data. From Table 1, the number of audio clips against box-like objects is smaller than the other type of objects. By

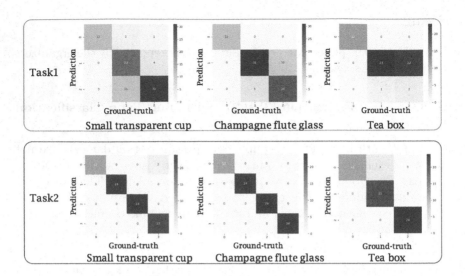

Fig. 6. Example confusion matrices of Task1 and Task2.

increasing the number of data against box-like container objects, the model can predict well against these objects. We also observe that the average inference time is highly related to the length of the inferred audio clip, but generally, the inference time is less than one second.

4.2   Container Capacity Estimation (Task3)

Next, we evaluate the accuracy of the container capacity estimation (Table 7). By employing re-projection process, the ACS scores of *small transparent cup*, *champagne flute glass*, *biscuit box*, and *tea box* are slightly improved. We confirmed that re-projection has the effect of improving the accuracy of capacity estimation by removing voxel points that are not included in the mask. However, if the volume of the cuboid is smaller than the ground truth, re-projection becomes a process that degrades the accuracy as shown in the scores of the other five containers.

There are several reasons for this low capacity estimation accuracy. First, we use only the RGB-D image from a single viewpoint so that the number of points is insufficient to generate an accurate 3D point cloud of the container. Second, when an objects is approximated to a cuboid, the orientation of the object is not considered. Lastly, we do not take into account transparent and opaque objects whose depth cannot be obtained from the infrared sensor.

Inference Time. As our proposed container capacity estimation method consists of instance segmentation of the container, best frame selection, and volume calculation, the inference time is mostly dependent on the video length, object

Table 7. The evaluation of Task3 (filling capacity estimation) using ACS metric for each container. Note that the higher value is better. *Before re-projection* denotes the volume of the 3D point cloud approximated by the cuboid. *After re-projection* denotes the volume after re-projecting the cuboid voxels to the image coordinates and excluding the parts not included in the mask.

Container	Before re-projection	After re-projection
Red cup	**0.533**	0.524
Small white cup	**0.518**	0.503
Small transparent cup	0.488	**0.495**
Green glass	**0.615**	0.598
Wine glass	**0.661**	0.649
Champagne flute glass	0.370	**0.373**
Cereal box	**0.508**	0.507
Biscuit box	0.460	**0.462**
Tea box	0.474	**0.478**

Table 8. Inference time of the container capacity estimation. The input image size is fixed to 1280720.

Container	# of pixels in mask	Video length [sec]	Instance segmentation [sec]	3D point processing [sec]	Total inference time [sec]
Red cup	5396	2.6	1.1	1.0	2.1
	3977	9.7	3.6	0.8	4.4
	4555	24.3	9.3	0.9	10.2
Cereal box	26936	2.6	1.2	3.0	4.1
	21305	3.9	1.6	2.2	3.8
	18382	3.0	1.3	2.1	3.4

mask size. Compared to filling level classification (Task1), filling type classification (Task2) using audio data, volume estimation takes a longer time to compute (Table 8). We assume that inference mostly consists of two major components: creating a Mask and selecting a frame by Mask R-CNN detection and volume calculation by 3D point cloud processing. As the object mask is extracted every frame in the video, the time of instance segmentation depends on the length of the video. On the other hand, as we select the best frame in the video to generate a 3D point cloud, the 3D point cloud processing step does not depend on the length of the video. As shown in the Table, our method cannot achieve a real-time system. However, if the faster instance segmentation method, such as SOLO [11], is employed instead of Mask R-CNN [1], the real-time capacity estimation can be achieved.

5 Conclusion

In this paper, we present our solutions for three different tasks of estimating the physical properties of containers with different fillings: Filling level classification (Task1), Filling type classification (Task2), and Container capacity estimation (Task3). As for Task1 and Task2, we utilize a neural network model with audio data, and as for Task3, we take a geometrical approach using visual data. The experimental results revealed that our method successfully predicts filling level, filling type, and container capacity for the unseen container. However, we also noticed that our solution still has room for improvement.

We are provided multi-modal sensory data containing audio and visual data such as infrared, depth, and RGB of multiple views, but we only used the data independently for each task, and also we could not make use of all the data. Therefore, in order to achieve higher accuracy, we will need to build a model that fuses multi-modal data.

References

1. He, K., Gkioxari, G., Dollár, P., Girshick, R.: Mask R-CNN. In: IEEE International Conference on Computer Vision (ICCV), pp. 2980–2988 (2017)
2. He, K., Zhang, X., Ren, S., Sun, J.: Deep residual learning for image recognition. In: IEEE Conference on Computer Vision and Pattern Recognition (CVPR), pp. 770–778 (2016)
3. Hochreiter, S., Schmidhuber, J.: Long short-term memory. Neural Comput. **9**, 1735–80 (1997)
4. Kingma, D.P., Ba, J.: Adam: a method for stochastic optimization. In: 3rd International Conference on Learning Representations (ICLR) (2015)
5. Lin, T.Y., et al.: Microsoft COCO: common objects in context. In: Fleet, D., Pajdla, T., Schiele, B., Tuytelaars, T. (eds.) ECCV 2014. LNCS, vol. 8693, pp. 740–755. Springer, Cham (2014). https://doi.org/10.1007/978-3-319-10602-1_48
6. Liu, F.T., Ting, K.M., Zhou, Z.: Isolation forest. In: Eighth IEEE International Conference on Data Mining (ICDM), pp. 413–422 (2008)
7. Logan, B.: Mel frequency cepstral coefficients for music modeling. In: International Symposium on Music Information Retrieval (2000)
8. Nair, V., Hinton, G.E.: Rectified linear units improve restricted Boltzmann machines. In: Proceedings of the 27th International Conference on International Conference on Machine Learning (ICML), pp. 807–814 (2010)
9. Paszke, A., et al.: Pytorch: an imperative style, high-performance deep learning library. In: Advances in Neural Information Processing Systems (Neurips), vol. 32, pp. 8026–8037. Curran Associates, Inc. (2019)
10. Simonyan, K., Zisserman, A.: Very deep convolutional networks for large-scale image recognition. In: 3rd International Conference on Learning Representations (ICLR) (2015)
11. Wang, X., Kong, T., Shen, C., Jiang, Y., Li, L.: SOLO: segmenting objects by locations. In: European Conference on Computer Vision (ECCV) (2020)
12. Xompero, A., Sanchez-Matilla, R., Mazzon, R., Cavallaro, A.: CORSMAL Containers Manipulation (2020)

VA2Mass: Towards the Fluid Filling Mass Estimation via Integration of Vision and Audio Learning

Qi Liu, Fan Feng, Chuanlin Lan, and Rosa H.M. Chan$^{(\boxtimes)}$ (iD)

Department of Electrical Engineering, City University of Hong Kong,
Hong Kong, China
rosachan@cityu.edu.hk

Abstract. Robotic perception of filling mass estimation via multiple sensors and deep learning approaches is still an open problem due to the diverse pouring durations, small pixel ratio for target objects and complex pouring scenarios. In this paper, we propose a practical solution to tackle this challenging task via estimating filling level, filling type and container capacity simultaneously. The proposed method is inspired by how humans observe and understand the pouring process via the cooperation among multiple modalities, i.e., vision and audio. In a nutshell, our proposed method is divided into three folds to help the agent shape a rich understanding of the pouring procedure. First, the agent obtains the prior of container categories (i.e., cup, glass or box) through the object detection framework. Second, we integrate the audio features with the prior to make the agent learn a multi-modal feature space. Finally, the agent infers the distribution of both the container capacity and fluid properties. The experimental results show the effectiveness of the proposed method, which ranked as 2nd runner-up in the CORSMAL Challenge of Multi-modal Fusion and Learning For Robotics in ICPR 2020.

Keywords: Multi-modal perception · Robotic learning · Deep learning

1 Introduction

Deep learning, especially Deep Neural Networks (DNNs) have achieved state-of-the-art performances in various tasks such as speech recognition, visual object recognition, and image classification [2,8,16,29]. There is increasing interest in using DNNs and learning techniques (i.e., meta learning, transfer learning, continual learning, reinforcement learning and their intersections) for robotic learning in different robotic tasks, including manipulation, SLAM, motion control,

The work described in this paper was partially supported by grant from Guangdong-Hong Kong-Macau Greater Bay Area Center for Brain Science and Brain-Inspired Intelligence Fund (No. 20019009).

© Springer Nature Switzerland AG 2021
A. Del Bimbo et al. (Eds.): ICPR 2020 Workshops, LNCS 12668, pp. 451–463, 2021.
https://doi.org/10.1007/978-3-030-68793-9_33

and image processing [12,17,22,27,32,36]. However, the environments and tasks are dynamic and complex for robotics. Thus how to construct a stable, efficient and robust robotic learning system is still an open challenge [3,33,34].

In this work, we focus on one specific challenging task in robotic learning: estimating the properties of containers with different fillings poured, which is crucial for human-robot cooperation. In fact, pick-and-place and pouring are the top 2 frequently executed motions in household chores [25,26]. The elders or disabilities can perform better on such daily activities like objects pick-up, place and handovers with the assistance of the smart robots. In this paper, we focus on the estimation of the mass of the filling. The task is divided into 3 folds:

- **Task (1)**: filling level classification;
- **Task (2)**: filling type classification;
- **Task (3)**: container capacity estimation.

The only prior information known to the robot is the container categories and the containers vary in their physical properties, i.e., shape, material, texture, transparency, and deformability. Task (1) is to classify how full are the containers. The containers can be either empty or filled with an unknown content at 50% or 90% of the whole capacity of the container. There are three classes: 0 (empty), 50 (half full), and 90 (full). Task (2) is to classify which content is filled in the containers. The containers can be either empty or filled with an unknown content. There are four filling type classes: 0 (empty), 1 (pasta), 2 (rice), 3 (water). Task (3) is to estimate the container capacity. The containers vary in shape and size.

There are three main challenges for filling mass estimation with CORSMAL Containers Manipulation dataset. Firstly, the duration of each recording in the dataset is different from each other (Fig. 1), which makes it extract inconsistent dimensions of the modality features. Secondly, the target objects (the container and the content) occupied small pixel ratio compared with the subject or desk in the recording (Fig. 2), so it is impossible to track the objects by common classification models (e.g., VGG-16 pre-trained with ImageNet) [35]. Thirdly, the scenarios in the dataset vary in target occlusion and subject motion (e.g., the container is held by the subject or not) (Fig. 5). These issue would compromise the estimation performance.

To this end, we propose a solution to reduce the above issues and improve the performance by leveraging the modality of RGB images and acoustics. Inspired by how humans judge the physical properties of the filling content and the containers with their vision and hearing, our solution is to obtain the container prior first, followed by classifying the filling level and filling type with audio vibration, and sampling the container capacity from the Gaussian process regression. Empirically, given the container type (e.g., cup, glass, food box), humans deal with filling level (i.e., empty, half full and full) prediction by hearing the changes of the vibrational frequency of the air in the container right after the pouring procedure, especially for the liquid or empty filling. Besides, under the same prerequisite, humans can distinguish the filling type (i.e., empty, pasta, rice and water) via the nature frequency of the filling content.

The main contributions of this work are summarized as follows:

1. We propose to tackle the estimation task for physical properties of the filling and its corresponding container (i.e., filling level, filling type and container capacity) in the perception of human pouring. We adopted YOLOv4 [5] to classify the container as a prior, followed by audio feature extraction and fitting of container capacity distribution.
2. We have done a lot of experiments on the CORSMAL Containers Manipulation dataset, which proves the effectiveness and competitiveness of our method.

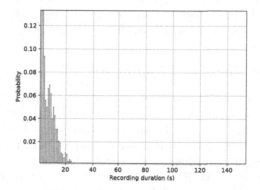

Fig. 1. Discrete probability mass function over the recording durations.

Fig. 2. The target object pixel ratios in the visual recording. The purple bounding box indicates the container, while the green bounding box indicates the filling content. (Color figure online)

2   Related Work

In this section, we focus on reviewing pouring tasks via different manipulation learning approaches.

2.1   Motion Trajectory Based Approaches

P. Pastor et al. learned dynamic motor primitives (DMPs) from human demonstrations for pouring tasks, and used these to generalize to different container (i.e., cup) placements [23]. Similarly, M. Muehlig et al. encoded demonstrated bimanual pouring trajectories using GMM [21]. In contract, S. Brandi et al. proposed learning in a feature space defined by the warped parameters, in order to automatically generalize between objects [6].

2.2   Modality Sensing Based Approaches

Vision, as the one of commonly used modality in our daily lives, has been explored to robotic learning, including perception of the pouring process. K.J. Pithadiya et al. [28] looked at different edge detection algorithms for detecting whether or not water bottles are over or under filled. However, instead of determining the actual liquid height, the detected edges are compared to a reference line to determine this. For the restaurant industry, R. Bhattacharyya et al. [4] use RFID tags for liquid level detection in beverage glasses and liquor bottles. Besides, RGB-D cameras are also adopted, as the extension of vision sensing, to tackle the robotic pouring [9,10]. The auditory information contributes to the pouring task when the filling interacts with the air column of the container [7,11,14,18]. For example, S. Griffith bootstraped classification learning about how objects interact with water with auditory and proprioceptive feature [11]. Recently, inspired by the phenomenon that the resonance frequencies implicitly relate to the length of the air column of the container, H. Liang et al. [18] designed a perception-based deep neural network to estimate the liquid filling level of the target containers. In addition to the vision and acoustic sensing, touch modality is also widely used in robotic pouring tasks, especially force and torque sensing [13,30,31].

3   Method

The overall pipeline of our method is shown in Fig. 3. All tasks is based on container prior, i.e., container category, by YOLOv4 [5]. After that, the process is divided into two parts. One part is for Task (1) and Task (2) by a multilayer perceptron (MLP) input with audio features, the other part is for Task (3) by using Gaussian process regression.

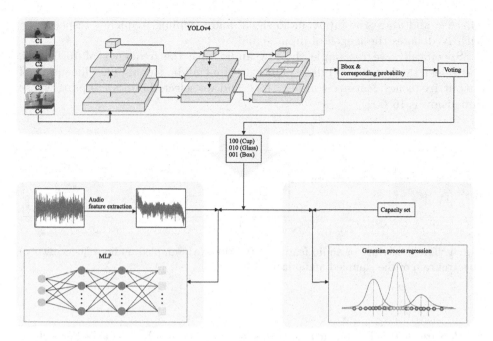

Fig. 3. The overall pipeline for filling mass estimation. C_i indicates the views from the ith camera (Intel RealSense D435i), C_1 is the view from the left side of the manipulator, C_2 is the view from the right side of the manipulator, C_3 is the front view with the camera mounted on the manipulator, C_4 is the view from the moving camera worn by the demonstrator (human).

3.1 Container Detection

To infer the container category, we first extract frames from recorded videos of four-view cameras (i.e., C_1, C_2, C_3 and C_4), then we conduct container detection via YOLOv4 pretrained on MS COCO dataset [19] for each frame, from which we obtain the bounding boxes and categories of the containers. Finally, we follow the majority rule, that votes for cup, glass and box among extracted frames, to decide the container category for each video. As shown in Fig. 2, the target container occupied small pixel ratio in the recording, YOLOv4 is capable to capture the small objects and predict reasonable category for the container.

3.2 Filling Level and Filling Type Classification (Task (1) and Task (2))

Audio Feature Extraction. As shown in Fig. 4, we use spectrogram as the audio feature by Discrete Fourier Transform (DFT):

$$F(u) = \sum_{x=0}^{N-1} f(x)e^{-j\frac{2\pi u x}{N}} \tag{1}$$

where x and u are the input audio signal and sampling frequency respectively, with N denotes the length of input signal.

Specifically, we re-sample the raw audio with the frequency of $16,600\,\mathrm{Hz}$, and select the last $32,000$ data points as input audio signal. The dimension of output frequency feature is also $32,000$, and we select the $u >= 0$ part, whose dimension is $16,001$.

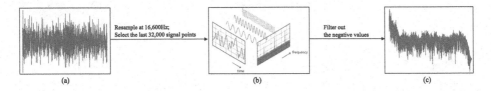

Fig. 4. The procedure of audio feature extraction. (a) Sampled audio sequence; (b–c) Spectrogram of the sampled audio using FFT.

Backbone Models. The utilized classification model is Multi-Layer Perceptron (MLP) with 2 hidden layers. Given the container category, we trained 6 MLP models for filling level and filling type classification. Specifically, we use 3 different MLPs for filling level classification, each of which belongs to each container category. Likewise 3 distinct MLPs are utilized for filling type classification. The loss function and optimizer are cross-entropy function and Adam [15]. Detailed experimental settings (i.e., learning rate, number of neurons, etc) are listed in Sect. 4.2.

3.3   Container Capacity Estimation (Task (3))

In this task, the objective is to estimate the container capacity from the data. We observe that for each category, the capacity distribution can be fit by Gaussian distribution well.

Thus we utilize the Gaussian process regression to learn the capacity distribution of each container. The pipeline can be divided into 3 steps:

- Step 1: Infer the category label x_i from the object detection model.
- Step 2: Construct the training set: $\mathcal{D} = (\mathbf{X}, \mathbf{y}) = \{(\mathbf{x}_i, y_i) \mid i = 1, \dots, N\}$, where each sample is (x_i, y_i), where x_i and y_i indicate the label of object category and its corresponding capacity. N is the number of samples.
- Step 3: Conduct the Gaussian process regression. For a new input X^* in test-set, we have $\hat{\mathbf{y}}^* = K\left(X^*, X\right) K(X, X)^{-1}\mathbf{y}$, where $\mathbf{y}^*$ is the predicted value and K is the covariance function defined by $K(A, B)_{ij} = \exp\left(-\frac{1}{2}|A_i - B_j|^2\right)$.

4   Experiments

4.1   CORSMAL Containers Manipulation Dataset

CORSMAL distributes an audio-visual-inertial dataset [1] of people interacting with containers, for example while pouring a filling into a glass or shaking a food box. The CORSMAL Container Manipulation dataset is collected with four multi-sensor devices (one on a robotic arm, one on the human chest and two third-person views) and a circular microphone array [1]. Each device is equipped with an RGB camera, a stereo infrared camera and an inertial measurement unit. In addition to RGB and infrared images, each device provides synchronised depth images that are spatially aligned with the RGB images. All signals are synchronised, and the calibration information for all devices, as well as the inertial measurements of the body-worn device, is also provided. Besides, the dataset is collected under three different scenarios (Fig. 5) with an increasing level of difficulty, caused by occlusions of the target objects or subject motion. In the first scenario, the subject sits in front of the robot, while a container is on a table. The subject pours the filling into the container, while trying not to touch the container (cup or glass), or shakes an already filled food box, and then initiates the handover of the container to the robot. In the second scenario, the subject sits in front of the robot, while holding a container. The subject pours the filling from a jar into a glass/cup or shakes an already filled food box, and then initiates the handover of the container to the robot. In the third scenario, a container is held by the subject while standing to the side of the robot, potentially visible from one third-person view camera only. The subject pours the filling from a jar into a glass/cup or shakes an already filled food box, takes a few steps to reach the front of the robot and then initiates the handover of the container to the robot. In our proposed solution, we used two modalities to tackle the filling mass estimation, which are RGB images from all views to classify the containers, and audio from the microphones to tackle Task (1) and Task (2).

4.2   Exeprimental Details

Here we list all the experimental details. Table 1 illustrates the hyper-parameters of MLP models used in Task (1) and Task (2). All the MLPs in the experiments are trained from scrach. For YOLOv4, we utilize the pre-trained model from MS COCO dataset [19]. Table 2 shows the model and library acquisitions in the experiments. All the methods are implemented using PyTorch [24] toolbox with an Intel Core i9 CPU and 8 Nvidia RTX 2080 Ti GPUs.

Table 1. Architecture & hyper-parameters of MLP used in Task (1) & Task (2).

Architecture & Hyper-parameters	Chosen values
# Hidden layers	2
# Neurons in the 1st hidden layer	3,096
# Neurons in the 1st hidden layer	512
# Epochs	200
Learning rate	0.05

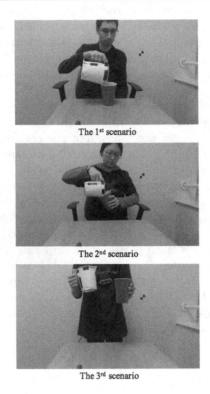

The 1st scenario

The 2nd scenario

The 3rd scenario

Fig. 5. The example visualization of three different scenarios in the CORSMAL Containers Manipulation dataset.

4.3   Evaluation Metric

For classification tasks (i.e., Task (1) and Task (2)), we used the Weighted Average F1-score (WAFS) as the evaluation metric. For the capacity estimation task (i.e., Task (3)), the Average Capacity Score (ACS) under the relative absolute error is employed in the experiments. For evaluating the filling mass estimation, the Average filling Mass Score (AMS) under the relative absolute error is used to evaluate the performance of our proposed method.

Table 2. Model and library acquisitions in the experiments.

Pre-trained models and libraries	Acquisition
YOLOv4 pre-trained model	https://github.com/kiyoshiiriemon/yolov4_darknet
Librosa lib [20]	https://librosa.org/doc/latest/index.html

4.4 Experimental Results

Table 3, Table 4, Table 5 and Table 6 show the performance results for the filling mass estimation, Task (1), Task (2) and Task (3) respectively. Though the Gaussian process regression showed effectiveness on container capacity estimation, we find that our method is relatively weak on filling level and filling type classification. The reason would lie in the audio feature extraction, which the number of signal points we select would be the background noise in the recordings of complex scenarios (i.e., the container is held by the subject, or the subject is potentially visible from one third-person view camera only). Therefore, the trained models would probably classify the filling level or filling type as the empty. In the future, we plan to extract the spectrogram based on the regular time windows (Fig. 6).

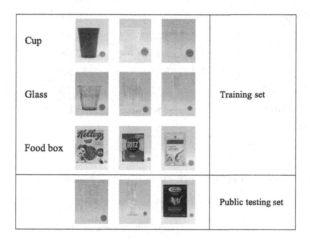

Fig. 6. Containers from training set and public testing set of CORSMAL Containers Manipulation dataset.

Table 3. Performance on filling mass estimation.

Team/Baseline	Performance		
	Public testset	Private testset	Overall
Because it's tactile	64.98	65.15	65.06
HVRL	63.32	61.01	62.16
Ours	52.80	54.14	53.47
NTNU-ERC	38.56	39.80	39.18
Baseline (Random)	38.47	31.65	35.06
Challengers	29.25	23.21	26.23
Baseline (SCC-Net)	28.02	22.92	25.47
Baseline (Mask R-CNN + RN18)	19.46	25.47	14.53

Table 4. Performance on filling level classification.

Team/Baseline	Performance		
	Public testset	Private testset	Overall
Baseline (SCC-Net)	84.21	80.98	82.66
Because it's tactile	78.14	78.14	79.65
HVRL	82.63	74.43	78.56
Challengers	50.73	47.08	48.71
Baseline (Mask R-CNN + RN18)	58.51	32.93	47.00
Ours	44.31	42.70	43.53
Baseline (Random)	38.47	31.65	35.06
NTNU-ERC	–	–	–

Table 5. Performance on filling type classification.

Team/Baseline	Performance		
	Public testset	Private testset	Overall
HVRL	97.83	96.08	96.95
Because it's tactile	93.83	94.70	94.26
Baseline (SCC-Net)	93.34	92.85	93.09
NTNU-ERC	81.97	91.67	86.89
Challengers	78.58	71.75	75.24
Ours	41.77	41.90	41.83
Baseline (Random)	21.24	27.52	27.52
Baseline (Mask R-CNN + RN18)	30.85	13.04	23.05

Table 6. Performance on container capacity estimation.

Team/Baseline	Performance		
	Public testset	Private testset	Overall
NTNU-ERC	66.92	67.67	67.30
Ours	63.00	62.14	62.14
Because it's tactile	60.56	60.58	60.57
HVRL	57.19	52.38	54.79
Baseline (Random)	31.63	17.53	24.58
NTNU-ERC	–	–	–
Challengers	–	–	–

5   Conclusion

In this paper, we present the solution for filling mass estimation. In our method, the container detection by YOLOv4 is served as the prior, then we extract the audio feature into MLPs for filling level and filling type classification, and conduct Gaussian process regression for container capacity estimation. The experimental results indicate the effectiveness of our proposed method for filling mass estimation task. The rank of our proposed method in the CORSMAL Challenge of Multi-modal Fusion and Learning For Robotics also indicates the effectiveness.

References

1. Xompero, R.A., Sanchez-Matilla,R.M., Cavallaro, A.: CORSMAL Containers Manipulation (1.0) [Data set]. https://doi.org/10.17636/101CORSMAL1
2. Abdel-Hamid, O., Mohamed, A.R., Jiang, H., Deng, L., Penn, G., Yu, D.: Convolutional neural networks for speech recognition. IEEE/ACM Trans. Audio Speech Lang. Process. **22**(10), 1533–1545 (2014)
3. Bae, H., et al.: Iros 2019 lifelong robotic vision: object recognition challenge [competitions]. IEEE Rob. Autom. Mag **27**(2), 11–16 (2020)
4. Bhattacharyya, R., Floerkemeier, C., Sarma, S.: Rfid tag antenna based sensing: does your beverage glass need a refill? In: 2010 IEEE International Conference on RFID (IEEE RFID 2010), pp. 126–133. IEEE (2010)
5. Bochkovskiy, A., Wang, C.Y., Liao, H.Y.M.: Yolov4: optimal speed and accuracy of object detection. arXiv preprint arXiv:2004.10934 (2020)
6. Brandi, S., Kroemer, O., Peters, J.: Generalizing pouring actions between objects using warped parameters. In: 2014 IEEE-RAS International Conference on Humanoid Robots, pp. 616–621. IEEE (2014)
7. Clarke, S., Rhodes, T., Atkeson, C.G., Kroemer, O.: Learning audio feedback for estimating amount and flow of granular material. Proc. Mach. Learn. Res. **87** (2018)
8. Deng, J., Dong, W., Socher, R., Li, L.J., Li, K., Fei-Fei, L.: Imagenet: a large-scale hierarchical image database. In: 2009 IEEE Conference on Computer Vision and Pattern Recognition, pp. 248–255. IEEE (2009)

9. Do, C., Burgard, W.: Accurate pouring with an autonomous robot using an RGB-D camera. In: Strand, M., Dillmann, R., Menegatti, E., Ghidoni, S. (eds.) IAS 2018. AISC, vol. 867, pp. 210–221. Springer, Cham (2019). https://doi.org/10.1007/978-3-030-01370-7_17

10. Do, C., Schubert, T., Burgard, W.: A probabilistic approach to liquid level detection in cups using an RGB-D camera. In: 2016 IEEE/RSJ International Conference on Intelligent Robots and Systems (IROS), pp. 2075–2080. IEEE (2016)

11. Griffith, S., Sukhoy, V., Wegter, T., Stoytchev, A.: Object categorization in the sink: Learning behavior-grounded object categories with water. In: Proceedings of the 2012 ICRA Workshop on Semantic Perception, Mapping and Exploration. Citeseer (2012)

12. Gu, S., Holly, E., Lillicrap, T., Levine, S.: Deep reinforcement learning for robotic manipulation with asynchronous off-policy updates. In: 2017 IEEE International Conference on Robotics and Automation (ICRA), pp. 3389–3396. IEEE (2017)

13. Huang, Y., Sun, Y.: Learning to pour. In: 2017 IEEE/RSJ International Conference on Intelligent Robots and Systems (IROS), pp. 7005–7010. IEEE (2017)

14. Ikeno, S., Watanabe, R., Okazaki, R., Hachisu, T., Sato, M., Kajimoto, H.: Change in the amount poured as a result of vibration when pouring a liquid. In: Kajimoto, H., Ando, H., Kyung, K.-U. (eds.) Haptic Interaction. LNEE, vol. 277, pp. 7–11. Springer, Tokyo (2015). https://doi.org/10.1007/978-4-431-55690-9_2

15. Kingma, D.P., Ba, J.: Adam: a method for stochastic optimization. arXiv preprint arXiv:1412.6980 (2014)

16. LeCun, Y., Bengio, Y., Hinton, G.: Deep learning. Nature **521**(7553), 436–444 (2015)

17. Lenz, I., Lee, H., Saxena, A.: Deep learning for detecting robotic grasps. Int. J. Rob. Res. **34**(4–5), 705–724 (2015)

18. Liang, H., et al.: Making sense of audio vibration for liquid height estimation in robotic pouring. arXiv preprint arXiv:1903.00650 (2019)

19. Lin, T.Y., et al.: Microsoft COCO: common objects in context. In: Fleet, D., Pajdla, T., Schiele, B., Tuytelaars, T. (eds.) ECCV 2014. LNCS, vol. 8693, pp. 740–755. Springer, Cham (2014). https://doi.org/10.1007/978-3-319-10602-1_48

20. McFee, B., et al.: librosa: audio and music signal analysis in python. In: Proceedings of the 14th Python in Science Conference, vol. 8, pp. 18–25 (2015)

21. Muhlig, M., Gienger, M., Hellbach, S., Steil, J.J., Goerick, C.: Task-level imitation learning using variance-based movement optimization. In: 2009 IEEE International Conference on Robotics and Automation, pp. 1177–1184. IEEE (2009)

22. Nair, A., Bahl, S., Khazatsky, A., Pong, V., Berseth, G., Levine, S.: Contextual imagined goals for self-supervised robotic learning. In: Conference on Robot Learning, pp. 530–539. PMLR (2020)

23. Pastor, P., Hoffmann, H., Asfour, T., Schaal, S.: Learning and generalization of motor skills by learning from demonstration. In: 2009 IEEE International Conference on Robotics and Automation, pp. 763–768. IEEE (2009)

24. Paszke, A., et al.: Pytorch: an imperative style, high-performance deep learning library. In: Neural Information Processing Systems (NeurIPS), pp. 8024–8035 (2019)

25. Paulius, D., Huang, Y., Milton, R., Buchanan, W.D., Sam, J., Sun, Y.: Functional object-oriented network for manipulation learning. In: 2016 IEEE/RSJ International Conference on Intelligent Robots and Systems (IROS), pp. 2655–2662. IEEE (2016)

26. Paulius, D., Jelodar, A.B., Sun, Y.: Functional object-oriented network: Construction & expansion. In: 2018 IEEE International Conference on Robotics and Automation (ICRA), pp. 1–7. IEEE (2018)
27. Pierson, H.A., Gashler, M.S.: Deep learning in robotics: a review of recent research. Adv. Rob. **31**(16), 821–835 (2017)
28. Pithadiya, K.J., Modi, C.K., Chauhan, J.D.: Selecting the most favourable edge detection technique for liquid level inspection in bottles. Int. J. Comput. Inf. Syst. Ind. Manag. Appl. (IJCISIM) ISSN, 2150–7988 (2011)
29. Redmon, J., Divvala, S., Girshick, R., Farhadi, A.: You only look once: unified, real-time object detection. In: Proceedings of the IEEE Conference on Computer Vision and Pattern Recognition, pp. 779–788 (2016)
30. Rozo, L., Jiménez, P., Torras, C.: Force-based robot learning of pouring skills using parametric hidden Markov models. In: 9th International Workshop on Robot Motion and Control, pp. 227–232. IEEE (2013)
31. Saal, H.P., Ting, J.A., Vijayakumar, S.: Active estimation of object dynamics parameters with tactile sensors. In: 2010 IEEE/RSJ International Conference on Intelligent Robots and Systems, pp. 916–921. IEEE (2010)
32. Sanchez-Matilla, R., et al.: Benchmark for human-to-robot handovers of unseen containers with unknown filling. IEEE Rob. Autom. Lett. **5**(2), 1642–1649 (2020)
33. She, Q., et al.: Openloris-object: a robotic vision dataset and benchmark for lifelong deep learning. In: 2020 IEEE International Conference on Robotics and Automation (ICRA), pp. 4767–4773. IEEE (2020)
34. Shi, X., et al.: Are we ready for service robots? the openloris-scene datasets for lifelong slam. In: 2020 IEEE International Conference on Robotics and Automation (ICRA), pp. 3139–3145. IEEE (2020)
35. Simonyan, K., Zisserman, A.: Very deep convolutional networks for large-scale image recognition. In: ICLR, vol. 2015 (2015)
36. Yang, P.C., Sasaki, K., Suzuki, K., Kase, K., Sugano, S., Ogata, T.: Repeatable folding task by humanoid robot worker using deep learning. IEEE Rob. Autom. Lett **2**(2), 397–403 (2016)

Pollen Grain Classification Challenge

Pollen Grain Classification Challenge (ICPR 2020)

Description

Pollen grain classification has a remarkable role in many fields from medicine, to biology and agronomy. Indeed, automatic pollen grain classification is an important task for all related applications and areas. The aim of the proposed challenge is the automatic classification of pollen grain images exploiting Pollen13K, the largest dataset of microscope pollen grain images, collected from aerobiological samples (https://iplab.dmi.unict.it/pollengraindataset/dataset). The microscope images of the samples have been digitalized and processed through a proper image processing pipeline to detect and extract four classes of objects, including three species of pollen grain and an additional class of objects that could be often mis-classified as pollen (e.g., air bubbles, dust, etc.). More than 13.000 objects have been detected and labelled by aerobiology experts.

Task Description

A set of images related to objects detected in microscope images have been given to participants, where each depicted object belongs to one of the defined classes. Segmentation mask of each object have been also be provided, to allow methods that exploit the localization of the salient regions in images or data augmentation. Participants have been requested to correctly classify the highest number of objects. Moreover, the proposed methods also addressed with the imbalance in the data, which represents one challenge of pollen grain classification in real-world scenarios. Test images have been released, without the ground truth classes, nor the segmentation masks.

Acknowledgement. The research has been carried out thanks to the collaboration with Ferrero HCo, that financed the project and allowed the collection of aerobiological samples from hazelnut plantations. We would like to thank ICPR 2020 organizers for hosting the challenge and its emerging community, and the ICPR 2020 challenge chairs for the valuable help and support.

November 2020

Organization

Challenge Chairs

Alessandro Ortis	Università degli Studi di Catania, Italy
Sebastiano Battiato	Università degli Studi di Catania, Italy
Francesco Guarnera	Università degli Studi di Catania, Italy
Francesca Trenta	Università degli Studi di Catania, Italy
Consolata Siniscalco	University of Turin, Italy
Lorenzo Ascari	University of Turin, Italy
Eloy Surez	Agri Competence Center, Ferrero HCo
Tommaso De Gregorio	Agri Competence Center, Ferrero HCo

Pollen Grain Classification Challenge 2020
Challenge Report

Sebastiano Battiato[1], Francesco Guarnera[1], Alessandro Ortis[1(✉)],
Francesca Trenta[1], Lorenzo Ascari[2], Consolata Siniscalco[2],
Tommaso De Gregorio[3], and Eloy Suárez[3]

[1] University of Catania, 95125 Catania, Italy
{battiato,ortis}@dmi.unict.it,
{francesco.guarnera,francesca.trenta}@unict.it
[2] University of Turin, 10125 Turin, Italy
{lorenzo.ascari,consolata.siniscalco}@unito.it
[3] Agri Competence Center – Ferrero HCo, Milan, Italy
{tommaso.degregorio,Eloy.SuarezHuerta}@ferrero.com

Abstract. This report summarises the *Pollen Grain Classification Challenge 2020*, and the related findings. It serves as an introduction to the technical reports that were submitted to the competition section at the *25th International Conference on Pattern Recognition (ICPR 2020)*, related to the Pollen Grain Classification Challenge. The challenge is meant to develop automatic pollen grain classification systems, by leveraging on the first large scale annotated dataset of microscope pollen grain images.

Keywords: Pollen grain classification · Computer vision · Machine learning

1 Introduction and Motivations

Aerobiology is a branch of biology that studies the dispersal into the atmosphere of microorganisms, such as viruses, bacteria, fungal spores, and pollen grains [17]. Despite being mainly applied for studying the effects of airborne biological agents on human health [28], aerobiology also plays an important role in other fields, such as in plant [32] and environmental sciences [18, 26]. In particular, monitoring airborne pollen dispersal is important for allergology [6], criminalistics [1], archaeobotany [25], biodiversity conservation [13] and crop modeling [9]. Despite its importance, the hard work required by the techniques currently used to identify and count the relevant entities in microscopy has hindered the application of aerobiology to those and new sectors. Standard palynological procedures rely on the manual classification of pollen grains by observing morphological traits on microscopy images [22]. Indeed, the identification and classification of pollen grains from different plant species require the intervention of qualified human

© Springer Nature Switzerland AG 2021
A. Del Bimbo et al. (Eds.): ICPR 2020 Workshops, LNCS 12668, pp. 469–479, 2021.
https://doi.org/10.1007/978-3-030-68793-9_34

Table 1. Comparison between the proposed dataset and the main datasets used in pollen grain classification.

Dataset	Number of grains	Image type	Resolution
Duller's Pollen Dataset [11]	630	Grayscale	25×25
POLEN23E [16]	805	Color	Minimum 250 pixel per dimension
Ranzato et al. [27]	3,686 (1,429 images)	Color	1024×1024 (multiple grains per image)
Pollen73S [2]	2,523	Color	Average size $\leqslant 512 \times 512$
Pollen13K [4]	>12,000 + ~1,000 examples of debris (e.g., dust, air bubbles)	Color	84×84

operators in a highly demanding process in terms of time and people training. Therefore, the importance of automation in the aerobiological field is crucial to provide valuable improvements, especially for the task of pollen grains classification. As a consequence, different automatic classification approaches have been investigated over the years [20,30]. Recent advances in Machine Learning methods based on deep neural networks have resulted in impressive performances on a variety of problems, such as facial recognition, motion detection, medical diagnosis, among many others. At present, Machine Learning approaches have been widely adopted in object classification applications, providing highly accurate results on large-scale Multi-class datasets [3]. The rapid progress of automatic methods for pollen grains classification will have great impacts on the development of low-cost tools for aerobiologists. Moreover, Machine Learning techniques require a large amount of data, promoting the definition of large-scale datasets. To this end, we collected a set of images related to pollen grains detected in microscope images from aerobiological samples, defining a large-scale dataset composed of more than 13,000 pollen grains [4] in 5 different categories. Previous studies on automatic pollen grain detection/classification are trained and evaluated on datasets which include from 65 to about 4,000 number of grains, and most of them report results obtained on self-collected databases. Three public databases are the Duller's Pollen Dataset [11], the POLEN23E [16] and the Pollen73S [2]. The first contains a total of 630 grayscale images of size 25×25, the second one includes 805 color images of 23 pollen species, with 35 images for each pollen type, and the latter is composed of 2,523 images from 73 pollen types. In Table 1, the main datasets used in pollen grain classification are reported.

2   Dataset Description

The provided dataset consists of more than 13 thousands per-object images collected from aerobiological samples, classified into five different categories: (1)

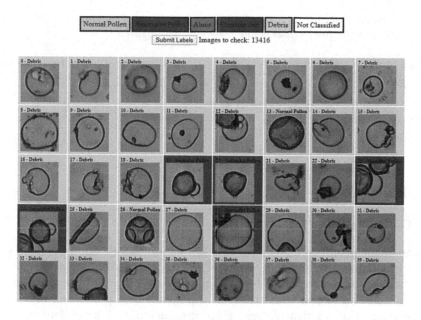

Fig. 1. Web-based tool used to label images

Corylus avellana (well-developed pollen grains), (2) *Corylus avellana* (anomalous pollen grains), (3) *Alnus*, (4) debris and (5) *Cupressaceae*. However, considering the small number of observations related to the class *Cupressaceae*, this has not included in the dataset used for the challenge. Airborne pollen grains were sampled by volumetric spore traps (Lanzoni VPPS®Hirst-type sampler), placed at plant canopy level, with an adhesive strip placed on a rotating drum, moved at 2 mm h-1 under a suction hole, for seven-day sampling autonomy. Thereafter, the sampling strip was collected weekly and cut into daily segments that were analyzed following standard staining procedures. The pollen grains placed on microscope slides were selectively stained with a mounting medium containing basic fuchsin (0.08 % gelatin, 0.44% glycerin, 0.015% liquefied phenol, 0.0015% basic fuchsin in aqueous solution). For image acquisition, the daily strip segments were inspected using a Leitz Diaplan bright-field microscope with a 5 MP CMOS sensor. Then, image patches depicting centered objects automatically extracted from microscope images were manually labeled by experts in aerobiology using a web-based tool (see Fig. 1). The dataset includes:

- 84×84 RGB images for each segmented object, for each of the four categories;
- binary masks for single object segmentation (84 × 84 resolution);
- segmented versions of the patches obtained by applying the segmentation mask and padding the background with all green pixels (84 × 84 resolution).

Table 2. Number of objects for each class on training and test set. Training objects represent 85% of the full dataset while test objects the 15%.

Class	Training objects	Test objects
Corylus avellana (well-developed pollen grains)	1,566	277
Corylus avellana (anomalous pollen grains)	773	136
Alnus (well-developed pollen grains)	8,216	1,450
Debris	724	128

3   Challenge

3.1   Description

The aim of the proposed challenge is the automatic classification of pollen grain images exploiting the largest dataset of microscope pollen grain images, collected from aerobiological samples. The microscope images of the samples have been digitalized and processed through a proper image processing pipeline [3] to detect and extract five classes of objects, including four pollen types and an additional class of objects that could be often misclassified as pollen (e.g., air bubbles, dust, etc.). Due to the very low number of examples of the class *Cupressaceae*, this class has been ignored for the classification task proposed by the challenge[1]. More than 13,000 objects have been detected and labeled by aerobiology experts. The challenge started officially on the 10th of May 2020, when the organizers opened the registration through the website https://iplab. dmi.unict.it/pollenclassificationchallenge. After ten days, when the training data have been released, the challenge counted 96 registered teams. Training data have been available for about one month, and on the 18th of June 2020 also test data have been released, together with an example template file (JSON format) for prediction results upload. The number of objects for each class in the training set and test set is described in Table 2.

3.2   Evaluation Criteria

Participants have been requested to upload the results of classification according to the specified submission format. The submitted classification results have been evaluated considering different metrics. Then, the ranking has been defined considering the F1 weighted score as the first metric, followed by the F1 macro and Accuracy respectively (i.e., F1 (weigh), F1 (macro) and Accuracy in Table 3).

The *F1 weighted score* computes the F1 for each label and returns their average with the number of instances of that class in the dataset. This alters the classic F1 score to account for label imbalance. The *F1 macro score* computes the F1 for each label and returns their average.

---

[1] More details about the full dataset can be found at: https://iplab.dmi.unict.it/ pollengraindataset/dataset.

3.3   Ranking

The submission page was open for five days: 50 teams submitted 87 files in JSON format representing the predicted labels of test data, as requested by the organizers. Four submissions have been removed because in the uploaded file some test instances were missing. Table 3 shows the final leaderboard. Each team was allowed to perform up to five attempts, however, this table shows only the best result for each team. The complete ranking of the accepted submissions listing all the 83 attempts is available at https://iplab.dmi.unict.it/pollenclassificationchallenge/results.

Table 3. Final leaderboard. For each team, only the best result of multiple attempts is reported.

Rank	Username	F1 (weigh)	F1 (macro)	Accuracy
1	zhangbaochang	0.975100	0.955361	0.975389
2	方超	0.973032	0.951970	0.973380
3	Penghui Gui	0.972592	0.951678	0.972877
4	jaideepm.111@gmail.com	0.972578	0.950828	0.972877
5	fangzhouzhao	0.972496	0.951796	0.972877
6	Chia Wei Chen	0.970588	0.950738	0.970868
7	Fangrui Liu	0.969953	0.948511	0.970366
8	Karan Pathak	0.968503	0.945373	0.968859
9	Yutao Hu	0.968093	0.947151	0.968357
10	Yuya Obinata	0.967979	0.946900	0.968357
11	jang_jian	0.967914	0.945436	0.968357
12	Xuihui Liu	0.967001	0.943794	0.967353
13	Vivek Mittal	0.966412	0.941226	0.966850
14	Andrinandrasana David Rasamoelina	0.965974	0.944739	0.966348
15	Nguyen Tu Nam	0.965447	0.940767	0.965846
16	dongdong	0.964497	0.939353	0.964841
17	Alvaro Gomez	0.964423	0.937687	0.964841
18	Alexander Gillert	0.964138	0.938476	0.964841
19	Zhao Qiuyang	0.963047	0.938714	0.963335
20	Amirreza Mahbod	0.962975	0.939495	0.962832
21	Wataru Miyazaki	0.962777	0.935647	0.963335
22	Jonathan Heras	0.961521	0.933872	0.962330
23	Pankaj Mishra	0.961169	0.936951	0.961325
24	Yufei Zhao	0.959996	0.932907	0.960321
25	Narek Maloyan	0.958624	0.928215	0.959316

(continued)

Table 3. (*continued*)

Rank	Username	F1 (weigh)	F1 (macro)	Accuracy
26	Gianluca Maguolo	0.957547	0.929319	0.958312
27	Bojan Batalo	0.955266	0.924223	0.955801
28	Bartosz Ptak	0.955024	0.922227	0.955801
29	Melinda Katona	0.954564	0.925895	0.955298
30	Alessandra Lumini	0.952579	0.924816	0.953289
31	Bartosz Ptak	0.951613	0.921605	0.951783
32	Soumyadeep Ghosh	0.951526	0.918610	0.952285
33	Xiaomin Lin	0.948412	0.910667	0.948769
34	Adriano D'Alessandro	0.947723	0.911103	0.947764
35	Soumyadeep Ghosh	0.939999	0.906203	0.940733
36	Umang Chaturvedi	0.939347	0.904577	0.939226
37	Jayasree Saha	0.938737	0.891418	0.941235
38	Umang Chaturvedi	0.931488	0.896115	0.930688
39	Michael Reed	0.916485	0.877608	0.913611
40	Nilesh Kumar	0.916437	0.850337	0.916122
41	Alessandra Crippa	0.911963	0.869167	0.910597
42	Silvio Barra	0.884577	0.841424	0.878955
43	Hussein Osman	0.872832	0.794640	0.874434
44	Abhijith Ragav	0.869042	0.808022	0.860873
45	Austin Lawson	0.797494	0.647156	0.823204
46	Xavier Anadn	0.690048	0.417303	0.735811
47	Oluwatobi Bello	0.518117	0.243847	0.473631
48	Julien Garnier	0.246656	0.321757	0.265193
49	Abhijith Ragav	0.109436	0.086493	0.118031
50	Oluwatoyin Popoola	0.052594	0.093299	0.089904

The leaderboard shows how almost all participants reached good results, with the 0.975 as the maximum F1 value. The average F1 is 0.885 and 82% of the teams outperform this score. Excluding some cases, the proposed methods have achieved slight differences between F1 weighted and F1 macro, which means that the performances of the proposed methods are good for all the classes included in the dataset, although the high imbalance in the data.

3.4   Top 3 Ranked

In this paragraph we summarise the reports for the top-3 ranked Pollen Grain Classification Challenge:

1. **Baochang Zhang et al.:** This is the top-ranking entry by Beihang University (Beijing China) and University at Buffalo (USA). The participants proposed an approach based on two different methods, fused by a proper blending strategy. The first method exploits a neural architecture search with a densely connected search space named DenseNAS [12], which is a neural architecture search method that defines a densely connected search space represented as a dense super network. The super network is composed of densely connected routing blocks that are selected in the search phase to find the best path between them and derive the final architecture. The second method implements a Destruction and Construction Learning architecture [7], which combines a shallow Convolutional Neural Network (CNN) classifier with an Adversarial Network, jointly trained to classify an augmented dataset which includes examples of the training data obtained by shuffling local regions of the original images (i.e., Region Confusion Mechanism). This approach aims at generalizing the classifier on sub-parts of the input image. The blending strategy consists of concatenating the DCL and DenseNAT output vectors to be used as the input of a Random Forest Classifier, which performs the final classification. The authors performed cross-validation tests using the provided train set data, achieving an accuracy of 98,35%. The proposed method obtained an accuracy score of 97,53% when evaluated on the challenge test set. This shows the high generalization capability of such an approach.

2. **Xuhui Liu et al.:** This is the second-ranked entry by Beihang University, Beijing China. Also, this method implements a fusion strategy over two independent pipelines. Specifically, Hierarchical Bilinear Pooling (HBP) [34] and Discriminative Filter Learning within a CNN (DFL-CNN) [31] models are employed. Then, the two outputs are jointly fed to a decision-level fusion model based on a Random Forest Classifier.

3. **Penghui Gui et al.:** Is the third-ranked entry by the College of Computer Science, Sichuan University, China. The solution proposed by this team implements a sophisticated data augmentation approach, which creates a large number of inputs starting from both the provided original and segmented images. In particular, besides common image processing data augmentation procedures, the authors further generated a number of images by applying the cut occlusion approach, which consists of augmenting the dataset with partially occluded versions of existing samples, to encourage the network to consider less prominent features by removing maximally activated features. The trained model is based on ResNet101 [19], followed by additional layers to map high dimensional features of ResNet101 to low dimensional output corresponding to the four classes. It worth mentioning that all three attempts uploaded by this team are ranked in the top-10 global leaderboard[2].

---

[2] Check the complete leaderboard ranking at https://iplab.dmi.unict.it/pollen classificationchallenge/results.

4   Relevance of the Results

Since the first applications of neural networks for the classification of pollen grains in light-microscopy [14,24], different machine learning approaches were tested for the scope by different authors (see [20] and [30] for review). Nevertheless, past research has mostly relied on relatively small databases for testing the performances of new classification algorithms [2,11,16,27]. Thanks to the challenge organization, several techniques based on deep neural networks for the classification of pollen grains on the same large scale benchmark database have been evaluated and compared. CNNs were first showed to achieve classification rates higher than 90% for solving pollen classification tasks in [10], where CNN transfer learning was used for both feature extraction and classification. In [30], AlexNet was used for transfer learning and feature extraction, while classification was performed by Linear Discriminative Analysis. This approach achieved an average F-score of 0.967 on the classification of pollen grains contained in the POLEN23E dataset [30]. In another study, the LeNet CNN was applied on a private collection of 1,900 pollen images from four plant taxa, reaching an F-score of 0.928 [23]. Recently, different CNNs were tested for the classification of the Pollen73S dataset, reaching an F-score of 0.964 with DenseNet-201 [2].

During this competition, the contenders had to develop a classifier able to separate instances in challenging conditions, as well-developed hazelnut and alder pollen have similar average dimensions and structures. Moreover, alder pollen was highly over-represented on the images, making correct classification of hazelnut pollen difficult, even for experienced human operators. In this context, the F1-scores obtained by the top competitors were therefore significant and better than what was found in recent studies. Besides, past research never included debris, i.e. bubbles created during the preparation of microscope slides and abiotic particulate matter, as part of the classification problem. This could be relevant especially for aerobiological samples where the abundance of debris can hinder correct pollen identification. CNN-based techniques were recently employed for pollen identification on microscope slides, showing promising results even in the presence of fungal spores, bubbles, debris and dust [15]. Future research should test for possible performance gains of such methods by the inclusion of disturbances in the identification procedure. Aerobiology has historically benefited from the use of simple and relatively low-cost techniques, that have allowed a extensive monitoring of airborne particles around the globe [5]. Its automation, by saving time in sample preparation and manual counting, while increasing the sampling rate, has the potential to open new research opportunities and address unanswered problems (for newly developed aerosol-sensing instrumentation see [8,21,29,33]). Nevertheless, for this to be true, new automated aerobiological tools should hold the cost-effectiveness typical of this discipline.

Acknowledgements. The research has been carried out thanks to the collaboration with Ferrero HCo, which financed the project and allowed the collection of aerobiological samples from hazelnut plantations.

References

1. Alotaibi, S.S., et al.: Pollen molecular biology: applications in the forensic paly-nology and future prospects: a review. Saudi J. Biol. Sci. **27**(5), 1185–1190 (2020). https://doi.org/10.1016/j.sjbs.2020.02.019
2. Astolfi, G., et al.: POLLEN73S: an image dataset for pollen grains classification. Ecol. Inf. **60**, 101165 (2020). https://doi.org/10.1016/j.ecoinf.2020.101165
3. Battiato, S., Ortis, A., Trenta, F., Ascari, L., Politi, M., Siniscalco, C.: Detection and classification of pollen grain microscope images. In: Proceedings of the IEEE/CVF Conference on Computer Vision and Pattern Recognition Workshops, pp. 980–981 (2020)
4. Battiato, S., Ortis, A., Trenta, F., Ascari, L., Politi, M., Siniscalco, C.: Pollen13k: a large scale microscope pollen grain image dataset. In: IEEE International Conference on Image Processing (ICIP), pp. 2456–2460. IEEE (2020)
5. Buters, J.T., et al.: Pollen and spore monitoring in the world. Clin. Transl. Allergy **8**(1), 1–5 (2018). https://doi.org/10.1186/s13601-018-0197-8
6. Caillaud, D., Martin, S., Segala, C., Besancenot, J.P., Clot, B., Thibaudon, M.: Effects of airborne birch pollen levels on clinical symptoms of seasonal allergic rhinoconjunctivitis. Int. Arch. Allergy Immunol. **163**(1), 43–50 (2014). https://doi.org/10.1159/000355630
7. Chen, Y., Bai, Y., Zhang, W., Mei, T.: Destruction and construction learning for fine-grained image recognition. In: Proceedings of the IEEE Conference on Computer Vision and Pattern Recognition, pp. 5157–5166 (2019)
8. Crouzy, B., Stella, M., Konzelmann, T., Calpini, B., Clot, B.: All-optical automatic pollen identification: towards an operational system. Atmos. Environ. **140**, 202–212 (2016). https://doi.org/10.1016/j.atmosenv.2016.05.062
9. Cunha, M., Ribeiro, H., Abreu, I.: Pollen-based predictive modelling of wine production: application to an arid region. Eur. J. Agron. **73**, 42–54 (2016). https://doi.org/10.1016/j.eja.2015.10.008
10. Daood, A., Ribeiro, E., Bush, M.: Pollen grain recognition using deep learning. In: Bebis, G., et al. (eds.) ISVC 2016. LNCS, vol. 10072, pp. 321–330. Springer, Cham (2016). https://doi.org/10.1007/978-3-319-50835-1_30
11. Duller, A., Guller, G., France, I., Lamb, H.: A pollen image database for evaluation of automated identification systems. Quat. Newsl. **89**, 4–9 (1999)
12. Fang, J., Sun, Y., Zhang, Q., Li, Y., Liu, W., Wang, X.: Densely connected search space for more flexible neural architecture search. In: Proceedings of the IEEE/CVF Conference on Computer Vision and Pattern Recognition, pp. 10628–10637 (2020)
13. Fernández-Llamazares, Á., Belmonte, J., Boada, M., Fraixedas, S.: Airborne pollen records and their potential applications to the conservation of biodiversity. Aerobiologia **30**(2), 111–122 (2013). https://doi.org/10.1007/s10453-013-9320-4
14. France, I., Duller, A.W., Duller, G.A., Lamb, H.F.: A new approach to automated pollen analysis. Quat. Sci. Rev. **19**(6), 537–546 (2000). https://doi.org/10.1016/S0277-3791(99)00021-9
15. Gallardo-Caballero, R., García-Orellana, C.J., García-Manso, A., González-Velasco, H.M., Tormo-Molina, R., Macías-Macías, M.: Precise pollen grain detection in bright field microscopy using deep learning techniques. Sensors (Switzerland) **19**(16), 1–19 (2019). https://doi.org/10.3390/s19163583
16. Goncalves, A.B., et al.: Feature extraction and machine learning for the classification of Brazilian savannah pollen grains. PLoS ONE **11**(6), e0157044 (2016). https://doi.org/10.1371/journal.pone.0157044

17. Haddrell, A.E., Thomas, R.J.: Aerobiology: experimental considerations, observations, and future tools. Appl. Environ. Microbiol. **83**(17), 1–15 (2017). https://doi.org/10.1128/AEM.00809-17
18. Hader, J.D., Wright, T.P., Petters, M.D.: Contribution of pollen to atmospheric ice nuclei concentrations. Atmos. Chem. Phys. **14**(11), 5433–5449 (2014). https://doi.org/10.5194/acp-14-5433-2014
19. He, K., Zhang, X., Ren, S., Sun, J.: Deep residual learning for image recognition. In: Proceedings of the IEEE Conference on Computer Vision and Pattern Recognition, pp. 770–778 (2016)
20. Holt, K.A., Bennett, K.: Principles and methods for automated palynology. New Phytol. **203**(3), 735–742 (2014). https://doi.org/10.1111/nph.12848
21. Huffman, J.A., et al.: Real-time sensing of bioaerosols: review and current perspectives. Aerosol Sci. Technol. **54**(5), 465–495 (2020). https://doi.org/10.1080/02786826.2019.1664724
22. Jackson, S.L., Bayliss, K.L.: Spore traps need improvement to fulfil plant biosecurity requirements. Plant Pathol. **60**(5), 801–810 (2011). https://doi.org/10.1111/j.1365-3059.2011.02445.x
23. Korobeynikov, A., Kamalova, Y., Palabugin, M., Basov, I.: The use of convolutional neural network LeNet for pollen grains classification. In: "Instrumentation Engineering, Electronics and Telecommunications" Proceedings of the IV International Forum, Izhevsk, Russia, pp. 38–44 (2018). https://doi.org/10.22213/2658-3658-2018-38-44
24. Li, P., Flenley, J., Empson, L.K.: Classification of 13 types of New Zealand pollen patterns using neural networks. In: IVCNZ (1998)
25. Mercuri, A.M.: Applied palynology as a trans-disciplinary science: the contribution of aerobiology data to forensic and palaeoenvironmental issues. Aerobiologia **31**(3), 323–339 (2015). https://doi.org/10.1007/s10453-015-9367-5
26. Pearce, D.A., et al.: Aerobiology over Antarctica-a new initiative for atmospheric ecology. Front. Microbiol. **7**, 16 (2016). https://doi.org/10.3389/fmicb.2016.00016
27. Ranzato, M., Taylor, P.E., House, J.M., Flagan, R.C., LeCun, Y., Perona, P.: Automatic recognition of biological particles in microscopic images. Pattern Recogn. Lett. **28**(1), 31–39 (2007). https://doi.org/10.1016/j.patrec.2006.06.010
28. Roy, C.J., Reed, D.S.: Infectious disease aerobiology: miasma incarnate. Front. Cell. Infect. Microbiol. **2**(December), 163 (2012). https://doi.org/10.3389/fcimb.2012.00163
29. Sauvageat, E., et al.: Real-time pollen monitoring using digital holography. Atmos. Meas. Tech. **13**(3), 1539–1550 (2020). https://doi.org/10.5194/amt-13-1539-2020
30. Sevillano, V., Aznarte, J.L.: Improving classification of pollen grain images of the POLEN23E dataset through three different applications of deep learning convolutional neural networks. PLoS ONE **13**(9), 1–18 (2018). https://doi.org/10.1371/journal.pone.0201807
31. Wang, Y., Morariu, V.I., Davis, L.S.: Learning a discriminative filter bank within a CNN for fine-grained recognition. In: Proceedings of the IEEE Conference on Computer Vision and Pattern Recognition, pp. 4148–4157 (2018)
32. West, J.S., Kimber, R.: Innovations in air sampling to detect plant pathogens. Ann. Appl. Biol. **166**(1), 4–17 (2015). https://doi.org/10.1111/aab.12191

33. Wu, Y.C., et al.: Air quality monitoring using mobile microscopy and machine learning. Light Sci. Appl. **6**(9), e17046 (2017). https://doi.org/10.1038/lsa.2017.46
34. Yu, C., Zhao, X., Zheng, Q., Zhang, P., You, X.: Hierarchical bilinear pooling for fine-grained visual recognition. In: Ferrari, V., Hebert, M., Sminchisescu, C., Weiss, Y. (eds.) ECCV 2018. LNCS, vol. 11220, pp. 595–610. Springer, Cham (2018). https://doi.org/10.1007/978-3-030-01270-0_35

The Fusion of Neural Architecture Search and Destruction and Construction Learning
First Classified

Chao Fang[1], Yutao Hu[1], Baochang Zhang[1,3(✉)], and David Doermann[2]

[1] Beihang University, Beijing, China
fangchaobuaa@foxmail.com, herman_hu1995@163.com, bczhang@buaa.edu.cn
[2] University at Buffalo, New York, USA
doermann@buffalo.edu
[3] Shenzhen Academy of Aerospace Technology, Shenzhen, China

Abstract. Object classification is a classic problem in the field of pattern recognition. The traditional deep neural networks have been able to achieve good results on some classification problems, however, there are still many difficulties to be overcome in the fine-grained identification task, whose performance are still baffled by practical problems. In this paper, we introduce neural architecture search (NAS) to search the appropriate network according to the specific data set, which do not need more engineering work to adjust parameters for the optimized performance. We further combine the Destruction and Construction Learning (DCL) network and the NAS-based network for pollen recognition. To this end, we use a fusion algorithm to implement the combination of different networks, and won the pollen recognition competition held at the international pattern recognition Conference (ICPR) 2020.

Keywords: Neural architecture search · Destruction and Construction Learning · Model fusion

1 Introduction

In recent years, deep learning has achieved great success in the field of computer vision, showing their value in various applications, such as speech recognition, natural language processing, image recognition, big data processing [13,19,27]. Fine grained image classification has a wide range of research needs and application scenarios in both industry and academia. For example, in ecological protection, effective identification of different species of organisms is an important prerequisite for ecological research. A low-cost fine-grained image recognition with the help of computer vision technology will be of great significance for both academic and industry. Due to the subtle differences between subcategories

---

C. Fang and Y. Hu—Contribute equally.

© Springer Nature Switzerland AG 2021
A. Del Bimbo et al. (Eds.): ICPR 2020 Workshops, LNCS 12668, pp. 480–489, 2021.
https://doi.org/10.1007/978-3-030-68793-9_35

and large intra-class differences [11], traditional classification algorithms have to rely on a large number of manual annotation information, but even the most professional researchers sometimes are difficult to distinguish them. With the development of deep learning, deep convolution neural networks (CNNs) bring new opportunities for fine-grained image classification. A large number of algorithms based on CNNs promote the rapid development of this field. The methods based on CNNs can learn a robust image feature representation. However, these methods usually need a lot of engineering works to adjust the parameters and optimize the performance. While neural architecture search (NAS) [2] is one of hot issues in deep learning, it can design a cost-effective search method. By NAS, neural network structure with strong generalization ability and hardware friendliness can be automatically obtained.

For the pollen identification challenge dataset, we regard it as a fine-grained recognition problem. Firstly, we choose NAS with densely connected search space (DenseNAS) [10] to deal with this problem. In DenseNAS, search space plays an indispensable role, which determines the performance of the searched model. In the search space design of DenseNAS, more blocks with different widths exist in one stage, and the blocks are closely connected with each other. Finally, an optimal path between blocks will be searched out. The network structure will be derived through this path, and the blocks that do not exist in this path will be discarded. In this way, the width and number of blocks in the network are automatically allocated. Densenas extends the depth search to a wider space, not only the number of layers in each block, but also the number and width of blocks in each stage can be searched.

For fine-grained image recognition, local details are more important than global structure [18]. In destruction and construction learning (DCL) [8], in addition to a standard classification backbone network, two branches "destruction and construction" are introduced to automatically learn the discriminant region. Firstly, the input image is destroyed to emphasize the discriminative local details, and then the semantic correlation between local regions is modeled to reconstruct the image. DCL can locate the discriminating region automatically, so there is no need for additional annotation during training. In addition, the DCL structure is only used in the training phase, so there is no additional computational overhead in the test phase.

We train our networks based on Cogradient descent [28] with a better performance than conventional gradient descent method. After that, we perform a decision-level fusion of these models. The fusion can combine different models via certain strategies, and then leads to better results than single models. Simple voting system can be regarded as the most primitive way of model fusion. In this paper, we first get a prediction vector from the test results, and then learn from the output vector to further exploit the decision of sub-networks and refine the raw prediction. At last, we use a blending strategy to fuse the predictions of each sub-network, and establish the relationship between each prediction and the comprehensive final prediction.

In the next section, we will introduce the related work. Section 3 presents the basic principles of the tested models and model fusion strategy. Section 4 presents the process of data preprocessing and test results of different models. In the last section, we will conclude our paper and show directions for the future research.

2   Related Works

2.1   NAS Methods

Neural structure search (NAS) is a kind of technology that can automatically design high-performance network structure according to the sample set [2,14,23]. In some tasks, it can even be comparable to the level of human experts and effectively reduce the use and implementation cost of neural network. But NAS is not a new field. As early as the 1990s, some researchers tried it [23]. Earlier, some NAS approaches [2] regarded neural network structure design as a reinforcement learning problem, and learns to obtain an optimal strategy for generating network structure. Zoph *et al.* [29] first proposed using a controller-based recurrent neural network to generate hyper-parameters of neural network and slaid the foundation for solving NAS problems with reinforcement learning. Evolutionary algorithms is another kind of optimization algorithm used in NAS and genetic algorithm is one of the most famous evolutionary algorithms. The idea of genetic algorithm is to encode the sub network structure into binary strings and run the genetic algorithm to get the network structure with the maximum fitness function, that is, the optimal structure. Among them, Xie *et al.* [25] decomposed each architecture into a representation of 'genes'. Real *et al.* [22] proposed aging evolution, which improved over standard tournament selection, and surpassed the best manually designed architectures developed to date. However, both evolutionary methods and reinforcement learning methods face the problem of large amount of computation and gradient based optimization algorithms [1,20] are gradually used by researchers. As a result, researchers started to search for blocks or cells [26] instead of the entire networks to reduce the overall computational costs. They introduce a one-shot strategy that designs an over-parameterized network or super-network covering all candidate operations, and then samples the sub-networks. As typical examples, Brock *et al.* [5] trained the over-parameterized network, and Pham *et al.* [21] proposed to make the discrete optimization problem continuous and utilize a gradient-based method to search for optimal neural architectures. They relax the architecture representation as a super network by assigning continuous weights to the candidate operations, then share parameters among child models to avoid retraining each candidate from scratch.

2.2   Fine-Grained Methods

Existing approaches to fine-grained visual categorization can be categorized into two lines. The first line is encoding based methods. Due to the subtle inter-class variations of fine-grained images, traditional Convolutional Neural Networks (CNNs) cannot satisfy the need of FGVC. To solve this problem, encoding based methods add an extra encoding module after the last convolution layer in CNNs to enhance the ability of feature learning and produce the more discriminative features. Specifically, bilinear pooling family [12,17,18] are widely utilized to learn pairwise interaction between deep channels, achieving convincing performance in FGVC. Besides that, some methods [6,24] have been proposed to collect statistic information in different feature spaces, in which *1st* order or high order relationship will be exploited.

Another line towards FGVC is localization based method. Due to the small inter-class differences in FGVC, localizing discriminative regions and extracting powerful feature is beneficial for FGVC. A straightforward way is utilizing manual object part annotations directly to localize discriminative parts [16], which however, costs much laborious work. With the development of attention mechanism, recent works in FGVC employ it to localize discriminative regions adaptively [11,15]. Furthermore, Chen *et al.* propose Destruction and Construction Learning (DCL) framework that destructs the global structure of the input image, which also shows powerful capacity in localizing discriminative local regions [8]. To be more specific, in DCL, the global information in the destructed image is destroyed and only the content in each patch is complete, forcing the network to learn useful information from each patch and localize the discriminative region. This destruction mechanism attracts considerable attention and achieves great success in the last two years [8,9]. Our method also employs the DCL as the basic network.

3 Methods

3.1 DenseNAS-Based Method

In the NAS method, search space plays an indispensable role, which not only determines the performance of the model to a large extent, but also leads to a more novel architecture, which further reduces human adjustment.

In our method, we employ a neural architecture search with densely connected search space (DenseNAS) [10]. The architecture is shown in Fig. 1. The search space is divided into three levels: layer, block and network. Each layer contains various operation candidates and each block is composed of layers and is divided into two parts: head layers and stacking layers. For the header layer, its input comes from the data of different channels and spatial resolution of the previous blocks. The head layer is parallel, which converts all input data to the same channel number and spatial resolution. The stack layer is serial, and the operation of each layer is searchable. For the whole layer, each candidate operation is given as a structure parameter, and the output of layer is obtained by the weighted sum of all candidate operations. At the block level, the whole search space contains multiple blocks with different widths. The data of each block will be output to its subsequent blocks and each output path will also be given a structure parameter. In the head layers section, the data from previous blocks will be weighted and summed by using the probability value of the path. In the end, only part of blocks are selected, which makes the search process more feasible.

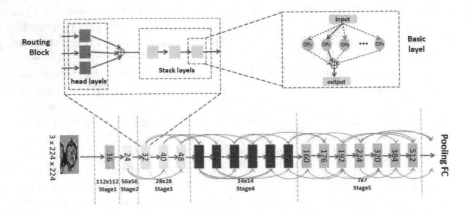

Fig. 1. Architecture of DenseNas.

The dense super network contains several stages, constructed with densely connected routing blocks. Besides, each stage corresponds to a range of width and spatial resolution. The width of the block in the super network increases gradually from the beginning to the end and architectures are searched within various path options in the super network. The whole search process is inspired by the previous work [7] and divided it into two parts. In the first part, only the weight parameters of operation are optimized; in the second part, the weight parameters and structural parameters of operation are alternately optimized according to epoch. After the whole search process, the structure parameters are used to derive the final structure. In the search process, Viterbi algorithm is used to select the path with the largest transmission probability, and then the probability sampling path is used to accelerate the parameter optimization process. In this way, not only the memory consumption can be accelerated, but also the coupling effect between different structures can be reduced.

3.2 Destruction and Construction Learning

DCL is proposed in [8], which achieves great performance in fine-grained classification task. In DCL, besides the standard classification backbone network, another "destruction and construction" stream is introduced to carefully "destruct" and then "reconstruct" the input image, which helps to localize extract discriminative features. Specifically, the whole stream is illustrated in Fig. 2. The framework of the proposed DCL method contains four parts: 1) Region Confusion Mechanism: a module to shuffle the local regions of the input image; 2) Classification Network: the standard classification backbone network that classifies images into different categories; 3) Adversarial Learning Network:

an adversarial loss is applied to distinguish regular images from destructed ones; 4) Region Alignment Network: appended after the classification network to induce backbone network to model the semantic correlation among regions.

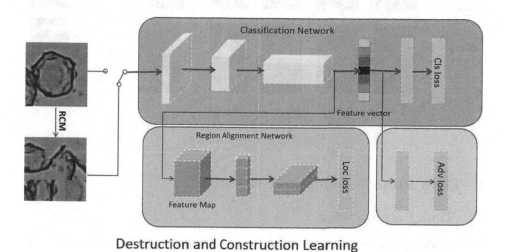

Destruction and Construction Learning

Fig. 2. The framework of Destruction and Construction Learning (DCL) method.

3.3 Blending Strategy

Model fusion is a method of combining base classifiers in a certain way to improve the overall performance. In the field of machine learning, data and features determine the upper limit of machine learning, while models and algorithms are only approaching this upper limit. So when data and features cannot improve performance, model fusion may be a powerful approach to increase accuracy on machine learning tasks. In our work, we use a blending strategy for its convenience and effectiveness. In the first stage, the whole pollen dataset had been split into a training set and a test set, so we split the training set into a new training set and validation set. Then the new training set is utilized to train the base models and make predictions on validation set. In the second stage, we takes the predictions on validation set to train a new model and evaluate its performance on the original test set. In this way, we obtain more independent features from single model. It should be noted that the second stage model should not be too complex, or it will lead to over-fitting.

Specifically, we employ the new training set to train the DCL models and DenseNAS, then concatenate their prediction vectors as the input of Random Forest Classifier, which is utilized as the classifier in the second stage. XGBoost and Multi-Output Regressor are also tested as the second stage models (Fig. 3).

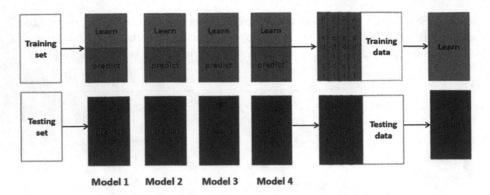

Fig. 3. Blending strategy.

4   Data Preprocessing and Results

4.1   Data Preprocessing

We test our methods on the dataset from the Pollen Challenge held at ICPR (2020) [4]. The challenge is to automatically classify pollen grain images from a large dataset of microscope pollen grain images collected from aerobiological samples. The microscope images have four classes of objects, including three species of pollen grains and an additional distractor class of objects, including air bubbles and dust that can be misclassified as pollen.

During the training phase, the number of training samples is limited, and the number of epochs is large, and neural networks will appear over-fitting the dataset. Furthermore, the number of images with different labels are very uneven. To address this, we use image enhancement technology to artificially extend the data set for some classes with few samples. We have tried to use grayscale images for training, but this approach does not improve the final performance. Besides, the segmentation of the pollen from the background is unnecessary because our networks can identify the important and non-important features based on training images. In the end, the dataset is divided into two parts and all images are reshaped to 224×224 pixels, then 80% for the training of the CNN models and the remaining 20% images for testing the classification performance on unseen images.

4.2   Results

At last, our group won the first Place in the Pollen Challenge. Compared with the previous work [3], the results further validate the effectiveness and generality of our method. It should be noticed that in DenseNAS, we use the resnet-based search space, while in DCL, we select reset101 as the backbone network. All result can be seen in Table 1. We achieve 1% improvement over the state-of-the-art DCL.

Table 1. The performances on Pollen Challenge

Model	Params (M)	Accuracy
ResNet18	11.21	93.84%
ResNet101	42.65	95.28%
DenseNet169	13.22	96.07%
DenseNAS	9.43	96.83%
DCL	22.0	97.31%
Blending	-	98.35%

5 Conclusion

In this paper, we combine NAS-based networks with manual networks to solve the pollen identification problem. Firstly, we use DenseNAS to create new networks and construct several different search spaces. Besides, we choose the DCL method, which can take the traditional network as the backbone, and get better results with a little more computation. Finally, a blending strategy is introduced to combine networks and achieve an enhanced performance. In the process of fusing these models, the best fusion effect can be obtained when the number of fused models is between four and nine. In the future work, we will apply our method to solve other classification problems.

Acknowledgement. The work was supported by the Natural Science Foundation of China (62076016, 61672079). Baochang Zhang is also with Shenzhen Academy of Aerospace Technology, Shenzhen, China, and he is corresponding author. He is in part supported by Shenzhen Science and Technology Program (No. KQTD20161125151346).

References

1. Ahmed, K., Torresani, L.: MaskConnect: connectivity learning by gradient descent. In: Ferrari, V., Hebert, M., Sminchisescu, C., Weiss, Y. (eds.) ECCV 2018. LNCS, vol. 11209, pp. 362–378. Springer, Cham (2018). https://doi.org/10.1007/978-3-030-01228-1_22
2. Baker, B., Gupta, O., Naik, N., Raskar, R. Designing neural network architectures using reinforcement learning. arXiv preprint arXiv:1611.02167 (2016)
3. Battiato, S., Ortis, A., Trenta, F., Ascari, L., Politi, M., Siniscalco, C.: Detection and classification of pollen grain microscope images. In: Proceedings of the IEEE/CVF Conference on Computer Vision and Pattern Recognition Workshops, pp. 980–981 (2020)
4. Battiato, S., Ortis, A., Trenta, F., Ascari, L., Politi, M., Siniscalco, C.: Pollen13K: a large scale microscope pollen grain image dataset. In: IEEE International Conference on Image Processing (ICIP), pp. 2456–2460. IEEE (2020)
5. Brock, A., Lim, T., Ritchie, J.M., Weston, N.: Smash: one-shot model architecture search through hypernetworks. arXiv preprint arXiv:1708.05344 (2017)

6. Cai, S., Zuo, W., Zhang, L. : Higher-order integration of hierarchical convolutional activations for fine-grained visual categorization. In: Proceedings of the IEEE Conference on Computer Vision and Pattern Recognition, pp. 511–520 (2017)

7. Chen, H., et al.: Binarized neural architecture search for efficient object recognition. Int. J. Comput. Vis. (2019). https://doi.org/10.1007/s11263-020-01379-y

8. Chen, Y., Bai, Y., Zhang, W., Mei, T.: Destruction and construction learning for fine-grained image recognition. In: Proceedings of the IEEE Conference on Computer Vision and Pattern Recognition, pp. 5157–5166 (2019)

9. Du, R., et al.: Fine-grained visual classification via progressive multi-granularity training of jigsaw patches. arXiv preprint arXiv:2003.03836 (2020)

10. Fang, J., Sun, Y., Zhang, Q., Li, Y., Liu, W., Wang, X.: Densely connected search space for more flexible neural architecture search. In: Proceedings of the IEEE Conference on Computer Vision and Pattern Recognition, pp. 10628–10637 (2020)

11. Fu, J., Zheng, H., Mei, T.: Look closer to see better: recurrent attention convolutional neural network for fine-grained image recognition. In: Proceedings of the IEEE Conference on Computer Vision and Pattern Recognition, pp. 4438–4446 (2017)

12. Gao, Y., Beijbom, O., Zhang, N., Darrell, T.: Compact bilinear pooling. In: Proceedings of the IEEE Conference on Computer Vision and Pattern Recognition, pp. 317–326 (2016)

13. Hu, J., Zhu, E., Wang, S., Wang, S., Liu, X., Yin, J.: Two-stage unsupervised video anomaly detection using low-rank based unsupervised one-class learning with ridge regression. In: 2019 International Joint Conference on Neural Networks (IJCNN), pp. 1–8. IEEE (2019)

14. Hu, Y., et al.: NAS-count: counting-by-density with neural architecture search. arXiv preprint arXiv:2003.00217 (2020)

15. Hu, Y., Yang, Y., Zhang, J., Cao, X., Zhen, X.: Attentional kernel encoding networks for fine-grained visual categorization. IEEE Trans. Circ. Syst. Video Technol. **31**, 301–314 (2020)

16. Huang, S., Xu, Z., Tao, D., Zhang, Y.: Part-stacked CNN for fine-grained visual categorization. In: Proceedings of the IEEE Conference on Computer Vision and Pattern Recognition, pp. 1173–1182 (2016)

17. Lin, T.-Y., Maji, S.: Improved bilinear pooling with CNNs. arXiv preprint arXiv:1707.06772 (2017)

18. Lin, T.-Y., RoyChowdhury, A., Maji, S.: Bilinear CNN models for fine-grained visual recognition. In: Proceedings of the IEEE International Conference on Computer Vision, pp. 1449–1457 (2015)

19. Luan, S., Chen, C., Zhang, B., Han, J., Liu, J.: Gabor convolutional networks. IEEE Trans. Image Process. **27**(9), 4357–4366 (2018)

20. Luo, R., Tian, F., Qin, T., Chen, E., Liu, T.-Y.: Neural architecture optimization. In: Advances in Neural Information Processing Systems, pp. 7816–7827 (2018)

21. Pham, H., Guan, M.Y., Zoph, B., Le, Q.V., Dean, J.: Efficient neural architecture search via parameter sharing. arXiv preprint arXiv:1802.03268 (2018)

22. Real, E., Aggarwal, A., Huang, Y., Le, Q.V.: Regularized evolution for image classifier architecture search. In: Proceedings of the AAAI Conference on Artificial Intelligence, vol. 33, pp. 4780–4789 (2018)

23. Saunders, G.M., Pollack, J.B.: The evolution of communication schemes over continuous channels. Anim. Animats **4**, 580–589 (1996)

24. Wang, Q., Li, P., Zhang, L.: G2DeNet: global gaussian distribution embedding network and its application to visual recognition. In: Proceedings of the IEEE Conference on Computer Vision and Pattern Recognition, pp. 2730–2739 (2017)

25. Xie, L., Yuille, A.: Genetic CNN. In: Proceedings of the IEEE International Conference on Computer Vision, pp. 1379–1388 (2017)
26. Zhong, Z., Yan, J., Wu, W., Shao, J., Liu, C.-L.: Practical block-wise neural network architecture generation. In: Proceedings of the IEEE Conference on Computer Vision and Pattern Recognition, pp. 2423–2432 (2018)
27. Zhuo, L., et al.: CP-NAS: child-parent neural architecture search for binary neural networks. arXiv preprint arXiv:2005.00057 (2020)
28. Zhuo, L., et al.: Cogradient descent for bilinear optimization. In: Proceedings of the IEEE/CVF Conference on Computer Vision and Pattern Recognition (CVPR), June 2020
29. Zoph, B., Le, Q.V.: Neural architecture search with reinforcement learning. arXiv preprint arXiv:1611.01578 (2016)

Improved Data Augmentation of Deep Convolutional Neural Network for Pollen Grains Classification
Third Classified

Penghui Gui, Ruowei Wang, Zhengbang Zhu, Feiyu Zhu, and Qijun Zhao[✉]

College of Computer Science, Sichuan University, Chengdu, China
penghuigui@stu.scu.edu.cn, wangruowei1027@qq.com, zbzhu.yz@gmail.com,
{feiyuz,qjzhao}@scu.edu.cn

Abstract. Traditionally, it is a time-consuming work for experts to accomplish pollen grains classification. With the popularity of deep Convolutional Neural Network (CNN) in computer vision, many automatic pollen grains classification methods based on CNN have been proposed in recent years. However, The CNN they used often focus on the most proniment area in the center of pollen grains and neglect the less discriminative local features in the surrounding of pollen grains. In order to alleviate this situation, we propose two data augmentation operations. Our experiment results on Pollen13K achieve a weighted F1 score of 97.26% and an accuracy of 97.29%.

Keywords: Deep convolutional neural network · Pollen grains classification · Data augmentation

1 Introduction

Pollen classification plays an important role in a wide range of applications, such as study of climate-change, honey quality control and allergy prevention. Traditionally, the predominant manner is performed by qualified palynology experts to analyze images in microscopy [3]. It is a time-consuming work for observing shape, size, texture features in images manually. Therefore, it is highly demanded to develop automatic methods for pollen grains classification.

Recently, with the development of computer vision technology, a lot of automated pollen classification methods are proposed [4,6,9,11,12]. Classical machine learning and deep learning are both used in pollen grains classification, but the deep learning approach often achieve better performance in large datasets. The POLLEN23E [6] datsaset is publicly available and consists of 23 pollen types in a total of 805 images. The authors in the paper [6] explore three automatic feature extractors, which are the "bag of visual words" (BOW), the "color, shape and texture" (CST), and a combination of BOW and CST (CST + BOW). The highest classification rate, 64%, is achieved using CST + BOW and support vector machines.

© Springer Nature Switzerland AG 2021
A. Del Bimbo et al. (Eds.): ICPR 2020 Workshops, LNCS 12668, pp. 490–500, 2021.
https://doi.org/10.1007/978-3-030-68793-9_36

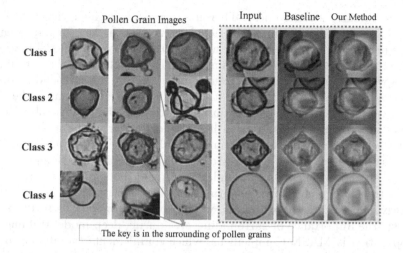

Fig. 1. Example pollen grain images in the left and visualized results in the right. The difference in the surrounding of pollen grains are important discriminative local features for pollen grains classification (for example, the aperture area of surrounding make class 1 seem like a triangle star and make class 3 seem like a pentagram; the pollen wall of surrounding in class 4 is more thinner than class 2). The Class Activation Map (CAM) results show that our method can attract model pay more attention to the surrounding features comparing to the baseline method. (Color figure online)

In [12], they reach up to an accuracy of 97% for classified samples after applying transfer learning to the AlexNet pre-trained network and then using a linear discriminant classifier to the extracted features. From the work above, we can realize that deep learning has more convenient and efficient feature extraction capability compared with classical machine learning methods. However, these deep learning approaches are still not inspire thorough to their potential due to limitation of the dataset size.

The Pollen13K proposed in [2] is a large dataset. It is composed of more than 13000 objects, identified by a segmentation pipeline applied on aerobiological samples. In [1], they augmented the dataset by including the segmented version of the training patches and trained on a SmallerVGGNET model using the augmented dataset and some additional data augmentations, which brings the best result with an accuracy of 0.8973 and an F1 score of 0.8914. In our proposed methods, we adopt two other data augmentation operations on these, which puts forward the best result by large margins.

As Fig. 1 shows, the Pollen13K dataset is more challenging than other datasets. Objects in different categories have similar appearance (for example, pollen images in class 1 and class 3 have similar pollen wall and apertural area) while objects in the same category have varying appearance in different images (for example, pollen images in class 1 have different shapes and sizes, and very similar with class 2 sometimes). Therefore, as a fine-grained visual classification task, getting the discriminative local features is the key for improvement. After experiments and observations, we find that the baseline model pays most attention to the center of pollen grains and merely focuses on the surrounding area, as we can see from visulized results in Fig. 1. But the surrounding area of pollen grains contains rich discriminative local features. For example, the difference between class 1 and class 3 is in the pattern of "bubble chamber" in the aperture area (most of class 1 seem like a triangle star in the inside of pollen grain but class 3 seem like a pentagram), and the difference between class 2 and class 4 is the pollen walls (class 2 are thicker and class 4 are thinner). So the aperture area and pollen wall around the center of pollen grains is the key to improve the performance of pollen grains classification.

Motivated by these observations, we propose two operations to utilize and emphasis the importance of surrounding area during deep model training. The first operation is MASK Complement, which complements the absence of surrounding area in the segmented images; the second operation is Cut Occlusion, which randomly cover up the equal cutting patch in train images. Both operations prompt the deep model to focus on the key areas of improvement. Our result on the Pollen Grain Classification Challenge show that two operations are impressive effective. Our experiments also prove the effectiveness of these two operation respectively. To sum up, our contributions are as follows:

- We find the key areas in pollen grains, and propose two data augmentation operations to urge the deep model pay more attention to the key areas.
- Evaluation results show that the proposed method achieves impressive performance on the Pollen Grain Classification Challenge. And extensive experiments demonstrate the effectiveness of the proposed methods.

2   Method

2.1   Overview

The flowchart of our proposed method is shown in Fig. 2. The first step is Mask Complement operation, which uses dilated mask images to complement the absence of aperture areas and pollen grains in the original SEGM images. The second step is Cut Occlusion operation for training data, which cuts image into patches around center point and makes these patches into black occlusion during the training phrase. In the third step, we use CNN model to train both OBJ and complemented SEGM images and to infer the class of pollen grains images in the test set. Some data augmentations and regularization mechanisms are used in the CNN model. In the rest of this section, we introduce these steps in detail.

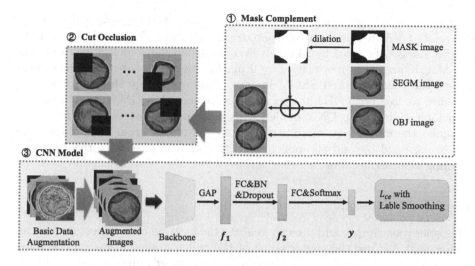

Fig. 2. Overview of the proposed method for pollen grains classification.

2.2 Mask Complement

As we mentioned in Sect. 1, the aperture area and pollen wall are very important features for distinguishing different classes of pollen grain. But the background information outside from pollen wall in the OBJ images are very redundant and disruptive, so the SEGM images that only contain texture of the pollen grain object are very useful to ease this trouble. However, we found some of the original SEGM images are not implement for the aperture area and pollen wall, as can be seen from Fig. 3, and the experiments also demonstrate that the original SEGM images will reduce the performance obviously.

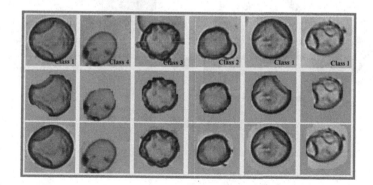

Fig. 3. Examples of OBJ images (the first row), related SEGM images (the second row) and complemented SEGM images (the last row). The aperture area and pollen wall in the surrounding of pollen grains are incomplete sometimes as the related SEGM images show.

In order to complement the absence of original SEGM images, we first amplify the related MASK images by morphological operation of dilation. We dilate the MASK images of class 1 by 24 pixels because of enormous mutilation, and dilate the MASK images of rest classes by 9 pixels. Then, we re-segment OBJ images to get the complemented SEGM images, some results are shown in Fig. 3. In the end, we feed both OBJ images and complemented SEGM images to the next step for training deep CNN model. This combination has two benefits: one is to make the model pay more attention to the pollen grain itself rather than the background beyond the pollen wall; the other is to enlarge the number of training samples.

2.3   Cut Occlusion

This operation simply and directly realizes the location of the aperture area and pollen wall. We use the center point of the pollen grains image approximately as the center point of the pollen grains, because most pollen grains are usually located in the center of images. Then, we cut the pollen grain into k patches of same size around the center point as shown in Fig. 4. The aperture area and pollen wall become the main discriminative features in these patches, which hence attract the model to learn more information of "bubble chamber" and cell wall areas. It is an exception when $k = 1$, which only cut out one patch of $1/16$ size of pollen grain image around the center point.

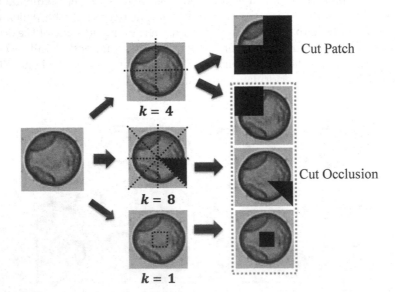

Fig. 4. Illustration of Cut Occlusion operation. An input image can be divided into k equal patches, the discriminative local features of the surrounding will become the leading parts in one patch.

Then how to use these patches? In early stage, we highlight these patches with an operation named Cut Patch. This operation randomly highlights a single patch by covering up the remaining $k - 1$ patches, as shown in Fig. 4. Later, we figure out another way to use these patches, named Cut Occlusion. This operation only covers up one patch among k patches, which brings two prominent advantages comparing to Cut Patch. One is that it preserves more information of pollen grains. Another is that we can apply it to smaller patches(for example, $k = 8$). When $k = 1$, the center of pollen grain will be drop out, and the surrounding of pollen grain will be taken into account. Due to the advantages of Cut Occlusion approach, we use it for all of our experiments.

The idea of Cut Occlusion is similar to CutOut [5] which aims to remove maximally activated features in order to encourage the network to consider less prominent features. It removes contiguous sections of input images, and hence augments the dataset with partially occluded versions of existing samples. Similarly, the Cut Occlusion destroys the maximally activated features in the center area and encourages the model to focus the surrounding area. By observing visualized results of test samples in Fig. 1, our approach successfully disrupts the model's attention in the central area and makes the model pay more attention to the occluded patch (surrounding area of pollen grains).

The Cut Occlusion operation can easily be applied using CPU along with any other data augmentations during data loading. By implementing this operation on the CPU in parallel with the main GPU training task, we can hide the computation and obtain performance improvements.

2.4 CNN Model

The input of CNN model are augmented images after above two operations and basic data augmentation. The basic data augmentations are used for increasing the diversity of training data, which has been proved to prevent overfitting problem. As pollen grain images have black and white dots, we add salt and pepper noise at random locations in input images. In addition, we use some common geometric transformations and color space transformations [13] in the basic data augmentation. Then the augmented images are resized as fixed size and normalized by the mean and variance of the pollen grain dataset. Detailed experimental setup is shown in Sect. 3.1.

The CNN Model employs ResNet101 [7] as the backbone. More specifically, the convolution layers from Layer 0 to Layer 4 of ResNet101 are used in our model. As we can see from Fig. 2, the feature maps of Layer4 are fed into a Global Average Pooling (GAP) [10] layer to generate a feature vector $f_1 \in R^{2048 \times 1}$, which is then transformed to another feature vector $f_2 \in R^{512 \times 1}$ via a fully connected (FC) layer followed by a batch normalization (BN) layer [8] and a dropout layer [14]. The reason why feature $f_2 \in R^{512 \times 1}$ is introduced here is to implement a transition about high-dim features (2048) mapping to low-dim classes (4). Based on f_2, the class value y of the input pollen grain image is predicted via softmax function with FC layer.

As [15] mentioned, the Label Smoothing regularization can be also obtained by considering the cross entropy. We integrate it into the cross-entropy loss function to prevent model from having too high a confidence for the larger predicted value.

3   Experiment

3.1   Experiment Setup

Datasets. We use a subset of Pollen13K which is a large-scale microscope pollen grain image dataset. The Pollen13K is composed of more than 13000 objects spanning over 5 different categories: (1) Corylus Avellana (well-developed pollen grains), (2) Corylus Avellana (anomalous pollen grains), (3) Alnus, (4) Debris, (5) and Cupressaceae. Every object in this dataset has the corresponding binary mask and the segmented object with green background. We name these three types of object as OBJ, MASK and SEGM images. Considering the small number of observations related to Cupressaceae class, we not use this class in the dataset for experiments. So the sub-Pollen13K dataset used for our experiments has 11,279 OBJ images in total, and a same number of related MASK and SEGM images.

In order to perform classification, we divide the sub-Pollen13K data into a training set of 80% and a test set of 20%. Only OBJ images are used for the test set, which includes 2,256 images.

Training and Testing Settings. Before training the deep model, we first use MASK Complement, which re-segments the OBJ images to obtain complemented SEGM images using amplified mask images. During training, we resize both OBJ images and complemented SEGM images to 244×244, and augment the training data online by Cut Occlusion strategy and basic data augmentations. The number of occlusion patches is set to $k = 4$ and probability is 0.3 in Cut Occlusion. The probability of adding salt and pepper noise to each training image is 0.75 and signal noise rate is set to 0.9. Geometric transformations in basic data augmentations are composed of horizontal flip, vertical flip and rotation. Color space transformations include grayscale, brightness, contrast, saturation and hue changes. The probability of Geometric transformations and Color space transformations are all set to 0.5. The rotation angle ranges from $-45°$ to $45°$.

We implement our model in Pytorch, and train it on a PC with four NVIDIA GeForce GTX 1080 GPUs. For the first three epochs, we fix the backbone network pretrained on ImageNet and warm up the rest layers with learning rate $lr = 0.0001$. We use Adam optimizer with basic learning rate $lr = 0.00001$ and weight decay $\lambda = 0.0001$ for rest epochs. The learning rate of model is set to $0.1 \times lr$ when the accuracy on test dataset did not increase for three consecutive times. This learning rate schedule can prevent the model from falling into local optimum. All the experiments use a batch size of 32, and total number of epochs is 100. The smoothing factor of label smoothing is set to 0.1.

In the testing phase, we use Test Time Augmentation (TTA) strategy to improve the performance of the trained model. We first augment every test image with all basic data augmentations used in training phase, and then predict these augmented images. In the end, we use the average of predict values to calculate the final accuracy.

Evaluation Criteria. We use weighted F1 score, macro F1 score, and Accuracy to evaluate our proposed methods following the official evaluation criteria. F1 score is used for quantitative evaluation considering the imbalance in the data.

3.2   Comparison with Other Teams

Table 1. The top 3 results of the Pollen Grain Classification challenge. A total of 79 submissions performed by 47 teams have been evaluated. The test set is another subset of Pollen13K with 1,006 OBJ images.

Rank	Submissions	F1 (weighted)	F1 (macro)	Acc.
1	zhangbaochang	97.5100	95.5361	97.5389
2	fangchao	97.3032	95.1970	97.3380
3	ours ($k = 4$)	97.2592	95.1678	97.2877

In Table 1, We show the top 3 results on the Pollen Grain Classification Challenge. The test set used in this challenge is another subset of Pollen13K, which includes 1006 OBJ images. As we can see from the results, our proposed method ($k = 4$) is very effective. We believe that the impressive results achieved by our method owes to the following factors. (1) Our method complements the absence of aperture area of pollen wall in the SEGM images and combine the new SEGM images with OBJ images for training. (2) Our method prompts the model learn more discriminative features around the pollen wall rather than the pollen centre, and uses occlusion instead of highlight to achieve this aim. (3) Our method uses rich and effective data augmentation mechanisms and tricks of train and test, which makes our method more robust to pollen grains classification.

3.3   Ablation Study

Contribution of Mask Complement and Cut Occlusion. We evaluate the contribution of the Mask Complement operation and the Cut Occlusion strategy to the superior performance of the proposed model by enabling or disabling these two parts. When Mask Complement is disabled, the train images only include OBJ images. The results are summarized in Table 2. The baseline method in Fig. 1 is obtained when both two parts are disabled. Obviously, the best F1 score and accuracy rate are obtained when both two parts are enabled. Note that the best result of 96.05% is less than the accuracy on the Pollen Grain

Classification Challenge test set (97.28%) because of the absence in training data. These results demonstrate the effectiveness of our proposed method for focusing on the aperture area and pollen wall. Due to the problem of class imbalance, there is an abnormal result of F1 (macro) score but the result is normal in F1 (weighted) score.

Table 2. Performance of the proposed method when Mask Complement operation and Cut Occlusion strategy are enabled or disabled.

Mask Complement	Cut Occlusion	F1 (weighted)	F1 (macro)	Acc.
✗	✗	93.62	89.26	93.79
✗	✓	95.73	**93.39**	95.79
✓	✗	95.05	91.90	95.12
✓	✓	**96.00**	93.37	**96.05**

Table 3. Effectiveness of Cut Occlusion comparing to Cut Patch on the test set with 2,256 OBJ images.

Cut strategies	F1 (weighted)	F1 (macro)	Acc.
Not Cut	93.62	89.26	93.79
Cut Patch	93.93	90.02	94.06
Cut Occlusion (k = 4)	95.73	93.39	95.79
Cut Occlusion (k = 8)	95.77	93.31	95.83
Cut Occlusion (k = 1)	**95.90**	**93.51**	**95.97**

Impact of Different Cut Strategies. As introduced in Sect. 2.3, Cut Patch and Cut Occlusion both can focuses the aperture area of pollen wall. Not surprisingly, the performance improved after highlighting the "bubble chamber" and cell wall according to Table 3. The results also indicate that Cut Occlusion is better than Cut Patch, because too many information lost in Cut Patch. On the contrary, the Cut Occlusion only loss one quarter and can loss less information when $k = 8$. It is worth noting that the performance of $k = 8$ is better than $k = 4$, which also declares the advantage of Cut Occlusion compare to Cut Patch. From the result of $k = 1$, we can demonstrate that the surrounding of pollen grains have important disciminative local features. The probabilities of $k = 4$, $k = 8$, and $k = 1$ are 0.3, 0.6, and 0.08.

Importance of Mask Complement. In this experiment, we evaluate the necessity of Mask Complement for pollen classification only using ResNet50 without any data augmentations and other tricks. According to Sect. 2.2, We need to

Table 4. Effectiveness of Mask Complement operation and combination of OBJ and SEGM images for training.

Training data type	F1 (weighted)	F1 (macro)	Acc.
OBJ	93.40	90.30	93.26
SEGM	66.18	35.37	74.47
Complemented SEGM	76.52	54.30	77.80
OBJ + SEGM	93.98	90.53	94.10
OBJ + Complemented SEGM	**94.79**	**91.39**	**94.86**

get rid of the redundant background information around pollen wall (e.g. using SEGM images for training). But the performance of training with SEGM images on OBJ images test set is an obvious disadvantage demonstrated by results in Table 4. Furthermore, We found some of the SEGM images provided by official are incomplete for aperture areas of pollen wall. So we use Mask Complement operation to obtain complemented SEGM images, and Table 4 has proved the effectiveness of this operation(from 74.47% to 77.80%). Finally, the accuracy of training with combination is better than single OBJ images by 1.6%.

4 Conclusion

In this paper, we find the key areas to improve the performance of pollen grains classification. For these key areas, we adopt two data augmentation operations to make deep model pay more attention to the surrounding of pollen grains. Moreover, we use many effective basic data augmentation and some regularization techniques to achieve an impressive performance on the Pollen Grain Classification Challenge. The method used in the challenge is improved again by us on the ablation study. In the future, We will use a more specific network model to separate the center and surrounding of pollen grains with attention map, and improve the performance by extracting complementary features of both areas. What's more, we will address the problem of class imbalance in pollen grains classification.

Acknowledgement. The authors would like to thank Mingbo Hong for his constructive discussion on the proposed method. All correspondences should be directed to Q. Zhao at qjzhao@scu.edu.cn.

References

1. Battiato, S., Ortis, A., Trenta, F., Ascari, L., Politi, M., Siniscalco, C.: Detection and classification of pollen grain microscope images. In: IEEE/CVF Conference on Computer Vision and Pattern Recognition, CVPR Workshops 2020, Seattle, WA, USA, 14–19 June 2020, pp. 4220–4227. IEEE (2020)

2. Battiato, S., Ortis, A., Trenta, F., Ascari, L., Politi, M., Siniscalco, C.: Pollen13k: a large scale microscope pollen grain image dataset (2020)
3. Buters, J.T.M.: Pollen and spore monitoring in the world. Clin. Transl. Allergy **8**(1), 9 (2018)
4. Daood, A., Ribeiro, E., Bush, M.: Pollen grain recognition using deep learning. In: Bebis, G., et al. (eds.) ISVC 2016. LNCS, vol. 10072, pp. 321–330. Springer, Cham (2016). https://doi.org/10.1007/978-3-319-50835-1_30
5. DeVries, T., Taylor, G.W.: Improved regularization of convolutional neural networks with cutout. arXiv preprint arXiv:1708.04552 (2017)
6. Gonçalve, A.B., et al.: Feature extraction and machine learning for the classification of Brazilian savannah pollen grains. Plos ONE **11**, e0157044 (2016)
7. He, K., Zhang, X., Ren, S., Sun, J.: Deep residual learning for image recognition. In: Proceedings of the IEEE Conference on Computer Vision and Pattern Recognition, pp. 770–778 (2016)
8. Ioffe, S., Szegedy, C.: Batch normalization: Accelerating deep network training by reducing internal covariate shift. arXiv preprint arXiv:1502.03167 (2015)
9. Khanzhina, N., Putin, E., Filchenkov, A., Zamyatina, E.: Pollen grain recognition using convolutional neural network. In: ESANN (2018)
10. Lin, M., Chen, Q., Yan, S.: Network in network. arXiv preprint arXiv:1312.4400 (2013)
11. Nguyen, N.R., Donalson-Matasci, M., Shin, M.C.: Improving pollen classification with less training effort. In: IEEE Workshop on Applications of Computer Vision (WACV), pp. 421–426. IEEE (2013)
12. Sevillano, V., Aznarte, J.L.: Improving classification of pollen grain images of the polen23e dataset through three different applications of deep learning convolutional neural networks. PloS ONE **13**(9), e0201807 (2018)
13. Shorten, C., Khoshgoftaar, T.M.: A survey on image data augmentation for deep learning. J. Big Data **6**(1), 60 (2019)
14. Srivastava, N., Hinton, G., Krizhevsky, A., Sutskever, I., Salakhutdinov, R.: Dropout: a simple way to prevent neural networks from overfitting. J. Mach. Learn. Res. **15**(1), 1929–1958 (2014)
15. Szegedy, C., Vanhoucke, V., Ioffe, S., Shlens, J., Wojna, Z.: Rethinking the inception architecture for computer vision. In: Proceedings of the IEEE Conference on Computer Vision and Pattern Recognition, pp. 2818–2826 (2016)

Author Index

Printed in the United States
by Bookmasters

Printed in the United States
By Bookmasters